Discussions on Disability Law and Policy

Discussions on Disability Law and Policy

Edited by

Patricia C. Kuszler

Christy Thompson Ibrahim

CAROLINA ACADEMIC PRESS

Durham, North Carolina

Library of Congress Cataloging-in-Publication Data

Kuszler, Patricia C., 1952-
  Discussions on disability law and policy / edited by Patricia C. Kuszler and
Christy Thompson Ibrahim.
      pages cm
  Includes bibliographical references and index.
  ISBN 978-1-61163-395-5 (alk. paper)
  1. People with disabilities--Legal status, laws, etc.--United
States. I. Ibrahim, Christy Thompson. II. Title.

  KF480.K89 2013
  346.7301'3--dc23

                        2013027048

Carolina Academic Press
700 Kent Street
Durham, North Carolina 27701
Telephone (919) 489-7486
Fax (919) 493-5668
www.cap-press.com

Printed in the United States of America

Contents

Table of Cases

Acknowledgments

Thank you to Vickie Parker, Jay Schulkin, and Jeanette Stengel for all of their help. Thanks also to Keith Sipe and the great people at Carolina Academic Press for being excited about this project and making it come to pass.

Reprint Permissions by Chapter

2. "Unspeakable Conversations" from the book *Too Late to Die Young* by Harriet McBryde Johnson. Copyright 2005 by Harriet McBryde Johnson. Reprinted by permission of Henry Holt and Company, LLC.

   "Politics" from the book *Always Looking Up* by Michael J. Fox. Copyright 2009 Michael J. Fox. Reprinted by permission of Hyperion. All rights reserved.

   "Sun Devils wrestler different, all right—extraordinarily so." Reprinted by permission of CBSSports.com.

   "Whether their perpetrators realize it or not, Disability Awareness Days send the wrong message." Reprinted by permission of The Advocado Press.

   "Christmas Cheer" by Karin Mango. Reprinted by permission of the author.

4. "'Baby, Look Inside Your Mirror'": The Legal Profession's Willful and Sanist Blindness to Lawyers with Mental Disabilities," by Michael Perlin. Reprinted by permission of the author.

6. "Teachers Caught on Tape Bullying Special Needs Girl." Reprinted by permission of msnbc.com.

   "Impairing Education: Corporal Punishment of Students with Disabilities in US Public Schools." Reprinted by permission of the ACLU.

   "Special ed teachers feeling unsafe in class." Reprinted by permission of *The Seattle Post-Intelligencer*.

   "School district pays $180,000 to be free of blind, autistic student it considers dangerous." Reprinted by permission of *The Seattle Times*.

7. "Mom Straps Herself To Flag Pole In Protest" and accompanying articles. Reprinted by permission of Inclusion Daily Express, www.InclusionDaily.com.

8. "Disabled Students Come Out: Questions without Answers" by Georgina Kleege. Reprinted by permission of the Modern Language Association of America.

   Michael Edward Slipsky, "Flagging Accommodated Testing on the LSAT and MCAT: Necessary Protections of the Academic Standards of the Legal and Medical Communities," 82 N.C.L. Rev. 811, January 2004. Reprinted with permission of the *North Carolina Law Review*, Vol.82 pp. 81, and with permission of the author.

9. "Persons with Disabilities and the U.S. Immigration System" by Rebecca Watson. Reprinted by permission of the author.

10. "The U.S. Ratification of the Convention on the Rights of Persons with Disabilities Fact Sheet" reprinted by permission of The United States International Council on Disabilities.

11. "Untitled," art piece by Tanya Temkin, reprinted by permission of the author.

12. "The Regulation of the Use of Seclusion and Restraints in Mental Disability Law" by Michael Perlin. Reprinted by permission of the author.

13. "The *Olmstead* Decision at Ten: Directions for Future Advocacy" by Ira A. Burnim and Jennifer Mathis. Reprinted by permission of Jennifer Mathis.

    "Behavioral Outcomes of Deinstitutionalization for People with Intellectual and/ or Developmental Disabilities: Third Decennial Review of U.S. Studies, 1977–2010" by the Research and Training Center on Community Living, Institute on Community Integration, University of Minnesota. Reprinted with their permission.

14. "Group Homes and Zoning Under the Fair Housing Act" by Michael Mirra. Reprinted with permission of the author, article found at http://www.hudhre.info/documents/ GroupHomesandZoning.pdf.

15. "Individuals with Disabilities Education Improvement Act (IDEA) of 2004: Provisions for Homeless Children and Youth with Disabilities" by the National Center for Homeless Education. Reprinted with their permission.

    "Ending Homelessness for People with Mental Illnesses and Co-Occurring Disorders," by the National Mental Health Association. Reprinted with their permission.

    "From Street Lawering to Systemic Lawyering: Meeting the Basic Needs of Unac-companied and Homeless Youth Through Systemic Legal Advocacy" from *Clearinghouse Review Journal of Poverty Law and Policy*. Reprinted with permission of the author.

16. "The Role of Mental Health Courts in System Reform." Used by permission of The Bazelon Center for Mental Health Law.

17. "Know Your Rights: Legal Rights of Disabled Prisoners." Reprinted by permission of the ACLU.

    "Expecting the Unreasonable: Why a Specific Request Requirement for ADA Title II Discrimination Claims Fails to Protect Those Who Cannot Request Reasonable Accommodations" by David A. Maas. Reprinted by permission of Harvard University Law School.

19. "Sharing the Dream: Is the ADA Accommodating All?" A report of the U.S. Commission on Civil Rights. Used with their permission.

21. "Sheltered Workshops Pay Equal to Sweatshops, Says Group," by Dave Reynolds, *Inclusion Daily Express*. This article is reprinted here with permission from Inclusion Daily Express www.InclusionDaily.com.

22. "Public Transit" from *Moving Violations* by John Hockenberry. Copyright 1995 by John Hockenberry. Reprinted by permission of Hyperion. All rights reserved.

    "Mean Streets" by Ed Eames. Reprinted by permission of Advocado Press.

23. "The Clint Eastwood Verdict Makes My Day," from *Business Week*. Reprinted by permission of Business Week.

    "Discrimination Lawsuit Filed Against Dorney" from *The Morning Call*. Reprinted with permission of The Morning Call. All rights reserved.

About the Editors

Patricia C. Kuszler is a graduate of Mayo Medical School (MD, 1978) and Yale Law School (JD, 1991). She joined the faculty of the School of Law at the University of Washington in 1994 and is currently the Associate Dean for Academic Administration in the School of Law and the Charles I. Stone Professor of Law. She also directs the School of Law's Center for Law, Science and Global Health. The center's major components include the J.D. concentration track in health law (1996–present), a Master of Laws (LL.M.) Program in Health Law (2009–present) major collaboration with the UW Institute for Public Health Genetics (1997–present), and concurrent J.D./M.P.H., J.D./M.H.A. and J.D./M..A programs. In addition to her law faculty appointment, Professor Kuszler is an Adjunct Professor in the UW School of Medicine (Department of Bioethics and Humanities), the School of Public Health, and core faculty in the University's Institute for Public Health Genetics. Professor Kuszler 's teaching and research interests include the impact of law and regulation on health care delivery, health care finance, health insurance fraud and abuse, research standards and misconduct, health and human rights, disability law, public health law in the age of bioterrorism, and the legal, ethical and policy issues presented by genetic information and the biotechnology industry.

Christy Thompson Ibrahim is a graduate of Brigham Young University and the University of Washington School of Law. She is a disability law attorney in Seattle, Washington, focusing on the legal needs and rights of people with intellectual disabilities and their families. Her brother had Down Syndrome and left a legacy of love and laughter. She is a part-time faculty lecturer at the University of Washington School of Law, where she has taught Disability Law, Interviewing and Counseling, and the course component for the Disability Law Clinic. She is the author of *An Anthology of Disability Literature* and will be co-teaching a Disability Literature and Philosophy course at the undergraduate level this year. She was inducted into the UW Law School's Public Interest Law Association Hall of Fame, and is a member of the board of the Arc of Washington.

Editors' Note

Several Disability Law texts exist on the market. Most of them are arranged by statute, and contain a short overview of the statute along with short excerpts of cases. This book's approach is different. This book is arranged topically, and contains full cases instead of snippets. Besides cases, this text is a trove of articles — some law review articles, some policy articles, some from the popular press, and some personal stories and essays. We hope you will enjoy the variety, and engage in many great discussions as a result.

Patricia C. Kuszler, M.D., J.D.

Christy Thompson Ibrahim, J.D.

Discussions on Disability Law and Policy

Discussion 1

An Overview of
Disability Rights

Recommended Background
Reading and Viewing

The Smithsonian National Museum of American History's website slideshow about the disability rights movement, retrieved May 15, 2012 at http://www.americanhistory.si.edu/disabilityrights/welcome.html.

UC Berkeley's overview of the disability rights movement, retrieved May 15, 2012 at http://bancroft.berkeley.edu/collections/drilm/introduction.html.

PBS Documentary, "Lives Worth Living." Clips available at pbs.org; DVDs available for purchase. Excellent hour-long documentary about the disability rights movement and some of its key players.

Shapiro, Joseph. *No Pity: People with Disabilities Forging a New Civil Rights Movement.* New York: Random House, 1993. A summary of the book is available at http://ddc.ohio.gov/Pub/Nopity.htm.

Levy, Robert and Leonard Rubenstein, *The Rights of People with Mental Disabilities.* Carbondale: ACLU Press, 1996.

Alan Macurdy, *Commentary: Disability Ideology and the Law School Curriculum*, 4 B.U. Pub. Int. L.J. 443 (1995).

Arlene S. Kanter, *The Law: What's Disability Studies Got to Do with It? Or, An Introduction to Disability Legal Studies*, 42 Colum. Hum. Rts. L. Rev. 403 (2011).

Readings for Class Discussion

What legal rights do people with disabilities have? The following document from the U.S. Department of Justice is an overview of federal rights laws. As you read it, consider which of these laws you were already familiar with and which are new to you.

A Guide to Disability Rights Laws

U.S. Department of Justice, July 2009

Reproduction of this document is encouraged.

This guide provides an overview of Federal civil rights laws that ensure equal opportunity for people with disabilities. To find out more about how these laws may apply to you, contact the agencies and organizations listed below.

 Americans with Disabilities Act (ADA)

The ADA prohibits discrimination on the basis of disability in employment, State and local government, public accommodations, commercial facilities, transportation, and telecommunications. It also applies to the United States Congress.

To be protected by the ADA, one must have a disability or have a relationship or association with an individual with a disability. An individual with a disability is defined by the ADA as a person who has a physical or mental impairment that substantially limits one or more major life activities, a person who has a history or record of such an impairment, or a person who is perceived by others as having such an impairment. The ADA does not specifically name all of the impairments that are covered.

ADA Title I: Employment

Title I requires employers with 15 or more employees to provide qualified individuals with disabilities an equal opportunity to benefit from the full range of employment-related opportunities available to others. For example, it prohibits discrimination in recruitment, hiring, promotions, training, pay, social activities, and other privileges of employment. It restricts questions that can be asked about an applicant's disability before a job offer is made, and it requires that employers make reasonable accommodation to the known physical or mental limitations of otherwise qualified individuals with disabilities, unless it results in undue hardship. Religious entities with 15 or more employees are covered under title I.

Title I complaints must be filed with the U. S. Equal Employment Opportunity Commission (EEOC) within 180 days of the date of discrimination, or 300 days if the charge is filed with a designated State or local fair employment practice agency. Individuals may file a lawsuit in Federal court only after they receive a "right-to-sue" letter from the EEOC.

Charges of employment discrimination on the basis of disability may be filed at any U.S. Equal Employment Opportunity Commission field office. Field offices are located in 50 cities throughout the U.S. and are listed in most telephone directories under "U.S. Government."

ADA Title II: State and Local Government Activities

Title II covers all activities of State and local governments regardless of the government entity's size or receipt of Federal funding. Title II requires that State and local governments give people with disabilities an equal opportunity to benefit from all of their programs, services, and activities (e.g. public education, employment, transportation, recreation, health care, social services, courts, voting, and town meetings).

State and local governments are required to follow specific architectural standards in the new construction and alteration of their buildings. They also must relocate programs or otherwise provide access in inaccessible older buildings, and communicate effectively with people who have hearing, vision, or speech disabilities. Public entities are not required to take actions that would result in undue financial and administrative burdens. They are required to make reasonable modifications to policies, practices, and procedures where necessary to avoid discrimination, unless they can demonstrate that doing so would fundamentally alter the nature of the service, program, or activity being provided.

Complaints of title II violations may be filed with the Department of Justice within 180 days of the date of discrimination. In certain situations, cases may be referred to a mediation program sponsored by the Department. The Department may bring a lawsuit where it has investigated a matter and has been unable to resolve violations.

Title II may also be enforced through private lawsuits in Federal court. It is not necessary to file a complaint with the Department of Justice (DOJ) or any other Federal agency, or to receive a "right-to-sue" letter, before going to court.

ADA Title II: Public Transportation

The transportation provisions of title II cover public transportation services, such as city buses and public rail transit (e.g. subways, commuter rails, Amtrak). Public transportation authorities may not discriminate against people with disabilities in the provision of their services. They must comply with requirements for accessibility in newly purchased vehicles, make good faith efforts to purchase or lease accessible used buses, remanufacture buses in an accessible manner, and, unless it would result in an undue burden, provide paratransit where they operate fixed-route bus or rail systems. Paratransit is a service where individuals who are unable to use the regular transit system independently (because of a physical or mental impairment) are picked up and dropped off at their destinations.

ADA Title III: Public Accommodations

Title III covers businesses and nonprofit service providers that are public accommodations, privately operated entities offering certain types of courses and examinations, privately operated transportation, and commercial facilities. Public accommodations are private entities who own, lease, lease to, or operate facilities such as restaurants, retail stores, hotels, movie theaters, private schools, convention centers, doctors' offices, homeless shelters, transportation depots, zoos, funeral homes, day care centers, and recreation facilities including sports stadiums and fitness clubs. Transportation services provided by private entities are also covered by title III.

Public accommodations must comply with basic nondiscrimination requirements that prohibit exclusion, segregation, and unequal treatment. They also must comply with specific requirements related to architectural standards for new and altered buildings; reasonable modifications to policies, practices, and procedures; effective communication with people with hearing, vision, or speech disabilities; and other access requirements. Additionally, public accommodations must remove barriers in existing buildings where it is easy to do so without much difficulty or expense, given the public accommodation's resources.

Courses and examinations related to professional, educational, or trade-related applications, licensing, certifications, or credentialing must be provided in a place and manner accessible to people with disabilities, or alternative accessible arrangements must be offered.

Commercial facilities, such as factories and warehouses, must comply with the ADA's architectural standards for new construction and alterations.

Complaints of title III violations may be filed with the Department of Justice. In certain situations, cases may be referred to a mediation program sponsored by the Department. The Department is authorized to bring a lawsuit where there is a pattern or practice of discrimination in violation of title III, or where an act of discrimination raises an issue of general public importance. Title III may also be enforced through private lawsuits. It is not necessary to file a complaint with the Department of Justice (or any Federal agency), or to receive a "right-to-sue" letter, before going to court.

ADA Title IV: Telecommunications Relay Services

Title IV addresses telephone and television access for people with hearing and speech disabilities. It requires common carriers (telephone companies) to establish interstate and intrastate telecommunications relay services (TRS) 24 hours a day, 7 days a week. TRS enables callers with hearing and speech disabilities who use TTYs (also known as TDDs), and callers who use voice telephones to communicate with each other through a third party communications assistant. The Federal Communications Commission (FCC) has set minimum standards for TRS services. Title IV also requires closed captioning of Federally funded public service announcements.

Telecommunications Act

Section 255 and Section 251(a)(2) of the Communications Act of 1934, as amended by the Telecommunications Act of 1996, require manufacturers of telecommunications equipment and providers of telecommunications services to ensure that such equipment and services are accessible to and usable by persons with disabilities, if readily achievable. These amendments ensure that people with disabilities will have access to a broad range of products and services such as telephones, cell phones, pagers, call-waiting, and operator services, that were often inaccessible to many users with disabilities.

Fair Housing Act

The Fair Housing Act, as amended in 1988, prohibits housing discrimination on the basis of race, color, religion, sex, disability, familial status, and national origin. Its coverage includes private housing, housing that receives Federal financial assistance, and State and local government housing. It is unlawful to discriminate in any aspect of selling or renting housing or to deny a dwelling to a buyer or renter because of the disability of that individual, an individual associated with the buyer or renter, or an individual who intends to live in the residence. Other covered activities include, for example, financing, zoning practices, new construction design, and advertising.

The Fair Housing Act requires owners of housing facilities to make reasonable exceptions in their policies and operations to afford people with disabilities equal housing opportunities. For example, a landlord with a "no pets" policy may be required to grant an exception to this rule and allow an individual who is blind to keep a guide dog in the residence. The Fair Housing Act also requires landlords to allow tenants with disabilities to make reasonable access-related modifications to their private living space, as well as to common use spaces. (The landlord is not required to pay for the changes.) The Act further requires that new multifamily housing with four or more units be designed and built to allow access for persons with disabilities. This includes accessible common use areas, doors that are wide enough for wheelchairs, kitchens and bathrooms that allow a person using a wheelchair to maneuver, and other adaptable features within the units.

Complaints of Fair Housing Act violations may be filed with the U.S. Department of Housing and Urban Development.

Additionally, the Department of Justice can file cases involving a pattern or practice of discrimination. The Fair Housing Act may also be enforced through private lawsuits.

Air Carrier Access Act

The Air Carrier Access Act prohibits discrimination in air transportation by domestic and foreign air carriers against qualified individuals with physical or mental impairments. It applies only to air carriers that provide regularly scheduled services for hire to the public. Requirements address a wide range of issues including boarding assistance and certain accessibility features in newly built aircraft and new or altered airport facilities. People may enforce rights under the Air Carrier Access Act by filing a complaint with the U.S. Department of Transportation, or by bringing a lawsuit in Federal court.

Voting Accessibility for the Elderly and Handicapped Act

The Voting Accessibility for the Elderly and Handicapped Act of 1984 generally requires polling places across the United States to be physically accessible to people with disabilities for federal elections. Where no accessible location is available to serve as a polling place, a political subdivision must provide an alternate means of casting a ballot on the day of the election. This law also requires states to make available registration and voting aids for disabled and elderly voters, including information by TTYs (also known as TDDs) or similar devices.

National Voter Registration Act

The National Voter Registration Act of 1993, also known as the "Motor Voter Act," makes it easier for all Americans to exercise their fundamental right to vote. One of the basic purposes of the Act is to increase the historically low registration rates of minorities and persons with disabilities that have resulted from discrimination. The Motor Voter Act requires all offices of State-funded programs that are primarily engaged in providing services to persons with disabilities to provide all program applicants with voter registration forms, to assist them in completing the forms, and to transmit completed forms to the appropriate State official.

Civil Rights of Institutionalized Persons Act

The Civil Rights of Institutionalized Persons Act (CRIPA) authorizes the U.S. Attorney General to investigate conditions of confinement at State and local government institutions such as prisons, jails, pretrial detention centers, juvenile correctional facilities, publicly operated nursing homes, and institutions for people with psychiatric or developmental disabilities. Its purpose is to allow the Attorney General to uncover and correct widespread deficiencies that seriously jeopardize the health and safety of residents of institutions. The Attorney General does not have authority under CRIPA to investigate isolated incidents or to represent individual institutionalized persons.

The Attorney General may initiate civil law suits where there is reasonable cause to believe that conditions are "egregious or flagrant," that they are subjecting residents to "grievous harm," and that they are part of a "pattern or practice" of resistance to residents' full enjoyment of constitutional or Federal rights, including title II of the ADA and section 504 of the Rehabilitation Act.

Individuals with Disabilities Education Act

The Individuals with Disabilities Education Act (IDEA) (formerly called P.L. 94-142 or the Education for all Handicapped Children Act of 1975) requires public schools to make available to all eligible children with disabilities a free appropriate public education in the least restrictive environment appropriate to their individual needs.

IDEA requires public school systems to develop appropriate Individualized Education Programs (IEPs) for each child. The specific special education and related services outlined in each IEP reflect the individualized needs of each student.

IDEA also mandates that particular procedures be followed in the development of the IEP. Each student's IEP must be developed by a team of knowledgeable persons and must be at least reviewed annually. The team includes the child's teacher; the parents, subject to certain limited exceptions; the child, if determined appropriate; an agency representative who is qualified to provide or supervise the provision of special education; and other individuals at the parents' or agency's discretion.

If parents disagree with the proposed IEP, they can request a due process hearing and a review from the State educational agency if applicable in that state. They also can appeal the State agency's decision to State or Federal court.

Rehabilitation Act

The Rehabilitation Act prohibits discrimination on the basis of disability in programs conducted by Federal agencies, in programs receiving Federal financial assistance, in Federal employment, and in the employment practices of Federal contractors. The standards for determining employment discrimination under the Rehabilitation Act are the same as those used in title I of the Americans with Disabilities Act.

Section 501

Section 501 requires affirmative action and nondiscrimination in employment by Federal agencies of the executive branch. To obtain more information or to file a complaint, employees should contact their agency's Equal Employment Opportunity Office.

Section 503

Section 503 requires affirmative action and prohibits employment discrimination by Federal government contractors and subcontractors with contracts of more than $10,000.

Section 504

Section 504 states that "no qualified individual with a disability in the United States shall be excluded from, denied the benefits of, or be subjected to discrimination under" any program or activity that either receives Federal financial assistance or is conducted by any Executive agency or the United States Postal Service.

Each Federal agency has its own set of section 504 regulations that apply to its own programs. Agencies that provide Federal financial assistance also have section 504 regulations covering entities that receive Federal aid. Requirements common to these regulations include reasonable accommodation for employees with disabilities; program accessibility; effective communication with people who have hearing or vision disabilities; and accessible new construction and alterations. Each agency is responsible for enforcing its own regulations. Section 504 may also be enforced through private lawsuits. It is not necessary to file a complaint with a Federal agency or to receive a "right-to-sue" letter before going to court.

Section 508

Section 508 establishes requirements for electronic and information technology developed, maintained, procured, or used by the Federal government. Section 508 requires Federal electronic and information technology to be accessible to people with disabilities, including employees and members of the public.

An accessible information technology system is one that can be operated in a variety of ways and does not rely on a single sense or ability of the user. For example, a system that provides output only in visual format may not be accessible to people with visual impairments and a system that provides output only in audio format may not be accessible to people who are deaf or hard of hearing. Some individuals with disabilities may need accessibility-related software or peripheral devices in order to use systems that comply with Section 508.

Architectural Barriers Act

The Architectural Barriers Act (ABA) requires that buildings and facilities that are designed, constructed, or altered with Federal funds, or leased by a Federal agency, comply with Federal standards for physical accessibility. ABA requirements are limited to architectural standards in new and altered buildings and in newly leased facilities. They do not address the activities conducted in those buildings and facilities. Facilities of the U.S. Postal Service are covered by the ABA.

* * *

Questions for Discussion

1. Which of these laws do you think are the most powerful for people with disabilities? Why?

2. Which laws in your state would supplement these laws?

3. What do you think of needing to get a "right to sue" letter? Why do you think this is a requirement?

_____

The following is a piece on "disability etiquette" for the media. It is written by the National Disability Rights Network and can be found at http://www.napas.org/en/media/disability-etiquette/435-words-matter.html.

Words Matter
The National Disability Rights Network

An important part of disability rights is using respectful language. The following list depicts phrases and terms that are generally considered appropriate, as well as terms and phrases to avoid using. Please keep in mind that language is constantly evolving and not everyone has the same preference, so the best guideline when referring to people is to *ASK*.

PREFERRED	AVOID
accessible parking/accommodations	handicapped accessible
children with disabilities	special children
individual without a disability	able-bodied; normal; whole
individual with a physical disability	crippled; handicapped; deformed; defective
individual with a spinal cord injury	quadriplegic; paraplegic; incapacitated
individual with multiple sclerosis (MS)	person who suffers from MS
individual who uses a wheelchair	wheelchair-bound/confined to a wheelchair
individual who is blind or has low vision	the blind
individual who is deaf or hard of hearing	the deaf; deaf and dumb; mute; hearing impaired
individual with burns	burn victim; disfigured
individual of short stature	dwarf or midget
individual who had a stroke	stroke victim/suffered from a stroke
individual with a cleft lip/cleft palate	hare lip
individual with a congenital disability	deformed/person with birth defect
individual with epilepsy or a seizure disorder	epileptic; spastic; person who has "fits" or "attacks"
individual living with HIV or AIDS	HIV or AIDS victim
individual with a learning disability	slow learner; retarded; stupid
individual with an intellectual disability	slow; retarded; dim-witted
individual with dyslexia	dyslexic
individual with a psychiatric disability or with a mental health diagnosis	crazy; maniac; lunatic; demented; schizo; psycho; feeble-minded

* * *

Questions for Discussion

1. Have you ever felt hesitant to address the issue of disability (either your own or someone else's) due to the awkwardness of language? What did you do?

2. Where have you seen or heard some of the outdated expressions listed above in the "avoid" column?

3. Can you think of other terms that could belong in the chart?

4. Do you think this terminology matters, or is it just political correctness taken too far?

5. In Joseph Shapiro's book *No Pity,* he talks about two stereotypes of disability: objects of pity and the supercrip/"inspirational disabled person." How do you think the media does at portraying disability? What recent examples have you seen of either of these stereotypes? His book also advocates the view that disability should be seen as

simply a difference and not something in need of a "cure." What do you think of this point of view?

———————

For Further Reading and Viewing

"Disability Rights Law: Roots, Present Challenges, and Future Collaborations," retrieved May 15, 2012 at http://www.dredf.org/publications/publications.shtml.

Check out www.thearc.org to learn about The Arc, the largest national community-based organization advocating for and serving people with intellectual and developmental disabilities and their families.

Check out www.nami.org to learn about the National Alliance on Mental Illness.

Check out www.adapt.org to learn about ADAPT.

"Disability rights protests bring Trafalgar Square traffic to a standstill," retrieved May 15, 2012 at http://www.guardian.co.uk/society/2012/apr/18/disability-benefits-cuts-protest-trafalgar-square?newsfeed=true. Wheelchair users chain themselves together to protest welfare cuts (includes video).

"China sentences disabled activist to more than two years in jail," CNN wire staff, retrieved May 15, 2012 at http://www.cnn.com/2012/04/10/world/asia/china-activist-sentence/index.html. A chilling reminder that disability rights are not universally accepted.

Read these two cases just for the purpose of contrasting the discourse used by the court: *Wolff v. South Colonie Central Sch. Dist.*, 534 F.Supp. 758 (N.D.N.Y. 1982) and *Coleman v. Zatechka*, 824 F. Supp. 1360 (D. Neb. 1993). Or, try these two: *Wyatt v. Stickney*, (found in chapter ___), and *Youngberg v. Romeo*, 457 U.S. 307 (1982). Or, these two, both found in chapter ___: *Hertz v. Arkay* and *Perkl v. CEC*.

"I Call Myself 'Survivor,'" retrieved May 15, 2012 at http://www.raggededgemagazine.com/departments/reflections/000652.html. A person with a physical disability suggests "survivor" as a better word than "disabled" or "handicapped."

Check out the "Campaign to "End the 'R' Word": http://www.r-word.org/.

"If People with Down Syndrome Ruled the World," retrieved May 15, 2012 at http://www.nads.org/pages_new/news/ruletheworld.html.

A National Geographic feature about having Down Syndrome: http://kids.nationalgeographic.com/kids/stories/peopleplaces/downsyndrome/, retrieved May 15, 2012.

"Bill O'Reilly discusses 'Family Guy' Eisode with Sarah Palin," retrieved May 15, 2012 at http://www.youtube.com/watch?v=KD5Dz7kPUtA.

"Barack Obama Special Olympics Insult," retrieved May 15, 2012 at http://www.youtube.com/watch?v=2HOBTUCv4o0.

Discussion 2

Personal Stories

Recommended Background Reading

Patrick Cooke, "A Genetic Test for Huntington's Let Colin MacAllister See His Future. And That's When His Free-Fall Began." Health Magazine, Vol. 7 No. 4, July 1993, p. 80.

Tammet, Daniel. *Born on a Blue Day: Inside the Extraordinary Mind of an Autistic Savant.* New York: Simon & Schuster, 2006; "A Look at an Autistic Savant's Brilliant Mind," NPR Interview of Daniel Tammet, retrieved May 15, 2012 at http://www.npr.org/templates/story/story.php?storyId=6860157.

Tan, Amy. *The Opposite of Fate.* Excerpt retrieved May 15, 2012 at http://amytan.net/, called "Lyme Disease."

Readings for Class Discussion

The following is a chapter from Harriet McBryde Johnson's book *Too Late to Die Young.* Ms. Johnson was a civil rights attorney and disability activist for many years, and passed away in 2008.

Unspeakable Conversations
Harriet McBryde Johnson

He insists he doesn't want to kill me. He simply thinks it would have been better, all things considered, to have given my parents the option of killing the baby I once was, and to let other parents kill similar babies as they come along and thereby avoid the suffering that comes with lives like mine and satisfy the reasonable preferences of parents for a different kind of child. It has nothing to do with me. I should not feel threatened.

Whenever I try to wrap my head around his tight string of syllogisms, my brain gets so fried it's ... almost fun. Mercy! It's like "Alice in Wonderland." Now, having leapt down the rabbit hole and landed in this place, I find things becoming curiouser and curiouser.

It is a chilly Monday in late March 2002. I'm at Princeton University. My host is Professor Peter Singer, often called—and not only by his book publicist—the most influential philosopher of our time. He's the man who wants me dead. No, not me. Babies who might come to be like me if allowed to live. He also believes that in some circumstances it should be lawful to kill, at any age, individuals with cognitive impairments so severe that he doesn't consider them "persons." What does it take to be a person? Awareness of one's own existence in time. The capacity to harbor preferences as to the future, including the preference for continuing to live.

At this stage of my life, he says, I am a person. However, as an infant, I wasn't. I, like all infants, was born without self-awareness. And eventually, assuming my brain finally gets so fried that I fall into that wonderland where self and other and present and past and future blur into one boundless, formless all or nothing, then I'll lose my personhood and therefore my right to life. Then, he says, I might be put out of my misery, or out of my bliss or oblivion, and no one count it murder.

I am the token cripple with an opposing view.

My reasons for accepting Singer's invitation are both political and personal. Politically, I see a rare opportunity to experiment with modes of discourse that might work with very tough audiences. Personally, I expect to get a great story, first for telling and then for writing down.

By now I've told the story to family and friends and colleagues on long car trips, over lunches and dinners, and in a couple of formal speeches. But it proves to be a story that won't settle down. It lacks structure; I'm miles away from a rational argument. The telling keeps getting interrupted by questions, like these, frequently asked:

Q: Was he totally grossed out by your physical appearance?

A: He gave no sign of it. None whatsoever.

Q: How did he handle having to interact with someone like you?

A: He behaved in every way appropriately, treated me as a respected professional acquaintance, was a gracious and accommodating host.

Q: Was it emotionally difficult for you to take part in a public discussion of whether your life should ever have happened?

A: It was very difficult. And horribly easy.

Q: Did he get that job at Princeton because they like his ideas on killing disabled babies?

A: Those ideas apparently didn't hurt, but he's most famous for animal rights. He's the author of *Animal Liberation*.

Q: How can he put so much value on animal life and so little value on human life?

That last question is the only one I avoid. I used to say, I don't know; it doesn't make sense. But now I've read some of Singer's writing, and I admit it does make sense — within the conceptual world of Peter Singer. But I don't want to go there, or at least not for long. It's only a place to visit.

I first meet singer in April 2001, when he is invited to the College of Charleston, not two blocks from my house, to lecture on "Rethinking Life and Death." I am dispatched by Not Dead Yet, the national organization that is leading the disability-rights opposition to legalized assisted suicide and disability-based killing.

I arrive almost an hour early to reconnoiter, to take in the scene as the scene is forming. I mark key locations: security, media. The scene is entirely peaceful; even the boisterous display of South Carolina spring is muted by gray wisps of Spanish moss and mottled oak bark.

I roll around the corner of the building and am confronted with the unnerving sight of two people I know sitting on a park bench eating veggie pitas with Singer. Sharon is a veteran activist for human rights. Herb is South Carolina's most famous atheist. Good people, I've always thought—now sharing veggie pitas and conversation with a proponent of genocide. I try to beat a retreat, but Herb and Sharon have seen me. Sharon gets up, tosses her trash, and comes over. After we exchange the usual courtesies, she asks, "Would you like to meet Professor Singer?"

She clearly doesn't have a clue. She probably likes his book on animal rights. "I'll talk to him in the Q & A."

But Herb, with Singer at his side, is fast approaching. They are looking at me and Herb is talking, no doubt saying nice things about me. He'll be saying that I gave a talk against assisted suicide at his secular humanist group a while back. He didn't agree with everything I said, he'll say, but I was brilliant. Singer appears interested, engaged. I sit where I'm parked. Herb makes an introduction. Singer extends his hand.

I hesitate. I shouldn't shake hands with the Evil One. But he is Herb's guest, and I simply can't snub Herb's guest at the college where Herb teaches. Hereabouts the rule is that if you're not prepared to shoot on sight, you have to be prepared to shake hands. I give Singer the three fingers on my right hand that still work. "Good afternoon, Mr. Singer. I'm here for Not Dead Yet."

I want to think he flinches just a little. Not Dead Yet disrupted his first week at Princeton University. I sent a check to the fund for the fourteen arrestees, who included comrades in power chairs. But if Singer flinches, he instantly recovers. He answers my questions about the lecture format. When he says he looks forward to an interesting exchange, he seems entirely sincere. What stands out in memory about that first meeting is Singer's apparent immunity to my looks, his lack of the visual discombobulation I expect, his immediate ability to deal with me as a person with a particular point of view.

I go into the hall with no plan. The flyer from Not Dead Yet has twenty good talking points, but they're secondhand. I know the people who wrote the flyer; they are scrupulously careful with their analysis. But if Singer claims he's been quoted out of context, I won't have much of a comeback. If he asks me which of his books or articles I've read in full, I'm in trouble. I'll have to say none. I need to glean something from the lecture itself, maybe some glint of disability prejudice, some whiff of the outrageous, that I can weave into the kind of withering cross-examination that happens in real life only when you're very lucky—and very well-prepared.

Singer makes it easy. He lays everything out. The basic assumptions of "Preference Utilitarianism." The illogic of allowing abortion but not infanticide, of allowing withdrawal of life support but not active killing. He weighs utilities [as] he spins out his bone-chilling argument for killing disabled babies and replacing them with nondisabled babies who have a greater chance at happiness. It's all about allowing as many people to fulfill as many of their preferences as possible.

As soon as he's done, I get the microphone. As a practicing lawyer, I disagree with his jurisprudential assumptions. Illogic is not a sufficient reason to change the law; law serves many competing needs an[d] interests. As an atheist, I object to his using religious terms ("the doctrine of the sanctity of human life") to characterize his critics. Singer takes a notepad out of his pocket and jots down my points, apparently eager to take them on, and I proceed to what I see as the heart of my argument: that the presence or absence of a disability doesn't predict quality of life. I question his replacement-baby theory, with its assumption of "other things equal," arguing that people are not fungible. I draw out a comparison of myself and my nondisabled brother Mac (the next-born after me), each of us with a combination of gifts and flaws so peculiar that we can't be measured on the same scale.

He responds to each point with clear and lucid counterarguments. He proceeds with the assumption that I am one of the people who might reasonably have been killed at birth. He sticks to his guns, conceding just enough to show himself open-minded and flexible. We go back and forth for ten long minutes. Even as I am horrified by what he says, and by the fact that I have been sucked into a civil discussion of whether I ought to exist, I can't help being dazzled by his verbal facility. He is so respectful, so free of condescension, so focused on the argument, that by the time the show is over, I'm not exactly angry with him. Yes, I am shaking, furious, enraged—but it's with the big room, two hundred of my fellow Charlestonians who have listened with polite interest, when in decency they should have run him out of town on a rail.

By the following December, a lot has happened—including September 11 and my fall from my chair—but my Sunday afternoon chat with Peter Singer still merits a bullet point in my annual canned December letter. But that causes a dilemma. It is part of my personal honor code that anyone mentioned by name in my canned letter gets a copy. The only exception is Jerry Lewis; I am sure Lewis wouldn't want to hear from me. Should the exception extend to Singer? I decide not. I write a brief note on a beautiful card that is entirely free of religion, and put it on the stack to mail.

In mid-January, I get the nicest possible e-mail from Singer. "Dear Harriet (if I may)." Just back from Australia, where he's from. Glad to hear from me. Hopes I've fully recovered from my fall. Agrees with my comments on the world situation. Supports my work against institutionalization. And then—some pointed questions to clarify my views on selective infanticide.

I reply. Fine, call me Harriet, and I'll reciprocate in the interest of equality, though I'm accustomed to more formality. Skipping agreeable preambles, I answer his questions on disability-based infanticide and pose some of my own. Answers, and more questions come back. Back and forth over several weeks it proceeds, an engaging discussion of baby killing, disability prejudice, and related points of law and philosophy. Dear Harriet. Dear Peter.

Singer wants to understand how someone who is not a religious fanatic—who is, indeed, as good an atheist as he is—could disagree with his entirely reasonable views. At the same time, I'm trying to plumb his theories. What has him so convinced it would be best to allow parents to kill babies with severe disabilities, and not other kinds of babies, if no infant is a "person" with a right to life? I learn it's partly that both biological and adoptive parents prefer healthy babies. But I have trouble with basing life-and-death decisions on market considerations when the market is structured by prejudice. I offer a comparison hypothetical: "What about mixed-race babies, especially when the combination is entirely nonwhite, who I believe are just about as unadoptable as babies with disabilities?" Wouldn't a law allowing the killing of these undervalued babies validate race prejudice? Singer agrees there is a problem. "It would be horrible," he says, "to see mixed-race babies being killed because they can't be adopted, whereas white ones could be." What's the difference? Preferences based on race are unreasonable. Preferences based on ability are not. Why? To Singer, it's pretty simple: disability makes a person "worse off."

Are we "worse off"? I don't think so. Not in any meaningful sense. There are too many variables. For those of us with congenital conditions, disability shapes all we are. Those disabled later in life adapt. We take constraints that no one would choose and build rich and satisfying lives within them. We enjoy pleasures other people enjoy, and pleasures peculiarly our own. We have something the world needs.

Pressing me to admit a negative correlation between disability and happiness, Singer presents a scenario: imagine a disabled child on the beach, watching the other children play.

It's right out of the telethon. I expected something more sophisticated from a professional thinker. I respond. "As a little girl playing on the beach, I was already aware that some people felt sorry for me, that I wasn't frolicking with the same level of frenzy as other children. This annoyed me, and still does." I take the time to write a detailed description of how I, in fact, had fun playing on the beach, without the need of standing, walking or running. But, I've had enough. I suggest that we have exhausted our topic and I'll be back in touch when I get around to writing about him.

He responds by inviting me to Princeton. I fire off an immediate maybe.

Of course I'm flattered. Mama will be impressed. But there are things to consider. Not Dead Yet has declared—and I completely agree—that Singer's views are so far beyond the pale that we should not legitimate them with a forum. We should not make our own lives subject to debate. Moreover, any spokesman chosen by the opposition is by definition a token, not my favorite role. Yet I'm thinking about it. Even if I'm a token, I won't have to act like one. Also, I'm kind of stuck. If I decline, Singer can make some hay: "I offered them a platform, but they refuse rational discussion." I've laid myself wide open.

Singer proposes two exchanges of views, one during his 10 A.M. undergraduate course on practical ethics and the other open to the whole university, later in the day. This sounds a lot like debating my right to exist—and on my opponent's turf, with my opponent moderating, to boot. I offer a counterproposal, to which Singer proves amenable. I will open the class with some comments on infanticide and related issues and then let Singer grill me as hard as he likes before we open it up for the students. Later in the day, I might take part in a discussion of some other disability issue in a neutral forum. Singer suggests a faculty-student discussion group sponsored by his department but with cross-departmental membership. The topic I select is "Assisted Suicide, Disability Discrimination and the Illusion of Choice: A Disability Rights Perspective." I inform a few movement colleagues of this turn of events, and advice starts rolling in. I decide to go with the advisers who counsel me to do the gig, lie low and get out of Dodge.

I ask Singer to refer me to the person who arranges travel at Princeton. I imagine some capable and unflappable woman like my sister, Beth, whose varied job description at a state university includes handling visiting artists. Singer refers me to his own assistant, who certainly seems capable enough. However, almost immediately Singer jumps back in via e-mail. It seems the nearest hotel has only one wheelchair-accessible double room, a suite that rents for $600 per night. What to do? I know I shouldn't be so accommodating, but I say I can make do with an inaccessible room if it has certain features. Other logistical issues come up. We go back and forth. Questions and answers. Do I really need a lift-equipped vehicle at the airport? Can't my assistant assist me into a conventional car?

By the time we're done, Singer knows I'm twenty-eight inches wide and don't fold up. I have trouble controlling my wheelchair if my hand gets cold. I can swallow purees, soft bread and grapes. I use a bedpan, not a toilet. None of this is a secret; none of it cause for particular angst, but I wonder whether Singer is jotting down my specs in his little notepad, as evidence of how "bad off" people like me really are.

At some point, I realize I must put one more issue on the table: etiquette. I was criticized within the movement when I confessed to shaking Singer's hand in Charleston, and some are appalled that I have agreed to break bread with him in Princeton. I think they have a very good point, but, again, I'm stuck. I'm engaged for a day of discussion, not a picket line. It's not in my power to marginalize Singer at Princeton; nothing would be accomplished by displays of personal disrespect. However, chumminess is clearly inappropriate. I tell Singer that in the lecture hall it can't be Harriet and Peter; it must be Ms. Johnson and Mr. Singer.

He seems genuinely nettled. Shouldn't it be Ms. Johnson and Professor Singer, if I want to be formal? To counter, I invoke the ceremonial Lowcountry usage, Attorney Johnson and Professor Singer, but point out that Mr./Ms. is the custom in American political debates and might seem more normal in New Jersey. All right, he says. Ms./Mr. it will be.

At the office, I describe this awkward social situation to Tim. He gives forth a full-body shudder. "That poor, sorry son of a b****! He has no idea what he's in for."

I feel like saying, Forget about Singer—I'm not headed into a forensic competition; I want to win hearts and minds, to connect with at least a student or two. But instead I accept a kind offer of solidarity. The Charleston bar takes pride in going for the jugular with courtly manners. I'm almost ready to go.

Being a disability rights lawyer lecturing at Princeton does confer some cachet at the Newark airport. I need all the cachet I can get. Delta Airlines has torn up my power chair. Again.

When they inform me of the damage in Atlanta, I throw a monumental fit and demand that a repair person meet me in Newark with new batteries to replace the ones inexplicably destroyed. Then I am told no new batteries can be had until the morning. It's Sunday night. On arrival in Newark, I'm told of a plan to put me up there for the night and get me repaired and driven to Princeton by ten a.m.

"That won't work. I'm lecturing at ten. I need to get there tonight, go to sleep, and be in my right mind tomorrow."

"What? You're lecturing? They told us it was a conference. We need to get you fixed tonight!"

Carla the gate agent relieves me of the need to throw any further fits by undertaking on my behalf the fit of all fits. "Don't tell me," she shouts into a cell phone, "that you don't know somebody who knows somebody who has a key to a store where they sell batteries. Get somebody to get somebody to open up a store and sell you those batteries and get over here! She's lecturing at Princeton at ten in the morning and we got to get her there tonight!"

Soon there is a promise of batteries tonight, and I'm beginning to be charmed by the shouting manners of Newark. Carla barks an order to Princeton's lift-equipped contract driver to wait and provides food vouchers, phone car[d]s, and the pass to the VIP lounge.

Carmen, the personal assistant I'm traveling with, pushes me in my disabled chair around the airport in search of a place to use the bedpan. However, instead of diaper-changing tables, which are functional though far from private, we find a flip-down plastic shelf that doesn't look like it would hold my 70 pounds of body weight. It's no big deal; I've restricted my fluids. But Carmen is a little freaked. It is her first adventure in power-chair air travel. I thought I prepared her for the trip, but I guess I neglected to warn her about the probability of wheelchair destruction. I keep forgetting that even people who know me well don't know much about my world.

We reach the hotel at ten-fifteen p.m., four hours late at the end of a very long day.

I wake up tired. I slept better than I would have slept in Newark with an unrepaired chair, but any hotel bed is a near guarantee of morning crankiness. I tell Carmen to leave the TV off because I don't want to hear the temperature. Whatever it is, it's bound to fill me with dread. I hate to be cold.

With the help of Carmen's hands, I do the morning stretch. I let myself be propped up to eat oatmeal and drink tea. Then there's the bedpan and then bathing and dressing, still in bed. As the caffeine kicks in, silence gives way to conversation about practical things. Carmen lifts me into my chair and straps a rolled towel under my ribs for comfort and stability and to placate my shoulder, which has been creaky since Tucson. She tugs at my clothes to remove wrinkles that could cause pressure sores. She switches on my motors and gives me the means of moving without anyone's help. They don't call it a power chair for nothing.

I drive to the mirror. I undo yesterday's braid, fix the part and comb the hair in front. Carmen combs where I can't reach. I divide the mass into three long hanks and start the braid behind my left ear. Section by section, I hand it over to her, and her unimpaired young fingers pull tight, crisscross, until the braid is fully formed. She binds the end with a rubber band and lets it fall past my knees. She hands me my earrings and I poke the wires in.

A big polyester scarf completes my costume. Carmen lays it over my back. I tie it the way I want it, but Carmen starts fussing with it, trying to tuck it down in the back. I tell her that it's fine and she stops.

On top of the scarf, she wraps the two big shawls that I hope will substitute for an overcoat. I don't own any real winter clothes. I stay out of the cold, such cold as we get in Charleston.

We review her instructions for the day. Keep me in view and earshot. Be instantly available but not intrusive. Be polite, but don't answer any questions about me. I'm glad that she has agreed to come. She's strong, smart, adaptable and very loyal. But now she's digging under the shawls, fussing with that scarf again.

"Carmen. What are you doing?"

"I thought I could hide this furry thing you sit on."

"Leave it," I say firmly. "Singer knows lots of people eat meat. Now he'll know some crips sit on sheepskin."

The walk is cold but mercifully short. The hotel is across the street from Princeton's wrought-iron gate and a few blocks from the building where Singer's assistant shows us to the elevator. The elevator doubles as the janitor's closet — the cart with the big trash can and all the accoutrements is rolled aside so I can get in. Evidently there aren't many wheelchair users in this building.

We ride the broom closet down to the basement. We are led down a long passageway to a door that admits us into the well of a big lecture hall. As students drift in, I engage in light badinage with the sound technician. My brother Mac complains about people who act cute when they're being miked, so I always do it, to tweak him by proxy. My cute little prima donna act is natural enough. "Get that lectern away! It might make me look small!" The cordless lavaliere is my mike of choice. The technician is squeamish about touching me; I invite him to clip the mike to the big polyester scarf.

The students enter from the rear door, way up at ground level, and walk down stairs to their seats. By the time the hall is full, I feel like an animal in the zoo. In a way, I can't complain; unlike the zoo residents, I've voluntarily agreed to be displayed as a pedagogical tool. But I didn't reckon on the architecture, those tiers of steps that separate me from a human wall of apparent physical and mental perfection and keep me confined down here in my pit.

It's five minutes before ten. Singer is loping down the stairs. I feel like signaling to Carmen to open the door, summon the broom closet and get me out of here. But Singer greets me pleasantly and hands me Princeton's check for $500, the fee he offered with apologies for its inadequacy.

So. On with the show.

My talk to the students is pretty Southern. I've decided to pound them with heart, hammer them with narrative, and say "y'all" and "folks." I give them peaks and valleys and play with the emotional tone, modulating three times in one forty-five-second patch. I talk about justice and even beauty and love. I figure they haven't been getting that kind of talk from Singer.

Of course, I give them some argument too. I mean to honor my contractual obligations. I lead with the hypothetical about mixed-race nonwhite babies and build the ending around the question of who should have the burden of proof as to the quality of disabled lives. Woven throughout the talk is the presentation of myself as a representative of a minority group that has been rendered invisible by prejudice and oppression, a participant in a discussion that would not occur in a just world.

I let it go longer than I should; their faces show they're going where I'm leading, and I don't look forward to letting them go. But the clock on the wall behind me reminds me of promises I mean to keep, and I stop talking and submit myself to examination and inquiry.

Singer's response is surprisingly soft; maybe after hearing that this discussion is insulting and painful to me, he doesn't want to exacerbate my discomfort. His reframing of the issues is almost pro forma, abstract, entirely impersonal. The students' inquiries are abstract and fairly predictable: anencephaly, permanent unconsciousness, eugenic abortion. I respond to some of them with stories, but mostly I give answers I could have e-mailed in.

I call on a young man near the top of the room.

"Do you eat meat?"

"Yes, I do."

"Then how do you justify—"

"I haven't made any study of animal rights, so anything I could say on the subject wouldn't be worth everyone's time."

The next student wants to work the comparison of disability and race, and Singer joins the discussion until he elicits a comment from me that he can characterize as racist. He scores a point, but that's all right. I've never claimed to be free of prejudice, just struggling against it.

When the class ends, Singer proposes taking me on a walk around campus, unless I think it would be too cold. What the hell? "It's probably warmed up some. Let's go out and see how I do."

He doesn't know how to get out of the building without using the stairs, so this time it's my assistant leading the way. When we get out of the building, Carmen falls behind a couple of paces, like a respectful chaperone, and Singer and I continue the conversation.

In the classroom there was a question about keeping alive the unconscious. In response, I told a story about a family I knew as a child who took loving care of a nonresponsive teenage girl, acting out their unconditional commitment to each other, making all the other children, and me as their visitor, feel safe. This doesn't satisfy Singer. "Let's assume we can prove, absolutely, that the individual is totally unconscious and that we can know, absolutely, that the individual will never regain consciousness."

I see no need to state an objection, with no stenographer present to record it; I'll play the game and let him continue.

"Assuming all that," he says, "don't you think continuing to take care of that individual would be a bit—weird?"

"No, done right, it could be profoundly beautiful."

"But what about the caregiver, a woman typically, who is forced to provide all this service to a family member, unable to work, unable to have a life of her own?"

"That's not the way it should be. Not the way it has to be. As a society we should pay workers to provide that care in the home. In some places, it's been done that way for years. That woman shouldn't be forced to do it, any more than my family should be forced to do my care."

Singer takes me around the architectural smorgasbord that is Princeton University by a route that includes not one step, unramped curb or turn on a slope. In the distance, through an archway, I see what look like acres of colonnaded steps featured in the recent film, *A Beautiful Mind*. I cringe to think how this pleasant walk would look on film, perhaps in some flattering documentary about Singer; I can almost hear the voice-over, explaining that the docile American disability rights movement respects Singer's ideas, unlike the uncivilized rabble who ran him out of Germany a few years ago. Before I came, Singer asked about videotaping the class for an Australian filmmaker; I declined but didn't think to say no to photos generally. Would Carmen have the presence of mind to block the shot? I don't know. But I'm not worried. Within the strange limits of this strange assignment, it seems Singer is doing all he can to make me comfortable.

He asks what I thought of the students' questions.

"They were fine, about what I expected. I was a little surprised by the question about meat eating."

"I apologize for that. That was out of left field."

"It's all right. I should have expected it."

"No, it wasn't your topic. But—I think what he wanted to know is how you can have such high respect for human life and so little respect for animal life."

"I'm sure that is what he wanted to know. People have lately been asking me the converse, how you can have so much respect for animal life and so little respect for human life."

"And what do you answer?"

"I say I don't know. It doesn't make a lot of sense to me."

"Well, in my view—"

"Look. I have lived in blissful ignorance all these years, and I'm not prepared to give that up today."

"Fair enough," he says and proceeds to recount bits of Princeton history. He stops. "This will be of particular interest to you, I think. This is where your colleagues with Not

Dead Yet set up their blockade." I'm grateful for the reminder. My brothers and sisters were here before me and behaved far more appropriately than I am doing.

Aaron, the coorganizer of the National Lawyers Guild Disability Rights Committee, has come by train from New York. At noon, we meet in the hotel lobby and go with Carmen to a restaurant nearby—my driving hand did get pretty frozen during the morning stroll. He asks about the morning class.

"It went fine, I suppose. They liked the talk, but I keep thinking of better things I could have said in the Q&A. I was tired."

Aaron assures me I was great, with all that confidence lawyers so effectively convey when we have no knowledge of the facts. "I'm looking forward to seeing you take on the ghoul tonight."

"It's not like that. We are monstrously civil. And you need to fall in with the program and be civil, too." I hear an unpleasant stridency in my voice. I've invited a card-carrying lunatic into a delicate situation and now I wonder if I should have.

Our conversation turns to other topics. Our committee business. Our work. Fees we're hoping to collect any minute now. How cool that "A Beautiful Mind," with its unstereotypical view of genius-in-madness, got the Academy Award. Our states' compliance—or non-compliance—with *Olmstead*'s civil rights challenge to disability institutions. I'm feeling better. Normally Aaron's big-city world seems far away from my life in a place that tourists call quaint. Here at Princeton University, Aaron seems like an old friend from my hometown: a place called Reality.

Heading back, Carmen and I tell Aaron about an interesting sign we've seen [at] the hotel. We decide to check it out. I roll up to the front desk, "tell me about the Christopher Reeve suite."

We learn that the actor has family in the area and often spends time at Princeton. After his injury, the hotel combined three rooms into one suite that is fully accessible. I ask if we can see it, and they give us the key.

There are two bedrooms, one with a king, one with two double beds. A sitting room with a Murphy bed, a dining area, a couch, chairs, and noncontroversial art books on the coffee table. A large ADA-compliant bathroom. I roll into the shower so I can say I've been in Christopher Reeve's shower. I invite Aaron to join me so I can say I've been in Christopher Reeve's shower with Aaron. Carmen pulls out a camera.

"Wait a second," Aaron says. He tidies his jacket and takes off his hat. "OK!"

A van delivers Carmen and me to the evening forum about an hour early. Singer comes down from his office with a manilla envelope, "some reading material that may be of interest." He drops it in the floppy bag that hangs on the back of my chair. He hopes I had a pleasant afternoon.

Yes, indeed. I report a pleasant lunch and a very pleasant nap and tell him about the Christopher Reeve Suite in the hotel.

"Do you suppose that's the six-hundred-dollar accessible suite they told me about?"

"Without doubt. And if I'd known it was the Christopher Reeve Suite, I would have held out for it."

"Of course you would have!" Singer laughs. "And we'd have had no choice, would we?"

I give him the short version of what it was like to be on the floor when Reeve spoke to the Democratic convention, and we talk about image and ritual in American politics, about Bill Clinton and the crew now in charge. Singer is easy to talk to, very good company. Such a pity that he regards lives like mine as avoidable mistakes.

The others arrive. I find I'm looking forward to the soft vegetarian meal that has been arranged; I'm hungry. Assisted suicide, as difficult as it is, doesn't cause the kind of agony I felt discussing disability-based infanticide. In this one, I understand and to some degree can sympathize with the opposing point of view—misguided though it is.

There are some awkward minutes when Aaron somehow sets off a frightening security alarm, but soon we settle into the conventions of an academic discussion. My opening sticks to the five-minute time limit. I introduce the issue as framed by academic articles Not Dead Yet recommended for my use. Law Professor Andrew Batavia argues for assisted suicide based on autonomy, a principle generally held high in the disability rights movement. He says that if we need assistance to effectuate our choices, we are entitled to that assistance, even if the choice is suicide. But Carol Gill says it's disability discrimination to try to prevent most suicides while facilitating the suicides of ill and disabled people. She asks whether such discrimination is justified and makes a case from the empirical evidence that it is not. The case for assisted suicide rests on stereotypes that our lives are inherently so bad that it is entirely rational if we want to die.

In the discussion that follows, I argue that choice is illusory in a context of pervasive inequality. Choices are structured by oppression. We shouldn't offer assistance with suicide until we all have the assistance we need to get out of bed in the morning and live a good life. Common causes of suicidality—dependence, institutional confinement, being a burden—are entirely curable. I tell them about the Olmstead Supreme Court decision that declared unwanted, unneeded institutional confinement a form of illegal segregation. It is unknown to everyone in the room except Aaron and Carmen.

Singer, seated on my right, participates in the discussion but doesn't dominate it. During the meal, I occasionally ask him to put things within my reach, and he competently complies.

I feel like I'm getting to a few of them when a student asks me a question. The words are all familiar, but they're strung together in a way so meaningless that I can't even retain them—it's like a long sentence in Tagalog. I can only admit my limitations. "That question's too abstract for me to deal with. Can you rephrase it?"

He indicates that it is as clear as he can make it, so I move on.

A little while later, my right elbow slips out from under me. This is awkward. Carmen is opposite me; to make the necessary adjustment, she'd need to stand up, walk around the table, and interrupt the flow of talk. Normally I get whoever is on my right to do this sort of thing. Why not now? I gesture to Singer. He leans over, and I whisper. "Grasp this wrist and pull forward one inch, without lifting." He looks a little surprised but follows my instructions to the letter. He sees that now I can again reach my food with my fork. And he may now understand what I was saying a minute ago, that most of the assistance disabled people need does not demand medical training.

A philosophy professor says, "It appears that your objections to assisted suicide are essentially tactical."

"Excuse me?"

"By that I mean they are grounded in current conditions of political, social and economic inequality."

"Exactly."

"What if we assume that such conditions do not exist?"

"Why would we want to do that?"

"I want to get to the real basis for the position you take."

"The real basis is that we're talking about making laws. Laws are made for societies. All societies have political, social, and economic conditions. Laws must be made with reference to those conditions. I don't see the point in assuming their nonexistence."

A few of the students seem to like this, but mostly I feel like I'm losing caste. It is becoming very clear that I'm not a philosopher. I'm like one of those old practitioners who used to visit my law school and bluster about life in the real world. Such a bore! A once-sharp mind gone muddy! That's how I regarded them then, but now I don't mind knowing I'm one of them. I've been changed by my years in the trenches.

The forum is ended and I've been able to eat very little of my pureed food. I ask Carmen to find the caterer and get me a container. Singer jumps up to take care of it. He returns with a box and obligingly packs my food to go.

In the hotel room, I ask Carmen to check out the reading material Singer dropped in my bag. It's a copy of Writings on an Ethical Life, varied selections from his previously published work. The cover photo is startling. His disembodied head is encased in a graphic black bubble. His face is lit from beneath, a cinematographer's cliché for the spooky. I wonder if Singer, apparently as oblivious to visual image as I am image-conscious, has noticed that his publisher is trading on the public perception that he is, to use Aaron's term, a ghoul.

On the flyleaf, Singer has written, "For Harriet Johnson, So that you will have better answers to questions about animals. And thanks for coming to Princeton. Peter Singer. March 25, 2002."

Under the crazy circumstances, I think the inscription is entirely appropriate.

When I get home, people are clamoring for the story. The lawyers want the blow-by-blow of my forensic triumph over the formidable foe; when I tell them it wasn't like that, they insist that it was. Within the disability rights community, the reaction is more tentative. It is generally assumed that I handled the substantive discussion well, but people worry that my civility may have given Singer a new kind of legitimacy. They're relieved that there were no photos and no press, but somewhat nervous when I say that one day I expect to write about the experience.

There is welcomed solidarity. I wouldn't have done it, says one comrade, but I'm glad you did. Thanks for putting your persona on the line. An elderly gent who tends to be a bit flirtatious, inquires, "Was your date with the professor consummated?" I reply, "Yes, if your definition of consummation includes civil academic discourse, pleasant strolling, and letting one's date pack one's doggie bag."

With others I can't be so flip. I hear from my movement sister Laura in Denver, who has written insightfully about power relationships and caregiving. She is appalled that I let Singer provide even minor physical assistance at the dinner. How could I put myself in a relationship with Singer that made him appear so human, even kind?

I struggle to explain. I didn't feel disempowered; quite the contrary, it seemed a good thing to make him do some useful work. And then, the hard part: I've come to believe that Singer actually is human, even kind in his way. The prejudice he represents isn't limited to monsters and ghouls. There ensues a discussion of good and evil and personal assistance and power and philosophy and tactics for which I'm profoundly grateful.

I e-mail Laura again. This time I inform her that I've changed my will—she'll get the book Singer gave me, with its peculiar inscription. "It will make a fine addition to your collection of books on disability, or nice fuel for a bonfire—whichever you prefer." She responds that she is changing her will, too. I'll get the autographed photo of Jerry Lewis she received as an M.D.A. poster child. We joke that each of us has given the other a "reason to live."

I have had a nice e-mail message from Singer, hoping Carmen and I and the chair got home without injury, relaying positive feedback from my audiences—and taking me to task for a statement that isn't supported by a relevant legal authority, which he looked up. I report that we got home exhausted but unharmed and concede that he has caught me in a generalization that should have been qualified. It's clear that the conversation will continue.

I am sucked into the daily demands of law practice, family, community and politics. In the closing days of the state legislative session, I help get a bill passed that I hope will move us one small step toward a world in which killing won't be such an appealing solution to the "problem" of disability. It is good to focus on this kind of work. But the conversations with and about Singer continue. Unable to muster the appropriate moral judgments, I ask myself a tough question: Am I in fact a silly little lady whose head is easily turned by a man who gives her a kind of attention she enjoys? I ask Laura, but in somewhat different terms: "Do you think I've been taken in by a sure-enough sociopath?"

"I don't think so," she answers, "but I wonder if your Southern politeness has dulled your righteous anger."

I have to confess—something about Laura draws me toward confession—that I can't seem to sustain righteous anger for more than about thirty minutes at a time. My view of life tends more toward tragedy.

The tragic view comes closest to describing how I now look at Peter Singer. He is a man of unusual gifts, reaching for the heights. As he has written, he wants a system of ethics derived from fact and reason, that largely throws off the perspectives of religion, place, family, tribe, community, maybe even species—to assume "the point of view of the universe." His is a grand, heroic undertaking.

But like the protagonist in a classical drama, Singer has his flaw, that unexamined prejudice—that all-too-common belief that disabled people are inherently "worse off," that we "suffer," that we have a ["]lesser chance of happiness." Because of this prejudice, and his rare courage in taking it to its logical conclusion, catastrophe looms. Here in the midpoint of the play, I can't look at him without fellow-feeling.

I am regularly confronted by people who tell me that Singer doesn't deserve my human sympathy. I should take the role of Nemesis and make him an object to be cut off, silenced, destroyed absolutely. And I find myself lacking a logical argument to the contrary.

I am talking to my sister Beth on the phone and Singer's name comes up. "You kind of like the monster, don't you?"

I find myself unable to evade, certainly unwilling to lie. "Yeah, in a way. And he's not exactly a monster."

"You know, Harriet, there were some very pleasant Nazis. They say the SS guards went home and played on the rug with their children every night."

"I suppose that's true."

Her harshness has come as a surprise. She isn't inclined to moralizing; in our family, I'm the one who always sets people straight. She can tell that I'm chastened; she changes the topic, lets me off the hook.

When I put the phone down, my argumentative nature feels frustrated. In my mind, I replay the conversation, but this time defend my position.

"He's not exactly a monster."

"He's advocating genocide."

"That's the thing. In his mind, he isn't. He thinks the humans he is talking about aren't people, aren't 'persons.'"

"But that's the way it always works, isn't it? Objects, not persons. He's repackaging some old ideas. Making them acceptable."

"I think his ideas are new, in a way. It's not old-fashioned hate. It's a twisted, misinformed, warped kind of beneficence. His motive is to do good."

"What do you care about motives?" she asks. "Doesn't this beneficent killing make your disabled brothers and sisters just as dead?"

"But he isn't killing anyone. It's just talk."

"Just talk? It's talk aimed at policy and law. Talk that's getting a receptive audience. You of all people know the power of that kind of talk."

"Well, sure, but—"

"If talk didn't matter, would you make it your life's work?"

"But," I say, "his talk won't matter in the end. He won't succeed in reinventing morality. He stirs the pot, brings things out into the open. But my side will win out. We'll make a world that's fit to live in, a society that has room for all its flawed creatures. If Singer is remembered by history, it will be as a curious example of the bizarre things that can happen when paradigms collide."

"What if you're wrong?"

"I'm not."

"But what if? Assume, arguendo—"

"Since when do you say arguendo?"

"Assume," she continues, "he convinces people that there's no morally significant difference between a fetus and a newborn, and just as disabled fetuses are routinely aborted now, so disabled babies are routinely killed. Assume, further, that some future decade takes it further than Singer wants to go. Might some say there's no morally significant line between a newborn and a 3-year-old?"

"Sure. Singer concedes that a bright line cannot be drawn. But he doesn't propose killing anyone who prefers to live."

"Ah, yes," she says, "that overarching respect for the individual's preference for life. Do you really think it holds up? Isn't it a bit naïve?"

"Yes. I'd call it a fiction or a quasi-religious belief. I think, logically, once you kill someone all preferences are moot."

"So what if you can't break disability prejudice? What if you wind up in a world where the disabled person's 'irrational' preference to live must yield to society's 'rational' interest in reducing the incidence of disability? Doesn't horror kick in somewhere? Maybe as you watch the door close behind whoever has wheeled you into the gas chamber?"

"That's not going to happen. It's just not going to happen."

"Do you have empirical evidence?" she asks. "A logical argument?"

"Of course not. And I know it's happened before, in what was considered the most progressive medical community in the world. But it won't happen. I have to believe that."

Belief. Is that what it comes down to? Am I a person of faith after all? Or is this just wishful thinking? Am I clinging to foolish hope that the tragic protagonist, this time, will shift course before it's too late—even though I know that's not how these dramas play out?

I don't think so. It's less about belief, less about hope, than about a practical need for definitions I can live with.

If I define Singer's kind of disability prejudice as an ultimate evil, and him as a monster, then I must so define all who believe disabled lives are inherently worse off or that a life without a certain kind of consciousness lacks value. That would make monsters of many of the people with whom I move on the sidewalks, do business, break bread, swap stories and share the grunt work of politics. It would reach some of my family and most of my nondisabled friends, people who show me enormous kindness and who somehow, sometimes manage to love me through their ignorance. I can't live with a definition of ultimate evil that encompasses all of them. I can't refuse the monster-majority basic courtesy, respect and human sympathy. It's not in my heart to deny every single one of them, categorically, my affection and my love.

The peculiar drama of my life has placed me in a world that by and large thinks it would be better if people like me did not exist. My fight has been for accommodation, the world to me, and me to the world.

As a disability-pariah, I have had to struggle for a place, for kinship, for community, for connection. I am still seeking acceptance of my humanity. Singer's call to get past species seems a luxury way beyond my reach. My goal isn't to shed the perspective that comes from my particular experience, but to give voice to it. I want to be engaged in the tribal fury that rages when opposing perspectives are let loose.

I can only trust in the fact that, while we struggle, we must also live with our theories and with one another. As a shield from the terrible purity of Singer's vision, I'll look to the corruption that comes from interconnectedness. To justify my hopes that Singer's theoretical world—and its entirely logical extensions—won't become real, I'll invoke the muck and mess and undeniable reality of disabled lives well lived. That's the best I can do right now.

* * *

Questions for Discussion

1. If you had been the author, would you have accepted the invitation to the debate at Princeton? Why or why not?

2. What do you think about discussions surrounding "life quality" issues for people with disabilities, particularly when those discussions are being held by those without disabilities? Consider searching for articles about Bree Walker Lampley, who faced media scrutiny about her decision to have children in light of an impairment she had.

3. What do you think of Peter Singer's ideas, as referenced in this article? What do you think of the author's responses?

4. Search the Internet for "Harriet McBryde Johnson" and enjoy watching some video clips of her.

The following is a letter written by Justin Dart, Jr., disability rights pioneer, shortly before his death.

I Am with You. I Love You. Lead On!
Justin Dart

Dearly Beloved:

Listen to the heart of this old soldier. As with all of us the time comes when body and mind are battered and weary. But I do not go quietly into the night. I do not give up struggling to be a responsible contributor to the sacred continuum of human life. I do not give up struggling to overcome my weakness, to conform my life—and that part of my life called death—to the great values of the human dream.

Death is not a tragedy. It is not an evil from which we must escape. Death is as natural as birth. Like childbirth, death is often a time of fear and pain, but also of profound beauty, of celebration of the mystery and majesty which is life pushing its horizons toward oneness with the truth of mother universe. The days of dying carry a special responsibility. There is a great potential to communicate values in a uniquely powerful way—the person who dies demonstrating for civil rights.

Let my final actions thunder of love, solidarity, protest—of empowerment.

I adamantly protest the richest culture in the history of the world, a culture which has the obvious potential to create a golden age of science and democracy dedicated to maximizing the quality of life of every person, but which still squanders the majority of its human and physical capital on modern versions of primitive symbols of power and prestige.

I adamantly protest the richest culture in the history of the world which still incarcerates millions of humans with and without disabilities in barbaric institutions, backrooms and worse, windowless cells of oppressive perceptions, for the lack of the most elementary empowerment supports.

I call for solidarity among all who love justice, all who love life, to create a revolution that will empower every single human being to govern his or her life, to govern the society and to be fully productive of life quality for self and for all.

I do so love all the patriots of this and every nation who have fought and sacrificed to bring us to the threshold of this beautiful human dream. I do so love America the beautiful and our wild, creative, beautiful people. I do so love you, my beautiful colleagues in the disability and civil rights movement.

My relationship with Yoshiko Dart includes, but also transcends, love as the word is normally defined. She is my wife, my partner, my mentor, my leader and my inspiration to believe that the human dream can live. She is the greatest human being I have ever known.

Yoshiko, beloved colleagues, I am the luckiest man in the world to have been associated with you. Thanks to you, I die free. Thanks to you, I die in the joy of struggle. Thanks to you, I die in the beautiful belief that the revolution of empowerment will go on. I love you so much. I'm with you always. Lead on! Lead on!

Justin Dart

* * *

Questions for Discussion

1. What do you know about Justin Dart? What is his legacy? Who are some other leaders in the disability rights movement?

2. What do you think of the content of his message?

———————

The following is an excerpt from the book *Always Looking Up* by Michael J. Fox, the actor. Michael J. Fox has Parkinson's Disease and has established a foundation to fund research.

Politics
Michael J. Fox

Choosing to invest time, energy, and identity in the political process is an expression of hope. If something in our personal experience has informed or inspired us to believe that one direction or outcome is preferable to another, for not only the individual, but society as a whole, we put that belief into action through activism, advocacy, financial support of a candidate, actually running for office, or by simply casting a vote. The American political experience can therefore be viewed as optimism in the collective. Naturally, unanimity is rare, as reasonable (and not so reasonable) people are bound to disagree. Take it from me, things get a little intense when the swords come out and all you're holding is a plowshare.

When I first felt the jab of the swords, [my assistant] Jackie and I had just arrived in Chicago on the morning flight out of New York. We were to head directly to a campaign appearance on behalf of Major Tammy Duckworth, a Democrat hoping to win Henry Hyde's soon-to-be-vacant seat in the staunchly conservative sixth congressional district outside Chicago. The plan was to stay over Tuesday night, attend an unrelated nonpolitical donor luncheon for the Michael J. Fox Foundation, and then return to New York Wednesday afternoon. As we deplaned, we were met by John Rogers, Kelly Boyle, and Alan McLeod. Throughout our handshakes and hellos, the three of them were like multimedia jugglers, responding to the cacophony of buzzes, trills, and ring tones emanating from their cell phones, BlackBerrys, and other various PDAs. Now off the plane, Jackie had activated hers as well, and instantly, it began clamoring for her attention. From the look on everyone's face, the urgent tone of their whispered questions and answers, and the furious flurry of their text messaging, it was obvious that something serious was in the wind.

We met up with a Duckworth staffer who led us to yet another rented campaign minivan. Hustling through the parking lot, John briefed me on the situation. There had been a conservative response to the campaign ads, the McCaskill ad in particular. We had anticipated this, but what we hadn't counted on was that no less an attack dog than Rush Limbaugh was leading the charge. Much of his previous day's broadcast had been devoted to not so much debunking the ad on its merits or plumbing the ethical complexities of stem cell research, but going after me specifically ad hominem and apparently ad nauseam. Up to this point, I had been completely unaware—my radio tastes tend toward classic rock and NPR. He'd been going on about it since the first McCaskill ad interrupted game one of the World Series, while he was no doubt enjoying his hometown Cardinals' domination of the Detroit Tigers. The gist of his complaint, I was learning from John and his staff, was that I was a faker, exaggerating, playing up, and manufacturing symptoms in order to stir sympathy and pity in the hearts and minds of voters.

"What the hell did you get me into, John?" I muttered.

John, who was sitting in the backseat of the latest campaign minivan on our way to our hotel in suburban Chicago, shrugged and said, "Well, pal, I'm not quite sure of that yet myself, but it's gonna be fun."

"For you maybe," I laughed.

"Let's just see where it goes," he said.

We poured the tepid dregs of our Starbucks coffees out of the van's windows as we pulled into the hotel parking lot. We had a busy morning ahead of us. I couldn't think of a more appropriate person than Major Tammy Duckworth to spend the morning with, given that I'd woken up to the fact that I was in for a hell of a fight. Tammy, after all, was no stranger to tough fights. Here she was, a political newcomer, a Democrat, with the guts to compete for the seat Henry Hyde was vacating in this most conservative of Chicago suburbs.

Less than two years earlier, Major Duckworkth, a thirty-eight-year old National Guard pilot, had lost both her legs in Iraq when the Black Hawk helicopter she was copiloting was hit by a rocket-propelled grenade and brought down. Ten days later she woke up in Walter Reed Army Medical Center in Washington, DC, and by August of 2005, she had decided to run for Congress. Not given a chance in the traditionally Republican district, she was now, less than two weeks before Election Day, engaged in an unexpectedly competitive race with her GOP opponent, Peter Roskam.

Before meeting with Tammy, still en route to the rally, I had the standard local interviews, one in print and one televised. My inner circle had moved from the van to a holding room within the hotel, where they would prep me for the interviews. Under normal circumstances this would involve refreshing myself on the issues of research and the point-counterpoint that developed between sides of the debate. But now there was this new element to the discussion. How to respond to Rush?

"Let me get this straight one more time. He said I did what?" I asked.

"That you were either faking your symptoms or that you purposefully didn't take your medication when you shot the ads so that your symptoms would be exaggerated," John answered.

"Wait, let's back up," I said. "Did he say anything about stem cells, about the merits of the research, or any inaccuracies in the statements we made in the ad?"

"Mostly just that you were a fraud," Kelly said. I detected a slight upturn at the corner of her mouth as she said it. *Was she actually smiling?*

"Oh," Alan joined in. "He also said you were pandering to Missouri voters by pronouncing Missouri *Missoura*."

Then I smiled too and half-laughed as I responded, "You've gotta be kidding."

A Duckworth aide tapped on the door. The local NBC reporter was ready to do the on-camera interview in another room of the hotel.

In my role as an advocate for Parkinson's-related issues, my key responsibility is to inform and educate, to promote understanding of what we go through as individuals and as a community. For the first time that I could remember, my message was being countered by someone equally visible and even more vocal than I, and to make matters worse, he was actively and enthusiastically disseminating misinformation, promoting ignorance.

"We don't know for sure that she's gonna bring this up in the interview," John said as I put on my jacket and he instinctively straightened my tie.

"And if she does?" I asked. I mean, this stuff was almost crazy. I decided that I'd just go with the truth, that I hadn't heard or read the exact comments yet and wasn't in a position to respond. As I was being escorted to the interview, I took stock of my physical condition. I was actually feeling pretty good this morning. My meds had kicked in nicely; my gait was smooth, my hands were steady, and as of yet, I had no pronounced dyskinesias. *Great. Or was it?*

I knew of course that to simply dismiss Limbaugh's allegations as crazy would be dangerous. If he was crazy, then he was, pardon the expression, crazy like a fox. It was a classic "when did you stop beating your wife?" provocation, based not on an accusation, but on a presumption that something sinister had been perpetrated. His diatribe had set out an array of traps for me to stumble into if I wasn't careful, the first of which lay immediately ahead.

Like I said, I was feeling good that morning. It's always the goal to be as comfortable as possible, particularly in public situations. But was there now suddenly such a thing as being too comfortable, too smooth — not symptomatic enough? I wasn't going to involve myself with circular thinking, manufacturing symptoms to prove I wasn't manufacturing symptoms.

It turned out that the two reporters I spoke to weren't entirely up to speed on Rush's attack, so his remarks were only referred to in passing and rather obliquely at that.

The morning received a much-need injection of class when I finally met Major Tammy Duckworth, just moments before the rally. Her warm smile and affable nature immediately put me at ease. Very quickly we were exchanging anecdotes about our respective experiences as political neophytes on the campaign trail. She was the first to mention the attention coming my way from the conservative Right; having heard Limbaugh on the radio, she found herself "in utter disbelief," though she had faced similar accusations herself. After brief inquiries about each other's health, she matter-of-factly showed me the prosthetics she wore on each leg, admitting with a smile that any height advantage she held over me, she acquired with her new prosthetic legs.

I had read Major Duckworth's campaign biographical materials and was familiar with her story. Be that as it may, meeting her was nothing short of inspirational. Her example — transforming a tragic circumstance into an opportunity for service — put into sharp relief the character of those detractors who claimed she was using her disability to evoke sympathy. I pity anyone who would make the mistake of having pity for Tammy Duckworth. She's the real deal. Even more obvious than her toughness is her positive spirit. In the first moment of eye contact, it is clear that she believes in what she's doing and has a real hope — an informed optimism — that given the opportunity, she can affect positive change, not only for disabled vets, from whom she drew the inspiration to run, but for people in her district, her country, and the world.

Never a "super-optimistic person" before she was injured, she says, "I'm more optimistic now than I was before." She points out that battlefield triage has advanced over the last ten years to such a degree that "I would not have survived if I had been injured in the first Gulf War."

Unfortunately, advances in our ability to treat victims on the battlefield haven't been matched by our capacity to care for them once they've returned stateside, to heal and rehabilitate. Military hospitals, the Veterans Administration, the entire system, already considered by many to be woefully impersonal and inefficient, are now buckling almost to the point of breaking under the strain. Tammy discovered this firsthand in the days, weeks, and months she spent in the hospital being treated for horrific injuries. "When I was at Walter Reed, I started doing advocacy work for other patients because I was the highest-ranking amputee there for a while," she told me. "So whenever anyone needed to speak as a representative for other patients, they sent me. I started talking about the bureaucracy that existed and how we need to get rid of it. I testified before the Senate and the House, and through that process I was sucked into being politically active even though I never was before. The army had assigned me to this post for the other patients and then I started calling Senator Durbin's office saying, look, we've got a problem here or a problem there, I need help. It was in the late summer when Senator Durbin called me and told me that if I'm this upset about things that are not happening, I should run for office. At that point he mentioned Henry Hyde's district to me."

The rally was held in one of the hotel's large banquet halls. The room was already packed and raucous with cheering and chanting as we entered, gauntlet-style, the Major proceeding through a phalanx of well-wishers and supporters on either side. It was hard to grasp what any individual was saying, but suffice it to say, I was hearing the name "Rush" a lot, usually accompanied by an expletive or two. Metal risers accommodated the media, which was out in force—a dozen or so TV cameras and two or three times as many still photographers. I kept my comments brief, with most of the focus on Tammy and stem cell research. As with the two interviews I had done earlier, I didn't mention Rush Limbaugh specifically. In fact, from that point on, with only one exception, I didn't say the guy's name in any public forum for the remainder of the campaign. I couldn't help but appreciate the enormous roar of approval when I made a passing reference to a certain "less than compassionate conservative" who had spoken out against our efforts. It was a good line, and I'd keep using it for the next two weeks.

That afternoon I checked into a hotel in downtown Chicago; I had a luncheon the next day for some Fox Foundation donors in the Chicago area. The political portion of my junket was now complete. But, of course, my mind was entirely occupied with politics.

There was no question that I was on edge. Having been retired for the most part from acting for the last few years, it had been a while since I had received a bad review, and I don't think I'd ever had one so surgically personal in nature. This was not disagreement, disapproval, or even distaste. This was disgust, that same sort of sharp rebuke I had seen dealt out to those over the past few years who had spoken out against government policy, although their comments had largely been about the war and the administration's actions leading up to it. I was being "Dixie Chicked."

This was new for me, and I suddenly realized how much I had always liked being liked. It is spooky to see that a contingent of society, vocal and connected to power, has worked up an antipathy toward you and is rallying this base to marginalize you and the threat you represent. Would I have still made the ads if I'd had some idea of what the stakes were for my public reputation?

Absolutely. The stakes for me as a patient and an advocate were infinitely higher. My options had been narrowed to the basic "fight or flight," and I wasn't about to run away, but I was anxious and a little unsure as to how to respond.

My immediate plan was to order some room service and watch the baseball game. While I was waiting for dinner time to roll around, I compulsively forged through the contents of the minibar, putting a large dent in the inventory. Not the booze, of course— after fifteen years of being sober, it would take more than a gust of hot air from Rush Limbaugh to blow me off the wagon. I did, however, polish off two bags of peanut M&M's at the inflated hotel price of about eight bucks each, some gelatinous lemon wedge-type things, coated in crystallized sugar, and some salty squares with wasabi peas from a bag labeled entirely in Japanese except for the single English word "SNACK."

There were a number of phone calls. The wider media, smelling blood in the water, were circling and looking for someone to feed them something. John called to gather a statement. I told him I wasn't sure yet.

"Tell ya what, pal, for today, I'm just gonna speak on your behalf and say something general, but accurate — express shock and disappointment at the ignorance of his statements and reaffirm your commitment to continue speaking out on behalf of stem cells."

That was cool with me.

The phone rang again. It was my mom. She didn't even ask if it was me, but instead, immediately led with the question "Are you okay?"

There's a way that people ask that question, teeming with the certainty that you aren't, that makes you do a quick scan of your extremities and put the back of your hand to your forehead just to make sure that indeed, you are, before answering in the affirmative.

"What an idiot that man is. I'm so mad I can't see straight."

"Mom, it's all right."

"He's just ignorant. He has no idea what he's talking about!"

"That's why it's okay. No serious person will take him seriously."

As we talked, it became clear that what had Mom especially fired up, aside from the natural maternal instinct to defend her kid, was her recollection of the day the ads were filmed, how upset she was to see me struggle with dyskinesias.

"I didn't even know you listened to his show."

"I don't," she said. "But other people do, and they've been calling. Then I saw him imitating you on TV and I was so livid."

"You saw him doing what?" I said. This was the first I'd heard of this.

"He was imitating you, making fun of you — wiggling, shaking, squirming around."

Hunter S. Thompson was right. When the going gets weird, the weird definitely do turn pro.

My subsequent telephone conversation with Tracy went a long way toward keeping my head in the right place. Sensibly, she was neither as angry as my mother nor as baffled as I still seemed to be.

"Congratulations," she said. "You got their attention."

Tracy, as she so often does, had hit the nail on the head. I had the attention not only of Rush Limbaugh and his "ditto heads," but also of those in the media and general public drawn to the sound of their complaints. The attention had created an opportunity to educate. I'd have to give a little more thought as to how to best capitalize on that opportunity. In the meantime, John's first public comment on my behalf was a step in the right direction: "It's a shameful statement. It's appallingly sad that people who don't understand Parkinson's disease feel compelled to make these comments. Anyone who understands the disease knows that it is because of the medications that Parkinson's sufferers experience dyskinesias."

... I was slack-jawed when I finally caught the video of the Limbaugh show before I left Chicago. He flapped his arms and wiggled his fingers while rocking his body, rolling his shoulders, and bobbing his head.

"[Michael J. Fox] is exaggerating the effects of the disease. He's moving all around and shaking and it's purely an act … This is really shameless of Michael J. Fox. Either he didn't take his medication or he's acting."

If his intention was only to mimic and mock what he maintained was my "shameless" performance, it went well beyond the personal—caricaturing the thousands of Parkinson's patients I'd met and worked with over the years. I saw it as an affront to them and their families, and I felt an obligation to defend them.

Predictably, my reception at the luncheon for the foundation was warm and supportive. Up to now, most of my focus had been on the extent to which Limbaugh and the Right had denounced the ads and the motive behind my involvement in them, but now I was getting a dose of the other side. The pro-research and patient communities were shocked and disgusted by the political attack. On the plane back home and at the airports on both ends of my journey, I discovered that my well-wishers extended beyond those with an interest in Parkinson's or stem cells. At the check-in counter, through security, and at the baggage claim, people approached me with words of encouragement. The consistent message I was getting was that I should fight back. While I appreciated the sentiment, I was wary of letting myself be distracted and engaging in the wrong fight. My battle was not with a conservative radio talk show host, whose intention among other things was to distract me and others from our message, but rather, against those in power who willfully sought to impede the progress of scientific research that could improve the life of millions.

Limbaugh wasn't alone in his objections to the ads and my participation in them. Predictably, representatives of the candidates whose anti-stem cell views I was effectively campaigning against took issue with our message, but what they had no way around was the indisputable effects and ravages of catastrophic illness. It's ironic that one answer for it could very well be the research they so strongly opposed.

Over the course of the few hours that it took to travel back from Chicago to New York, the controversy only intensified. Limbaugh apparently was feeling the force of a backlash. His allegation that I had been manufacturing symptoms to manipulate voters had been effectively countered by John's explanation about dyskinesias.

....

Slightly chastened, Limbaugh allowed that he would "bigly, hugely, admit that I was wrong, and I will apologize to Michael J. Fox if I am wrong in characterizing his behavior in this commercial as an act." Surprisingly, perhaps benefiting from low expectations in general, this was widely regarded as an apology from the talk show host, or as close as he was going to get to one.

His next salvo was, I think, intended to work on two levels. Having already alluded to my being an actor and, therefore, a con man, he now made the next logical connection. If my being an actor didn't necessarily mean that I was faking my symptoms, it was a pretty safe bet that I was a liberal and, therefore, a de facto Democrat. He went on to say, "Michael J. Fox is allowing his illness to be exploited and in the process is shilling for a Democratic politician."

Friends and associates from every corner of my life—professional, personal, and medical—were quick to correct him at every turn, loudly and convincingly. Moreover, members of the media were themselves having fun poking holes in his accusations. Keith Olbermann on MSNBC took glee in responding to the Democratic "shill" comment by pointing out that I had, in fact, supported and campaigned on behalf of pro-stem cell Republicans in the past.

What I needed to do, I decided, more than anything else, was to seize the opportunity that had presented itself, to use this spotlight that had been fixed upon me right up to Election Day. The only acceptable counter to all of this negativity was positivity.

Late in the evening after I returned from Chicago, Tracy found me standing at the fridge, door open, staring vacantly at a jar of mayonnaise, as men are wont to do. Intuiting that I wasn't really looking for anything but just filling the moment with an instinctive activity, she gently closed the door and pulled me in for a hug.

"You must be exhausted," she said.

"Yeah, I guess so," I replied. "But I feel really calm, ya know? This whole thing, the ads, Limbaugh, stem cells, the elections—it's like a perfect storm. And I'm right in the center of it, the eye, I mean. I just feel so weirdly relaxed."

"I know. It's great," she said. "I think this is the first time since I've known you that you haven't worried about ticking somebody off. You're always such a diplomat. But when it comes to this, you have such conviction, you truly don't care about what anybody else thinks—especially Rush Limbaugh."

"I care what you think," I said.

"I think you should get some sleep."

Good thinking.

Wanting me to slam Rush Limbaugh, preferably on their air, requests ran the gamut from talk radio shows—liberal and conservative—to the seeming thousands of cable news programs. Two names that stood out on the list of potential interviewers were Katie Couric and George Stephanopoulos. I have already mentioned George, and besides having been interviewed many times by Katie when she was on *The Today Show*, we live in the same neighborhood and often pass each other as we walk our kids to the bus stop on school-day mornings. I wouldn't characterize either as a close friend, but I knew that they would be intelligent and fair, and were informed on stem cell research.

I'm old enough to remember Walter Cronkite, the most trusted man in America (he had a pretty solid rep in Canada too), so stepping onto the set of the *CBS Evening News* in midtown Manhattan gained me a further appreciation for the history and tradition of the institution. I heard Katie's voice, and turned as she approached to welcome me. I could sense the enormity of the weight that had been placed upon this diminutive but determined broadcaster. I understood that I was the day's hot topic and therefore a good "get," but what Katie and her producers had proposed was extraordinary, the first seven and last six minutes of their broadcast. While we did have a personal connection, I was prepared for her to be as tough as she needed to be.

As if to confirm this, in the seconds before tape rolled—the floor director literally counting down—Katie leaned toward me and quietly allowed, "Now I have to forget how much I like you." After opening remarks to the camera, she turned to me, polite but professional, and asked, "How are you?"

Let's see. I was already sweating; my assistant, Jackie, had talked me into a sports coat over a blue cashmere sweater over a T-shirt. My fashion deference to the women in my life, dating back to Mom laying out clothes at the end of my bed, prevented me from protesting that we were in the middle of a heat wave. Now, under the studio lights, aesthetics became less important than absorbency. Shaking uncontrollably, I sought in vain to establish and maintain a single, consistent physical attitude, like a gate swinging in the wind, waiting for the latch to catch. Partly at my urging, partly on its own initiative, my right arm, in a semi-controlled flail, tried to catch and contain my left leg, the ankle of which crossed my right knee. And I knew that if my hand wasn't there to police it, a violent spasm could cause a painful kick to Katie's shin. If this was distracting to her, she didn't let on. I was also occupied by what I call a "central body tremor"; it feels as though someone has punched through my torso, grabbed a hold of my spine, and is waving me like a flag.

"I'm fine, thank you."

Katie began asking about symptoms, allowing a chance to correct the mistaken ideas and address willful ignorance. It took four questions for Katie to invoke Limbaugh's name and his allegations of fakery. She played the role of devil's advocate, albeit a more polite version, in deference to the sensibilities of others, putting Limbaugh's attack in more reasonable terms.

"Could you have waited to do that ad when you had less dyskinesias, for example?"

My answer was immediate. "Well, when do you know when that's going to be? … It's just not that simple." I saw this as an opportunity to correctly and necessarily take it away from the personal—this was not just about me.

That's why we're doing this. Not only people with Parkinson's. People who have spinal cord injuries. People who have the ticking clock of ALS, where they waste away, kids who are born with juvenile diabetes. I mean, potentially there's answers for those people. We're not interested in being exhibitionists with our symptoms or asking for pity or anything else. We're just resolved to get moving with this science. It's been a long time. It's not a time-neutral situation.

We moved on to explaining the disease, and, more importantly, why I had chosen this moment to speak up. Aside from being the first of several high-profile interviews that I would do over the next couple of weeks, two things about the *CBS Evening News* stand out in my mind. It was my first and only time, on the campaign before or after, that I uttered Rush Limbaugh's name. (I believe the quote was "I don't give a damn about Rush Limbaugh's pity.") And the second was something Katie did later in the interview, as the drugs kicked in and the tremors segued into the jerkiness of dyskinesias. Somewhere in the contortions of making a point, my left arm detached the microphone clip from my jacket lapel. With no fuss and hardly a break in conversation or eye contact, she calmly leaned over and refastened it. Neither of us commented on it, but it was such an empathetic gesture, so far from anything patronizing or pitying, a simple kindness that allowed me the dignity to carry on making a point more important than the superficiality of my physical circumstance.

I was aware of Katie's familial connection to Parkinson's disease—her father had PD. She disclosed this information as well as her previous support for the foundation at the end of the interview. Still, it would be hard for any objective viewer to judge the exchange as anything but fair. One thing was clear though, whether or not she was able to forget how much she liked me: with that single act of consideration, she made it abundantly clear how much she loved her father.

The impact of the Couric piece was immediate and powerful. My voice mail and e-mail were full. Not surprisingly, the Parkinson's and patient advocacy communities were supportive and gratified by the measured tone of our response. By neither appearing defensive nor firing back with inflammatory rhetoric, we were taking the high road, effectively a passive resistance sort of approach. In fact, Meg Ryan, an old friend of Tracy's, called her and jokingly asked, "What's it like to be married to Gandhi?" That's me, Mahatma J. Ghandi.

The show was widely watched and the *CBS Evening News* registered a significant bump in its overnight numbers. (A recent *New York* magazine article chronicling Katie's tenure as a news anchor pointed to our segment as both a ratings and editorial highlight). Personally, I felt a real sense of relief.

I certainly hadn't been at my best physically. I admitted to Katie, "It's not pretty when it gets bad … but I've had enough years of people thinking I was pretty, and teen-age girls hanging my picture on the wall. I'm over that now." Watching the playback, I was confronted by the physical price I was paying for my efforts and the certainty that it was a bargain for the privilege. The forum Katie provided, to state our position passionately yet with a calm diplomacy, provided a sharp contrast to the belligerence of those attempting to confuse the issue. It helped shift the tone.

Later that afternoon, John and I and our retinue were at ABC's Manhattan studios for the next stop on our schedule of appearances. George Stephanopoulos had flown up from his Washington base, no doubt wishing that I was still on the Vineyard. I anticipated, correctly, that George would be after the political angle more than the personal. As I endured the rituals of paint and powder in the makeup room, George and I kidded around, talking politics and family. Physically, true to formless form, I had given up any pretense of control or calibration of symptoms and went before the cameras feeling at ease, if not anywhere close to being comfortable.

George started off with the rantings of Mr. Limbaugh. Still loose from the joviality of the backstage conversation, I went right away to the ridiculousness of Limbaugh's premise: "When I heard his response, I was like, 'What, are you kidding me?'… It just seemed so 'No, it can't be.'"

"But your mom was mad," George countered.

I said yes, then alluded to "the way Irish moms can get."

"Or Greek moms," he replied.

Much of the remaining conversation was nuts-and-bolts politics, detailing campaign positions, methods, and tactics. But a later reference to Limbaugh returned me to a theme that I had touched upon before and that would become a major part of my message in the coming days—the intrinsic faith we have in ourselves as Americans to do the right thing. I also touched upon how ironic it is that sometimes the greatest believers in the possibilities for the future are the very people who have cause to doubt.

"I'm going to bring up Rush Limbaugh one more time," George warned. "One of the things he says is that when you're talking about all these cures, you're giving people false hope and that is cruel."

"Which is crueler," I responded, "to not have hope or to have hope? And it's not a false hope. It's an informed hope. But two steps forward, one step back, you know? It's a process. It's how this country was built. It's what we do. It seems to me that in the last few years, eight, ten years, we've just stopped. We've become incurious and unambitious. And hope, I mean, hope is …" My enthusiasm had now carried me to a patriotic reference that would make Emma Lazarus twist in her grave, "… I don't want to get too corny about it, but isn't that what the person in the harbor with the thing—?" I made an emphatic flourish with my arm and held aloft an imaginary torch indicating the Statue of Liberty, and then finished my point. "To characterize hope as some sort of malady or some kind of flaw of character or national weakness is, to me, really counter to what this country is about."

Even as the interview was winding down, Rush Limbaugh was in the rearview mirror. He had given us a significant push, and we were ready to take to the road. Let's face it, the whole episode, unpleasant though it may have been, was a gift in the same way that

I have described Parkinson's as a gift. You suffer the blow, but you capitalize on the opportunity left open in its wake. "The notion of hiding—this is what struck a nerve. Feeling the need to hide symptoms is so key to what patients of all kinds of conditions, but particularly Parkinson's, have to face. We have to hide—don't let anybody see, don't let them think you're drunk, don't let them think you're incapable, don't let them think you're unstable, you're unsteady, you're flawed, you're devalued. Mask it. Hide it. Cover it up … We'd be better to take other things into account. We take our responsibility as citizens very seriously and our sense of ethics and, again, our spirituality and our participation in government, we take it very seriously. It's not made sinister by the fact that we have an affliction that may drive us down a certain path of activism."

Wrapping up, George inquired, "And you're campaigning next week?"

"Yes," I replied, "I'll be out there."

* * *

Questions for Discussion

1. Search YouTube for videos related to this story, particularly regarding Rush Limbaugh's comments and Michael J. Fox's responses.

2. How do disability and politics intersect? How was this evident in this chapter, and in what other areas have you seen it? What are your thoughts about stem cell research? What do you think of the argument that it is cruel to raise people's hopes of a cure, and what did you think of Michael J. Fox's response?

3. What did you think of Michael J. Fox's comments to George Stephanopoulos about masking symptoms? What other types of disabilities might have symptoms that people try to mask? What do you think about masking symptoms versus just letting them be obvious?

4. How and why do various celebrities support various causes? What is your opinion about this? Which celebrities come to your mind in this regard?

5. Michael J. Fox says he views Tammy Duckworth as an inspiration. Some disability rights activists do not like feeling like they have to be "supercrips" or "inspirational people," but just wish to lead their own lives and be seen for who they are. Can you see both sides of this issue, or what is your opinion?

————————

The following is an article from *Ragged Edge Online* magazine, a disability rights publication.

Whether Their Perpetrators Realize It or Not, Disability Awareness Days Send the Wrong Message

Valerie Brew-Parrish,* *Ragged Edge Online*

Hey, Hey, Hey, it's Disability Awareness Day! Everyone gets a chance to see what it's really like to have a disability! Yank out those blindfolds, grab cotton to stuff in your

————————

* Valerie Brew-Parrish is a polio survivor and a longtime disability activist. She has an M.S. degree from Southern Illinois University and writes a column on disability issues for her local paper.

ears, and plop yourself in a wheelchair to navigate around an obstacle course! To get the most out of Disability Awareness Day, it is important to try almost all the disabilities on for size.

Now it is time to tie one of your arms behind you so you can fully appreciate a paralyzed limb.

No doubt about it, life with a disability is a tragedy! Why these poor gimps, blinks, and others would be better off dead! They are so courageous and yet pitiful as they go about their daily routines. Yep, I'm so glad it is their fate and not mine …

Sadly, these are the misconceptions that the public holds about those of us who live with disabilities. Disability simulations do nothing but reinforce these negative stereotypes about persons with disabilities.

Like the Jerry Lewis Telethon, disability simulations should be abolished. The disability community should be as outraged by disability simulations as they are over the negative implications of telethons. Overwhelming feelings of pity well up in those who simulate a disability—and pity does not equate with dignity. Disability simulations rob persons with disabilities of their dignity and self respect.

Simulations are phony. To "simulate" means to assume the mere appearance of—without the reality. The reality is this: nondisabled persons can never understand what it is like to have a disability. Jumping in a wheelchair for a few minutes, wearing a blindfold, and stuffing cotton in one's ears does not make a person understand life with a disability.

People who have never been disabled who simulate a disability are often terrified. Many of the "simulators" even cheat a little. Haven't we all observed a person standing up in their wheelchair in order to lift the chair over a curb? They breathe a collective sigh of relief knowing full well that their charade will soon come to an end and their momentary disability will gratefully vanish.

Agencies purportedly serving disabled clients frequently advocate disability simulations, with fancy brochures encouraging the public to assume a disability with blindfolds and wheelchairs. The pamphlets gleefully expound the theory that disability simulations are useful for teaching family members and others what the person with a disability is really experiencing.

What these rehab professionals fail to realize is that the public does not have the coping skills or strategies developed by people who actually have disabilities.

This point was clearly illustrated a few years ago when airline personnel decided to blindfold themselves to test evacuation procedures in case of an airline crash. The results were disastrous. Naturally. The airline staff had no training in mobility or orientation. Therefore, they erroneously concluded that blind persons could never safely evacuate a plane. Nothing could be further from the truth.

When I'm disoriented in a dark place, I let my blind husband lead the way! The National Federation of the Blind has long argued that disability simulations are destructive. Other disability groups should follow their lead and speak out against these sordid attempts to empathize with us by becoming gimp for a day.

For several years, I was employed at a large university that sponsored an annual "Disability Awareness Day." Despite protests from students and staff with disabilities, the nondisabled sponsors of the event continued the spectacle.

I was told by participants that I was an inspiration because I coped so well with my disability. Others told me they would rather be dead than live with a disabling condition. The participants of the simulation debacle now looked at me with pity. In their eyes, I was no longer on an equal basis with them; they felt superior because all of their limbs were in proper working condition.

Regrettably, it seems every annual celebration of the passage of the Americans with Disabilities Act, every disability awareness event, is combined with a tasteless display of disability simulations. In many instances, persons with disabilities are actually participating and perpetuating these contemptible attempts to make the public aware.

Awareness Days can be beneficial if it they are done properly; it is important for the public to meet with persons with disabilities and to interact with us. Why not have people who use wheelchairs discuss obstacles and the need for accessibility? Deaf persons can demonstrate sign language skills, and blind persons can show proper travel techniques. The public needs to know we exist; that we are professionals, parents and homeowners just like them.

But disability simulations need to die a quick death. There are more effective and positive ways to educate the public. Come on folks, we can do a better job getting our messages across. We do not need people to pretend they have disabilities and simulate our disabilities to understand us. All of us need to demand to be treated with dignity. When disability simulations become extinct, perhaps the flood of pity will dry up and be replaced with respect.

A 2004 Update from Valerie Brew-Parrish: The Wrong Message — Still
Posted August 9, 2004

HEY, HEY, HEY it's Disability Awareness Day! Still. Even in the 21st century!

Schools, government agencies, and sometimes, deplorably, gimp groups, are still offering the public "try on a disability" programs — exercises in which nondisabled people are blindfolded, put into wheelchairs or given earplugs to "simulate" having a disability.

When I first wrote my article, The Wrong Message, back in 1997 for the *Ragged Edge*, I never imagined the stir it would cause. I am proud that the article has made people think about the harm simulations can do.

I still consider simulations an atrocity perpetuated — mostly — by nondisabled professionals. Disabled folks are sometimes involved though, as well.

> My muscles started to hurt from sitting all day.
> — Joliet (IL) Central High School student

I don't know who dreamed up the concept of "disability simulations" but they have been around for a mighty long time. My lifelong friend, Michael A. Winter, now the Director of Civil Rights for the U.S. Department of Transportation, first exposed me to the shameful practice. Michael and I were classmates at a segregated school for crips and met in 6th grade. We attended the same university. As undergrads, Michael formed a group called Wheelchair Action. When the Rehabilitation Institute at Southern Illinois University sponsored a disability simulation, Michael and members of his group stormed into the classroom and tried in vain to halt the fiasco.

Professionals who are nondisabled rarely stop to listen to the people who live with disabilities. I was proud of Michael for trying to get people to understand how destructive these simulations can be.

Nondisabled people usually come away from disability simulations

- thinking life is a tragedy for persons with disabilities,
- thanking the good Lord they are not saddled with a disability,
- or falling prey to the "amazing" syndrome: "Ohhhhh just lookie at what disabled people can do! They're better than us at (getting around in the dark, popping wheelies, reading hand signs …)"

When I wrote "The Wrong Message," I was angry. My daughter Tara had come home from school in tears. It was Disability Simulation Day at Greenwood High. Blindfolded students were being led around by sighted students, others were bumping into walls. The students were terrified of their newly created disabilities. Some had told Tara they thought persons with disabilities had horrible lives; a few thought they might be better off dead.

School personnel knew that both Tara's parents had disabilities. She was quizzed about her home life: did she have to take care of us? Was she resentful? Were we a burden to her? Did she miss out on having a childhood? Sometimes the questions were implied; at other times they were quite direct.

Her answers always warmed my heart and brought tears to my eyes. She told them she had been taught from infancy to accept people of all colors, creeds, and disabilities. She told them about going along with her parents to conferences all over the country. She told them about meeting Ed Roberts when she was little, and, later, meeting Justin Dart. She reminded them that she participated in soccer and ballet and had even attended a Neil Diamond concert.

I contacted the school's psychology teacher once and tried to get Disability Simulation Day stopped. It was a lost cause. She liked having Disability Simulation Day featured in the local newspaper, and saw no need for me or my husband—or anyone from our local independent living center—to come to her classroom to talk with the students.

Although Greenwood High often needed substitute teachers, they refused to hire my husband Rick, because he's blind. Rick holds a teaching certificate and an advanced degree. He applied to the school system to work as a substitute, but was never called to Greenwood High. Many a day Tara would come home to tell us that her school had been unable to locate enough substitute teachers for the day.

After two years of this, Rick filed a complaint with the U.S. Department of Education Office of Civil Rights, noting as well in his complaint that the school had hired a phys ed teacher who held no teaching certificate whatsoever.

The investigator found merit in his complaint (school administrators had held meetings to debate letting a blind person teach), and Rick was awarded back pay for all the days it was determined he would have been able to teach had he not been excluded—close to $5,000.

Every March, the Indiana Governor's Planning Council for People With Disabilities does a really stupendous job providing materials for people in celebration of Disability Awareness month. Their posters are excellent, as are their public service announcements.

But their "Disability Awareness Activities" booklet, one of their handouts, is horrendous.

Here are a couple of excerpts from their publication. You decide:

"All Thumbs" (physical disabilities, group activity)

Materials: masking tape, raisins, nuts, pudding.

Activity: Sometimes people with physical disabilities don't have good muscle control. With masking tape, tape together the fingers of the participant's weaker hand, leaving only the thumb free. Give each participant a cup of raisins or a dish of pudding to eat using only that hand. Divide participants into pairs. Let one in each pair feed the other a dish of pudding. Trade places.

Discussion: How did you feel during these experiments? Did you find ways to overcome the problems of eating when you had less control of your hands? How does it feel to be fed by someone else?

"Thick Hands"

Materials: thick socks, shirts, sweaters, shoes, beads, string and ruler.

Activity: Some people have trouble with fine motor coordination. This is because their muscles are weaker, and they need more time and practice to learn how to move. To help participants understand this condition, have them put a pair of thick socks on each hand and try to tie shoes, button a shirt and string beads. Tie a ruler between the students' ankles so that their legs are stiff and apart from each other. Have them walk down the hall and back, slowly. How would they feel if people laughed or stared at them or imitated the way they walked?

Discussion: Some people who have these kinds of difficulties have mental retardation. Their muscles are weaker and their coordination is poor. But not everyone with these difficulties has mental retardation. Discuss this assumption. Can you assume that someone who can't use his or her hands has mental retardation?

Because I have paralyzed arms, I never wear tie shoes, a simple fashion decision that compensates for my inability to tie shoes. There's nothing demeaning about it. There are many such things students could learn. The activities detailed above, though, cannot help but suggest helplessness. They evoke pity and disgust. The raisins and pudding dribble out of participants' mouths and get splattered across their clean faces. Being fed, they can't help but conclude, is a demeaning experience.

Even the exercises' titles are offensive. "All Thumbs" is a cliche — for clumsiness. Suggesting that someone who can't use their hands has mental retardation, even if made ostensibly to prove it wrong, seems to beg the question. Would it not be more instructive to show a physics video of Stephen Hawking?

On May 5, in Joliet, IL, Joliet Central High School journalism students, turned loose on a "Disabled for a day" article in the local newspaper, had this to say: "My muscles started to hurt from sitting all day ... although I was in physical pain, the worst part was knowing that many people have to endure this pain on a daily basis for the rest of their lives."

And, "I briefly felt how it would feel to be wheelchair bound for life. I couldn't keep the tears in my eyes."

And, "People with mental disabilities don't comprehend and learn like others, but they're carefree. I would love to be carefree at times."

And, "Trembling and shaking, I took my first steps blind ... I felt like I was in a small, dark room ... At the end of the day, I took off the blindfold. I was so grateful because so many people do not have the option of taking off the blindfold."

These were the honest feelings the students got from participating in an Awareness Day. Is this the message we really want to send about living with a disability?

I AM BAFFLED AS TO WHY nondisabled people see a need to simulate a disability in order to understand our situation. Across our nation in February, we celebrate Black History Month. Is it necessary for people with white skin to paint their faces black to better understand this minority? Should heterosexuals be asked to experience homosexuality so we are not homophobic?

Should I expect to be able to teach someone how to drive a car, diaper and dress a baby and make the bed with their feet as I do? Am I amazing? No; I am just living my life.

We, the people who live with disabilities, we who have so long advocated for being treated as full members of society, must reclaim our dignity and say "No!" to simulations. I long for the day when disability simulations are dumped into the trash cans of oblivion.

WHAT CAN BE DONE to help the nondisabled masses understand the disability experience?

Talk to us and ask us questions. Ask persons who have had a disability from birth (or a longtime disability) to come to your class or organization.

Read publications written BY persons with disabilities: *Ragged Edge*, *Mouth* magazine, *Braille Monitor*.

There are some really excellent books out there, too. Here are some of my favorites:

- *Reflections from a Different Journey: What Adults with Disabilities Wish All Parents Knew* by Stanley D. Klein & John D. Kemp
- *Make Them Go Away: Clint Eastwood, Christopher Reeve & the Case Against Disability Rights* by Mary Johnson
- *Moving Violations: War Zones, Wheelchairs, and Declarations of Independence* by John Hockenberry
- *By Trust Betrayed* by Hugh Gregory Gallagher
- *FDR's Splendid Deception* by Hugh Gregory Gallagher
- *Don't Laugh At Me* by Steve Seskin and Allen Shamblin/Illustrations by Glin Dibley. Afterword by Peter Yarrow (ages 4–8)
- *No Pity* by Joseph P. Shapiro
- *Awakening To Disability: Nothing About Us Without Us* by Karen G. Stone
- *Extraordinary People With Disabilities* by Deborah Kent. Short essays profile 48 famous people—John Milton, Helen Keller, FDR, Tom Cruise—who have disabilities.

* * *

Questions for Discussion

1. Have you ever participated in a Disability Awareness Day? What did you think of it? What do you think this author would have thought of it?

2. Do you think Disability Awareness Days can be effective or do you think they should be abolished? Why?

3. What did you think of the authors' ideas about changing or abolishing Disability Awareness Days?

The following is a media piece from CBSSports.com about Anthony Robles, a wrestler with one leg.

Sun Devils Wrestler Different, All Right — Extraordinarily So

Gregg Doyel, CBSSports.com, Feb. 10, 2008

Judy Robles knew her son was different when he tore off his right leg and started to hop around the house on his left. Well, she had known he was different since birth, when he came into this world first with the head and shoulders, and one arm and then another arm, and one leg and then … well, there wasn't another *then*. Anthony Robles came into the world with one leg.

But that didn't make him different. Not to Anthony's parents. He was born the way he was born. Missing a leg? That wasn't different. That was life. And so the Robles family adjusted to their oldest son's life by having him fitted with an elaborate prosthetic that allowed him to walk despite being born without even a hip bone on his right side.

Anthony didn't want to walk. Not like that. Not if it meant going through all sorts of gyrations every morning to put the prosthetic on, and then repeating those gyrations in reverse to take it off at night. The heck with that. Anthony Robles was just 3 years old when he tore it off and contented himself with crutches, or with hopping on one leg.

He wouldn't take no for an answer, this kid. His father, Ron Robles, was into power-lifting and had a weight set in the garage, and Anthony wanted to lift weights, too. Ron said no, Anthony, you're too young. It wasn't the leg—it was his age. So one day Ron Robles was resting between sets when he heard someone else breathing heavily. It was Anthony, on the floor, doing push-ups.

A few years later, Anthony broke his school's sixth-grade record for push-ups. Today, a wrestler at Arizona State and one of the highest-rated freshmen in the country, he can do pushups until he loses count. When you're born without a leg, you compensate with your arms, which become like legs. They become thicker, stronger, than a regular kid's arms.

But then, what's a "regular" kid anyway? Anthony was a regular kid. He played football with kids his age, and he tagged along with older kids. And so there was Anthony in the eighth grade, tagging along with an older cousin on the high school wrestling team, when he hopped onto the mat and started rolling with a team member.

And right then it became apparent that Anthony Robles wasn't regular at all. He was different: He was gifted, almost supernaturally so, at wrestling.

All those supposed weaknesses that come from missing a leg, well, those became strengths on the mat. His upper body was enormous for his size. So was his strength. And his grip? Like a hand from hell.

"That kid has a super grip," Judy Robles says. "He's always had that. Once he latches on, he's not letting you go."

All that was left for Anthony was to figure out an individual style that would work best. Conventional wrestling was of no use, because there's nothing conventional about a one-legged wrestler. His high school coach, Bobby Williams, studied Robles for days before coming up with the idea that this low-to-the-ground kid should get even lower.

Robles started wrestling from his left knee, with his foot behind him, poised to push off. Anthony Robles can't run a long way very quickly—although he can crutch a mile in 10 minutes—but in the short space of a wrestling mat, he has explosive quickness. He crouches low on his knee and pushes off with his foot like a sprinter coming out of a starting block, and then he's under you, pulling you down to his level. Wrestlers call the technique the "ball and chain." The opponent becomes the ball, and Robles reels him in.

Ball-and-chain is a fine name for it, but I've seen Robles wrestle and I'd suggest calling it "the Alligator." He pulls his opponent down to the mat, below his foe's comfort zone, and starts grabbing and spinning and mauling. It's like watching an alligator roll with a piece of meat.

"It's hard for people because I am so low like that, and I take advantage of my upper-body strength," Robles says. "That's what I love about wrestling—whatever your strengths are, you build your style around those. The best wrestler wins. Whoever works harder and wants it more is going to win. Everybody's going to lose once in a while, it's just going to happen, but this is a sport where anybody has a chance."

The first time Robles participated in organized wrestling was his freshman year of high school in Mesa, Ariz. He finished sixth in the city. As a sophomore he was sixth in the state. He won state titles as a junior and senior, going a combined 96–0, and capped his high school career with the 112-pound title at the 2006 High School Senior Nationals and a scholarship to Arizona State.

After redshirting his first season at ASU, Robles is 19–7 and ranked No. 14 in the country at 125 pounds, including pins over veteran Joey Lucas of Oregon and 15–7 Joey Fio of Oklahoma in 82 seconds. Of Robles' 19 wins, 14 have earned bonus points, which is the wrestling equivalent of a blowout victory. A freshman season like that has people in the wrestling community wondering just how far Anthony Robles can go. Robles wonders himself.

"I want to be a (collegiate) national champion first, but then I'd like to be on the Olympic team," Robles says. "Maybe try to go once or twice and win a gold medal."

Lucas, a fifth-year senior with 44 career victories, hadn't been pinned this year before Robles did it to him on Jan. 27. And it was no fluke. Robles led 8–0 before alligator-rolling Lucas into a bad spot and finishing him off.

"I knew what he was going to do, but I still couldn't figure out how to stop it," Lucas says. "Wrestling him is … I don't know how to describe it. It's extremely different, and he's extremely talented. Almost everything conventional is out the window because you're put in positions you're not used to being in, and there are times you're going to reach for a leg and it's not there. You reach for it and you're reaching for air."

Anthony Robles is as unconventional as it gets. He bench-presses 300 pounds, enormous for someone who weighs 125. That would be like an NFL linebacker benching 600 pounds. Impossible. Robles can do 50 pull-ups on command, and he can flip upside down and walk on his hands back and forth across the wrestling mat.

And he can do greater things. Earlier this season a woman approached Robles as he was hanging out with his parents after a match. This woman, this stranger, was crying—and because she knew ahead of time she would be crying, she had a hand-written note already prepared. Robles read the note and excused himself, going up into the crowd to speak for several minutes with a teenage boy. When he came back, he handed his parents the note.

"It said (the woman's) son had been fighting cancer and had to have his leg amputated," Judy Robles says. "Anthony had inspired him to wrestle."

* * *

Questions for Discussion

1. What do you think of this piece? What do you think of the discourse?

2. Search YouTube for "Anthony Robles" and watch several media clips about him. What do you think of the tone of the coverage? What does Anthony Robles's response to the coverage seem to be?

———————

The following is a piece written by Karin Mango, a writer and editor.

Christmas Cheer

Karin Mango

Maybe the best idea would be to pack a small bag with books and Hershey bars and go away to an isolated cottage somewhere in the wilds. Peacefully alone over Christmas. It was tempting, even if I were accidentally to pack junk mail and Proust instead of James Michener and Agatha Christie.

No straining to hear above a hubbub of voices. No explaining: "I have a hearing loss — would you say that again, please? And again? Just one more time, in different words?" No resentment over yet again being the "odd man out" in a holiday group of chatting people. What good was "Hark, the Herald Angels Sing" when you couldn't hark to them yourself? And when all the family was gathered together so rarely and it was so important to hear them, not to understand two connected sentences. Christmas cheer? Not that way.

It wouldn't have to be anywhere exotic like Bermuda or the Bahamas. I'd even take New Jersey — a stone's throw from home in New York — if it was quiet.

The feeling started soon after Thanksgiving. "Panic" was too strong a word, and it wasn't depression. "Mixed feelings" was more like it. Very mixed. I love festivals and traditions, and Christmas has always been my favorite. But with my hearing loss creeping annually down the scale from mild to moderate to severe and now severe to profound, all the things I had loved — people, festivities, carol-singing, getting together — were being slowly and inexorably pulled from my resisting grasp. As I saw the signs of Christmas appearing all around, in store decorations, Christmas tree vendors with their "forests" at street corners, the first cards arriving … the sensation intensified in my mind — and in my stomach — as I thought, How will I manage with so little intelligible sound? I miss such a lot. It's not worth the effort. Why not just say, "See you after the New Year" and even leave my TT behind?

I have thought about it quite seriously. First, I would leave the festive food ready for my husband and for Nick and Helen when they arrived from out of town. Then, we simply wouldn't give a party that year. I wouldn't get angry and resentful at the various gatherings of the season. I wouldn't have to be frustrated by the carol service at the church — a small thing, but emblematic of the whole season. I wouldn't get so tired by the sheer effort to communicate that all I wanted was escape.

Escape from the thick glass wall behind which so many of us hearing impaired people live. On the other side we see the lips moving, the easy communication, the connections with our fellow men and women, the laughter, the conversation, the discussions. All the things we sweat to get a mere inkling of. Outsiders at the window, looking in.

If you allow yourself to look at it that way.

It can be very easy to get into that frame of mind. It does seem a solution to escape and be safely, quietly alone. But as I went on thinking, it was clear I had to look at it differently. Not "escape," because it wasn't that at all. What I might be starting was the easy, deadly path to withdrawal and isolation, losing the ground so carefully achieved through adapting to the hearing loss and learning to live with it as best I could.

And what I'd been thinking of certainly wouldn't do much for my family's Christmas spirit. Not a brave "escape," merely a self-centered, cowardly running away.

Now that I was no longer looking through a haze of anxiety, common sense started to reassert itself. I didn't have to hear everything or struggle beyond reason. People would help me. What I didn't hear, I wouldn't hear. It wasn't only words that were important.

I sat down with my husband, Tony, and we planned our party. "Let's make it an open house," he suggested. "People will come in smaller groups and that will mean less noise to try to hear through. Easier for everyone." It was easier already.

It was a good party, with neighbors from our brownstone area. Truthfully, I didn't hear much, and yes, I did read a lot. But it wasn't either junk mail or Agatha Christie. It was the conversations carried on in writing to supplement my hearing aids and keep my friends from going mad with repetition. I had also forgotten that they were friends, who knew about my hearing loss, knew how to help me and were willing to do so.

Before Christmas, my son Nick brought his girlfriend to dinner. She is thoughtful and patient and in the quiet of home we managed quite passably. Then my daughter Helen brought her new boyfriend for us to meet. I looked at the beard hopelessly. How would I ever lipread him? I wanted to be at least minimally intelligent and communicative with someone who's important to her.

"What can I do to make conversation easier?" He asked the perfect question.

"Shave off the beard!" was my sincere but unspoken wish. But that was not what he meant and anyway it looked good on him. Instead, I took him into good light, asked him to speak slowly, Helen helped, and we could — sort of — talk. And "sort of" didn't matter.

The carol service is on Christmas Eve. Poinsettias were on the altar, a huge Christmas tree beside it; candles filled the church with their gentle light. Over the past years I have been going for the family company and the beauty of the scene. Forget the service, forget the minister speaking, forget the carols.

Well, this year it was still forget the first two items (and now I thought, common sense uppermost at last, how about getting a loop installed?), but surely carols are meant to be sung! The music, distorted and cacophonous to my damaged ears, was still familiar inside my head. I sang along, inaudible to myself, but no heads turned. I went on singing happily.

Christmas Day. We always take the festive lunch to a tetchy and touchy old aunt who never leaves her house. We all helped her celebrate in spite of herself, heading off her impatience with my hearing difficulties. She has her own problems of failing hearing and sight and arthritic legs. I have only one thing wrong with me.

But still, the next evening, invited to a gathering across the street from our house, with people overflowing the rooms, with the noise and effort and straining to catch a minimal something, I nearly despaired. I couldn't hear Tony's familiar voice trying to help me, no quiet place, no room for paper messages. I reminded myself firmly of a couple of things. Sometimes it's not a defeat to withdraw, but common sense. You don't have to be a part of everything—and you can also be part in various ways. It isn't only words that matter; it's people. I rested my ears and relaxed.

On the day both Nick and Helen had to leave, we all sat around the kitchen table eating Christmas leftovers. I looked at the faces around me. I no longer wanted to be in New Jersey or wherever it was by myself. With gratitude, love, and a small but definite feeling of success, I raised my glass: "*Christmas cheers!*"

* * *

Questions for Discussion

1. What does this piece say about withdrawing versus putting forth effort to interact with others? What do you think of the author's philosophy on this subject? The author says escaping for the holidays might start her on "the easy, deadly path to withdrawal and isolation." Do you agree or disagree, or why?

2. Near the end of the story the author comments, "Sometimes it's not a defeat to withdraw, but common sense. You don't have to be a part of everything—and you can also be part in various ways. It isn't only words that matter; it's people." Do you agree or disagree, and why?

For Further Reading and Viewing

Grandin, Temple. *Thinking in Pictures.* New York: Random House, 1995. Memoir by an author with autism, well-known for her work with designing livestock facilities.

Hockenberry, John. *Moving Violations.* New York: Hyperion, 1995. Memoir by an NPR reporter about his career and his paraplegia.

Montalambert, Hugues de. *Invisible: A Memoir.* New York: Simon & Schuster, 2010. Memoir by an artist who loses his vision to an assault.

Simon, Rachel. *Riding the Bus with My Sister: A True Life Journey.* New York: Houghton Mifflin, 2002. Memoir by a professor whose sister with disabilities loves to ride buses.

Walker, Cami. *29 Gifts: How a Month of Giving Can Change Your Life.* Philadelphia: Perseus, 2009.

Robert F. Molsberry, "More Than an Inspiration," anthologized in *Disability: The Social, Political, and Ethical Debate.* Amherst: Prometheus Books, 2009. An essay about Christopher Reeve and the controversy he incited in the disability community with his search for cure.

Consider the media stories about Oscar Pistorius, the sprinter and double-amputee: "An Amputee Sprinter: Is He Disabled or Too-Abled?" retrieved May 15, 2012 at http://www.nytimes.com/2007/05/15/sports/othersports/15runner.html?_r=1; "Blade Runner," retrieved May 15, 2012 at http://www.youtube.com/watch?v=c-fbSHENjHc. What do you think of the discourse used in these pieces? What do you think about the substance of the debate?

"Girl in Wheelchair Wants to Be Cheerleader, School Says No," retrieved May 15, 2012 at http://www.opposingviews.com/i/health/girl-wheelchair-wants-be-cheerleader-school-says-no.

"Disabled kids show host draws criticism, praise," retrieved May 15, 2012 at http://www.cnn.com/2009/WORLD/europe/02/28/bbc.disabled.host/index.html. A CNN article about a children's TV host with a disability and the audience's response:

"Stroke survivors inspired by Dick Clark," retrieved May 15, 2012 at http://www.usatoday.com/news/health/2006-01-03-clark-stroke-survivors_x.htm. An article about the media's response to Dick Clark's hosting of the New Year's Eve celebration after his stroke.

A blog by the dad of a child with Down Syndrome: http://noahsdad.com/target-down-syndrome/.

"At First Glance," retrieved May 15, 2012 at http://health.groups.yahoo.com/group/Sotosyndrome/message/24712. What do you think about the stereotypes in this story (pity, supercrip)? The ideas about cure?

O'Brien, Mark, "The Unification of Stephen Hawking," in *Staring Back: The Disability Experience From the Inside Out* by Kenny Fries, ed. New York: Penguin Group, 1997. A reporter with disabilities gets to meet Stephen Hawking—but how does it go?

"The Woman in the Mirror," retrieved May 15, 2012 at http://www.nytimes.com/2001/01/21/magazine/lives-the-woman-in-the-mirror.html. An article about a blind woman who regained some of her sight.

"Famous (and not-so-famous) people with disabilities," retrieved May 15, 2012 at http://www.disabilityhistory.org/people.html.

"Reading Between the Lines," a comment on disability fiction, retrieved May 15, 2012 at http://www.raggededgemagazine.com/departments/fiction/000851.html.

"Harry Potter and the Allure of Separatism," retrieved May 15, 2012 at http://www.raggededgemagazine.com/focus/potter0604.html. In imagining an ideal world for disability rights, can we learn anything from the setup of Harry Potter's magical world?

Discussion 3

Advising Clients with Capacity Issues

Recommended Background Reading

U.S. Const. Amend. VI.

Massey v. Moore, 348 U.S. 105 (1954), holding that convictions should not stand for "mentally deficient" or "insane" people who went to trial without counsel.

Jackson v. Indiana, 406 U.S. 715 (1972), holding that indefinite involuntary commitment on the basis of lack of competency to stand trial violates due process.

Clark v. Arizona, 548 U.S. 735 (2006), upholding the state of Arizona's insanity defense.

Readings for Class Discussion

Consider the following model Rule of Professional Conduct and its comment:

Rule 1.14 Client with Diminished Capacity

(a) When a client's capacity to make adequately considered decisions in connection with a representation is diminished, whether because of minority, mental impairment or for some other reason, the lawyer shall, as far as reasonably possible, maintain a normal client-lawyer relationship with the client.

(b) When the lawyer reasonably believes that the client has diminished capacity, is at risk of substantial physical, financial or other harm unless action is taken and cannot adequately act in the client's own interest, the lawyer may take reasonably necessary protective action, including consulting with individuals or entities that have the ability to take action to protect the client and, in appropriate cases, seeking the appointment of a guardian ad litem, conservator or guardian.

(c) Information relating to the representation of a client with diminished capacity is protected by Rule 1.6. When taking protective action pursuant to paragraph (b), the lawyer is impliedly authorized under Rule 1.6(a) to reveal information about the client, but only to the extent reasonably necessary to protect the client's interests.

Comment to the rule:

Client-Lawyer Relationship

Rule 1.14 Client With Diminished Capacity—Comment

[1] The normal client-lawyer relationship is based on the assumption that the client, when properly advised and assisted, is capable of making decisions about important matters. When the client is a minor or suffers from a diminished mental capacity, however, maintaining the ordinary client-lawyer relationship may not be possible in all respects. In particular, a severely incapacitated person may have no power to make legally binding decisions. Nevertheless, a client with diminished capacity often has the ability to understand, deliberate upon, and reach conclusions about matters affecting the client's own well-being. For example, children as young as five or six years of age, and certainly those of ten or twelve, are regarded as having opinions that are entitled to weight in legal proceedings concerning their custody. So also, it is recognized that some persons of advanced age can be quite capable of handling routine financial matters while needing special legal protection concerning major transactions.

[2] The fact that a client suffers a disability does not diminish the lawyer's obligation to treat the client with attention and respect. Even if the person has a legal representative, the lawyer should as far as possible accord the represented person the status of client, particularly in maintaining communication.

[3] The client may wish to have family members or other persons participate in discussions with the lawyer. When necessary to assist in the representation, the presence of such persons generally does not affect the applicability of the attorney-client evidentiary privilege. Nevertheless, the lawyer must keep the client's interests foremost and, except for protective action authorized under paragraph (b), must to look to the client, and not family members, to make decisions on the client's behalf.

[4] If a legal representative has already been appointed for the client, the lawyer should ordinarily look to the representative for decisions on behalf of the client. In matters involving a minor, whether the lawyer should look to the parents as natural guardians may depend on the type of proceeding or matter in which the lawyer is representing the minor. If the lawyer represents the guardian as distinct from the ward, and is aware that the guardian is acting adversely to the ward's interest, the lawyer may have an obligation to prevent or rectify the guardian's misconduct. See Rule 1.2(d).

Taking Protective Action

[5] If a lawyer reasonably believes that a client is at risk of substantial physical, financial or other harm unless action is taken, and that a normal client-lawyer relationship cannot be maintained as provided in paragraph (a) because the client lacks sufficient capacity to communicate or to make adequately considered decisions in connection with the representation, then paragraph (b) permits the lawyer to take protective measures deemed necessary. Such measures could include: consulting with family members, using a reconsideration period to permit clarification or improvement of circumstances, using voluntary surrogate decisionmaking tools such as durable powers of attorney or consulting with support groups, professional services, adult-protective agencies or other individuals or entities that have the ability to protect the client. In taking any protective action, the lawyer should be guided by such factors as the wishes and values of the client to the extent known, the client's best interests and the goals of intruding into the client's decisionmaking autonomy to the least extent feasible, maximizing client capacities and respecting the client's family and social connections.

[6] In determining the extent of the client's diminished capacity, the lawyer should consider and balance such factors as: the client's ability to articulate reasoning leading to a decision, variability of state of mind and ability to appreciate consequences of a decision; the substantive fairness of a decision; and the consistency of a decision with the known long-term commitments and values of the client. In appropriate circumstances, the lawyer may seek guidance from an appropriate diagnostician.

[7] If a legal representative has not been appointed, the lawyer should consider whether appointment of a guardian ad litem, conservator or guardian is necessary to protect the client's interests. Thus, if a client with diminished capacity has substantial property that should be sold for the client's benefit, effective completion of the transaction may require appointment of a legal representative. In addition, rules of procedure in litigation sometimes provide that minors or persons with diminished capacity must be represented by a guardian or next friend if they do not have a general guardian. In many circumstances, however, appointment of a legal representative may be more expensive or traumatic for the client than circumstances in fact require. Evaluation of such circumstances is a matter entrusted to the professional judgment of the lawyer. In considering alternatives, however, the lawyer should be aware of any law that requires the lawyer to advocate the least restrictive action on behalf of the client.

Disclosure of the Client's Condition

[8] Disclosure of the client's diminished capacity could adversely affect the client's interests. For example, raising the question of diminished capacity could, in some circumstances, lead to proceedings for involuntary commitment. Information relating to the representation is protected by Rule 1.6. Therefore, unless authorized to do so, the lawyer may not disclose such information. When taking protective action pursuant to paragraph (b), the lawyer is impliedly authorized to make the necessary disclosures, even when the client directs the lawyer to the contrary. Nevertheless, given the risks of disclosure, paragraph (c) limits what the lawyer may disclose in consulting with other individuals or entities or seeking the appointment of a legal representative. At the very least, the lawyer should determine whether it is likely that the person or entity consulted with will act adversely to the client's interests before discussing matters related to the client. The lawyer's position in such cases is an unavoidably difficult one.

Emergency Legal Assistance

[9] In an emergency where the health, safety or a financial interest of a person with seriously diminished capacity is threatened with imminent and irreparable harm, a lawyer may take legal action on behalf of such a person even though the person is unable to establish a client-lawyer relationship or to make or express considered judgments about the matter, when the person or another acting in good faith on that person's behalf has consulted with the lawyer. Even in such an emergency, however, the lawyer should not act unless the lawyer reasonably believes that the person has no other lawyer, agent or other representative available. The lawyer should take legal action on behalf of the person only to the extent reasonably necessary to maintain the status quo or otherwise avoid imminent and irreparable harm. A lawyer who undertakes to represent a person in such an exigent situation has the same duties under these Rules as the lawyer would with respect to a client.

[10] A lawyer who acts on behalf of a person with seriously diminished capacity in an emergency should keep the confidences of the person as if dealing with a client, disclosing them only to the extent necessary to accomplish the intended protective action. The lawyer should disclose to any tribunal involved and to any other counsel involved the nature of

his or her relationship with the person. The lawyer should take steps to regularize the relationship or implement other protective solutions as soon as possible. Normally, a lawyer would not seek compensation for such emergency actions taken.

* * *

Questions for Discussion

1. What do you think of this rule and comment?

2. Review the analogous rule for your state. What differences do you find?

———————

The following is a court decision about Ted Kaczynski, the "Unabomber." The dissent and most footnotes have been omitted.

United States v. Kaczynski
239 F.3d 1108 (9th Cir. 2000)

RYMER, Circuit Judge:

Theodore John Kaczynski, a federal prisoner, appeals the district court's denial of his motion under 28 U.S.C. § 2255 to vacate his conviction. In that motion, Kaczynski alleges that his guilty plea to indictments returned against him as the "Unabomber" in the Eastern District of California and in the District of New Jersey, in exchange for the United States renouncing its intention to seek the death penalty, was involuntary because his counsel insisted on presenting evidence of his mental condition, contrary to his wishes, and the court denied his *Faretta* request to represent himself. Having found that the *Faretta* request was untimely and not in good faith, that counsel could control the presentation of evidence, and that the plea was voluntary, the district court denied the § 2255 motion without calling for a response or holding a hearing.

This court issued a certificate of appealability. The government submits that Kaczynski is foreclosed from raising the voluntariness of his plea on collateral review because he did not do so on direct appeal, but we conclude on the merits that the district court did not err. Therefore, we affirm.

I

The facts underlying Kaczynski's arrest (April 3, 1996) and indictment for mailing or placing sixteen bombs that killed three people, and injured nine others, are well known and we do not repeat them here. Rather, we summarize the pre-trial proceedings that bear on the voluntariness of Kaczynski's plea.

The California Indictment (returned June 18, 1996) charged Kaczynski with four counts of transporting an explosive in interstate commerce with intent to kill or injure in violation of 18 U.S.C. § 844(d); three counts of mailing an explosive device with intent to kill or injure, in violation of 18 U.S.C. § 1716; and three counts of using a destructive device during and in relation to a crime of violence, in violation of 18 U.S.C. § 924(c). The New Jersey Indictment (returned October 1, 1996) charged one count of transporting an explosive device in interstate commerce with intent to kill or injure, in violation of 18 U.S.C. § 844(d); one count of mailing an explosive device with intent to kill or injure, in violation of 18 U.S.C. § 1716; and one count of using a destructive device during and in relation to a crime of violence, in violation of 18 U.S.C. § 924(c). The government gave notice of its intent to seek the death penalty under both indictments on May 15, 1997.

The California Indictment was assigned to the calendar of the Hon. Garland E. Burrell, Jr. Quin Denvir, the Federal Public Defender for the Eastern District of California, and Judy Clarke, the Federal Public Defender for Eastern Washington and Idaho, were appointed to represent Kaczynski. They filed motions to suppress evidence in March, 1997, which were denied.

On June 24, 1997, Kaczynski filed a notice under Fed. R. Crim. P. 12.2(b) of his intent to introduce expert testimony of his mental condition at trial. According to his § 2255 motion, Kaczynski consented to the notice reluctantly and only to allow evidence relating to his "mental condition" — not to a "mental disease or defect." He also avers that the purpose of the notice was to allow psychologist Julie Kriegler, who did not think that he suffered from serious mental illness, to testify.

Jury selection began November 12. Six hundred veniremen were summoned, and 450 questionnaires were filled out. Voir dire of 182 prospective jurors took sixteen days over the course of six weeks.

Kaczynski alleges that he learned in the courtroom on November 25 that his attorneys intended to portray him as suffering from major mental illness (schizophrenia), but that he was deterred from bringing his conflict with counsel to the court's attention as counsel were in plea negotiations with the government. Evidently by December 17 it had become clear that Kaczynski would not go for an unconditional plea and the government would not accept a conditional one. In the mean time, Kaczynski was giving thought to whether he wanted Tony Serra, a San Francisco lawyer whom he believed would not employ a mental state defense, to represent him. On December 16, he received a letter indicating that Serra would be available, but on December 17 Serra withdrew from consideration.

On December 18, Kaczynski's counsel gave the district court three letters in which Kaczynski explained that he had a conflict with his attorneys over the presentation of a mental status defense.[1] The next day the court held an ex parte, in camera conference with Kaczynski and counsel, as a result of which he and they undertook to confer over the weekend. On December 22, Clarke and Denvir advised the court that a compromise had been worked out: they agreed to withdraw the Rule 12.2(b) notice and not to present any expert mental health testimony at the guilt phase of the trial, while Kaczynski accepted their control over the presentation of evidence and witnesses to be called, including mental health expert witnesses and members of Kaczynski's family, in order to put on a full case of mitigation at the penalty phase. Kaczynski told the court that he was willing to proceed with his attorneys on this basis, and that "the conflict at least is provisionally resolved." In response to the court's query, Kaczynski also said that he did not want to represent himself. Jury selection was then completed and (to allow for the holidays) opening statements were set to begin January 5, 1998.

On January 5, Kaczynski told the court that he wished to revisit the issue of his relations with his attorneys. He said that he had learned from a preview of the opening statement

---

1. In a letter to the court, Kaczynski wrote:
   Your Honor, I recognize that you are an unusually compassionate judge, and that you sincerely believe yourself to be acting in my best interest in seeking to prevent me from representing myself. In an ordinary case your course would be the most compassionate one, and the one most likely to preserve the defendant's life. But I beg you to consider that you are dealing with an unusual case and an unusual defendant and that preventing me from representing myself is not the most compassionate course or the one most likely to preserve my life.

the evening before (January 4) that counsel intended to present non-expert evidence of his mental state in the guilt phase. Clarke and Denvir explained that they intended to introduce evidence of Kaczynski's physical state, living conditions, life-style, and writings to show the deterioration of his mental state over the 25 years he lived in Montana. Kaczynski also raised for the first time with the court the possibility that he might want to have Serra replace Denvir and Clarke. The district court continued the trial to January 8, and appointed Keven Clymo as "conflicts" counsel for Kaczynski.

Another hearing was held January 7. Kaczynski withdrew his January 5 request for Serra to represent him because Clymo had convinced him it would not be in his best interests; however, later the same day, Serra "faxed" a letter indicating that if Kaczynski's present lawyers were recused, he was willing to substitute in. Kaczynski told the court that he would like to be represented by Serra, but said: "As to the question of when he would be able to start, he stated that, of course, he will not be able to start trial tomorrow. He would need a considerable time to prepare." The court refused to allow Serra to take over because of the delay it would cause. After discussing Kaczynski's continuing differences with counsel over mental status evidence, the court also ruled that counsel could control the defense and present evidence of his mental condition over Kaczynski's objection. Again in response to a question from the court, Kaczynski said that he did not want to represent himself. He explained that "if this had happened a year and a half ago, I would probably have elected to represent myself. Now, after a year and a half with this, I'm too tired, and I really don't want to take on such a difficult task. So far I don't feel I'm up to taking that challenge at the moment, so I'm not going to elect to represent myself."

However, the next day (January 8), Kaczynski's counsel informed the court that Kaczynski wanted to proceed as his own counsel. Clarke explained that Kaczynski believed he had no choice, given presentation of a mental illness defense which he "cannot endure." Clarke also indicated that Kaczynski had advised her that he was prepared to proceed pro se that day, without delay. Both sides thought that a competency examination should be conducted, given defense counsels' view that his mental condition was Kaczynski's only viable defense. The court also noted that it had learned from the U.S. Marshals office that Kaczynski might have attempted suicide the night before. Accordingly, it ordered a competency examination, to be completed before ruling on the *Faretta* request. The trial was continued to January 22. A court-appointed psychiatrist examined Kaczynski and concluded that he was competent. All parties agreed on January 20 that this resolved the issue.

On January 21, Kaczynski again asked to represent himself. The court denied the request on January 22, finding that it was untimely because it came after meaningful trial proceedings had begun and the jury had been empaneled. The court also found that Kaczynski's request to represent himself was a tactic to secure delay and that delay would have attended the granting of the motion given the complexity of the capital prosecution. Although Kaczynski did not request a continuance, the court found "it was impossible to conceive" that he could immediately assume his own defense without considerable delay for preparation of an adequate defense. This, in turn, would risk losing jurors and having again to go through the arduous process of selecting a new jury. The court also found that Kaczynski's conduct was not consistent with a good faith assertion of his right to represent himself, as he had long known of his attorneys' intention to present mental health evidence and had agreed on December 22 that they could do so at the penalty phase. Accordingly, the court concluded, Kaczynski's conflict with counsel turned solely on the moment when mental evidence would be presented. Finally, the court declined to exercise its discretion to permit Kaczynski to represent himself in spite of the untimely request, noting that to do so would result in Kaczynski's foregoing "the only defense that is likely to prevent his conviction and execution."

The district court issued another order May 4, 1998, the day of sentencing, in which it further detailed its reasons for finding that Kaczynski was competent (not at issue on appeal) and had not asserted his request for self-representation in a timely manner or consistent with a good faith invocation of the *Faretta* right.

Immediately after the *Farreta* request was denied from the bench, Denvir informed the court that Kaczynski would unconditionally plead guilty to both the California and New Jersey Indictments if the government would withdraw its notices of intent to seek the death penalty. (Kaczynski alleges that this condition was counsels' idea, not his.) A written plea agreement was entered into shortly thereafter, and the plea was taken by the court the same day.

Kaczynski was sentenced May 4, 1998 to four consecutive life sentences, plus 30 years imprisonment. He was ordered to pay $ 15,026,000 in restitution to his victims. Pursuant to the terms of the plea agreement, Kaczynski did not appeal.

On April 23, 1999, he filed a motion under 28 U.S.C. § 2255 seeking to vacate his conviction. The district court denied the motion without calling for a response or holding a hearing. It also denied a certificate of appealability. This appeal followed. We certified three issues: (1) whether Kaczynski's guilty plea was voluntary; (2) whether Kaczynski properly was denied the right to self-representation; and (3) whether a criminal defendant in a capital case has a constitutional right to prevent his appointed defense counsel from presenting evidence in support of an impaired mental state defense at trial.

II

We must first consider whether Kaczynski is barred from raising these claims in a collateral attack under § 2255, for the government argues that he procedurally defaulted by failing to raise them on direct appeal. See *Bousley v. United States*, 523 U.S. 614, 621, 140 L. Ed. 2d 828, 118 S. Ct. 1604 (1998) ("Even the voluntariness and intelligence of a guilty plea can be attacked on collateral review only if first challenged on direct review. Habeas review is an extraordinary remedy and will not be allowed to do service for an appeal.") (internal quotations omitted). Kaczynski counters that the government waived its right to raise the issue of procedural default by having not done so in the district court. We disagree, because the district court summarily denied Kaczynski's § 2255 motion without giving the government an opportunity to be heard. As the government had no chance to argue default, we allow it to do so now. Cf. *United States v. Barron*, 172 F.3d 1153 (9th Cir. 1999) (en banc) (government's failure to raise petitioner's procedural default in district court waives the defense in the absence of extraordinary circumstances suggesting that the omission should be overlooked).

Kaczynski acknowledges that his § 2255 motion raises only one claim—that his guilty plea was involuntary. Therefore, it is unnecessary to consider default with respect to his *Faretta* request or control over the mental state defense. These issues are only points upon which Kaczynski relies to show that his guilty plea was involuntary; he does not now (nor, as he also recognizes, could he) raise these claims independently. See *Tollett v. Henderson*, 411 U.S. 258, 267, 93 S. Ct. 1602, 36 L. Ed. 2d 235 (1973) (criminal defendant who has admitted guilt in guilty plea may not thereafter raise independent claims relating to deprivation of constitutional rights that occurred prior to entry of plea).

Kaczynski argues that even if he did procedurally default his voluntariness claim, there were two causes to excuse it: first, that he waived the right to appeal in the plea agreement, and second, that his attorneys failed to consult with him about the possibility of direct appeal. The government maintains that the plea agreement waiver cannot justify bypassing direct review of his current claims, see *United States v. Pipitone*, 67 F.3d 34, 39 (2d Cir.

1995) (so holding with respect to agreement not to appeal a sentence within the guideline range), but it fails to argue how we can resolve counsels' possible ineffectiveness without a more fully developed record. *Bousley*, 523 U.S. at 621–22; *Waley v. Johnston*, 316 U.S. 101, 86 L. Ed. 1302, 62 S. Ct. 964 (1942) (per curiam) (coercion of plea appropriately raised on collateral review when facts relied on are dehors the record and not open to consideration and review on direct appeal). Accordingly, we cannot say that Kaczynski procedurally defaulted his involuntariness claim without cause.

III

On the merits, Kaczynski contends that his plea was involuntary because he was improperly denied his *Faretta* right, or because he had a constitutional right to prevent his counsel from presenting mental state evidence. Even if neither deprivation suffices, still the plea was involuntary in his view because it was induced by the threat of a mental state defense that Kaczynski would have found unendurable.

It goes without saying that a plea must be voluntary to be constitutional. We review whether it was de novo, *United States v. Littlejohn*, 224 F.3d 960, 964 (9th Cir. 2000), and the district court's findings for clear error. *United States v. Signori*, 844 F.2d 635, 638 (9th Cir. 1988).

The general principles are well settled. To determine voluntariness, we examine the totality of the circumstances. *Iaea v. Sunn*, 800 F.2d 861, 866 (9th Cir. 1986). A plea is voluntary if it "represents a voluntary and intelligent choice among the alternative courses of action open to the defendant." *North Carolina v. Alford*, 400 U.S. 25, 31, 27 L. Ed. 2d 162, 91 S. Ct. 160 (1970); *Hill v. Lockhart*, 474 U.S. 52, 56, 88 L. Ed. 2d 203, 106 S. Ct. 366 (1985). "[A] plea of guilty entered by one fully aware of the direct consequences ... must stand unless induced by threats (or promises to discontinue improper harassment), misrepresentation (including unfulfilled or unfulfillable promises), or perhaps by promises that are by their nature improper as having no proper relationship to the prosecutor's business (e.g. bribes)." *Brady v. United States*, 397 U.S. 742, 755, 25 L. Ed. 2d 747, 90 S. Ct. 1463 (1970). In sum, "a guilty plea is void if it was 'induced by promises or threats which deprive it of the character of a voluntary act.'" *Sanchez v. United States*, 50 F.3d 1448, 1454 (9th Cir. 1995) (quoting *Machibroda v. United States*, 368 U.S. 487, 493, 7 L. Ed. 2d 473, 82 S. Ct. 510 (1962)).

A

Here, the plea was both written and oral. In the written agreement, Kaczynski admitted guilt on each of the offenses charged in both indictments and agreed to plead guilty "because he is in fact guilty"; waived his constitutional trial and appellate rights; acknowledged he understood that by pleading guilty he was waiving these rights, that his attorney had explained both the rights and the consequences of his waiver, and that he freely and voluntarily consented to the waiver; and agreed to waive all rights to appeal the plea and sentence including legal rulings made by the district court. In a separate, "approval" section of the plea agreement, Kaczynski affirms that he had reviewed the agreement with his attorneys, and that "I understand it, and I voluntarily agree to it and freely acknowledge that I am guilty of the crimes charged." Also, that: "No other promises or inducements have been made to me, other than those contained in this agreement. In addition, no one has threatened or forced me in any way to enter into this Plea Agreement. Finally, except as otherwise reflected in the record, I am satisfied with the representation of my attorneys in this case."

During the Rule 11 colloquy, Kaczynski stated under oath that he was "entering [the] plea of guilty voluntarily because it is what [he] wanted to do"; that he was satisfied with his attorneys' representation, except for the mental defect defense as reflected in the record; and that no one had forced or threatened him to plead guilty. He stated that he was willing to proceed for sentencing with present counsel. The district court found that "the defendant is fully competent and capable of entering an informed plea and that his plea of guilty is a knowing and voluntary plea supported by an independent basis in fact containing each of the essential elements of the offense."

In its order denying the § 2255 motion, the court found that Kaczynski was aware of the basis on which his motion challenged the plea at the time of the plea colloquy, yet affirmatively answered the court's inquiry about whether he was entering his guilty plea voluntarily and responded negatively when asked whether anyone had attempted to force or threaten him to plead guilty. The court noted that Kaczynski specifically referred to the disagreement with his attorneys about a mental status defense, but did not suggest in any way that he believed this disagreement affected the voluntariness of his plea. Further, the court found that Kaczynski showed no signs of anxiety or distress when he stated that he was voluntarily entering into the plea; that nothing about his demeanor indicated he endured any coercion; that he admitted the charges with no sign of reservation; and that his sworn plea statements were "lucid, articulate, and utterly inconsistent with his present claim that he did not voluntarily plead guilty."

We give "substantial weight" to Kaczynski's in-court statements, *United States v. Mims*, 928 F.2d 310, 313 (9th Cir. 1990), and we accept the district court's findings as we are not firmly convinced they are wrong. Kaczynski was clearly aware of the consequences of his plea (and does not contend otherwise). The decision to plead guilty in exchange for the government's giving up its intent to seek the death penalty and to continue prosecuting him was rational given overwhelming evidence that he committed the Unabomb crimes and did so with substantial planning and premeditation, lack of remorse, and severe and irreparable harm. While Kaczynski does contend that his attorneys deceived him about their intentions to present a mental status defense, he knew what they planned to do before deciding to plead guilty, and he does not claim that he was persuaded to plead guilty by threats or misrepresentations of his attorneys, the government, or the court. Thus, there is no basis for concluding that his decision to plead guilty was influenced by improper threats, promises, or deceits, and no reason not fully to credit Kaczynski's sworn statements in the plea agreement, as well as during the plea colloquy, that he was pleading voluntarily.

This would normally end the enquiry, for being forced to choose between unpleasant alternatives is not unconstitutional. See *Brady*, 397 U.S. at 750. However, since the district court ruled on Kaczynski's § 2255 motion, we held in *United States v. Hernandez*, 203 F.3d 614 (9th Cir. 2000), that the erroneous denial of a *Faretta* request renders a guilty plea involuntary. We reasoned that wrongly denying a defendant's request to represent himself forces him "to choose between pleading guilty and submitting to a trial the very structure of which would be unconstitutional." *Id.* at 626. Because this deprives the defendant "of the choice between the only two constitutional alternatives—a plea and a fair trial," we concluded that a district court's improper *Faretta* ruling "imposed unreasonable constraints" on the defendant's decision making, thus making a guilty plea involuntary. *Id.* at 627. Therefore, we must consider whether Kaczynski's plea was rendered involuntary on account of a wrongful refusal to grant his request for self-representation.

B

Following *Faretta*, our court has developed the rule that "[a] criminal defendant's assertion of his right to self-representation must be timely and not for purposes of delay;

it must also be unequivocal, as well as voluntary and intelligent." *Hernandez*, 203 F.3d at 620 (summarizing prior law).

Kaczynski argues that there must be an affirmative showing that he intended to delay the trial by asking to represent himself, and that none was made here. See *Fritz v. Spalding*, 682 F.2d 782, 784 (9th Cir. 1982). Rather, he asserts, the facts show that his purpose was to avoid the mental state defense. Kaczynski also contends that his *Faretta* request was timely, which we assume (without deciding) that it was for purposes of appeal. This leaves only the question whether he had bona fide reasons for not asserting his right of self-representation until he did. In making this determination, a court may consider the effect of delay as evidence of a defendant's intent, along with events preceding the motion, "to determine whether they are consistent with a good faith assertion of the *Faretta* right and whether the defendant could reasonably be expected to have made the motion at an earlier time." *Id.* at 784–85.

We review the district court's factual findings for clear error, but we have not yet clarified whether denial of a *Faretta* request is reviewed de novo or for abuse of discretion. See *United States v. George*, 56 F.3d 1078, 1084 (9th Cir.), cert. denied, 516 U.S. 937, 133 L. Ed. 2d 247, 116 S. Ct. 351 (1995). We conclude that under either standard, the propriety of denying Kaczynski's request necessarily follows from the district court's finding that he asserted the right to represent himself as a tactic to delay trial proceedings and lacked bona fide reasons for failing to assert it before January 8, 1998.

The court found that Kaczynski "clearly and unambiguously permitted his lawyers to adduce mental status evidence at trial, and his complaints to the contrary, asserted on the day trial was set to commence, evidence his attempt to disrupt the trial process." Further, the court found that although Kaczynski contended he made his January 8 request to represent himself only because he could not endure his attorneys' strategy of presenting mental status evidence in his defense, the record belied this contention because Kaczynski had authorized its use. The court also found that Kaczynski was well aware before January 8 that evidence of his mental status would be adduced at trial. In addition to the December 22 accord, Kaczynski was present during all but one day of the seventeen days of voir dire, during which the court observed that he conferred amicably with his attorneys while they openly and obviously selected jurors appearing receptive to mental health evidence about him. Finally, the court found that Kaczynski could not have immediately assumed his own defense without considerable delay, given the large amount of technical evidence and more than 1300 exhibits that the government intended to offer.

These findings are well grounded in the record, and support the court's conclusion that Kaczynski's request for self-representation was tactically made for dilatory purposes. Kaczynski knew from at least November 25 that he and his attorneys disagreed about a mental status defense, but he agreed on December 22 to let Denvir and Clarke proceed with both expert and lay testimony on his mental condition in the penalty phase so long as they presented no such expert testimony in the guilt phase. Although he knew then that evidence of his mental condition would be presented, Kaczynski expressly said that he did not want to represent himself. As he agreed to evidence of his mental state, it cannot be for this reason that he later invoked the right; otherwise, he could have done so on December 22. 12 Instead, on January 5, when opening statements were supposed to start, Kaczynski renewed complaints about the mental status evidence his counsel planned to present in the guilt phase and mentioned to the court for the first time his interest in being represented by Tony Serra. This caused the trial to be continued to January 8. On January 7 Kaczynski said that he would like Serra to represent him, knowing that it would take Serra months to get ready. When the court refused to substitute Serra because of the substantial continuance that would be required, and ruled that appointed counsel could control the timing of when mental status evidence was introduced, Kaczynski repeated that he did not want to represent himself. However, that evening he may have attempted suicide and the next day (when the continued trial was set to start), Kaczynski informed the court that given presentation of a mental illness defense which he could not endure, he wanted to go forward as his own counsel. This triggered a competency examination and another delay in the start of trial, until January 22.

Kaczynski contends that he could not have been influenced by delay, given that he was incarcerated for the long haul in any event. However, the district court found that he was simultaneously pursuing strategies to delay the trial, to project a desired image of himself, and to improve his settlement prospects with the government. Kaczynski also argues that it should not matter whether he agreed to let evidence of his mental state be presented in the penalty phase, because the trial might never have gotten that far. We disagree, for Kaczynski never did—and does not now suggest—that he is actually innocent or that there was any realistic chance that the jury would not unanimously find him guilty beyond a reasonable doubt.

As the events preceding Kaczynski's *Faretta* request show, he knew about and approved use of mental state evidence without invoking his right to represent himself. Accordingly, the court could well determine that Kaczynski's avowed purpose of invoking the right in order to avoid a defense he could not endure was not "consistent with a good faith assertion of the *Faretta* right," and that he "could reasonably be expected to have made the motion at an earlier time." *Fritz*, 682 F.2d at 784–85. Having found that the request for self-representation was for tactical reasons and not for any good faith reason other than delay, the court properly denied Kaczynski's *Faretta* request. His Sixth Amendment rights were not violated. Thus, his guilty plea was not, on this account, rendered involuntary under *Hernandez*.

C

For essentially the same reasons, neither was Kaczynski's plea rendered involuntary on account of the threat of a mental state defense that he did not want presented. The government argues that Kaczynski's guilty plea waived his right to challenge the district court's ruling that his attorneys could put on mental state evidence at the guilt phase, and it unquestionably does. *United States v. Reyes-Platero*, 224 F.3d 1112, 1114 (9th Cir. 2000) (unconditional guilty plea "cures all antecedent constitutional defects") (quoting *United States v. Floyd*, 108 F.3d 202, 204 (9th Cir. 1997)). Kaczynski does not contend otherwise, but instead argues that he was coerced into pleading guilty by his counsel's insistence on a mental state defense, that his counsel deceived him in order to gain his cooperation with some such defense, and that he was induced to plead guilty by a choice (being unable to represent himself or to proceed without the mental state defense) that was constitutionally offensive.

Even if Kaczynski were misled by his counsel about the degree to which evidence of his mental state would be adduced in the guilt phase, he learned for sure what their plans were on January 4 when they previewed their opening statement for him and he does not allege, nor does the record show, that they in any way threatened or misled him with respect to the plea or its consequences. Cf. *Iaea*, 800 F.2d at 867–68 (attorney's threat to withdraw if defendant continued to refuse to plead guilty may, along with other factors, have coercive impact on voluntariness of plea). Kaczynski hypothesizes that counsel may have used mental state evidence as a threat to pressure him into an unconditional plea bargain as a means of saving him from the risk of a death sentence, but admits that this is speculative and that no proof for it is possible. Beyond this, he contends that the *Hernandez* rationale applies also to the right to proceed to trial without the presentation of mental state evidence. He points out that "the accused has the ultimate authority to make certain fundamental decisions regarding the case, as to whether to plead guilty, waive a jury, testify in his or her own behalf, or take an appeal," *Jones v. Barnes*, 463 U.S. 745, 751, 77 L. Ed. 2d 987, 103 S. Ct. 3308 (1983), and argues that evidence about mental status is of the same order of magnitude. The government, on the other hand, submits that it is equally "clear that appointed counsel, and not his client, is in charge of the choice of trial tactics and the theory of defense." *United States v. Wadsworth*, 830 F.2d 1500, 1509 (9th Cir. 1987); *New York v. Hill*, 528 U.S. 110, 120 S. Ct. 659, 664, 145 L. Ed. 2d 560 (2000) ("the lawyer has—and must have—full authority to manage the conduct of the trial") (quoting *Taylor v. Illinois*, 484 U.S. 400, 417–18, 98 L. Ed. 2d 798, 108 S. Ct. 646 (1988)). We need not decide where along this spectrum control of a mental defense short of insanity lies, because Kaczynski agreed that his counsel could control presentation of evidence and witnesses to be called (including expert witnesses and members of his family who would testify that he was mentally ill) in order to put on a full case of mitigation at the penalty phase. Thus, as the district court found, Kaczynski's claim that his plea was involuntary due to his aversion to being portrayed as mentally ill is inconsistent with his willingness to be so portrayed for purposes of avoiding the death penalty. This leaves only the pressure that Kaczynski personally felt on account of his wish to avoid the public disclosure of evidence about his mental state sooner rather than later. We agree with the district court that this does not transform his plea into an involuntary act. See *Brady*, 397 U.S. at 749–50.

Accordingly, as Kaczynski's guilty plea was voluntary and was not rendered involuntary on account of the wrongful denial of his *Faretta* request or because of anticipation of evidence about his mental condition, his habeas petition was properly denied.

AFFIRMED.

* * *

Questions for Discussion

1. Should defendants be permitted to represent themselves, even if they have a mental illness?

2. What do you think of the reasoning of this opinion?

3. What do you think about the policy issues surrounding plea bargaining? How might the plea bargaining system disfavor people with intellectual disabilities and/or mental illness?

For Further Reading

Arthur Garwin, *Questioning Competence: Mentally incapacitated clients still can tell their lawyers what to do*, 81 A.B.A.J. 84 (1995).

Discussion 4

Disabilities in the Legal Profession

Recommended Background Reading

"ABA Disability Statistics Report," ABA Commission on Mental and Physical Disability Law, retrieved May 15, 2012 at http://www.americanbar.org/content/dam/aba/uncategorized/2011/20110314_aba_disability_statistics_report.pdf.

Donald Stone, "The Disabled Lawyers Have Arrived; Have They Been Welcomed with Open Arms into the Profession? An Empirical Study of the Disabled Lawyer." *Law & Inequality: A Journal of Theory and Practice* (2009).

Mary T. Robinson, "The Professional Cost of Untreated Addiction and Mental Illness in Practicing Lawyers," *Journal of the Professional Lawyer* (2009).

Readings for Class Discussion

The following is an article by Michael Perlin, Professor of Law at New York Law School and Director of the International Mental Disability Law Reform Project. Footnotes have been omitted.

"Baby, Look Inside Your Mirror":
The Legal Profession's Willful and Sanist Blindness to
Lawyers with Mental Disabilities
69 U. Pitt. L. Rev. 589 (2008)

Introduction

The legal profession has notoriously ignored the reality that a significant number of its members exhibit signs of serious mental illness (and become addicted or habituated to drugs or alcohol at levels that are statistically significantly elevated from levels of the public at large). This is no longer news. What has not been explored is why so much of the bar has remained willfully ignorant of these realities, and why it refuses to confront the depths of this problem—one which appears to be exacerbated in the cases of lawyers in large, high-powered firms.

Paradoxically, there has been increased attention paid to related issues: the extent to which the Americans with Disabilities Act (ADA) is a factor to consider in bar disciplinary proceedings brought against lawyers with a diagnosis of mental illness, and the extent to which an attorney's mental illness might be a cognizable factor in a criminal post-conviction application alleging ineffective assistance of counsel at trial. Yet there has been no consideration of the paradox that our responses in these cohorts of cases are utterly dissonant with our responses to the crisis in the profession mentioned above.

I believe that the roots of this puzzle are found in the social attitude of sanism, an irrational prejudice of the same quality and character of other irrational prejudices that cause (and are reflected in) prevailing social attitudes of racism, sexism, homophobia, and ethnic bigotry, infecting both our jurisprudence and our lawyering practices. Sanism is largely invisible and largely socially acceptable, is based predominantly upon stereotype, myth, superstition, and deindividualization, and is sustained and perpetuated by our use of alleged "ordinary common sense" (OCS) and heuristic reasoning in an unconscious response to events both in everyday life and in the legal process. Just as lawyers are sanist towards clients with mental disabilities, they are sanist towards their peers with mental disabilities. And this sanism manifests itself in utterly inconsistent ways (ignoring the reality of mental illness in the practicing bar, blaming attorneys for their mental illness in disciplinary matters, and, again, ignoring the impact of mental illness on representation in the criminal trial process), an inconsistency that is a common mechanism that allows us to avoid confronting both the realities of mental disability and the stereotypical ways that we seek to deal with it in legal contexts. As I have argued elsewhere, "We tend to ignore, subordinate or trivialize behavioral research in this area, especially when acknowledging that such research would be cognitively dissonant with our intuitive—albeit empirically flawed views."

I have written frequently about the ways that therapeutic jurisprudence (TJ)—a means of studying the law as a therapeutic agent, recognizing that substantive rules, legal procedures and lawyers' roles may have either therapeutic or antitherapeutic consequences—might be a redemptive tool in efforts to combat sanism, as a means of "strip[ping] bare the law's sanist façade" and as a "powerful tool that will serve as a means of attacking and uprooting the we/they distinction that has traditionally plagued and stigmatized the mentally disabled." My friend, colleague, and co-presenter Susan Daicoff has already done a herculean job of looking at lawyer-stress issues through a TJ filter; I hope in this paper to add to that by considering squarely the impact of sanism on the underlying dilemmas.

This paper (1) briefly reviews the evidence as to rates of mental disability among practicing lawyers, the state of ADA law as it relates to lawyers with mental disability, and the caselaw that has emerged in the criminal procedure context with regard to ineffectiveness of counsel issues; (2) explains sanism and describes its impact upon the legal system with special attention paid to the narrow but important issue of its impact on lawyers with mental disabilities; (3) speculates as to why lawyers are as susceptible (or more susceptible) to sanism's pernicious power as others; and then (4) considers how an application of TJ principles to this problem may eventually have a redemptive effect.

My title for this paper comes from Bob Dylan's "Mama, You Been on My Mind," a song written in 1964 but not released officially by Dylan until 1991. Characterized by Oliver Trager in his definitive Dylan encyclopedia as "simply a great love song" with "gorgeous melody and cascading almost incantatory lyrics of romance and inevitable separation," the song includes this verse:

When you wake up in the mornin', baby, look inside your mirror.

You know I won't be next to you, you know I won't be near.

I'd just be curious to know if you can see yourself as clear

As someone who has had you on his mind.

Lawyers and the legal system fail miserably at "looking inside [their own] mirror," and lawyers do not see themselves "as clear." Perhaps it is time that we have ourselves on our collective minds.

I. What the Evidence Tells Us

Lawyers, as a group, are twice as likely to commit suicide as the general public. Practicing lawyers ranked highest in major depressive disorders among 104 occupational groups studied. The rate of alcoholism among practicing lawyers is generally estimated at being twice that of the rate of the general public, and even more startlingly, nearly 70% of lawyers are likely to have an alcohol problem at some time during their career. Estimates of substance abuse rates range from 9–20%. These statistics hold true for law students as well, and some evidence suggests that rates of clinical depression as well as alcohol and substance abuse rise regularly while students continue their legal education. These figures are appalling and appear to be higher for lawyers than for other professionals (presumably under like levels of stress). And they are made even more appalling by what appears to be widespread denial that there is anything wrong; the reality that less than .1% of practicing attorneys have reported "having a disability" suggests the enormity of this problem. I recognize that many states have compulsory or optional continuing legal education dealing with alcoholism and substance abuse issues among attorneys. But my sense — based on a combination of research and anecdote — suggests to me that this remains an issue that is still, at best, under the radar for many or, at worst, the subject of a "don't ask, don't tell" attitude.

There is no doubt that these are frightening statistics, and at this point in time they should be a surprise to no one. But what is perhaps more frightening is the reality that very few of us seem to notice or care. It is not a coincidence, I think, that one of the bar journal articles — about impaired judges — is titled The Worst Kept Secret in the Courthouse. There are multiple articles in state-level bar journals calling attention to our abysmal record, but I see no evidence that this is an issue that has grabbed the attention of the practicing bar, the academy, or the judiciary, notwithstanding the great publicity that attended the first ABA National Conference on the Employment of Lawyers with Disabilities. To paraphrase a more famous Bob Dylan song: something's happening, but we don't care what it is.

What we are paying attention to, however, is the intersection between mental disability and a cluster of other issues: the impact of such mental disability on bar disciplinary proceedings; the application of the ADA to such matters, and to the bar examination process; and the role of a lawyer's mental disability in a defendant's appeal of a criminal conviction in which the defendant alleges he was denied effective assistance of counsel under *Strickland v. Washington*.

In each of these scenarios, questions of mental disability are raised and evaluated, often with apparently inconsistent results. Bar discipline cases often talk about mental illness as if it were curable in precisely the same way that a sore throat or cold is curable and reject mitigation arguments unless lawyers can "prove that the risk of continued substance abuse causing future acts of misconduct is virtually nonexistent." Underlying the cases is a powerful current of blame: claims of mitigation are rejected on the basis that the initial use of alcohol and drugs was voluntary. Decisions in these cases eerily track decisions under the Federal Sentencing Guidelines that reject arguments seeking mitigation in the sentencing process unless the defendant's mental disability mimics that of an insanity defense (usually, that he cannot tell right from wrong). In short, the assessment by a student author — "[u]ntil recently, the profession has preferred to ignore the possibility of rehabilitation for mentally ill attorneys[; i]nstead, courts have drummed them out of the profession" — appears to be frighteningly accurate.

The phrase "until recently" used by the author in the article just cited refers to a (partial) change that has followed the passage of the ADA. Yet, virtually without exception, ADA claims have been rejected by the courts. Notwithstanding Professor Laura Rothstein's bold and optimistic prediction that the ADA "will permit individuals with disabilities to have a level playing field in … the practice of law," nearly two decades of practice under the ADA has made it clear that, in the words of one commentator, "courts have consistently held that the ADA does not prevent courts from taking disciplinary action against attorneys with disabilities." In a Florida case, the court concluded that, even if any of the respondent's "actions occurred when he could not distinguish right from wrong, the ADA would not necessarily bar this [c]ourt from imposing sanctions," thus establishing a more stringent standard in ADA cases than in criminal insanity defense cases! Not coincidentally, the same case raised the tiresome and shopworn specter of fakery, a cliched, though ubiquitous, fear that continues to resonate with many, including, notoriously, Supreme Court Justice Antonin Scalia.

The bar admission and testing cases are somewhat different. A significant percentage of all ADA cases involving questions of mental disability involve this cohort of cases, most narrowing the scope of acceptable questions on the bar admission application form, but some sustaining the use of such questions. In discussing this topic, commentators have voiced concern that intensive questioning on this topic "may encourage applicants with true psychological problems to avoid seeking psychiatric treatment in fear of not obtaining a license, which will pose a greater risk to the public." In general, however, there is probably little question that ADA litigation on these bar admission and testing issues has had more of an impact on practice than such litigation has had on bar discipline issues. The question here remains: Has the ADA been successful in meeting the challenge of "eradicating stereotypes and misconceptions regarding qualified individuals with disabilities?" More to the point, can we or should we continue "[t]o label lawyers with non-visible disabilities as the probable class of incompetent lawyers?"

The application of *Strickland v. Washington* to cases involving lawyers with mental disability has been, to be charitable, bizarre. In the lead case, *Smith v. Ylst*, the court rejected a defendant's *Strickland*-based appeal in a case where his lawyer, in opening statements, discussed a conspiracy theory that purportedly endangered the lawyer's life. In coming to its decision, the court analogized to cases involving competency to stand trial, and relying on, in part, the Supreme Court's 1966 decision in *Pate v. Robinson*, it found that a hearing would be required "when there is substantial evidence that an attorney is not competent to conduct an effective defense." Based on the evidence before it, and notwithstanding psychiatric affidavits submitted to the court that the lawyer, at that time, was undergoing a "paranoid psychotic reaction," and notwithstanding other evidence that "created a doubt as to [trial counsel]'s mental stability," the Ninth Circuit concluded that the decision to not hold such a hearing was not "erroneous."

Other state and federal courts have held that abuse of alcohol, cocaine, or prescription medication does not create per se ineffectiveness. Perhaps the most stunning example is the case of *Bellamy v. Cogdell*. In *Bellamy*, a death penalty case, counsel — who was subject to a disciplinary hearing to determine whether he should still be able to practice law (because of his incapacity) — was allowed to continue representing his client. Due to a finding of mental impairment, trial counsel was thus initially disqualified from defending himself in his own disciplinary hearing. To be able to continue representing his client in *Bellamy*, he promised he would only serve in an advisory capacity to competent lead counsel. However, as that lead counsel was unable to attend the trial, the same attorney who was mentally incompetent to defend himself was allowed to defend someone else charged with murder, and that representation in that trial was deemed effective assistance of counsel under the *Strickland* test. These decisions are consistent with other decisions affirming convictions involving defendants whose attorneys fell asleep in court, came to court inebriated, etc.

Judges' refusals to consider the meaning and realities of mental illness cause them to act in what appears, at first blush, to be contradictory and inconsistent ways, and teleologically, to privilege (where that privileging serves what they perceive as a socially-beneficial value) and subordinate (where that subordination serves what they perceive as a similar value) evidence of mental illness. Thus, it is no surprise that courts that regularly engage in gross stereotyping with regard to the impact of mental illness on behavior in the context of the sentencing of persons convicted of crime or facing involuntary civil commitment, similarly minimize it in cases where recognition of that impact might lead to a socially-undesirable result, such as an insanity acquittal, where this tactic allows them to engage in greater social control. In this instance, sanist behavior leads to pretextual outcomes.

When these cohorts of cases are read together, some common threads can be teased out: there is absolutely no indication that the statistics regarding the high incidence of lawyer dysfunction discussed earlier are known (or, if known, are of interest) to the judges deciding the cases; there is substantial blame of lawyers with mental disabilities, often accompanied by thinly-veiled suggestions that their disability was their fault; courts simply do not want to acknowledge that the non-discrimination principles of the ADA apply to attorney discipline matters, though they are grudgingly beginning to "get" that they apply to bar application questionnaire cases; and the desire to uphold criminal convictions against *Strickland* attacks leads to behavior that is—there is no other descriptor—utterly pretextual.

In an article about the Federal Sentencing Guidelines that I co-authored with Professor Keri Gould some twelve years ago, this was our conclusion: The cases reported so far reflect no coherent reading of the Guidelines and no real understanding of the role of mental disability, short of an exculpating insanity defense, in criminal behavior. Federal judges are remarkably inconsistent in their reading of mental disability. The caselaw suggests that federal judges have not seriously considered the way mental disability should be assessed in sentencing decisions, and that random decisions generally reflect a judge's "ordinary common sensical read" of whether an individual defendant "really" could have overcome his disability. We contend that this is caused by several factors:

> (1) a lack of understanding on the part of federal judges and defense counsel as to the meaning of mental disability and its potential interrelationship with criminal behavior;

> (2) the structure of the insanity defense as an all-or-nothing alternative, causing many to believe that lesser evidence of mental disorder is simply an insufficient factor to consider in sentencing decisions.

I believe that judicial (and social) attitudes in the sorts of cases that I am discussing here track these attitudes almost precisely. In that context, we concluded then that the "pernicious forces" of sanism and pretextuality drove the developments on which we reported. I believe the same forces are at play here.

II. On Sanism

Sanism permeates all aspects of mental disability law and affects all participants in the mental disability law system—litigants, fact finders, counsel, and expert and lay witnesses. Its corrosive effects have warped mental disability law jurisprudence in involuntary civil commitment law, institutional law, tort law, and all aspects of the criminal process (pretrial, trial, and sentencing). It reflects what civil rights lawyer Florynce Kennedy has characterized as the "pathology of oppression."

We must consider sanism hand-in-glove with pretextuality. "Pretextuality" means that courts accept (either implicitly or explicitly) testimonial dishonesty and engage similarly in dishonest (and frequently meretricious) decision-making, specifically where witnesses, especially expert witnesses, show a high propensity to purposely distort their testimony in order to achieve desired ends. "This pretextuality is poisonous; it infects all participants in the judicial system, breeds cynicism and disrespect for the law, demeans participants, and reinforces shoddy lawyering, blase judging, and, at times, perjurious and/or corrupt testifying."

In another article (dealing primarily with the impact of sanism on clinical education), I asserted that sanism permeates the legal representation process both in cases in which mental capacity is a central issue and those in which such capacity is a collateral question. I found that "[s]anist lawyers (1) distrust their mentally disabled clients, (2) trivialize their complaints, (3) fail to forge authentic attorney-client relationships with such clients and reject their clients' potential contributions to case-strategizing, and (4) take less seriously case outcomes that are adverse to their clients."

The pretexts of the forensic mental health system are reflected both in the testimony of forensic experts and in the decisions of legislators and fact-finders. Experts frequently testify in accordance with their own self-referential concepts of "morality" and openly subvert statutory and case-law criteria that impose rigorous behavioral standards as predicates for commitment or that articulate functional standards as prerequisites for an incompetency-to-stand-trial finding. Often this testimony is further warped by a heuristic bias. Expert witnesses—like the rest of us—succumb to the seductive allure of simplifying cognitive devices in their thinking and employ such heuristic gambits as the vividness effect or attribution theory in their testimony. This testimony is then weighed and evaluated by frequently sanist fact-finders. Judges and jurors, both consciously and unconsciously, often rely on reductionist, prejudice-driven stereotypes in their decision-making, thus subordinating statutory and case law standards as well as the legitimate interests of the mentally disabled persons who are the subject of the litigation. Judges' predispositions to employ the same sorts of heuristics as do expert witnesses further contaminate the process.

As I have previously noted:

> I believe that these two concepts have controlled—and continue to control—modern mental disability law. Just as importantly (perhaps, more importantly), they continue to exert this control invisibly. This invisibility means that the most important aspects of mental disability law—not just the law "on the books," but, more importantly, the law in action and practice—remains hidden from the public discussions about mental disability law.

These attitudes corrupt the entire process of dealing with lawyers who have mental disabilities. Because, socially, we encourage punishment for those who demonstrate a "lack of effort" or are "responsible" for their failure, we blind ourselves willfully to the realities of mental illness, to the "gray areas" of human behavior, and to behavioral, scientific, cultural, and empirical realities. As a result of this self-inflicted blindness, we blame lawyers with mental disabilities for their status, we minimize the impact of mental disabilities on their actions, and we—in criminal cases—allow this minimization to pretextually affirm convictions of defendants whose trials did not meet the minimum levels of decency that the criminal justice system demands. It is no coincidence that, in the bar cases, we employ language that reflects the most sanist language employed in criminal cases.

There is a massive database that tells us of the extent to which the problem of stigma continues to pervade all aspects of society. Our refusal to confront the extent to which mental disability (and alcoholism and substance abuse) affect the bar, the inevitable impact those conditions have on legal practice and the lives of practitioners continue to reflect sanist behaviors and attitudes, as do decisions that impute blame to those with such disabilities. Our abject failure to acknowledge the ways that this willful blindness corrupts the criminal justice system exacerbates this shameful state of affairs.

III. Lawyers' Susceptibility to Sanism

There is, to be sure, some irony in all this. Lawyers—whose job it is to provide effective representation to all their clients—fall prey to the same sanist and pretextual contaminants that distort the actions of other players in the judicial system. Just as judges and jurors "frequently rely on reductionist, prejudice-driven stereotypes in their decision-making, thus subordinating statutory and caselaw standards as well as the legitimate interests of the mentally disabled persons who are the subject of the litigation," so do lawyers. I have argued elsewhere that lawyers who represent persons with mental disabilities reflect "sanist practices." If lawyers who serve as professors and supervisors in clinical programs reflect ongoing sanist biases, it should not surprise us that other members of the bar and the judiciary are susceptible to the same prejudice. It is a problem that cries out for remediation.

IV. Therapeutic Jurisprudence

TJ questions whether legal rules, procedures, and roles can or should be reshaped so as to enhance their therapeutic potential while preserving due process principles. Elsewhere, I have suggested that TJ has the capacity to "expose pretextuality and strip bare the law's sanist façade." To what extent might TJ be a tool to serve this end in this particular context? Susan Daicoff argues that one way to counteract the "rampant" dissatisfaction on the part of lawyers with their work is an adaptation of what she calls a "TJ/PL [preventative law] practice." She argues:

> Because of its emphasis on psychological well-being, interpersonal dynamics and relationships, and human behavior, TJ/PL offers [dissatisfied] lawyers a way to optimize their strengths, to use their special humanistic and caring skills, and to practice law in an ultimately satisfying way that has beneficial effects on all involved. With TJ/PL, the lawyer can finally "do good," help people, prevent harm, avoid interpersonal conflict, build and maintain relationships instead of tear them asunder, and become a positive force in people's lives rather than a necessary and often-hated evil.

Furthermore, at least some, if not all, lawyers and clients desperately need to experience the lawyer-client interaction as a positive, healing experience. TJ/PL offers one avenue to this end because it explicitly values mental health concerns, emotional consequences, and interpersonal relationships inherent in many legal matters.

There is no question that the current state of affairs is abjectly anti-therapeutic to virtually all who are touched by the legal system—lawyers, clients, the general public. I believe there are several remedial steps we can take—in addition to the ones initially set out so clearly and eloquently a decade ago by Professor Daicoff—to ameliorate current conditions. Consider the following:

1. We must acknowledge—openly and candidly—the extent to which disability and addiction permeate the profession and affect the practice of law. Acknowledgment of this reality should not be limited to articles in local bar journals. The topic should be added to scholarly agendas of academics, and national bar leaders should take the lead in initiating a national, top-priority conversation on this question.

2. In bar disciplinary hearings, decision-makers should abandon the culture of blame that they have embraced; should avoid parallels to insanity defense standards, burdens of proof in criminal trials, malingering fears, and federal sentencing guideline mitigation standards; and should rather seek to enter orders in such cases that are at once protective of the public, but also sensitive to the realities of mental illness and addiction-driven behavior.

3. These approaches should be implemented in ADA cases in this area of law and practice as well.

4. It is hard to imagine a more anti-therapeutic case than *Strickland*. Criminal defendants whose lawyers fall asleep in court or come to court inebriated, and who are then convicted, and whose appeals are rejected perfunctorily on the basis of *Strickland*, will not likely find the criminal trial process one that makes rehabilitation easy or acceptance of responsibility likely. Cases in which defendants with a lawyer who assumes representation while in the midst of a serious psychotic episode are, for these purposes, no different. If courts were to acknowledge the pretextual bases of such decisions as *Smith v. Ylst* or *Bellamy v. Cogdell*, the first step toward a more therapeutic jurisprudence would be taken. Courts continually and routinely ignore the reality that defendants represented by lawyers with serious mental disabilities—even lawyers deemed incompetent to represent themselves in civil actions—may have valid *Strickland* claims. Such actions bespeak pretextuality.

I am not so naive as to think that these changes would serve as full amelioration. But they would be a valuable series of first steps.

Conclusion

I shared the statistics that I discuss in this paper with a heterogeneous group (in terms of age, gender, politics, area of practice) of lawyer friends. Many assumed the statistics were skewed, biased, artificial, etc. Others questioned the methodology ("Does it include someone who graduated law school but didn't practice law?" "Maybe they were this way before they started to practice law?"). Only a few truly "got it." I do not think that this denial is in any way atypical of the bar as a whole, and I think it flows in large part from the extent to which sanism—even unconscious sanism—affects individuals who are otherwise thoughtful, intelligent, politically articulate, and nuanced. Like the judges in many of the cases I have discussed, though, they decline to, in Dylan's words, "look inside [their] mirror." I hope that the publication of this paper inspires a few, at least, to do so.

* * *

Questions for Discussion

1. Why do you think there is a widespread alcohol and substance abuse problem among lawyers? What do you think can be done about this, if anything?

2. What do you think of the idea of "sanism"?

3. What do you think of the author's suggested list of remedial steps? Can you think of other possible steps?

4. Should issues surrounding substance abuse be considered in the same way as issues surounding mental health?

The following is a case about law students with disabilities applying to the Texas State bar. Some footnotes have been omitted, and some of the decision has been edited for length.

Applicants v. The Texas State Board of Law Examiners

No. A 93 CA 740 SS
UNITED STATES DISTRICT COURT FOR THE WESTERN
DISTRICT OF TEXAS, AUSTIN DIVISION
U.S. Dist. LEXIS 21290 (W.D. Tx 1994);
4 Am. Disabilities Cas. (BNA) 165

SAM SPARKS, District Judge.

The plaintiffs, individually and on behalf of those similarly situated, allege that the Texas Board of Law Examiners' inquiries and investigation into the mental health history of applicants seeking to practice law in the State of Texas violate the Americans with Disabilities Act (ADA), 42 U.S.C. Sections 12101–12213 (West Pamph. 1993). The defendants are the Texas Board of Law Examiners and Rachel Martin, its executive director, collectively referred to as the defendants or the Board.

The plaintiffs, three law students who wish to be admitted to the Texas Bar, specifically challenge Section 82.027(b)(2) of the Texas Government Code requiring applicants to verify they are not mentally ill, the Texas Rules of Court governing admission that require applicants to execute an authorization for release of psychiatric records, and the Board's inquiries concerning treatment or hospitalization for mental illness in the preceding ten years and the follow-up investigations and hearings. The plaintiffs contend the statute, rules, inquiries, and investigations violate the ADA's prohibitions of discrimination against individuals on the basis of mental disability, a history of mental disability, or perceived mental disability. For these alleged violations, the plaintiffs seek injunctive and declaratory relief.

This cause was tried before the Court, without a jury, on July 7, 1994. For the reasons set forth below, the Court finds the Board's narrowly focused inquiries and investigation into the mental fitness of applicants to the Texas Bar who have been diagnosed or treated for bipolar disorder, schizophrenia, paranoia, or any other psychotic disorder do not violate the ADA.

I. FINDINGS OF FACT

Pursuant to Texas Government Code Section 82.022(b), the Texas Supreme Court adopted the Texas Rules of Court that "govern the administration of the (Board's) functions relating to the licensing of lawyers." Tex. Gov't Code Ann. Section 82.022 (West 1988). The Texas Government Code further requires each person intending to apply for admission to the Texas Bar to file with the Board a declaration of intention to study law and, before taking the bar examination, an application for examination. Sections 82.023, 82.027.

The Board is charged with assessing each applicant's moral character and fitness to practice law based on its investigation of the character and fitness of applicants. Sections 82028(a), 82.030(a). The Board, in fulfilling its statutory duties, must recommend denial of a license if the Board finds "a clear and rational connection between the applicant's present mental or emotional condition and the likelihood that the applicant will not discharge properly the applicant's responsibilities to a client, a court, or the legal profession if the applicant is licensed to practice law." Section 82.028(c)(2).

The Board's investigation is limited to areas "clearly related to the applicant's moral character and present fitness to practice law." Section 82.028(d). The rules promulgated by the Texas Supreme Court that govern admission to the Texas bar define fitness as "the assessment of mental and emotional health as it affects the competence of a prospective lawyer." Rules Governing Admission to the Bar of Texas, Rule IV. The fitness requirement is designed to exclude from the practice of law in Texas those persons having a mental or emotional condition that "would prevent the person from carrying out duties to clients, courts, or the profession." Id. The fitness requirement is limited to present fitness; "prior mental or emotional illness or conditions are relevant only so far as they indicate the existence of a present lack of fitness." Id.

Persons intending to seek admission to the Texas Bar usually file their declarations during the first year of law school. The rules require each applicant filing a declaration to provide extensive information about his or her background, including a history of mental illness. Rules Governing Admission to the Bar of Texas, Rule VI(D). The Rules also provide that the Board may require the applicant to execute a consent form authorizing the release of records to the Board. Id.

The questions formulated by the Board to seek information about an applicant's mental health history have been substantially revised since 1992 in efforts to comply with the ADA. Question 11, the question the Board used in the declaration before April 1992, asked whether the applicant had been treated for any mental, emotional, or nervous condition in the past ten years and if the condition had resulted in either voluntary or involuntary admission to a hospital or institution.[1] Between April 1992 and July 1993, the Board used a version of question 11 that narrowed the focus to mental illness as defined by the Texas Health and Safety Code.[2] The current version of question 11 further

---

1. The version of question 11 the Board used before April 1992 asked:
   11. Have you, within the last ten (10) years:
   a) Been examined or treated for any mental, emotional or nervous conditions? (You may exclude marriage counseling.)
   b) Been voluntarily or involuntarily admitted to a hospital or institution as a result of mental, emotional or nervous conditions?
   If you answered "YES" to 11a. or b., give details on the Supplemental Form. Include dates of treatment or confinement, name and current mailing address of the person(s) who treated you (or the facility where you received treatment), and the reason for treatment.
2. The version of question 11 used between April 1992 and July 1993 asked:
   11. a) Have you, within the last ten (10) years, been treated for any mental illness? b) Have you, within the last ten (10) years, been admitted to any hospital or other facility for the treatment of any mental illness? Section 571.033, Texas Health and Safety Code, defines mental illness, as follows: "Mental illness" means an illness, disease, or condition other than epilepsy, senility, alcoholism, or mental deficiency, that: (A) substantially impairs a person's

narrows the inquiry to the diagnosis of certain specified mental illnesses that may bear on an applicant's present fitness to practice law.[3] Dr. Richard Coons, one of the experts who testified on the Board's behalf and who is educated as a lawyer, medical doctor, and psychiatrist, was a consultant to the Board in the Board's formulation of the current version of question 11.

An affirmative answer to any part of question 11 triggers a requirement that the applicant provide a detailed description of the diagnosis or treatment and identify and provide the address of each individual that has treated the applicant. The current declaration also includes a general authorization and release for records that each applicant must sign. The current authorization limits the release of mental health records to only those pertaining to diagnosis of the conditions specified in question 11.

As part of the investigation process, each applicant must identify employers or clients and provide character references. The Board then sends forms to the identified references requesting information about the applicant. The current form sent to individuals listed in the declaration by the applicant as character references, employers, or former clients includes a question regarding the reference's knowledge about whether the applicant has been diagnosed or treated in the past ten years for bipolar disorder, schizophrenia, paranoia, or any psychotic disorder.

In addition to the declaration, each person wishing to take the Bar exam must file an application not later than 180 days before the examination. By law, the application is to consist of a verified affidavit that requires, among other statements, an assertion that the applicant is not mentally ill. This statutory requirement is implemented in the Board's current application by requiring each applicant to sign a verified affidavit stating, among other things, that the applicant has not been diagnosed, treated, or hospitalized since the filing of the declaration for bipolar disorder, schizophrenia, or any psychotic disorder.

Bipolar disorder, schizophrenia, paranoia, and psychotic disorders are serious mental illnesses that may affect a person's ability to practice law. People suffering from these illnesses may suffer debilitating symptoms that inhibit their ability to function normally. The fact that a person may have experienced an episode of one of these mental illnesses in the past but is not currently experiencing symptoms does not mean that the person will not experience another episode in the future or that the person is currently fit to practice law. Indeed, a person suffering from one of these illnesses may have extended periods between episodes, possibly as much as ten years for bipolar disorder or schizophrenia.

---

thought, perception of reality, emotional process, or judgment; or (B) grossly impairs behavior as demonstrated by recent disturbed behavior.

If you answered "YES" to any part of this question, provide details on the Supplemental Form. Include dates of treatment, name, current mailing address, and telephone number of each person who treated you, each facility where you received treatment, and the reason for each treatment.

3. The current version of question 11 asks:

11. a) Within the last ten years, have you been diagnosed with or have you been treated by bipolar disorder, schizophrenia, paranoia, or any other psychotic disorder?

b) Have you, since attaining the age of eighteen or within the last ten years, whichever period is shorter, been admitted to a hospital or other facility for the treatment of bipolar disorder, schizophrenia, paranoia, or any other psychotic disorder?

If you answered "YES" to any part of this question, please provide details on a Supplemental Form, including date(s) of diagnosis or treatment, a description of the course of treatment, and a description of your present condition. Include the name, current mailing address, and telephone number of each person who treated you, as well as each facility where you received treatment, and the reason for treatment.

Although a past diagnosis of the mental illness will not necessarily predict the applicant's future behavior, the mental health history is important to provide the Board with information regarding the applicant's insight into his or her illness and degree of cooperation in controlling it through counseling and medication. In summary, inquiry into past diagnosis and treatment of the severe mental illnesses is necessary to provide the Board with the best information available with which to assess the functional capacity of the individual.

The plaintiffs are law students in ABA-approved law schools. Applicant A, a first year law student, was hospitalized in the past five years in a psychiatric facility for the treatment of depression with psychotic features and currently takes anti-depressant medication. Applicant A has not filed a declaration, pending resolution of this lawsuit. Under the current question, applicant A would be required to answer "yes."

Applicant B, a first-year law student, received out-patient mental health services in the past ten years for the treatment of a depressive disorder and is currently involved in group therapy. Applicant B filed a declaration on November 15, 1993, in which Applicant B, who has not been treated for the mental illnesses specified in the current version of question 11, answered the question "no."

Applicant C, a second-year law student, received out-patient mental health services in the past ten years for the treatment of a depressive disorder, currently takes anti-depressant and anti-anxiety medications, and received therapy. Applicant C completed the declaration before the Board's 1993 amendments to the questions concerning mental health treatment, answering "yes" to the preceding question used from April 92 to July 93. Applicant C has not been treated or hospitalized for bipolar disorder, schizophrenia, paranoia, or any other psychotic condition in the past ten years and, therefore, would answer the current question 11 "no."

None of the plaintiffs have a history of criminal activity, financial irresponsibility, or academic discipline. At this time, none of the applicants have filed the application to take the Bar exam.

Before the current wording of question 11, if an applicant answered any part of the question affirmatively, the staff technician screening the file generally would order the treatment records. Marshall depo. at 47. In many cases, the technician would then forward the file and records to the director of fitness and character, Jack Marshall, or his assistant.[4] If after his review, Marshall was concerned about the mental health history of the person, he would place the person's name on the "Potentials Hearing Report" and discuss the file with Board's executive director or a staff attorney.[5] Thus, following the conclusion of the investigation of the applicant, one of three things occurred: 1) the person's technician certified the person's present fitness; 2) if the person's name had been placed on the "Potential Hearings List," Marshall, following discussion with the executive director or staff attorney, would instruct the technician to certify the person's present fitness; or 3)

---

4. Marshall has served as the Board's director of fitness and character since November 1986. He is not a lawyer and has not had formal training in the area of mental health. Marshall depo. at 5, 12. Although in most cases, the file was forwarded to Marshall or his assistant, there have been cases in which, after review of the records, the technician was able to clear the problem with no review from supervisory staff. Id. at 49–50. Marshall estimated during his tenure, he has reviewed approximately 35 files as a result of affirmative responses to question 11. Id. at 60–62.

5. Id. at 51. Two circumstances often triggered Marshall's concern about the present mental fitness of applicants: 1) if an applicant was currently in treatment or hospitalized; and 2) if an applicant's history included numerous hospitalizations, including a recent hospitalization. Id. at 52–53. If, however, the Board received a statement from an applicant's treating physician that the individual had the mental fitness to practice law, Marshall generally would not forward the file to the executive director. Id. at 54–55.

Marshall, in consultation with the executive director or a staff attorney, made a preliminary determination that the applicant did not possess the present fitness to practice law, necessitating consideration of the matter by the actual Board. The Board sent persons in the third category a preliminary determination letter detailing the results of the investigation and giving them thirty days to respond to the letter. Id. The applicant also had the right to request a hearing, unless the Board had already determined a hearing was necessary. Id. Following the hearing, the Board could require an applicant to be evaluated by a mental health professional. Marshall depo. at 71–73.

In practice, very few applicants are actually placed on the "Potential Hearings Report." Id. at 62. In fact, the treating physicians of approximately half the applicants answering question 11 affirmatively indicated comfort with the applicant's fitness to practice law. Id.

Because of the narrowed focus of the current question 11, the Board's current policy is that Marshall will review all affirmative responses to the mental health question. Marshall will determine, based on the information provided in the declaration, whether direct inquiries for additional information to mental health professionals who have treated the applicant are necessary. If Marshall deems it necessary to receive additional information, he, in consultation with the executive director and a staff attorney, will review the response. If they are not convinced the person's mental health problem is completely under control, Marshall will request complete records of treatment and send the applicant to an expert chosen by the Board for evaluation. If the expert recommends that the Board continue to investigate the person and if after that continued investigation a determination is made that the person may pose potential harm to clients, the person will be sent a preliminary determination of lack of present fitness and notice of a right to a hearing before the Board. P-32 at 4.

The Board has received only one affirmative response to the current mental health question. Id. at 2. In that case, Marshall has requested a summary of treatment from the treating professional. Id.

As a result of this litigation, Marshall researched the issue of the number of applicants whose files raised mental health concerns. See D-7. Since August 1987, the earliest "Potential Hearings Report" Marshall could find, thirty cases involved mental health issues. Of the thirty cases, nineteen raised serious mental health concerns. In thirteen of the cases, the information provided by the applicant was the only source of mental health information. Twenty-one of the cases were set for hearing, and in ten cases, the Board required a psychiatric evaluation or psychiatric review of the record following the hearing.

Of the nineteen cases involving serious mental heath concerns, one remains under investigation and two were cleared either by the staff following a review of recent psychological evaluations. The sixteen remaining cases were set for hearing with the following dispositions: one was denied admission to the Bar on mental health grounds; one was denied but not on mental health grounds; seven were approved by Board; two had hearings set but not held, and the applicants have taken no further action; one applicant's file was terminated for failure to execute a release for mental health records; one was approved by the Board with the caveat that a mental health update may be required upon filing of the application; one file was terminated for failure to complete a Board-required examination; one was approved for a temporary license that included a condition requiring mental health counseling; and one has been required to submit to a post-hearing psychological evaluation, the results of which are pending.

Eight of these cases resulted in either denial or inconclusive results. In five of the eight cases, the Board would have been unaware of mental health concerns absent the applicant's disclosure. In the three remaining cases in this group, mental health concerns were developed as a result of the applicant's disclosure and information received from other sources.

CONCLUSIONS OF LAW

1. As a preliminary matter, the defendants have challenged the plaintiffs' standing to bring this cause of action, claiming none of the plaintiffs have sustained an injury—in-fact. Title II of the ADA provides that "no qualified individual with a disability shall, by reason of such disability, be excluded from participation in or be denied the benefits of the services, programs, or activities of a public entity or be subjected to discrimination by any such entity." ADA Section 12122. Although none of the plaintiffs have been denied a license, Applicant A will be required to answer question 11 affirmatively and, as a result of that question, will be subjected to further investigation. Further, at the time this suit was filed, the Board's application affidavit required applicants to state whether they had been mentally ill since the filing of the declaration. Both Applicants B and C have received treatment for mental illness in the past ten years and, therefore, would have to state on the application that they had been mentally ill. In fact, Applicant C was required to respond affirmatively to the question in force at the time Applicant C filed the declaration. The Board has voluntarily revised both the question on the declaration and, subsequent to the filing of this suit, the application question. Additionally, the Board's counsel ac-knowledged at trial that the previous versions of the question were not in compliance with the ADA. However, the Texas statute allows the Board, at its discretion, to inquire into an applicant's mental illness and, therefore, the Board could, theoretically, return to use of the broader form question. Accordingly, the Court finds the Applicants have standing to bring this suit.

The ADA defines a "public entity" as "any department, agency or other instrumentality of a State ... or local government." 42 U.S.C. Section 12131(1)(B). The Board as the state governmental agency responsible for licensing attorneys in the State of Texas is a public entity within the ADA definition.

Under the ADA, "disability" is defined as a physical or mental impairment that substantially impairs a major life activity, a record of such impairment, or being regarded as having such impairment. ADA Section 12102(2). If an individual meets any one of these three tests, he or she is considered to be an individual with a disability for the purposes of ADA coverage. A mental impairment includes "[a]ny mental or psychological disorder such as emotional or mental illness...." 28 C.F.R. Section 35.104 (1993). Thus, individuals not currently impaired but who have a history of mental illness or emotional disorder may fit within the second and third elements of the statutory definition. Applicants A, B, and C come within one or more prongs of the definition and, therefore, are disabled, as defined by the ADA.

The prohibition against discrimination extends to "qualified individual[s] with a disability." A person is a "qualified individual with a disability" in the context of licensing or certification if the person can meet the essential eligibility requirements for receiving a license or certification. The regulations prohibit the imposition of eligibility criteria that "screen out or tend to screen out" a disabled individual from "fully and equally enjoying any service, program, or activity, unless such criteria can be shown to be necessary for the provision or the service, program, or activity being offered." Section 35.130(b)(8). When, as in this case, questions of public safety are involved, the determination of whether an applicant meets "essential eligibility requirements" involves consideration of whether the individual with a disability poses a direct threat to the health and safety of others. 28

C.F.R. pt. 35, app. A, at 448. However, a determination that a person poses such a threat may not be based on generalizations or stereotypes about the effects of a particular disability but must be based on an individualized assessment, based on reasonable judgment that relies on current medical evidence or on the best available objective evidence, to determine: the nature, duration, and severity of the risk; the probability that the potential injury will actually occur; and whether reasonable modifications of policies, practices, or procedures will mitigate the risk. Id.

2. The plaintiffs argue that the all the mental health questions the Board has used, including the present narrow inquiry, inquire into an individual's status as mentally ill rather than focusing on behaviors that would affect the individual's ability to practice law. They contend such inquiry is not necessary, the standard required by the ADA to justify the application of criteria that "screen out or tend to screen out," because the same information can be ascertained through other sources and means. In support of their position, the plaintiffs direct the Court's attention to recent court orders holding that mental health questions asked on other states' licensing applications violate the ADA. See *Medical Soc'y v. Jacobs*, No. 93-3670 [2 Am. Disabilities Cas. (BNA) 1318] (U.S.D.C. N.J. Oct. 5, 1993) (question whether physicians seeking renewal of licenses had ever suffered or been treated for mental illness violated ADA); *In re applications of Plano and Underwood*, No. BAR-93-21 [3 Am. Disabilities Cas. (BNA) 573] (Me. Dec. 7, 1993) (questions regarding whether applicants had ever been diagnosed with "an emotional, nervous or mental disorder" and whether they had received treatment of the disorder in the past ten years were invalid under ADA).

The plaintiffs suggest that applicants to the Board have already been extensively screened by virtue of successfully completing college and achieving admission to law school. Further, any aberrant behavior that might bear on their present mental fitness would be apparent from a criminal, educational, or employment history. The plaintiffs presented evidence that, in fact, the current question was imperfect in that some who suffer from the specified mental illnesses may be missed by current question because they have not sought diagnosis or treatment. The plaintiffs suggest reliance on other facets of the investigatory process applied to all applicants or a series of question aimed at behavior would comply with the ADA and would be just as effective as the process the Board currently employs. Alternatively, the plaintiffs suggest asking applicants to voluntarily disclose if they suffer from any mental illness that could affect their ability to perform the functions essential to being a lawyer.

The ADA prohibits the use of licensing procedures that "screen out or tend to screen out" individuals defined as disabled under the ADA unless the screening criteria are necessary to the service being offered. The defendant's expert testified that a direct mental health inquiry like the current question 11 is necessary in the licensing process to get a full understanding of the functional capacity of the applicant's mental fitness. The defendant's expert further testified that the inquiry should go back a minimum of five years and optimally ten years because of the chronic nature of the severe mental illnesses specified in the current question 11, which often have an onset during adolescence. Although relying on past behavior in other areas may reveal behavior relevant to mental fitness, the evidence reflected that in the majority of cases already reviewed by the Board, this was not the case. Further, self-disclosure-type questions suffer, possibly to a greater degree, from some of the same defects the plaintiffs criticize in the current question— those who answer untruthfully or who do not recognize or understand the nature and extent of their illness will not be identified.

The plaintiffs further contend that because only one person has been denied admission to the bar since 1986 based on mental health concerns, the question serves no useful purpose. The Court finds this contention also to be without merit. The plaintiffs' argument ignores the fact that other applicants subjected to investigation as a result of an affirmative answer to question 11 have not pursued the process, have had their files terminated for failure to comply with requirements, and have received temporary licenses contingent upon continued counseling. Further, for those applicants answering the mental health question affirmatively, the Board engages in an individualized, case-by-case investigation. In fact, the evidence reflects that many of the applicants answering the mental health question affirmatively are ultimately cleared by the Board and certified to have the present fitness to practice law. This highlights the Board's efforts to avoid improper generalization or stereotyping of mentally disabled individuals, as defined by the ADA, and to apply objective criteria on an individualized basis to determine if an applicant poses a threat to the public if licensed. The Court, therefore, finds the Board discharges its duty in a responsible manner while making every effort not to discriminate against those who have suffered a mental illness but have the present fitness to practice law.

The inquiries courts in other states have held prohibited by the ADA were virtually identical to the previous broad-based forms of question 11 used by the Board that intruded into an applicant's mental health history without focusing on only those mental illnesses that pose a potential threat to the applicant's present fitness to practice law. The Court concurs that such a broad-based inquiry violates the ADA.

As stated above, however, the ADA does not preclude a licensing body from any inquiry and investigation related to mental illness, instead allowing for such inquiry and investigation when they are necessary to protect the integrity of the service provided and the public. The Court recognizes that no perfect question can be formulated that will ensure all individuals suffering mental illnesses affecting their fitness to practice will be detected. As the plaintiff's expert testified, some may defer treatment to avoid having to answer affirmatively and others may not recognize that they suffer from a mental illness, thereby precluding diagnosis or treatment. However, reliance on "behaviors" occurring in other facets of an individual's life as triggers to indicate a mental illness affecting present fitness may be present is a much more inexact and potentially unreliable method of ascertaining mental fitness.[6]

The plaintiffs, seeking to vindicate the rights of the mentally disabled, fail to account for the awesome responsibility with which the Board is charged. The Board has a duty not to just the applicants, but also to the Bar and the citizens of Texas to make every effort to ensure that those individuals licensed to practice in Texas have the good moral character and present fitness to practice law and will not present a potential danger to the individuals they will represent. The Board has a limited opportunity to accomplish this task—the time of the filing of the declaration and application. The Board, therefore, must make every effort to investigate each applicant as thoroughly as possible and as efficiently as possible during this limited time.

Although a negative light is often cast upon the legal profession in the information that the general public receives and hears, in reality, lawyers serve the important role in our

---

6. Even the plaintiff's expert agreed that employment histories would not be perfect indicators because many employers may not be totally forthcoming about an employee's performance and behavior for fear of legal reprisal. Additionally, many applicants to law school do not have extensive employment histories because of their relatively young age. Further, the Court has concerns about the practical application of a "behavior" based method of ascertaining mental fitness and what difficulties the Board would encounter under the ADA in defining "behavior" sufficient to trigger a mental fitness investigation.

society of assisting people in the management of the most important of their affairs. Therefore, as a practical concern, the Board must evaluate each applicant's ability in light of the important responsibilities lawyers assume. Lawyers counsel individuals contemplating everything from divorce, bankruptcy, and the disposal of assets to the institutionalization of a loved one. Is it necessary that the Board inquire whether an applicant has been diagnosed or treated for bipolar disorder, schizophrenia, paranoia, or other psychosis before licensing the individual to assume these responsibilities? Before licensing the individual to write wills, manage trusts set up for minors and disabled individuals, or draft contracts affecting parties' rights and finances? Before licensing the individual to represent a parent in a proceeding to determine if the parent will maintain or lose custody of a child? Before licensing the individual to represent a [sic] individual charged with a crime who faces loss of liberty or even life? In each of these proceedings, the lawyer must be prepared to offer competent legal advice and representation despite the stress of understanding the responsibility the lawyer has assumed while balancing other clients' interests and time demands. The rigorous application procedure, including investigating whether an applicant has been diagnosed or treated for certain serious mental illnesses, is indeed necessary to ensure that Texas' lawyers are capable, morally and mentally, to provide these important services.

* * *

III. CONCLUSION

The purpose of the ADA is to protect disabled individuals from discrimination and to promote integration of disabled individuals into the mainstream of society. It is ludicrous, however, to propose that this purpose can only be accomplished by prohibiting a state from directly investigating and assessing an applicant's emotional and mental fitness to determine if the applicant has sufficient competence to discharge the responsibilities of a lawyer before the state warrants by licensing to the citizens that the individual has the mental and emotional fitness to fulfill a lawyer's legal, ethical, and moral responsibilities. The Board would be derelict in its duty if it did not investigate the mental health of prospective lawyers. It has made every effort to do so in the least intrusive, least discriminatory manner possible, focusing on only those serious mental illnesses that experts have indicated are likely to affect present fitness to practice law. It has limited the inquiry to a specified time frame, primarily spanning late adolescence and adult life. Although affirmative answers do trigger investigation that applicants answering negatively do not have to undergo, the affirmative answer does not result in an immediate denial of a license to practice law. The ensuing investigation serves two purposes: protection of the Bar and public as well as an opportunity for the applicant to indicate present fitness. Therefore, the Court finds, by a preponderance of the evidence that the Board's use of the current question 11, a narrowly focused question, and the subsequent investigation based on an affirmative response to the question are necessary to ensure the integrity of the Board's licensing procedure, as well as to provide a practical means of striking an appropriate balance between important societal goals. The Board's process furthers the goal of the ADA to integrate those defined as mentally disabled into society while ensuring that individuals licensed to practice law in Texas are capable of practicing law in a competent and ethical manner.

To the extent any finding of fact is a conclusion of law and any conclusion of law is a finding of fact, it should be considered as such.

In accordance with the above findings of fact and conclusions of law, the Court denies the injunctive and declaratory relief sought by the plaintiffs. Judgment shall be entered in favor of the defendant.

* * *

Questions for Discussion

1. What conflicting policies are evident in this case? What do you think the best resolution is?

2. What do you think of the various versions of "question 11"? Do you believe the current version (litigated in the case) is satisfactory?

3. What does your state's bar exam application ask about mental health issues? How does it compare to the application in this case?

For Further Reading

"Sara Granda '09 Passes California State Bar Exam after Legal Fight," retrieved May 15, 2012 at http://www.law.ucdavis.edu/news/news.aspx?id=2444. News story about a law student with disabilities whose bar exam application was rejected because she had no credit card.

Alexis Anderson and Norah Wylie, "Beyond the ADA: How Clinics Can Assist Law Students with Non-Visible Disabilities to Bridge the Accommodations Gap Between Classroom and Practice," *Clinical Law Review, Inc.* (2008).

Discussion 5

Inclusion and Exclusion of Kids at School

Recommended Background Reading

Board of Education of the Hendrick Hudson Central School District v. Rowley, 458 U.S. 176 (1982), holding that all students are allowed to attend school.

Cedar Rapids Community School Dist. v. Garret F., 526 U.S. 66 (1999), holding that even children with significant health issues must be allowed to attend school.

Readings for Class Discussion

The following case explores the issue of "least restrictive environment" in the elementary school setting. Footnotes and string citations have been omitted.

Sacramento City Unified School District v. Rachel H.

14 F.3d 1398; 1994 U.S. App. LEXIS 1124;
94 Cal. Daily Op. Service 482; 94 Daily Journal DAR 799
UNITED STATES COURT OF APPEALS FOR THE NINTH CIRCUIT
August 12, 1993, Argued, Submitted, San Francisco, California
January 24, 1994, Filed

SNEED, Circuit Judge:

The Sacramento Unified School District ("the District") timely appeals the district court's judgment in favor of Rachel Holland ("Rachel") and the California State Department of Education. The court found that the appropriate placement for Rachel under the Individuals with Disabilities Act ("IDEA") was full-time in a regular second grade classroom with some supplemental services. The District contends that the appropriate placement for Rachel is half-time in special education classes and half-time in a regular class. We affirm the judgment of the district court.

I. FACTS AND PRIOR PROCEEDINGS

Rachel Holland is now 11 years old and is moderately mentally retarded. She was tested with an I.Q. of 44. She attended a variety of special education programs in the District from 1985–89. Her parents sought to increase the time Rachel spent in a regular classroom, and in the fall of 1989, they requested that Rachel be placed full-time in a regular classroom for the 1989–90 school year. The District rejected their request and proposed a placement that would have divided Rachel's time between a special education class for academic subjects and a regular class for non-academic activities such as art, music, lunch, and recess. The district court found that this plan would have required moving Rachel at least 6 times each day between the two classrooms. The Hollands instead enrolled Rachel in a regular kindergarten class at the Shalom School, a private school. Rachel remained at the Shalom School in regular classes and at the time the district court rendered its opinion, was in the second grade.

The Hollands and the District were able to agree on an Individualized Education Program ("IEP") for Rachel. Although the IEP is required to be reviewed annually, see 20 U.S.C. § 1401(20)(B), because of the dispute between the parties, Rachel's IEP has not been reviewed since January 1990.

An IEP is prepared for each child eligible for special education at a meeting between a representative from the school district, the child's teacher, and the child's parents. *Board of Educ. v. Rowley*, 458 U.S. 176, 182, 73 L. Ed. 2d 690, 102 S. Ct. 3034 (1982). The purpose of the IEP is to tailor the child's education to her individual needs. Id. at 181.

The 1990 IEP objectives include: speaking in 4 or 5 word sentences; repeating instructions of complex tasks; initiating and terminating conversations; stating her name, address and phone number; participating in a safety program with classmates; developing a 24 word sight vocabulary; counting to 25; printing her first and last names and the alphabet; playing cooperatively; participating in lunch without supervision; and identifying upper and lower case letters and the sounds associated with them.

The Hollands appealed the District's placement decision to a state hearing officer pursuant to 20 U.S.C. § 1415(b)(2). They maintained that Rachel best learned social and academic skills in a regular classroom and would not benefit from being in a special education class. The District contended Rachel was too severely disabled to benefit from full-time placement in a regular class. The hearing officer concluded that the District had failed to make an adequate effort to educate Rachel in a regular class pursuant to the IDEA. The officer found that (1) Rachel had benefitted from her regular kindergarten class—that she was motivated to learn and learned by imitation and modeling; (2) Rachel was not disruptive in a regular classroom; and (3) the District had overstated the cost of putting Rachel in regular education—that the cost would not be so great that it weighed against placing her in a regular classroom. The hearing officer ordered the District to place Rachel in a regular classroom with support services, including a special education consultant and a part-time aide.

The District appealed this determination to the district court. Pursuant to 20 U.S.C. § 1415(e)(2), the parties presented additional evidence at an evidentiary hearing. The court affirmed the decision of the hearing officer that Rachel should be placed full-time in a regular classroom.

In considering whether the District proposed an appropriate placement for Rachel, the district court examined the following factors: (1) the educational benefits available to Rachel in a regular classroom, supplemented with appropriate aids and services, as compared with the educational benefits of a special education classroom; (2) the non-academic benefits of interaction with children who were not disabled; (3) the effect of Rachel's presence on the teacher and other children in the classroom; and (4) the cost of mainstreaming Rachel in a regular classroom.

1. Educational Benefits

The district court found the first factor, educational benefits to Rachel, weighed in favor of placing her in a regular classroom. Each side presented expert testimony which is summarized in the margin. The court noted that the District's evidence focused on Rachel's limitations, but did not establish that the educational opportunities available through special education were better or equal to those available in a regular classroom. Moreover, the court found that the testimony of the Hollands' experts was more credible because they had more background in evaluating children with disabilities placed in regular classrooms, and they had a greater opportunity to observe Rachel over an extended period of time in normal circumstances. The district court also gave great weight to the testimony of Rachel's current teacher, Nina Crone, who the court found to be an experienced, skillful teacher. Ms. Crone stated that Rachel was a full member of the class and participated in all activities. Ms. Crone testified that Rachel was making progress on her IEP goals — that Rachel was learning one-to-one correspondence in counting, could recite the English and Hebrew alphabets, and that her communication abilities and sentence lengths were also improving.

The district court found that Rachel received substantial benefits in regular education and that all of her IEP goals could be implemented in a regular classroom with some modification to the curriculum and with the assistance of a part-time aide.

2. Non-academic Benefits

The district court next found that the second factor, non-academic benefits to Rachel, also weighed in favor of placing her in a regular classroom. The court noted that the Hollands' evidence indicated that Rachel had developed her social and communications skills as well as her self-confidence from placement in a regular class, while the District's evidence tended to show that Rachel was not learning from exposure to other children and that she was isolated from her classmates. The court concluded that the differing evaluations in large part reflected the predisposition of the evaluators. The court found the testimony of Rachel's mother and her current teacher to be the most credible. These witnesses testified regarding Rachel's excitement about school, learning, and her new friendships, and Rachel's improved self-confidence.

3. Effect on the Teacher and Children in the Regular Class

The district court next addressed the issue of whether Rachel had a detrimental effect on others in her regular classroom. The court looked at two aspects, (1) whether there was detriment because the child was disruptive, distracting or unruly, and (2) whether the child would take up so much of the teacher's time that the other students would suffer from lack of attention. The witnesses of both parties agreed that Rachel followed directions, was well-behaved and not a distraction in class. The court found the most germane evidence on the second aspect came from Rachel's second grade teacher, Nina Crone, who testified that Rachel did not interfere with her ability to teach the other children and in the future would require only a part-time aide. Accordingly, the district court determined that the third factor weighed in favor of placing Rachel in a regular classroom.

4. Cost

Finally, the district court found that the District had not offered any persuasive or credible evidence to support its claim that educating Rachel in a regular classroom with appropriate services would be significantly more expensive than educating her in the District's proposed setting.

The District contended that it would cost $109,000 to educate Rachel full-time in a regular classroom. This figure was based on a full-time aide for Rachel and an estimate that it would cost over $ 80,000 to provide school-wide sensitivity training. The court found that the District did not establish that such training was necessary, and if it was, the court noted that there was evidence from the California Department of Education that the training could be had at no cost. Moreover, the court found it would be inappropriate to assign the total cost of the training to Rachel when other children with disabilities would benefit. In addition, the court concluded that the evidence did not suggest that Rachel required a full-time aide.

In addition, the court found that the comparison should have been between, on the one hand, the cost of placing Rachel in a special class with a full-time special education teacher and two full-time aides with approximately 11 other children, and, on the other hand, the cost of placing her in a regular class with a part-time aide. It noted, however, that the District had provided no evidence of this cost comparison.

The court also was not persuaded by the District's argument that it would lose significant funding if Rachel did not spend at least 51% of her time in a special education class. The court noted that a witness from the California Department of Education testified that waivers were available if a school district sought to adopt a program that did not fit neatly within the funding guidelines. The District had not applied for a waiver, however.

Thus, by inflating the cost estimates and failing to address the true comparison, the District did not meet its burden of proving that regular placement would burden the District's funds or adversely affect services available to other children. Therefore, the court found that the cost factor did not weigh against mainstreaming Rachel.

The district court concluded that the appropriate placement for Rachel was full-time in a regular second grade classroom with some supplemental services and affirmed the decision of the hearing officer.

II. JURISDICTION

The district court had jurisdiction pursuant to 20 U.S.C. § 1415(e)(2). We have jurisdiction pursuant to 28 U.S.C. § 1291.

III. STANDARDS OF REVIEW

The appropriateness of a special education placement under the IDEA is reviewed de novo. The clearly erroneous standard applies to the district court's factual determinations regarding (1) whether Rachel was receiving academic and non-academic benefits in the regular classroom; (2) whether her presence was a detriment to others in the classroom; and (3) whether the District demonstrated that the cost of placing her in a regular classroom would be significantly more expensive.

IV. DISCUSSION

A. Mootness

It has been over a year since the district court rendered its decision. The court concluded that the appropriate placement at that time was full-time in a regular classroom. It noted that Rachel and the educational demands on her may change, and the IDEA had foreseen such changes in providing for an annual IEP review.

This court cannot determine what would be the appropriate placement for Rachel at the present time. However, we conclude that this case presents a live controversy, because the conduct giving rise to the suit is capable of repetition, yet evading review. As the district court noted, the District and the Hollands have conflicting educational philosophies and perceptions of the District's mainstreaming obligation. The District has consistently taken the view that a child with Rachel's I.Q. is too severely disabled to benefit from full-time placement in a regular class, while the Hollands maintain that Rachel learns both social and academic skills in a regular class and would not benefit from being in a special education class. This conflict is a continuing one and will arise frequently. Moreover, it is likely to evade review since the nine month school year will not provide enough time for judicial review.

B. Mainstreaming Requirements of the IDEA

1. The Statute

The IDEA provides that each state must establish:

> Procedures to assure that, to the maximum extent appropriate, children with disabilities ... are educated with children who are not disabled, and that special classes, separate schooling, or other removal of children with disabilities from the regular educational environment occurs only when the nature or severity of the disability is such that education in regular classes with the use of supplementary aids and services cannot be achieved satisfactorily....

20 U.S.C. § 1412 (5)(B).

This provision sets forth Congress's preference for educating children with disabilities in regular classrooms with their peers.

2. Burden of Proof

There is a conflict regarding which party bears the burden of proof. The Third Circuit has held that a school district has the initial burden of justifying its educational placement at the administrative level and the burden in the district court if the student is challenging the agency decision. See *Oberti*, No. 92-5462 at 28. Other circuits have held that the burden of proof in the district court rests with the party challenging the agency decision. Under either approach, in this case the District, which was challenging the agency decision, had the burden of demonstrating in the district court that its proposed placement provided mainstreaming to "the maximum extent appropriate."

3. Test for Determining Compliance with the IDEA's Mainstreaming Requirement

We have not adopted or devised a standard for determining the presence of compliance with 20 U.S.C. § 1412(5)(B). The Third, Fifth and Eleventh Circuits use what is known as the *Daniel R.R.* test. *Oberti*, No. 92-5462 at 19–20; *Greer*, 950 F.2d at 696; *Daniel R.R.*, 874 F.2d at 1048. The Fourth, Sixth and Eighth Circuits apply the Roncker test. *Devries v. Fairfax County Sch. Bd.*, 882 F.2d 876, 879 (4th Cir. 1989); *A.W. v. Northwest R-1 Sch. Dist.*, 813 F.2d 158, 163 (8th Cir.), cert. denied, 484 U.S. 847 (1987); *Roncker v. Walter*, 700 F.2d 1058, 1063 (6th Cir.) cert. denied, 464 U.S. 864, 98 L. Ed. 2d 100, 108 S. Ct. 144 (1983).

Although the district court relied principally on *Daniel R.R.* and *Greer*, it did not specifically adopt the *Daniel R.R.* test over the *Roncker* test. Rather, it employed factors found in both lines of cases in its analysis. The result was a four factor balancing test in which the court considered (1) the educational benefits of placement full-time in a regular class; (2) the non-academic benefits of such placement; (3) the effect Rachel had on the teacher and children in the regular class, and (4) the costs of mainstreaming Rachel. This analysis directly addresses the issue of the appropriate placement for a child with disabilities under the requirements of 20 U.S.C. § 1412(5)(b). Accordingly, we approve and adopt the test employed by the district court.

4. The District's Contentions on Appeal

The District strenuously disagrees with the district court's findings that Rachel was receiving academic and non-academic benefits in a regular class and did not have a detrimental effect on the teacher or other students. It argues that the court's findings were contrary to the evidence of the state Diagnostic Center, and that the court should not have been persuaded by the testimony of Rachel's teacher, particularly her testimony that Rachel would need only a part-time aide in the future. The district court, however, conducted a full evidentiary hearing and made a thorough analysis. The court found the Hollands' evidence to be more persuasive. Moreover, the court asked Rachel's teacher extensive questions regarding Rachel's need for a part-time aide. We will not disturb the findings of the district court.

The District is also not persuasive on the issue of cost. The District now claims that it will lose up to $ 190,764 in state special education funding if Rachel is not enrolled in a special education class at least 51% of the day. However, the District has not sought a waiver pursuant to California Education Code § 56101. This section provides that (1) any school district may request a waiver of any provision of the Education Code if the waiver is necessary or beneficial to the student's IEP, and (2) the Board may grant the waiver when failure to do so would hinder compliance with federal mandates for a free appropriate education for children with disabilities.

Finally, the District, citing *Wilson v. Marana Unified Sch. Dist.*, 735 F.2d 1178 (9th Cir. 1984), argues that Rachel must receive her academic and functional curriculum in special education from a specially credentialed teacher. *Wilson* does not stand for this proposition. Rather, the court in *Wilson* stated:

> The school district argues that under state law a child who qualifies for special education must be taught by a teacher who is certificated in that child's particular area of disability. We do not agree and do not reach a decision on that broad assertion. We hold only, under our standard of review, that the school district's decision was a reasonable one under the circumstances of this case.

735 F.2d at 1180. More importantly, the District's proposition that Rachel must be taught by a special education teacher runs directly counter to the congressional preference that children with disabilities be educated in regular classes with children who are not disabled. See 20 U.S.C. § 1412(5)(B).

We affirm the judgment of the district court. While we cannot determine what the appropriate placement is for Rachel at the present time, we hold that the determination of the present and future appropriate placement for Rachel should be based on the principles set forth in this opinion and the opinion of the district court.

AFFIRMED.

* * *

Questions for Discussion

1. Do you agree with IDEA's "least restrictive environment" policy as it is written? Do you think the "four factor test" in this case would be a useful way of helping courts reach decisions?

2. What did you think of the district's arguments in this case?

3. Should special education students be taught only by special education teachers? What training do general education teachers have in working with students with disabilities?

The following case deliberates the issue of whether a student with disabilities should be allowed to go on school-sponsored trips. Footnotes and string citations have been omitted.

Wolff v. South Colonie Central School District

No. 82-CV-235
UNITED STATES DISTRICT COURT FOR THE
NORTHERN DISTRICT OF NEW YORK
534 F. Supp. 758; 1982 U.S. Dist. LEXIS 12542
March 25, 1982

OPINION BY: MINER

I.

Plaintiffs, Phyllis Wolff and her handicapped infant daughter Jean, bring this action under section 504 of the Rehabilitation Act, 29 U.S.C. § 794, to enjoin the South Colonie Central School District from preventing Jean's participation in an upcoming school-sponsored trip to Spain. Jurisdiction is pursuant to 28 U.S.C. § 1331. Plaintiff's application for a preliminary injunction was consolidated, by stipulation of the parties, with the trial of the action on the merits pursuant to Fed.R.Civ.P. 65(a)(2). The following are the findings of fact and conclusions of law mandated by Fed.R.Civ.P. 52.

II. FINDINGS OF FACT

1. Plaintiff, Jean Wolff, a 15½ year old student attending the 10th grade at South Colonie High School, has a congenital limb deficiency. Her legs are approximately 1 foot in length; her right arm has been amputated above the elbow and fitted with a prosthetic device. At the end of her left arm, which is shorter than normal, are two partially functional digits. Jean is approximately 3½ feet in height.

2. Defendant South Colonie Central School District (hereinafter "School District"), a municipal corporation organized pursuant to the laws of the State of New York, operates the high school Jean attends and is an entity receiving federal financial assistance.

3. In September, 1979, plaintiff Phyllis Wolff contacted School District officials concerning Jean's attendance in the South Colonie school system and requested that a van or automobile be supplied to transport Jean to and from school. She also requested that an "aide" be supplied to help Jean in school to perform her daily school activities.

4. At a meeting of the South Colonie Board of Education on September 18, 1979, a resolution was passed approving the creation of a 6½ hour school monitor position (hereinafter "aide") at the Sand Creek Jr. High School to provide for Jean's individual safety and welfare. In addition, arrangements were made for a special van to transport Jean to and from school. The School District has continued to supply the special van and aide during Jean's attendance at the High School and plaintiff Phyllis Wolff has not applied to discontinue these services.

5. The special van, which has no riders other than Jean, transports Jean daily from the door of her house to the school entrance. The van is specially equipped with lower than usual access steps.

6. The aide, Mrs. Dorothy Kulzer, meets Jean at the entrance of the school. During the school day she takes Jean's books out of a locker and carries them from class to class. She also protects Jean from inadvertent harm from her fellow classmates by walking behind Jean and to her left, thereby blocking any onrushing students. In addition, the aide guards against slipping or falling when Jean ascends or descends stairways.

7. However, there are occasions when students have bumped into Jean in the hallways during the passing of classes as well as occasions when she has stumbled and fallen. Jean is allowed to use a "short cut" to class through normally restricted hallways. She usually is late for the class to which she has the longest walk with a stairway en route.

8. In order to climb stairs, Jean must place one foot on the next level step and then, using the bannister for leverage, haul the rest of her body up to that level. This procedure is repeated until she reaches the top. Jean descends stairs in the same manner, hopping from stair to stair if no bannister is available.

9. Jean is capable of walking at a speed of approximately one half that of a normal adult for at least three miles, and is capable of "running" for between 5 and 10 minutes. On a short field trip through the Pine Bush, Jean was unable to keep up with the class.

10. This Court has had the opportunity to observe Jean during the course of these proceedings and notes the difficulties she encountered with such tasks as seating herself on the witness chair. Otherwise, Jean appears to be above average in intelligence, friendly and highly motivated for a child of her years.

11. In October, 1981, an announcement was made in Jean's Spanish class concerning a forthcoming trip to Spain. Wishing to participate, Jean fulfilled all the preliminary requirements, including demonstration of a serious interest in languages, completion of Level I Spanish studies, stipulating to certain school and trip policies, obtaining a medical release, attendance at certain planning meetings, paying a deposit of $100, and obtaining her mother's consent and signature. At some point, the balance of the cost of the trip was paid in full.

12. A meeting attended by Jean, her mother, and various school officials and teachers was held thereafter to discuss the itinerary, city by city, in light of problems which might develop for Jean. In January 1982, plaintiffs were informed that Jean would not be allowed to participate in the program without being accompanied by an aide. When plaintiffs made no attempt to obtain such an aide, all payments were returned to plaintiffs and Jean was dropped from the program.

13. The itinerary of the trip includes various Spanish cities, and the tour is to last for approximately twenty days. Much of the trip will include extensive walking tours of the cities, including the crossing of congested highways, ascending and descending stairs, and exploring various sites and monuments of historic significance. Many of the tours would be conducted by a "guide" at a brisk pace. During most of their stay in Madrid, the students will be residing with Spanish families who will accompany the children on additional excursions. Madrid, during the tour, will be particularly crowded due to the Easter holidays.

14. On the day of arrival in Madrid, the Colonie School group is scheduled to take a five mile walking tour of the City. Later that day, there will be a two mile walking tour to dinner. On another day, the students will travel to the outskirts of Madrid, where they will tour El Escorial, involving the descent of a steep and narrow stairway to the tombs of the Spanish Kings, and the Valley of the Fallen, involving the ascent of numerous flights of stairs to the monument dedicated to those who died in the Spanish Civil War.

15. The trip will also include a walking tour of Toledo, lasting almost an entire day. Toledo's streets are uneven and cobblestoned. In addition, the group will spend two days

in Seville, including an extensive walking tour of much of the city. It is anticipated that Seville will be particularly crowded due to the upcoming annual spring fair. Generally, past school tours have included a day at the bullfights. The bullfight is particularly crowded and frenzied, and is apparently on the upcoming tour's agenda for Seville. Attending the bullfight will entail the climbing of numerous stone stairways.

16. In Granada, the group will visit the Alhambra Palace. The tour bus will stop at some distance from the Palace, which contains numerous steps. The group will also take extensive walking tours of other Spanish cities.

17. Given her present physical limitations, Jean would be unable to maintain the brisk and physically demanding pace of the group's walking tours and would be unable to ascend and descend the myriad stairways, many of which, as part of historically preserved sites, do not contain bannisters or guardrails necessary for her locomotion and safety.

18. In addition, the throngs of people encountered in many cities, the heavy urban traffic and the crowds gathered at events such as the bullfight, constitute significant hazards to the well-being and safety of the infant plaintiff.

III. CONCLUSIONS OF LAW

1. This action arises under section 504 of the Rehabilitation Act of 1973, 29 U.S.C. § 794, which provides that no otherwise qualified handicapped individual, as defined in section 706(6) of title 29, shall, solely by reason of his handicap, be excluded from participation in any program or activity receiving Federal financial assistance.

2. Section 706(6) defines a handicapped individual as any person who has a physical impairment which substantially limits one or more of such person's major life activities.

3. Under section 504 of the Rehabilitation Act, therefore, a tripartite inquiry must be made:

(a) whether plaintiff is a handicapped individual as defined by § 706(6);

(b) whether the activity or program receives Federal financial assistance; and

(c) whether plaintiff is an otherwise qualified handicapped individual excluded from participation in the activity or program solely by reason of his handicap.

4. Plaintiff Jean Wolff is a handicapped individual within the meaning of this Act.

5. The trip to Spain can be considered an activity or program receiving Federal financial assistance within the meaning of the Act since, although the students pay for a substantial portion of the expenses of the trip, regular salaried teachers will be attending as chaperones while school is in session, the School District has sponsored and planned the program, and students will be under the supervision of teacher and School District personnel during this trip.

6. For a determination of whether plaintiff Jean Wolff is "otherwise qualified" within the meaning of the Act, the Court may consider whether the program requires applicants to possess certain physical qualifications necessary for participation, *Southeastern Community College v. Davis*, 442 U.S. 397, 99 S. Ct. 2361, 60 L. Ed. 2d 980 (1979), and the Court may also consider a state's parens patriae interest in protecting the disabled against physical harm when the state has shown a risk to safety in a particular activity.

7. Since Jean is unable to fulfill the physical requirements of the trip, and since a substantial degree of physical risk to her safety has been demonstrated were she to participate in the program, plaintiff Jean Wolff is not otherwise qualified within the meaning of § 504 of the Act.

8. Accordingly, the relief sought by plaintiffs is denied in all respects and the complaint is dismissed.

* * *

Questions for Discussion

1. Is this outcome fair to the plaintiff? Do you think the court could have found that she was qualified for the trip? Might the outcome be different under the ADA?

2. What do you think of the discourse in the case?

3. Do you think other students with different types of disabilities might have been allowed on this trip?

_____

The following is an article about a statute that was passed to allow students with disabilities to walk in graduation ceremonies.

States to Allow All High School Seniors to Celebrate Commencement

Dave Reynolds, *Inclusion Daily Express*, May 5, 2006

HARRISBURG, PENNSYLVANIA & BOSTON, MASSACHUSETTS—There's good news this week for students with disabilities in Pennsylvania.

Governor Ed Rendell signed "Ashley's Law" Monday allowing all special education students in the state to participate in graduation ceremonies at the end of 12th grade, the Pittsburgh Post-Gazette reported.

Under the measure, which passed unanimously in both the state Senate and House, such students will be able to receive what amounts to a certificate of completion rather than a diploma. They would then be able to continue to receive special education services through age 21.

One senior to benefit from the new law is Ashley Brubaker, for whom the new law is named. Her mother, Deb, personally advocated for a change in the law after officials at Selinsgrove Area School District informed her that Ashley—who has cerebral palsy, autism, anxiety disorder, and speech problems—would not be able to participate in commencement ceremonies.

In Massachusetts, a state representative announced that the House has unanimously passed a measure that would allow special education students in the state to participate in graduation whether or not they have passed the mandatory Massachusetts Comprehensive Assessment System exam.

* * *

Questions for Discussion

1. Does your state have such a statute?

2. Should such a statute be necessary? What might be a district's motivation for refusing to allow students with disabilities to participate in graduation?

_____

For Further Reading

Southern Poverty Law Center, "Children with Disabilities Face Discrimination in New Orleans Schools," retrieved June 11, 2012 at http://www.splcenter.org/get-informed/news/splc-complaint-children-with-disabilities-face-discrimination-in-new-orleans-school.

"Schools on the Move: Stories of Urban Schools Engaged in Inclusive Journeys of Change: Benito Martinez Elementary, El Paso, Texas." Retrieved June 11, 2012 at http://www.urbanschools.org/pdf/Benito.pdf?v_document_name+Benito%20Martinez%20Elementary.

"Advocates accuse D.C. charter schools of excluding the disabled," retrieved June 9, 2012 at http://www.washingtonpost.com/local/education/dc-charter-schools-exclude-the-disabled-advocates-say/2011/05/12/AFVgcV1G_story.html.

"Do charter schools wreck it for special needs kids?" Retrieved June 9, 2012 at http://www.thefastertimes.com/specialneeds/2011/04/26/do-charter-schools-wreck-it-for-special-needs-kids/.

"Girl with no arms and legs says cheerleading try-out is unfair after she fails to make school squad," retrieved June 9, 2012 at http://www.dailymail.co.uk/news/article-2014508/Girl-arms-legs-says-Nebraska-school-cheerleading-try-unfair.html#ixzz1xMfIZxUO.

"Update: Student Excluded From Field Trip Because of Autism," retrieved June 9, 2012 at http://www.nbc15.com/news/headlines/85158897.html.

"School Can Ban Boy From Playground, Judge Says," retrieved June 9, 2012 at http://www.inclusiondaily.com/archives/04/09/01/090104meplayground.htm.

Discussion 6

Bullying & Violence at School

Recommended Background Reading

Doe v. Honig, 484 U.S. 305 (1988); 20 U.S.C. § 1415(k)(1)(G).

David Ellis Ferster, *Deliberately Different: Bullying as a Denial of a Free Public Education under the Individuals with Disabilities Education Act*, 43 Ga. L. Rev. 191 (2008).

Readings for Class Discussion

The following is an online article about a story that was on the TODAY show. A video clip of the show may still be available online.

Teachers Caught on Tape Bullying Special Needs Girl
Scott Stump,* TODAY.com, November 15, 2011

When a 14-year-old special needs student in Ohio told her father she was being bullied at school, he figured it was something that many teenagers endure.

Then he realized it was his daughter's teachers doing the bullying.

"We were shocked," he tearfully said. "We couldn't know. We didn't know."

After being told repeatedly by school administrators that his daughter was lying about being harassed and bullied, he outfitted her with a hidden tape recorder under her clothes. For the next four days, she recorded a series of abusive and cutting remarks from a teacher and a teacher's aide at Miami Trace Middle School in Washington Courthouse, Ohio.

The father, Brian, and his daughter, Cheyanne (their last names were withheld in the interview), appeared on TODAY with their attorneys Tuesday as snippets from the secret audio tapes were played.

When asked by Ann Curry how all of this made her feel, Cheyanne simply replied, "Sad."

---

* Scott Stump is a Today.com contributor.

'Are you that damn dumb?'

The tapes reveal teacher Christie Wilt and her teacher's aide, Kelly Chaffins, saying disturbing things to Cheyanne in the classroom. Cheyanne, who is now in high school, was in Wilt's class for three years of middle school. Chaffins has since resigned, while Wilt had to undergo eight hours of anti-bullying and child abuse training. On Monday, Wilt was put on unpaid leave for the rest of the school year, but Cheyanne's family is hoping to prevent her from ever teaching or working with special needs students again.

Wilt, who did not respond to requests for an interview, can be heard on the recordings alongside Chaffins calling Cheyanne "lazy" and "dumb."

"Cheyanne, are you kidding me? Are you that damn dumb? You are that dumb?" Chaffins can be heard saying in one instance. "Oh my God. You are such a liar. You told me you don't know. It's no wonder you don't have friends. No wonder nobody likes you because you lie, cheat."

On another occasion, Chaffins can be heard poking fun at Cheyanne's appearance.

"Cheyanne, don't you want to do something to get rid of that belly? Well evidently you don't because you don't do anything at home. You sit at home and watch TV. All night. All weekend."

In one instance, Wilt informs Cheyanne she has failed a test before Wilt even takes a glance at it.

"You know what? Just keep it," Wilt can be heard saying. "You failed it. I know it. I don't need your test to grade. You failed it."

Punished on treadmill

"Listening to seven hours' worth of stuff on this tape, we were up all night, crying, upset, because we didn't understand why," Cheyanne's father said tearfully. "Why would they do this?"

On another day, Chaffins forced Cheyanne to walk on a treadmill as a punishment for getting a question wrong. The school district claimed the treadmill is just there to "refocus" students and not punish them. Chaffins later declares that Cheyanne has broken the treadmill and should run in place.

The problems for Cheyanne began in fifth grade and became progressively worse until culminating in an eighth-grade year that was "just terrible," according to her father.

"She got to where she didn't want to go to school," Brian told Curry. "Cheyanne's always loved school. We never had a problem with her. She was doing things, (and) starting to harm herself to keep from going to school, so we knew we had to do something at that point."

Cheyanne's parents repeatedly contacted the school, only to be consistently rebuffed.

"We weren't getting anywhere," Brian said. "Every time we called, it was always, 'Cheyanne's lying, Cheyanne's making up stories. She's taking parts of this story, parts of that story, and making her own story.'"

Her parents then went to the school's principal, whose investigation consisted of speaking to Wilt and Chaffins, according to Brian. Feeling they were getting nowhere, Cheyanne's parents then met with Miami Trace superintendent Dan Roberts.

"[That was] the first time we ever spoke with the man," Brian said, "and he told us we were bordering on slander and harassment so [we should] let it go and he would guarantee me the best education possible," Brian said.

After the damning evidence on the tapes was brought to school administrators' attention, Chaffins was asked to resign, while Wilt, who was in charge of the classroom as the teacher, had to undergo the anti-bullying training. Roberts told a local television station that Wilt's role in the incidents "did not meet what the educational aide (Chaffins) had done."

'I just hope they do something'

The family filed a civil lawsuit against the school district and were awarded $300,000 in damages. But Brian felt he needed to go public with the story to prevent Wilt from being allowed back in the classroom. The family's attorneys indicated that they would like Wilt to be terminated from her position.

"I just hope they do something with this teacher," Brian said. "She doesn't need to be around kids at all. She participated in it, she was right there. I'm looking out for [Cheyanne], but also I'm worried about the other children in that class and what they went through.

"She's [Wilt] just as much to blame, if not more, because she's the one who takes that oath to protect our children. She has more education than the teacher's aide."

As for Cheyanne, the full effects of the harassment on her are not yet known.

"Cheyanne right now, she's doing OK," her father said. "She's trying to forget. She knows that they did something bad to her, but we don't know years down the road what's going to happen."

* * *

Questions for Discussion

1. What do you think should be the disciplinary action for this teacher and aide? Do you think they should be civilly liable? Should the district be "on the hook" as well?

2. What could be done to lessen the possibility of special needs students being treated poorly by teachers?

3. What other issues of teacher-student bullying have you seen or heard about in the media?

The following case grapples with the intersection of Least Restrictive Environment and behavior problems.

Clyde K. v. Puyallup School District

35 F.3D 1396 (9th Cir. 1994)

Appeal from the United States District Court for the Western District of Washington.

Before: WRIGHT, KOZINSKI and FERNANDEZ, Circuit Judges.

KOZINSKI, Circuit Judge.

Under the Individuals with Disabilities Education Act (IDEA), 20 U.S.C. Sec. 1400 et seq., parents and school officials must try to reach agreement on the appropriate educational program for a disabled student. We consider what happens when they fail.

Ryan K. is a fifteen-year-old student with Tourette's Syndrome and Attention Deficit Hyperactivity Disorder (ADHD). Prior to the events giving rise to this litigation, Ryan received special education services while enrolled in mainstream schools in the Puyallup

School District. Between mid-January and mid-March 1992, Ryan's behavioral problems at Ballou Junior High School escalated dramatically. He frequently disrupted class by taunting other students with name-calling and profanity, insulting teachers with vulgar comments, directing sexually-explicit remarks at female students, refusing to follow directions, and kicking and hitting classroom furniture. In addition, Ryan was involved in several violent confrontations. On January 27, he received a one-day suspension for punching another student in the face. On February 10, he received a second suspension for pushing another student's head into a door. Finally, on March 12, Ryan was removed from school pursuant to an emergency expulsion order after he assaulted a school staff member.[1]

Ryan's parents, Clyde and Sheila K., agreed with school officials that it was no longer safe for Ryan to remain at Ballou. Ryan's teachers and school administrators met shortly after his expulsion to discuss available alternatives. They suggested placing Ryan temporarily in an off-campus, self-contained program called Students Temporarily Away from Regular School (STARS), where Ryan would be in a more structured environment and receive more individualized attention. On March 17, 1992, the school notified Ryan's parents of its recommendation that Ryan be placed in STARS on an interim basis until he could be safely reintegrated into regular school programs.

Though Ryan's parents initially agreed with the school's proposed change of placement, they subsequently had second thoughts. On March 27, 1992, they requested a due process hearing under Wash.Admin.Code Sec. 392-171-531; on April 6, they formally rejected placement at STARS until a new Individualized Education Program (IEP) had been drafted. After efforts to draft a new IEP broke down, Ryan's parents insisted that he return to Ballou for the remainder of the school year. Over the summer, a ten-day due process hearing was held pursuant to 20 U.S.C. Sec. 1415(b)(2). The administrative law judge issued her ruling on September 14, 1992, concluding that the school fully complied with the IDEA. The parents appealed to the district court, which, after hearing additional testimony and reviewing the record of the administrative proceedings, affirmed the ALJ's decision in all material respects on March 23, 1993.[2]

As a preliminary matter, the parties disagree over who should have borne the burden of proof in the district court. The school clearly had the burden of proving at the administrative hearing that it complied with the IDEA. Ryan's parents contend the burden of proof remained on the school in the district court as well, even though they were the ones appealing the administrative ruling. Generally, the party challenging an agency's decision bears the burden of proof. Whether the IDEA calls for an exception to this general principle has yet to be decided in this circuit.

The parents rely on *Oberti v. Board of Educ.*, 995 F.2d 1204 (3d Cir.1993), which held that the burden of proof remains on the school even if the school prevails at the administrative hearing. The court in *Oberti* stated that placing the burden of proof on the school is essential to ensure that parents' rights under the IDEA aren't undermined. Id. at 1219. We note, however, that merely because a statute confers substantive rights

---

1. Though the school contended below that Ryan's disruptive behavior wasn't related to his disability, Ryan's doctors disagreed. The district court found that Ryan's behavioral problems did stem from Tourette's Syndrome and ADHD. That finding is not clearly erroneous and, indeed, the school district doesn't challenge it.

2. Judge Bryan was already familiar with both the IDEA and Puyallup's programs. See *Parents of Student W v. Puyallup Sch. Dist.*, No. 3, 31 F.3d 1489 (9th Cir.1994) (affirming summary judgment for school district on validity of ten-day suspension guidelines).

on a favored group does not mean the group is also entitled to receive every procedural advantage. Absent clear statutory language to the contrary, procedural questions are resolved by neutral principles that are independent of any particular statute's substantive policy objectives. Allocation of the burden of proof has long been governed by the rule that the party bringing the lawsuit must persuade the court to grant the requested relief. Because we find nothing in the IDEA suggesting that a contrary standard should apply here, we join the substantial majority of the circuits that have addressed this issue by placing the burden of proof on the party challenging the administrative ruling. See *Roland M. v. Concord Sch. Comm.*, 910 F.2d 983, 991 (1st Cir.1990); *Kerkam v. McKenzie*, 862 F.2d 884, 887 (D.C.Cir.1988); *Spielberg v. Henrico County Pub. Sch.*, 853 F.2d 256, 258 n. 2 (4th Cir.1988).

Ryan's parents allege various procedural violations of the IDEA. We address each of these in turn.

A. On March 11, 1992, after Ryan had been suspended twice for assaulting other students, the school hired an aide to observe Ryan's behavior over a three-day period. The aide was hired at the urging of Ryan's doctors, who suggested that a first-hand report on his behavioral problems would be helpful in evaluating appropriate responses. Ryan's parents claim the school violated 34 C.F.R. Sec. 300.504(a) because it failed to give them written notice before hiring the aide.

The parents contend that hiring the aide constituted a change of Ryan's educational program, thus triggering the prior notice requirement of section 300.504(a). We agree with the district court that hiring the aide did not change Ryan's educational program. The aide merely observed Ryan's behavior; he didn't provide educational services or any other type of assistance. As a result, prior written notice was not required. See *Doe v. Maher*, 793 F.2d 1470, 1487 (9th Cir.1986), aff'd sub nom. *Honig v. Doe*, 484 U.S. 305, 108 S.Ct. 592, 98 L.Ed.2d 686 (1988).

B. In the wake of Ryan's emergency expulsion on March 12, school officials met to consider their options.[3] Ryan's multi-disciplinary team concluded that his increasingly aggressive behavior posed a clear danger to others at the school and was significantly disrupting the educational process for other students. The team reviewed Ryan's current IEP — which had taken effect in October 1991 and remained valid through the end of the school year — and concluded that its objectives could be met satisfactorily at STARS. On March 17, the school sent Ryan's parents a Notice of Proposed Placement Change, suggesting that Ryan attend STARS on a temporary basis while the parents and school officials developed a plan to reintegrate him into a mainstream setting. Ryan's parents allege that the school violated IDEA procedural requirements by failing to draft a new IEP before attempting to move Ryan to STARS.

We reject this contention. The district court found that Ryan's parents initially agreed with the school's recommended placement, including the determination that Ryan's current IEP could be implemented at STARS. Though Ryan's parents vigorously contend they never consented to this change of placement, we cannot conclude, after reviewing the record, that the district court's contrary finding is clearly erroneous. Since the primary goals and objectives of Ryan's current IEP could be achieved in the proposed placement,

---

3. Schools can temporarily remove a disabled student from a mainstream placement only if the child poses an immediate threat to the safety of himself or others. Absent a court order or parental consent, the student can't be suspended for more than ten school days if his misconduct stems from a protected disability. See *Honig*, 484 U.S. at 325, 108 S.Ct. at 605.

the school was not obligated to draft a new IEP prior to making its recommendation. See *Daniel R.R. v. State Bd. of Educ.*, 874 F.2d 1036, 1042 (5th Cir.1989).[4]

C. After preparations had been made for Ryan's arrival at STARS, Ryan's parents informed the school they wouldn't let him attend until a new IEP was drafted. Though school officials continued to believe Ryan's current IEP could be implemented satisfactorily at STARS, they agreed to work with the parents in drafting a new one. Ryan's parents contend the school violated the IDEA when it failed to bring teachers from Ballou to the IEP meetings.

The record reveals that the school complied with its obligations under the IDEA. Under 34 C.F.R. Sec. 300.344(a)(2), Ryan's teacher had to attend the meetings. The school saw to this by having a teacher and a behavioral specialist from STARS attend the IEP meeting on May 1. Ryan's parents claim this didn't suffice because Ryan's teachers were those from Ballou, not those from STARS. By May 1, however, Ryan hadn't attended Ballou for 45 days; in accordance with the earlier agreement reached between the school and Ryan's parents, he had been removed from Ballou and enrolled in the STARS program. Thus, as the district court found, the school complied with section 300.344 by having teachers from STARS attend the IEP meeting. See 34 C.F.R. Sec. 300.344, note 1(b) (noting that teacher required to be present at meeting can be either teacher from student's current placement, or teacher from student's future placement).[5]

IV

We turn next to the alleged substantive violations of the IDEA.

A. Ryan's parents claim the district court erred when it held that STARS was the "stay-put" placement under 20 U.S.C. Sec. 1415(e)(3), which provides that during the pendency of any proceedings under the IDEA, "the child shall remain in the then current educational placement." As noted above, when Ryan's parents requested a due process hearing on March 27, 1992, Ryan's current educational placement was STARS; with the parents'

---

4. Ryan's parents also allege a violation of 34 C.F.R. Sec. 300.534(b), claiming the school should have reassessed Ryan's special education needs before recommending a change of placement. Because they failed to raise the issue at either the administrative hearing or in the district court, we decline to consider it here.

5. Though Ryan's parents were frustrated by the absence of Ballou teachers at the May 1 meeting, this did not justify the singularly counterproductive stance taken by their attorney, Neil Martinson. Instead of at least initiating discussions with the school, he abruptly ended the meeting, declaring that further negotiations would be pointless. He then announced that Ryan would be returning to Ballou on the next school day, May 4. When school officials pleaded with the parents to stay and help prepare for Ryan's return to Ballou, Martinson insisted they leave the meeting with him at once.

Judge Bryan, who remained composed and patient throughout the proceedings in the district court, cogently asked, "[W]hat happened there? All we know is that [Ryan's parents] did not participate very actively. Their participation was through Mr. Martinson. Mr. Martinson's approach was rigid, it was one way only, 'my way or the highway,' so to speak. It was not realistic."

If Martinson was concerned that the parents might be waiving their statutory rights by staying, he surely knew how to make a record indicating that the parents were staying under protest. But it is difficult to imagine what interests of Ryan's were served by thrusting him back into a school environment where he was having significant difficulty and then refusing even to discuss how these problems might be ameliorated. Such hard-ball tactics are seldom productive even in ordinary civil litigation, and are particularly ill-advised in this context. Working out an acceptable educational program must, in the end, be a cooperative effort between parents and school officials; the litigation process is simply too slow and too costly to deal adequately with the rapidly changing needs of children. See, e.g., nn. 6 & 10 infra. In addition, litigation tends to poison relationships, destroying channels for constructive dialogue that may have existed before the litigation began. This is particularly harmful here, since parents and school officials must—despite any bad feelings that develop between them—continue to work closely with one another. As this case demonstrates, when combat lines are firmly drawn, the child's interests often are damaged in the ensuing struggle.

consent, the school had already removed him from Ballou. That Ryan's parents later withdrew their consent on April 6 and pursued administrative remedies doesn't change this reality. We agree with the district court that STARS was the stay-put placement under section 1415(e)(3).

B. Ryan's parents also contend the district court erred in concluding that STARS was the least restrictive environment in which Ryan could be educated satisfactorily. See 20 U.S.C. Sec. 1412(5)(B). They claim Ryan can be educated in a mainstream setting if the school provides a personal classroom aide to assist him.

We've recently adopted a four-part test to determine whether a disabled student's placement represents the least restrictive environment. See *Sacramento City Unified Sch. Dist. v. Rachel H.*, 14 F.3d 1398 (9th Cir.1994). In applying this test, we consider: (1) the academic benefits of placement in a mainstream setting, with any supplementary aides and services that might be appropriate; (2) the non-academic benefits of mainstream placement, such as language and behavior models provided by non-disabled students; (3) the negative effects the student's presence may have on the teacher and other students; and (4) the cost of educating the student in a mainstream environment. Id. at 1401, 1404. We review for clear error the district court's factual findings as to each of these elements; we review de novo its conclusion as to the appropriateness of a student's educational placement under the IDEA. Id. at 1402.

Applying these elements to the case before us, we conclude that STARS was the least restrictive environment.[6] First, it is undisputed that by March 1992, Ryan no longer received any academic benefit from his mainstream placement at Ballou. Ryan's disruptive classroom behavior largely prevented him from learning; indeed, test results indicate that his level of academic achievement actually declined during the 1991–92 school year. Nor is it likely—given the severity of Ryan's behavioral problems—that a personal aide would have made a meaningful difference.[7] Second, Ryan derived at best only minimal non-academic benefits from his placement at Ballou. No evidence in the record suggests that Ryan modelled his behavior on that of his non-disabled peers. Moreover, Ryan's doctors found that he was socially isolated at Ballou, had few friends, and suffered a great deal of stress from the teasing he was subjected to by other students.

With respect to the third element, the record indicates that Ryan's presence in classes at Ballou had an overwhelmingly negative effect on teachers and other students. By March 1992, Ryan's behavior had become dangerously aggressive: he violently attacked two students before being expelled for assaulting a school staff member. These are not incidents school officials can dismiss lightly; they have a special obligation to ensure that students entrusted to their care are kept out of harm's way. In addition to posing a danger to others at Ballou, Ryan's behavioral problems regularly disrupted class. The record discloses that

6. We note the limited scope of our decision: STARS was intended to be a temporary placement; the parties agreed Ryan should be reintegrated into mainstream programs as soon as that became feasible. We cannot determine on the record before us whether Ryan's behavioral problems abated during the 1992–93 and 1993–94 school years. Consequently, we reach no conclusion as to whether STARS or a similar self-contained program will be Ryan's least restrictive environment during 1994–95. Cf. *Rachel H.*, 14 F.3d at 1405; *Greer v. Rome City Sch. Dist.*, 950 F.2d 688, 699 (11th Cir.1991).

7. This is not a case where school officials failed to provide supplementary services or make reasonable adjustments to accommodate a student's disability. Prior to Ryan's enrollment at Ballou, teachers and staff attended special training sessions designed to educate them about Tourette's Syndrome. ER 120. Ryan received maximum support from the school's special education staff, attending small group "resource classes" for each of his academic subjects. ER 119-20. In addition, Ryan received the assistance of the school's behavioral specialist, who secured standing permission for Ryan to leave class whenever he needed time to relieve his "tics" in private. The school designated a special area in the nurse's office for this purpose. ER 123.

he frequently taunted other students with name-calling and profanity, and that on several occasions he made vulgar and insulting comments to teachers.

Ryan also directed sexually-explicit remarks at female students, another legitimate cause for concern among school officials. Given the extremely harmful effects sexual harassment can have on young female students, public officials have an especially compelling duty not to tolerate it in the classrooms and hallways of our schools. See Monica L. Sherer, Comment, No Longer Just Child's Play: School Liability Under Title IX for Peer Sexual Harassment, 141 U.Pa.L.Rev. 2119, 2133–35 (1993) (noting that targets of peer sexual harassment often experience embarrassment, fear, anxiety and loss of self-confidence, which in turn can lead to diminished opportunities for social and educational growth). Moreover, school officials might reasonably be concerned about liability for failing to remedy peer sexual harassment that exposes female students to a hostile educational environment.[8]

The record supports the district court's finding that Ryan's behavioral problems interfered with the ability of other students to learn. Disruptive behavior that significantly impairs the education of other students strongly suggests a mainstream placement is no longer appropriate. See 34 C.F.R. Sec. 300.552, Comment. While school officials have a statutory duty to ensure that disabled students receive an appropriate education, they are not required to sit on their hands when a disabled student's behavioral problems prevent both him and those around him from learning.

Weighing these elements together, we conclude that STARS was Ryan's least restrictive environment. See Daniel R.R., 874 F.2d at 1050–51.[9]

Conclusion

Though the doors to federal courts are always open, the slow and tedious workings of the judicial system make the courthouse a less than ideal forum in which to resolve disputes over a child's education. See Perry A. Zirkel, Over-Due Process Revisions for the Individuals with Disabilities Education Act, 55 Montana L.Rev. 403, 406–07 (1994) (noting that parties are often unable to achieve satisfactory results through litigation under the IDEA). Ryan's experience offers a poignant reminder that everyone's interests are better served when parents and school officials resolve their differences through cooperation and compromise rather than litigation.[10]

The judgment of the district court is AFFIRMED.

---

8. See, e.g., *Doe v. Petaluma City Sch. Dist.*, 830 F.Supp. 1560, 1571 (N.D.Cal.1993) (holding that, where intentional discrimination is shown, schools can be held liable for monetary damages under Title IX, 20 U.S.C. Sec. 1681 et seq., for failing to eradicate hostile environment caused by peer sexual harassment); Kristina Sauerwein, A New Lesson in Schools: Sexual Harassment Is Unacceptable, L.A. Times, Aug. 1, 1994, at E1 (noting that plaintiff in Doe will seek $1 million in damages at trial set for early next year); see also Tamar Lewin, Students Seeking Damages for Sex Bias, N.Y. Times, July 15, 1994, at B7 (suit for peer sexual harassment filed against school district in Albany, N.Y., by 12-year-old female student).

9. Though the parties didn't specify the cost of hiring a classroom aide for Ryan, this fourth factor is irrelevant in light of the district court's finding that an aide would not have materially improved Ryan's ability to benefit from his placement at Ballou.

10. Ryan has now spent two years in a self-contained program originally intended to serve as a short-term interim placement. The parties' unfortunate inability to reach agreement has resulted in legal expenses of over $100,000 for the school district alone—money that might have been better spent improving educational opportunities for Ryan and other disabled students. This is surely a case where the lawyers would have better served their clients—and the interests of society—had they concentrated their efforts on being healers and mediators rather than warriors. See, e.g., Warren E. Burger, The Role of the Lawyer Today, 59 Notre Dame L.Rev. 1, 2 (1983) ("In their highest role, lawyers

* * *

Questions for Discussion

1. How does this case highlight the importance of IDEA's "stay-put provision"?

2. What did you think of the application of the ninth circuit's four-factor test for "least restrictive environment"? What do you think of the test itself?

3. What do you think of the final footnote?

4. What do you think about having students with significant behavior issues in mainstream classroom settings?

The following is an article from the ACLU about corporal punishment of students with disabilities.

Impairing Education: Corporal Punishment of Students with Disabilities in U.S. Schools[1]

August 11, 2009

Students with disabilities face corporal punishment in public schools at disproportionately high rates according to a new report by the ACLU and Human Rights Watch. Corporal punishment—ranging from paddling to smacking to throwing children into walls—can worsen these students' medical conditions and undermine their education. Students with disabilities are entitled to appropriate, inclusive educational programs that give them the opportunity to thrive. No child should be hit, especially the most vulnerable.

Corporal punishment causes pain, humiliation, and in some cases deep bruising or other serious injury; it also can have long-lasting psychological consequences. Students with disabilities may see their underlying conditions worsened as a result. Furthermore, it creates a violent, degrading school environment in which all students—and particularly students with disabilities—may struggle to succeed. The American Civil Liberties Union and Human Rights Watch call on the federal government and US states to prohibit corporal punishment. School districts should replace corporal punishment with effective, positive forms of discipline, so that children's human rights are protected, and so that every student throughout the United States can maximize his or her academic potential.

* * *

Questions for Discussion

1. What do you think about corporal punishment as a form of discipline in schools?

2. How might corporal punishment disproportionately impact students with disabilities?

3. There have been (thus far unsuccessful) attempts to pass federal legislation barring corporal punishment in schools. Are any such attempts pending?

---

should be the healers of conflicts and, as such, should help the diverse parts of a complex, pluralistic social order function with a minimum of friction.").

1. For an interactive map, see http://www.hrw.org/sites/default/files/features/us_map_esed/index.html. The map shows statistics for corporal punishment meted out to both students with disabilities and students without disabilities during the 2006–2007 school year.

The following is an article about teacher safety.

Special Ed Teachers Feeling Unsafe In Class: Educators, Saying Risk of Attacks Is Growing, Are Turning to Lawsuits

Debera Carlton Harrell, *Seattle Post-Intelligencer Reporter*,
January 11, 2002

When police charged a Federal Way teenager with assaulting his special education teacher last month, it became the most recent example of a disturbing trend that has caused eight special education teachers or aides to file claims against their school districts in the past year.

The educators, whose claims range from death threats to bites, claim they are not being adequately protected in the classroom. Their districts are spread across Western Washington and include Issaquah, Puyallup, Tacoma, Clover Park and Ferndale.

"It's a serious problem. Special education teachers are like cannon fodder," said Hal Hodgins, a Seattle attorney who filed the lawsuits pending against the school districts.

Next week, a 15-year-old Federal Way student, charged with second-degree assault for slamming his special education teacher's head onto a desk, will appear in juvenile court. While his teacher struggles to heal from her injuries, the incident has thrown a grenade into the state's special education system.

The case is the most egregious publicized example of a problem that has been quiet for too long, say some special education teachers.

The teachers, parents and legal experts emphasize that the vast majority of the state's 120,000 special ed students pose no harm. Kids with speech, vision or hearing problems, developmental delays, physical birth defects, or other disabilities deserve to be educated in the least restrictive environment possible, as federal and state laws require, they say. For most, this means mainstream classrooms or other suitable district programs during the school day.

But some teachers say they are being hurt by a small minority of extremely troubled students who should not be in public schools. Worn out by being head-butted, kicked, punched and in some cases knocked out, teachers and teaching aides are leaving special education, already suffering an acute national and state shortage.

"I was never trained to be a lion tamer," said Joyce Burtch, a former Puyallup School District special ed teacher who has sued the district for injuries suffered while trying to restrain kids who "went into rages."

"You have to be on your guard all the time—and even then they can hurt you," she said.

Christie Perkins, past president of the Washington State Special Education Coalition, an advocacy organization for parents of special ed students, said she is worried about a backlash in the wake of the publicized cases.

"Violence in schools is still more of a general education problem than a special ed problem," Perkins said.

The organization has long pushed for including special education students in public education and time has shown this works, she said.

But she believes the law does not require a district to put those students back into a regular or even special ed classroom if they are violent; they are required to reassess the student and modify his or her individual educational plan accordingly.

"We are not saying it's OK for teachers to get hurt or for kids to hurt other students," Perkins said. "Our kids get victimized first if they're in a classroom with other non- or special ed kids with violent tendencies."

But lately, compliance with federal and state special education laws has meant a delicate balancing act in light of teacher and student safety concerns, costly litigation, higher academic expectations of all students, and taxpayer accountability.

The situation is aggravated by what many educators and special education experts consider an inadequate state system of alternative placements for the most violent kids—and inadequate federal funding for special education.

Meanwhile, teachers are grappling with the day-to-day reality of working with high-needs kids. Some of those who have filed civil lawsuits say they love working with most special education kids, but are leaving the profession because they have been hurt and unnerved by extreme students in their care.

"Autistic kids are my first love, and most are extremely sweet, harmless," said Linda Roselle, who has sued the Issaquah School District after injuring herself while trying to catch a boy who suddenly bolted from the classroom. "But it hits you one day: Some kids are violent. They chase you with broomsticks and scissors.... These kids cannot remain in the district. There has to be a place where they can get better treatment."

Hodgins, the attorney, said he believes many districts are so afraid of being sued by parents that they are not adequately protecting their teachers and other students from students known to be dangerous.

Some of his clients, he said, told superiors they were afraid to work with certain students for fear of being hurt by them, but were ignored.

In the Federal Way case, the district has said it did not receive documentation of the 15-year-old boy's violent tendencies from the California school he attended before transferring to Washington.

Pat Steinberg of the Washington Education Association recalls teaching special education years ago and being kicked down the stairs by one student. Steinberg, like many of her colleagues, figured it was an "occupational hazard" she was duty-bound to accept—and she was attached to kids who had no other place to go. She didn't report the incident.

"But things are shifting," Steinberg said. "Teachers are calling now, asking for protection from some of these kids."

Doug Gill, director of special education operations for the state Office of the Super-intendent of Public Instruction, said the number of special education students has risen in past years while the number of teachers for them has decreased.

That trend, coupled with what some consider inadequate teacher training and legal requirements, has led to clashing needs, Gill said.

"Parents want inclusion; they want their children in the least restrictive environment," Gill said. "But special ed and the issue of individual entitlement needs to be looked at in a greater context. You don't want to punish someone for being disabled, but you don't want to jeopardize someone else because of another's disability. That's the quintessential dilemma districts face."

And districts are troubled.

Janet Barry, a 33-year educator and superintendent of the Issaquah School District, said that over the years the federal law has been expanded to include some forms of mental health and behavioral problems that schools must serve—but can't. She cited a school district where one high school student is so violent, he is transported to school by police car every day, with a bodyguard.

"Under IDEA (the federal Individuals with Disabilities in Education Act), schools do not have the right to decline services to anybody," Barry said. "You can't blame the kids or the parents, but some of these issues are beyond the capacity of a public school to meet. We don't have the training, the specialized services, the resources."

Special education parents can—and have—sued to ensure their children receive maximum school services under IDEA. A court ordered Issaquah to pay $240,000 a year for one violent student to go to school in Texas when the parents refused a lower-cost, in-state placement.

Last year, the Seattle Public Schools reached a $180,000 settlement with the mother of a violent special ed student who the district claimed it could no longer accommodate.

Jeanette Vallandingham is a former teacher in the Clover Park School District who sued the district after being head-butted by a student. She said she was knocked backward and fell, hitting her head on the end of a counter and knocked unconscious.

"This can happen to anybody; violent students just act out," said Vallandingham, echoing other teachers. "But part of my concern is for other students. One of our students was blind and in a wheelchair; the (violent) student shoved her wheelchair, nearly tipping it over."

Concerns of the districts have heightened since the Federal Way case, but have been growing since a 1999 state Supreme Court ruling found in favor of two Stanwood special education aides who alleged the district was negligent in not protecting them from students known to be violent. They were awarded a total of $455,000. A departure from previous workers' compensation law, the ruling cleared the way for current civil litigation.

Dan Steele, governmental relations director for the Washington State School Directors Association, which represents school boards, said the organization will ask the Legislature to pass a law offering immunity to districts sued by special education teachers. The organization also plans to seek more funding for special ed, Steele said.

James Rosenfeld, visiting clinical professor of law at Seattle University and an expert in national special education law, said he is disturbed by what he fears is a national trend—schools trying to expel or otherwise remove some special education students. Rosenfeld said the biggest needs in special education nationwide are more funding to provide better services for troubled youths and better special education training for teachers.

"There's no doubt that some kids who misbehave need special services, but what good is throwing them out? The law says these kids must be served (by the schools)," Rosenfeld said. "Even if a student poses physical danger, he can be isolated, but it doesn't mean all services can be cut off."

* * *

Questions for Discussion

1. Did anything surprise you about this article?

2. What other examples of workplace injury for special education teachers have you heard about in the media? Are such viewpoints underrepresented, overrepresented, or valid?

3. What solutions do you see to these issues?

The following is an article about a district's decisions surrounding one student.

School District Pays $180,000 to Be Free of Blind, Autistic Student It Considers Dangerous

Ray Rivera, *Seattle Times*, April 8, 2001

Seattle School District officials called him the toughest special education case they'd seen in decades.

Students at Chief Sealth High School called him the "kid in the cage."

The blind, developmentally disabled 16-year-old could throw a tantrum so fierce school officials placed him in a padded basement room for months, isolated from other students. Then they paid to make him go away. In a settlement that special-education experts say is both rare and troubling, the district has agreed to pay Kathy Harris $180,000 on condition she keep her son out of the district. School officials say it's the first time in memory they've paid to remove a student from Seattle schools.

The agreement ends a bitter struggle between the district and Harris over how best to serve her son.

"They treated him like a monster," Harris said. "For all the money they spent trying to get him out, they could have made a perfect program for him. They never even tried."

District officials say they faced an impossible situation: trying to serve a boy with an extraordinary combination of disabilities while protecting staff and other students from his violent, unpredictable outbursts.

"To conclude this district did not want to serve this student is to ignore the very complex set of disabilities—the dangerousness—this student represents," said Christopher Hirst, an outside attorney who represented the district.

In addition to blindness, the boy has been diagnosed with autism and intermittent explosive disorder, which causes difficulty controlling aggressive behavior. He has the cognitive age of a toddler.

Hirst said the boy presented "easily" the most difficult set of challenges he has seen in 20 years of handling special-education cases.

But court documents, school records and interviews with special-education experts and those involved in the boy's care raise questions about the district's efforts.

Last summer an administrative-hearing officer found the district had violated multiple provisions of the Individual with Disabilities Education Act (IDEA), a federal law that sends billions of dollars to public schools to care for children with disabilities.

Among her findings, she said the district:

- Improperly suspended the boy, then went months providing "virtually no services."
- Failed to train teachers and instructional aides to safely deal with him.
- Made inadequate efforts to design a program for him before deciding he belonged in a special institution.

And late last month, Karen Marie Thompson, a guardian ad litem assigned to protect the boy's interests in court, wrote in her approval of the settlement, "… It is crystal clear that the Seattle School District simply did not want to serve this student."

District officials said the settlement was the best—and least costly—way to resolve an impossible situation.

Serving special-education students is never cheap. Caring for the boy, identified as I.H. in court documents, was especially expensive because he required constant one-on-one supervision. In the boy's last month at Sealth, for example, the district paid more than $10,000 to a private company that provided instructional assistants and transportation—$1,100 of it to repair van upholstery torn by the boy on his way to school.

The law requires public schools to provide special-education services to age 21, and often year-round. Seattle school officials considered sending the boy to a private institution, costing more than $100,000 a year, at district expense. But the facility had no beds available and said the boy's blindness would put him at risk from other students.

The settlement stipulates that most of the money be placed in an educational trust for the boy. It also wards off a discrimination suit threatened but never filed by his mother.

"This is the first time I've ever heard of a district essentially purchasing a child's removal," said University of Kansas Professor Rud Turnbull, commonly recognized as the nation's top expert on special-education law. "From the point of view of the district, it's probably a very inexpensive way to go, but I would not like to see school districts begin to do this kind of thing because they are really discharging their responsibilities."

The district's payoff also drew concern from the Council for Exceptional Children, a Washington, D.C.-based advocacy group that consults with the U.S. Department of Education.

"Basically, they're admitting their negligence and liability," said Beth Foley, a policy specialist for the council.

District officials say it wasn't a matter of avoiding responsibility, it was a matter of finding the best place for him. The law says students must be served in the "least restrictive environment." The district felt that was a residential institution, where he could have a consistent environment 24 hours a day.

"Whether this child appeared in Seattle or Omak, he deserved to be served," said Superintendent Joseph Olchefske.

But the boy's mother disagreed. And district officials claimed they couldn't find a residential program to take him.

Before arriving in Seattle in the fall of 1999, I.H. spent years in the Edmonds district safely sharing a classroom with other disabled students. He's now in the Shoreline district, where, according to records there, he is in a class with two other boys, where staff is working to improve his communication and daily-living skills.

As the state's largest school district, Seattle also has the state's largest number of special-education students—about 6,000—presenting it with enormous financial and educational challenges. And for the most part, it receives few complaints about how it handles these students, and is credited with creating numerous programs to serve them.

Next fall it will add six new autism centers to the seven it now has.

"Federal law obligates us to serve all kids regardless of the complexity of their needs or disabilities, while at the same time balancing the safety needs of the other students and staff," said Mark Green, the district's general counsel. "Obviously in this case we struggled."

For centuries, students like I.H. were often shunted into private institutions or hospitals, or left at home. But in 1975, Congress enacted the federal law now known as IDEA, which requires public schools to serve children with physical, mental and emotional disabilities, even when those disabilities pose a potential danger to themselves, staff and students.

I.H.'s 14-month enrollment in the Seattle School District provides a window into the dilemma public schools face in serving special-needs children. It also raises questions over the measures the district took to shift care of I.H. elsewhere.

Kathy Harris, a single mother who runs a résumé business out of her home, declined to be interviewed at length. But she allowed a *Times* reporter to view her son's school and court records, pages numbering into the thousands, and allowed district officials to discuss the case.

She also shared photographs of her only son, but asked that he be identified only as I.H., as he is in court records.

Diagnosed as totally blind at 3 months, I.H. lives in a world of sounds.

When happy, he croons to Garth Brooks and flaps his arms. He jangles bells and pulls a plastic bucket over his head to listen to his voice reverberate.

His speech is limited to utterances and a few words. He pats his chest for "yes" and responds to simple cues such as "lay down," "give," and "time for snack."

When agitated, he is prone to pinch, bite or head-butt anyone around him. His forehead has a permanent ridge from being hammered against walls and windows.

Little things can set him off: an unfamiliar voice, an unwelcome demand.

The state Department of Social and Health Services (DSHS), which has worked with I.H. through various programs over the years, traces some of his behavioral problems to misdiagnosed ear problems when he was 5. Because doctors told his mother nothing was wrong, she disciplined him for his tantrums, "when in reality he was in pain," according to a 1998 DSHS report.

Apart from three years in a residential program at the Washington State School for the Blind, I.H. spent most of his school years at Maplewood Center, a facility for children with disabilities in the Edmonds School District. He shared a classroom there in a separate building with other severely disabled children, who get close to one-on-one supervision from teachers and aides.

The curriculum there focused on the most basic life skills: dressing, communicating, using the toilet. He was assigned to crush cans and shred paper to increase his attention span. He swam, received speech therapy and sang.

Though progress was slow, staffers reported his outbursts fell from three a day to fewer than three a week, court records show. And though teachers and assistants occasionally suffered cuts and bruises, I.H. never showed aggression toward other children, employees said in court testimony. He once inadvertently injured a student when he threw a toy, court records show.

"He's a sweetheart," said Sherry Stephenson, an instructional assistant who worked with I.H. the last five years he was at Maplewood. "He has another side of him that is very loving and affectionate and playful."

In 1999, Harris moved to West Seattle and enrolled her son at Sealth.

He got off to a stormy start, head-butting a special-education teacher on his first visit. The teacher said the boy also grabbed a knife from a table and went after his mother, who wrestled it away from him. Harris says her son picked up the knife out of curiosity and released it on her cue, "give."

His first day was intentionally short to help him adjust to his new surroundings. But as an aide walked him back to the school bus, I.H. took a swipe at him, scratching him under the eye. The aide, who was hired to work one-on-one with the boy, quit that day.

District officials believed his transition into adolescence, the jolt of moving to a new school and changes in his sleep cycle made him more volatile than he had been at Maplewood.

Over the next three months, I.H. spent fewer than 10 fragmented hours in school as the district searched for a new aide, then slowly reintroduced him to school. Part of that process involved bus rides in which he wasn't allowed to leave the bus.

On March 28, he wriggled free from his harness on a parked bus and injured another aide and the driver. The district refused to allow him back on campus.

Harris immediately filed for a due-process hearing with the Office of the State Super-intendent of Public Instruction, claiming the district was violating her son's right to an education. In return, the district obtained a preliminary injunction in May in King County Superior Court to keep the boy off campus.

After three days of testimony at a due-process hearing in mid-June, Administrative Law Judge Janice L. Shave found the district's efforts to serve I.H. "inadequate" and in violation of IDEA.

"The school district has not made an adequate effort to devise, implement or provide special-education and related services to the student," Shave wrote in her 30-page decision. "The services the district did provide were too limited to afford any educational benefit."

Pending an appeal to federal court, the district in September took I.H. back on Shave's order. A boy who all say needed consistency had now been out of school for the better part of 10 months.

A basement room was modified for him, the walls and floors covered with protective mats. The room was well lighted, had a bed, a beanbag chair, toys, children's books and a desk where I.H. ate meals. The district prepared an individual education plan for the boy, as required by law. But execution of that plan was largely left to a revolving door of ill-prepared substitute teachers—a dozen of them over a period of four months—and employees of a private firm who said their job was to provide security, not education.

Michelle Corker-Curry, a district special-education supervisor, said the firm, Professional Network Inc. (PNI) of Lynnwood, was supposed to help substitutes teach the boy from a "menu" of educational exercises.

PNI officials declined comment, except to give a description of the company as a provider of social services.

However, three PNI employees—Richard Essex and Phillip Forsell, former long-time police officers; and Peter Verburg-Sachs, who had experience in mental-health counseling but none in special education for the disabled—said they were told to guard the boy and the substitutes, who they said were given no lesson plans. While a special-education consultant to the district, Michael Sanford, occasionally dropped in and offered hints, the teachers were often exasperated, wondering how to reach the child, the men said. Daily logs and summaries kept by PNI staff and teachers support those views.

"Some teachers read to him and one got him so far as to throw a ball back," Forsell said. "But he had needs and desires and I think part of his aggression was not being able to communicate these things."

One of the substitutes, Jim Michael, said the only instructions he received were to monitor and record I.H.'s behavior. He was left on his own to determine how to teach the boy.

"My whole reason for being there was to document his failure," Michael said. "At the very least give me something specific to try. A game, an exercise … something that has a chance to reach him."

Another substitute, who worked with I.H. for several weeks and asked not to be identified, said: "They told me to sit, observe and record."

Michael said he sympathized with the district's challenge, and came to believe the boy belonged in a special institution. But he also said the district was not doing all it could to serve the boy.

"I kept saying to myself, 'Why is this kid in school? He's not learning anything,'" he said.

Substitute Gloria Loveless said a Sealth assistant principal told her she would be "crazy" to take the assignment. She did anyway.

Some of the substitutes assigned to I.H. suffered scratches and quit after one day.

The boy's mother and her lawyer objected to the isolation, lack of instruction and constant change of teachers, noting that I.H. missed at least nine days when there was either no teacher or no transportation available.

"When (I.H.) attends school, he's not engaged in tasks or activities," wrote attorney Carol Vaughn of the Northwest Justice Project, a free legal-services group that represented Harris, in a letter to the district. "(I.H.) is 'learning' to associate school with unstructured nap and play time."

"We've learned if we isolate students from each other, we lose a tremendous opportunity for them to learn from each other," said University of Oregon special-education professor Robert Horner, a leader in the study of children with violent behavioral problems. "We've got to get over the hubris that children only learn when they receive individual instruction from adults."

Jeannette Cohen, an educational consultant hired by Harris, said in court the boy wasn't the threat the district made him out to be. His blindness precludes him from obtaining weapons, unless by chance, or from targeting his acts of aggression, she said.

But district officials said their own expert, psychologist Stephen Sulzbacher of the Children's Hospital & Regional Medical Center in Seattle, said that placing I.H. among other students would be "ludicrous." The district would have preferred a permanent special-ed teacher to work with I.H., but without one, had to use substitutes, said Green, the district's counsel.

Explosive as the boy could be, those who worked with him said they saw glimpses of hope, especially on the few occasions when Sanford, a trained special-education professional employed by the district, worked with him.

"It was awesome to watch," Forsell said. "If a person with training like that had worked with the kid for a long period of time, he probably would have achieved what he's capable of."

* * *

Questions for Discussion

1. What did you think of the district's decision to buy this student's absence? If you were his parent, what factors might you consider when deciding whether to accept this "deal"?

2. What aspects do you consider "broken" about the special education system as a whole? What remedies would you propose? Is inadequate funding the culprit? Inadequate teacher training?

For Further Reading

Witte v. Clark Co. Sch. Bd., 197 F.3d 1271 (9th Cir. 1999).

Charlie F. v. Board of Education of Skokie School District, 98 F.3d 989 (7th Cir. 1996).

"U.S. Education Department Releases Analysis of State Bullying Laws and Policies," U.S. Department of Education, retrieved May 15, 2012 at http://www.ed.gov/news/press-releases/ us-education-department-releases-analysis-state-bullying-laws-and-policies.

"Not going to be bullied," retrieved May 15, 2012 at http://www.aapd.com/what-we-do/ education/safe-schools/.

Discussion 7

Parents and the IDEA: Could We Get Some Help Here?

Recommended Background Reading

Board of Ed. v. Rowley, 458 U.S. 176 (1982).

"When Parents & Schools Disagree," retrieved May 15, 2012 at http://www.wrightslaw.com/info/advo.disagree.heitin.htm.

"Why Do Schools Draw Lines in the Sand?" retrieved May 15, 2012 at http://www.wrightslaw.com/howey/power.mtgs.ltrs.htm.

Readings for Class Discussion

Mom Straps Herself to Flag Pole in Protest

Dave Reynolds, *Inclusion Daily Express*, August 30, 2000

WASHINGTON COUNTY, PENNSYLVANIA—All children who have Down syndrome within the McGuffey School District are educated outside the district. All, that is, except Ryan "Max" Lesneski, 7, who attends Blain-Buffalo Elementary School. Max's mother Deanna says she wants her son to attend classes in his home district, where she and the boy's four older siblings went to school. And she wants for Max, who has a hearing disability, to receive the services she feels he needs—services which the district had agreed to provide.

About 9:30 Monday morning, Deanna demonstrated her resolve to make sure he gets those services by tying herself to a flagpole in front of the school.

Deanna says the school informed her that they would no longer administer asthma medication for Max. It is a claim district officials dispute. They say they have no problem giving Max any of his medicine.

Deanna says this is only one the many problems she has had with the district in getting them to comply with the Individuals With Disabilities Education Act (IDEA) in serving her son. She claims that they also failed to modify a computer for Max, to assign a qualified sign language interpreter for him, and to provide an adequate summer school. She says

111

these were part of a 13-point plan the district agreed to follow in February. A judge is expected to review the case this morning.

District officials say they are meeting Max's needs and don't understand why his mother is protesting. And even though they are concerned about the effect the public spectacle will have on their students, the district says it has no plans to arrest Deanna.

By Monday afternoon, about 20 members of a local independent living disability rights group organization had joined the protest. The protesters, many in wheelchairs, had to park about a mile away from the campus. They spent the night with Deanna and were expected to continue the vigil through last night.

Mom Leaves Flag Pole

Dave Reynolds, *Inclusion Daily Express*, September 5, 2000

WASHINGTON COUNTY, PENNSYLVANIA—At 10:00 a.m. last Monday, Deanna Lesneski, 47, tied a lawn chair to the flag pole in front of her son's school and sat down in it. At about 4:30 p.m. Friday, she got up and went home, declaring victory for the five-day protest.

"I want to get a shower so bad I can't stand it," said Lesneski.

The end to the dramatic protest came a few minutes after McGuffy School District officials announced their intention to contract with a woman who has a Master's degree in Deaf Education and has taught deaf students for several years to be a teaching assistant at the school. The contract would mean the district had decided to abide by an agreement it signed in February, to provide an appropriately trained aide for Lesneski's son Max. The seven-year-old has Down syndrome, asthma, and uses sign language to communicate.

Lesneski began her vigil, she says, after school staff members told her they were not going to administer the boy's asthma medication. What she thought would have been a small demonstration grew as disability rights advocates from the local area and several states came to the rural elementary school to show their support.

Late on Friday, the district also agreed to have a meeting to discuss Max's Individualized Education Plan during a meeting with Lesneski on Tuesday morning. More than 25 people were scheduled to attend that meeting.

Mom Back at Flagpole

Dave Reynolds, *Inclusion Daily Express*, September 6, 2000

WASHINGTON COUNTY, PENNSYLVANIA—Claiming her son's school did not follow through with pledges it made on Friday, Deanna Lesneski once again tied a lawn chair to the flag pole in front of the school last night, then sat down to resume a protest she started over a week ago.

. . . .

Lesneski was back at the flag pole last night, saying the new teacher apparently had been hired to observe her son but not educate him. She said that during one class yesterday, Max got no help from the teacher when he had difficulty communicating with others.

Acting Superintendent Frank Zito explained yesterday that the district hired the teacher at a rate of $70 per day, to act as a mediator between Max and others if communication problems came up. A nurse or other qualified person also will be on hand at the school to administer Max's medications, Zito said.

Lesneski was better prepared for her vigil last night, showing up with a sleeping bag and blankets. Overnight temperatures were expected to be below 50 degrees.

Parents Object to Lesneski's Flag Pole Protest

Dave Reynolds, *Inclusion Daily Express*, September 7, 2000

WASHINGTON COUNTY, PENNSYLVANIA—During a meeting at Blaine-Buffalo Elementary School last night, about 70 parents expressed outrage at the mother who has drawn attention to their school by demonstrating in front of it.

Some of the parents criticized Deanna Lesneski, 46, demanding she be removed from the area. Others complained about her seven-year-old son Max, saying he had been aggressive with fellow students and that meetings regarding him took the teacher away from their children.

Lesneski spent the 7th day of her vigil sitting in a lawn chair strapped to a flag pole, protesting what she says is the district's lack of responsiveness to her son's needs. She says the school has repeatedly failed to provide the supports for Max which they agreed to provide in February. Max has Down syndrome and asthma and uses sign language to communicate. Other McGuffy School District students with Down syndrome are educated outside the district, but Lesneski wants Max to attend the same school his siblings attended, and to get the supports he needs to be successful.

At one point during the meeting, acting district superintendent Frank Zito had to physically come between one enraged parent and an advocate defending Lesneski.

"We don't need you in here," one man yelled at the advocate. "Get out."

Zito went on to answer questions and concerns from the crowd. Zito also announced the resignation of the Master's level teacher of deaf students who had been hired to work with Max. The teacher worked for less than a day after Lesneski discovered that the woman was hired to observe her son, not work with him directly. The district is continuing the search for a qualified teacher to fill the job.

According to today's Pittsburgh Post-Gazette, the district also wants a court to order Lesneski and her supporters—advocates for people with disabilities—removed from the flagpole area to a spot at the edge of school property.

Flag Pole Mom Victorious in Protest for Son's Education

Dave Reynolds, *Inclusion Daily Express*, September 20, 2000

WASHINGTON COUNTY, PENNSYLVANIA—Satisfied that her son's educational needs will be met in his classroom—at least for now—Deanna Lesneski yesterday ended her three-week long protest tied to the flagpole in front of Blaine-Buffalo Elementary School. Her decision came after a four-hour meeting with state and school officials, and a meeting with the aide who is to begin working with her son on Monday.

"This is all I've ever wanted," said Lesneski, after she untied her lawn chair from the flag pole, hopefully for the last time.

The mother of 7-year-old Ryan "Max" Lesneski, who has Down syndrome, asthma and uses sign language to communicate, met with about 20 officials from McGuffey School

District, Washington County Intermediate Unit One and the state Department of Health. Joining her were two of Max's therapists, her attorneys and a representative from Tri-County Patriots for Independent Living, a local disability rights organization.

The group yesterday developed an Individualized Education Plan (IEP) for Max, which outlines expected education outcomes and how services will be delivered. One of the main points which had remained—the hiring of an aide who is proficient in sign language to work with Max—was addressed to Lesneski's satisfaction during the meeting. Lesneski met for some time with the aide, who will work with Max on a one-on-one basis, seven hours a day, five days a week. Some of aide's salary will come from the Washington County Intermediate Unit One, which receives federal money for special education programs.

Another issue, regarding Max's medication, was worked out during a meeting with a Department of Health mediator last week. The school's medication policy had only allowed the district's registered nurse, who travels between five schools in the rural district, to administer medications. A new policy will allow a licensed nurse, who currently works as a clerical aide, to administer medications to Max.

Lesneski's protest, which began on the morning of August 28, had to do in part with Max's last IEP, written in February. In that IEP, a 13-point agreement was worked out with the district, calling for the hiring of an aide proficient in sign language, an extended school year for Max, along with "inclusion training" for the community and district employees. After the district failed to implement provisions of the agreement, Lesneski took her fight to federal court in March, asking a U.S. District Court Judge to enforce it.

Lesneski had stopped her vigil on September 1, after the school superintendent told her they had hired an aide to work with Max. She resumed her protest the following school day upon learning that the aide was only to observe the boy and not work directly with him.

Within a day of beginning her protest, disability rights activists from the local area and surrounding states worked in shifts to keep Lesneski company.

Lesneski told the Pittsburgh Post-Gazette that if the district does not abide by the new agreement, she would be strapping herself to a flagpole at the state's capitol in Harrisburg.

* * *

Questions for Discussion

1. What do you think of this mom's methods? Of the school district's response?

2. What other avenues do parents have available if they are dissatisfied with the education their child with a disability is receiving? How do these differ from avenues available to "typically developing" children?

_____

The following case is about an educational advocate who was brought before the Board on the Unauthorized Practice of Law. Some footnotes and string citations have been omitted.

In the Matter of Marilyn Arons

No. 440, 1999
Supreme Court of Delaware
756 A.2d 867; 2000 Del. LEXIS 284
May 23, 2000, Submitted
July 6, 2000, Decided

This is an appeal from a decision of the Board on the Unauthorized Practice of Law (the "Board"), an arm of the Supreme Court of Delaware, concluding that the appellants had engaged in the unauthorized practice of law. The appellants, supported by the United States Department of Justice as amicus curiae, contend that the Board erred in not recognizing their entitlement under federal law to represent parents of children with disabilities before State administrative agencies. That entitlement, it is argued, preempts state law and is supported by due process considerations. We conclude, however, that the Board's decision is supported by the evidence and free of any error of law. Accordingly, we affirm.

I

The appellants, Marilyn Arons and Ruth Watson, are, respectively, the founder and Executive Director of Parent Information Center of New Jersey, Inc. (collectively "Appellants"). The Parent Information Center is a non-profit organization founded in 1977 that provides advice, counseling and advocacy services to families of children with disabilities. On five occasions, the Center has represented families of children with disabilities in "due process" hearings held by the Delaware Department of Public Instruction pursuant to the federal Individuals with Disabilities Education Act ("IDEA"), 20 U.S.C. § 1400 et seq. Four of these five hearings were handled by Arons, while the other hearing was handled by Watson. Although neither Arons nor Watson is an attorney, both possess special knowledge and training with respect to the problems of children with disabilities.

The IDEA is intended to "ensure that children with disabilities and their parents are guaranteed procedural safeguards with respect to the provision of free appropriate public education." 20 U.S.C. § 1415(a). Under the IDEA, the parents of a disabled child are entitled to challenge any proposal to change or initiate, or refusal to change or initiate, the identification, evaluation, educational placement or any other aspect of the provision of a free appropriate public education service to that child. See id. at § 1415(b)(3). When complaints are received, "the parents involved in such complaint shall have the opportunity for an impartial due process hearing." Id. at § 1415(f).

Due process hearings in Delaware are conducted in a manner typical of contested, adjudicatory hearings. The parties include the parent(s), the local school board and the Department of Public Instruction. The hearing is conducted by a three-member panel consisting of an attorney admitted to practice in Delaware; an educator who is either certified in the area of special education or who has been a post-secondary educator in the area of programs for students with disabilities; and a lay person with demonstrated interest in the education of students with disabilities from an approved list compiled by the Governor's Advisory Counsel for Exceptional Citizens. Hearings are chaired by the attorney member of the panel.

Due process hearings usually last from two to four days. The school board and the Department of Public Instruction are always represented by counsel. The hearing begins with opening statements from each party. Evidence is then presented through witnesses, who are subjected to direct and cross-examination. Although the rules of evidence do not apply strictly, the Chair rules on legal issues, the qualification of experts and objections to relevance, materiality and admissibility. Following the presentation of evidence, the parties make closing statements and may be asked to file written submissions on key questions.

On August 8, 1996, the Office of Disciplinary Counsel ("ODC") filed a petition with the Board requesting that Arons, Watson and the Parent Information Center be declared to have engaged in activities constituting the unauthorized practice of law by representing families of children with disabilities in due process hearings. While admitting the representation of at least five such families in Delaware due process hearings, Appellants denied that their activities, even if amounting to the practice of law, constitute the unauthorized practice of law. They argued that section 1415(h)(1) of the IDEA permits the representations in which they have engaged and preempts any state-law proscription against the unauthorized practice of law that might otherwise apply. That section provides that any party to a due process hearing "shall be accorded.... the right to be accompanied and advised by counsel and by individuals with special knowledge or training with respect to the problems of children with disabilities." They also claimed that Delaware is alone among the fifty states in precluding non-lawyer representation in these circumstances.

The matter was submitted to the Board on a stipulation of facts, including transcripts of due process hearings, briefs, oral argument and post-hearing correspondence. On September 24, 1999, the Board issued a written opinion concluding that the IDEA does not authorize the practice of law by non-lawyers, including Appellants, in due process hearings. This appeal followed. Following the entry of this appeal, the United States Department of Justice sought leave to appear as an amicus curiae. Leave was granted and the Department has filed a brief in support of Appellants' position.

II

The present appeal poses the first occasion for this Court to exercise its power of review of decisions of the Board. Under Supreme Court Rule 86(e), this Court will accept factual findings by the Board so long as they are supported by substantial evidence. We review on a de novo basis findings by the Board related to legal issues. See Supr. Ct. R. 86(e). Because the parties stipulated to the facts in this matter and the only dispute relates to matters of law, this Court's review on all issues is de novo.

Appellants' principal argument is that the IDEA guarantees parents the right to have trained non-lawyers advocate on their behalf in due process hearings. They contend that the IDEA could hardly be clearer because it draws no distinction between counsel and "individuals with special knowledge or training with respect to the problems of children with disabilities." To the extent that Delaware law conflicts with federal law, the argument runs, Delaware law is displaced and federal law governs.

The ODC responds that the IDEA unambiguously supports its position. It argues that counsel have inherent and presumptive representational ability and authority, while educational consultants do not, and that the statutory language of section 1415(h) neither creates nor implies an equivalence of permissible roles for "counsel" and for "individuals with special knowledge or training."

Appellants and the ODC each argue that the pertinent language of the IDEA in dispute—"the right to be accompanied and advised by counsel and by individuals with special knowledge or training with respect to the problems of children with disabilities"—unambiguously supports their respective positions. We do not share the parties' vision of clarity. In our view, section 1415(h)(1) is ambiguous to the extent it appears to confer joint authority on lawyers and non-lawyers to accompany and advise parents and others affected by the operation of the due process hearings provided under the IDEA. That being said, however, case law as well as statutory history support the ODC's interpretation.

The pertinent language of section 1415(h)(1) has been discussed by the United States Court of Appeals for the Third Circuit in *Arons v. New Jersey State Board of Education*, 3d. Cir., 842 F.2d 58 (1988). In that case, Appellant Arons sought an award of fees for her successful representation of parents in a due process hearing in New Jersey, where state law allows non-lawyers to represent parents in due process hearings. In affirming a decision of the United States District Court for New Jersey that held that the New Jersey regulation authorizing such fees permitted payment of only legal fees and not those of lay advocates, the court of appeals rejected the statutory intent argument advanced by Appellants here. The court explained:

> The carefully drawn statutory language does not authorize these specially qualified individuals to render legal services. Although the [IDEA] does give "any party to any hearing" the right to "present evidence and confront, cross-examine, and compel the attendance of witnesses," those functions are not designated to be performed by lay advocates. Furthermore, the statute does not use the word "represent" in subsection (d)(1), as would be expected if Congress intended to place expert and legal counsel on the same footing.

Our search through the legislative history has failed to uncover any indication that Congress contemplated that the "individuals with special knowledge" would act in a representative capacity. The Senate Report describes the "individual's" role as one of consultation, with emphasis on the responsibility to identify educational problems, evaluate them, and determine proper educational placement.

The provisions's [sic] text and history thus cast substantial doubt on the plaintiff's statement in her brief that "Congress intended that no distinction be drawn between lawyers and lay advocates." 842 F.2d at 62–63 (citations omitted).

Because the sole issue presented in *Arons* was whether a lay advocate, whose authority to represent parents in the IDEA proceedings was unchallenged, was entitled to seek fees for her services, the *Arons* holding is contextually distinct from the issue posed in this appeal. We find the analysis of the federalism issue articulated by the court of appeals to be persuasive. That court's reference to a 1975 Senate Report discussing the IDEA is arguably dicta. Nevertheless, the contents of the Senate Report describing the nonlawyer's role as one of consultation is compelling evidence that Congress did not intend non-lawyers to advocate on behalf of parents in due process hearings. See *Arons*, 842 F.2d at 62 (citing S. Rep. No. 94-168 (1975)).

Also supportive of the ODC's proposed interpretation of the IDEA are a Senate Conference Report addressing the statute and remarks made by the original author of the Senate bill, Senator Harrison Williams of New Jersey. The Conference Report states that in administrative due process hearings a party is entitled to "the right to counsel and to be advised and accompanied by individuals with special knowledge, training or skills with respect to the problems of handicapped children." S. Conf. Rep. No. 94-455 (1975). Senator Williams, in providing a detailed analysis of the legislation before the Senate on November 19, 1975, echoed those words verbatim. See 121 Cong. Rec. 37416. This language confirms the clear distinction that Congress envisioned between the representational role of counsel and the advisory role of non-lawyers.

Recent amendments to the IDEA further bolster the ODC's position. Pursuant to these amendments, one of the safeguards required for agencies receiving federal funds under the IDEA is the adoption of procedures by the agency "that require the parent of a child with a disability, or the attorney representing the child, to provide notice" to the state or local educational agency of certain information in connection with a complaint. 20 U.S.C. § 1415(b)(6) and (7). The word "attorney" is an indisputable reference to a member of the Bar and not a layperson, even if that layperson possesses "special knowledge or training with respect to the problems of children with disabilities." Equally supportive of the ODC's position is the fact that while the IDEA has been amended several times since *Arons* was decided, Congress has not attempted to overrule that judicial interpretation.

Finally, Congress has explicitly included language in other federal statutes to permit lay representation where such a result was intended. See, e.g., 7 U.S.C. § 2020(e)(7) (Food Stamp Act provision allowing households in certification process to "be represented by a person other than a member of the household so long as that person has been clearly designated as the representative.... and.... is an adult."). Congress obviously knows how to provide such authority when it wishes to do so. The absence of similar language in the IDEA strongly suggests that Congress chose not to create a right to lay representation in due process hearings.

Appellants place great reliance on, and request our deference to, an interpretation of section 1415(h)(1) contained in an April 8, 1981 letter of Theodore Sky, the then acting General Counsel of the United States Department of Education. That letter was written in response to a request by the Superintendent of Public Instruction for the State of Washington for a "legal analysis regarding the role of lay advocates in educational agency administrative hearings" conducted under the IDEA. The superintendent suggested that the IDEA's language indicates that non-lawyers are not in fact authorized to engage in activities conventionally viewed as legal representation, such as examining and cross-examining witnesses. In its response, the Department of Education rejected the superintendent's reading of the IDEA, concluding that notwithstanding the Senate Conference Report and the absence in section 1415(h)(1) of the term "represent," lay advocates are permitted to represent parties at due process hearings and appeals under the IDEA.

In reaching its conclusion that section 1415(h)(1) authorizes lay representation in due process hearings, the Department of Education relied on three factors. First, it reasoned that because no "bifurcation of function" is set forth in the statute between counsel on the one hand and individuals with special knowledge or training on the other, the permissible roles of the two must be the same. Second, the Department looked to the remarks of Congressman George Miller and Senator Alan Cranston, both of California. Congressman Miller, a member of the Subcommittee on Select Education which prepared the House bill, explained section 1415(h)(1) to his colleagues by observing that parents "will have the right to be accompanied by counsel or other qualified individuals who possess 'special knowledge or training with respect to the education of handicapped children.'" 121 Cong. Rec. 25539 (1975). Senator Cranston noted that the "procedural requirements [of the IDEA] are consistent with the existing California statutory and master plan requirements on this subject," which, at the time, permitted the lay representation of parties in California due process hearings. 121 Cong. Rec. 37419 (1975). Third, the Department relied upon the fact that lay representation had been authorized by Congress for certain other types of administrative proceedings.

Because section 1415(h)(1) is arguably ambiguous, the Department's interpretation of that section is entitled to some level of deference by this Court. See *Chevron, U.S.A., Inc. v. Natural Resources Defense Council, Inc.*, 467 U.S. 837, 843–45, 81 L. Ed. 2d 694, 104

S. Ct. 2778 (1984). Here, however, that level of deference is modest. Where Congress has not expressly delegated "authority to an agency to elucidate a specific provision of the statute by regulation," deference is due only to a "reasonable" administrative interpretation. 467 U.S. at 843–44. Further, less deference is due to informal agency interpretations, such as that expressed in the Sky letter, than to formal agency regulations adopted after a notice and comment period. See *Cleary v. Waldman*, 3d Cir., 167 F.3d 801, 807–08 (1999).

Even if this Court were required to give greater deference to the Department of Education's interpretation of section 1415(h)(1), it is doubtful whether that interpretation could withstand the sheer weight of the legal and factual support for the opposite conclusion. The Department's analysis of the statute is subject to criticism. First, in concluding that the permissible roles of counsel and individuals with special knowledge or training with respect to the problems of children with disabilities must be the same, the Department overlooked the inherent and presumptive representational authority with which counsel are cloaked and non-lawyers are not. Second, the Department selectively chose statements made by two lawmakers, while placing no weight on the Senate Report, the Senate Conference Report, or the remarks of Senator Williams. Such an approach renders that aspect of the Department's analysis questionable. See generally *Consumer Prod. Safety Comm'n v. GTE Sylvania, Inc.*, 447 U.S. 102, 118, 64 L. Ed. 2d 766, 100 S. Ct. 2051 (1980) ("Contemporaneous remarks of a single legislator who sponsors a bill are not controlling in analyzing legislative history."). Finally, the Department's reliance upon the fact that lay representation had been authorized by Congress for certain other types of administrative proceedings is puzzling because as previously noted, that factor actually supports the opposite conclusion — that Congress knew how to authorize lay representation when it wished to do so.

III

In addition to their statutory interpretation argument, Appellants contend even if the IDEA does not expressly entitle them to represent parents in due process hearings, due process would be violated by forbidding parents from having non-lawyer representation in hearings under the IDEA. They note that due process hearings are formal adversarial proceedings in which the State of Delaware funds the attorneys who argue for the parents' adversaries. Denying parents and children access to "the only assistance available to them," the argument goes raises "unyielding due process problems."[1]

The parties agree that *Mathews v. Eldridge*, 424 U.S. 319, 47 L. Ed. 2d 18, 96 S. Ct. 893 (1976), governs the determination of what process is due to safeguard a child's fundamental right to education. Under *Mathews*, courts must consider: (i) the importance of the individual interest involved; (ii) the value of specific procedural safeguards to that interest; and (iii) the governmental interest in fiscal and administrative efficiency. See id. at 335.

The ODC acknowledges that the individual liberty interest at stake in due process hearings under the IDEA is substantial. It also concedes that some parents will forego their statutory right to contest changes to their child's education plan because they cannot afford legal counsel and will opt not to proceed pro se due to the complexity of the hearings

---

1. This Court has some difficulty understanding the applicability of this argument to the matter at hand. It is not alleged that forbidding parents from having non-lawyer assistance in hearings under the IDEA will deprive the Appellants of their due process rights, nor are the parents, whose rights are purportedly abridged, parties to this action. Appellants appear to be acting as surrogates in pressing the due process claim. We will address Appellants' argument, however, in the context of adopting a statutory construction that will avoid constitutional entanglements.

and the prospect of facing two sets of government lawyers. The ODC submits, however, that Appellants "grossly and unfairly" exaggerate the risk that Delaware will deprive children of that interest unless the children and their parents are allowed to be represented by lay advocates. In this regard, the ODC notes that Delaware's Community Legal Aid Society has, on occasion, provided representation at IDEA due process hearings to parents and children whose cases satisfy the organization's case acceptance criteria. The ODC further contends that the State of Delaware has a compelling interest in regulating the practice of law within its boundaries, and that this interest significantly outweighs any potential benefit that some individual parents and children may obtain through the services of lay advocates.

We agree. A balancing of the *Mathews* factors suggests that procedural due process would not be violated by forbidding parents from having non-lawyer representation in hearings under the IDEA. While there is no question of the importance of the individual interests involved, it seems clear that parties to an IDEA hearing are already provided with substantial procedural safeguards. The hearings are conducted in a manner typical of contested, adversarial adjudicatory hearings, including the direct and cross-examination of witnesses and the required exchange of witness lists and documents in advance of the hearing.[2] While we recognize that Appellants possess some expertise in the area of the educational needs of disabled children, they admittedly lack the training and skills that lawyers are expected to exhibit in matters of evidence and procedure. Second, it seems logical that the third *Mathews* factor, i.e., "governmental interest in fiscal and administrative efficiency," would encompass this State's exclusive authority to regulate the practice of law. It would also implicate the ODC's argument that lay advocates are unregulated and, unlike members of the Bar, are not answerable to the disciplinary process that operates as an arm of this Court. This Court does not exercise its inherent authority to regulate the practice of law for the purpose of protecting the financial interests of the lawyer. Our role is to insure that the public will enjoy the representation of individuals who have been found to possess the necessary skills and training to represent others.

Finally, the record does not support Appellants' assertion that parents and children will be denied access to "the only assistance available to them." The stipulation of the parties does state that the five families represented by the Appellants looked diligently to find legal counsel to represent them on a reduced-cost or pro bono basis prior to obtaining Appellants' services. But the record also reflects that Delaware's Community Legal Aid Society has in the past provided representation at IDEA due process hearings to parents and children whose cases satisfy the organization's case acceptance criteria. The record further reflects that the State Superintendent of Public Instruction and the district involved are required to provide information to parents regarding the availability of free or low-cost legal services which may be available. If it could be demonstrated that an unmet need exists and that the local bar could not adequately respond, this Court would consider the adoption of a rule allowing lay representation in a certain limited class of cases. See, e.g., Supr. Ct. R. 57 (permitting civil actions before Justice of the Peace Courts in which an artificial entity or public body is a party to be prosecuted and/or defended by an officer or employee of that artificial entity or public body, who need not be an attorney duly licensed to practice law in this State). At present, however, such a need has not been demonstrated.

---

2. We also believe that the three member panel consisting of an attorney, an educator in the area of special education, and a lay person with demonstrated interest in the education of students with disabilities, affords parents an unbiased hearing and, coupled with the above mentioned safeguards, adequate structural protection.

IV

For the foregoing reasons, the language of section 1415(h)(1) cannot be interpreted as granting any clear right to lay representation. This conclusion renders moot Appellants' claim that the IDEA preempts any state-law proscription against the unauthorized practice of law that might otherwise apply to the activities of such individuals with special knowledge or training in this context. Accordingly, we affirm the decision of the Board.

* * *

Questions for Discussion

1. When you read the IDEA provision about representation for the first time, what did you think it meant?

2. Do you think only attorneys should be able to represent people in due process hearings under the IDEA? What are the competing policies involved? Might an educational consultant like Ms. Arons be substantially more knowledgeable than a brand-new lawyer, or than a lawyer who has never practiced in this area?

3. What do you think of the court's statement that a lack of legal aid resources has not been demonstrated? What such resources exist in your state?

Must parents have legal counsel to pursue IDEA claims in federal court? The following case tackles that question.

Winkelman v. Parma City School District

550 US 516 (2007)

Justice Kennedy delivered the opinion of the Court.

Some four years ago, Mr. and Mrs. Winkelman, parents of five children, became involved in lengthy administrative and legal proceedings. They had sought review related to concerns they had over whether their youngest child, 6-year-old Jacob, would progress well at Pleasant Valley Elementary School, which is part of the Parma City School District in Parma, Ohio.

Jacob has autism spectrum disorder and is covered by the Individuals with Disabilities Education Act (Act or IDEA), 84 Stat. 175, as amended, 20 U. S. C. § 1400 *et seq.* (2000 ed. and Supp. IV). His parents worked with the school district to develop an individualized education program (IEP), as required by the Act. All concede that Jacob's parents had the statutory right to contribute to this process and, when agreement could not be reached, to participate in administrative proceedings including what the Act refers to as an "impartial due process hearing." § 1415(f)(1)(A) (2000 ed., Supp. IV).

The disagreement at the center of the current dispute concerns the procedures to be followed when parents and their child, dissatisfied with the outcome of the due process hearing, seek further review in a United States District Court. The question is whether parents, either on their own behalf or as representatives of the child, may proceed in court unrepresented by counsel though they are not trained or licensed as attorneys. Resolution of this issue requires us to examine and explain the provisions of IDEA to determine if it accords to parents rights of their own that can be vindicated in court proceedings, or alternatively, whether the Act allows them, in their status as parents, to represent their child in court proceedings.

I

Respondent Parma City School District, a participant in IDEA's educational spending program, accepts federal funds for assistance in the education of children with disabilities. As a condition of receiving funds, it must comply with IDEA's mandates. IDEA requires that the school district provide Jacob with a "free appropriate public education," which must operate in accordance with the IEP that Jacob's parents, along with school officials and other individuals, develop as members of Jacob's "IEP Team." Brief for Petitioners 3 (internal quotation marks omitted).

The school district proposed an IEP for the 2003–2004 school year that would have placed Jacob at a public elementary school. Regarding this IEP as deficient under IDEA, Jacob's nonlawyer parents availed themselves of the administrative review provided by IDEA. They filed a complaint alleging respondent had failed to provide Jacob with a free appropriate public education; they appealed the hearing officer's rejection of the claims in this complaint to a state-level review officer; and after losing that appeal they filed, on their own behalf and on behalf of Jacob, a complaint in the United States District Court for the Northern District of Ohio. In reliance upon 20 U.S.C. § 1415(i)(2) (2000 ed., Supp. IV) they challenged the administrative decision, alleging, among other matters: that Jacob had not been provided with a free appropriate public education; that his IEP was inadequate; and that the school district had failed to follow procedures mandated by IDEA. Pending the resolution of these challenges, the Winkelmans had enrolled Jacob in a private school at their own expense. They had also obtained counsel to assist them with certain aspects of the proceedings, although they filed their federal complaint, and later their appeal, without the aid of an attorney. The Winkelmans' complaint sought reversal of the administrative decision, reimbursement for private-school expenditures and attorney's fees already incurred, and, it appears, declaratory relief.

The District Court granted respondent's motion for judgment on the pleadings, finding it had provided Jacob with a free appropriate public education. Petitioners, proceeding without counsel, filed an appeal with the Court of Appeals for the Sixth Circuit. Relying on its recent decision in *Cavanaugh v. Cardinal Local School Dist.*, 409 F. 3d 753 (2005), the Court of Appeals entered an order dismissing the Winkelmans' appeal unless they obtained counsel to represent Jacob. See Order in No. 05-3886 (Nov. 4, 2005), App. A to Pet. for Cert. 1a. In *Cavanaugh* the Court of Appeals had rejected the proposition that IDEA allows nonlawyer parents raising IDEA claims to proceed pro se in federal court. The court ruled that the right to a free appropriate public education "belongs to the child alone," 409 F. 3d, at 757, not to both the parents and the child. It followed, the court held, that "any right on which the [parents] could proceed on their own behalf would be derivative" of the child's right, ibid., so that parents bringing IDEA claims were not appearing on their own behalf, *ibid*. See also 28 U. S. C. § 1654 (allowing parties to prosecute their own claims pro se). As for the parents' alternative argument, the court held, nonlawyer parents cannot litigate IDEA claims on behalf of their child because IDEA does not abrogate the common-law rule prohibiting nonlawyer parents from representing minor children. 409 F. 3d, at 756. As the court in *Cavanaugh* acknowledged, its decision brought the Sixth Circuit in direct conflict with the First Circuit, which had concluded, under a theory of "statutory joint rights," that the Act accords to parents the right to assert IDEA claims on their own behalf. See *Maroni v. Pemi-Baker Regional School Dist.*, 346 F. 3d 247, 249, 250 (CA1 2003).

Petitioners sought review in this Court. In light of the disagreement among the Courts of Appeals as to whether a nonlawyer parent of a child with a disability may prosecute IDEA actions pro se in federal court, we granted certiorari. 549 U. S. ___ (2006). Compare

Cavanaugh, supra, with *Maroni, supra*; see also *Mosely v. Board of Ed. of Chicago,* 434 F. 3d 527 (CA7 2006); *Collinsgru v. Palmyra Bd. of Ed.,* 161 F. 3d 225 (CA3 1998); *Wenger v. Canastota Central School Dist.,* 146 F. 3d 123 (CA2 1998) (per curiam); *Devine v. Indian River Cty. School Bd.,* 121 F. 3d 576 (CA11 1997).

II

Our resolution of this case turns upon the significance of IDEA's interlocking statutory provisions. Petitioners' primary theory is that the Act makes parents real parties in interest to IDEA actions, not "mer[e] guardians of their children's rights." Brief for Petitioners 16. If correct, this allows Mr. and Mrs. Winkelman back into court, for there is no question that a party may represent his or her own interests in federal court without the aid of counsel. See 28 U. S. C. § 1654 ("In all courts of the United States the parties may plead and conduct their own cases personally or by counsel ..."). Petitioners cannot cite a specific provision in IDEA mandating in direct and explicit terms that parents have the status of real parties in interest. They instead base their argument on a comprehensive reading of IDEA. Taken as a whole, they contend, the Act leads to the necessary conclusion that parents have independent, enforceable rights. Brief for Petitioners 14 (citing *Koons Buick Pontiac GMC, Inc. v. Nigh,* 543 U. S. 50, 60 (2004)). Respondent, accusing petitioners of "knit[ting] together various provisions pulled from the crevices of the statute" to support these claims, Brief for Respondent 19, reads the text of IDEA to mean that any redressable rights under the Act belong only to children, id., at 19–40.

We agree that the text of IDEA resolves the question presented. We recognize, in addition, that a proper interpretation of the Act requires a consideration of the entire statutory scheme. See *Dolan v. Postal Service,* 546 U. S. 481, 486 (2006). Turning to the current version of IDEA, which the parties agree governs this case, we begin with an overview of the relevant statutory provisions.

A

The goals of IDEA include "ensur[ing] that all children with disabilities have available to them a free appropriate public education" and "ensur[ing] that the rights of children with disabilities and parents of such children are protected." 20 U. S. C. §§ 1400(d)(1)(A)–(B) (2000 ed., Supp. IV). To this end, the Act includes provisions governing four areas of particular relevance to the Winkelmans' claim: procedures to be followed when developing a child's IEP; criteria governing the sufficiency of an education provided to a child; mechanisms for review that must be made available when there are objections to the IEP or to other aspects of IDEA proceedings; and the requirement in certain circumstances that States reimburse parents for various expenses. See generally §§ 1412(a)(10), 1414, 1415. Although our discussion of these four areas does not identify all the illustrative provisions, we do take particular note of certain terms that mandate or otherwise describe parental involvement.

IDEA requires school districts to develop an IEP for each child with a disability, see §§ 1412(a)(4), 1414(d), with parents playing "a significant role" in this process, *Schaffer v. Weast,* 546 U. S. 49, 53 (2005). Parents serve as members of the team that develops the IEP. § 1414(d)(1)(B). The "concerns" parents have "for enhancing the education of their child" must be considered by the team. § 1414(d)(3)(A)(ii). IDEA accords parents additional protections that apply throughout the IEP process. See, e.g., § 1414(d)(4)(A) (requiring the IEP Team to revise the IEP when appropriate to address certain information provided by the parents); § 1414(e) (requiring States to "ensure that the parents of [a child with a disability] are members of any group that makes decisions on the educational placement of their child"). The statute also sets up general procedural safeguards that protect the informed involvement of parents in the development of an education for their child. See, e.g., § 1415(a) (requiring States to "establish and maintain procedures ... to ensure that children with disabilities and their parents are guaranteed procedural safeguards with respect to the provision of a free appropriate public education"); § 1415(b)(1) (mandating that States provide an opportunity for parents to examine all relevant records). See generally §§ 1414, 1415. A central purpose of the parental protections is to facilitate the provision of a " 'free appropriate public education,' " § 1401(9), which must be made available to the child "in conformity with the [IEP]," § 1401(9)(D).

The Act defines a "free appropriate public education" pursuant to an IEP to be an educational instruction "specially designed ... to meet the unique needs of a child with a disability," § 1401(29), coupled with any additional "related services" that are "required to assist a child with a disability to benefit from [that instruction]," § 1401(26)(A). See also § 1401(9). The education must, among other things, be provided "under public supervision and direction," "meet the standards of the State educational agency," and "include an appropriate preschool, elementary school, or secondary school education in the State involved." Ibid. The instruction must, in addition, be provided at "no cost to parents." § 1401(29). See generally *Board of Ed. of Hendrick Hudson Central School Dist., Westchester Cty. v. Rowley*, 458 U. S. 176 (1982) (discussing the meaning of "free appropriate public education" as used in the statutory precursor to IDEA).

When a party objects to the adequacy of the education provided, the construction of the IEP, or some related matter, IDEA provides procedural recourse: It requires that a State provide "[a]n opportunity for any party to present a complaint ... with respect to any matter relating to the identification, evaluation, or educational placement of the child, or the provision of a free appropriate public education to such child." § 1415(b)(6). By presenting a complaint a party is able to pursue a process of review that, as relevant, begins with a preliminary meeting "where the parents of the child discuss their complaint" and the local educational agency "is provided the opportunity to [reach a resolution]." § 1415(f)(1)(B)(i)(IV). If the agency "has not resolved the complaint to the satisfaction of the parents within 30 days," § 1415(f)(1)(B)(ii), the parents may request an "impartial due process hearing," § 1415(f)(1)(A), which must be conducted either by the local educational agency or by the state educational agency, ibid., and where a hearing officer will resolve issues raised in the complaint, § 1415(f)(3).

IDEA sets standards the States must follow in conducting these hearings. Among other things, it indicates that the hearing officer's decision "shall be made on substantive grounds based on a determination of whether the child received a free appropriate public education," and that, "[i]n matters alleging a procedural violation," the officer may find a child "did not receive a free appropriate public education" only if the violation

"(I) impeded the child's right to a free appropriate public education;

"(II) significantly impeded the parents' opportunity to participate in the decisionmaking process regarding the provision of a free appropriate public education to the parents' child; or

"(III) caused a deprivation of educational benefits." §§ 1415(f)(3)(E)(i)–(ii).

If the local educational agency, rather than the state educational agency, conducts this hearing, then "any party aggrieved by the findings and decision rendered in such a hearing may appeal such findings and decision to the State educational agency." § 1415(g)(1). Once the state educational agency has reached its decision, an aggrieved party may commence suit in federal court: "Any party aggrieved by the findings and decision made [by the hearing officer] shall have the right to bring a civil action with respect to the complaint." § 1415(i)(2)(A); see also § 1415(i)(1).

IDEA, finally, provides for at least two means of cost recovery that inform our analysis. First, in certain circumstances it allows a court or hearing officer to require a state agency "to reimburse the parents [of a child with a disability] for the cost of [private school] enrollment if the court or hearing officer finds that the agency had not made a free appropriate public education available to the child." § 1412(a)(10)(C)(ii). Second, it sets forth rules governing when and to what extent a court may award attorney's fees. See § 1415(i)(3)(B). Included in this section is a provision allowing an award "to a prevailing party who is the parent of a child with a disability." § 1415(i)(3)(B)(i)(I).

B

Petitioners construe these various provisions to accord parents independent, enforceable rights under IDEA. We agree. The parents enjoy enforceable rights at the administrative stage, and it would be inconsistent with the statutory scheme to bar them from continuing to assert these rights in federal court.

The statute sets forth procedures for resolving disputes in a manner that, in the Act's express terms, contemplates parents will be the parties bringing the administrative complaints. In addition to the provisions we have cited, we refer also to § 1415(b)(8) (requiring a state educational agency to "develop a model form to assist parents in filing a complaint"); § 1415(c)(2) (addressing the response an agency must provide to a "parent's due process complaint notice"); and § 1415(i)(3)(B)(i) (referring to "the parent's complaint"). A wide range of review is available: administrative complaints may be brought with respect to "any matter relating to … the provision of a free appropriate public education." § 1415(b)(6)(A). Claims raised in these complaints are then resolved at impartial due process hearings, where, again, the statute makes clear that parents will be participating as parties. See generally *supra*, at 7–8. See also § 1415(f)(3)(C) (indicating "[a] parent or agency shall request an impartial due process hearing" within a certain period of time); § 1415(e)(2)(A)(ii) (referring to "a parent's right to a due process hearing"). The statute then grants "[a]ny party aggrieved by the findings and decision made [by the hearing officer] … the right to bring a civil action with respect to the complaint." § 1415(i)(2)(A).

Nothing in these interlocking provisions excludes a parent who has exercised his or her own rights from statutory protection the moment the administrative proceedings end. Put another way, the Act does not *sub silentio* or by implication bar parents from seeking to vindicate the rights accorded to them once the time comes to file a civil action. Through its provisions for expansive review and extensive parental involvement, the statute leads to just the opposite result.

Respondent, resisting this line of analysis, asks us to read these provisions as contemplating parental involvement only to the extent parents represent their child's interests. In respondent's view IDEA accords parents nothing more than "collateral tools related to the child's underlying substantive rights—not freestanding or independently enforceable rights." Brief for Respondent 25.

This interpretation, though, is foreclosed by provisions of the statute. IDEA defines one of its purposes as seeking "to ensure that the rights of children with disabilities and parents of such children are protected." § 1400(d)(1)(B). The word "rights" in the quoted language refers to the rights of parents as well as the rights of the child; otherwise the grammatical structure would make no sense.

Further provisions confirm this view. IDEA mandates that educational agencies establish procedures "to ensure that children with disabilities and their parents are guaranteed procedural safeguards with respect to the provision of a free appropriate public education." § 1415(a). It presumes parents have rights of their own when it defines how States might provide for the transfer of the "rights accorded to parents" by IDEA, § 1415(m)(1)(B), and it prohibits the raising of certain challenges "[n]otwithstanding any other individual right of action that a parent or student may maintain under [the relevant provisions of IDEA]," §§ 1401(10)(E), 1412(a)(14)(E). To adopt respondent's reading of the statute would require an interpretation of these statutory provisions (and others) far too strained to be correct.

Defending its countertextual reading of the statute, respondent cites a decision by a Court of Appeals concluding that the Act's "references to parents are best understood as accommodations to the fact of the child's incapacity." *Doe v. Board of Ed. of Baltimore Cty.*, 165 F. 3d 260, 263 (CA4 1998); see also Brief for Respondent 30. This, according to respondent, requires us to interpret all references to parents' rights as referring in implicit terms to the child's rights—which, under this view, are the only enforceable rights accorded by IDEA. Even if we were inclined to ignore the plain text of the statute in considering this theory, we disagree that the sole purpose driving IDEA's involvement of parents is to facilitate vindication of a child's rights. It is not a novel proposition to say that parents have a recognized legal interest in the education and upbringing of their child. See, e.g., *Pierce v. Society of Sisters*, 268 U. S. 510, 534–535 (1925) (acknowledging "the liberty of parents and guardians to direct the upbringing and education of children under their control"); *Meyer v. Nebraska*, 262 U. S. 390, 399–401 (1923). There is no necessary bar or obstacle in the law, then, to finding an intention by Congress to grant parents a stake in the entitlements created by IDEA. Without question a parent of a child with a disability has a particular and personal interest in fulfilling "our national policy of ensuring equality of opportunity, full participation, independent living, and economic self-sufficiency for individuals with disabilities." § 1400(c)(1).

We therefore find no reason to read into the plain language of the statute an implicit rejection of the notion that Congress would accord parents independent, enforceable rights concerning the education of their children. We instead interpret the statute's references to parents' rights to mean what they say: that IDEA includes provisions conveying rights to parents as well as to children.

A variation on respondent's argument has persuaded some Courts of Appeals. The argument is that while a parent can be a "party aggrieved" for aspects of the hearing officer's findings and decision, he or she cannot be a "party aggrieved" with respect to all IDEA-based challenges. Under this view the causes of action available to a parent might relate, for example, to various procedural mandates, see, e.g., *Collinsgru*, 161 F. 3d, at 233, and reimbursement demands, see, e.g., § 1412(a)(10)(C)(ii). The argument supporting this conclusion proceeds as follows: Because a "party aggrieved" is, by definition, entitled to a remedy, and parents are, under IDEA, only entitled to certain procedures and reimbursements as remedies, a parent cannot be a "party aggrieved" with regard to any claim not implicating these limited matters.

This argument is contradicted by the statutory provisions we have recited. True, there are provisions in IDEA stating parents are entitled to certain procedural protections and reimbursements; but the statute prevents us from placing too much weight on the implications to be drawn when other entitlements are accorded in less clear language. We find little support for the inference that parents are excluded by implication whenever a child is mentioned, and vice versa. Compare, e.g., § 1411(e)(3)(E) (barring States from using certain funds for costs associated with actions "brought on behalf of a child" but failing to acknowledge that actions might also be brought on behalf of a parent) with

§ 1415(i)(3)(B)(i) (allowing recovery of attorney's fees to a "prevailing party who is the parent of a child with a disability" but failing to acknowledge that a child might also be a prevailing party). Without more, then, the language in IDEA confirming that parents enjoy particular procedural and reimbursement-related rights does not resolve whether they are also entitled to enforce IDEA's other mandates, including the one most fundamental to the Act: the provision of a free appropriate public education to a child with a disability.

We consider the statutory structure. The IEP proceedings entitle parents to participate not only in the implementation of IDEA's procedures but also in the substantive formulation of their child's educational program. Among other things, IDEA requires the IEP Team, which includes the parents as members, to take into account any "concerns" parents have "for enhancing the education of their child" when it formulates the IEP. § 1414(d)(3)(A)(ii). The IEP, in turn, sets the boundaries of the central entitlement provided by IDEA: it defines a "free appropriate public education" for that parent's child. § 1401(9).

The statute also empowers parents to bring challenges based on a broad range of issues. The parent may seek a hearing on "any matter relating to the identification, evaluation, or educational placement of the child, or the provision of a free appropriate public education to such child." § 1415(b)(6)(A). To resolve these challenges a hearing officer must make a decision based on whether the child "received a free appropriate public education." § 1415(f)(3)(E). When this hearing has been conducted by a local educational agency rather than a state educational agency, "any party aggrieved by the findings and decision rendered in such a hearing may appeal such findings and decision" to the state educational agency. § 1415(g)(1). Judicial review follows, authorized by a broadly worded provision phrased in the same terms used to describe the prior stage of review: "[a]ny party aggrieved" may bring "a civil action." § 1415(i)(2)(A).

These provisions confirm that IDEA, through its text and structure, creates in parents an independent stake not only in the procedures and costs implicated by this process but also in the substantive decisions to be made. We therefore conclude that IDEA does not differentiate, through isolated references to various procedures and remedies, between the rights accorded to children and the rights accorded to parents. As a consequence, a parent may be a "party aggrieved" for purposes of § 1415(i)(2) with regard to "any matter" implicating these rights. See § 1415(b)(6)(A). The status of parents as parties is not limited to matters that relate to procedure and cost recovery. To find otherwise would be inconsistent with the collaborative framework and expansive system of review established by the Act. Cf. *Cedar Rapids Community School Dist. v. Garret F.*, 526 U. S. 66, 73 (1999) (looking to IDEA's "overall statutory scheme" to interpret its provisions).

Our conclusion is confirmed by noting the incongruous results that would follow were we to accept the proposition that parents' IDEA rights are limited to certain nonsubstantive matters. The statute's procedural and reimbursement-related rights are intertwined with the substantive adequacy of the education provided to a child, see, e.g., § 1415(f)(3)(E), see also § 1412(a)(10)(C)(ii), and it is difficult to disentangle the provisions in order to conclude that some rights adhere to both parent and child while others do not. Were we nevertheless to recognize a distinction of this sort it would impose upon parties a confusing and onerous legal regime, one worsened by the absence of any express guidance in IDEA concerning how a court might in practice differentiate between these matters. It is, in addition, out of accord with the statute's design to interpret the Act to require that parents prove the substantive inadequacy of their child's education as a predicate for obtaining, for example, reimbursement under § 1412(a)(10)(C)(ii), yet to prevent them from obtaining a judgment mandating that the school district provide their child with an educational program demonstrated to be an appropriate one. The adequacy of the educational program is, after all, the central issue in the litigation. The provisions of IDEA do not set forth these distinctions, and we decline to infer them.

The bifurcated regime suggested by the courts that have employed it, moreover, leaves some parents without a remedy. The statute requires, in express terms, that States provide a child with a free appropriate public education "at public expense," § 1401(9)(A), including specially designed instruction "at no cost to parents," § 1401(29). Parents may seek to enforce this mandate through the federal courts, we conclude, because among the rights they enjoy is the right to a free appropriate public education for their child. Under the countervailing view, which would make a parent's ability to enforce IDEA dependant on certain procedural and reimbursement-related rights, a parent whose disabled child has not received a free appropriate public education would have recourse in the federal courts only under two circumstances: when the parent happens to have some claim related to the procedures employed; and when he or she is able to incur, and has in fact incurred, expenses creating a right to reimbursement. Otherwise the adequacy of the child's education would not be regarded as relevant to any cause of action the parent might bring; and, as a result, only the child could vindicate the right accorded by IDEA to a free appropriate public education.

The potential for injustice in this result is apparent. What is more, we find nothing in the statute to indicate that when Congress required States to provide adequate instruction to a child "at no cost to parents," it intended that only some parents would be able to enforce that mandate. The statute instead takes pains to "ensure that the rights of children with disabilities and parents of such children are protected." § 1400(d)(1)(B). See, e.g., § 1415(e)(2) (requiring that States implement procedures to ensure parents are guaranteed procedural safeguards with respect to the provision of a free appropriate public education); § 1415(e)(2)(A)(ii) (requiring that mediation procedures not be "used to deny or delay a parent's right to a due process hearing ... or to deny any other rights afforded under this subchapter"); cf. § 1400(c)(3) (noting IDEA's success in "ensuring children with disabilities and the families of such children access to a free appropriate public education").

We conclude IDEA grants parents independent, enforceable rights. These rights, which are not limited to certain procedural and reimbursement-related matters, encompass the entitlement to a free appropriate public education for the parents' child.

C

Respondent contends, though, that even under the reasoning we have now explained petitioners cannot prevail without overcoming a further difficulty. Citing our opinion in *Arlington Central School Dist. Bd. of Ed. v. Murphy*, 548 U.S. ___ (2006), respondent argues that statutes passed pursuant to the Spending Clause, such as IDEA, must provide " 'clear notice' " before they can burden a State with some new condition, obligation, or liability. Brief for Respondent 41. Respondent contends that because IDEA is, at best, ambiguous as to whether it accords parents independent rights, it has failed to provide clear notice of this condition to the States. See id., at 40–49.

Respondent's reliance on *Arlington* is misplaced. In *Arlington* we addressed whether IDEA required States to reimburse experts' fees to prevailing parties in IDEA actions. "[W]hen Congress attaches conditions to a State's acceptance of federal funds," we explained, "the conditions must be set out 'unambiguously.' " 548 U. S., at ___ (slip op., at 3) (quoting *Pennhurst State School and Hospital v. Halderman*, 451 U. S. 1, 17 (1981)). The question to be answered in *Arlington*, therefore, was whether IDEA "furnishes clear notice regarding the liability at issue." 548 U. S., at ___ (slip op., at 4). We found it did not.

The instant case presents a different issue, one that does not invoke the same rule. Our determination that IDEA grants to parents independent, enforceable rights does not impose any substantive condition or obligation on States they would not otherwise be required by law to observe. The basic measure of monetary recovery, moreover, is not expanded by recognizing that some rights repose in both the parent and the child. Were we considering a statute other than the one before us, the Spending Clause argument might have more force: A determination by the Court that some distinct class of people has independent, enforceable rights might result in a change to the States' statutory obligations. But that is not the case here.

Respondent argues our ruling will, as a practical matter, increase costs borne by the States as they are forced to defend against suits unconstrained by attorneys trained in the law and the rules of ethics. Effects such as these do not suffice to invoke the concerns under the Spending Clause. Furthermore, IDEA does afford relief for the States in certain cases. The Act empowers courts to award attorney's fees to a prevailing educational agency whenever a parent has presented a "complaint or subsequent cause of action ... for any improper purpose, such as to harass, to cause unnecessary delay, or to needlessly increase the cost of litigation." § 1415(i)(3)(B)(i)(III). This provision allows some relief when a party has proceeded in violation of these standards.

III

The Court of Appeals erred when it dismissed the Winkelmans' appeal for lack of counsel. Parents enjoy rights under IDEA; and they are, as a result, entitled to prosecute IDEA claims on their own behalf. The decision by Congress to grant parents these rights was consistent with the purpose of IDEA and fully in accord with our social and legal traditions. It is beyond dispute that the relationship between a parent and child is sufficient to support a legally cognizable interest in the education of one's child; and, what is more, Congress has found that "the education of children with disabilities can be made more effective by ... strengthening the role and responsibility of parents and ensuring that families of such children have meaningful opportunities to participate in the education of their children at school and at home." § 1400(c)(5).

In light of our holding we need not reach petitioners' alternative argument, which concerns whether IDEA entitles parents to litigate their child's claims pro se.

The judgment of the Court of Appeals is reversed, and the case is remanded for further proceedings consistent with this opinion.

It is so ordered.

* * *

Questions for Discussion

1. The court leaves unanswered the question whether parents are entitled to litigate their children's IDEA claims pro se. What do you think the answer to this question should be? How have lower courts answered this question?

2. Is there merit to the idea that parents should be provided with an attorney in IDEA litigation because districts are represented by counsel? As district counsel, what are the ethical obligations in dealing with pro se litigants? Might binding arbitration be a good solution?

For Further Reading and Listening

Patricia C. Hagdorn, *Comment: Winkelman v. Parma City School District: A Major Victory for Parents or More Ambiguity?* 39 Seton Hall L. Rev. 981, 2009.

For streaming audio from oral arguments at the U.S. Supreme Court in the *Winkelman* case: http://www.clevelandmemory.org/legallandmarks/winkelman/index.html, retrieved May 15, 2012.

*Arlington Central School Dist. v. Murphy,*548 U.S. 291 (2006) — discusses whether school districts must reimburse parents for expert fees when parents win IDEA cases.

Check http://www.govtrack.us/congress/bill.xpd?bill=h110-4188 to see if further action has been taken on The IDEA Fairness Restoration Act, proposed legislation that would overturn *Arlington Central School Dist. v. Murphy.*

Discussion 8

Higher Education: Seeking Accommodations, Flagging Test Scores, and Trying to "Make It Work"

Recommended Background Reading

Coleman v. Zatcheka, 824 F.Supp. 1360 (D. Neb. 1993).

Kristan S. Mayer, *Flagging Nonstandard Test Scores in Admissions to Institutions of Higher Education*, 50 Stan. L. Rev. 469 (1998).

Jennifer Jolly-Ryan, *The Fable of the Timed and Flagged LSAT: Do Law School Admissions Want the Tortoise or the Hare?* 38 Cumb. L. Rev. 33 (2007).

Readings for Class Discussion

The following is an essay by Georgina Kleege, Ph.D., author and professor.

Disabled Students Come Out: Questions without Answers
Georgina Kleege

Once, in an undergraduate fiction-writing workshop, a student wrote a story about a Deaf woman. The woman was married to a hearing man and had two hearing children. In the central scene, the couple was discussing having a third child, and the woman announced that she hoped the child would be Deaf. A distinctive feature of the story was the way the author handled the characters' dialogue. The characters were using American Sign Language, and the author had, in effect, transcribed their conversation without translating it. She was trying to capture the flavor of ASL while making the language comprehensible to an English-speaking reader.

The story generated a lot of discussion. It turned out there was another student in the class who knew ASL because her mother was deaf. The story's author had learned ASL in high school so she could interpret at assemblies and theatrical events. Together they introduced the class to basic elements of the language and did an impromptu performance of some of the story's dialogue as a demonstration. As we discussed this dialogue, I reminded the class of discussions we had previously about how such authors as William Faulkner and D. H. Lawrence rendered dialect. Was this the same or different?

A student said that he found the story convincing because he'd heard on a segment of "Sixty Minutes" that all Deaf people want to have Deaf children so they can all speak the same language. The generalization made me uneasy, so I asked, "Can we say all Deaf people?" This question sparked some discussion about deafness, the physical condition, versus Deafness, the linguistic and cultural minority.

I was pleased that the class wanted to talk about these issues but felt compelled to guide the discussion back to the student's story. This was a fiction-writing workshop after all, not a class in disability studies. I kept asking questions about elements of fiction we'd discussed all term. We talked about the sequence of scenes (Did that flashback work?), about narration (Could she have written the story in the first person?), about characterization (Was there a need for more background information and, if so, how much and where?).

As the discussion was beginning to wane, a student, who had been uncharacteristically quiet so far, began a sentence with the phrase "Speaking as a disabled person" and raised the question of whether a hearing person could or should write from the perspective of a Deaf person. We'd talked about similar issues before: Could a male author write from a female point of view? Could an African American represent an Asian American's experience? Was this the same situation or different?

Naturally class ended before we could answer all the questions we'd raised. Still, I felt the story's author had received some useful feedback. I left the classroom making a mental list of additional points I wished to bring up at our next meeting. Distracted by these thoughts, I was a little surprised when the student with the disability followed me back to my office. He seemed agitated, a little out of breath. Before we even sat down, he said, "That's the first time I ever did that."

"Did what?" I asked, because I genuinely did not know.

"You know," he said. "The first time I ever said it in front of people like that. The first time I ever called myself disabled."

Many people might have been startled by his statement. His disability was readily apparent to everyone in the class. Everyone but me, that is, because I am legally blind. Still, I knew he was disabled. He rocked from side to side when he walked, and he dragged one foot. I could not tell if he used a cane or wore leg braces and would not hazard to put a name to his condition. Even if I had been unaware of these traits, however, I knew he was disabled because we'd talked about it. He'd explained to me that sometimes he used a wheelchair, in museums or the grocery store, but generally he did not. He'd also referred to operations he'd undergone and mentioned that he'd been a poster child and appeared on a telethon. On these occasions we'd also talked about my disability: When did my condition develop? How did I handle all the reading I had to do? And we talked about the differences between having a visible disability like his and an invisible one like mine, which is apparent only when I use a white cane or read Braille.

These conversations were always comfortable—matter-of-fact exchanges of information. Furthermore, I knew he'd talked about his disability with other instructors. So why was it such a big deal for him to identify himself as disabled on this occasion? The question I asked was "Why haven't you ever said it before?"

"I don't know," he said. "I guess I didn't want to be one of those whiny wheelies."

His reluctance reminded me of the reluctance of some women to identify themselves as feminists even though they have beliefs and expectations that could be defined as feminist, for fear they would seem strident and unfeminine. Was he worried that calling himself disabled would make him appear abrasive and militant? In fact, he had a chip on his shoulder and could be rather edgy, argumentative, defensive. He was also smart, quick-witted, prone to make ironic asides. These were all traits that conform to a stereotypical disabled personality—the cranky cripple rather than the cheerfully stoic kind. These facets of his personality may well have evolved as ways to counter playground taunts or to repel patronizing pity. But he might have turned out this way because he'd grown up without a father or for some other reason I didn't know.

In any case, he did not seem like someone who worried about offending people. Before I could ask another question, he said, "You should have seen the way they looked when I said it."

I almost cautioned him against being oversensitive, but I stopped myself. I had noticed a pause after he spoke, but since I can't make eye contact or read people's expressions, I had no idea what sort of nonverbal communication might have occurred. Still, I told him that I didn't think his classmates' response to his word came from hostility or prejudice. Rather, they had been brought up not to stare at people with disabilities, not to call them names, not to ask rude questions. For him to bring it up forced them to violate all those parental admonitions, to look at his disabled body and give it a name.

Of course they should have been used to this simply because they had a professor with a disability. From the first day of class my presence challenged many of their assumptions. In my class, they were obliged to break the cardinal rule of classroom decorum and speak without raising their hands, since I cannot see this gesture. Also, since I read tape-recorded versions of their written work, they were obliged to think about how their writing would sound out loud. Eventually they'd got used to what's different about my classes; they even learned to tease me about it. When I asked, "Who's not here today?," someone was bound to say, "Please raise your hand if you're absent."

Although my students had a greater awareness of disability issues than the general nondisabled public, when the student with the disability "came out" in my class, it was still startling, subversive, perhaps even revolutionary. For many, a disabled person is a unique individual with a specific physical, perceptual, or cognitive problem marked by a distinct set of characteristics or behaviors. Thus, a person with a mobility impairment seems to have little in common with someone who is visually impaired. The student in my class was not merely identifying an obvious physical fact about himself. He was claiming identity with the Deaf woman in the story; with me, his blind professor; and with numerous other people who had various deficits, impairments, and anomalies. He was saying, "I speak for all these."

Did he have the right to do this? Is there really such a thing as a disabled perspective? Did this student and I share common beliefs and values that transcended all other identity categories? I admit these questions make me uneasy. Every female is not a feminist. Similarly, every disabled person is not a disability rights activist or an expert in disability studies. I write and think about disability issues, but I write and think about a lot of other things too. Of all the adjectives I can use to describe myself, disabled is only one of many and not always the first I mention. When I encounter such phrases as "blind lust" or "lame response" in a student's writing, I will probably mark it as a cliche. When I encounter a disabled character in a work of literature, I may analyze the cultural attitudes connected to that representation. A nondisabled instructor could do the same. Do my students find it more memorable when I do it, because they perceive me as speaking from personal experience? Did this student feel comfortable coming out in my class because I have a disability, or would he have done it anywhere? Did the student who wrote the story about the Deaf woman feel I would be more receptive to it than a nondisabled teacher?

I don't have all the answers. I do resent any inference that the mere fact of my disability augments my teaching qualifications or that there is a pedagogical value in exposing my disability to nondisabled students. This practice smacks too much of the freak show and casts me in the role of goodwill ambassador sharing the quaint beliefs and customs of my alien world.

While I resist displaying myself as an exotic species, I am also a reluctant role model for students with disabilities. I'm unconvinced that the ways I deal with my disability are worthy of emulation. Furthermore, I am not always as sensitive and sympathetic as I could be. I have a chip on my shoulder too. Like many disabled people who went through school before IDEA (Individuals with Disabilities Education Act) and ADA (Americans with Disabilities Act), I must quell the urge to say, "You kids today have it so easy." While they may enjoy the advantages of legally mandated access and new assistive technologies, the world continues to be far from perfect.

Still, my disabled students and I have much in common. We do not, for instance, take for granted that the university environment and practices were designed with us in mind. This can make us cranky, but it can also make us resilient and adaptable. These are qualities we need, since legally mandated access does not eliminate all barriers. The student who came out in my class had told me on a previous occasion that another professor once asked him, "What's wrong with you?"

"I didn't know what he meant at first," he said. "I thought maybe my nose was bleeding or something."

"What did you tell him?" I asked.

"I told him what he wanted to know," he said. "I should have told him it was none of his business. I mean, if I was blind or deaf, I would have had to explain things to him. What's 'wrong' with me makes no difference to how I read or write or talk."

I asked him if he wanted me to do something, to speak to the professor or take some other action. He said he did not. Perhaps he sensed that my anger with my colleague would have made me an ineffective advocate. Instead, we talked about what we found wrong with the question, articulating a response for the next time it was asked. What was wrong with the question was not the way it violated contemporary codes of political correctness, not to mention older codes of common courtesy. What was wrong with the question was the way it assumed that we people with disabilities perceive ourselves to be defective, deficient, substandard, that we long for the abilities we lack, experiencing eye envy, leg envy, ear envy. A better though more challenging answer to the question would be to say, "There is nothing wrong with being disabled." Disability is a fact of life for some of us. It demands our attention and effort in certain situations. If we long for anything, it is better assistive technologies, better architecture, better attitudes among the nondisabled.

When this student came out in my class, it was unclear how the event would affect his future life. Had he now appointed himself official spokesperson for disability issues? Would his spin on things be the same as mine? We disagreed about many things. I told him that a lot of Deaf people reject the disability label, preferring to be identified as a linguistic or cultural minority. Then we argued about identity politics. I said, "I don't think it's a question of whether a nondisabled person has the right to write about a disabled person. It's a matter of whether or not the writing seems genuine and doesn't conform to stereotypes."

"I hate the way they always want us to be inspirational," he said.

I wanted to caution him against divisive generalizations and thought of asking, "Can we really say always?" But in this instance I found myself on his side of the divide, so I said, "I hate it, too."

Sometimes, the consequences of coming out as disabled are more practical than philosophical. In a sophomore-level literature class, a student stayed after the first session to ask a question. From the way she let other students go before her, I sensed that she wanted to speak to me privately. When everyone else was gone, she pointed to a line in my syllabus and said, "It says here that this is available in large print."

I noticed that she was making a statement, not a request. I also noticed that she made no mention of herself, as if she were asking for a friend who wasn't there. I gave her the large-print syllabus and explained that I could produce all the course materials—handouts, quizzes, exams—in this or other formats.

I had already explained to the class about my disability. Now I told her that to the extent that I can read print at all, it must be very large. I showed her some pages of notes I had and some other materials, naming the different font sizes. She seemed a little overwhelmed by the range of options. Although we were still not talking about her or her disability, I finally asked, "Which one would you prefer?"

"Whatever's easiest," she blurted, as if it required extra effort to produce a text in 18- rather than 14-point type. I surmised she was new at this, perhaps newly disabled. She was uncertain how to ask for what she needed, uncertain how much was permitted. But the ice was broken now, and she volunteered that she was in her forties, a returning student. She'd dropped out of college when she was twenty to get married and raise her children, and now she was back. Then finally, she told me that she was deaf in one ear and blind in one eye, which was why she was asking about the large print. She could read standard print, but it was a slow and difficult process. So for my course she'd bought the textbooks as soon as they showed up in the campus bookstore and had been reading ahead during the term break.

I asked her if she'd ever been to the university's Office of Disability Services. Perhaps they could offer some additional assistance.

"But I'm not disabled," she said.

I guessed it was the word disabled that made her balk. Yes, she had "something wrong" with her, but she was not disabled. She was normal, a normal person with a problem.

Though "deaf in one ear and blind in one eye" sounded like a disability to me, I wasn't going to argue with her. Instead, I gave her some basic information about what an office of disability services does. I said it was a resource, a place to ask questions, to try out technologies and techniques. I also said that it could be helpful to make contact with other students with disabilities, who might offer additional advice, even if they had different disabilities. I have learned a lot about reading audio books from a dyslexic and about crossing streets from a paraplegic. I sensed the phrase "other students with disabilities" was presumptuous on my part. It forced her to picture herself as part of a group she'd always perceived as alien—people in wheelchairs, people with garbled speech, people with missing limbs. So I hastened to add that many people with disabilities develop their own adaptive strategies without others' advice, such as buying the textbook early in order to give themselves extra reading time.

"Or like sitting in the front row," she said. "And I always sit on this side, so I can use my good ear to hear."

I was pleased that I hadn't offended her, but I sent her to Disability Services with some trepidation. At their worst, such offices exist merely to protect the institution from lawsuits. In other cases they may offer only those accommodations experts deem appropriate for a particular disability without fully assessing the student's individual needs. A student who fails to benefit from the prescribed accommodation or asks for something else can be labeled a malingerer or troublemaker. I didn't tell her all this, however. She was an adult and could decide for herself. I didn't want to poison her with my paranoia. My own bad experiences with the Evil Custodial Oppressor might scare her away from possibly valuable services.

Two weeks later she was back, breathless with gratitude. "Disability Services was so helpful," she told me. They had calibrated and certified her impairments and offered all sorts of visual and audio aids. She was going to try a hearing aid, magnification devices, audio books. I offered to share the taped versions of my texts and gave her a few tips about aural reading.

"It's such a relief," she told me. "I've been this way all my life, but I never really talked about it before." Because she had always thought of herself as an individual with a unique problem, it was a revelation to discover not only that there were other people with similar conditions but also that there were others who had thought up ways of dealing with them. She was learning to shift her attention from what was wrong with her to what was wrong with the educational environment that barred her access to it. I was glad for her, glad that coming out was a positive experience, glad that her transition from "normal person with something wrong" to "person with a disability" was going smoothly.

But by the end of the term she was angry. There was trouble with Disability Services. They refused to order recorded books for the next term until all the other students had turned in their requests. I gave her a phone number and told her she could order the books on her own, warning that if she did this, she might be viewed as subversive.

She took this advice without comment. Was she developing a chip on her shoulder? She was still angry, about something else. "When I dropped out of college, I thought there was something wrong with me," she said. "If I'd known all this before, I never would have dropped out of school. Why did I have to wait so long for this help? Why did everybody think it was better to say I was 'not college material' than to say I was disabled?"

I had no answer to this question. I offered some personal history, telling her that though I was diagnosed as legally blind when I was eleven, I didn't really talk about it until I was well into adulthood and first started teaching. We talked about the nature of an invisible disability, about stoicism, about the temptations and risks of passing. I did not presume to advise her about dealing with her past, but I wanted her to know that my own disabled identity has evolved over many years and continues to evolve.

I was reminded that I had only one disabled professor during my entire college career, though he did not identify himself as such. His disability affected his use of one arm, and, as far as I could tell, he was able to write, type, and carry things with the other, so he did not need to speak about his disability to his classes as I do. He was not the sort of person who invited personal disclosures, and though I must have had a conversation with him about my disability, I cannot imagine the possibility of any discussion of our shared experiences as disabled people. I had "something wrong" with my eyes, he had "something wrong" with his arm; we had nothing in common. For me to claim otherwise would have been as shocking to him as it was unthinkable to me.

The world has changed a lot since then, and the change manifests itself in university classrooms. As more and more students with disabilities pursue higher education, disability becomes a central topic for scholars not only in the social sciences, medicine, and law but also in history, literature, even creative writing. Social evolution seldom follows a smoothly linear path. It can create discomfort and discord. It can raise more questions than it answers. And while I have few answers, I believe that as long as disability remains a taboo topic, progress is impossible. When disabled students come out, they assert that there is nothing wrong with being disabled. We have a right to a place in the classroom, as students and teachers. As we come out, we demonstrate that there is more than one way to move through space, to access a text, to process information, to communicate— more than one way to be a human being.

"It's better now than it used to be," I told my student. "Now at least there are more of us around."

"Us" was presumptuous, pushing her to the other side of the us/them divide. But I sensed she was moving in that direction anyway.

Then she said, "I guess sooner or later they'll have to get used to us."

* * *

Questions for Discussion

1. What might be the pros and cons of asking for accommodations versus "self-accommodating"?

2. What stories have you heard from students who have asked for various accommodations from either professors or disability services' offices?

3. The author's class had a discussion about whether a hearing person could or should write from the perspective of a Deaf person. What do you think about this issue? Also, what about the issue that is raised by this piece about whether a disabled person can speak for people with all kinds of disabilities, not just their own particular kind of disability?

4. What did you think of the female student who was visually and hearing impaired saying that she wasn't disabled? What did you think of her interactions with Disability Services?

5. What did you think of the author's views of herself as a mentor?

The following is a case about a student seeking accommodations. What can be learned from this case about the accomodations process?

Hartnett v. Fielding Graduate Institute

198 Fed. Appx. 89; 2006 U.S. App. LEXIS 24128;
18 Am. Disabilities Cas. (BNA) 804
UNITED STATES COURT OF APPEALS FOR THE SECOND CIRCUIT
September 21, 2006, Decided

JUDGES: PRESENT: HON. CHESTER J. STRAUB, HON. SONIA SOTOMAYOR, HON. ROBERT A. KATZMANN, Circuit Judges.

OPINION

Plaintiff-Appellant Joyce Hartnett appeals the judgment of the District Court for the Southern District of New York (Colleen McMahon, Judge), granting summary judgment in favor of defendant The Fielding Graduate Institute ("FGI") and dismissing Hartnett's claims under the Americans with Disabilities Act of 1990 ("ADA") and the Rehabilitation Act of 1973.

We review the District Court's grant of summary judgment de novo. *Back v. Hastings on Hudson Union Free Sch. Dist.*, 365 F.3d 107, 122 (2d Cir. 2004). "To justify summary judgment, the defendants must show that 'there is no genuine issue as to any material fact' and that they are 'entitled to a judgment as a matter of law.'" Id.(quoting Fed. R. Civ. P. 56(c)). We resolve all ambiguities, and credit all rational factual inferences, in favor of the non-moving party, in this case Hartnett. Id. However, "the existence of a mere scintilla of evidence in support of nonmovant's position is insufficient to defeat the motion; there must be evidence on which a jury could reasonably find for the nonmovant." *Powell v. Nat'l Bd. of Med. Exam'rs*, 364 F.3d 79, 84 (2d Cir. 2004).

We assume the parties' familiarity with the facts and arguments on appeal. Briefly summarized, the facts of this case are as follows. FGI is a "distance learning" graduate institution. Among other things, FGI offers a PhD program in clinical psychology ("the PhD Program"). The PhD program is primarily a distance learning program; the majority of the program consists of online courses. However, students are required to meet a 300 hour residency requirement. This requirement can be satisfied in a number of ways, of which the primary method is the "cluster meeting"—monthly group meetings between students and their faculty advisors.

Hartnett was accepted to FGI's PhD program in December 2000. In her application materials, Hartnett informed FGI that she suffers from lupus, which causes her severe physical exhaustion, muscle pain and weakness, headaches and nausea. Hartnett requested that FGI make a number of accommodations to her disability. FGI ultimately refused her requests, and, in October 2001, Hartnett withdrew from the program.

Both the Rehabilitation Act and the ADA "prohibit discrimination against qualified disabled individuals by requiring that they receive 'reasonable accommodations' that permit them to have access to and take a meaningful part in public services and public accommodations." *Powell*, 364 F.3d at 85. For present purposes, the requirements of the two statutes are identical, and we will consider them together. See id. In order to establish a prima facie case under either statute, Hartnett must show that: (1) that she is a "qualified individual" with a disability; (2) that FGI is subject to one of the Acts; and (3) that she was "denied the opportunity to participate in or benefit from defendants' services, programs, or activities, or was otherwise discriminated against by defendants, by reason of her disability." Id.

While FGI is required to make "reasonable accommodations" to allow for Hartnett's disability, it "is not required to offer an accommodation that imposes an undue hardship on its program's operation." Id. at 88 (citing 28 C.F.R. §41.53 (2002)). "In addition, a defendant need not make an accommodation at all if the requested accommodation 'would fundamentally alter the nature of the service, program, or activity.'" Id. (quoting 28 C.F.R. §35.130(b)(7)). Finally, "[t]he obligation to make reasonable accommodation ... does not extend to the provision of adjustments or modifications that are primarily for the personal benefit of the individual with a disability." 29 C.F.R. Pt. 1630.9, App.; see also *Felix v. N.Y. City Transit Auth.*, 324 F.3d 102, 107 (2d Cir. 2003) ("The ADA mandates reasonable accommodation of people with disabilities in order to put them on an even playing field with the non-disabled; it does not authorize a preference for disabled people generally.").

There is no dispute here that FGI is subject to the ADA and the Rehabilitation Act, or that Hartnett is qualified to take part in the PhD program. The critical question is whether the accommodations sought by Hartnett were reasonable. We will consider each of Hartnett's requests in turn.

Principally, Hartnett sought to be transferred from the cluster group to which she had been assigned, headed by a Dr. Ruffins, to another cluster group, headed by a Dr. Freimuth. FGI refused this request, on the ground that Dr. Freimuth's cluster group was over-subscribed and Dr. Ruffins' was under-subscribed. We must give Dr. Freimuth's determination that her cluster was over-subscribed great deference. See *Powell*, 364 F.3d at 88 (2d Cir. 2004) ("When reviewing the substance of a genuinely academic decision, courts should accord the faculty's professional judgment great deference."). Although Hartnett presented evidence that FGI student Adrienne Vogel withdrew from Dr. Freimuth's cluster around the time Hartnett requested a transfer, this alone does not establish that the cluster did not remain oversubscribed.

Hartnett identifies two ways in which a transfer to Dr. Freimuth's group would have accommodated her disability—and specifically, the additional difficulty she suffers as a result of her lupus when commuting long distances. First, Hartnett observes that the commute from her home to Dr. Freimuth's Manhattan office is shorter than the commute to Dr. Ruffins' Manhattan office. Given the absence of medical evidence that a two to three mile difference in Hartnett's commute would have made a difference to her health, we agree with the District Court that no reasonable trier of fact could find the two to three mile difference between the two offices significant, in the context of plaintiff's forty-five mile commute into Manhattan from Yorktown Heights, New York.

Second, Hartnett observes that Dr. Freimuth's home office, in Bedford, New York, is significantly closer to Hartnett's home than is either Manhattan office, and suggests that she could have fulfilled her residency requirement through face-to-face meetings at Dr. Freimuth's home office. It appears from the record that some FGI faculty met with students, or held some of their cluster meetings, at their home offices. However, Dr. Freimuth denied that she herself ever did so, and no evidence in the record contradicts that assertion. The mere fact that Dr. Freimuth listed her home office telephone number—alongside her Manhattan office number—on FGI's website, does not suffice to raise an inference that she used the office to meet face-to-face with students. In the absence of any showing that it was Dr. Freimuth's practice to meet with students at her home office, we do not think that the ADA or the Rehabilitation Act compels her to do so. To impose such a re-quirement would not only be a severe burden on faculty, but would work a substantial change in the nature of the teaching program of those faculty who prefer not to use their home offices for face-to-face student meetings. See *Powell*, 364 F.3d at 88. The undisputed evidence thus establishes that re-assignment to Dr. Freimuth's cluster would not reasonably have accommodated Hartnett's disability.

Hartnett's second request was for part-time status. As the District Court correctly observed, FGI is already effectively a part-time program: students are free to take FGI's courses at their own pace. Hartnett's request for part-time status was essentially a request for a reduction in tuition, and would not have accommodated her disability in any way.

Hartnett's third request was that the start of her program be deferred until September 2001, and that a space be reserved for her in Dr. Freimuth's cluster at that time. The District Court interpreted Hartnett's request as motivated solely by her desire for a place in Dr. Freimuth's cluster. Accordingly, the District Court, having found that a transfer to Dr. Freimuth's cluster was not a reasonable accommodation to her disability, found that it was reasonable for FGI to deny this request as well. We agree with the District Court that it was reasonable for FGI to deny Hartnett's request insofar as she sought a transfer, in

September 2001, to Dr. Freimuth's cluster. However, in her request for the deferral, Hartnett also explained that she had suffered a "setback" in her treatment, and was "to begin a new treatment in mid-January. The benefits will not be realized for about six months." A rational jury could conclude that FGI did not properly consider Hartnett's request to delay the start of her coursework in order to allow her treatment to progress, and could conclude that such a delay would have been a reasonable accommodation to her illness. We therefore reverse and remand for further proceedings with respect to this claim.

Finally, Hartnett requested that she be allowed to fulfill her residency requirement through video-conferencing. FGI's Associate Dean Nancy Leffert testified to the reason for FGI's denial of this request:

> The requirement that residency hours be accrued by face-to-face contact with faculty members is rigid.... This requirement was put in place in order to obtain accreditation from the American Psychological Association ("APA"). The APA ... requires that doctoral graduate programs in Clinical Psychology require a minimum of 3 full-time academic years, at least one year of which must be in full-time residence (or the equivalent thereof) at that same institution. In 1991, the APA permitted [FGI] to satisfy the one-year residency requirement through 300 hours of face-to-face student-faculty contact, as the equivalent of one year of full-time residency. The APA only accepted this proposal on the condition that there be actual face-to-face contact with the faculty member for the 300 hours.... If [FGI] were to make an exception to this requirement, it would jeopardize its accreditation.

Nothing in the record before us indicates that video-conferencing would, absent the APA'srequirements, pose an undue burden for FGI. We agree with the District Court that FGI is not required to jeopardize its accreditation in order to accommodate Hartnett's disability. However, it appears that FGI never contacted the APA to determine whether an exception could be made in Hartnett's case, in light of her illness. In the absence of any such inquiry, FGI cannot rely on the APA's presumed refusal to permit such an exception. We therefore reverse and remand with respect to this request.

Finally, Hartnett argues that FGI failed to engage in an "interactive process" in an attempt to accommodate her. In the employment context, we have held that "the ADA envisions an 'interactive process' by which employers and employees work together to assess whether an employee's disability can be reasonably accommodated." *Lovejoy-Wilson v. NOCO Motor Fuel, Inc.*, 263 F.3d 208, 218 (2d Cir. 2001). We have yet to determine, however, whether an employer's failure to carry out such an interactive process gives rise to an independent cause of action, see id. at 219 (declining to address the question), or whether any such duty applies in the educational as opposed to the employment context.

The District Court did not reach these questions, finding that "the undisputed evidence shows that FGI did engage in an 'interactive process' with [Hartnett]." We disagree. The District Court relied primarily on the evidence of a meeting between Hartnett and faculty members at a March 2001 orientation session, at which Hartnett's disability was discussed. Hartnett testified that this meeting, far from being a good-faith attempt to reach an accommodation, was "hostile, "intimidating," and "upsetting." Moreover, this meeting came after FGI had already, by e-mail, denied Hartnett's requests. A reasonable trier of fact could credit Hartnett's testimony, and could conclude from the course of dealings between Hartnett and FGI that no effort was made to accommodate her. We therefore reverse the District Court's grant of summary judgment on this question because material issues of fact exist as to whether FGI engaged in an interactive process. On remand, the District

Court should consider, in the first instance, whether the duty to engage in an interactive process is applicable in the educational context, and whether the failure to engage in such a process gives rise to an independent cause of action under the ADA.

We have considered all of the parties' arguments. For the foregoing reasons, we affirm with respect to Hartnett's request for reassignment to Dr. Friemuth's cluster, and with respect to her request for part-time status. With respect to her remaining requests, and to the District Court's finding that an interactive process occurred, we reverse and remand for further proceedings in accordance with this order. All motions for costs, fees, and sanctions are denied.

* * *

Questions for Discussion

1. What do you think of the possibility of the "interactive process" between parties applying to the educational setting? Have other courts addressed this issue?

2. Do you think the plaintiff's requests were reasonable? If you had been on this court, what do you think you would have decided?

The following article discusses the practice of flagging standardized tests. For the full text of the article, including footnotes, look at the original source.

Flagging Accommodated Testing on the LSAT and MCAT: Necessary Protections of the Academic Standards of the Legal and Medical Communities

Michael Edward Slipsky

82 N.C.L. Rev. 811 (Jan 2004)

In 1999, Mark Breimhorst filed a lawsuit against Educational Testing Services ("ETS"), alleging that its practice of "flagging" the scores of persons who took the Graduate Management Admission Test ("GMAT") under accommodated circumstances violated the Americans With Disabilities Act of 1990 ("ADA"), section 504 of the Rehabilitation Act of 1973, and various state statutes.

After surviving ETS's motion to dismiss, the parties settled, with ETS agreeing to discontinue flagging all tests it owned. This settlement did not include the Scholastic Aptitude Test ("SAT"), which ETS administers but which is created and owned by the College Board.

This discrepancy was resolved when, not long after the ETS settlement, Disability Rights Associates and the College Board agreed to submit the issue of flagging on College Board-owned tests to a blue ribbon panel. Upon consideration of policy concerns and data gleaned from empirical studies, the panel voted four to two to discontinue the practice on all College Board tests beginning in October 2003. On July 26, 2002, the American College Testing Program ("ACT"), the administrator of the eponymously named admissions test, announced that, effective September 2003, it too would discontinue flagging the scores of accommodated test-takers.

As it stands, the only major standardized admissions tests not affected by the Breimhorst settlement and its progeny are the law and medical school admissions tests—the LSAT and MCAT. Both of these tests continue to flag the scores of accommodated test-takers. This Recent Development examines the legal and public policy aspects of flagging for the purpose of determining whether the professional school admissions tests must, or should, discontinue the practice. After engaging in the aforementioned analysis, this Recent Development concludes that flagging is both legally permissible and sound policy with respect to professional school admissions tests. Specifically, it is the author's contention that (1) flagging by the testing companies does not amount to a per se violation of federal disability laws; (2) available evidence tends to show that law and medical school admissions committees give flagged scores the same consideration as non-flagged scores, thus making a potential plaintiff's "injury-in-fact" highly questionable; (3) because of the demonstrated statistical invalidity of scores obtained under non-standard conditions, admissions committees would be justified in discounting flagged scores by the amount of statistical overprediction (even though data show that they do not engage in this behavior); and (4) public policy is best served by maintaining the flagging system until the validity gap between standard and accommodated scores can be sufficiently narrowed.

I. Does Flagging by Testing Services Violate Federal Law?

In order to determine whether flagging constitutes a violation of federal disability law, one must first determine which statutes, and sections thereof, are applicable. The ADA and the Rehabilitation Act of 1973 are the primary sources of federal disability discrimination law and the application of each to flagging accommodations will be considered in turn.

A. Title III of the ADA

The ADA is divided into five titles, three of which deal with specific categories of prospective defendants: Title I governs discrimination in the employment context; Title II relates to state and local government entities; and Title III applies to "places of public accommodation." There is little doubt that the employment-related provisions of Title I and the public entity provisions of Title II would be inapplicable to the issue of flagging academic admissions tests by private testing services; therefore, they can be safely ignored. Title III, however, merits further examination.

While testing services are not treated as public accommodations subject to the general requirements of Title III, 12,189 specifically addresses admissions testing, stating:

> Any person that offers examinations or courses related to applications, licensing, certification, or credentialing for secondary or postsecondary education, professional, or trade purposes shall offer such examinations or courses in a place and manner accessible to persons with disabilities or offer alternative accessible arrangements for such individuals.

The U.S. Department of Justice promulgated the following regulation in order to implement 12,189:

> The examination ... [shall be] administered so as to best ensure that ... the examination results accurately reflect the individual's aptitude or achievement level.... rather than reflecting the individual's impaired sensory, manual, or speaking skills.... Required modifications may include changes in the length of time permitted for the completion of the examination, substitution of specific requirements and adaptation of the manner in which the examination is given.

Since both the LSAT and MCAT offer accommodated testing upon presentation of certain required documentation, a plaintiff's complaint under Title III would not concern a failure to accommodate pursuant to 12,189 or its implementing regulations, but rather the failure to keep the non-standard testing conditions secret from the law or medical school admissions committee. Thus, the issue is not whether the test administrators have a legal obligation to provide extra time (or other accommodations)—since it would seem from the above-quoted statutes and regulations that they unquestionably do—but whether the ADA requires that the non-standard nature of the testing conditions be kept secret from law and medical schools' admissions committees. Under both 12,189 and 28 C.F.R. 36.309, it is clear that they do not owe such a duty.

If testing services were held to be public accommodations, most likely because a plaintiff could establish the necessary nexus between the place and the service being offered, then it would be appropriate to consider Title III's general definitions regarding illegal discrimination in the provision of public accommodations. Title III defines discrimination in two ways. First, the general definition involves:

> [A] failure to make reasonable modifications in policies, practices, or procedures, when such modifications are necessary to afford such goods, services, facilities, privileges, advantages, or accommodations to individuals with disabilities, unless the entity can demonstrate that making such modifications would fundamentally alter the nature of such goods, services, facilities, privileges, advantages, or accommodations.

The statute then provides another definition of discrimination:

> [A] failure to take such steps as may be necessary to ensure that no individual with a disability is excluded, denied services, segregated or otherwise treated differently than other individuals because of the absence of auxiliary aids and services, unless the entity can demonstrate that taking such steps would fundamentally alter the nature of the good, service, facility, privilege, advantage, or accommodation being offered or would result in an undue burden.

A plaintiff could employ either or both of these definitions in order to establish a cause of action.

One could argue, under the first definition, that the failure to modify the flagging policy renders the service or good unavailable to disabled persons. Additionally, one could contend that flagging the scores of tests taken under non-standard conditions amounts to treating disabled persons "differently than other individuals," which appears to be proscribed under the second definition of discrimination. However, the second definition also states that the differential treatment becomes discrimination when it occurs "because of the absence of auxiliary aids and services," not because of the presence of auxiliary aids and services, as would be the case when the testing entity flags an accommodated score.

Whatever the merits of these initial arguments, a plaintiff would have a difficult time making a case because of the "fundamentally alter" clause common to both definitions. A plaintiff could argue that accommodations do not fundamentally change the standardized nature of the test because, theoretically, such accommodations only "level the playing field" for the disabled test-taker. However, at least with respect to the LSAT, available empirical data shows that accommodated scores significantly overpredict future success in law school. That being the case, the testing entity could convincingly argue that accommodations "fundamentally alter" the nature of the good or service being provided— a statistically valid predictor of future success in professional school—and therefore scores obtained under non-standard conditions could be flagged without constituting illegal discrimination under Title III.

Doe v. National Board of Medical Examiners is currently the only federal appellate case directly on point. In Doe, Chief Judge Becker analyzed the issue of flagging the scores of a medical student who took the United States Medical Licensing Exam with extra time and special seating. In so doing, the court followed an analysis similar to that outlined in this Section, ultimately holding that flagging is not a violation of Title III:

> In the absence of a statutory proscription against annotating the test scores of examinees who receive accommodations, we do not view the annotation on Doe's score ... as itself constituting a denial of access. If Doe were to establish either that his scores are psychometrically comparable to the scores of candidates who take the test under standard time conditions, or that his scores will be ignored by the programs to which they are reported, he might have demonstrated a reasonable likelihood of success on this claim. He has not met these evidentiary burdens. It may be that Doe will be able to develop a fuller record at final hearing. On the current record, however, he has not shown a reasonable likelihood that he will prevail.

Thus, it would appear that under current federal case law, flagging, without more, does not constitute a per se violation of the ADA.

B. The Rehabilitation Act of 1973

Title V of the Rehabilitation Act of 1973 marked the federal government's first attempt to protect disabled persons from discrimination, and, not surprisingly, it was fairly modest in scope. Specifically, section 504 provides that any program receiving federal funds is prohibited from discriminating against "otherwise qualified" applicants on the basis of their disabilities. While this provision undoubtedly applies to both public and private institutions of higher education, it is less certain that it would apply to testing services such as LSAC and the American Association of Medical Colleges ("AAMC").

The Office of Civil Rights ("OCR") directly addressed the issue of flagging while interpreting an enforcement regulation that accompanies section 504. In so doing, the OCR appears to have effectively settled the question of whether 504 would apply to LSAC and AAMC. According to the regulation promulgated by the Department of Health, Education, and Welfare, postsecondary educational institutions are prohibited from making a "preadmission inquiry as to whether an applicant for admission is a handicapped person." Despite this prohibition, schools receiving flagged scores could easily, and no doubt correctly, surmise that the applicant was disabled based on the presence of the flags. When combined with the fact that the vast majority of professional schools require submission of test scores as part of an application, flagging could be characterized as an indirect preadmission inquiry.

The OCR responded to this concern by endorsing an interim policy permitting testing services to "continue to notify their users that tests were taken under non-standard conditions." Despite the fact that this "interim policy" was issued in the late 1970s, it has yet to be changed or repealed. In fact, the OCR impliedly reaffirmed flagging of accommodated scores in several subsequent letters of finding issued in response to complaints filed against law and medical schools. As long as the OCR continues to adhere to this policy, it appears that flagging, or receiving flagged scores, does not constitute a per se violation of the Rehabilitation Act.

The conclusion that flagging per se does not constitute a violation of disability law should not be taken to suggest that the Rehabilitation Act, or the ADA, might not be important in assessing the treatment of flagged scores. Indeed, the OCR seems to support the position that giving unequal weight to flagged scores in the admissions process is a touchstone of discriminatory treatment. Accepting the OCR's position for the sake of argument, the following Section focuses on what the empirical evidence and case law indicate about the treatment actually afforded flagged scores in professional school admissions.

II. Does Flagging Actually Injure Accommodated Test-takers?

The previous discussion explored whether flagging constitutes a per se violation of federal disability law. Under current law, it appears that it does not. While this conclusion would not necessarily end a plaintiff's case, it would raise the issue of standing, specifically, whether an injury-in-fact could be alleged that would survive a defendant's motion for summary judgment. The Supreme Court set forth this standard in *Lujan v. Defenders of Wildlife*, stating "the irreducible constitutional minimum of standing" requires, inter alia, that the plaintiff have suffered an injury-in-fact that is both "concrete and particularized" and "actual or imminent, not 'conjectural' or 'hypothetical.'"

The plaintiff has the burden of establishing the injury-in-fact "with the manner and degree of evidence required at the successive stages of the litigation." While the plaintiff might successfully carry the burden at the pleading stage with general factual allegations, a response to a defendant's motion for summary judgment must establish, by averments or other evidence, "specific" facts. Finally, in order to avoid a directed verdict for the defendant, the plaintiff must present adequate evidence at trial in support of the allegations made in the complaint.

These requirements are not unique to disability discrimination cases, but they do highlight the difficulty a plaintiff would face in winning, or even surviving, the initial stages of a case against law and medical schools that receive flagged scores. After all, in the hypothetical case, there are at least two possible injuries: (1) the act of flagging, and (2) the schools' discriminatory treatment of flagged scores resulting in unwarranted and illegal denials of admission.

Establishing the former "injury" is quite easy: the testing services openly admit that they flag the scores of accommodated test-takers. Thus, in such a case, the focus would be on legal analysis, not fact-finding. However, as established in the previous discussion, the mere act of flagging does not appear to constitute an invasion of a legally protected interest. Thus, the plaintiff has a sole remaining cause of action — discriminatory treatment of the flagged score. This injury, however, would be more difficult to establish than the former per se injury, because while testing services readily admit to flagging scores, admissions committees, it would seem safe to assume, would be loathe to admit to violating federal law by treating flagged scores in a discriminatory manner. Unlike the hypothetical lawsuit against the testing entities, in which the facts are largely uncontested, the plaintiff alleging discriminatory treatment would need to allege specific facts and adequately support them with evidence adduced at trial. Unfortunately for the plaintiff, the currently available empirical research and the facts developed in other cases indicate that discriminatory treatment of flagged scores is rare.

Although empirical research on the relationship between flagged scores and admission rates is scant and apparently limited to the LSAT, the available data indicate that applicants with flagged scores are admitted to law school at the same rate as applicants with similar undergraduate grade point averages and the same, but non-flagged, LSAT scores. There have been, on the other hand, a number of cases alleging discriminatory treatment by professional school admissions committees. In adjudicating these disputes, the courts, the OCR, and the litigants have had numerous opportunities to investigate the admissions procedures of law and medical schools. Consistent with Professor Linda F. Wightman's empirical findings, virtually all of these cases and investigations indicate that professional schools give flagged scores the same consideration as those achieved under standard conditions.

The overwhelming majority of these cases involved complainants who, even with accommodation, attained very low scores on the LSAT and MCAT. This suggests that in the universe of disappointed disabled applicants, very few actually achieved test scores which, flagged or not, would have placed them within the normal admissions range. While admittedly anecdotal, this evidence also suggests that applicants with flagged, but otherwise competitive, scores are not being discriminated against (or at least not to an extent worthy of filing complaints with the OCR) by law and medical school admissions committees.

This Part does not suggest that a lawsuit against a professional school for discriminatory treatment of flagged scores could not be successful, or that such discrimination never occurs, but simply that such a lawsuit would be much more difficult to win because of the necessity of proving the facts alleged. Two additional factors further complicate the plaintiff's burden. First, available evidence suggests that discrimination against flagged scores is exceptionally infrequent, making it difficult to prove that such discrimination is widespread or inevitable. Second, because professional school admissions decisions are not made on the basis of test scores alone and often involve a complex calculus utilizing multiple factors, a given test score, flagged or not, generally does not guarantee admission to a professional school.

For the purposes of analyzing a plaintiff's likelihood of success under current law, the preceding discussion assumed the truth of the OCR's previous statements regarding differential treatment of flagged scores as being per se illegal. However, Part III explores the possibility that in the proper circumstances, a certain amount of differential treatment of flagged scores would be both appropriate and legal.

III. If Professional Schools Were to Treat Flagged Scores Differently, Would This Necessarily Violate Federal Disability Laws?

The applicable law for analyzing the differential treatment of flagged scores by professional schools is found in Title II of the ADA and section 504 of the Rehabilitation Act. Due to the substantive similarities between Title II and section 504, the following analysis considers them simultaneously.

Title II prohibits the exclusion of "qualified individuals with a disability ... by reason of such disability," from participation in the programs of a public entity. "Discrimination by any such entity" against the otherwise qualified disabled individual on the basis of the individual's disability is likewise prohibited under Title II. Reflecting the high degree of similarity between the statutes, section 504 states that "no otherwise qualified individual with a disability ... shall, solely by reason of her or his disability, be excluded from the participation in, be denied the benefits of, or be subjected to discrimination under any program or activity receiving Federal financial assistance...."

The quoted language suggests two important limitations on the prohibitions against discrimination. First, the individual alleging discrimination must be an individual "with a disability" to receive protection under the statutes. Second, in order to be violative, the discrimination or exclusion must be based upon the individual's disability and not, presumably, on permissible criteria for differential treatment. The following subsections address these limitations and how each might be implicated in an argument for differential treatment of flagged test scores.

A.

"An Individual with a Disability"

Both the ADA and the Rehabilitation Act define an "individual with a disability" to be: "any person who: (i) has a physical or mental impairment which substantially limits one or more of such person's major life activities; (ii) has a record of such an impairment; or

(iii) is regarded as having such an impairment." The Equal Employment Opportunity Commission's regulations shed some light on what the meaning of "physical or mental impairment," "major life activities," and "substantially limits":

> Physical or mental impairment means: (1) Any physiological disorder, or condition ... affecting ... the ... body ...; or (2) Any mental or psychological disorder, such as mental retardation, organic brain syndrome, emotional or mental illness, and specific learning disabilities. Major Life Activities means functions such as caring for oneself, performing manual tasks, walking, seeing, hearing, speaking, breathing, learning, and working. The term substantially limits means: (i) Unable to perform a major life activity that the average person in the general population can perform; or (ii) Significantly restricted as to the condition, manner or duration under which an individual can perform a particular major life activity as compared to the condition, manner, or duration under which the average person in the general population can perform that same major life activity.

Even if an applicant establishes that he has a documented mental or physical impairment and that it affects a major life activity, he still must establish that the impairment is so severe that it "substantially limits" his ability to perform the major life activity so as to render him "unable" or "significantly restricted" as compared to the "average person in the general population."

The "substantially limits" requirement might be easier to fulfill for some categories of disabilities than others. For example, being legally blind would almost certainly render one unable to read conventionally printed words. Similarly, a person lacking hands would be significantly restricted as compared to the average person in any number of tasks associated with the major life activity of caring for oneself. In the case of persons with learning disabilities, especially those applying to professional schools, however, the substantial limitation may not be easy to establish. Simply stated, a person may have a learning disability and yet still outperform the average person in the major life activity of learning. This seems particularly likely with regard to learning disabled persons who already attained undergraduate degrees, in light of the fact that in so doing they have already attained educational superiority *vis-a-vis* the "average person."

Assuming arguendo that every person has strengths and weaknesses, both physical and mental, the "substantially limits" requirement makes public policy sense. For instance, one might discover, upon being tested, a discrepancy between one's raw I.Q. and one's reading ability, suggesting the presence of dyslexia. However, the fact that an individual possesses a 99th percentile I.Q. but due to dyslexia exhibits only an 80th percentile reading ability does not justify giving the individual legal protection. Indeed, it would be ludicrous to describe a person with reasoning ability better than ninety-nine out of one hundred of her fellow citizens and reading ability superior to eighty out of one hundred as "disabled" simply because she is stronger in some cognitive capacities than in others. Implicitly recognizing this, the law instead protects persons with impairments so severe that their ability to perform affected life activities falls below the 50th percentile of the general population—the "average person" standard.

Applying these principles to the professional school admissions context, and specifically to the treatment of flagged scores, it seems that a certain amount of discounting for accommodations is permissible, if the school can be certain that the applicant was not substantially limited in the major life activity that formed the basis for the accommodation. The paradigmatic situation in which the school could be so certain would involve a recently-diagnosed learning disabled applicant who took the LSAT or MCAT with accommodations, but who previously demonstrated relatively high levels of academic achievement prior to diagnosis and without accommodation. Given such a situation, the applicant most likely would not be considered disabled for the purposes of the Title II or section 504, and the admissions committee could justifiably treat the applicant and the applicant's flagged score as being more closely comparable to the vast majority of test-takers who would, no doubt, benefit from a grant of extra time while taking the LSAT or MCAT.

B. Discrimination on the Basis of Disability

Not only must an individual satisfy the ADA and the Rehabilitation Act shared definition of "disabled" in order to fall within the scope of Title II and section 504, but the discrimination alleged must be, on the basis of the individual's disability. One can imagine all sorts of retrograde and repulsive examples of discrimination that would violate the spirit and the letter of federal disability law. However, if the statistical evidence shows that scores achieved under non-standard conditions are consistently and significantly overpredictive of future success in professional school, then discounting such scores by the known factor of overprediction would not constitute discrimination on the basis of disability. In fact, such a practice would be non-discriminatory in the sense that all applicants' scores, both standard scores and properly adjusted flagged scores, would thereby acquire equal statistical validity.

At this point, it should be emphasized that the preceding discussion merely attempts to delineate the outermost limits to which schools might attempt to push current law, should they find it necessary or desirable to give flagged scores less weight than their non-flagged counterparts. As mentioned previously, available data suggest that professional schools do not currently discount flagged scores, even if there are viable arguments for doing so. The next Part of this Recent Development departs from the legal analysis of flagging and instead argues that sound public policy mandates continuing the practice so long as a validity gap exists between accommodated and standard test scores.

IV. What Are the Policy Arguments for Continuing to Flag Accommodated LSAT and MCAT Scores?

Under the current system of competitive admissions, it seems fair to assume that the primary objective of the admissions committees of most professional schools is to enroll the most academically-qualified student body possible while maintaining a fair admissions process. If this is indeed the case, then flagging is not only legally permissible, but also the most prudent, fair, and realistic way to deal with the fact that testing accommodations tend to produce scores of significantly decreased statistical validity.

A. Flagging as a Disincentive for Fraud

Under the current system, the professional school applicant has an incentive to explain to the school the reason for the flagged accommodation, thereby giving the admission committee a more complete picture of the applicant's abilities and likelihood of success in professional school. Of course, this also puts the onus on the admissions committee to refrain from discriminating against the applicant on the basis of the disability. This might seem like a large risk to ask the applicant to bear, but it pales in comparison to the risks posed by the discontinuation of flagging.

Whereas the current danger is that professional admissions committees will use the flag as a signal to discriminate, which has been shown to be unlikely, the potential danger of failing to flag accommodated scores is that every applicant (or at least every applicant who thinks extra time would be advantageous) will have a strong incentive to obtain a "learning disabled" diagnosis. The number of requests for accommodation on the LSAT grew by 37 percent from 1993 to 1996; one can only imagine how many people will "discover"—with the help of a well-compensated expert's opinion—that they have a learning disability if flagging were to be discontinued.

B. Issues of Fairness

The discontinuation of flagging raises two serious issues of fairness, both of which indicate the improvidence of taking such action. First, the discontinuation of flagging would give applicants receiving testing accommodations an unfair advantage over non-accommodated applicants because the accommodated scores are overly optimistic about their future academic success yet would appear to be as statistically valid as standard scores. Until the testing companies and psychometricians can develop more accurate methods for determining the amount of accommodation required for each disabled individual—which would be shown by a closing of the validity gap between standard and accommodated scores—flagging of LSAT and MCAT scores is the fairest method for ensuring equal access to professional education.

Second, by creating an incentive to become classified as disabled, the end of flagging would benefit chiefly those applicants sophisticated and wealthy enough to obtain a diagnosis. Educators and college administrators have already voiced this concern in the aftermath of the Breimhorst settlement agreements. The Dean of Admissions at Pomona College recently observed, "it's very clear who's been getting extended-time: the highest-income communities have the highest rates of accommodations." A guidance counselor in an affluent Boston suburb echoed the dean's concerns: "this will open the floodgates to families that think they can beat the system by buying a diagnosis, and getting their kid extra time."

Buying a diagnosis is not cheap. The New York Times recently reported that an evaluation by educational psychologists starts at $ 2,400 and can cost hundreds more if the doctor has to lobby the testing service on behalf of the client. Thus a poor, non-disabled applicant would be doubly hurt by discontinuing flagging. The genuinely disabled student would receive an inflated (but unblemished) score, and the wealthy student could buy a diagnosis for $ 2,400, but the poor student would be left to take the test as best she could.

While this immediate effect is undoubtedly regressive, the long-term effects of an erosion of the standardized admissions tests as a valid predictor could be even more damaging to poor law and medical school applicants. Without a reliable tool for predicting the applicant's likelihood for future academic success, law and medical schools may be forced to give other elements of the application greater weight. Since undergraduate GPA is the second-strongest predictor of success in professional school, it would be logical for admissions committees to look more closely at the academic strength of the applicant's undergraduate program. Presumably they would give greater weight to grades earned at elite undergraduate programs, again disproportionately favoring economically and educationally privileged applicants.

C. Professional Concerns

As gatekeepers of their respective professions, law and medical schools ultimately must consider whether an applicant will be able to serve competently as a doctor or lawyer. Certainly, this concern might not loom as large at the top echelon schools (where a near-perfect, but flagged, LSAT or MCAT would nonetheless probably indicate future professional competency) as it would at less academically selective schools where serious thought must be given to each applicant's potential for professional competence. Yet, it is at the margin where the schools must be particularly free to exercise their judgment about whether it is in the best interests of the applicant, the school, and the public to admit a particular individual.

There are many situations in which a physician or an attorney is expected to work quickly and accurately: while performing surgery, when reading a critically ill patient's charts, during oral arguments, during litigation, and during negotiations, just to name a few. In many of these instances a person's liberty, property, or life itself hangs in the balance, and quite often can be protected only if the proper action is taken within a given span of time. No "extra time" accommodation is reasonable when one's death-row client is relying upon the filing of a last-minute brief. Similarly, no doctor who takes twice as long to read an emergent patient's chart could be reasonably accommodated when doing so would result in a significantly higher mortality rate. These are real concerns of public safety that law and medical schools should, indeed must, take into account when selecting a class of students. Discontinuing flagging would tend to conceal, at least at the margin, some applicants whose disabilities could pose a danger to the public, especially if real world circumstances make accommodation impossible.

Conclusion

A lawsuit filed against the administrators of the LSAT and MCAT, on the theory that flagging violates federal disability law, would likely fail. Under current case law and regulatory interpretation, the inclusion of flagged scores in professional school admissions decisions is not a per se violation of federal disability law, but negative treatment of flagged scores on the basis of the test-taker's disability does constitute a violation. However, there is little evidence that negative treatment of flagged scores actually occurs, and there is a small, but strong, body of evidence suggesting that it typically does not. Moreover, one could argue that discounting accommodated scores only to the extent that they tend to overpredict future academic success does not constitute invidious discrimination on the basis of disability, but rather is a legitimate response to the lower validity of accommodated scores relative to those achieved under standard conditions.

In the final analysis, flagging may be an imperfect solution, but it is the only one currently available to correct for the even greater imperfections of disability diagnosis and accommodation. Flagging may cause disabled students to feel stigmatized as intellectually inferior. It may, on rare occasions, cause a disabled applicant to be refused admission to academic programs which, but for the flag, would have accepted the individual. These are truly unfortunate, though remediable, outcomes. However, the pertinent question is not whether these collateral ill effects are "bad," but whether they are bad enough to outweigh the risk of harm that the discontinuation of flagging would create.

These potential harms, especially the erosion of the integrity of professional school admissions, might be brushed aside as too speculative to merit consideration. Yet the temptation to disregard the potential for, and the magnitude of, unintended consequences must be resisted. The desire to do the "right" thing and thereby achieve the "right" outcomes, without regard to other, perhaps negative, consequences of the course of conduct has been termed "the imperious immediacy of interest" problem. In the case of post-secondary admissions, the ETS, College Board, and ACT settlements indicate that the imperious immediacy of interest in achieving the appearance of non-discriminatory admissions testing has outweighed any concern that doing so will create newer and greater problems of fairness and accuracy. Robert Merton explained this phenomenon succinctly: "intense interest often tends to preclude [objective] analysis precisely because strong concern with the satisfaction of the immediate interest is a psychological generator of emotional bias, with consequent lopsidedness or failure to engage in the required calculations." When the issue of flagging on the LSAT and MCAT is litigated, as it inevitably will be, the law and medical school communities would be wise to heed Merton's words and thereby prevent the imperious immediacy of interest from overwhelming the rational, objective analysis that this important issue deserves.

* * *

Questions for Discussion

1. What do you think about this issue? Do you agree that flagging of LSAT and MCAT scores is necessary, as the title suggests? What policy issues can you see on both sides?

2. What should students be required to show in order to be given accommodations on a test? Should students have to pay for their own evaluations/testing to "prove" their disability exists?

3. How should an admissions committee treat a "flagged" test?

———————

For Further Reading and Discussion

Cory, R. C. *Disability services offices for students with disabilities: A campus resource.* New Directions for Higher Education, 27–36 (2011).

"Campus Mental Health," Bazelon Center for Mental Health Law, retrieved May 15, 2012 at http://bazelon.org.gravitatehosting.com/Where-We-Stand/Community-Integration/Campus-Mental-Health/Campus-Mental-Health-Legal-Action.aspx.

"Justice Department Reaches Three Settlements Under the Americans with Disabilities Act Regarding the Use of Electronic Book Readers," U.S. Dept. of Justice, retried May 15, 2012 at http://www.justice.gov/opa/pr/2010/January/10-crt-030.html.

Brenda G. Hameister, et al., *College Students with Disabilities and Study Abroad: Implications for International Education Staff,* Frontiers: The Interdisciplinary Journal of Study Abroad, http://www.frontiersjournal.com/issues/vol5/vol5-04_Hameister.htm.

Jeanne M. Kincaid, "Highlights of ADA/Section 504 Decisions As Applied To Institutions of Higher Education," 2009.

Helia Garrido Hull, *Equal Access to Post-Secondary Education: The Sisyphean Impact of Flagging Test Scores of Persons with Disabilities"* 55 Clev. St. L. Rev. 15 (2007).

Nancy Leong, *Beyond Breimhorst: Appropriate Accommodation of Students with Learning Disabilities on the SAT,* 57 Stan. L. Rev. 2135 (2005).

Ben-Moshe, L., Feldbaum, M., Cory, R. and Sagendorf, K. (eds.) (2005). *Building Pedagogical Curb Cuts: Incorporating Disability in the University Classroom and Curriculum.* Syracuse, NY: Graduate School, Syracuse University (distributed and sold by SU Press).

Discussion 9

Disability Discrimination in Immigration

Recommended Background Reading

"Deportation by Default: Mental Disability, Unfair Hearings, and Indefinite Detention in the U.S. Immigration System," Human Rights Watch & the ACLU, retrieved May 15, 2012 at http://www.hrw.org/en/reports/2010/07/26/deportation-default-0.

Readings for Class Discussion

The following article considers issues legal surrounding people with disabilities and the immigration system in the U.S.

Persons with Disabilities and the U.S. Immigration System

Rebecca Watson, J.D.

Introduction

Immigrants who have disabilities face both obvious and subtle barriers within the U.S. immigration system. The U.S. immigration system is composed of a complex array of laws, procedures, and institutions and it is a challenge for even a trained legal practitioner to understand it. It is even more difficult for individuals who represent themselves in an immigration process. Individuals with disabilities face additional barriers within the immigration system in the form of specific laws and procedures that may discriminate against individuals with disabilities or place individuals at a disadvantage due to their disability. This can be particularly true where an individual has an intellectual disability or a mental health issue. Although immigration laws have improved since the time that it was legal to turn away a potential immigrant based purely on the existence of a disability, barriers nonetheless remain despite recent agency efforts to improve procedures. This article attempts to illustrate these barriers through a discussion of three different aspects of the immigration system: (1) inadmissibility criteria, (2) credibility determinations in asylum proceedings, and (3) immigration court treatment of the mentally ill. In order to explain how disability may factor into each of these parts of the immigration system, it is first necessary to give a brief overview of what is meant by the "U.S. immigration system."

Overview of the U.S. Immigration System

What is referred to as the U.S. "immigration system" is actually composed of several separate entities that are responsible for making decisions related to different immigration processes. When an individual applies for a visa from outside of the U.S., the consular offices of the U.S. Department of State are charged with making the decision as to whether an individual (an "alien") is admissible. An eligible[1] individual within the U.S. who applies for immigration status has his affirmative[2] application reviewed by U.S. Citizenship and Immigration Services ("USCIS"). USCIS and its twin agency, Immigration and Customs Enforcement ("ICE"), are a part of the Department of Homeland Security and together share[3] the responsibilities of the former Immigration and Naturalization Service. A third entity is the immigration courts housed within the Department of Justice's Executive Office of Immigration Review. These courts, overseen by administrative judges, conduct hearings and review cases on issues such as deportation. An immigrant awaiting his hearing in Immigration Court may be detained in an immigration detention facility or may be released on bond. The complexity of the immigration system is deepened by the fact that each of these entities—consulates, USCIS offices, and immigration courts—have different procedures. However, they are all responsible for deciding cases based on the same laws contained within the Immigration and Nationality Act.

There are many different decision-makers operating in the immigration system and these decision-makers are often granted broad discretion. Additionally, not all decisions made in the immigration system are reviewable such as with decisions made by consular officers abroad. Even where decisions are appealable, such as with decisions made by the Immigration Court,[4] it is difficult to challenge a discretionary decision on appeal. This is significant for any analysis of how a disability may impact an individual in the immigration process because, where a disability was improperly used as a basis to deny an application or appeal, it can be challenging to prove that this was actually the basis for a discretionary decision. The quantity and diversity of decision-makers is also significant because it makes it more challenging to ensure that all decision-makers are receiving proper training and following consistent procedures when working with individuals with disabilities. As will be discussed below, these aspects of the decision-making structure in the immigration system create risks that an individual's disability will negatively impact that individual's immigration application or status. The lack of an appeal right, or the difficulty of reversing a discretionary decision on appeal, further the risk that this negative impact cannot be corrected even if a disability was erroneously used as a basis to deny an immigration benefit. In order to explain how this can occur in more concrete terms, three different

---

1. Not all individuals residing within the U.S. are eligible to apply through USCIS. For example, even though an individual resides within the U.S., he nonetheless may not be eligible to apply for a visa, or other immigration benefit, from within the U.S. if he has been unlawfully present within the U.S. for a certain amount of time.

2. Immigration practitioners distinguish between affirmative applications for an immigration benefit and defensive actions where, for example, an immigrant presents a defense to deportation. Some types of claims, such as a claim of asylum, can be presented either in an affirmative application or as a defense to deportation.

3. The agencies have disparate responsibilities. Very generally, ICE handles investigations and enforcement of customs and immigration laws within the U.S. (along with Customs and Border Protection), whereas USCIS is responsible for reviewing immigration applications.

4. Immigration Court decisions are reviewable through the Board of Immigration Appeals (BIA) and then through the Courts of Appeals and the Supreme Court.

aspects of the immigration system will be described with a discussion of how an individual's disability might factor into the decision-making process in each.

Grounds of Inadmissibility

In order to contextualize current immigration law as it relates to individualizes with disabilities, it is important to understand that, until relatively recently, an individual could be denied entry to the U.S. based solely on the presence of a disability. Until 1986, classes of immigrants that could be excluded from entry included individuals that were "mentally retarded," "insane," or those "having a physical defect, disease or disability ... of such a nature that it may affect the ability of the alien to earn a living, unless the alien affirmatively establishes that he will not have to earn a living."[5] These disability-specific classes of inadmissibility[6] applied not only to individuals seeking non-immigrant visas (like a tourist visa) but to all individuals seeking to enter the U.S. including those otherwise eligible to be permanent residents. Individuals who were likely to become a "public charge" were separately inadmissible.[7] This meant that an individual could be excluded from entry by an officer either under the disability-specific grounds or on the grounds that he was likely to become a public charge. As part of the Immigration and Reform Control Act of 1986, the law was changed allowing some individuals with disabilities to obtain waivers of the public charge exclusion provided that they met the standard of disability needed to qualify for Supplemental Security Income benefits.[8] Finally, through amendments to the immigration law in 1990, Congress deleted the provisions allowing for exclusion based solely on the presence of a disability.[9] However, not all grounds related to disability were removed. An individual may still be inadmissible under the public charge exclusion or under health-related exclusions. The health-related grounds for inadmissibility include where the individual has "a communicable disease of public health significance,"[10] or where the individual has or had "a physical or mental disorder and behavior associated with the disorder that may pose, or has posed, a threat to the property, safety, or welfare of the alien or others."[11] Because of the provisions that remain, an individual may still be declared inadmissible as a result of having a disability.

Although the presence of a disability is no longer a categorical bar to entering the U.S., the health-related and public charge grounds of inadmissibility that remain a part of immigration law can still be a barrier to individuals with disabilities. This can occur directly because of the disability or due to the effects of an underlying disability. One prominent, and much critiqued, example of how the health-related grounds have been used to discriminate directly against individuals with disabilities was in the case of HIV-positive individuals. Beginning in 1987, HIV-positive individuals were inadmissible to the U.S. due to the classification of HIV as a communicable disease of public health significance.[12] Although an individual could seek a waiver of these grounds in order to still enter the U.S., the presumption was that any HIV-positive individual was inadmissible. It was not

---

5. Mark C. Weber, *Opening the Golden Door: Disability and the Law of Immigration*, 8 J. Gender & Just. 153, 161 (2004).

6. Inadmissibility is a term of art in immigration law that refers to grounds on which an individual may be denied "admission" to the U.S.

7. Weber, *Opening the Golden Door* at 162.

8. *Id.*

9. *Id.*

10. Immigration and Nationality Act, 8 U.S.C. § 1182(a)(1)(A)(i).

11. 8 U.S.C. § 1182(a)(1)(A)(iii).

12. See Human Rights Campaign, *U.S. Senate Approves Repeal of Discriminatory HIV Travel and Immigration Ban* (Jul. 7, 2008), http://www.hrc.org/10832.htm.

until January 2010 that being HIV-positive was removed from the statute as a ground for inadmissibility.[13] The fact that this was not removed until 2010 demonstrates that, unfortunately, discrimination against individuals with disabilities is still a reality in immigration law. For example, although an individual may not be barred from the U.S. solely on the basis of a disability, he may be barred if his "physical or mental disorder" results in behaviors that have caused or may cause harm to himself or others. On its face, this provision can be used to exclude individuals with disabilities even if that disability has not actually caused any harm. In a less direct way, individuals with disabilities may also be excluded from entering the U.S. due to the potential impacts of their disability on their ability to work. This is due to the public charge grounds for inadmissibility. For purposes of determining inadmissibility, a public charge means an individual who is likely to become "primarily dependent on the government for subsistence, as demonstrated by either the receipt of public cash assistance for income maintenance, or institutionalization for long-term care at government expense."[14] A number of factors are considered in this determination, including health,[15] which presumably could take into account the presence of a disability. In summary, although immigration law has improved its treatment of immigrants with disabilities by removing disability-specific grounds for inadmissibility, including the HIV-positive grounds, the presence of a disability may still be used as a factor in denying an individual admission to the U.S.

The highly-discretionary nature of inadmissibility decisions can heighten the risk that individual officers may use evidence of a disability to deny admission to an individual. Individual consular officers are vested with enormous discretion and there are few options for challenging a consular officer's decision. For example, if an individual is applying for a U.S. visa, he will submit an application and attend an interview at a U.S. consulate overseas. At the interview, a consular officer makes the decision, based on the facts before him, whether or not the applicant is admissible.[16] Although this decision may be reviewed internally by the Department of State,[17] it is not reviewable in court. An individual may be denied admission based on a disability under the health-related or public charge grounds, and practically speaking will have no recourse to challenge this decision. If an individual is applying for admission from within the U.S., a USCIS officer will be charged with making the decision on admissibility. As in the case of a consular officer, the USCIS officer will have broad discretion in determining whether or not the individual is admissible. Unlike decisions made by consular offices, decisions made by USCIS officers are appealable.[18]

---

13. USCIS Memorandum, *Public Law 110-293, 42 CFR 34.2(b), and Inadmissibility Due to Human Immunodeficiency Virus (HIV) Infection* (Nov. 24, 2009), http://www.uscis.gov/USCIS/New%20Structure/Laws%20and%20Regulations/Memoranda/2009/HIVInadmissibilityFinalHHSRule.pdf.

14. USCIS, *Public Charge Fact Sheet* (Nov. 6, 2009), http://www.uscis.gov/USCIS/New%20Structure/Press%20Releases/2009%20Press%20Releases/Oct%202009/public_charge_fact_%20sheet_11_06_09.pdf.

15. *Id.*

16. U.S. Department of State, *Visa Denials* (Last accessed May 28, 2011), http://www.travel.state.gov/visa/frvi/denials/denials_1361.html.

17. *Id.* ("Immigration law delegates the responsibility for issuance or refusal of visas to consular offices overseas. They have the final say on all visa cases. By regulation the U.S. Department of State has authority to review consular decisions, but this authority is limited to the interpretation of law, as contrasted to determinations of facts.")

18. Generally, appeals of family-based immigration petitions denied by a USCIS office are appealed to the USCIS Administrative Appeals Office, whereas USCIS denial of other types of petitions are appealed through the BIA. See, USCIS, *Denied Immigration Petitions and Appeals* (Sep. 2, 2010), http://www.uscis.gov/portal/site/uscis/.

Of course, even if the individual has a right to appeal, it is difficult to reverse a discretionary decision. And, it is important to remember that these officers are explicitly allowed to take a disability into account under the health-related grounds of inadmissibility. An individual officer may erroneously believe that the presence of a certain disability, such as schizophrenia, is sufficient evidence to refuse admission on health-related grounds. This decision, even if erroneous, would be difficult to challenge whether made by a consular or USCIS officer. Under these circumstances, there is a great risk that officers may be interpreting current immigration law in a way that disadvantages individuals with disabilities.

Asylum and Credibility Determination

An individual with a disability can face barriers in the asylum process due to the importance of credibility determinations to the decision of whether to grant asylum. In order to be granted asylum, an applicant has to prove that he meets the statutory definition of refugee,[19] which is that he is unable or unwilling to return to his country, "because of persecution or a well-founded fear of persecution."[20] An applicant can meet his burden of proving this through documentary evidence and testimony. Testimony is, "often the critical core of the asylum determination, since refugees generally are unable to produce external corroborating evidence."[21] The individual deciding whether to grant asylum, either a USCIS asylum officer or an Immigration Judge,[22] assesses the individual's testimony to determine if it "is credible, is persuasive, and refers to specific facts sufficient to demonstrate that the applicant is a refugee."[23] The credibility of the applicant, as determined by the decision-maker, is central to the decision whether to grant asylum. Many factors may be considered in assessing credibility, including "the demeanor, candor, and or responsiveness of the applicant," "the inherent plausibility" of the account, consistency between written and oral statements, "the internal consistency of each statement," and "any inaccuracies or falsehoods in such statements."[24] Because so many factors may be taken into account in assessing credibility and these assessments are primarily based on first-person observation of the applicant and/or witnesses, these assessments are highly subjective. In this subjective assessment, disabilities can form a hidden barrier to successfully demonstrating credibility, particularly in cases where the disability is unrecognized.

There are many ways in which a cognitive disability or a mental health issue may make an asylum applicant appear to not be credible. Because demonstrating credibility is often the key to a successful asylum application, an applicant may be denied asylum due to the effect of a disability. For example, an asylum applicant may have suffered a traumatic brain injury, and even mild TBIs can cause, "cognitive problems such as …

---

19. A refugee is an individual who applies for permission to enter the U.S. from outside the U.S. based on this standard, whereas an asylum-seeker is someone who applies at a U.S. port-of-entry or from within the U.S.

20. 8 U.S.C. § 1101(a)(42)(A).

21. Daniel Forman, Comment, *Improving Asylum-Seeker Credibility Determinations: Introducing Appropriate Dispute Resolution Techniques into the Process*, 16 Cardozo J. Int'l & Comp. L. 207, 213 (2008).

22. *Id.* at 211–12. (An affirmative application is filed with an asylum officer of USCIS whereas a defensive application is offered as a defense to removal in Immigration Court. "An affirmative application results in an interview with an asylum officer that is non-adversarial and may be private … A defensive application goes to immigration court and is adjudicated by an IJ, a DOJ employee.")

23. 8 U.S.C. § 1158(b)(1)(B)(ii) (2008).

24. 8 U.S.C. § 1158(b)(1)(B)(iii) (2008).

difficulty thinking, memory problems, attention deficits, mood swings, and frustration."[25] Any of these cognitive problems could impact the content of the applicant's testimony by making it appear disjointed or lacking in detail. These problems could also impact the applicant's demeanor due to frustration or mood swings caused by the injury. In a similar way, other cognitive or intellectual disabilities may make the applicant appear not to be credible. Mental health issues may also negatively impact the credibility determination. For example, "medical conditions that result from traumatic events, including depression and disassociation, have … fragmenting effects on memory, which can also lessen an asylum-seeker's credibility."[26] Although an individual with a disability or mental health issue could present evidence on this issue to explain these problems, they may not even be aware that they have this problem due to lack of medical and mental health care in their home country. The risk that a mental health issue will be present, and will negatively impact credibility, is increased for asylum applicants as they have a higher rate of psychological problems than the general population.[27] If an asylum applicant has been detained while awaiting his hearing, this detention may exacerbate the individual's mental health issues[28] and increase the risk. In these ways, a cognitive or intellectual disability or a mental health issue could cause an asylum applicant to lose his case where behaviors or problems associated with the disability make him appear not credible.

Although there is a strong chance that an applicant's disability or mental health issue may impact a credibility determination in any asylum case, specific guidance does not appear to exist for asylum officers or Immigration Judges[29] on the impact of this issue. Very generally, USCIS states that it is committed to providing accommodations for disabilities so that applicants with disabilities may participate in immigration processes.[30] However, the examples given on the USCIS website all reference physical disabilities and do not provide guidance on accommodations for cognitive disabilities or mental health issues. In more specific guidance directed at asylum officers, USCIS directs officers to take into account such issues as trauma, the length of time since the described events, certain cultural factors, detention, or interpretation problems when assessing credibility.[31] Not mentioned in this list of factors are mental health issues or any cognitive or intellectual disabilities that the individual may have. Without specific guidance or training on how to identify when these issues are present and how they may impact testimony, it seems likely that decision-makers in the asylum process will fail to accommodate individuals with disabilities. Unfortunately, this means that asylum applicants with a disability may be found not credible due solely to the effects their disability has on their testimony.

---

25. Traumatic Brain Injury.Com, *What are the Effects of TBI?* (Last accessed May 28, 2011), http://www.traumaticbraininjury.com/content/understandingtbi/effectsoftbi.html.

26. Daniel Forman, *Improving Asylum-Seeker Credibility Determinations* at 225.

27. Physicians for Human Rights, *From Persecution to Prison: The Health Consequences of Detention for Asylum Seekers* (Jun. 2003), at 9–10, http://www.pegc.us/archive/Organizations/PHR_detention.pdf.

28. *Id.*

29. There are specific regulations that Immigration Judges must follow in cases where the individual may not be competent. This will be discussed in the below section.

30. USCIS, *Requesting Accommodations for Disabilities* (Feb. 10, 2011), http://www.uscis.gov/portal/site/uscis/.

31. USCIS Asylum Division, *Asylum Officer Basic Training Course: Credible Fear* (Apr. 14, 2006), at 17, http://www.uscis.gov/USCIS/Humanitarian/Refugees%20&%20Asylum/Asylum/AOBTC%20Lesson%20Plans/Credible-Fear-31aug10.pdf.

Immigration Courts and Mental Health Issues

Immigration Courts are perhaps the most widely-criticized entity of the U.S. immigration system. They have come under attack both from immigrant legal advocates and from Court of Appeals judges who are tasked with reviewing their decisions. Seventh Circuit Judge Richard Posner declared that, "the adjudication of these cases at the administrative level has fallen below the minimum standards of legal justice."[32] Immigration courts have been critiqued for their lack of attention to due process rights, disrespectful treatment of immigrants, and their failure to adequately document decisions. In part, the problems that exist are undoubtedly due to the high number and wide variety of cases that pass through Immigration Courts. These courts are, without a doubt, overloaded.[33] Commenting on the high stakes of the cases in Immigration Court and the lack of resources, the leader of the immigration judge union has said that, "We're doing death penalty cases in traffic court settings."[34] Unsurprisingly, given this background, mentally ill individuals do not fare well in the Immigration Court system.

Mentally ill individuals have few protections in the Immigration Court system or while they are held in detention. The specific problems they face in Immigration Court are the lack of a standard for competency and the lack of established procedures for requiring psychological or competency evaluations.[35] Immigration Courts instead rely on individuals to self-identify. One exhaustive report identified the myriad ways in which mental health issues, or other mental disabilities, can undermine or destroy an individual's case in Immigration Court.[36] These problems are exacerbated by the fact that individuals have no right to a state-funded attorney in Immigration Court, even where the Immigration Judge is concerned that competency is an issue.[37] This is true even in cases where it is clear that competency is an issue, such as where an individual cannot state their name or date of birth. The problem is so severe that there have been several well-publicized cases in which U.S. citizens with mental disabilities were erroneously deported when they were unable to effectively defend themselves in immigration proceedings.[38] If it is possible for an Immigration Court to wrongfully deport a U.S. citizen because he is unable to explain his case, it is clear that individuals with mental disabilities who have

---

32. Eliot Walker, *Asylees in Wonderland: A New Procedural Perspective on America's Asylee System*, 2 Nw. J. L. & Soc. Pol'y 1 (2007) (quoting *Benslimane v. Gonzalez*, 430 F. 3d 828, 830 (7th Cir. 2005)).

33. Immigration Policy Center, *Non-Citizens with Mental Disabilities* (Nov. 2010), www.immigrationpolicy.org/special-reports/non-citizens-mental-disabilities. ("The 55 immigration courts in the United States have about 230 judges, who heard a record 391,829 cases in 2009.... if all the cases were evenly distributed amongst Immigration Judges, each would have to decide seven cases per day, five days per week, with no vacation.")

34. Jacqueline Stevens, *Lawless Courts*, THE NATION, Oct. 20, 2010, http://www.thenation.com/article/155497/lawless-courts (quoting Dana Marks).

35. IPC, *Non-Citizens with Mental Disabilities*.

36. Human Rights Watch and ACLU, *Deportation by Default: Mental Disability, Unfair Hearings, and Indefinite Detention in the US Immigration System* (Jul. 2010), http://www.hrw.org/en/reports/2010/07/26/deportation-default-0.

37. See *Franco-Gonzalez v. Holder*, No. 10-02211 (C.D. Cal. filed March 26, 2010) (Plaintiffs with mental disabilities seek to require the government to provide attorneys for individuals in Immigration Court who have been found incompetent.)

38. In one case, a mentally ill U.S. citizen who was born in North Carolina, spoke no Spanish, and had no family ties in Mexico, was deported to Mexico. See, Kristin Collins, *N.C. Native Wrongly Deported to Mexico*, CHARLOTTE OBSERVER, Aug. 30, 2009, http://www.charlotteobserver.com/2009/08/30/917007/nc-native-wrongly-deported-to.html.

more complex cases have little hope of effectively defending themselves. It is also clear that if Immigration Courts are failing to create procedures to protect individuals with even severe mental disabilities, protections for less severe, or more hidden, disabilities must also not exist.

The problems individuals with mental disabilities face in Immigration Court are sometimes also tied to problems with conditions of detention. Many individuals are held in immigration detention facilities while they await their hearing. The wait can be long. Detention can lead to deterioration in their mental condition both because detention itself can be a destabilizing or traumatic experience and because of inadequate medical and psychological care while in detention. One report summarized that, "the lack of proper diagnosis and treatment protocols, and understaffing or staffing with inadequately trained or unqualified facility staff—combined with ineffective enforcement of existing standards—all contribute to insufficient care for immigrants with mental disabilities."[39] When immigrants with mental disabilities are separated from their families and held in detention without adequate care, they may become less able to defend themselves in Immigration Court than if they were released and receiving community-based treatment. This can have a feedback effect as Immigration Judges who recognize that an individual before him may not be competent have the option to "administratively close" the case and keep the individual detained.[40] In one case, "two men in southern California remained in detention more than four years while waiting for their immigration hearings after an IJ determined they were not competent to proceed with their hearings and administratively closed their cases."[41] Mentally disabled individuals in immigration detention can be detained indefinitely with no means to defend themselves. And, even where they are not detained, they will still face myriad problems in defending themselves in Immigration Court due to the lack of protections for individuals with mental disabilities in that system.

Conclusion

This summary of the barriers that individuals with disabilities may face in the immigration system is not meant to describe all potential barriers. There are undoubtedly many other ways that individuals are disadvantaged in the immigration system because of the presence of a disability. Nonetheless, from this discussion, it is apparent that barriers exist in the form of discriminatory statutes, inadequate procedures, and the lack of resources in Immigration Court and immigration detention facilities. Significant changes in law and procedure will need to be made in the immigration system before individuals with disabilities have equal access and equal protection.

* * *

Questions for Discussion

1. What changes do you think are needed in our immigration system on behalf of people with disabilities? What agents for change might such improvements require?

2. As far as people with disabilities are concerned, how are issues in the immigration system similar to and different from issues in the criminal system?

---

39. Texas Appleseed, *Justice for Immigration's Hidden Population: Protecting the Rights of Persons with Mental Disabilities in the Immigration Court and Detention System* (Mar. 2010), at 15–16.
40. HRW, *Deportation by Default* at 74.
41. *Id.* at 75.

For Further Reading

"Immigration: ICE Detainees in State and Local Facilities Resource Materials," TASC (a division of National Disability Rights Network), retrieved May 15, 2012 at http://www.ndrn.org/images/Images/Issues/Ice_Detainees/Immigration_ICEdetainees_11-2011.pdf.

Mark C. Weber, *Opening the Golden Door: Disability and the Law of Immigration*, 8 J. Gender Race & Just. 153 (2004).

"Noncitizens with Mental Competency Issues in Removal Proceedings," Legal Action Center, retrieved May 15, 2012 at http://www.legalactioncenter.org/clearinghouse/litigation-issue-pages/immigrants-mental-disabilities-removal-proceedings.

Nina Bernstein, "Mentally Ill and in Immigration Limbo," *N.Y. Times*, May 4, 2009, at A21.

Emily Ramshaw, "Mentally Ill Immigrants Have Little Hope for Care When Detained," *Dallas Morning News*, July 13, 2009.

Helen Eisner, *Disabled, Defenseless, and Still Deportable: Why Deportation Without Representation Undermines Due Process Rights of Mentally Disabled Immigrants*, 14 U. Pa. J. Const. L. 511 (2011).

Discussion 10

Convention on the Rights of Persons with Disabilities

Suggested Background Reading

"The U.S. Ratification of the Convention on the Rights of Persons with Disabilities Fact Sheet," United States International Council on Disabilities, retrieved May 15, 2012 at www.usicd.org/doc/CRPDToolkit.pdf.

http://en.wikipedia.org/wiki/Convention_on_the_Rights_of_Persons_with_Disabilities. A map showing countries' responses to the Convention.

Readings for Class Discussion

The following is the text of the convention.

Convention on the Rights of Persons with Disabilities

Preamble

The States Parties to the present Convention,

(a) *Recalling* the principles proclaimed in the Charter of the United Nations which recognize the inherent dignity and worth and the equal and inalienable rights of all members of the human family as the foundation of freedom, justice and peace in the world,

(b) *Recognizing* that the United Nations, in the Universal Declaration of Human Rights and in the International Covenants on Human Rights, has proclaimed and agreed that everyone is entitled to all the rights and freedoms set forth therein, without distinction of any kind,

(c) *Reaffirming* the universality, indivisibility, interdependence and interrelatedness of all human rights and fundamental freedoms and the need for persons with disabilities to be guaranteed their full enjoyment without discrimination,

(d) *Recalling* the International Covenant on Economic, Social and Cultural Rights, the International Covenant on Civil and Political Rights, the International Convention on the Elimination of All Forms of Racial Discrimination, the Convention on the Elimination of All Forms of Discrimination against Women, the Convention against Torture and Other Cruel, Inhuman or Degrading Treatment or Punishment, the Convention on the Rights of the Child, and the International Convention on the Protection of the Rights of All Migrant Workers and Members of Their Families,

(e) *Recognizing* that disability is an evolving concept and that disability results from the interaction between persons with impairments and attitudinal and environmental barriers that hinders their full and effective participation in society on an equal basis with others,

(f) *Recognizing* the importance of the principles and policy guidelines contained in the World Programme of Action concerning Disabled Persons and in the Standard Rules on the Equalization of Opportunities for Persons with Disabilities in influencing the promotion, formulation and evaluation of the policies, plans, programmes and actions at the national, regional and international levels to further equalize opportunities for persons with disabilities,

(g) *Emphasizing* the importance of mainstreaming disability issues as an integral part of relevant strategies of sustainable development,

(h) *Recognizing also* that discrimination against any person on the basis of disability is a violation of the inherent dignity and worth of the human person,

(i) *Recognizing further* the diversity of persons with disabilities,

(j) *Recognizing* the need to promote and protect the human rights of all persons with disabilities, including those who require more intensive support,

(k) *Concerned* that, despite these various instruments and undertakings, persons with disabilities continue to face barriers in their participation as equal members of society and violations of their human rights in all parts of the world,

(l) *Recognizing* the importance of international cooperation for improving the living conditions of persons with disabilities in every country, particularly in developing countries,

(m) *Recognizing* the valued existing and potential contributions made by persons with disabilities to the overall well-being and diversity of their communities, and that the promotion of the full enjoyment by persons with disabilities of their human rights and fundamental freedoms and of full participation by persons with disabilities will result in their enhanced sense of belonging and in significant advances in the human, social and economic development of society and the eradication of poverty,

(n) *Recognizing* the importance for persons with disabilities of their individual autonomy and independence, including the freedom to make their own choices,

(o) *Considering* that persons with disabilities should have the opportunity to be actively involved in decision-making processes about policies and programmes, including those directly concerning them,

(p) *Concerned* about the difficult conditions faced by persons with disabilities who are subject to multiple or aggravated forms of discrimination on the basis of race, colour, sex, language, religion, political or other opinion, national, ethnic, indigenous or social origin, property, birth, age or other status,

(q) *Recognizing* that women and girls with disabilities are often at greater risk, both within and outside of the violence, injury or abuse, neglect or negligent treatment, maltreatment or exploitation,

(r) *Recognizing* that children with disabilities should have full enjoyment of all human rights and fundamental freedoms on an equal basis with other children, and recalling obligations to that end undertaken by States Parties to the Convention on the Rights of the Child,

(s) *Emphasizing* the need to incorporate a gender perspective in all efforts to promote the full enjoyment of human rights and fundamental freedoms by persons with disabilities,

(t) *Highlighting* the fact that the majority of persons with disabilities live in conditions of poverty, and in this regard recognizing the critical need to address the negative impact of poverty on persons with disabilities,

(u) *Bearing in mind* that conditions of peace and security based on full respect for the purposes and principles contained in the Charter of the United Nations and observance of applicable human rights instruments are indispensable for the full protection of persons with disabilities, in particular during armed conflicts and foreign occupation,

(v) *Recognizing* the importance of accessibility to the physical, social, economic and cultural environment, to health and education and to information and communication, in enabling persons with disabilities to fully enjoy all human rights and fundamental freedoms,

(w) *Realizing* that the individual, having duties to other individuals and to the community to which he or she belongs, is under a responsibility to strive for the promotion and observance of the rights recognized in the International Bill of Human Rights,

(x) *Convinced* that the family is the natural and fundamental group unit of society and is entitled to protection by society and the State, and that persons with disabilities and their family members should receive the necessary protection and assistance to enable families to contribute towards the full and equal enjoyment of the rights of persons with disabilities,

(y) *Convinced* that a comprehensive and integral international convention to promote and protect the rights and dignity of persons with disabilities will make a significant contribution to redressing the profound social disadvantage of persons with disabilities and promote their participation in the civil, political, economic, social and cultural spheres with equal opportunities, in both developing and developed countries,

Have agreed as follows:

Article 1

Purpose

The purpose of the present Convention is to promote, protect and ensure the full and equal enjoyment of all human rights and fundamental freedoms by all persons with disabilities, and to promote respect for their inherent dignity.

Persons with disabilities include those who have long-term physical, mental, intellectual or sensory impairments which in interaction with various barriers may hinder their full and effective participation in society on an equal basis with others.

Article 2

Definitions

For the purposes of the present Convention:

"Communication" includes languages, display of text, Braille, tactile communication, large print, accessible multimedia as well as written, audio, plain-language, human-reader and augmentative and alternative modes, means and formats of communication, including accessible information and communication technology;

"Language" includes spoken and signed languages and other forms of non-spoken languages;

"Discrimination on the basis of disability" means any distinction, exclusion or restriction on the basis of disability which has the purpose or effect of impairing or nullifying the recognition, enjoyment or exercise, on an equal basis with others, of all human rights and fundamental freedoms in the political, economic, social, cultural, civil or any other field. It includes all forms of discrimination, including denial of reasonable accommodation;

"Reasonable accommodation" means necessary and appropriate modification and adjustments not imposing a disproportionate or undue burden, where needed in a particular case, to ensure to persons with disabilities the enjoyment or exercise on an equal basis with others of all human rights and fundamental freedoms;

"Universal design" means the design of products, environments, programmes and services to be usable by all people, to the greatest extent possible, without the need for adaptation or specialized design. "Universal design" shall not exclude assistive devices for particular groups of persons with disabilities where this is needed.

Article 3

General principles

The principles of the present Convention shall be:

(a) Respect for inherent dignity, individual autonomy including the freedom to make one's own choices, and independence of persons;

(b) Non-discrimination;

(c) Full and effective participation and inclusion in society;

(d) Respect for difference and acceptance of persons with disabilities as part of human diversity and humanity;

(e) Equality of opportunity;

(f) Accessibility;

(g) Equality between men and women;

(h) Respect for the evolving capacities of children with disabilities and respect for the right of children with disabilities to preserve their identities.

Article 4

General obligations

1. States Parties undertake to ensure and promote the full realization of all human rights and fundamental freedoms for all persons with disabilities without discrimination of any kind on the basis of disability. To this end, States Parties undertake:

(a) To adopt all appropriate legislative, administrative and other measures for the implementation of the rights recognized in the present Convention;

(b) To take all appropriate measures, including legislation, to modify or abolish existing laws, regulations, customs and practices that constitute discrimination against persons with disabilities;

(c) To take into account the protection and promotion of the human rights of persons with disabilities in all policies and programmes;

(d) To refrain from engaging in any act or practice that is inconsistent with the present Convention and to ensure that public authorities and institutions act in conformity with the present Convention;

(e) To take all appropriate measures to eliminate discrimination on the basis of disability by any person, organization or private enterprise;

(f) To undertake or promote research and development of universally designed goods, services, equipment and facilities, as defined in article 2 of the present Convention, which should require the minimum possible adaptation and the least cost to meet the specific needs of a person with disabilities, to promote their availability and use, and to promote universal design in the development of standards and guidelines;

(g) To undertake or promote research and development of, and to promote the availability and use of new technologies, including information and communications technologies, mobility aids, devices and assistive technologies, suitable for persons with disabilities, giving priority to technologies at an affordable cost;

(h) To provide accessible information to persons with disabilities about mobility aids, devices and assistive technologies, including new technologies, as well as other forms of assistance, support services and facilities;

(i) To promote the training of professionals and staff working with persons with disabilities in the rights recognized in this Convention so as to better provide the assistance and services guaranteed by those rights.

2. With regard to economic, social and cultural rights, each State Party undertakes to take measures to the maximum of its available resources and, where needed, within the framework of international cooperation, with a view to achieving progressively the full realization of these rights, without prejudice to those obligations contained in the present Convention that are immediately applicable according to international law.

3. In the development and implementation of legislation and policies to implement the present Convention, and in other decision-making processes concerning issues relating to persons with disabilities, States Parties shall closely consult with and actively involve persons with disabilities, including children with disabilities, through their representative organizations.

4. Nothing in the present Convention shall affect any provisions which are more conducive to the realization of the rights of persons with disabilities and which may be contained in the law of a State Party or international law in force for that State. There shall be no restriction upon or derogation from any of the human rights and fundamental freedoms recognized or existing in any State Party to the present Convention pursuant to law, conventions, regulation or custom on the pretext that the present Convention does not recognize such rights or freedoms or that it recognizes them to a lesser extent.

5. The provisions of the present Convention shall extend to all parts of federal states without any limitations or exceptions.

Article 5

Equality and non-discrimination

1. States Parties recognize that all persons are equal before and under the law and are entitled without any discrimination to the equal protection and equal benefit of the law.

2. States Parties shall prohibit all discrimination on the basis of disability and guarantee to persons with disabilities equal and effective legal protection against discrimination on all grounds.

3. In order to promote equality and eliminate discrimination, States Parties shall take all appropriate steps to ensure that reasonable accommodation is provided.

4. Specific measures which are necessary to accelerate or achieve de facto equality of persons with disabilities shall not be considered discrimination under the terms of the present Convention.

Article 6

Women with disabilities

1. States Parties recognize that women and girls with disabilities are subject to multiple discrimination, and in this regard shall take measures to ensure the full and equal enjoyment by them of all human rights and fundamental freedoms.

2. States Parties shall take all appropriate measures to ensure the full development, advancement and empowerment of women, for the purpose of guaranteeing them the exercise and enjoyment of the human rights and fundamental freedoms set out in the present Convention.

Article 7

Children with disabilities

1. States Parties shall take all necessary measures to ensure the full enjoyment by children with disabilities of all human rights and fundamental freedoms on an equal basis with other children.

2. In all actions concerning children with disabilities, the best interests of the child shall be a primary consideration.

3. States Parties shall ensure that children with disabilities have the right to express their views freely on all matters affecting them, their views being given due weight in accordance with their age and maturity, on an equal basis with other children, and to be provided with disability and age-appropriate assistance to realize that right.

Article 8

Awareness-raising

1. States Parties undertake to adopt immediate, effective and appropriate measures:

(a) To raise awareness throughout society, including at the family level, regarding persons with disabilities, and to foster respect for the rights and dignity of persons with disabilities;

(b) To combat stereotypes, prejudices and harmful practices relating to persons with disabilities, including those based on sex and age, in all areas of life;

(c) To promote awareness of the capabilities and contributions of persons with disabilities.

2. Measures to this end include:

(a) Initiating and maintaining effective public awareness campaigns designed:

(i) To nurture receptiveness to the rights of persons with disabilities;

(ii) To promote positive perceptions and greater social awareness towards persons with disabilities;

(iii) To promote recognition of the skills, merits and abilities of persons with disabilities, and of their contributions to the workplace and the labour market;

(b) Fostering at all levels of the education system, including in all children from an early age, an attitude of respect for the rights of persons with disabilities;

(c) Encouraging all organs of the media to portray persons with disabilities in a manner consistent with the purpose of the present Convention;

(d) Promoting awareness-training programmes regarding persons with disabilities and the rights of persons with disabilities.

Article 9

Accessibility

1. To enable persons with disabilities to live independently and participate fully in all aspects of life, States Parties shall take appropriate measures to ensure to persons with disabilities access, on an equal basis with others, to the physical environment, to transportation, to information and communications, including information and communications technologies and systems, and to other facilities and services open or provided to the public, both in urban and in rural areas. These measures, which shall include the identification and elimination of obstacles and barriers to accessibility, shall apply to, inter alia:

(a) Buildings, roads, transportation and other indoor and outdoor facilities, including schools, housing, medical facilities and workplaces;

(b) Information, communications and other services, including electronic services and emergency services.

2. States Parties shall also take appropriate measures to:

(a) Develop, promulgate and monitor the implementation of minimum standards and guidelines for the accessibility of facilities and services open or provided to the public;

(b) Ensure that private entities that offer facilities and services which are open or provided to the public take into account all aspects of accessibility for persons with disabilities;

(c) Provide training for stakeholders on accessibility issues facing persons with disabilities;

(d) Provide in buildings and other facilities open to the public signage in Braille and in easy to read and understand forms;

(e) Provide forms of live assistance and intermediaries, including guides, readers and professional sign language interpreters, to facilitate accessibility to buildings and other facilities open to the public;

(f) Promote other appropriate forms of assistance and support to persons with disabilities to ensure their access to information;

(g) Promote access for persons with disabilities to new information and communications technologies and systems, including the Internet;

(h) Promote the design, development, production and distribution of accessible information and communications technologies and systems at an early stage, so that these technologies and systems become accessible at minimum cost.

Article 10

Right to life

States Parties reaffirm that every human being has the inherent right to life and shall take all necessary measures to ensure its effective enjoyment by persons with disabilities on an equal basis with others.

Article 11

Situations of risk and humanitarian emergencies

States Parties shall take, in accordance with their obligations under international law, including international humanitarian law and international human rights law, all necessary measures to ensure the protection and safety of persons with disabilities in situations of risk, including situations of armed conflict, humanitarian emergencies and the occurrence of natural disasters.

Article 12

Equal recognition before the law

1. States Parties reaffirm that persons with disabilities have the right to recognition everywhere as persons before the law.

2. States Parties shall recognize that persons with disabilities enjoy legal capacity on an equal basis with others in all aspects of life.

3. States Parties shall take appropriate measures to provide access by persons with disabilities to the support they may require in exercising their legal capacity.

4. States Parties shall ensure that all measures that relate to the exercise of legal capacity provide for appropriate and effective safeguards to prevent abuse in accordance with international human rights law. Such safeguards shall ensure that measures relating to the exercise of legal capacity respect the rights, will and preferences of the person, are free of conflict of interest and undue influence, are proportional and tailored to the person's circumstances, apply for the shortest time possible and are subject to regular review by a competent, independent and impartial authority or judicial body. The safeguards shall be proportional to the degree to which such measures affect the person's rights and interests.

5. Subject to the provisions of this article, States Parties shall take all appropriate and effective measures to ensure the equal right of persons with disabilities to own or inherit property, to control their own financial affairs and to have equal access to bank loans, mortgages and other forms of financial credit, and shall ensure that persons with disabilities are not arbitrarily deprived of their property.

Article 13

Access to justice

1. States Parties shall ensure effective access to justice for persons with disabilities on an equal basis with others, including through the provision of procedural and age-appropriate accommodations, in order to facilitate their effective role as direct and indirect participants, including as witnesses, in all legal proceedings, including at investigative and other preliminary stages.

2. In order to help to ensure effective access to justice for persons with disabilities, States Parties shall promote appropriate training for those working in the field of administration of justice, including police and prison staff.

Article 14

Liberty and security of the person

1. States Parties shall ensure that persons with disabilities, on an equal basis with others:

> (a) Enjoy the right to liberty and security of person;

> (b) Are not deprived of their liberty unlawfully or arbitrarily, and that any deprivation of liberty is in conformity with the law, and that the existence of a disability shall in no case justify a deprivation of liberty.

2. States Parties shall ensure that if persons with disabilities are deprived of their liberty through any process, they are, on an equal basis with others, entitled to guarantees in

accordance with international human rights law and shall be treated in compliance with the objectives and principles of this Convention, including by provision of reasonable accommodation.

Article 15

Freedom from torture or cruel, inhuman or degrading treatment or punishment

1. No one shall be subjected to torture or to cruel, inhuman or degrading treatment or punishment. In particular, no one shall be subjected without his or her free consent to medical or scientific experimentation.

2. States Parties shall take all effective legislative, administrative, judicial or other measures to prevent persons with disabilities, on an equal basis with others, from being subjected to torture or cruel, inhuman or degrading treatment or punishment.

Article 16

Freedom from exploitation, violence and abuse

1. States Parties shall take all appropriate legislative, administrative, social, educational and other measures to protect persons with disabilities from all forms of exploitation, violence and abuse, including their gender-based aspects.

2. States Parties shall also take all appropriate measures to prevent all forms of exploitation, violence and abuse by ensuring, inter alia, appropriate forms of gender- and age-sensitive assistance and support for persons with disabilities and their families and caregivers, including through the provision of information and education on how to avoid, recognize and report instances of exploitation, violence and abuse. States Parties shall ensure that protection services are age-, gender- and disability-sensitive.

3. In order to prevent the occurrence of all forms of exploitation, violence and abuse, States Parties shall ensure that all facilities and programmes designed to serve persons with disabilities are effectively monitored by independent authorities.

4. States Parties shall take all appropriate measures to promote the physical, cognitive and psychological recovery, rehabilitation and social reintegration of persons with disabilities who become victims of any form of exploitation, violence or abuse, including through the provision of protection services. Such recovery and reintegration shall take place in an environment that fosters the health, welfare, self-respect, dignity and autonomy of the person and takes into account gender- and age-specific needs.

5. States Parties shall put in place effective legislation and policies, including women- and child-focused legislation and policies, to ensure that instances of exploitation, violence and abuse against persons with disabilities are identified, investigated and, where appropriate, prosecuted.

Article 17

Protecting the integrity of the person

Every person with disabilities has a right to respect for his or her physical and mental integrity on an equal basis with others.

Article 18

Liberty of movement and nationality

1. States Parties shall recognize the rights of persons with disabilities to liberty of movement, to freedom to choose their residence and to a nationality, on an equal basis with others, including by ensuring that persons with disabilities:

(a) Have the right to acquire and change a nationality and are not deprived of their nationality arbitrarily or on the basis of disability;

(b) Are not deprived, on the basis of disability, of their ability to obtain, possess and utilize documentation of their nationality or other documentation of identification, or to utilize relevant processes such as immigration proceedings, that may be needed to facilitate exercise of the right to liberty of movement;

(c) Are free to leave any country, including their own;

(d) Are not deprived, arbitrarily or on the basis of disability, of the right to enter their own country.

2. Children with disabilities shall be registered immediately after birth and shall have the right from birth to a name, the right to acquire a nationality and, as far as possible, the right to know and be cared for by their parents.

Article 19

Living independently and being included in the community

States Parties to this Convention recognize the equal right of all persons with disabilities to live in the community, with choices equal to others, and shall take effective and appropriate measures to facilitate full enjoyment by persons with disabilities of this right and their full inclusion and participation in the community, including by ensuring that:

(a) Persons with disabilities have the opportunity to choose their place of residence and where and with whom they live on an equal basis with others and are not obliged to live in a particular living arrangement;

(b) Persons with disabilities have access to a range of residential and other community support services, including personal assistance necessary to support living and inclusion in the community, and to prevent isolation or segregation from the community;

(c) Community services and facilities for the general population are available on an equal basis to persons with disabilities and are responsive to their needs.

Article 20

Personal mobility

States Parties shall take effective measures to ensure personal mobility with the greatest possible independence for persons with disabilities, including by:

(a) Facilitating the personal mobility of persons with disabilities in the manner and at the time of their choice, and at affordable cost;

(b) Facilitating access by persons with disabilities to quality mobility aids, devices, assistive technologies and forms of live assistance and intermediaries, including by making them available at affordable cost;

(c) Providing training in mobility skills to persons with disabilities and to specialist staff working with persons with disabilities;

(d) Encouraging entities that produce mobility aids, devices and assistive technologies to take into account all aspects of mobility for persons with disabilities.

Article 21

Freedom of expression and opinion, and access to information

States Parties shall take all appropriate measures to ensure that persons with disabilities can exercise the right to freedom of expression and opinion, including the freedom to seek, receive and impart information and ideas on an equal basis with others and through all forms of communication of their choice, as defined in article 2 of the present Convention, including by:

(a) Providing information intended for the general public to persons with disabilities in accessible formats and technologies appropriate to different kinds of disabilities in a timely manner and without additional cost;

(b) Accepting and facilitating the use of sign languages, Braille, augmentative and alternative communication, and all other accessible means, modes and formats of communication of their choice by persons with disabilities in official interactions;

(c) Urging private entities that provide services to the general public, including through the Internet, to provide information and services in accessible and usable formats for persons with disabilities;

(d) Encouraging the mass media, including providers of information through the Internet, to make their services accessible to persons with disabilities;

(e) Recognizing and promoting the use of sign languages.

Article 22

Respect for privacy

1. No person with disabilities, regardless of place of residence or living arrangements, shall be subjected to arbitrary or unlawful interference with his or her privacy, family, or correspondence or other types of communication or to unlawful attacks on his or her honour and reputation. Persons with disabilities have the right to the protection of the law against such interference or attacks.

2. States Parties shall protect the privacy of personal, health and rehabilitation information of persons with disabilities on an equal basis with others.

Article 23

Respect for and the family

1. States Parties shall take effective and appropriate measures to eliminate discrimination against persons with disabilities in all matters relating to marriage, family, parenthood and relationships, on an equal basis with others, so as to ensure that:

(a) The right of all persons with disabilities who are of marriageable age to marry and to found a family on the basis of free and full consent of the intending spouses is recognized;

(b) The rights of persons with disabilities to decide freely and responsibly on the number and spacing of their children and to have access to age-appropriate information, reproductive and family planning education are recognized, and the means necessary to enable them to exercise these rights are provided;

(c) Persons with disabilities, including children, retain their fertility on an equal basis with others.

2. States Parties shall ensure the rights and responsibilities of persons with disabilities, with regard to guardianship, wardship, trusteeship, adoption of children or similar institutions, where these concepts exist in national legislation; in all cases the best interests of the child shall be paramount. States Parties shall render appropriate assistance to persons with disabilities in the performance of their child-rearing responsibilities.

3. States Parties shall ensure that children with disabilities have equal rights with respect to family life. With a view to realizing these rights, and to prevent concealment,

abandonment, neglect and segregation of children with disabilities, States Parties shall undertake to provide early and comprehensive information, services and support to children with disabilities and their families.

4. States Parties shall ensure that a child shall not be separated from his or her parents against their will, except when competent authorities subject to judicial review determine, in accordance with applicable law and procedures, that such separation is necessary for the best interests of the child. In no case shall a child be separated from parents on the basis of a disability of either the child or one or both of the parents.

5. States Parties shall, where the immediate family is unable to care for a child with disabilities, undertake every effort to provide alternative care within the wider family, and failing that, within the community in a family setting.

Article 24

Education

1. States Parties recognize the right of persons with disabilities to education. With a view to realizing this right without discrimination and on the basis of equal opportunity, States Parties shall ensure an inclusive education system at all levels and life long learning directed to:

(a) The full development of human potential and sense of dignity and self-worth, and the strengthening of respect for human rights, fundamental freedoms and human diversity;

(b) The development by persons with disabilities of their personality, talents and creativity, as well as their mental and physical abilities, to their fullest potential;

(c) Enabling persons with disabilities to participate effectively in a free society.

2. In realizing this right, States Parties shall ensure that:

(a) Persons with disabilities are not excluded from the general education system on the basis of disability, and that children with disabilities are not excluded from free and compulsory primary education, or from secondary education, on the basis of disability;

(b) Persons with disabilities can access an inclusive, quality and free primary education and secondary education on an equal basis with others in the communities in which they live;

(c) Reasonable accommodation of the individual's requirements is provided;

(d) Persons with disabilities receive the support required, within the general education system, to facilitate their effective education;

(e) Effective individualized support measures are provided in environments that maximize academic and social development, consistent with the goal of full inclusion.

3. States Parties shall enable persons with disabilities to learn life and social development skills to facilitate their full and equal participation in education and as members of the community. To this end, States Parties shall take appropriate measures, including:

(a) Facilitating the learning of Braille, alternative script, augmentative and alternative modes, means and formats of communication and orientation and mobility skills, and facilitating peer support and mentoring;

(b) Facilitating the learning of sign language and the promotion of the linguistic identity of the deaf community;

(c) Ensuring that the education of persons, and in particular children, who are blind, deaf or deafblind, is delivered in the most appropriate languages and modes and means of communication for the individual, and in environments which maximize academic and social development.

4. In order to help ensure the realization of this right, States Parties shall take appropriate measures to employ teachers, including teachers with disabilities, who are qualified in sign language and/or Braille, and to train professionals and staff who work at all levels of education. Such training shall incorporate disability awareness and the use of appropriate augmentative and alternative modes, means and formats of communication, educational techniques and materials to support persons with disabilities.

5. States Parties shall ensure that persons with disabilities are able to access general tertiary education, vocational training, adult education and lifelong learning without discrimination and on an equal basis with others. To this end, States Parties shall ensure that reasonable accommodation is provided to persons with disabilities.

Article 25

Health

States Parties recognize that persons with disabilities have the right to the enjoyment of the highest attainable standard of health without discrimination on the basis of disability. States Parties shall take all appropriate measures to ensure access for persons with disabilities to health services that are gender-sensitive, including health-related rehabilitation. In particular, States Parties shall:

(a) Provide persons with disabilities with the same range, quality and standard of free or affordable health care and programmes as provided to other persons, including in the area of sexual and reproductive health and population-based public health programmes;

(b) Provide those health services needed by persons with disabilities specifically because of their disabilities, including early identification and intervention as appropriate, and services designed to minimize and prevent further disabilities, including among children and older persons;

(c) Provide these health services as close as possible to people's own communities, including in rural areas;

(d) Require health professionals to provide care of the same quality to persons with disabilities as to others, including on the basis of free and informed consent by, inter alia, raising awareness of the human rights, dignity, autonomy and needs of persons with disabilities through training and the promulgation of ethical standards for public and private health care;

(e) Prohibit discrimination against persons with disabilities in the provision of health insurance, and life insurance where such insurance is permitted by national law, which shall be provided in a fair and reasonable manner;

(f) Prevent discriminatory denial of health care or health services or food and fluids on the basis of disability.

Article 26

Habilitation and rehabilitation

1. States Parties shall take effective and appropriate measures, including through peer support, to enable persons with disabilities to attain and maintain maximum independence,

full physical, mental, social and vocational ability, and full inclusion and participation in all aspects of life. To that end, States Parties shall organize, strengthen and extend comprehensive habilitation and rehabilitation services and programmes, particularly in the areas of health, employment, education and social services, in such a way that these services and programmes:

(a) Begin at the earliest possible stage, and are based on the multidisciplinary assessment of individual needs and strengths;

(b) Support participation and inclusion in the community and all aspects of society, are voluntary, and are available to persons with disabilities as close as possible to their own communities, including in rural areas.

2. States Parties shall promote the development of initial and continuing training for professionals and staff working in habilitation and rehabilitation services.

3. States Parties shall promote the availability, knowledge and use of assistive devices and technologies, designed for persons with disabilities, as they relate to habilitation and rehabilitation.

Article 27

Work and employment

1. States Parties recognize the right of persons with disabilities to work, on an equal basis with others; this includes the right to the opportunity to gain a living by work freely chosen or accepted in a labour market and work environment that is open, inclusive and accessible to persons with disabilities. States Parties shall safeguard and promote the realization of the right to work, including for those who acquire a disability during the course of employment, by taking appropriate steps, including through legislation, to, inter alia:

(a) Prohibit discrimination on the basis of disability with regard to all matters concerning all forms of employment, including conditions of recruitment, hiring and employment, continuance of employment, career advancement and safe and healthy working conditions;

(b) Protect the rights of persons with disabilities, on an equal basis with others, to just and favourable conditions of work, including equal opportunities and equal remuneration for work of equal value, safe and healthy working conditions, including protection from harassment, and the redress of grievances;

(c) Ensure that persons with disabilities are able to exercise their labour and trade union rights on an equal basis with others;

(d) Enable persons with disabilities to have effective access to general technical and vocational guidance programmes, placement services and vocational and continuing training;

(e) Promote employment opportunities and career advancement for persons with disabilities in the labour market, as well as assistance in finding, obtaining, maintaining and returning to employment;

(f) Promote opportunities for self-employment, entrepreneurship, the development of cooperatives and starting one's own business;

(g) Employ persons with disabilities in the public sector;

(h) Promote the employment of persons with disabilities in the private sector through appropriate policies and measures, which may include affirmative action programmes, incentives and other measures;

(i) Ensure that reasonable accommodation is provided to persons with disabilities in the workplace;

(j) Promote the acquisition by persons with disabilities of work experience in the open labour market;

(k) Promote vocational and professional rehabilitation, job retention and return-to-work programmes for persons with disabilities.

2. States Parties shall ensure that persons with disabilities are not held in slavery or in servitude, and are protected, on an equal basis with others, from forced or compulsory labour.

Article 28

Adequate standard of living and social protection

1. States Parties recognize the right of persons with disabilities to an adequate standard of living for themselves and their families, including adequate food, clothing and housing, and to the continuous improvement of living conditions, and shall take appropriate steps to safeguard and promote the realization of this right without discrimination on the basis of disability.

2. States Parties recognize the right of persons with disabilities to social protection and to the enjoyment of that right without discrimination on the basis of disability, and shall take appropriate steps to safeguard and promote the realization of this right, including measures:

(a) To ensure equal access by persons with disabilities to clean water services, and to ensure access to appropriate and affordable services, devices and other assistance for disability-related needs;

(b) To ensure access by persons with disabilities, in particular women and girls with disabilities and older persons with disabilities, to social protection programmes and poverty reduction programmes;

(c) To ensure access by persons with disabilities and their families living in situations of poverty to assistance from the State with disability-related expenses, including adequate training, counselling, financial assistance and respite care;

(d) To ensure access by persons with disabilities to public housing programmes;

(e) To ensure equal access by persons with disabilities to retirement benefits and programmes.

Article 29

Participation in political and public life

States Parties shall guarantee to persons with disabilities political rights and the opportunity to enjoy them on an equal basis with others, and shall undertake to:

(a) Ensure that persons with disabilities can effectively and fully participate in political and public life on an equal basis with others, directly or through freely chosen representatives, including the right and opportunity for persons with disabilities to vote and be elected, inter alia, by:

(i) Ensuring that voting procedures, facilities and materials are appropriate, accessible and easy to understand and use;

(ii) Protecting the right of persons with disabilities to vote by secret ballot in elections and public referendums without intimidation, and to stand for elections, to effectively hold office and perform all public functions at all levels of government, facilitating the use of assistive and new technologies where appropriate;

(iii) Guaranteeing the free expression of the will of persons with disabilities as electors and to this end, where necessary, at their request, allowing assistance in voting by a person of their own choice;

(b) Promote actively an environment in which persons with disabilities can effectively and fully participate in the conduct of public affairs, without discrimination and on an equal basis with others, and encourage their participation in public affairs, including:

(i) Participation in non-governmental organizations and associations concerned with the public and political life of the country, and in the activities and administration of political parties;

(ii) Forming and joining organizations of persons with disabilities to represent persons with disabilities at international, national, regional and local levels.

Article 30

Participation in cultural life, recreation, leisure and sport

1. States Parties recognize the right of persons with disabilities to take part on an equal basis with others in cultural life, and shall take all appropriate measures to ensure that persons with disabilities:

(a) Enjoy access to cultural materials in accessible formats;

(b) Enjoy access to television programmes, films, theatre and other cultural activities, in accessible formats;

(c) Enjoy access to places for cultural performances or services, such as theatres, museums, cinemas, libraries and tourism services, and, as far as possible, enjoy access to monuments and sites of national cultural importance.

2. States Parties shall take appropriate measures to enable persons with disabilities to have the opportunity to develop and utilize their creative, artistic and intellectual potential, not only for their own benefit, but also for the enrichment of society.

3. States Parties shall take all appropriate steps, in accordance with international law, to ensure that laws protecting intellectual property rights do not constitute an unreasonable or discriminatory barrier to access by persons with disabilities to cultural materials.

4. Persons with disabilities shall be entitled, on an equal basis with others, to recognition and support of their specific cultural and linguistic identity, including sign languages and deaf culture.

5. With a view to enabling persons with disabilities to participate on an equal basis with others in recreational, leisure and sporting activities, States Parties shall take appropriate measures:

(a) To encourage and promote the participation, to the fullest extent possible, of persons with disabilities in mainstream sporting activities at all levels;

(b) To ensure that persons with disabilities have an opportunity to organize, develop and participate in disability-specific sporting and recreational activities and, to this end, encourage the provision, on an equal basis with others, of appropriate instruction, training and resources;

(c) To ensure that persons with disabilities have access to sporting, recreational and tourism venues;

(d) To ensure that children with disabilities have equal access with other children to participation in play, recreation and leisure and sporting activities, including those activities in the school system;

(e) To ensure that persons with disabilities have access to services from those involved in the organization of recreational, tourism, leisure and sporting activities.

Article 31

Statistics and data collection

1. States Parties undertake to collect appropriate information, including statistical and research data, to enable them to formulate and implement policies to give effect to the present Convention. The process of collecting and maintaining this information shall:

(a) Comply with legally established safeguards, including legislation on data protection, to ensure confidentiality and respect for the privacy of persons with disabilities;

(b) Comply with internationally accepted norms to protect human rights and fundamental freedoms and ethical principles in the collection and use of statistics.

2. The information collected in accordance with this article shall be disaggregated, as appropriate, and used to help assess the implementation of States Parties' obligations under the present Convention and to identify and address the barriers faced by persons with disabilities in exercising their rights.

3. States Parties shall assume responsibility for the dissemination of these statistics and ensure their accessibility to persons with disabilities and others.

Article 32

International cooperation

1. States Parties recognize the importance of international cooperation and its promotion, in support of national efforts for the realization of the purpose and objectives of the present Convention, and will undertake appropriate and effective measures in this regard, between and among States and, as appropriate, in partnership with relevant international and regional organizations and civil society, in particular organizations of persons with disabilities. Such measures could include, inter alia:

(a) Ensuring that international cooperation, including international development programmes, is inclusive of and accessible to persons with disabilities;

(b) Facilitating and supporting capacity-building, including through the exchange and sharing of information, experiences, training programmes and best practices;

(c) Facilitating cooperation in research and access to scientific and technical knowledge;

(d) Providing, as appropriate, technical and economic assistance, including by facilitating access to and sharing of accessible and assistive technologies, and through the transfer of technologies.

2. The provisions of this article are without prejudice to the obligations of each State Party to fulfil its obligations under the present Convention.

Article 33

National implementation and monitoring

1. States Parties, in accordance with their system of organization, shall designate one or more focal points within government for matters relating to the implementation of the present Convention, and shall give due consideration to the establishment or designation of a coordination mechanism within government to facilitate related action in different sectors and at different levels.

2. States Parties shall, in accordance with their legal and administrative systems, maintain, strengthen, designate or establish within the State Party, a framework, including one or

more independent mechanisms, as appropriate, to promote, protect and monitor implementation of the present Convention. When designating or establishing such a mechanism, States Parties shall take into account the principles relating to the status and functioning of national institutions for protection and promotion of human rights.

3. Civil society, in particular persons with disabilities and their representative organizations, shall be involved and participate fully in the monitoring process.

Article 34

Committee on the Rights of Persons with Disabilities

1. There shall be established a Committee on the Rights of Persons with Disabilities (hereafter referred to as "the Committee"), which shall carry out the functions hereinafter provided.

2. The Committee shall consist, at the time of entry into force of the present Convention, of twelve experts. After an additional sixty ratifications or accessions to the Convention, the membership of the Committee shall increase by six members, attaining a maximum number of eighteen members.

3. The members of the Committee shall serve in their personal capacity and shall be of high moral standing and recognized competence and experience in the field covered by the present Convention. When nominating their candidates, States Parties are invited to give due consideration to the provision set out in article 4.3 of the present Convention.

4. The members of the Committee shall be elected by States Parties, consideration being given to equitable geographical distribution, representation of the different forms of civilization and of the principal legal systems, balanced gender representation and participation of experts with disabilities.

5. The members of the Committee shall be elected by secret ballot from a list of persons nominated by the States Parties from among their nationals at meetings of the Conference of States Parties. At those meetings, for which two thirds of States Parties shall constitute a quorum, the persons elected to the Committee shall be those who obtain the largest number of votes and an absolute majority of the votes of the representatives of States Parties present and voting.

6. The initial election shall be held no later than six months after the date of entry into force of the present Convention. At least four months before the date of each election, the Secretary-General of the United Nations shall address a letter to the States Parties inviting them to submit the nominations within two months. The Secretary-General shall subsequently prepare a list in alphabetical order of all persons thus nominated, indicating the State Parties which have nominated them, and shall submit it to the States Parties to the present Convention.

7. The members of the Committee shall be elected for a term of four years. They shall be eligible for re-election once. However, the term of six of the members elected at the first election shall expire at the end of two years; immediately after the first election, the names of these six members shall be chosen by lot by the chairperson of the meeting referred to in paragraph 5 of this article.

8. The election of the six additional members of the Committee shall be held on the occasion of regular elections, in accordance with the relevant provisions of this article.

9. If a member of the Committee dies or resigns or declares that for any other cause she or he can no longer perform her or his duties, the State Party which nominated the member shall appoint another expert possessing the qualifications and meeting the re-

quirements set out in the relevant provisions of this article, to serve for the remainder of the term.

10. The Committee shall establish its own rules of procedure.

11. The Secretary-General of the United Nations shall provide the necessary staff and facilities for the effective performance of the functions of the Committee under the present Convention, and shall convene its initial meeting.

12. With the approval of the General Assembly, the members of the Committee established under the present Convention shall receive emoluments from United Nations resources on such terms and conditions as the Assembly may decide, having regard to the importance of the Committee's responsibilities.

13. The members of the Committee shall be entitled to the facilities, privileges and immunities of experts on mission for the United Nations as laid down in the relevant sections of the Convention on the Privileges and Immunities of the United Nations.

Article 35

Reports by States Parties

1. Each State Party shall submit to the Committee, through the Secretary-General of the United Nations, a comprehensive report on measures taken to give effect to its obligations under the present Convention and on the progress made in that regard, within two years after the entry into force of the present Convention for the State Party concerned.

2. Thereafter, States Parties shall submit subsequent reports at least every four years and further whenever the Committee so requests.

3. The Committee shall decide any guidelines applicable to the content of the reports.

4. A State Party which has submitted a comprehensive initial report to the Committee need not, in its subsequent reports, repeat information previously provided. When preparing reports to the Committee, States Parties are invited to consider doing so in an open and transparent process and to give due consideration to the provision set out in article 4.3 of the present Convention.

5. Reports may indicate factors and difficulties affecting the degree of fulfilment of obligations under the present Convention.

Article 36

Consideration of reports

1. Each report shall be considered by the Committee, which shall make such suggestions and general recommendations on the report as it may consider appropriate and shall forward these to the State Party concerned. The State Party may respond with any information it chooses to the Committee. The Committee may request further information from States Parties relevant to the implementation of the present Convention.

2. If a State Party is significantly overdue in the submission of a report, the Committee may notify the State Party concerned of the need to examine the implementation of the present Convention in that State Party, on the basis of reliable information available to the Committee, if the relevant report is not submitted within three months following the notification. The Committee shall invite the State Party concerned to participate in such examination. Should the State Party respond by submitting the relevant report, the provisions of paragraph 1 of this article will apply.

3. The Secretary-General of the United Nations shall make available the reports to all States Parties.

4. States Parties shall make their reports widely available to the public in their own countries and facilitate access to the suggestions and general recommendations relating to these reports.

5. The Committee shall transmit, as it may consider appropriate, to the specialized agencies, funds and programmes of the United Nations, and other competent bodies, reports from States Parties in order to address a request or indication of a need for technical advice or assistance contained therein, along with the Committee's observations and recommendations, if any, on these requests or indications.

Article 37

Cooperation between States Parties and the Committee

1. Each State Party shall cooperate with the Committee and assist its members in the fulfilment of their mandate.

2. In its relationship with States Parties, the Committee shall give due consideration to ways and means of enhancing national capacities for the implementation of the present Convention, including through international cooperation.

Article 38

Relationship of the Committee with other bodies

In order to foster the effective implementation of the present Convention and to encourage international cooperation in the field covered by the present Convention:

(a) The specialized agencies and other United Nations organs shall be entitled to be represented at the consideration of the implementation of such provisions of the present Convention as fall within the scope of their mandate. The Committee may invite the specialized agencies and other competent bodies as it may consider appropriate to provide expert advice on the implementation of the Convention in areas falling within the scope of their respective mandates. The Committee may invite specialized agencies and other United Nations organs to submit reports on the implementation of the Convention in areas falling within the scope of their activities;

(b) The Committee, as it discharges its mandate, shall consult, as appropriate, other relevant bodies instituted by international human rights treaties, with a view to ensuring the consistency of their respective reporting guidelines, suggestions and general recommendations, and avoiding duplication and overlap in the performance of their functions.

Article 39

Report of the Committee

The Committee shall report every two years to the General Assembly and to the Economic and Social Council on its activities, and may make suggestions and general recommendations based on the examination of reports and information received from the States Parties. Such suggestions and general recommendations shall be included in the report of the Committee together with comments, if any, from States Parties.

Article 40

Conference of States Parties

1. The States Parties shall meet regularly in a Conference of States Parties in order to consider any matter with regard to the implementation of the present Convention.

2. No later than six months after the entry into force of the present Convention, the Conference of the States Parties shall be convened by the Secretary-General of the United Nations. The subsequent meetings shall be convened by the Secretary-General of the United Nations biennially or upon the decision of the Conference of States Parties.

Article 41

Depositary

The Secretary-General of the United Nations shall be the depositary of the present Convention.

Article 42

Signature

The present Convention shall be open for signature by all States and by regional integration organizations at United Nations Headquarters in New York as of 30 March 2007.

Article 43

Consent to be bound

The present Convention shall be subject to ratification by signatory States and to formal confirmation by signatory regional integration organizations. It shall be open for accession by any State or regional integration organization which has not signed the Convention.

Article 44

Regional integration organizations

1. "Regional integration organization" shall mean an organization constituted by sovereign States of a given region, to which its member States have transferred competence in respect of matters governed by this Convention. Such organizations shall declare, in their instruments of formal confirmation or accession, the extent of their competence with respect to matters governed by this Convention. Subsequently, they shall inform the depositary of any substantial modification in the extent of their competence.

2. References to "States Parties" in the present Convention shall apply to such organizations within the limits of their competence.

3. For the purposes of article 45, paragraph 1, and article 47, paragraphs 2 and 3, any instrument deposited by a regional integration organization shall not be counted.

4. Regional integration organizations, in matters within their competence, may exercise their right to vote in the Conference of States Parties, with a number of votes equal to the number of their member States that are Parties to this Convention. Such an organization shall not exercise its right to vote if any of its member States exercises its right, and vice versa.

Article 45

Entry into force

1. The present Convention shall enter into force on the thirtieth day after the deposit of the twentieth instrument of ratification or accession.

2. For each State or regional integration organization ratifying, formally confirming or acceding to the Convention after the deposit of the twentieth such instrument, the Convention shall enter into force on the thirtieth day after the deposit of its own such instrument.

Article 46

Reservations

1. Reservations incompatible with the object and purpose of the present Convention shall not be permitted.

2. Reservations may be withdrawn at any time.

Article 47

Amendments

1. Any State Party may propose an amendment to the present Convention and submit it to the Secretary-General of the United Nations. The Secretary-General shall communicate any proposed amendments to States Parties, with a request to be notified whether they favour a conference of States Parties for the purpose of considering and deciding upon the proposals. In the event that, within four months from the date of such communication, at least one third of the States Parties favour such a conference, the Secretary-General shall convene the conference under the auspices of the United Nations. Any amendment adopted by a majority of two thirds of the States Parties present and voting shall be submitted by the Secretary-General to the General Assembly for approval and thereafter to all States Parties for acceptance.

2. An amendment adopted and approved in accordance with paragraph 1 of this article shall enter into force on the thirtieth day after the number of instruments of acceptance deposited reaches two thirds of the number of States Parties at the date of adoption of the amendment. Thereafter, the amendment shall enter into force for any State Party on the thirtieth day following the deposit of its own instrument of acceptance. An amendment shall be binding only on those States Parties which have accepted it.

3. If so decided by the Conference of States Parties by consensus, an amendment adopted and approved in accordance with paragraph 1 of this article which relates exclusively to articles 34, 38, 39 and 40 shall enter into force for all States Parties on the thirtieth day after the number of instruments of acceptance deposited reaches two thirds of the number of States Parties at the date of adoption of the amendment.

Article 48

Denunciation

A State Party may denounce the present Convention by written notification to the Secretary-General of the United Nations. The denunciation shall become effective one year after the date of receipt of the notification by the Secretary-General.

Article 49

Accessible format

The text of the present Convention shall be made available in accessible formats.

Article 50

Authentic texts

The Arabic, Chinese, English, French, Russian and Spanish texts of the present Convention shall be equally authentic.

In witness thereof the undersigned plenipotentiaries, being duly authorized thereto by their respective Governments, have signed the present Convention.

* * *

Questions for Discussion

1. Do you feel that this text is well-drafted? Why or why not? Are there issues that you feel are missing?

2. What methods are available to enforce the convention? How does the convention interact with local or national human rights laws?

3. What could be done to increase awareness about the convention?

The following document, found at http://www.whitehouse.gov/the-press-office/ remarks-president-rights-persons-with-disabilities-proclamation-signing, reports President Obama's remarks when signing the convention. Note that the U.S. has not ratified the convention.

Remarks by President Obama on Signing of U.N. Convention on the Rights of Persons with Disabilities Proclamation

East Room
July 24, 2009 5:58 P.M. EDT

THE PRESIDENT: Thank you. Please, everybody be seated. Thank you. First of all, how about my Secretary of State? (Applause.) Give it up for Senator Hillary Clinton. She is doing an unbelievable job. She's traveling all around the world delivering a message that America is back and ready to lead. And everywhere she goes she is representing us with grace and strength and we are very fortunate to have her.

I'm also lucky to have an outstanding Attorney General in Eric Holder—(applause)—so I wanted to make sure that we thank him for being here. My Secretary of Labor, who is committed to these issues, Hilda Solis. (Applause.) We've got a couple of governors in the house, at least I see one of them over here, Governor David Paterson of New York. (Applause.) And I think that Christine Gregoire was here—there she is, right here—from Washington State. (Applause.)

I want to thank the outstanding members of Congress who are on the stage. Senator Dan Inouye, Representative Steny Hoyer, Representative Robert Andrews, Representative James Sensenbrenner, Representative Jim Langevin. Thank you so much. Please give them a big round of applause. (Applause.)

And not on the stage, but extraordinarily important are three key figures who helped to get the original ADA passed. I want to acknowledge them. First of all, not able to attend, but this guy is a fierce warrior on behalf of the disabilities community, Tom Harkin. (Applause.) He couldn't be here, but give him a round of applause. (Applause.) Another person who could not be here but was instrumental in guiding the passage of this landmark legislation, Bob Dole, but his wonderful partner, Elizabeth Dole, Senator Elizabeth Dole is here, so please give her a round of applause on behalf of Bob Dole. (Applause.) And Attorney General and somebody who worked very hard on this issue, Richard Thornburgh. Please give him a big round of applause. (Applause.) Where's Richard? There he is.

Well, welcome to the White House. We are thrilled to have you all here for an historic announcement regarding our global commitment to fundamental human rights for persons with disabilities. I'm also honored to mark the anniversary of a historic piece of civil rights legislation with so many of the people who helped make it possible, and I'd like to reflect on that for a few moments.

I'm reminded today of my father-in-law—some of you have heard his story—Fraser Robinson. He was Michelle's hero—when you talk to her about her dad even today she just lights up. He was a vibrant and athletic man who provided for his family as a shift worker at a water treatment plant in Chicago. And in his early 30s, he was diagnosed with multiple sclerosis. And even as it progressed, even as he struggled to get dressed in the morning and used two canes to get himself to work every day, despite the fact that he had to wake up a little bit earlier and work a little harder to overcome the barriers he faced every day—he never complained. He never asked for special treatment. He just wanted to be given the opportunity to do right by his family. Never missed a day of work. Would have trouble buttoning his own shirts, but he would make sure that he woke up in time to do it.

And by the time I met him he would struggle with those two canes, but even if he had to go over a bumpy patch of grass to watch his son's ball games or go up a flight of stairs so that he could see his daughter dance, he would do it. This was before the ADA passed. And I think about him all the time when I think about these issues.

It's a reminder of the very promise of the ADA. Nineteen years ago this weekend, Democrats and Republicans, advocates and ordinary Americans, came together here at the White House to watch President George H.W. Bush sign the ADA into law. Folks traveled from all across America to witness a milestone in the long march to achieve equal opportunity for all.

But like all great movements, this one did not begin or end in Washington, D.C. It began in small towns and big cities across this country. It began with people like Fraser Robinson showing that they can be full contributors to society regardless of the lack of awareness of others. It began when people refused to accept a second-class status in America. It began when they not only refused to accept the way the world saw them, but also the way they had seen themselves.

And when quiet acts of persistence and perseverance were coupled with vocal acts of advocacy, a movement grew, and people marched and organized and testified. And parents of children with disabilities asked why their children, who had the same hopes and dreams as children everywhere else, were left out and left behind. And wounded veterans came home from war only to find that, despite their sacrifice for America, they now felt excluded from America's promise.

We had a little meeting before we came out and Tony Coelho, who was instrumental on this issue, spoke in just incredibly moving terms about what it meant for him to be an epileptic and the fact that discrimination was rife—he was rejected from the priesthood because that was considered unacceptable; he was rejected from the Army because that was considered unacceptable.

Those experiences could have just been internalized and people could have felt doubt, but instead it became a source of strength. And step by step, progress was won. Laws were changed. Americans with disabilities were finally guaranteed the right to vote—a right that only carries real meaning when you can enter the voting booth to cast that vote. Folks were extended certain protections from discrimination, and given the needed rehabilitation and training to go to the job. And even though we still have a long way to go with regard to education, children with disabilities were no longer excluded, no longer kept separate, and then no longer denied the opportunity to learn the same skills in the same classroom as other children.

Now, even two decades ago, too many barriers still stood. Too many Americans suffered under segregation and discrimination. Americans with disabilities were still measured by what folks thought they couldn't do—not by what can. Employers often assumed disabled meant unable. Millions of Americans with disabilities were eager to work, but couldn't find a job. An employer could have told a person with a disability, "No, we don't hire your kind." That person then could have tried to find recourse at the courthouse, only to find that she couldn't enter the building—and wouldn't find a receptive audience even if she did.

What was needed was a bill of rights for persons with disabilities, and that's what the ADA was. It was a formal acknowledgment that Americans with disabilities are Americans first, and they are entitled to the same rights and freedoms as everybody else: a right to belong and participate fully in the American experience; a right to dignity and respect in the workplace and beyond; the freedom to make of our lives what we will.

In a time when so many doubted that people with disabilities could participate in our society, contribute to our economy, or support their families, the ADA assumed they could. Americans with disabilities didn't ask for charity or demand special treatment— they only wanted a fair shot at opportunity. They didn't want to be isolated, they wanted to be integrated; not dependent, but independent. And allowing all Americans to engage in our society and our economy is in our national interest, especially now, when we all have a part to play to build a new foundation for America's lasting prosperity.

So the ADA showed the world our full commitment to the rights of people with disabilities—and now we have an opportunity to live up to that commitment. Today, 650 million people—10 percent of the world's population—live with a disability. In developing countries, 90 percent of children with disabilities don't attend school. Women and girls with disabilities are too often subject to deep discrimination.

Disability rights aren't just civil rights to be enforced here at home; they're universal rights to be recognized and promoted around the world. And that's why I'm proud to announce that next week, the United States of America will join 140 other nations in signing the United Nations Convention on the Rights of Persons with Disabilities—(applause)—the first new human rights convention of the 21st century.

This extraordinary treaty calls on all nations to guarantee rights like those afforded under the ADA. It urges equal protection and equal benefits before the law for all citizens; reaffirms the inherent dignity and worth and independence of all persons with disabilities worldwide. I've instructed Ambassador Susan Rice to formally sign the Convention at the United Nations in New York next week, and I hope that the Senate can give swift consideration and approval to the Convention once I submit it for their advice and consent.

And even as we extend our commitment to persons for—with disabilities around the world, we're working to deepen that commitment here at home. We've lifted the ban on stem cell research. We've reauthorized the Children's Health Insurance Program, continuing coverage for 7 million children and covering an additional 4 million children in need, including children with disabilities. I was proud to sign the landmark Christopher and Dana Reeve Paralysis Act, the first piece of comprehensive legislation specifically aimed at addressing the challenges that are faced by Americans living with paralysis.

We've nearly doubled funding for the Individuals with Disabilities Education Act. (Applause.) We're strengthening anti-discrimination enforcement at the Justice Department. We're creating a new special assistant position at the Department of Transportation just to focus on accessible transportation. (Applause.) We've launched the "Year of Community

Living" to affirm the fundamental right of people with disabilities to live with dignity and respect wherever they choose. (Applause.)

So I'm proud of the progress we've made. But I'm not satisfied, and I know you aren't either. Until every American with a disability can learn in their local public school in the manner best for them, until they can apply for a job without fear of discrimination, and live and work independently in their communities if that's what they choose, we've got more work to do. As long as we as a people still too easily succumb to casual discrimination or fear of the unfamiliar, we've still got more work to do.

As we continue that work, we should remember just who it was that the ADA was all about. It was about the young girl with cerebral palsy who just wanted to see a movie at her local theater, but was turned away. It was about the Vietnam veteran who returned home paralyzed and said he felt like he'd fought for everyone but himself. It was about the thousands of people with disabilities who showed up at public hearings all across the country to share their stories of exclusion and injustice—and the millions more they spoke up for.

Because they did, we live in a country where our children can grow up with every opportunity to learn and compete, where our disabled veterans returning from Iraq and Afghanistan can navigate public places more easily, and where 54 million Americans with disabilities can pursue their full measure of happiness. And what we've learned—what we've—what they have taught us is that it is far more noble and worthwhile and valuable to make it possible for these Americans to live up to their full potential. Because when we do, it makes all of us more whole, it makes our union more perfect, it makes the United States of America strong.

Every morning, I walk along the Colonnade that connects this house to the Oval Office. And there's something you might not notice unless you're really paying attention—and I'll be honest, when I take that walk, I usually have a lot on my mind. (Laughter.) But there's a gentle slope at the end of that Colonnade, a ramp that was installed during a renovation of the West Wing 75 years ago, making it much easier for one of my predecessors to get to work.

Back then, fear and prejudice towards Americans with disabilities was the norm, but most Americans didn't even know that President Roosevelt had a disability. That means that what most Americans also didn't know was that President Roosevelt's disability made absolutely no difference to his ability to renew our confidence, or rescue our economy, and mobilize our greatest generation to save our way of life.

Let me correct that—I actually think it did make a difference in a positive way. What he told us was that "further progress must of necessity depend on a deeper understanding on the part of every man and woman in the United States." I believe we're getting there. And today, because more than one in five Americans live with a disability—and chances are, the rest of us love somebody with one—we remember our obligation to ensuring their every chance to pursue the American Dream. We celebrate the courage and commitment of those who brought us to this point. And we recommit ourselves to building a world free of unnecessary barriers and full of that deeper understanding.

So thank you, all, for being here. Let's sign this bill. (Applause.)

(The proclamation is signed.)

THE PRESIDENT: There we go. (Applause.) Thank you, everybody.

END 6:15 P.M. EDT

* * *

Questions for Discussion

1. What do you think of the President's discourse in this address?

2. Do you agree with the President's assessment of the impact of the ADA and IDEA? Why or why not?

3. Why do you think the U.S. has not yet ratified the convention? Do you think it should? Is there any current movement in that direction?

4. What is the function of the Committee on the Rights of Persons with Disabilities? If you were thinking of Americans to sit on that committee, whom might you nominate?

———————

For Further Reading

Michelle Diament, "Obama Urges Senate to Ratify Disability Treaty," retrieved June 11, 2012 at http://www.disabilityscoop.com/2012/05/18/obama-urges-senate-treaty/15654/.

"Ratify Now FAQ," retrieved May 15, 2012 at http://www.ratifynow.org/ratifynow-faq/.

Arlene S. Kanter, *The Promise and Challenge of the United Nations Convention on the Rights of Persons with Disabilities*, 34 Syracuse J. Int'l L. & Com 287 (2007).

Don MacKay, *The U.N. Convention on the Rights of Persons with Disabilities*, 34 Syracuse J. Int'l L. & Com (2007).

Discussion 11

Institutional Conditions &
The *Wyatt* Case

Untitled by Tanya Temkin.

Recommended Background Reading

Estelle v. Gamble, 429 US 97 (1976) (discussing conditions in jails).

Youngberg v. Romeo, 102 S.Ct. 2452 (1982) (setting forth the "professional judgment" standard).

Levy, Robert M. and Leonard S. Rubenstein. *The Rights of People with Mental Disabilities*, chapter VII, "Rights in Everyday Life in Institutions and the Community." Southern Illinois University Press: Carbondale, 1996.

Readings for Class Discussion

The following is a landmark opinion from 1972, and an additional opinion in the same case.

Wyatt v. Stickney

344 F.Supp. 373 (N.D. Al. 1972)

ORDER AND DECREE

JOHNSON, Chief Judge.

This class action originally was filed on October 23, 1970, in behalf of patients involuntarily confined for mental treatment purposes at Bryce Hospital, Tuscaloosa, Alabama. On March 12, 1971, in a formal opinion and decree, this Court held that these involuntarily committed patients "unquestionably have a constitutional right to receive such individual treatment as will give each of them a realistic opportunity to be cured or to improve his or her mental condition." The Court further held that patients at Bryce were being denied their right to treatment and that defendants, per their request, would be allowed six months in which to raise the level of care at Bryce to the constitutionally required minimum. *Wyatt v. Stickney*, 325 F.Supp. 781 (M.D.Ala.1971). In this decree, the Court ordered defendants to file reports defining the mission and functions of Bryce Hospital, specifying the objective and subjective standards required to furnish adequate care to the treatable mentally ill and detailing the hospital's progress toward the implementation of minimum constitutional standards. Subsequent to this order, plaintiffs, by motion to amend granted August 12, 1971, enlarged their class to include patients involuntarily confined for mental treatment at Searcy Hospital and at Partlow State School and Hospital for the mentally retarded.

On September 23, 1971, defendants filed their final report, from which this Court concluded on December 10, 1971, 334 F.Supp. 1341, that defendants had failed to promulgate and implement a treatment program satisfying minimum medical and constitutional requisites. Generally, the Court found that defendants' treatment program was deficient in three fundamental areas. It failed to provide: (1) a humane psychological and physical environment, (2) qualified staff in numbers sufficient to administer adequate treatment and (3) individualized treatment plans. More specifically, the Court found that many conditions, such as nontherapeutic, uncompensated work assignments, and the absence of any semblance of privacy, constituted dehumanizing factors contributing to the degeneration of the patients' self-esteem. The physical facilities at Bryce were overcrowded and plagued by fire and other emergency hazards. The Court found also that most staff members were poorly trained and that staffing ratios were so inadequate as to render the administration of effective treatment impossible.

The Court concluded, therefore, that whatever treatment was provided at Bryce was grossly deficient and failed to satisfy minimum medical and constitutional standards. Based upon this conclusion, the Court ordered that a formal hearing be held at which the parties and amici would have the opportunity to submit proposed standards for constitutionally adequate treatment and to present expert testimony in support of their proposals.

Pursuant to this order, a hearing was held at which the foremost authorities on mental health in the United States appeared and testified as to the minimum medical and constitutional requisites for public institutions, such as Bryce and Searcy, designed to treat the mentally ill. At this hearing, the parties and amici submitted their proposed standards, and now have filed briefs in support of them. Moreover, the parties and amici have stipulated to a broad spectrum of conditions they feel are mandatory for a constitutionally acceptable minimum treatment program. This Court, having considered the evidence in the case, as well as the briefs, proposed standards and stipulations of the parties, has concluded that the standards set out in Appendix A to this decree are medical and constitutional minimums. Consequently, the Court will order their implementation. In so ordering, however, the Court emphasizes that these standards are, indeed, both medical and constitutional minimums and should be viewed as such. The Court urges that once this order is effectuated, defendants not become complacent and self-satisfied. Rather, they should dedicate themselves to providing physical conditions and treatment programs at Alabama's mental institutions that substantially exceed medical and constitutional minimums.

In addition to asking that their proposed standards be effectuated, plaintiffs and amici have requested other relief designed to guarantee the provision of constitutional and humane treatment. Pursuant to one such request for relief, this Court has determined that it is appropriate to order the initiation of human rights committees to function as standing committees of the Bryce and Searcy facilities. The Court will appoint the members of these committees who shall have review of all research proposals and all rehabilitation programs, to ensure that the dignity and the human rights of patients are preserved. The committees also shall advise and assist patients who allege that their legal rights have been infringed or that the Mental Health Board has failed to comply with judicially ordered guidelines. At their discretion, the committees may consult appropriate, independent specialists who shall be compensated by the defendant Board. Seven members shall comprise the human rights committee for each institution, the names and addresses of whom are set forth in Appendix B to this decree. Those who serve on the committees shall be paid on a per diem basis and be reimbursed for travel expenses at the same rate as members of the Alabama Board of Mental Health.

This Court will reserve ruling upon other forms of relief advocated by plaintiffs and amici, including their prayer for the appointment of a master and a professional advisory committee to oversee the implementation of the court-ordered minimum constitutional standards. Federal courts are reluctant to assume control of any organization, but especially one operated by a state. This reluctance, combined with defendants' expressed intent that this order will be implemented forthwith and in good faith, causes the Court to withhold its decision on these appointments. Nevertheless, defendants, as well as the other parties and amici in this case, are placed on notice that unless defendants do comply satisfactorily with this order, the Court will be obligated to appoint a master.

Because the availability of financing may bear upon the implementation of this order, the Court is constrained to emphasize at this juncture that a failure by defendants to comply with this decree cannot be justified by a lack of operating funds. As previously established by this Court:

> "There can be no legal (or moral) justification for the State of Alabama's failing to afford treatment—and adequate treatment from a medical standpoint—to the several thousand patients who have been civilly committed to Bryce's for treatment purposes. To deprive any citizen of his or her liberty upon the altruistic theory that the confinement is for humane therapeutic reasons and then fail to provide adequate treatment violates the very fundamentals of due process." *Wyatt v. Stickney*, 325 F.Supp. at 785.

From the above, it follows consistently, of course, that the unavailability of neither funds, nor staff and facilities, will justify a default by defendants in the provision of suitable treatment for the mentally ill. Despite the possibility that defendants will encounter financial difficulties in the implementation of this order, this Court has decided to reserve ruling also upon plaintiffs' motion that defendant Mental Health Board be directed to sell or encumber portions of its land holdings in order to raise funds.[1]

Similarly, this Court will reserve ruling on plaintiffs' motion seeking an injunction against the treasurer and the comptroller of the State authorizing expenditures for nonessential State functions, and on other aspects of plaintiffs' requested relief designed to ameliorate the financial problems incident to the implementation of this order. The Court stresses, however, the extreme importance and the grave immediacy of the need for proper funding of the State's public mental health facilities. The responsibility for appropriate funding ultimately must fall, of course, upon the State Legislature and, to a lesser degree, upon the defendant Mental Health Board of Alabama. For the present time, the Court will defer to those bodies in hopes that they will proceed with the realization and understanding that what is involved in this case is not representative of ordinary governmental functions such as paving roads and maintaining buildings. Rather, what is so inextricably intertwined with how the Legislature and Mental Health Board respond to the revelations of this litigation is the very preservation of human life and dignity. Not only are the lives of the patients currently confined at Bryce and Searcy at stake, but also at issue are the well-being and security of every citizen of Alabama. As is true in the case of any disease, no one is immune from the peril of mental illness. The problem, therefore, cannot be overemphasized and a prompt response from the Legislature, the Mental Health Board and other responsible State officials, is imperative.

In the event, though, that the Legislature fails to satisfy its well-defined constitutional obligation, and the Mental Health Board, because of lack of funding or any other legally insufficient reason, fails to implement fully the standards herein ordered, it will be necessary for the Court to take affirmative steps, including appointing a master, to ensure that proper funding is realized and that adequate treatment is available for the mentally ill of Alabama.[2]

This Court now must consider that aspect of plaintiffs' motion of March 15, 1972, seeking an injunction against further commitments to Bryce and Searcy until such time as adequate treatment is supplied in those hospitals. Indisputably, the evidence in this case reflects that no treatment program at the Bryce-Searcy facilities approaches constitutional standards. Nevertheless, because of the alternatives to commitment commonly utilized in Alabama, as well as in other states, the Court is fearful that granting plaintiffs' request at the present time would serve only to punish and further deprive Alabama's mentally ill.

Finally, the Court has determined that this case requires the awarding of a reasonable attorneys' fee to plaintiffs' counsel. The basis for the award and the amount thereof will be considered and treated in a separate order. The fee will be charged against the defendants as a part of the court costs in this case.

---

1. The evidence presented in this case reflects that the land holdings and other assets of the defendant Board are extensive.

2. The Court understands and appreciates that the Legislature is not due back in regular session until May, 1973. Nevertheless, special sessions of the Legislature are frequent occurrences in Alabama, and there has never been a time when such a session was more urgently required. If the Legislature does not act promptly to appropriate the necessary funding for mental health, the Court will be compelled to grant plaintiffs' motion to add various State officials and agencies as additional parties to this litigation, and to utilize other avenues of fund raising.

To assist the Court in its determination of how to proceed henceforth, defendants will be directed to prepare and file a report within six months from the date of this decree detailing the implementation of each standard herein ordered. This report shall be comprehensive and shall include a statement of the progress made on each standard not yet completely implemented, specifying the reasons for incomplete performance. The report shall include also a statement of the financing secured since the issuance of this decree and of defendants' plans for procuring whatever additional financing might be required.

Upon the basis of this report and other available information, the Court will evaluate defendants' work and, in due course, determine the appropriateness of appointing a master and of granting other requested relief.

Accordingly, it is the order, judgment and decree of this Court:

1. That defendants be and they are hereby enjoined from failing to implement fully and with dispatch each of the standards set forth in Appendix A attached hereto and incorporated as a part of this decree;

2. That human rights committees be and are hereby designated and appointed. The members thereof are listed in Appendix B attached hereto and incorporated herein. These committees shall have the purposes, functions, and spheres of operation previously set forth in this order. The members of the committees shall be paid on a per diem basis and be reimbursed for travel expenses at the same rate as members of the Alabama Board of Mental Health;

3. That defendants, within six months from this date, prepare and file with this Court a report reflecting in detail the progress on the implementation of this order. This report shall be comprehensive and precise, and shall explain the reasons for incomplete performance in the event the defendants have not met a standard in its entirety. The report also shall include a financial statement and an up-to-date timetable for full compliance.

4. That the court costs incurred in this proceeding, including a reasonable attorneys' fee for plaintiffs' lawyers, be and they are hereby taxed against the defendants;

5. That jurisdiction of this cause be and the same is hereby specifically retained.

It is further ordered that ruling on plaintiffs' motion for further relief, including the appointment of a master, filed March 15, 1972, be and the same is hereby reserved.

APPENDIX A

MINIMUM CONSTITUTIONAL STANDARDS FOR ADEQUATE TREATMENT OF THE MENTALLY ILL

I. Definitions:

a. "Hospital"—Bryce and Searcy Hospitals.

b. "Patients"—all persons who are now confined and all persons who may in the future be confined at Bryce and Searcy Hospitals pursuant to an involuntary civil commitment procedure.

c. "Qualified Mental Health Professional"—

(1) a psychiatrist with three years of residency training in psychiatry;

(2) a psychologist with a doctoral degree from an accredited program;

(3) a social worker with a master's degree from an accredited program and two years of clinical experience under the supervision of a Qualified Mental Health Professional;

(4) a registered nurse with a graduate degree in psychiatric nursing and two years of clinical experience under the supervision of a Qualified Mental Health Professional.

d. "Non-Professional Staff Member"—an employee of the hospital, other than a Qualified Mental Health Professional, whose duties require contact with or supervision of patients.

II. Humane Psychological and Physical Environment

1. Patients have a right to privacy and dignity.

2. Patients have a right to the least restrictive conditions necessary to achieve the purposes of commitment.

3. No person shall be deemed incompetent to manage his affairs, to contract, to hold professional or occupational or vehicle operator's licenses, to marry and obtain a divorce, to register and vote, or to make a will solely by reason of his admission or commitment to the hospital.

4. Patients shall have the same rights to visitation and telephone communications as patients at other public hospitals, except to the extent that the Qualified Mental Health Professional responsible for formulation of a particular patient's treatment plan writes an order imposing special restrictions. The written order must be renewed after each periodic review of the treatment plan if any restrictions are to be continued. Patients shall have an unrestricted right to visitation with attorneys and with private physicians and other health professionals.

5. Patients shall have an unrestricted right to send sealed mail. Patients shall have an unrestricted right to receive sealed mail from their attorneys, private physicians, and other mental health professionals, from courts, and government officials. Patients shall have a right to receive sealed mail from others, except to the extent that the Qualified Mental Health Professional responsible for formulation of a particular patient's treatment plan writes an order imposing special restrictions on receipt of sealed mail. The written order must be renewed after each periodic review of the treatment plan if any restrictions are to be continued.

6. Patients have a right to be free from unnecessary or excessive medication. No medication shall be administered unless at the written order of a physician. The superintendent of the hospital and the attending physician shall be responsible for all medication given or administered to a patient. The use of medication shall not exceed standards of use that are advocated by the United States Food and Drug Administration. Notation of each individual's medication shall be kept in his medical records. At least weekly the attending physician shall review the drug regimen of each patient under his care. All prescriptions shall be written with a termination date, which shall not exceed 30 days. Medication shall not be used as punishment, for the convenience of staff, as a substitute for program, or in quantities that interfere with the patient's treatment program.

7. Patients have a right to be free from physical restraint and isolation. Except for emergency situations, in which it is likely that patients could harm themselves or others and in which less restrictive means of restraint are not feasible, patients may be physically restrained or placed in isolation only on a Qualified Mental Health Professional's written order which explains the rationale for such action. The written order may be entered only after the Qualified Mental Health Professional has personally seen the patient concerned and evaluated whatever episode or situation is said to call for restraint or isolation. Emergency use of restraints or isolation shall be for no more than one hour, by which time a Qualified Mental Health Professional shall have been consulted and shall have entered an appropriate order in writing. Such written order shall be effective for no more than 24 hours and must be renewed if restraint and isolation are to be continued. While in restraint or

isolation the patient must be seen by qualified ward personnel who will chart the patient's physical condition (if it is compromised) and psychiatric condition every hour. The patient must have bathroom privileges every hour and must be bathed every 12 hours.

8. Patients shall have a right not to be subjected to experimental research without the express and informed consent of the patient, if the patient is able to give such consent, and of his guardian or next of kin, after opportunities for consultation with independent specialists and with legal counsel.

Such proposed research shall first have been reviewed and approved by the institution's Human Rights Committee before such consent shall be sought. Prior to such approval the Committee shall determine that such research complies with the principles of the Statement on the Use of Human Subjects for Research of the American Association on Mental Deficiency and with the principles for research involving human subjects required by the United States Department of Health, Education and Welfare for projects supported by that agency.

9. Patients have a right not to be subjected to treatment procedures such as lobotomy, electro-convulsive treatment, adversive reinforcement conditioning or other unusual or hazardous treatment procedures without their express and informed consent after consultation with counsel or interested party of the patient's choice.

10. Patients have a right to receive prompt and adequate medical treatment for any physical ailments.

11. Patients have a right to wear their own clothes and to keep and use their own personal possessions except insofar as such clothes or personal possessions may be determined by a Qualified Mental Health Professional to be dangerous or otherwise inappropriate to the treatment regimen.

12. The hospital has an obligation to supply an adequate allowance of clothing to any patients who do not have suitable clothing of their own. Patients shall have the opportunity to select from various types of neat, clean, and seasonable clothing. Such clothing shall be considered the patient's throughout his stay in the hospital.

13. The hospital shall make provision for the laundering of patient clothing.

14. Patients have a right to regular physical exercise several times a week. Moreover, it shall be the duty of the hospital to provide facilities and equipment for such exercise.

15. Patients have a right to be outdoors at regular and frequent intervals, in the absence of medical considerations.

16. The right to religious worship shall be accorded to each patient who desires such opportunities. Provisions for such worship shall be made available to all patients on a nondiscriminatory basis. No individual shall be coerced into engaging in any religious activities.

17. The institution shall provide, with adequate supervision, suitable opportunities for the patient's interaction with members of the opposite sex.

18. The following rules shall govern patient labor:

A. Hospital Maintenance

No patient shall be required to perform labor which involves the operation and maintenance of the hospital or for which the hospital is under contract with an outside organization. Privileges or release from the hospital shall not be conditioned upon the performance of labor covered by this provision. Patients may voluntarily engage in such labor if the labor is compensated in accordance with the minimum wage laws of the Fair Labor Standards Act, 29 U.S.C. § 206 as amended, 1966.

B. Therapeutic Tasks and Therapeutic Labor

(1) Patients may be required to perform therapeutic tasks which do not involve the operation and maintenance of the hospital, provided the specific task or any change in assignment is:

> a. An integrated part of the patient's treatment plan and approved as a therapeutic activity by a Qualified Mental Health Professional responsible for supervising the patient's treatment; and

> b. Supervised by a staff member to oversee the therapeutic aspects of the activity.

(2) Patients may voluntarily engage in therapeutic labor for which the hospital would otherwise have to pay an employee, provided the specific labor or any change in labor assignment is:

> a. An integrated part of the patient's treatment plan and approved as a therapeutic activity by a Qualified Mental Health Professional responsible for supervising the patient's treatment; and

> b. Supervised by a staff member to oversee the therapeutic aspects of the activity; and

> c. Compensated in accordance with the minimum wage laws of the Fair Labor Standards Act, 29 U.S.C. § 206 as amended, 1966.

C. Personal Housekeeping

Patients may be required to perform tasks of a personal housekeeping nature such as the making of one's own bed.

D. Payment to patients pursuant to these paragraphs shall not be applied to the costs of hospitalization.

19. Physical Facilities

A patient has a right to a humane psychological and physical environment within the hospital facilities. These facilities shall be designed to afford patients with comfort and safety, promote dignity, and ensure privacy. The facilities shall be designed to make a positive contribution to the efficient attainment of the treatment goals of the hospital.

A. Resident Unit

The number of patients in a multi-patient room shall not exceed six persons. There shall be allocated a minimum of 80 square feet of floor space per patient in a multi-patient room. Screens or curtains shall be provided to ensure privacy within the resident unit. Single rooms shall have a minimum of 100 square feet of floor space. Each patient will be furnished with a comfortable bed with adequate changes of linen, a closet or locker for his personal belongings, a chair, and a bedside table.

B. Toilets and Lavatories

There will be one toilet provided for each eight patients and one lavatory for each six patients. A lavatory will be provided with each toilet facility. The toilets will be installed in separate stalls to ensure privacy, will be clean and free of odor, and will be equipped with appropriate safety devices for the physically handicapped.

C. Showers

There will be one tub or shower for each 15 patients. If a central bathing area is provided, each shower area will be divided by curtains to ensure privacy. Showers and tubs will be equipped with adequate safety accessories.

D. Day Room

The minimum day room area shall be 40 square feet per patient. Day rooms will be attractive and adequately furnished with reading lamps, tables, chairs, television and other recreational facilities.

They will be conveniently located to patients' bedrooms and shall have outside windows. There shall be at least one day room area on each bedroom floor in a multi-story hospital. Areas used for corridor traffic cannot be counted as day room space, nor can a chapel with fixed pews be counted as a day room area.

E. Dining Facilities

The minimum dining room area shall be ten square feet per patient. The dining room shall be separate from the kitchen and will be furnished with comfortable chairs and tables with hard, washable surfaces.

F. Linen Servicing and Handling

The hospital shall provide adequate facilities and equipment for handling clean and soiled bedding and other linen. There must be frequent changes of bedding and other linen, no less than every seven days to assure patient comfort.

G. Housekeeping

Regular housekeeping and maintenance procedures which will ensure that the hospital is maintained in a safe, clean, and attractive condition will be developed and implemented.

H. Geriatric and Other Nonambulatory Mental Patients

There must be special facilities for geriatric and other nonambulatory patients to assure their safety and comfort, including special fittings on toilets and wheelchairs. Appropriate provision shall be made to permit nonambulatory patients to communicate their needs to staff.

I. Physical Plant

(1) Pursuant to an established routine maintenance and repair program, the physical plant shall be kept in a continuous state of good repair and operation in accordance with the needs of the health, comfort, safety and well-being of the patients.

(2) Adequate heating, air conditioning and ventilation systems and equipment shall be afforded to maintain temperatures and air changes which are required for the comfort of patients at all times and the removal of undesired heat, steam and offensive odors. Such facilities shall ensure that the temperature in the hospital shall not exceed 83°F nor fall below 68°F.

(3) Thermostatically controlled hot water shall be provided in adequate quantities and maintained at the required temperature for patient or resident use (110°F at the fixture) and for mechanical dishwashing and laundry use (180°F at the equipment).

(4) Adequate refuse facilities will be provided so that solid waste, rubbish and other refuse will be collected and disposed of in a manner which will prohibit transmission of disease and not create a nuisance or fire hazard or provide a breeding place for rodents and insects.

(5) The physical facilities must meet all fire and safety standards established by the state and locality. In addition, the hospital shall meet such provisions of the Life Safety Code of the National Fire Protection Association (21st edition, 1967) as are applicable to hospitals.

19A. The hospital shall meet all standards established by the state for general hospitals, insofar as they are relevant to psychiatric facilities.

20. Nutritional Standards

Patients, except for the non-mobile, shall eat or be fed in dining rooms. The diet for patients will provide at a minimum the Recommended Daily Dietary Allowances as developed by the National Academy of Sciences. Menus shall be satisfying and nutritionally adequate to provide the Recommended Daily Dietary Allowances. In developing such menus, the hospital will utilize the Low Cost Food Plan of the Department of Agriculture. The hospital will not spend less per patient for raw food, including the value of donated food, than the most recent per person costs of the Low Cost Food Plan for the Southern Region of the United States, as compiled by the United States Department of Agriculture, for appropriate groupings of patients, discounted for any savings which might result from institutional procurement of such food. Provisions shall be made for special therapeutic diets and for substitutes at the request of the patient, or his guardian or next of kin, in accordance with the religious requirements of any patient's faith. Denial of a nutritionally adequate diet shall not be used as punishment.

III. Qualified Staff in Numbers Sufficient to Administer Adequate Treatment

21. Each Qualified Mental Health Professional shall meet all licensing and certification requirements promulgated by the State of Alabama for persons engaged in private practice of the same profession elsewhere in Alabama. Other staff members shall meet the same licensing and certification requirements as persons who engage in private practice of their speciality elsewhere in Alabama.

22. a. All Non-Professional Staff Members who have not had prior clinical experience in a mental institution shall have a substantial orientation by Qualified Mental Health Professionals trained in particular disciplines.

b. Staff members on all levels shall have regularly scheduled in-service training by members of other disciplines.

23. Each Non-Professional Staff Member shall be Court upon a clear and convincing demonstration that under the direct supervision of a Qualified Mental the proposed deviation from this staffing structure Health Professional. will enhance the treatment of the patients.

24. Staffing Ratios

The hospital shall have the following minimum numbers of treatment personnel per 250 patients.

Classification	Number of Employees
Unit Director	1
Psychiatrist (3 years' residency training in psychiatry)	2
MD (Registered physicians)	4
Nurses (RN)	12
Licensed Practical Nurses	6
Aide III	6
Aide II	16
Aide I	70
Hospital Orderly	10
Clerk Stenographer II	3
Clerk Typist II	3

Unit Administrator	1
Administrative Clerk	1
Psychologist (Ph.D.) (doctoral degree from accredited program)	1
Psychologist (M.A.)	1
Psychologist (B.S.)	2
Social Worker (MSW) (from accredited program)	2
Social Worker (B.A.)	5
Patient Activity Therapist (M.S.)	1
Patient Activity Aide	10
Mental Health Technician	10
Dental Hygienist	1
Chaplain	.5
Vocational Rehabilitation Counselor	1
Volunteer Services Worker	1
Mental Health Field Representative	1
Dietitian	1
Food Service Supervisor	1
Cook II	2
Cook I	3
Food Service Worker	15
Vehicle Driver	1
Housekeeper	10
Messenger	1
Maintenance Repairman	2

IV. Individualized Treatment Plans

25. Each patient shall have a comprehensive physical and mental examination and review of behavioral status within 48 hours after admission to the hospital.

26. Each patient shall have an individualized treatment plan. This plan shall be developed by appropriate qualified Mental Health Professionals, including a psychiatrist, and implemented as soon as possible-in any event no later than five days after the patient's admission.

Each individualized treatment plan shall contain:

a. a statement of the nature of the specific problems and specific needs of the patient;

b. a statement of the least restrictive treatment conditions necessary to achieve the purposes of commitment;

c. a description of intermediate and long-range treatment goals, with a projected timetable for their attainment;

d. a statement and rationale for the plan of treatment for achieving these intermediate and long-range goals;

e. a specification of staff responsibility and a description of proposed staff involvement with the patient in order to attain these treatment goals;

f. criteria for release to less restrictive treatment conditions, and criteria for discharge;

g. a notation of any therapeutic tasks and labor to be performed by the patient in accordance with Standard 18.

27. As part of his treatment plan, each patient shall have an individualized post-hospitalization plan. This plan shall be developed by a Qualified Mental Health Professional as soon as practicable after the patient's admission to the hospital.

28. In the interests of continuity of care, whenever possible, one Qualified Mental Health Professional (who need not have been involved with the development of the treatment plan) shall be responsible for supervising the implementation of the treatment plan, integrating the various aspects of the treatment program and recording the patient's progress. This Qualified Mental Health Professional shall also be responsible for ensuring that the patient is released, where appropriate, into a less restrictive form of treatment.

29. The treatment plan shall be continuously reviewed by the Qualified Mental Health Professional responsible for supervising the implementation of the plan and shall be modified if necessary. Moreover, at least every 90 days, each patient shall receive a mental examination from, and his treatment plan shall be reviewed by, a Qualified Mental Health Professional other than the professional responsible for supervising the implementation of the plan.

30. In addition to treatment for mental disorders, patients confined at mental health institutions also are entitled to and shall receive appropriate treatment for physical illnesses such as tuberculosis. In providing medical care, the State Board of Mental Health shall take advantage of whatever community-based facilities are appropriate and available and shall coordinate the patient's treatment for mental illness with his medical treatment.

31. Complete patient records shall be kept on the ward in which the patient is placed and shall be available to anyone properly authorized in writing by the patient. These records shall include:

a. Identification data, including the patient's legal status;

b. A patient history, including but not limited to:

(1) family data, educational background, and employment record;

(2) prior medical history, both physical and mental, including prior hospitalization;

c. The chief complaints of the patient and the chief complaints of others regarding the patient;

d. An evaluation which notes the onset of illness, the circumstances leading to admission, attitudes, behavior, estimate of intellectual functioning, memory functioning, orientation, and an inventory of the patient's assets in descriptive, not interpretative, fashion;

e. A summary of each physical examination which describes the results of the examination;

f. A copy of the individual treatment plan and any modifications thereto;

g. A detailed summary of the findings made by the reviewing Qualified Mental Health Professional after each periodic review of the treatment plan which analyzes the successes and failures of the treatment program and directs whatever modifications are necessary;

h. A copy of the individualized post-hospitalization plan and any modifications thereto, and a summary of the steps that have been taken to implement that plan;

i. A medication history and status, which includes the signed orders of the prescribing physician. Nurses shall indicate by signature that orders have been carried out;

j. A detailed summary of each significant contact by a Qualified Mental Health Professional with the patient;

k. A detailed summary on at least a weekly basis by a Qualified Mental Health Professional involved in the patient's treatment of the patient's progress along the treatment plan;

l. A weekly summary of the extent and nature of the patient's work activities described in Standard 18, *supra,* and the effect of such activity upon the patient's progress along the treatment plan;

m. A signed order by a Qualified Mental Health Professional for any restrictions on visitations and communication, as provided in Standards 4 and 5, *supra*;

n. A signed order by a Qualified Mental Health Professional for any physical restraints and isolation, as provided in Standard 7, *supra*;

o. A detailed summary of any extraordinary incident in the hospital involving the patient to be entered by a staff member noting that he has personal knowledge of the incident or specifying his other source of information, and initialed within 24 hours by a Qualified Mental Health Professional;

p. A summary by the superintendent of the hospital or his appointed agent of his findings after the 15-day review provided for in Standard 33 *infra.*

32. In addition to complying with all the other standards herein, a hospital shall make special provisions for the treatment of patients who are children and young adults.

These provisions shall include but are not limited to:

a. Opportunities for publicly supported education suitable to the educational needs of the patient. This program of education must, in the opinion of the attending Qualified Mental Health Professional, be compatible with the patient's mental condition and his treatment program, and otherwise be in the patient's best interest.

b. A treatment plan which considers the chronological, maturational, and developmental level of the patient;

c. Sufficient Qualified Mental Health Professionals, teachers, and staff members with specialized skills in the care and treatment of children and young adults;

d. Recreation and play opportunities in the open air where possible and appropriate residential facilities;

e. Arrangements for contact between the hospital and the family of the patient.

33. No later than 15 days after a patient is committed to the hospital, the superintendent of the hospital or his appointed, professionally qualified agent shall examine the committed patient and shall determine whether the patient continues to require hospitalization and whether a treatment plan complying with Standard 26 has been implemented. If the patient no longer requires hospitalization in accordance with the standards for commitment, or if a treatment plan has not been implemented, he must be released immediately unless he agrees to continue with treatment on a voluntary basis.

34. The Mental Health Board and its agents have an affirmative duty to provide adequate transitional treatment and care for all patients released after a period of involuntary con-

finement. Transitional care and treatment possibilities include, but are not limited to, psychiatric day care, treatment in the home by a visiting therapist, nursing home or extended care, out-patient treatment, and treatment in the psychiatric ward of a general hospital.

V. Miscellaneous

35. Each patient and his family, guardian, or next friend shall promptly upon the patient's admission receive written notice, in language he understands, of all the above standards for adequate treatment. In addition a copy of all the above standards shall be posted in each ward.

APPENDIX B

BRYCE HUMAN RIGHTS COMMITTEE [Editor's note: names omitted.]

Wyatt v. Sawyer

United States District Court, M.D. Alabama, Northern Division, 2000
MEMORANDUM OPINION

MYRON H. THOMPSON, District Judge.

In October 1999, as this case challenging conditions in the Alabama Mental Health and Mental Retardation System approached its 30th birthday, this court wrote with some optimism:

> "[I]t is apparent that this litigation is steadily progressing toward its final resolution. Contributing to these efforts, newly appointed Commissioner of Mental Health and Mental Retardation Kathy E. Sawyer has, as this court recently observed, directly addressed one of the primary concerns of the court: the past unwillingness of the Mental Health and Mental Retardation Department to address rather than hide serious problems. As this court stated in its order of October 7, 1999: 'Commissioner Sawyer has made clear that all problems will be "aired" and that all will be directly and forcefully addressed. Therefore, it appears now within sight that, under the leadership of Commissioner Sawyer, this litigation will come to an end in the near future, and certainly within her stint as Commissioner.'" *Wyatt v. Sawyer*, 190 F.R.D. 685, 689 (M.D.Ala.1999)

(Thompson, J.) (quoting *Wyatt v. Sawyer*, 67 F.Supp.2d 1331, 1358 (M.D.Ala.1999) (Thompson, J.)). Just a few months later, on January 20, 2000, the parties reached a settlement agreement, and, on January 27, filed a joint motion for judicial approval of the agreement. On May 4, 2000, the court conducted a fairness hearing, and, based on a close examination of the agreement, the objections and other responses filed by plaintiff-class members and other interested persons, and the testimony offered at the fairness hearing, the court entered an order the next day approving the agreement, and promised that a memorandum opinion would follow later. This is the promised opinion.

I. BACKGROUND

This litigation has traveled a long, winding, and often quite bumpy course, which the court has described at length in prior opinions and need not recount here. However, a brief overview of the case's general trajectory and major turning points will serve as a useful foundation for consideration of the matter currently before the court.

1970–1974: The first phase of this litigation featured "expansive and landmark opinions," *Wyatt*, 985 F.Supp. at 1361, of Judge Frank M. Johnson, Jr., finding "that conditions in the facilities operated by the Alabama Department of Mental Health and Mental Retardation violated patients' constitutional rights," id., and enjoining the defendants "to bring the facilities into compliance with certain minimum constitutional standards." Id. More specifically, in 1972, the court entered injunctions requiring the defendants to bring state facilities into compliance with certain minimum constitutional standards, now commonly referred to as the 'Wyatt standards,' see *Wyatt v. Stickney*, 344 F.Supp. 373 (M.D.Ala.1972) (standards for mentally ill) (Johnson, J.), aff'd in relevant part, 503 F.2d 1305 (5th Cir.1974); Wyatt v. Stickney, 344 F.Supp. 387 (M.D.Ala.1972) (standards for mentally retarded) (Johnson, J.), aff'd in relevant part, 503 F.2d 1305 (5th Cir.1974).

1975–1980: In the second phase, the parties focused on the defendants' non-compliance with these minimum constitutional standards. The plaintiffs and amicus curiae United States of America petitioned the court to appoint a special master or receiver to assure compliance, and both opposed a petition by the Governor of Alabama to be appointed as receiver of the State Mental Health and Mental Retardation System. Ultimately, following extensive hearings and appeals on the issue, the court appointed the Governor as receiver.

1981–1990: The plaintiffs triggered the third phase with their motion for sufficient state funding to ensure implementation of the Governor's plan of compliance with the *Wyatt* standards; in response, the Governor moved for termination of the receivership while the defendants moved to eliminate all of the *Wyatt* standards and to substitute in their place a requirement that the defendants achieve accreditation of the State's mental-illness facilities by the Joint Commission on the Accreditation of Healthcare Organizations (JCAHO) and certification of the mental-retardation facilities through Title XIX of the Social Security Act, 42 U.S.C.A. § 1396, et seq. The parties settled these conflicts, and, on September 22, 1986, this court approved a five-page consent decree which reflected a resolution of three issues, among others: (1) the defendants' desire to terminate court supervision of the state system; (2) the plaintiffs' concern about the continued viability of the *Wyatt* standards; and (3) the plaintiffs' efforts to focus the litigation on the provision of community facilities and programs and the placement of qualified patients in those facilities and programs. See *Wyatt v. Wallis*, 1986 WL 69194 (M.D.Ala. Sept. 22, 1986) (Thompson, J.).

1991–1997: The next round of litigation focused on the defendants' attempts to terminate this lawsuit upon a judicial finding that they had met their obligations under the 1986 consent decree. At the conclusion of a 35-day trial spanning several months in 1995, the court found that the defendants had acted in good faith with regard to some but not the whole 1986 consent decree, and it concluded that they should be released from the decree to the extent of their compliance with 17 of the mental-illness standards and 35 of the mental-retardation standards, as well as the requirement of JCAHO accreditation at all mental-illness facilities and Title XIX certification at all mental-retardation facilities. At this time the court also directed the parties to shift their focus to a standard-by-standard approach. See *Wyatt v. Rogers*, 985 F.Supp. 1356 (M.D.Ala.1997) (Thompson, J.).

1998–present: The parties devoted much of 1998 and 1999 to discovery, including facility inspections by the plaintiffs' experts, on disputed compliance issues, several of which were either resolved or narrowed for the trial that had been scheduled for May and June 2000. See, e.g., *Wyatt v. Rogers*, 1998 WL 213779 (M.D.Ala. Apr. 21, 1998); *Wyatt v. Rogers*, 1998 WL 264783 (M.D.Ala. May 14, 1998); *Wyatt v. Rogers*, 1998 WL 862920 (M.D.Ala. Dec.9, 1998); *Wyatt v. Sawyer*, 1999 WL 805285 (M.D.Ala.

Oct.4, 1999). Regularly scheduled status conferences with the court kept the parties focused. Negotiations intensified in 1999 when both parties retained settlement counsel independent of litigation counsel, which culminated in the settlement agreement now submitted for judicial approval.

II. SUMMARY OF THE SETTLEMENT AGREEMENT

The settlement agreement executed on January 20, 2000, proposes to dissolve the 1986 consent decree, settle the compliance disputes which have persisted since 1986, and finally bring to an end the federal court's long-term monitoring and control of the Alabama Department of Mental Health and Mental Retardation. Included in the settlement agreement are important provisions which guarantee that the State of Alabama will maintain its commitment to minimum constitutional standards for treatment and habilitation and significantly enhance and expand its services to the mentally ill and mentally retarded. Following is a summary of the settlement agreement's most significant provisions.

Accreditation: All of the State's mental-illness facilities are accredited by the JCAHO and all of the developmental centers are certified by the Health Care Financing Administration. These accreditations and certifications will be maintained.

Advocacy Program: The State Mental Health and Mental Retardation Department will maintain a trained staff of at least 26 full-time equivalent advocates for the effective operation of its internal advocacy program, which is designed to educate persons about client rights, to review or investigate complaints of rights violations, and to monitor conditions in mental illness and mental-retardation facilities and in certified community programs.

Census Reduction: During the three-year period between October 1, 2000, and September 30, 2003, the department shall reduce by a total of 300 the number of extended-care mental-illness beds at Bryce Hospital, Searcy Hospital, and Thomasville Mental Health Rehabilitation Center and by a total of 300 the number of extended-care mental-retardation beds at Partlow Developmental Center, Albert P. Brewer Developmental Center, J.S. Tarwater Developmental Center, and Lurleen B. Wallace Developmental Center. The settlement agreement does not require closure of any state facilities.

Community Placement: By September 1, 2000, the department shall develop a plan, to be implemented between October 1, 2000, and September 30, 2003, to identify consumers to be out-placed from mental-illness facilities and to increase community-based placements and community-based services for them. By the same deadlines, the department shall also develop and implement a plan to identify consumers to be out-placed from mental-retardation facilities and to increase community-based placements and community-based services for them.

Public Education: The Department of Mental Health and Mental Retardation and the Alabama Disabilities Advocacy Program ("ADAP") have agreed to develop and implement a comprehensive, statewide plan to enhance the public's appreciation for the abilities, rights, and needs of the persons with mental illness and the persons with mental retardation who are served by the department.

Quality Improvement: The department has incorporated into its Policy and Procedures Manual compliance mechanisms and structures related to client treatment, care, rights, and services required by the 1986 consent decree and the Wyatt standards for adequate treatment of persons with mental illness and for adequate habilitation of persons with mental retardation. The settlement agreement requires the department to maintain its system-wide policy commitment to these minimum constitutional standards, to require that all facilities utilize the Policy Manual and expressly adhere to and implement all of these policies. Additionally, the settlement agreement requires that the department continue operating its Continuous Quality Improvement ("CQI") systems in order to monitor the quality of mental-health and mental-retardation services provided to persons served in state-operated psychiatric facilities and developmental centers. The department must maintain at least one full-time, trained CQI employee in the mental-illness divisional office, in the mental-retardation divisional office, and at each facility.

Safety and Protection: When there are allegations of abuse and neglect in mental-health and mental-retardation facilities, the department must conduct timely investigations, using standard operating procedures and trained employees. ADAP shall have a representative on each facility's investigation committee, and the department must provide specified notice and reports to ADAP concerning deaths, major personal injuries, suspected neglect, mistreatment, sexual assault, exploitation or abuse involving a departmental consumer.

Treatment and Habilitation: The department must develop, review, and permit ADAP to have input concerning individualized treatment plans for each resident at Bryce, Searcy, and Thomasville facilities.

The department agrees to hire qualified professional consultants to study, and to recommend policies and procedures regarding treatment and discharge plans for all juveniles and for adults who have special needs relating to these diagnoses: a dual diagnosis of mental illness and mental retardation; traumatic or organic brain injury; self-injurious behavior; HIV/AIDS/ARC; deafness, blindness, or serious physical impairments. The department also agrees to hire qualified professional consultants to study and to make recommendations concerning the use of seclusion and restraint for consumers with self-injurious behavior at Bryce and Searcy Hospitals and the use and administration of psychiatric medications.

For residents at Wallace, Partlow, Brewer, and Tarwater facilities, the department must develop, implement, and permit ADAP to have input concerning individualized habilitation plans. The department also agrees to secure professional assessments and recommendations regarding both systemic and clinical matters relevant to the habilitation of persons with mental retardation.

Term of the Settlement Agreement: The settlement agreement became effective immediately upon entry of the court's May 5, 2000, order. The projected ending date for the agreement is not later than September 30, 2003, which is the final deadline for the State to complete certain obligations undertaken in the agreement. The court retains jurisdiction over this case for the limited purpose of enforcing the settlement agreement, and the agreement outlines procedures to resolve any compliance dispute.

III. DISCUSSION

Judicial policy favors voluntary settlement as the means of resolving class-action cases. See *Cotton v. Hinton*, 559 F.2d 1326, 1331 (5th Cir.1977). However, "the settlement process is more susceptible than the adversarial process to certain types of abuse and, as a result, a court has a heavy, independent duty to ensure that the settlement is 'fair, adequate, and reasonable.'" *Paradise v. Wells*, 686 F.Supp. 1442, 1444 (M.D.Ala.1988) (Thompson, J.) (quoting *Pettway v. American Cast Iron Pipe Co.*, 576 F.2d 1157, 1214 (5th Cir.1978), cert. denied, 439 U.S. 1115, 99 S.Ct. 1020, 59 L.Ed.2d 74 (1979)). This abuse can occur when, for example, "the interests of the class lawyer and the class may diverge, or a majority of the class may 'wrongfully compromise, betray or 'sell-out' the interests of the minority.'" Id. Besides evaluating the fairness of the settlement agreement, the court has the duty to make sure that the settlement is not illegal or against public policy. See *Piambino v. Bailey*,

757 F.2d 1112, 1119 (11th Cir.1985), cert. denied, 476 U.S. 1169, 106 S.Ct. 2889, 90 L.Ed.2d 976 (1986).

A. Class Notice

As a preliminary matter, Rule 23(e) of the Federal Rules of Civil Procedure requires that the court ensure that all interested parties were informed of the settlement and had the opportunity to voice their objections. This issue is particularly salient in the instant litigation because so many members of the plaintiff class lack the capacity to advocate effectively on their own behalf. The court must therefore take special care to ensure not only that the class members themselves, but also their guardians, advocates, and other interested persons were notified of the proposed settlement agreement and given adequate opportunities to voice their opinions on the class members' behalf. The court-approved notice was directed to "patients, residents, clients, and consumers served by the Alabama Department of Mental Health and Mental Retardation, their families, and legal guardians; individuals, groups, and organizations involved in advocacy or support for the rights of Alabama's citizens with mental illness and mental retardation; and interested members of the general public."

The notice advised that the settlement agreement proposed "to dissolve the 1986 consent decree, settle the compliance disputes which have persisted since 1986, and finally bring to an end the federal court's long-term monitoring and control of the Alabama Department of Mental Health and Mental Retardation." In plain and simple language, the notice highlighted substantive terms and requirements, stated the projected effective date and ending date for the settlement agreement, and outlined the federal court's role. Most importantly, the notice detailed alternative means for reviewing and securing copies of the complete agreement, identified official representatives for questions, specified the process for making objections, stated the date, time, and place for the fairness hearing, and authorized discretionary attendance or participation in the fairness hearing.

As shown by the joint evidentiary submission regarding notice of settlement agreement and timely filed responses, the parties disseminated the notices as stipulated in the court-approved plan. Notices were posted prominently in the living areas of all facilities covered by this agreement, and notices were hand-delivered to approximately 1,083 patients and residents while departmental advocates consulted with another 450 for whom hand-delivery was deemed clinically inappropriate. Mail-delivery notice was given to 695 persons identified as legal guardians or responsible parties for patients and residents while 17 notices were mailed to consumer and advocacy organizations with statewide constituencies.

The evidence also reflects newspaper publication of the notice in each of the cities housing a mental-health facility. Additionally, Commissioner Sawyer and counsel for the plaintiff class maximized the interested public's understanding of the settlement agreement with their joint presentations to advocacy groups in these same cities along with several individual presentations across the State as well as news releases and written communications.

The adequacy of the notice is reflected, in part, by the substantial number of written responses timely filed before the fairness hearing and by the attendance and participation at the fairness hearing. Forty-five comments were timely received, nine of which are in the nature of objections. The court also conducted a fairness hearing on May 4, 2000, which many class members and their advocates attended, and at which many took the opportunity to voice objections to the proposed settlement. The court concludes that these measures, taken together, were sufficient to satisfy the notice requirements of Rule 23(e).

B. Plaintiffs' Objections and Comments

"In determining whether a settlement is fair, adequate, and reasonable, the obvious first place a court should look is to the views of the class itself." *Paradise*, 686 F.Supp. at 1444. Determining those views and quantifying them in a manner that enables the court to determine whether the settlement is fair is, however, not always easy. The court should be careful "not [to] allow a majority, no matter how large, to impose its decision on the minority," *Pettway*, 576 F.2d at 1217; the court should be certain "that the burden of the settlement is not shifted arbitrarily to a small group of class members." Id. However, where the settlement provides for structural changes, with each class member having a virtually equivalent stake in the changes, and where there are no conflicts of interest among class members or among definable groups within the class, then the decision to approve the settlement "may appropriately be described as an intrinsically 'class' decision in which majority sentiments should be given great weight." Id.

As noted above with respect to the notice issue, the court must take special care in this case to consider carefully the opinions of those who filed objections or otherwise responded to the notice of settlement agreement. This is because many of the class members, as consumers of mental-health services, are not well-equipped to advocate on their own behalf in this litigation. The court must therefore rely on family, friends, other advocates, and those class members who are capable of voicing their opinions to communicate the interests of those who cannot. For this reason, the court takes the opinions of these advocates very seriously.

The timely-filed comments in response to notice of the parties' settlement agreement reflect a substantial sentiment in favor of the settlement. As stated, of the 45 submissions, only nine are in the nature of objections, 10 are statements of support from consumer and advocacy organizations, 23 are letters of support from mental-health consumers and relatives, and three are too vague and generalized to categorize.

The objectors fall into three categories. First, three relatives of mental-illness or mental-retardation patients express alarm at the prospect of having their loved ones transferred from institutional facilities to community placements, fearing a reduced quality of care in the latter. A second category consists of three objectors whose concerns either lack specificity or relate only generally to the issues in controversy. The last category of objectors consists of three advocacy groups, and the court deems it appropriate to address their thoughtful concerns.

On behalf of the Patrons of Partlow, a support organization for 214 parents or guardians of Partlow residents, President William Haas first expresses a viewpoint with which the court and the parties cannot disagree: that the settlement should "promot[e] the best possible care and quality of life for the Partlow [and other plaintiff class] residents." His organization's chief objection is to the provision of the agreement that requires that "a specific number [300]" of "persons with mental retardation receiving services at the four state institutions will be transferred to community facilities" over the term of the agreement. His organization proposes that the number, 300, be replaced with this: "those individuals who would benefit from community placement in terms of receiving care, services, and security that are better than that which they are currently receiving in an institution."

Vandy J. Copeland, the second objector, is parent of a resident at Tarwater as well as president of two support groups, Friends of Tarwater and Advocates for the Retarded. His objection, which he characterized at the fairness hearing as a "concern" rather than a true "objection," echoes those of Mr. Haas. Believing that many residents of Tarwater receive excellent and appropriate services in that institution, Copeland is concerned about the push toward outplacement, and seeks "guidelines and protection" to ensure the safety of mental-health consumers and the appropriate use of the projected census reduction in state facilities.

In contrast to Haas and Copeland, who worry about the over-use of community placement, the Arc of Morgan County—an 180-member advocacy organization for persons with mental retardation and developmental disabilities—complains that the settlement should address community placement for all 650 mental-retardation residents rather than only the 300 targeted. An additional concern, shared by all three objectors, relates to the possibility that insufficient funding will doom the projected census reduction in facilities and community placements, and transitional services.

C. Judgment of Counsel

"In addressing whether a settlement is fair, adequate, and reasonable, a court should also consider the judgment of experienced counsel for the parties." *Paradise*, 686 F.Supp. at 1446. Here, counsel for the plaintiffs argue strongly in favor of approval of the settlement agreement, and their views carry great weight with the court. The plaintiffs' attorneys have a significant background in disability law, and especially in mental-health law. Each of the two attorneys who have been the plaintiffs' liaison counsel in the last 15 years has extensive experience in litigating, negotiating, and implementing structural reforms on behalf of individuals with disabilities in institutional settings. The parties' settlement counsel are also experienced counsel with reputable records in federal class-action litigation. No one has questioned in any manner these attorneys' dedication to the plaintiff class. Counsel for amicus curiae United States also supports the settlement agreement, and the court takes their views, supported by many years of experience in this type of litigation, very strongly into consideration.

D. Assessment of the Settlement Agreement

"Finally, with the above considerations in mind, the court should itself assess whether the consent decree is fair, adequate, and reasonable," *Paradise*, 686 F.Supp. at 1446, as well as legal. See id. at 1448. The court finds that the proposed settlement meets these standards. The agreement imposes requirements and provides avenues for the outplacement of Alabama's mental-health consumers into the community, while ensuring that such decisions are made on an individualized basis and with adequate safeguards of each consumer's health and safety. The agreement is supported by commitments from Governor Don Siegelman and Commissioner Sawyer to put the agreement in place and to secure the funding necessary to do so. The court is also reassured of the agreement's fairness by the role it affords both to the plaintiffs' families and guardians to participate in placement decisions for each patient, and to the plaintiffs' counsel to remain active in monitoring implementation efforts over the course of the next three years. Thus, while the court appreciates the concerns voiced by Mr. Haas and Mr. Copeland, the court is convinced by Commissioner Sawyer's representation that the figures of "300" in the settlement reflect a reasonable assessment of the number of patients that should be eligible for community placement and that the actual placement of a patient in a community facility will not be driven by numbers but rather will be based on an individual assessment and approved only when it is in the best interest of the patient. Finally, the court also finds that the settlement agreement complies with state and federal law.

IV. CONCLUSION

For the foregoing reasons, the court concluded that the proposed settlement agreement is fair, adequate, and reasonable, and the joint motion for judicial approval of this agreement and termination of the litigation was granted. An appropriate judgment approving the settlement and granting the motion was, therefore, entered on May 5, 2000.

* * *

Questions for Discussion

1. Why was the first opinion such a landmark decision? What do you think of the court's discourse? Did anything surprise you about the standards themselves?

2. What does the second piece show about the nature of class action litigation? What does it show about the nature of settlement agreements?

For Further Reading

"A Patient's Bill of Rights," American Hospital Association Management Advisory, retrieved May 15, 2012 at http://www.patienttalk.info/AHA-Patient_Bill_of_Rights.htm.

Civil Rights of Institutionalized Persons Act, 42 U.S.C. § 1997 et seq.

Shapiro, Joseph. *No Pity*, chapter 10, "Crossing the Luck Line."

Discussion 12

Seclusion and Restraints

Recommended Background Reading

Wyatt v. Stickney, 344 F.Supp. 373 (in this text at p. 192).
Wyatt v. Sawyer, 105 F.Supp.2d 1234 (in this text at p. 204).
Youngberg v. Romeo, 102 S.Ct. 2452 (1982).

Readings for Class Discussion

The Regulation of the Use of Seclusion and Restraints in Mental Disability Law

Professor Michael L. Perlin, New York Law School

I. Introduction

The past two decades have seen the development of a robust and contentious body of caselaw in the area of the right of institutionalized persons to refuse antipsychotic medication, an area of the law that has been the subject of intense judicial and academic scrutiny. On the other hand, there has been virtually *no* attention paid to the constitutional dimensions of the potential right to refuse other modalities of treatment—such as seclusion and restraint—that are frequently used in public psychiatric hospitals. Although the use of these methods of control diminished markedly with the advent of the "psychotropic drug era," they remain in regular use in virtually all large psychiatric hospital facilities.

Only once has the Supreme Court decided a case that presented a question of seclusion and restraint. And while that case—*Youngberg v. Romeo*—is perhaps the Court's most important decision on the overarching question of how professional liability is to be assessed in *all* institutional rights litigation, it has had (as I'll discuss later) remarkably little impact on subsequent developments in this specific subject-matter area.

On the other hand, a substantial body of case law has developed in the more traditional area of tort law as it applies to both the regulation of seclusion and restraint, and to claims alleging negligence in the *failure* to restrain. These cases are based mostly on standard legal principles that have developed over the centuries: principles involving standards of care, proximate cause, duty, and other factors familiar to anyone who has ever read a survey article about medical malpractice. And what is especially interesting here is that the constitutional principles that I've been discussing are virtually never mentioned in any of this litigation.

In fact, if you read all the reported seclusion and restraint cases decided in the past 15 years, you'll see that cases quickly cluster into categories that appear to have little in common with each other (save the fact that litigation was initiated when someone complained about a seclusion and restraint practice). Some are constitutional. Some are based on tort principles. Yet others are statutory (based on so-called state "Patients' Bills of Rights," legislation enacted to comport with a series of court cases that established a broad constitutional right to treatment for psychiatric inpatients). Some are individual; some are class-based. Some complain about the *fact* of seclusion or restraint; some about the way seclusion or restraint was carried out; at least two about how staff *taunted* a secluded patient; yet others complain about the failure to restrain (either by the non-restrained patient but, rather or by an individual who alleges that she was injured because of the failure to restrain). And the decisions in each "category" of these cases rarely allude to decisions in other "categories." And I haven't yet mentioned the Americans with Disabilities Act and its potential impact on all of this.

What I am going to do here is try to offer you a structure through which seclusion and restraint cases can be analyzed, and to suggest to you some overarching principles that apply to the different categories.

But that's not all I'm planning to do, because I believe that *this* explanation would only be half of an answer. I also want to try to shed some light on the more difficult (and, to me, at least), more interesting question of *why* has the law developed as it has? To answer this latter question, I need to look at other more difficult questions: What factors *really* matter to the fact-finders hearing seclusion and restraint cases? What *really* happens when a facility seeks to involuntarily seclude or restrain certain kinds of patients? What bundle of social attitudes *really* dominates the landscape upon which most of this litigation is brought? And, mostly, why do we *really* feel the way that we do about these issues?

In the remainder of my time, then, I will do the following: first, I will offer a brief history of the development of seclusion and restraint law, looking at the sources of the law, and the way that courts often weigh rights and remedies in right-to-refuse treatment cases of all sorts by considering a "continuum of intrusivity," and then locating seclusion and restraint on that continuum. Next, I will discuss the different major categories of cases that have been litigated (both those seeking to stop unwanted seclusion and/or restraint and those claiming that a failure to seclude or restrain caused the injury in question). Then, I will apply the concepts of sanism and pretextuality to this area of the law (and I will explain what these terms mean in a few minutes), and will reconsider it by an application of therapeutic jurisprudence principles. I will end by offering some modest conclusions.

II. Sources of regulation

The authority to regulate seclusion and restraint practice derives from a cluster of sources: the constitution, statutory law, and common law. This is, of course, not unique to this area of the law. but, given the disparate categories into which seclusion and restraint cases can be "slotted," it probably makes sense to spend just a few minutes discussing these sources to seek to clarify this significance.

First, seclusion and restraint practices in public psychiatric hospitals implicate the constitution. And, once implicated, the Constitution is relevant to a potential variety of different claims. It may be argued that as an aspect of a patient's *substantive* right to *treatment*, a facility must establish seclusion and restraint policies that limit the use of these methods to "prevent a patient from physically injuring himself/herself or others." It may be argued that, as a part of a patient's *substantive* right to *refuse* treatment, that a patient cannot be restrained or secluded unnecessarily or punitively or for the convenience of staff or where a less restrictive alternative is available, or "in a manner that causes undue physical discomfort, harm or pain to the patient." It may also be argued that as an aspect of a patient's *procedural* right to *due process*, that the patient has a right to some sort of notice or hearing prior to the imposition of seclusion and restraint, save, perhaps in emergency situations. And when the United States Supreme Court articulates a substantive or procedural constitutional right, a potentially aggrieved patient can seek redress (for what are generally called "constitutional torts") by filing suit under the federal Civil Rights Act (known to court buffs as "section 1983 actions").

Seclusion and restraint may also be governed or regulated by statutory provisions. In the wake of the first generation of Constitutional decisions in the early 1970's, most states enacted Patients' Bills of Rights so as to provide institutionalized individuals with basically the same panoply of civil and constitutional rights mandated by federal courts in such cases as *Wyatt v. Stickney*, the Alabama case that transformed institutional care, and had a "dramatic influence" on constitutional and case law developments in other jurisdictions. More recently, Congressional enactment of the Americans with Disabilities Act—banning discrimination against persons with mental disabilities in virtually every aspect of public and private life—provides yet another potential source of legislative regulation (though one that remains practically dormant to this day).

But the most significant regulation of seclusion and restraint practice comes from the common law source of tort law. To reduce this whole body of law to an index card, there are five basic elements in a negligence case: an act, a duty of care, a breach of duty, causation, and damages. To prevail, a plaintiff must thus show that the defendant's action—or inaction—breached a present of duty to care, exposing him to an unreasonable risk of harm, and that that breach was the proximate cause of the harm that he suffered. These principles are millennia old, and can obviously be used in cases involving both improper seclusion or, conversely, claims arising from a failure to seclude.

In short, there are a variety of potential legal sources of legal authority for "seclusion and restraint actions," and it is important to keep that "in memory" as I discuss the various decisions. It is also important to turn our attention to a "sidebar" issue that may provide some clues to how we assess legal standards in seclusion and restraint cases, and to the ultimate case outcomes: the vexing question of where this modality falls on a spectrum of psychiatric hospital treatments. How intrusive is it? Is it *more* intrusive than the administration of antipsychotic drugs? Less? The same? Is there a difference between the use of seclusion and the use of restraint (they are discussed virtually interchangeably in the legal literature)?

As you might expect, experts, bureaucrats and clinicians differ. Professor Dix assumes that forced medication is more intrusive than seclusion or restraint. Arizona state policies categorize emergency medication as less restrictive than seclusion; Dr. Soloff agrees. New Hampshire guidelines rate seclusion as less restrictive than physical restraints which are, in turn, less restrictive than drugs. A survey of California hospital staff revealed that medication was felt to be less restrictive than seclusion or restraint.

Making this problem even more difficult is the literature on staff and patient preference. A survey of doctors at the same hospital revealed a nearly 2–1 preference for medications rather than seclusion or restraint; these numbers were nearly identical to percentages in a poll of patients at a different California hospital. And nearly 3/4 of patients found restraints more restrictive than seclusion. Generally, staff and patients who rated seclusion or restraint as more intrusive found medications to be less physically intrusive, and to allow patients to remain in common hospital living areas and to participate in other treatment modalities. Those who found it less intrusive found it to be less intrusive and "more apt to lead to immediate control of violent behaviors."

Interestingly, as to the choice *between* seclusion and restraint, 38% of staff polled felt seclusion would be more effective and 62% rated restraints as more effective. Those who favored seclusion made that choice largely because it allowed patients to "release more energy than restraints," was less physically restrictive, and less "demeaning"; those who preferred restraints focused on the likelihood that restraint would better prevent physical injury and would prevent "escalation" more effectively than would seclusion.

And making it all even *more* complicated are the rate variances that have been found. Rates of usage at state hospitals range from 1.9% to 51%, at university hospitals from 4% to 36.6%, and at other facilities from 3.6% at a military hospital to 66% at the research unit of an NIMH facility. In addition, persons with diagnoses of mental retardation are more likely to be secluded or restrained than those without such a diagnosis. On the other hand, no differences were found in one study of usage rates between civil and forensic hospitals, although *restraints* were used more often in forensic cases while *seclusion* was more often used in civil cases.

Seclusion and restraint are ordered for a wide range of behaviors. The most important finding here is that violence is *not* cited as the most frequent precipitant of physical control. Three out of five uses of seclusion or restraint follow "violations of community of administrative limits" (e.g., "inappropriate" behavior, "uncoooperativeness"). This, of course, flies in the face of those cases and statutes (that I will be discussing in a moment) limiting its use to "prevent[ing] a patient from physically injuring himself/herself or others."

In short, this is a very complicated area of psychiatric practice. It should be no wonder that it is just as complicated an area of law.

III. Categories of cases

Contemporaneous seclusion and restraint law has developed (or can potentially develop) from at least six different sources:

1. Class action or "law reform cases" seeking to mandate certain constitutional standards in litigation seeking a declaration of a constitutional right to treatment and/or adequate care and/or safe conditions of confinement (usually litigated in federal court settings),

2. Class action or "law reform cases" seeking to mandate certain constitutional standards in litigation seeking a declaration of a constitutional right to refuse treatment (also usually litigated in federal court settings),

3. Individual cases brought under the federal Civil Rights Act (§ 1983) seeking redress (usually in damages) for violations of previously-articulated constitutional rights,

4. State statutes (generally called "Patients' Bills of Rights") that regulate and control the way that treatment is provided at public psychiatric hospitals, and individual cases seeking to enforce, limit, or interpret such state statutes,

5. Federal statutes (e.g., the Americans with Disabilities Act) that prohibit discrimination against persons with mental disability,

6. Individual tort cases seeking monetary damages from allegedly improper use of seclusion and/or restraint, or failure to use seclusion and/or restraint (usually litigated in state court settings).

What I'm going to do now is to look at each of these categories separately, highlighting some of the important decisions in each one, with an eye toward discovering points in common that might be of help to us in understanding what the law is and how we can expect the law to reasonably develop.

First, as I've already noted, the constitutionally-driven *Wyatt* standards established limits on seclusion and restraint as part of the right to treatment: seclusion could not be used for punishment or staff convenience, and could only be used "to prevent a patient from physically injuring himself/herself or others," after alternative treatment interventions were unsuccessful or after determining alternative treatment interventions would not be practicable, and when authorized by a written order of a qualified physician who is physically present and has examined the patient, in all cases seclusion/restraint orders being limited to eight hours. Other courts quickly followed in the wake of *Wyatt*,and as recently as two years ago, federal courts continued to find that a state hospital's failure to "take adequate action to investigate and curb harm, abuse and undue use of seclusion and restraint" violated Constitutional guarantees of a right treatment.

Other constitutional cases have considered seclusion and restraint issues in the context of the patient's right to refuse treatment. The most important decision here is *Rogers v. Okin*, the trial court opinion that eventually led to the *Mills* decision in the Supreme Court that I mentioned earlier in this talk. There, the plaintiffs had argued that seclusion was routinely used by defendants in non-emergency situations for the purposes "[both] of treatment and punishment," and the federal district court agreed. It found that "the indiscriminate use of seclusion PRNs, the failure to properly fill out seclusion order and observation forms, and the failure to review incidents of seclusion within eight hours [as required by state law]," resulted in a violation of plaintiffs' liberty interest under the due process clause, and, to remedy this violation, enjoined seclusion use, "except in emergency situations where there is an occurrence of serious threat of extreme violence, personal injury or attempted suicide." In a much more recent case, a federal court rejected an (insanity acquittee) plaintiff's argument that a mental health facility must use restraints prior to the administration of antipsychotic medication in light of the parties' failure to develop the record on the question of "how effective alternative restraints will be and what risks, if any, their use poses to the staff."

Next to consider are the constitutional dimensions of cases seeking primarily (or at least, significantly) money damages. Here I start with the *Youngberg* case, as it is, as I've said, the only Supreme Court case to consider any of the underlying issues, and because its holding has had, and will continue to have, a major impact on all subsequent constitutional litigation in this area. *Youngberg* began as a damages action on behalf of a profoundly retarded resident of a Pennsylvania state institution, alleging that the plaintiff had suffered a series of over 70 significant injuries (some self-inflicted, some inflicted by other residents, some by staff), and that the defendants' failure to protect him from such injuries violated the Constitution. He subsequently amended his complaint to enjoin the defendants' use of physical restraints "for prolonged periods on a routine basis." In the course of its opinion, the Supreme Court found that patients have a constitutionally protected liberty interest in "conditions of reasonable care and safety," "freedom from bodily restraint" and such minimally adequate or reasonable training [as is needed] to ensure safety and freedom from undue restraint." In determining whether there has been a violation of these rights, the Court imposed a "professional judgment" test: "liability may only be imposed when the decision by the professional is such a substantial departure from accepted professional judgment, practice or standards as to demonstrate that the person responsible actually did not base the decision on such a judgment." There is no subsequent mention in the opinion of the question of the restraints that were used in the case.

Many constitutional cases have since considered seclusion and restraint issues, using the *Youngberg* standard as their guidepost, and the range of decisions in such cases appear to seek to take that standard seriously. Where professional judgment was apparently used, cases are dismissed; where it was apparently lacking, cases are allowed to proceed to a jury trial. In other cases, courts have allowed plaintiffs to proceed against certain defendants (usually those in line-level positions) but not against others (generally the supervisors).

Yet another set of cases are statutory. Again, as I've noted, in the wake of *Wyatt* and its progeny, most states adopted "Patients' Bills of Rights" that generally tracked the substantive rights provisions in the initial *Wyatt* decisions, and at least eight specifically adopted the language that seclusion could never be used as punishment or for staff convenience. What is not clear is what sort of prophylactic effect the *presence* of these statutes has had on patient treatment and staff attitude. At the least, though, these laws provide some support for the notion that some state legislatures have given some thought to *Wyatt*'s constitutional admonitions.

The bulk of litigation that has taken place, however, has flowed from traditional tort principles. And, as can be expected, decisions in these cases have been intensely fact-dependent. The paradigm successful (from a plaintiff's perspective, that is) case is *Pisel v. Stamford Hospital*, a case where an agitated and psychotic patient (who had been locked in a seclusion room) was later found unconscious and without a pulse, her head wedged between her bed's mattress and steel railing. There, the Connecticut Supreme Court affirmed a $3.6 million jury verdict, finding that the plaintiff had offered competent expert testimony indicating that the treatment violated the appropriate standard of care. The mirror opposite "successful" case is *Clark v. Ohio Dep't of Mental Health*. There, the court held that the plaintiff was entitled to nominal damages in the amount of one dollar for the improper use of restraints and seclusion by defendant's staff. In *Clark*, the plaintiff had been placed in restraints or in seclusion on numerous occasions due to her smoking habits, and her propensity for starting fires; however, the court found that restraining the plaintiff was a punitive response to her behavior, and less restrictive alternatives could have been utilized. But because the plaintiff had not shown any substantial damages, the court found nominal damages (in the amount of $1) to be appropriate.

In other cases, recovery has been denied, usually where plaintiffs failed to sustain the burden of proof that they were improperly restrained or that defendant's actions were responsible for their in their injuries. *Coltraine v. Pitt County Memorial Hospital* is illustrative of this category of cases. In *Coltraine*, the decedent was admitted to the hospital for "acute bronchitis and acute alcoholism." After he "became confused," the treating doctor ordered him to be placed in restraints, and ordered registered, private duty nurses around the clock. As none were available, a nursing student placed the restraints on Coltraine. About 15 minutes later, Coltraine was seen without his restraints standing on the ledge of the second floor and holding the bottom of the third floor. He subsequently fell and died.

The state Court of Appeals affirmed the trial court's directed verdict on behalf of defendants, finding there was no evidence that the hospital breached a duty of care, and that there was no evidence that the hospital personnel negligently applied the restraints, and that the hospital fulfilled its duty to the patient when it informed the doctor that there was no registered nurses available. In addition, it found the plaintiff had failed to prove that the death was foreseeably related to the use of restraints, as he had not been considered suicidal at the time restraints were ordered.

Other restraint cases present the inverse question: should there be liability when hospitals and/or mental health professionals *fail* to restrain? There is no question that it is fear over *this* sort of suit that often impels the use of restraints (at least in acute care hospitals), and, anecdotally, when I've discussed this topic with psychiatrist friends, this is the only category of case that seems to be of much interest (I leave any deconstruction of that to my more-analytical friends). Again, here, the responses are mixed and intensely-fact dependent. In one case, an unrestrained patient (in the neurological unit of a general hospital) was successful in suing for damages resulting from injuries he sustained in a fall, but generally such suits are *unsuccessful* (often because of immunity principles) unless the negligence is so profound as to not raise much of a debatable question, such as cases in which unsupervised patients jumped into vats of boiling soap in hospital laundries, or jumped through unlocked laundry chute doors. Professor Elyn Saks has thus suggested that doctors should not be held liable for injuries resulting from a failure to restrain patients, unless "a person of the most common understanding would have foreseen serious injuries."

The vast majority of failure-to-protect cases are decided in favor of defendants; as I will discuss subsequently, the extent to which the fear of *this* sort of litigation has captured the mental health professional community—in Stanley Brodsky's wonderful neologism, "litigaphobia" (On litigaphobia in *this* context, *see* Timothy Gammon & John Hulston, *The Duty of Mental Health Care Providers to Restrain Their Patients or Warn Third Parties*, 60 Mo. L. Rev. 749, 780–81 (1995))—is perhaps the overarching issue for us to ponder.

IV. Sanism and pretextuality

A. Sanism

1. Introduction

"Sanism" is an irrational prejudice of the same quality and character of other irrational prejudices that cause (and are reflected in) prevailing social attitudes of racism, sexism, homophobia and ethnic bigotry. It infects both our jurisprudence and our lawyering practices. Sanism is largely invisible and largely socially acceptable. It is based predominantly upon stereotype, myth, superstition and deindividualization, and is sustained and perpetuated by our use of alleged "ordinary common sense" (OCS) and heuristic reasoning in an unconscious response to events both in everyday life and in the legal process. Judges are not immune from sanism. "[E]mbedded in the cultural pre-suppositions that engulf us all," they express discomfort with social science (or any other system that may appear to challenge law's hegemony over society) and skepticism about new thinking; this discomfort and skepticism allows them to take deeper refuge in heuristic thinking and flawed, non-reflective OCS, both of which continue the myths and stereotypes of sanism.

2. Sanism and the court process in mental disability law cases

Judges reflect and project the conventional morality of the community, and judicial decisions in all areas of civil and criminal mental disability law continue to reflect and perpetuate sanist stereotypes.

C. Pretextuality

1. In general

The entire relationship between the legal process and mentally disabled litigants is often pretextual. By this, I mean simply that courts accept (either implicitly or explicitly) testimonial dishonesty and engage similarly in dishonest (frequently meretricious) decisionmaking, specifically where witnesses, especially *expert* witnesses, show a "high propensity to purposely distort their testimony in order to achieve desired ends." This pretextuality is poisonous; it infects all participants in the judicial system, breeds cynicism and disrespect for the law, demeans participants, and reinforces shoddy lawyering, blasé judging, and, at times, perjurious and/or corrupt testifying.

The pretexts of the forensic mental health system are reflected both in the testimony of forensic experts and in the decisions of legislators and fact-finders. Experts frequently testify in accordance with their own self-referential concepts of "morality" and openly subvert statutory and caselaw criteria that impose rigorous behavioral standards as predicates for commitment or that articulate functional standards as prerequisites for an incompetency to stand trial finding. Often this testimony is further warped by a heuristic bias. Expert witnesses—like the rest of us—succumb to the seductive allure of simplifying cognitive devices in their thinking, and employ such heuristic gambits as the vividness effect or attribution theory in their testimony.

D. Sanism, pretextuality, seclusion and restraint

It is clear that seclusion and restraint are often used for sanist and pretextual reasons. Kirk Heilbrun's research demonstrates that, in three out of five instances, it is used to control patients who are "uncooperative" or have engaged in "inappropriate behavior" (rather than patients whose violence makes them a danger to self or others). Reported cases reflect this: patients are restrained because they are "rude" and "disrespectful," because they are "disruptive" or a "thorn in everybody's side" (thus fostering staff resentment), because they shouted obscenities, or where administrators expressed fear of being sued if they failed to restrain. As I have already noted, patients in restraints are taunted by staff. Others have been forced to urinate in their clothes because of staff policies that patients in seclusion could only use bathroom facilities for 15 minutes during every hour, and then subject to "brutal beatings" for refusing to clean up their urine. And cases have been reported where patients have been restrained for years.

The case of *Alt v. John Umstead Hospital* is instructive. There, the North Carolina Court of Appeals upheld an award under the State Tort Claims Act to a patient who had been placed in seclusion and restraints for shouting obscenities and throwing his dinner tray against a wall of the hospital ward. Said the court:

> The decision of Dr. Parker and Nurse DeBerry to place plaintiff into seclusion and restraints at about 5:25 p.m. on February 22nd, 1990 was not in keeping with community standards of medical practice and was not justified by plaintiff's behavior, the state rules, or hospital policies. Throwing a tray and shouting obscenities do not constitute imminent danger to others or to a patient so as to justify the use of seclusion and restraint under psychiatric and medical standards of practice in February 1990. The behavior of Nurse DeBerry, smarting from being called names by her patient and unable to get her patient to be compliant, was one of punishment rather than treatment. Dr. Parker aided and abetted in this punishment. Irrational actions by a psychiatric patient are to be expected, and what might call for punishment in a mentally stable patient does not justify punishment of a mentally deficient patient.

Where the use of restraints is motivated by fear of litigation it is clearly pretextual. Writing about the use of restraints in nursing homes, Professor Marshall Kapp is clear on this point:

> One of the major impediments slowing down progress toward [the] goal [of bringing about a greatly reduced reliance on the use of nursing homes] is a widespread anxiety among many long-term care providers about potential legal liability resulting from injuries associated with the non-restraint of a resident. Apprehension of liability, or at least of being caught as an involuntary party in litigation, is frequently cited as a pretext for actions actually based more on a professional bias toward paternalism on behalf of older disabled persons, staff convenience, and desire for resident behavior control.

In short, the use of seclusion and restraints in psychiatric hospitals is often sanist and it is often pretextual. It is absolutely essential that we integrate these findings in any consideration of the issues that are before us today.

V. Therapeutic jurisprudence

A. Introduction

One potential solution is to turn to therapeutic jurisprudence (TJ) for some answers. TJ studies the role of the law as a therapeutic agent, recognizing that substantive rules, legal procedures and lawyers' roles may have either therapeutic or antitherapeutic consequences, and questioning whether such rules, procedures and roles can or should be reshaped so as to enhance their therapeutic potential, while not subordinating due process principles. Therapeutic jurisprudence looks at a variety of mental disability law issues in an effort to both shed new light on past developments and to offer new insights for future developments. Until now, however, there has been no consideration of the TJ implications of seclusion and restraint policies.

B. TJ and seclusion and restraint

I can identify at least five clusters questions to be considered if we look at seclusion and restraint from a TJ perspective.

First, are seclusion and restraint being used therapeutically? Certainly, there is a robust psychiatric literature that has expressed concern that seclusion and restraint techniques are often used punitively rather than for legitimate treatment purposes, that they are used more frequently on understaffed shifts or in poorly staffed facilities, and that there are potential psychological and physical risks associated with their use. The case law that I have discussed certainly demonstrates that these fears are not limited to a dark and distant past. This is not to say that there is no room for seclusion and restraint in a psychiatric hospital; indeed, there is impressive empirical support for the proposition that both can serve to effectively manage violent behavior in a way accompanied by few side-effects. But it *is* to say that—apparently, as it is employed in a significant number of psychiatric hospitals—it is *not* being used therapeutically.

Next, are constitutional decisions and Patients' Bills of Rights statutes therapeutic? If they are not, is this, nonetheless, an area where civil liberties/civil rights should still "trump" therapeutic ends? There is no research with which I am familiar that has looked at this precise question. On the other hand, studies of both the important right to treatment and right to refuse treatment law reform litigation suggests that both have had important therapeutic effects. Certainly, there is no research that suggests that these statutes have had the opposite effect.

Also, it is necessary to consider the role that lawyers play in this area of the law. I have written extensively about the "myth of advocacy" in related contexts; bluntly stated, most lawyers who represent persons with mental disabilities perform a sub-standard job, and fail to measure up to even the most minimal standards of adequacy. Indeed, in the taunting case to which I have already referred, the patient's lawyer—inexplicably—failed to specify to the court the section of the Patients' Bill of Rights under which he was bringing his claim, a blunder that led the trial judge to initially dismiss the complaint. Yet, a recent computer LISTSERV posting (on FORENSIC-PSYCH) by the medical director of a mental health facility in the same state blames patients' rights lawyers for the increased use of restraints (arguing that this increase is directly related to court decisions seeking to enforce the right to refuse antipsychotic medications). This is a fertile area for additional therapeutic jurisprudence analysis.

The legal literature about seclusion and restraints is negligible. I have found no articles on any of the related questions by law professors since Professor Wexler focused on this question some 15 years ago. The legal academy is generally disinterested in many important questions of mental disability law, but this inattention is truly glaring. A TJ inquiry into the relationship between this lack of interest and the seemingly-random way that seclusion and restraint cases have developed would be valuable to us all.

Finally, we are faced with the reality that seclusion and restraint are often used not because they are clinically indicated, but because of fear of litigation. We are just beginning to understand the role of "litigaphobia" in all mental disability law, and I expect that it is areas like this—areas that are generally of disinterest to the legal practitioner and scholar— that its impact is the most pernicious.

V. Conclusion

Mental disability law has always been a poor stepchild of the law, and seclusion and restraint law is a poor stepchild of mental disability law. Although it is of major significance to patients and providers alike, it remains "off the screen" to most academics and members of the bar. Because it arises from so many different sources (and these sources appear, on the surface, to bear little interrelationship), it is virtually impossible to create a unitary standard or methodology through which all seclusion and restraint cases can be read, analyzed and deconstructed.

At least partially for these reasons, I believe that it is impossible for us to make any true sense of the ways that the law regulates seclusion and restraint unless we look at the issues that i have been discussing through the filters of sanism and pretextuality, and under the filter of therapeutic jurisprudence. If we do this, then, and only then, will we be able to begin our understanding of this area of the law.

* * *

Questions for Discussion

1. As a policy matter, do you think these issues should be litigated in a constitutional framework, a statutory framework, or a tort framework? Why?

2. What can be done to decrease the incidence of of seclusion and restraint for staff convenience?

3. How do seclusion and restraint cases compare to cases about the right to refuse medication?

———————

For Further Reading

"Senator Harkin Introduces Keeping All Students Safe Act, NDRN Urges Senate Passage,"
National Disability Rights Network, retrieved May 15, 2012 at http://www.napas.org/
en/component/content/article/5/478-press-release-senate-introduces-keeping-all-
students-safe-act.html. Article about legislation aimed at solving problems caused
by the use of restraints and seclusion in schools.

Discussion 13

Moving Towards Closure of DD Institutions

Recommended Background Reading

Olmstead v. L.C. 527 U.S. 581, 119 S.Ct. 2176, 144 L.Ed.2d 540 (1999).

NYSARC & Parisi v. Carey: 706 F.2d 956 (2d. Cir. 1983).

Pennhurst State School & Hospital v. Halderman, 465 U. S. 89 (1984).

Youngberg v. Romeo, 457 U.S. 307 (1982).

Joseph Shapiro, *No Pity*, chapter 10.

Readings for Class Discussion

This article discusses the impact of *Olmstead* ten years later. The original article should be consulted for footnotes.

The *Olmstead* Decision at Ten:
Directions for Future Advocacy

Ira A. Burnim and Jennifer Mathis, Bazelon Center for Mental Health Law
43 Clearinghouse Rev. 386 (2009)

June 2009 marked the tenth anniversary of the U.S. Supreme Court's decision in *Olmstead v. L.C.*, making this an apt time to take stock of the decision's impact on service systems for individuals with disabilities and of directions for *Olmstead* advocacy. The unnecessary institutionalization of people with disabilities is a form of discrimination prohibited by the Americans with Disabilities Act of 1990 (ADA), and a public entity must administer services to individuals with disabilities in the most integrated setting appropriate to their needs unless doing so would fundamentally alter the entity's service system, the Court held in *Olmstead*.

As a result of the *Olmstead* decision and subsequent litigation, many states have been taking advantage of temporary federal incentives to expand community-based services for individuals with disabilities—for example, federal Nursing Home Transition grants, Real Choice Systems Change grants for community infrastructure development, and the Money Follows the Person initiative providing a one-year increased Medicaid match for individuals transitioning to community settings. States have also been continuing to expand Medicaid home- and community-based waivers to enable individuals to move to more integrated settings from nursing homes and from institutions for individuals with developmental disabilities. These state efforts, however, generally result in small, piecemeal expansion of community settings rather than large-scale systemic change.

Millions of people with disabilities remain institutionalized, although, with new service approaches, people with even the most challenging needs can now be served in integrated community settings. The heavy reliance on institutions continues in part because of states' reluctance to close institutional beds and reallocate dollars to more integrated settings. Such reliance continues also because the privately operated facilities, such as nursing homes and board-and-care homes, on which states rely, typically operate on a for-profit basis and have little incentive to identify residents as qualified for more integrated care. Neither these facilities nor states are making much effort to give residents information about more integrated settings. Often these private facilities—particularly board-and-care homes—receive little attention in state *Olmstead* planning efforts because they have been labeled as "in the community" even though many are large, segregated facilities serving hundreds of residents with disabilities. Even smaller board-and-care homes have features of larger institutional settings, diminishing residents' opportunities to interact with people without disabilities.

Here we envision future *Olmstead* litigation and policy efforts to achieve real change and ensure that people with disabilities have opportunities to live in settings that maximize their integration into community life. To drive disability service systems in this direction, *Olmstead* implementation efforts should focus on ensuring that

- institutional beds are closed and funding is reallocated to develop integrated community settings;
- privately operated facilities used as part of disability service systems are included in *Olmstead* compliance efforts;
- people with disabilities are truly integrated into community life, through technologies such as scattered-site supportive housing, and not resegregated in private facilities or housing projects; and
- people with disabilities have meaningful and informed choices about where to live.

Reallocation of Funds Is at the Heart of Olmstead's Integration Mandate

Many states' *Olmstead* planning does not consider closure of institutional beds or reallocation of funds to develop more integrated settings. Budgeting funds for *Olmstead* compliance is viewed as a drain on budgets rather than an opportunity for cost savings. When new money must be found to develop additional community-based settings, development remains modest. As long as individuals with disabilities have insufficient community options, they will continue to be placed in or steered toward institutional settings.

Even though states tend not to do so, tying development of community-based services to closure of institutional beds is at the heart of *Olmstead*'s analysis. The Court made clear that the possibility of closing institutional beds and reallocating funds must be considered as part of the fundamental alteration defense. In determining whether requested relief would be a fundamental alteration, cost savings from closing institutional beds must be analyzed and quantified. Indeed, the integration mandate would be hollow if states were allowed to keep unneeded institutional beds instead of reallocating funding to expand community settings. If a state cannot demonstrate that closing institutional beds and shifting resources to community-based services would compel cutbacks in services to other individuals with disabilities, then shifting resources in this way is not a fundamental alteration.

To achieve the promise of *Olmstead*, state service systems must commit to closing institutional beds and reallocating funds to develop more integrated settings.

Private Facilities Must Be Part of Olmstead Compliance Efforts

Increasing numbers of individuals with disabilities are served in privately operated facilities, including nursing homes and board-and-care homes. Often these facilities are considered permanent-living settings, and no discharge planning is done for residents. Some states insist that *Olmstead* does not apply to individuals in such facilities; they argue that *Olmstead* and the statutory provision that it interprets (the ADA's Title II, which prohibits state and local government entities from discriminating based on disability) apply only to government-operated facilities. Courts have consistently rejected this position when the private facilities are part of a larger, publicly planned and financed system of services. Title II covers all programs, services, and activities of a state or local government entity "without any exception." Hence the ADA applies to the way a state plans and administers its service systems for individuals with disabilities. In planning, organizing, and funding service systems, states must comply with the ADA's integration mandate.

Disability Advocates Incorporated v. Paterson contains an extensive and thoughtful discussion of *Olmstead*'s application to private facilities. The plaintiff—a nonprofit organization that advocates the rights of people with disabilities—challenged under *Olmstead* New York's use of large, segregated "adult homes" as service settings for individuals with mental illness. The state argued that *Olmstead* did not apply because the homes were private and the state played no role in admission and discharge decisions. The court rejected New York's argument and held that "[t]he statutory and regulatory framework governing the administration, funding, and oversight of New York's mental health services—including the allocation of State resources for the housing programs at issue here—involves 'administration' on the part of defendants," to which the ADA applies. The court found that the plaintiff's *Olmstead* claims did not challenge the conduct of the adult-home operators but rather "the State's choice to plan and administer its mental health services in a manner that results in thousands of individuals with mental illness living and receiving services in allegedly segregated settings." The court barred the state from evading its obligation to comply with the ADA by using private entities to deliver services.

The court also rejected New York's contention that Title II was inapplicable because the state did not require that anyone live or receive services in an adult home and individuals were free to move out or receive services elsewhere. As the court explained, the state determines the settings in which it will provide and fund mental health services: "Defendants do so by controlling the State's funding for services in various settings, including adult homes and [the more integrated setting of] supported housing, and effectively control how many adults receive services in any particular setting."

Despite the clear application of *Olmstead* to states' use of privately operated facilities as part of their disability service systems, large numbers of these private facilities remain outside state efforts to promote compliance with *Olmstead*.

Compliance with Olmstead's Integration Mandate Is
Best Achieved Through Supportive Housing

Olmstead is frequently described as requiring states to offer individuals living in "institutions" the opportunity to live "in the community." However, this characterization does not fully capture *Olmstead*'s meaning. *Olmstead* and the ADA's integration mandate require that states administer services to individuals with disabilities in the most integrated setting appropriate to their needs. The attorney general's regulations implementing Title II define the "most integrated setting" as "a setting that enables individuals with disabilities to interact with non-disabled persons to the fullest extent possible." The Disability Advocates decision concluded that the regulations "mean what they say," and the court set forth the proper inquiry. The decision rejected New York's argument that *Olmstead* required simply an inquiry into whether individuals had any opportunities to interact with nondisabled individuals.

The plaintiff in *Disability Advocates* sought to compel New York to make "supported housing" available to individuals residing in large, segregated adult homes. This type of housing is permanent housing where individuals with disabilities live in their own apartments or homes, with the rights and responsibilities of tenants and with services delivered according to the individuals' preferences and needs. Such housing typically provides a rental subsidy as well as a flexible array of services varying with the individual's needs. One important aspect of integrated supportive housing programs is that the housing is not conditioned on the individual's compliance with treatment—an approach known as "housing first." Another is that the housing units are "scattered site"—that is, units are scattered throughout the community rather than congregated in a single building where all tenants are people with disabilities.

The plaintiff in *Disability Advocates* sought "supported housing" because it was the most integrated setting for its constituents (individuals with mental illness living in adult homes), is effective in serving even people with the most challenging needs, and is less costly than other alternatives. Having one's own home is a powerful motivator for people to seek and continue treatment. Supportive housing gives people their own home, where they can focus on recovery from mental illness and rebuild their lives. Supportive housing participants choose their own apartments, in neighborhoods where they want to live, and receive services that they need and want. Participants' having housing and service choices correlates not only with satisfaction but also with greater housing stability. "Housing first" programs produce more long-term housing stability than programs in which housing is conditioned on compliance with treatment.

Supportive housing is also more cost-effective than other types of publicly financed housing for individuals with disabilities, even for people with significant needs. Supportive housing reduces costs by using apartments or houses available for rent on the market, thereby eliminating the need for rehabilitation or construction costs. The use of scattered-site units avoids the difficulties and expense of fighting neighborhood opposition to siting of housing developments or group homes. Supportive housing also saves money by focusing on teaching participants independent-living skills and reducing their use of costly resources such as shelters, day programs, inpatient hospitals, prisons, and jails.

Despite its successes, supportive housing remains unavailable to most people with disabilities because states have not developed sufficient amounts of supportive housing. Instead states rely on nursing homes, board-and-care homes, and traditional group homes as housing and service settings. None of them is the most integrated setting for individuals with disabilities, and hence serving people in these settings represents a form of "transinstitutionalization" or moving individuals from one type of institution into another type of institution.

Group-home settings were once considered state of the art. However, as our understanding of the capabilities of individuals with disabilities has evolved and as new service approaches have developed, we now know that even people with extremely significant needs can live in their own homes with appropriate supports. Congregate settings—those that house multiple people with disabilities—thus should no longer be considered the "most integrated setting" for individuals with disabilities. Because congregate settings amount to transinstitutionalization, some states are no longer developing new congregate capacity and are instead focusing on development of supportive housing.

With the development of supportive housing and the recognition that even people with the most challenging needs can be served in their own homes with services and supports, the answer to the question of what is the most integrated setting appropriate has changed. While nursing homes, board-and-care homes, and group homes may be more integrated than state psychiatric hospitals or state institutions for individuals with intellectual disabilities, today they are not the most integrated setting appropriate to the needs of a person with a disability. *Olmstead* implementation should focus on true integration through technologies such as scattered-site supportive housing. Otherwise scarce resources will continue to be wasted on settings that deprive individuals with disabilities of the full lives that they deserve and to which they are legally entitled.

People with Disabilities Must Have Opportunities to Make
Meaningful and Informed Choices About Where to Live

Individuals with disabilities must have an opportunity to make fully informed choices about where to live. Frequently people with disabilities express concerns about leaving institutional settings because they are unfamiliar with the full range of living options and services available outside the institution; among the options and services is the financial support that they will receive for community living. Many people assume that a return to the community will mean a return to what they had experienced before—often homelessness, restrictive or regimented programs, or independent living without services or resources to meet basic needs. Some assume that they would receive in the community only the same small "personal-needs allowance" that they receive in the institution from their Supplemental Security Income checks. Many lack confidence in their own abilities because they are told that they are incapable of living on their own.

Thus both education and active engagement must be part of the effort made to identify individuals who have disabilities and who want to live in more integrated settings. For individuals who are reluctant to make such a move, efforts must be made to explore the reasons and to give accurate information—and opportunities to visit integrated settings—to help overcome misperceptions. Also, community providers must build trust; many people with disabilities are understandably skeptical that service systems will keep their promises to provide adequate support for community living. Without such efforts, numerous individuals will continue to be excluded inappropriately from community life.

Progress in implementing the ADA's integration mandate has been disappointingly slow and is likely to remain so unless policy makers and advocates embrace a broader vision for change. We do not attempt here to set forth a comprehensive agenda for *Olmstead* implementation. Instead we identify a few fundamental principles that should be part of any effort to give people with disabilities a real chance to live, as much as possible, "like everyone else"—the fundamental goal of the ADA.

Court Decision in New York Advances Community
Living for People with Psychiatric Disabilities

New York violated the Americans with Disabilities Act of 1990 (ADA) by denying thousands of adult home residents with mental illness the opportunity to receive services in the most integrated setting appropriate to their needs, according to a federal district court deciding *Disability Advocates Incorporated v. Paterson* on September 8, following a five-week trial (No. 03-CV-3209 (NGG), 2009 WL 2872833, at *1 (E.D.N.Y. Sept. 8, 2009), www.bazelon.org/pdf/DAIruling9-8-09.pdf.

Disability Advocates Inc.—a nonprofit organization that advocates the rights of people with disabilities—brought claims under *Olmstead v. L.C.* (527 U.S. 581 (1999)) and the ADA's integration mandate on behalf of approximately 4,300 people with mental illness living in privately operated "adult homes" in New York City with more than 120 beds (*Disability Advocates Incorporated*, 2009 WL 2872833, at *1). Adult homes, the court found in a 210-page decision, are "segregated, institutional settings that impede integration in the community and foster learned helplessness" (id. at *18). These homes, the court wrote, bear little resemblance to the homes in which people without disabilities normally live (id.). The court found that virtually all of the constituents of Disability Advocates were qualified for supported housing, a setting that is far more integrated than adult homes and in which people with mental illness live in their own apartments with flexible support services, including, in some cases, assertive community treatment, an intensive service delivery model that provides, through a multidisciplinary team, comprehensive, individualized services for people with serious mental illness (id. at *28). The court also found that the constituents, as a whole, were not opposed to living in more integrated settings and would choose to live in an independent setting such as supported housing if given an informed choice (id. at *47).

Defendants, according to the court, failed to show that offering constituents of Disability Advocates the opportunity to live in more integrated settings would fundamentally alter the state's service system (id. at *51–85). The court found that the state had no comprehensive or effective plan to enable adult home residents to receive services in more integrated settings and that the requested relief would not increase costs to the state (id. at *53–83). In fact, according to the court, the state could redirect funds as individuals moved from adult homes to supported housing, and serving individuals in supported housing would be less costly (id. at *68–69).

The court concluded that Disability Advocates was entitled to declaratory and injunctive relief; the court will order an injunctive remedy following additional briefing from the parties. The decision's detailed and thorough analysis—of, among other issues, why the ADA's integration mandate applies to publicly funded but privately operated facilities—is likely to have an impact on *Olmstead* litigation across the country.

* * *

Questions for Discussion

1. Try to find information about the "*Olmstead* plan" in your state, and compare it to the plan in other states. What data are available for the numbers of people in DD institutions in your state today, versus the number in 1999? What about nationwide?

2. What suggestions does this article make about effective *Olmstead* planning? What other ideas do you have on this subject?

3. Which states have closed their DD institutions entirely? Why do you think some states have not done so?

For Further Reading and Viewing

Go to http://www.stateofthestates.org/ and explore the website. It allows you to create charts, study statistics by state, or read various articles about trends in developmental disabilities spending and services.

Research and Training Center on Community Living, "Behavioral Outcomes of Deinstitutionalization for People with Intellectual and/or Developmental Disabilities: Third Decennial Review of U.S. Studies, 1977–2010," Policy Research Brief, Volume 21, Number 2, April 2011, found at http://rtc.umn.edu/rtc/index.php?seriesID=10.

Information about the Willowbrook State School litigation, *NYSARC & Parisi v. Carey*:

http://www.clearinghouse.net/detail.php?id=478 (a brief overview)

http://www.mncdd.org/extra/wbrook/wbrook-timeline.htm (a timeline)

http://www.arcmass.org/StateHousePolicy/RegulationandPolicyDebates/FernaldSchoolClosingandRICCIClass/FernaldNews/WhyTheFernaldCenterShouldClose/ChristmasinPurgatoryWillowbrook/WillowbrookStateSchool/tabid/695/Default.aspx (general information)

http://www.mncdd.org/extra/wbrook/willowbrook.html (photo essay)

http://abandonedusa.com/site/willowbrook-state-school-staten-island-ny (current pictures)

"Serving Retarded: Some Are More Equal. Those Who Once Endured A Notorious Institution Get A Cornucopia Of Care In Philadelphia. But Others, In The Arms Of Their Families, Struggle. And Wait" retrieved May 15, 2012 at http://articles.philly.com/1997-11-02/news/25542192_1_severely-retarded-residents-retarded-people-pennhurst-state-school/6.

Discussion 14

Group Homes? Not in My Back Yard!

Recommended Background Reading

Cleburne v. Cleburne Living Center, Inc., 473 U.S. 432 (1985).

Children's Alliance v. City of Bellevue, 950 F.Supp. 1491 (W.D. Wash. 1997).

Laura C. Bornstein, *Contextualizing Cleburne*, 41 Golden Gate U.L. Rev. 91 (2010).

Readings for Class Discussion

The following article was written in 1998 as an overview. While caselaw has changed, the major tenets of the law are the same.

Group Homes and Zoning under the Fair Housing Act

Michael Mirra, Columbia Legal Services, Tacoma, WA

This outline is only a cursory review of the topics it covers. It cannot substitute for legal advice. Persons with a particular legal problem may wish to consult an attorney. Attorneys should supplement this outline with their own legal research. This outline reviews what the Fair Housing Act (FHA) has to say about governmental regulation or restriction of group homes, both their siting and operation. In general, the FHA provides group homes, their residents and developers with important protection. This protection results from the application to group homes of basic and longstanding principles of FHA adjudication. For that reason, this outline will begin by reviewing those basics. The original article contains many detailed footnotes. Readers should be aware that the law may have changed since time of publication.

I. SOME BACKGROUND

Much of the nation's housing segregation resulted from overt policies and practices of the public and private entities that controlled or influenced the housing market, *e.g.* realtors, housing lenders, federally assisted housing programs, local and state laws governing residential use or public enforcement of private restrictive covenants. These institutionalized efforts created or fortified a pervasive white racism in the housing market against African-Americans and other persons identified by race, ethnicity or religion.By 1968, the nation's housing was thoroughly segregated by race. In this century, the effort to promote fair housing began in the courts. The Supreme Court began using the Civil Rights Act of 1866 and the 14th amendment's guarantee of equal protection to restrict racial discrimination by local governments. In 1917, it issued its first ruling against racial zoning ordinances. In 1948, the Court prohibited judicial enforcement of racially restrictive covenants governing the use of land. Soon afterward, the Federal Housing Administration and the Veteran's Administration stopped insuring mortgages on property encumbered with racially restrictive covenants. Racial zoning and covenants continued in place, however, until the passage of effective affirmative legislation.

State and federal anti-discrimination laws generally followed a pattern. First, the laws outlawed discrimination in public accommodations and publicly financed activities. Employment laws then followed. Laws then outlawed discrimination in public housing. The last laws to be enacted restricted discrimination in the private housing market. By 1968, about half the states, including Washington, had some form of fair housing law. In 1968, Congress enacted Title VIII of the Civil Rights Act of 1968 — the Fair Housing Act. The turbulent events of the time spurred its passage. The urban riots of 1967 and the subsequent Kerner Commission report caused some to attribute many social afflictions to residential segregation. On April 4, 1968, Martin Luther King, Jr. was assassinated. The Fair Housing Act became law on April 11, 1968. In many respects, however, the 1968 Fair Housing Law has not been a success. As a source of legal enforcement it fell far short of its counterpart laws governing public accommodations or employment. The number of private and public prosecutions was comparably few. More importantly, its effect on patterns of residential use disappointed its proponents. Discriminatory barriers became more sophisticated if less overt. Most communities remained segregated for reasons that appeared directly related to discriminatory conduct.

One of the Act's shortcomings was its lack of effective enforcement. Efforts soon began in Congress to strengthen it. After nearly twenty years of debate, the Congress passed the Federal Fair Housing Amendments Act of 1988. Among its major provisions: it greatly strengthened the administrative enforcement of the Act, making its remedies available to people without lawyers; it eliminated the $ 1,000 cap on punitive damages available in private lawsuits; it provided for civil penalties and damages in lawsuits brought by the United States. Despite these enhancements, the racial segregation America's housing markets continues. The 1988 amendments also added handicap and "familial status" to the list of protected characteristics under the Fair Housing Act (FHA). These additions are meant to protect disabled persons and households with minor children from pervasive discriminatory practices that excluded them from large segments of the residential housing markets. Disabled persons have traditionally faced widespread public and private discrimination based on erroneous and destructive stereotypes. The Act was "a clear pronouncement of a national commitment to end the unnecessary exclusion of persons with handicaps from the American mainstream." *Helen L. v. DiDario*, 46 F.3rd 325, 333 n. 14 (3d Cir.) (quoting H.R.Rep. No. 711, 100th Cong., 2d Sess. 18, *reprinted in* 1988 U.S.C.C.A.N. 2173, 2179). At the same time, Congress recognized that large portions of the private rental market excluded households with minor children. These practices, combined with increasingly unaffordable housing prices, have contributed to a housing emergency for large segments of the American public for whom affordable, decent or secure housing remains unavailable.

II. PROMINENT PROVISIONS OF THE FAIR HOUSING ACT GENERALLY

A. Protected Characteristics

The FHA outlaws or restricts housing discrimination because of: race; color; religion; sex; "familial status;" national origin; handicap.

B. The Act's Scope is Broad

With few exceptions, the FHA governs nearly every type of housing, including mobile homes, shelters, vacant land intended for housing, and group homes. This is clear from its definition of "dwelling:" 'Dwelling' means any building, structure, or portion thereof which is occupied as, or designed or intended for occupancy as, a residence by one or more families, and any vacant land which is offered for sale or lease for the construction or location thereon of any such building, structure, or portion thereof. 42 USC § 3602(b). (The exceptions are narrow and refer to owner-occupied apartment complexes of 4 or less units, religious organizations, and private clubs. *See* 42 USC § 3603.) The FHA also governs nearly every aspect of a housing transaction, including financing, brokering, appraising, and marketing. It also applies to land-use and zoning practices of government. The FHA applies to a broad range of discriminatory behavior, including: (1) refusing to sell, rent, negotiate for "or otherwise make unavailable or deny" a dwelling; (2) discriminating in the "term, conditions, or privileges of a sale or rental" of a dwelling or in the "provision of services or facilities in connection therewith"; (3) making or publishing any discriminatory statement in regard to a sale or rental; (4) misrepresenting the availability of a dwelling; (5) inducing a person to sell or rent any dwelling by representations about the presence of members of a protected class in the neighborhood; (6) discriminating in the access to real estate services; (7) discrimination in the residential real estate related transactions and in the terms or conditions of such transactions, including the making of loans for the purchase of a dwelling, the making of loans secured by residential units and the "selling, brokering, or appraising of residential real property." 42 U.S.C. § 3604. There are limits, however, to the scope of the FHA's coverage. The FHA protects not only racial minorities or other protected classes of people. It gives a cause of action to any person or entity who is harmed by an act of illegal discrimination. Zoning laws that unlawfully discriminate against handicapped persons seeking group home living, for example, would give rise to claims not only by the prospective residents who are handicapped but also by the developers or financiers of the group home.

C. The Definition of Disability is Broad

The definition of "handicap" is very broad: (h) 'Handicap' means, with respect to a person — (1) a physical or mental impairment which substantially limits one or more of such person's major life activities, (2) a record of having such an impairment, or (3) being regarded as having such an impairment, but such term does not include current, illegal use or addiction to a controlled substance as defined in section 802 of Title 21. 42 USC § 3602. This definition includes mental illness, developmental disabilities, physical impairments, persons who test positive for HIV, persons who have AIDS, wet or dry alcoholics and persons recovering from addiction to an illegal drug as long as they are not currently using illegal drugs. The need to live in a group home, by itself, may denote a disability to the extent it results from an inability to live independently. Note: The definition of "disability" under Washington's Law Against Discrimination may be somewhat broader than the definition under the FHA.

D. Protections for Handicapped Persons and Children are Equivalent to Those Provided Against Racial Discrimination

The terms "handicap" and "familial status" appear in the FHA alongside those of "race" and the other protected characteristics. Thus, the law treats discrimination on the basis of "handicap" and "familial status" as it treats racial discrimination. "[F]amilies with children [and handicapped persons] must be provided the same protections as other [protected] classes of persons." 24 C.F.R. Ch. 1, Subch. A. App. I at 931 (1995).

E. Violations and Requirements of the FHA

Violations of the FHA include not only acts of intentional discrimination but other acts or policies that have a discriminatory effect even without any intent to discriminate.

1. Intentional Discrimination

A person or entity violates the FHA when it denies or conditions or impairs a housing opportunity intentionally because of race, color, religion, sex, familial status, national origin or handicap. Intentional discrimination can violate the law even if the defendant also had other legal reasons for his or her conduct. In relation to discrimination on the basis of handicap, the Act is intended to repudiate the use of stereotypes and requires that persons with handicaps be considered as individuals.

2. Unintended but Disparate Discriminatory Effects

The FHA also outlaws or restricts practices that have an unintended but disproportionate effect on protected persons. In these cases, the defendant must show a legitimate reason that is important enough to justify the practice despite its disproportionate effect. Courts have allowed such claims because of a practical view of fair housing enforcement:

> Effect, and not motivation, is the touchstone, in part because clever men may easily conceal their motivations, but more importantly, because … '[w]hatever our law was once, … we now firmly recognize that the arbitrary quality of thoughtlessness can be as disastrous and unfair to private rights and the public interest as a perversity of a willful scheme.'

United States v. City of Black Jack, Missouri, 508 F.2d 1179 (8th Cir 1974): Id. at 1185 (8th Cir. 1974), cert. den. 422 U.S. 1042 (1975). The legislative history of the 1988 Amendments strongly endorses this analysis as applied to handicapped persons.

Some common examples of practices or policies found to violate the FHA because of their unintended but disproportionate exclusion of protected persons include: exclusion of families with children found to constitute racial discrimination; exclusion of subsidized housing found to constitute race discrimination; occupancy maximums and siting restrictions on group homes found to constitute familial status discrimination.

3. Denial of Reasonable Accommodation of Handicaps

In addition to prohibiting discriminatory practices on the basis of handicap, the FHA goes further and limits the application of neutral rules that have no discriminatory intent or effect. The FHA requires owners to make "reasonable accommodation" in such rules, policies, practices, or services, when such accommodations may be necessary to afford such person equal opportunity to use and enjoy a dwelling. 42 U.S.C. § 3604(f)(3)(B). The FHA imposes an "affirmative duty upon landlords reasonably to accommodate the needs of handicapped persons." *U.S. v. California Mobile Home Park Management Co.,* 29 F.3rd 1413, 1416 (9th Cir. 1994), appeal after remand 107 F.3rd 1374 (9th Cir. 1997). This duty receives a " 'generous construction' in order to carry out a 'policy that Congress considered to be of the highest priority.' The generous spirit with which we are to interpret the FHA guides our [reasonable accommodation] analysis here." 29 F.3rd at 1416. *See Also, Shapiro v. Cadman Towers, Inc.,* 51 F.3rd 328, 335 (2d. Cir. 1995).

In general, a requested accommodation is reasonable and therefore required, if (i) it is necessary for the handicapped persons' equal opportunity to use and enjoy a dwelling and (ii) it does not impose undue administrative or financial burdens or require a fundamental alteration in the nature of the housing program. *E.g., U.S. v. California Mobile Home Park Management Co.,* 29 F.3rd 1413, 1416 (9th Cir. 1994), *appeal after remand* 107 F.3rd 1374 (9th Cir. 1997); *Hovsons, Inc. v. Township of Brick,* 89 F.3d 1096 (3rd Cir. 1996).

As a reasonable accommodation for handicapped persons, courts have required waivers in leases, contracts, rules, ordinances, restrictive covenants, zoning codes and otherwise reasonable rules of many types when necessary to accommodate a disability. Examples of lease rules that courts have waived include: first come, first serve rule for assignment of parking spaces; rule against pets; rule against threatening behavior; lease provision for charges and penalties. In requiring a waiver of rules, the FHA can also oblige a landlord to spend or forego money. Reasonable accommodation concerning group homes can include the waiver of otherwise applicable zoning restrictions.

The FHA also requires owners to permit, at the expense of the handicapped person, reasonable modifications of existing premises occupied or to be occupied by such person if such modification may be necessary to afford such person full enjoyment of the premises. A landlord may, where it is reasonable to do so, condition permission for a modification on the renter agreeing to restore the interior of the premises to the condition that existed before the modification, reasonable wear and tear excepted. 42 USC § 3604(f)(3)(A). (The FHA also requires that most multi-family buildings that are first occupied after March 15, 1991 meet certain adaptability and accessibility requirements. State law has imposed similar requirements for several years already.)

4. The "Dangerousness" Exception

The FHA makes an exception for the protections offered to "handicapped" persons to account for dangerous persons:

> Nothing in this subsection requires that a dwelling be made available to an individual whose tenancy would constitute a direct threat to the health or safety of other individuals or whose tenancy would result in substantial physical damage to the property of others.

42 U.S.C. § 3604(f)(9). Dangerous persons or persons with criminal histories are not, by virtue of that history, protected from discrimination. This remains the case even if they are handicapped. However, the criteria and process by which people are screened or excluded for dangerousness cannot itself by discriminatory. Several concepts are likely to govern a court's review of such procedures. First, the FHA requires that the "direct threat" restrictions be based on individual assessments. *Bangerter v. Orem City Corp.,* 46 F.3rd 1491, 1503 (10th Cir. 1995). Generalized conclusions about groups based upon their handicap are not permissible. *See Also* 54 FR 3245 (January 23, 1989).

Second, a process to screen out dangerous people cannot be applied only to handicapped people. See House Report at 30; 53 FR 45001 (November 7, 1988).

Third, a criteria or process that excludes people because of a dangerous history may be amenable to waiver as a reasonable accommodation to a person's disability. A reasonable accommodation, for example, may include treatment or controls that provide adequate assurance that threatening behavior will not recur.

F. Enforcement

Victims of FHA violations have several enforcement options:

1. Private Litigation

A victim can sue in state or federal court. 42 U.S.C. § 3613. The court can order the defendant to stop the illegal activity and to take affirmative measures to insure against repeated violations. The court can also require the defendant to pay money to compensate the victim for harm, including psychological and emotional injury. The court will also normally order the defendant to pay the attorney's fees of the prevailing victim. The court can also punish the defendant by requiring further payment of punitive damages. The FHA imposes a two year statute of limitations for filing such a lawsuit.

2. Administrative Enforcement

A victim can file an administrative complaint with an enforcement agency responsible for the jurisdiction. 42 U.S.C. § 3612. He or she must file within one year of the alleged violation. Under the Act, HUD can delegate this enforcement authority to a local agency whose laws are "substantially equivalent" to the FHA. In that case, the local enforcement agency contracts with HUD to handle complaints. Presently, HUD has contracts with four jurisdictions in Washington State: King County; Seattle; Tacoma; Washington State. As a result, HUD refers most administrative complaints arising from within Washington State either to the Washington State Human Rights Commission or to the fair housing enforcement agencies for King County, Seattle or Tacoma.

An agency, if it finds a violation, can order the defendant to stop the illegal activity. It can order the defendant to pay the victim's attorney's fees. In order "to vindicate the public interest," the agency can also impose a civil penalty of up to $50,000 depending on the number of the defendant's prior violations.

3. United States as Plaintiff

The United States Government can also sue to remedy violations of the Act that result from a "pattern or practice" of illegal activity or from conduct that otherwise "raises an issue of general public importance." 42 U.S.C. § 3614. The court may impose penalties of up to $100,000.

G. Courts Will Interpret the FHA Expansively

The court will give the FHA a generous and expansive construction "in order to carry out a 'policy that Congress considered to be of the highest priority.'" *U.S. v. California Mobile Home Park Management Co.*, 29 F.3d 1413 (9th Cir. 1994) (referring to the FHA, quoting from *Trafficante v. Metropolitan Life Ins.*, 409 U.S. 205, 212, 93 S.Ct. 364, 368, 34 L.Ed.2d 415 (1972).

III. FHA'S APPLICATION TO GROUP HOMES

A. The FHA Governs Local Zoning Regulation

Courts have long applied the FHA to local zoning codes. It governs not only behavior specified in the law but actions, like zoning, that "otherwise make unavailable or deny" a dwelling. §§ 42 U.S.C. § 3604(a),(f)(1). The FHA has been "construed to reach 'every practice which has the effect of making housing more difficult to obtain on prohibited grounds.'" *United States v. Yonkers Board of Education*, 624 F.Supp. 1276, 1291, n. 9. (S.D.N.Y. 1985), *aff'd*, 837 F.2d 1181 (2d Cir. 1987), *cert. denied*, 486 U.S. 1055 (1988). Additional sections of the FHA particularly govern local laws. The 1988 amendments adding "handicap" protections targeted zoning laws especially:

> These new subsections [protecting handicapped persons] would also apply to state or local land use and health and safety laws, regulations, practices or decisions which discriminate against individuals with handicaps.

House Report at 24.

Note: Other laws prohibiting discrimination on the basis of handicap also apply to zoning codes. *E.g.* Section 504 of the Rehabilitation Act of 1973, 29 U.S.C. § 794(a) (Section 504 applies to zoning codes of cities that receive federal money;) Americans with Disabilities Act, 42 U.S.C. § 12132 (The ADA applies to "public entities," defined to include cities. § 42 U.S.C. § 12131(1)(A)).

B. The FHA Protects Group Homes

Courts have further applied the FHA to protect group homes. Group homes fit the FHA's definition of dwelling. § 42 U.S.C. § 3602. The FHA's protection for group homes became particularly clear with the 1988 amendments for handicapped persons:

> This provision [protecting handicap persons] is intended to prohibit special restrictive covenants or other terms of conditions, or denials of services because of an individual's handicap and which have the effect of excluding, for example, congregate living arrangements for persons with handicaps.... While state and local governments have authority to protect safety and health, and to regulate use of land, that authority has sometimes been used to restrict the ability of individuals with handicaps to live in communities. This has been accomplished by such means as the enactment or imposition of health, safety or land-use requirements on congregate living arrangements among non-related persons with disabilities....

House Report at 23–24. Group homes are generally covered because their residents are handicapped. In one case, the court also applied the FHA to group homes for children under the Act's "familial status" provision.

C. Some Particular Issues Arising from Municipal Regulation of Group Homes

1. Occupancy Maximums:

Municipalities have commonly restricted the number of residents allowed in group homes. These restrictions appear in various forms. Some apply particularly to group homes, raising questions of direct and intentional discrimination. Other restrictions apply to all households of unrelated persons, raising questions of their discriminatory effect that results because handicapped people, more than others, require group home living.

The FHA expressly allows "any reasonable local, State, or Federal restrictions regarding the maximum number of occupants permitted to occupy a dwelling." 42 U.S.C. § 3607(b)(1). However, this exemption applies only if the maximums apply to everyone in a dwelling, generally for the purpose of avoiding overcrowding. *City of Edmonds v. Oxford House, Inc.,* U.S., 115 S.Ct. 1776, 131 L.Ed.2d 801 (1995) (generally applicable occupancy limits like the Uniform Housing Code designed to prevent overcrowding fall within exemption from FHA). The FHA does not exempt limits "designed to preserve the family character of a neighborhood, fastening on the composition of households rather than on the total number of occupants living quarters can contain, do not." *Id.* at 1782. Such limits that purport to define "families" have been found to discriminate against residents of group homes.

Some courts have struck down these limits relying either on their discriminatory intent or discriminatory effect. Other courts have reviewed requests to waive neutral occupancy maximums as a reasonable accommodation for the disability of residents of group homes.

2. Size and Bulk Limitations

In general, the FHA does not require a city to waive nondiscriminatory limitations on the size or bulk of buildings or their nonresidential use. E.g. *Gamble v. City of Escondido,*

104 F.3rd 300 (9th Cir. 1997) (City could reject proposal for a large complex for disabled adults, including non-housing services, in a single family residence.)

3. Dispersal Requirements

With some notable exceptions, courts have generally struck down requirements that group homes maintain minimum distances from other group homes. *E.g., The Children's Alliance et al. v. City of Bellevue*, 950 F.Supp. 1491 (W.D. Wash. 1997) (striking down 1,000 foot dispersal requirement for group homes); *Horizon House Developmental Services, Inc. v. Township of Upper Southampton*, 804 F.Supp. 683, 693, aff'd 995 F.2d 217 (3rd. Cir. 1993) (same); *But see, Familystyle of St. Paul v. City of St. Paul, Minn.*, 923 F.2d 91 (8th Cir. 1991) (The court permitted application of a dispersal requirement to prevent cluster of 21 group homes within one and one-half block area.)

4. Notice and Permit Requirement

Courts have also struck down requirements that group homes register with municipal authorities or notify their neighbors. *E.g. Stewart B. McKinney v. Town Plan and Zoning Com'n*, 790 F.Supp. 1197 (D.Conn. 1992) (neighbor notification); *Potomac Group Home Corp. v. Montgomery County, Maryland*, 823 F.Supp. 1285 (D. Md. 1993) (hearing and notification requirement); *Larkin v. State of Michigan*, 89 F.3d 285 (6th Cir. 1996) (notification of neighbors requirements); *The Children's Alliance et al. v. City of Bellevue*, 950 F.Supp. 1491 (W.D. Wash. 1997) (requirement for city permit and community hearing process).

Some courts, however, have allowed procedural requirements by which group home developers can be made to seek waivers of exclusionary rules as a reasonable accommodation to the disability of their prospective residents. *E.g., Elderhaven, Inc. v. City of Lubbock*, 98 F.3rd 175 (5th Cir. 1996).

Most courts have ruled that a city cannot justify a discriminatory rule merely by providing a process by which a group home may seek its waiver. Reasonable accommodation procedures are applicable only to consider a waiver of a nondiscriminatory rule.

5. Requirement for Permanent Residency

Courts have also rejected requirements that residents of group homes remain as occupants for minimum periods of time. The court in *North Shore-Chicago Rehab. v. Village of Skokie*, 827 F.Supp. 497 (N.D. Ill. 1993) struck down a requirement that group home residents be "permanent." Similarly, the court in *Oxford House, Inc. v. Township of Cherry Hill*, 799 F.Supp. 450 (D.N.J. 1992) barred enforcement of a requirement that all households of unrelated persons meet a standard of "permanency and stability"; *Oxford House,Inc. v. Town of Babylon*, 819 F.Supp. 1179, 1183 (E.D.N.Y. 1993) (barred town's eviction of the group home "due to the size or transient nature of plaintiffs' group living arrangement"); *The Children's Alliance et al. v. City of Bellevue*, 950 F.Supp. 1491 (W.D. Wash. 1997) (court voided exclusion of group homes for children who stayed less than 30 days).

6. Benign Intentions Do Not Excuse Adverse Discriminatory Regulation

Municipalities commonly justify adverse discriminatory regulation of group homes by claiming a benign motive to assist or protect the residents from harm. Several points are pertinent to such discussions. First, plaintiffs in a FHA claim do not have to prove malice or animus to show a violation:

> Specifically with regard to housing discrimination, a plaintiff need not prove the malice or discriminatory animus of a defendant to make out a case of intentional

discrimination where the defendant expressly treats someone protected by the FHAA in a different manner than others.

Bangerter v. Orem City Corp., 46 F.3rd 1491, 1500 (10th Cir. 1995). Second, good intentions do not cure discrimination. Third, discriminatory intentions are illegal even if the city also had non-discriminatory intentions.

7. Some Possible Grounds for Different Treatment of Handicapped Persons

Some courts, upon finding intentional discrimination, then consider possible reasons that could justify the discrimination. *Bangerter v. Orem City Corp.,* 46 F.3rd 1491, 1502–1504 (10th Cir. 1995); *Marbrunak, Inc v. City of Stow,* 974 F.2d 43 (6th Cir. 1992). The courts stated that the FHA may not prohibit overt discrimination beneficial to handicapped persons or to fair housing goals in the same way that racial categories designed to insure integration are sometimes permissible. Id. at 1504–1505. In *Alliance for the Mentally Ill v. City of Naperville,* 923 F.Supp. 1057, 1073 (N.D. Ill 1996), the court stated that any intentionally discriminatory rule must fulfill the "FHAA, which mandates that any such [facially discriminatory] requirements correspond to the 'unique and specific needs and abilities of [the] handicapped persons' affected." Any differential treatment must be based on a scrutiny of individual needs. *The Children's Alliance et al. v. City of Bellevue,* 950 F.Supp. 1491, 1499 (W.D. Wash. 1977). Even under these decisions, the possible justifications for overt discrimination are very narrow and provoke great judicial skepticism.

> We should be chary about accepting the justification that a particular restriction upon the handicapped really advances their housing opportunities rather than discriminates against them in housing. Restrictions that are based upon unsupported stereotypes or upon prejudice and fear stemming from ignorance or generalizations, for example, would not pass muster.

Bangerter, 46 F.3rd at 1504. Under the standard analysis and in the normal case, there is no reason that can justify overt intentional and adverse discrimination. Instead, discrimination must benefit the disabled residents and must be tailored to their needs.

One court, however, has expanded the grounds for permissible discrimination to include discrimination reasonably necessary to serve a city's legitimate interests. *Family-Style of St. Paul, Inc. v. City of St. Paul,* 923 F.2d 91 (8th Cir. 1991). In that case, the court permitted a city to prevent the addition of more group homes to a one and one-half block area that already had 21 such homes. The court ruled that dispersal benefited handicapped persons and FHA goals of integration. The court's use of a "rational basis" standard to review the city's overtly discriminatory ordinance is anomalous among the reported decisions. It has been rejected by courts in other Circuits. *E.g., Larkin v. State of Michigan,* 89 F.3d 285 (6th Cir. 1996); *The Children's Alliance et al. v. City of Bellevue,* 950 F.Supp. 1491, 1498 (W.D. Wash. 1997).

* * *

Questions for Discussion

1. What can be done to lessen discrimination against people with disabilities by local zoning boards?

2. If a new group home for people with disabilities were to be sited in your neighborhood, what do you think your neighbors' reaction would be?

3. What other examples of "NIMBY" attitudes have you seen?

4. What cases on this topic have been decided since the time this article was written?

———————

For Further Reading and Viewing

http://stopstigma.samhsa.gov/publications/combatingNIMBY.aspx.

http://www.hudhre.info/nimby/index.cfm?do=viewNimbyTopResponding.

Moira J. Kinnally, *Not in My Backyard: The Disabled's Quest for Rights in Local Zoning Disputes Under the Fair Housing, the Rehabilitation, and the Americans with Disabilities Acts*, 33 Val. U.L. Rev. 581 (1999).

Katherine Brinson, *Justifying Discrimination: How the Ninth Circuit Circumvented the Intent of the Fair Housing Act*, 38 Golden Gate U.L. Rev. 489 (2008).

Stephen F. Hayes, *The Usual Incidents of Citizenship: Rethinking When People With Disabilities Must Participate in Public Variance Proceedings*, 109 Colum. L. Rev. 2044 (2009).

"Condo Owners Say They're Not NIMBYs, They Just Don't Want 'Special People' Around," retrieved May 15, 2012 at http://www.raggededgemagazine.com/drn/08_04.html#754.

"Panther Creek Neighborhood Association Discriminates against the Disabled," retrieved May 15, 2012 at http://www.youtube.com/watch?v=b32XpJQBSrA.

Discussion 15

Homelessness and Disability

Suggested Background Reading

"Homelessness and Students with Disabilities: Educational Rights and Challenges," retrieved
   May 15, 2012 at http://www.cde.state.co.us/cdeprevention/download/Homeless%20
   Education%202010/NEW%20CDE%20WEB%20SITE%202010/4%20Resource%20
   and%20Training%20Materials/quick_forum_article_SPED.pdf.

"It's Madness: the Incarceration of Disabled Homeless People in the US," retrieved May
   15, 2012 at http://www.huffingtonpost.com/paul-boden/its-madness-the-incarcera_
   b_952431.html.

Readings for Class Discussion

The following is an article by the National Center for Homeless Education (NCHE),
found at http://center.serve.org/nche/downloads/briefs/idea.pdf.

Individuals with Disabilities Education
Improvement Act (IDEA) of 2004: Provisions for
Homeless Children and Youth with Disabilities

Over 1.35 million children and youth experience homelessness each year (Burt &
Laudan, 2000). These children and youth face educational challenges that include a lack
of basic necessities, such as food, clothing, and medical services; discontinuity of education
due to mobility; and trauma caused by the chaos, poverty, and instability of their family's
circumstances or, in the case of unaccompanied youth, their own circumstances.

Children and youth who are homeless face additional educational challenges when
they have disabilities. Studies indicate that children who are homeless are twice as likely
to have learning disabilities and three times as likely to have an emotional disturbance as
children who are not homeless (Better Homes Fund, 1999). Yet children and youth who
are homeless and have disabilities may not receive the special education services for which
they are eligible. Barriers to access these children and youth face include:

- Not being identified as needing special education services
- Difficulty with diagnosis due to mobility and other stressors

- Lack of timely assessment, diagnosis, or service provision
- Lack of continuity of services due to school transfers
- Lack of timely or efficient records transfer when enrolling in a new school
- Lack of an available parent or surrogate to represent the child or unaccompanied youth

Federal Response

Two federal laws that address the needs of homeless children and youth with disabilities are the McKinney-Vento Homeless Education Assistance Improvements Act and the Individuals with Disabilities Education Improvement Act (IDEA).

The McKinney-Vento Homeless Education Assistance Improvements Act

The McKinney-Vento Act, reauthorized in 2002 as part of the No Child Left Behind Act, ensures access to a free, appropriate public education (FAPE) for children experiencing homelessness.

The McKinney-Vento Act mandates:

Who is Homeless?

(McKinney-Vento Homeless Assistance Act of 2001—Title X, Part C, of the No Child Left Behind Act—Sec 725)

The term "homeless children and youth"—

A. means individuals who lack a fixed, regular, and adequate nighttime residence ...; and

B. includes—

> i. children and youths who are sharing the housing of other persons due to loss of housing, economic hardship, or similar reason; are living in motels, hotels, trailer parks, or camping grounds due to the lack of alternative accommodations; are living in emergency or transitional shelters; are abandoned in hospitals; or are awaiting foster care placement;

> ii. children and youths who have a primary nighttime residence that is a public or private place not designed for or ordinarily used as a regular sleeping accommodation for human beings ...

> iii. children and youths who are living in cars, parks, public spaces, abandoned buildings, substandard housing, bus or train stations, or similar settings; and

> iv. migratory children ... who qualify as homeless for the purposes of this subtitle because the children are living in circumstances described in clauses (i) through (iii).

- Immediate school enrollment and full participation in all school activities for eligible children, even when records normally required for enrollment are not available [Sec. 722(g)(3)(C)]
- The right of children and youth experiencing homelessness to remain in their school of origin (the school the student attended when permanently housed or the school in which the student was last enrolled) [Sec. 722(g)(3)(A)]
- Transportation to the school of origin [Sec. 722(g)(1)(J)(iii)]
- Access to programs and services, including special education services, preschool services, free school meals, Title I services, services for English language learners, vocational/technical education, gifted and talented services, and before- and after-school care [Sec. 722(g)(4)]

- The appointment of a local homeless education liaison in every school district to ensure that homeless children and youth are identified and given full and equal access to all educational services for which they are eligible in order to succeed in school [Sec. 722 (g)(6)(A)]

The Individuals with Disabilities Education Improvement Act

The purpose of IDEA, amended in 2004, is to ensure that all children with disabilities receive a FAPE, including special education and related services, to prepare them for further education, employment, and independent living [Part A, Sec. 601(d)(1)(A)]. Special education is defined as specially designed instruction, provided at no cost to the parents, to meet the unique needs of a child with a disability [Part A, Sec. 602(29)].

To be eligible, the child must have a disability and require specialized instruction to benefit from school. Special education instruction may take place in a general education classroom, special education classroom, specialized school, home, hospital, or institution [Part A, Sec. 602(29)(A)] and may include academic or behavioral support, speech and language pathology services, vocational education, and many other services. Related services may include transportation, physical therapy, psychological services, social work services, and counselling. Also included are certain medical services, parent counselling and training, recreation, and other support services if students need them to benefit from a special education program [Part A, Sec. 602(26)]. Eligibility and services are determined through evaluation and the development of an Individual Education Plan (IEP) [Part A, Sec. 614(d)]. Students who have not graduated from high school are eligible through age 21 [Part A, Sec. 612(a)(1)(A)]. Services are available to individuals with disabilities beginning at birth through Part C, Infants and Toddlers. Children under three are served under an Individualized Family Services Plan (IFSP) [Part C, Sec. 636].

Federal Guarantees for Children Who are Homeless and Have Disabilities

The McKinney-Vento Act and IDEA mandate protections and services for children and youth who are homeless and children and youth with disabilities. Moreover, both the McKinney-Vento Act and IDEA address serving children and youth who are homeless and have disabilities, ensuring that their complex and unique needs are met. In reviewing the needs of homeless children and youth with disabilities, educators should bring to bear the full range of both laws to optimize the educational access and success of these children. It is important to note that the two laws do not operate exclusively of one another, nor does one law supersede the other.

The 2004 reauthorization of IDEA in particular includes amendments that reinforce the timely assessment, appropriate service provision and placement, and continuity of services for children and youth with disabilities who experience homelessness and high mobility. Coordination and compliance with the McKinney-Vento Act are mandated specifically. The general requirements for a FAPE, evaluations, and IEPs are unchanged.

Following is a listing of the amendments in the reauthorized IDEA and implementing regulations from the U.S. Department of Education as related to the education of homeless children and youth with disabilities, pointing out the changes from prior law.

Definitions

• IDEA now mentions specifically and observes the McKinney-Vento definition of "homeless children and youth."

• The definition of "parent" has been changed, so that the statute now contains a similar definition to that contained in the federal regulations since 1999, with the notable addition of foster parents to the list of persons considered to be "parents." For the purpose of special education, "parents" now include biological, adoptive or foster parents, guardians, surrogate parents, individuals legally responsible for the child's welfare, or individuals acting in the place of a parent and with whom the child lives (specifically including grandparents, step-parents or other relatives).

• IDEA now contains a definition of "ward of the state."

Identification

• The Child Find requirements in the statute now include a specific requirement that states ensure that homeless children with disabilities are identified, located, and evaluated. (This requirement has been in federal regulations since 1999.)

Coordination/Compliance with the McKinney-Vento Act

• Any state receiving IDEA funds must ensure that the requirements of the McKinney-Vento Act are met for all homeless children and youth with disabilities in the state.

• IDEA requires every state receiving IDEA funds to maintain a State Advisory Panel to advise the State Educational Agency (SEA) on unmet needs in the state; to comment publicly on proposed rules and regulations; to advise the SEA on self-evaluation, data reporting and ensuring compliance; and to improve service coordination. IDEA now requires states to include state and local McKinney-Vento personnel on the Panel, as well as a representative of the state child welfare agency responsible for foster care.

Evaluations and IEPs

• IDEA now requires Local Educational Agencies (LEAs) to complete initial special education evaluations within 60 days of a parent's request, or within time frames established by the state.

• IDEA now specifically requires LEAs to ensure that assessments of children who change LEAs during the school year are coordinated with prior schools "as necessary and as expeditiously as possible, to ensure prompt completion of full evaluations."

• IDEA states specifically that the same time frame for completing initial evaluations applies if a child changes LEAs while the evaluations are pending, unless the new LEA "is making sufficient progress to ensure a prompt completion of the evaluation, and the parent and LEA agree to a specific time when the evaluation will be completed."

• When children with current IEPs change LEAs during the school year, the new LEA is now specifically required to provide the children with a FAPE immediately, "including services comparable to those described" in the previous IEP, in consultation with the parents. The LEA can then either adopt the old IEP or implement a new IEP. If the LEA is in a new state, the LEA can conduct new evaluations, if determined necessary, and develop a new IEP; but the LEA must still provide a FAPE, including services comparable to those described in the previous IEP, until the evaluations are completed and the new IEP is implemented.

• To facilitate the provision of a FAPE for students who change LEAs during the school year, IDEA now specifically requires enrolling schools to obtain the child's records from the previous school promptly, and previous schools to respond to such records requests promptly.

Unaccompanied Youth

• IDEA now requires each public agency to ensure that the rights of unaccompanied homeless youth are protected.

• The definition of "parent" includes individuals acting in the place of a biological or adoptive parent (including a grandparent, stepparent, or other relative) with whom the child lives. The regulations specify that "include" means that the items named are not all of the possible items that are covered, whether like or unlike the ones named. Thus, both relatives and non-relatives of unaccompanied homeless youth may be considered a parent if they are acting in the place of a biological or adoptive parent and the youth is living with them.

• For unaccompanied youth, IDEA specifically requires LEAs to appoint surrogate parents, and to make reasonable efforts to complete the appointment process within 30 days. In the interim, LEAs are to appoint temporary surrogate parents for unaccompanied youth. Temporary surrogates may be appropriate staff members of emergency shelters, transitional shelters, independent living programs, street outreach programs, the State, the LEA, or another agency involved in the education or care of the child, as long as the staff member has adequate knowledge and skills and does not have a personal or professional interest that conflicts with the interest of the youth.

• For wards of the state, IDEA now does not require an LEA to obtain parental consent for an initial evaluation, if the LEA cannot find the parent, the parent's rights have been terminated, or a judge has removed the parent's educational decision-making rights and appointed another person to represent the child.

• For wards of the state, IDEA now explicitly permits judges to appoint surrogate parents.

Services

• IDEA now allows LEAs to use up to 15% of their grants to develop and implement programs to intervene with K–12 students who have not been found eligible for special education but who need additional academic and behavioral support, with an emphasis on primary grades. (This provision should assist children experiencing homelessness with overcoming barriers to accessing services expeditiously.)

Resolution of Disputes

• When requesting a mediation or due process hearing under IDEA, families and youth experiencing homelessness do not need to provide a residential address; only available contact information is required.

Infants and Toddlers (Part C)

• Any state receiving a Part C grant must make early intervention services available to homeless infants and toddlers with disabilities and their families.

• States must ensure that appropriate early intervention services using scientifically based research are available, to the extent practicable, to homeless infants and toddlers with disabilities and their families.

• States must ensure the meaningful involvement of homeless families and wards of the state in the planning and implementation of the Part C program.

• In the report accompanying Part C, Congress stated that states should conduct public awareness programs about the Part C program in homeless family shelters, health service offices, public schools and the child welfare system.

• Any state receiving a Part C grant must establish a State Interagency Coordinating Council, which must include a representative of the State McKinney-Vento Coordinator and the state child welfare agency responsible for foster care.

* * *

Questions for Discussion

1. How does the statutory language of the IDEA attempt to help eligible students who are homeless? How does it interact with the McKinney-Vento Act?

2. What else could be done to ensure that homeless children with disabilities receive a free and appropriate education?

———————

The following is an article by the National Mental Health Association, found at http://homeless.samhsa.gov/resource/ending-homelessness-for-people-with-mental-illnesses-and-co-occurring-disorders-33718.aspx.

Ending Homelessness for People with Mental Illnesses and Co-Occurring Disorders

Homelessness is a growing social injustice in the United States. On any given night, approximately 600,000 Americans are homeless and more than 2 million people are homeless throughout the year. According to conservative estimates, one-third of people who are homeless have serious mental illnesses, and more than one-half also have substance use disorders.

Despite the grim statistics, studies show that supported housing is an effective option for communities working to meet the needs of people with mental health disorders who are homeless. In fact, people who are homeless and have mental illnesses or co-occurring disorders are more likely to recover and stay off the streets if they have access to supported housing programs.

Supported housing offers stable homes and services such as mental and physical health treatment, supported education and employment, peer support, daily living skills training, and money management instruction.

What Makes a Program Successful?

Many supported housing programs offer people a place to sleep, but effective programs for people who are homeless and have mental illnesses or co-occurring disorders share several crucial elements:

Access to Diverse Funding Streams. Accessing funding, deciphering funding application requirements, and understanding a fragmented funding and services system are just a few of the obstacles communities face when trying to secure funding for supported housing. To successfully expand housing and service options, it is vital to leverage funding from various sources such as Mental Health Services Block Grant and McKinney-Vento Homeless Assistance Funds.

Outreach and Engagement. Outreach and engagement workers attempt to build trust in neutral settings with people who are homeless. Although experts admit that some people who are homeless may initially view outreach workers as intrusive and suspect, they also contend that through continued face-to-face contact, outreach workers eventually build a sense of trust with clients that is essential to successfully linking them to effective treatment and support services.

Reintegration. People who are homeless and have mental illnesses should have access to the same opportunities as anyone else. This includes access to education, job training and housing opportunities that enable people to live, work and become fully participating members of the community. Although some people who are accustomed to living on the street may find reintegration difficult, access to appropriate services can help them successfully reintegrate into their communities.

Choice. The freedom to make treatment and service choices is vital to making a successful transition from homelessness to housing. It is important to respect people's decisions, to move at their pace, and to provide a variety of treatment options.

Flexibility. Providers can best help service recipients by offering an array of flexible treatment options that are designed to serve the largest number of people who have a variety of treatment needs. For example, some people may live independently but decide they feel more comfortable receiving services at home. A mobile team of healthcare workers, case managers and daily living skills trainers should be available to meet these types of requests. Flexibility involves eliminating the traditional one-size-fits-all approach to health care.

What Are Some Housing Options?

According to experts, a true supported housing program is defined by three principles: (1) people must live as members of the community in integrated, stable housing—not in mental health programs; (2) people must receive flexible services and supports that help maximize their opportunities for success over time; and (3) people must be free to exercise choices regarding their housing and support services.

Many housing options across the country value and respect individual choice. Although not all of them are considered "true" supported housing, many do serve as viable options.

Safe Havens. Safe Havens incorporate aspects of the supported housing philosophy. They serve hard-to-reach people who are homeless and have mental illnesses or co-occurring disorders but are unable or unwilling to participate in support services. The Stewart B. McKinney Homeless Assistance Act, the first and most extensive piece of homeless legislation, has specified that Safe Havens include the following features: (1) 24-hour residence for eligible people who may reside for an unspecified period of time; (2) private or semi-private accommodations; (3) overnight occupancy that is limited to 25 people; (4) access to low-demand services and referrals; and (5) access to supportive services on a drop-in basis for eligible people who are not residents.

Transitional Housing. Transitional housing provides services for limited periods of time (usually up to two years), including housing, food, transportation, training and psychiatric services, with the goal of moving residents into long-term housing. Transitional housing raises concerns about the fate of people who grow accustomed to living in one home but must transition to different housing to receive more or less intensive services.

When making decisions about implementing or expanding housing options, communities should consider the following aspects of transitional housing: (1) program participants may plateau at a stage of recovery in an effort to remain in their current housing, (2) people may be moved from one housing program to another to receive less intensive services before they are fully prepared to do so, and (3) recovery and wellness are not always linear and predictable, which could lead to many "transitional" moves.

Designated Apartments. Designated apartment buildings usually have eight to twenty-five individual rental apartments that are available only to people who meet specific qualifications. For example, some apartments may be available only to people who are homeless and have mental illnesses. Support services may be available on the property site or elsewhere in the community. Designated living has become increasingly popular as individual apartment units have become more difficult to obtain due to high rents and tight rental markets. Many people who need less intensive support than in-patient care but more support than complete independent living often feel comfortable in this living arrangement.

Independent Living. Many people who have mental illnesses live independently in the community. This includes people who rent apartments or condominiums as well as those who own homes. Independent living truly qualifies as supported housing because the living situation is not of limited duration, people live in places that are not designated for a specific type of population, and people may choose the services they want. NMHA envisions a society in which all people with psychiatric disabilities and co-occurring disorders have the option of living independently and being fully integrated in their communities.

How Can We Bring Supported Housing to Our Communities?

Convene a coalition of stakeholders including consumers and family members. Work collaboratively to create a plan for eliminating homelessness through improved housing and support services. Ask the state to appoint a task force — that includes consumers and stakeholders — to make concrete recommendations for improving services for people who are homeless. Advocate for increased federal and state funding to expand supported housing options. Research local foundations that fund programs designed to eliminate homelessness and apply for grants. Educate state governments about the cost-effectiveness of supported housing programs compared to the high costs of homelessness (see NMHA's fact sheet, "Homelessness: Reviewing the Facts" at http://www.nmha.org/homeless/ homelessnessfacts). Participate on state planning councils that determine how mental health funding is spent.

Where Can We Apply for Funding?

Various sources fund housing programs and support services that are designed to assist people with mental illnesses or co-occurring disorders who are homeless. Nonprofit organizations can apply directly for some funding to support such programs and activities, but other funding sources require advocacy efforts to ensure that public community entities apply for the funding. The Department of Housing and Urban Development (HUD), for example, is a major provider for supportive housing programs but is not the sole source of funding in this area. The following list of funding sources will help you get started.

HUD — Shelter Plus Care (S+C)

S+C provides rental assistance combined with social service supports service for people who are homeless and have disabilities — particularly for those who have serious mental illnesses, substance use disorders, and AIDS or related diseases, and their families. S+C supports a variety of housing options such as apartments, group homes and individual units for those who do not have families.

HUD — The Supportive Housing Program (SHP)

SHP provides supportive housing and/or supportive services to people who are homeless. SHP funds can be used to create transitional housing, to implement permanent supportive housing for people who have disabilities, and to provide supportive services that are not provided in conjunction with SHP-funded housing.

HUD — Section 811 Supportive Housing for Persons With Disabilities

Section 811 is designed to increase rental opportunities and supportive services for very low-income people who have disabilities and enable them to live independently in the community. The program provides interest-free capital advances to nonprofit organizations to build or rehabilitate rental housing, and offers support services to adults with disabilities and very low incomes. The advance does not need to be repaid as long the housing remains available to the specified population for a minimum of 40 years. In addition, the program provides rental assistance to supportive housing residents. Resident pay 30 percent of their adjusted gross income in rent, and Section 811 pays the difference between the monthly approved operating costs and the rent the tenant pays.

HUD—Section 8 Moderate Rehabilitation for Single Room Occupancy (SRO)

HUD contracts directly with local public housing authorities to fund the rehabilitation of residential properties and develop more standard SRO units for people who are homeless. The SRO program provides rental assistance to people who are homeless and compensates SRO property owners for some of the costs of rehabilitating, owning and maintaining the pro perty.

HUD/Continuum of Care (CoC)

CoC encourages communities to develop comprehensive plans that address the needs of people who are homeless. Jurisdictions may apply for these funds by submitting CoC plans that demonstrate broad participation by community stakeholders, that identify resources, and that point to gaps in the community's current approach to providing services to people who are homeless.

HUD—Section 8 Housing Choice Vouchers

Housing Choice Vouchers constitute the federal government's major program for assisting very low-income families, older adults and people with disabilities to obtain decent, safe and sanitary housing in the private market. Participants are free to choose any type of housing that meets program requirements and is not limited to units located in subsidized housing projects. The federal government determines annually how many vouchers will be distributed; however, to receive Section 8 Vouchers, individual public housing authorities must apply for them. Although vouchers are distributed according to community needs, not enough vouchers are distributed each year to meet the overwhelming demand.

HUD—Home Investment Partnership Program (HOME)

HOME provides grants to states and localities to fund activities such as building, buying and rehabilitating affordable housing for rent or ownership, and offering direct rental assistance to low-income individuals and families. HOME is the largest federal block grant, allocating $1 billion per year to state and local governments. It requires grant recipients to match 25 cents of every dollar in program funds to mobilize community resources that support affordable housing. HOME is designed exclusively to create affordable housing for low-income households.

HUD—Public Housing Program

Public housing was established to provide decent, safe rental housing for eligible low-income families, older adults and people with disabilities. HUD administers federal aid to local housing agencies (HAs) that manage housing for low-income residents at rents they can afford. HUD furnishes technical and professional assistance in planning, developing and managing these developments.

HUD Supported Housing Program (HUD-VASH)

HUD-VASH is a joint supported housing program between HUD and the Department of Veterans Affairs (VA). Its goal is to provide permanent housing and ongoing treatment services to veterans who are homeless and who have mental illnesses, substance use disorders or both.

CMHS — Projects for Assistance in Transition from Homelessness (PATH)

PATH is a grant program administered by the Center for Mental Health Services (CMHS) within the Substance Abuse and Mental Health Services Administration. PATH provides funds to states and territories to offer community-based services for people who are homeless or at risk of becoming homeless. Providers can use PATH funds to offer essential services such as outreach, screening and diagnostic treatment, community mental health services, case management, alcohol or drug treatment, rehabilitation, supportive and supervisory services in residential settings, and referrals to other needed services. In addition, PATH funding may be used to fund limited housing assistance such as minor renovations and repairs to existing housing, and one-time rental payments to prevent eviction.

This article has been edited for length. To read the full article and footnotes, see http://www.columbialegal.org/Resources/Publications.

* * *

Questions for Discussion

1. What examples of supportive housing (as defined by this article) exist in your community? Which housing agencies are operating as resources in your community?

2. What can be done to improve housing options for people with disabilities?

For Further Reading

"Beds Not Buses: Housing vs. Transportation For Homeless Students: A Report of the National Law Center on Homelessness & Poverty In Collaboration With Columbia Legal Services," retrieved May 15, 2012 at http://www.nlchp.org/content/pubs/HousingvTransport.pdf.

"Homelessness and Disability," retrieved May 15, 2012 at http://news.change.org/stories/homelessness-disability.

"Reading Between the Lines for Homeless People with Disabilities," retrieved May 15, 2012 at http://www.povertyinsights.org/2010/03/24/import-1482/.

Discussion 16

Mental Health Courts

Recommended Background Reading

"Improving Outcomes for Youth in the Juvenile Justice System: A Review of Alameda County's Collaborative Mental Health Court," National Center for Youth Law, retrieved May 15, 2012 at www.youthlaw.org/fileadmin/ncyl/youthlaw/health/ACCCFinal.pdf.

Readings for Class Discussion

This article is produced by the Bazelon Center for Mental Health Law. To read the full document, including footnotes, see http://bazelon.org.gravitatehosting.com/News-Publications/Publications/List/1/CategoryID/7/Level/a/ProductID/42.aspx?SortField=ProductNumber%2CProductNumber.

The Role of Mental Health Courts in System Reform
Bazelon Center for Mental Health Law

Introduction

In a recent report based on two years of study and meetings of hundreds of individuals involved in criminal justice or mental health systems at the state and local levels, the Council of State and Local Governments ("CSG") found that "people with mental illness are falling through the cracks of this country's social safety net and are landing in the criminal justice system at an alarming rate." The report noted that many people with mental illnesses are "[o]verlooked, turned away or intimidated by the mental health system" and "end up disconnected from community supports." As a result, and "not surprisingly, officials in the criminal justice system have encountered people with mental illness with increasing frequency."

Contact with the criminal and juvenile justice systems obviously has significant negative consequences for anyone who is subject to arrest, booking and incarceration. It can be doubly traumatic for people with mental illnesses, and the resulting criminal record can impede their later access to housing and mental health services. Their increasing "criminalization" is generating concern among policy-makers, criminal and juvenile justice administrators, families and advocates. A great many of the individuals arrested are charged with only minor offenses for which others are not usually subject to arrest. For most, the underlying issue is their need for basic services and supports that public systems have failed to deliver in meaningful ways. In the past few years, this concern has led a number of communities to establish some form of mental health court to process criminal cases involving people with serious mental illnesses. These specialty courts strive to reduce the incarceration and recidivism of people with mental illnesses by linking them to the mental health services and supports that might have prevented their arrest in the first place.

Mental health courts straddle the two worlds of criminal law and mental health, requiring collaboration and consideration from practitioners in both fields. They typically involve judges, prosecutors, defense attorneys and other court personnel who have expressed an interest in or possess particular mental health expertise. Today there are 25 to 30 of these courts, depending on the definition used, and more are being planned. Congress addressed the issue in 2000, passing America's Law Enforcement and Mental Health Project Act, which makes federal funds available to local jurisdictions seeking to establish or expand mental health specialty courts and diversion programs. This paper examines efforts in a growing number of concerned communities to respond to the immediate problem by establishing mental health courts to promote court-imposed treatment as a substitute for incarceration. It presents issues that arise when a mental health court is being contemplated—issues that apply, for the most part, to *all* courts because all courts share an obligation under the Americans with Disabilities Act ("ADA") to accommodate individuals with mental illnesses.

Part I illustrates the scope of the problem facing courts and communities. Part II describes the Bazelon Center's review of information about 20 of these mental health courts and makes recommendations for improving the functioning of such courts.

I. Scope of the Problem

Policymakers' concern stems from the shockingly high percentage of jail and prison inmates who have mental illnesses, the incarceration of people with mental illnesses typically for much longer periods than other offenders, the fact that while incarcerated these inmates become especially vulnerable to assault and other forms of intimidation by other inmates and the awareness that mental health treatment in prison is rarely successful and usually not even adequate to combat the worsening of psychiatric conditions caused by incarceration itself. The following statistics illustrate the scope of the problem that needs to be addressed:

- Approximately a quarter million individuals with severe mental illnesses are incarcerated at any given moment—about half arrested for non-violent offenses, such as trespassing or disorderly conduct. This does not include more than half a million probationers with serious mental illnesses.

- Sixteen percent of state and local inmates suffer from a mental illness and most receive no treatment beyond medication.

- During street encounters, police officers are almost twice as likely to arrest someone who appears to have a mental illness. A Chicago study of thousands of police encounters found that 47 percent of people with a mental illness were arrested, while only 28 percent of individuals without a mental illness were arrested for the same behavior.

In 1999, in response to requests from state government officials for recommendations to improve the criminal justice system's response to people with mental illnesses, the Council of State Governments (CSG) convened a small, national, bipartisan working group of leading criminal justice and mental health policymakers from across the country. The group identified key issues affecting people with mental illnesses who were involved with the criminal justice system. That meeting was the genesis of the Criminal Justice/Mental Health Consensus Project, a two-year effort to prepare recommendations that local, state and federal policymakers and criminal justice and mental health professionals can use to improve the criminal justice system's response to people with mental illnesses. Guided by a steering committee of six organizations and advised by more than 100 of the most respected criminal justice and mental health practitioners in the United States, the Consensus Project provides concrete practical approaches that can be tailored to the unique needs of communities.

II. Special Courts for Offenders with Mental Illness: The Bazelon Center Review

Under the Americans with Disabilities Act, states and municipalities cannot discriminate against people with disabilities and must make reasonable accommodations in their programs and services. These legal obligations apply to courts as well as to diversion and alternative sentencing programs and practices administered by law enforcement, prosecutors and pretrial services. All jurisdictions have some ability to divert offenders from the criminal justice system, either by exercising discretion not to arrest or prosecute or by providing formal diversion programs or alternative sentencing. However, in practice many courts do not even consider such options for people with mental illnesses. This may occur because of stereotypes about mental illness, such as the erroneous belief that people with mental illnesses are more dangerous than others, or for lack of information about how people with mental illnesses could be successfully accommodated in these programs.

During the CSG development process, some judges, prosecutors and defense attorneys observed that defendants with mental illnesses are treated more harshly in court—that they are more likely to be remanded without the opportunity to post bail and given harsher sentences. According to the Consensus Project, "the court should never enhance a sentence solely because of the offender's mental illness. Rather, the sentence should be based on the behavior that brought the offender to court."

In 2001, the Bazelon Center for Mental Health Law embarked on a project of assessing the effectiveness of mental health courts as an alternative to criminal courts. The Center, founded in 1972, is the leading national legal-advocacy organization representing people with mental disabilities. Through precedent-setting litigation in the public-policy arena and by assisting legal advocates across the country, it works to define and uphold the rights of adults and children who rely on public services and ensure them equal access to health and mental health care, education, housing and employment.

A. Bazelon Center Review of 20 Mental Health Courts

The Bazelon Center reviewed information relating to 20 mental health courts around the country and, through interviews with judges, public defenders and other stakeholders, studied a dozen more intensively. From the study, the center reached the following conclusions:

- There is no single "model" of a mental health court; each court operates under its own, mostly unwritten, rules and procedures and has its own way of addressing service issues.

- Many of the existing courts include practices that are unnecessarily burdensome to defendants, that make it harder for them to reintegrate into the community and that may compromise their rights.

- Few of the courts are part of any comprehensive plan to address the underlying failure of the service system to reach and effectively address the needs of people at risk of arrest.

  Substantial numbers of mental health court participants are people who should not have been arrested in the first place. However, some courts are beginning to accept defendants who are more appropriate for such a program, such as people who have committed serious felonies.

- Addressing the issues raised by the escalating number of contacts between individuals with serious mental illnesses and the criminal justice system requires a broad and comprehensive approach that should include mechanisms giving all police, prosecutors and judges effective options for alternatives to arrest or incarceration. These options should be available to offenders with mental illnesses just as they are available to all other offenders, with reasonable accommodations provided as necessary to ensure fair access and improve opportunities for their successful completion.

- No diversion or alternative disposition program, whether prosecutor-driven, court-based, within law enforcement or jail-based, can be effective unless the services and supports that individuals with serious mental illnesses need to live in the community are available.

  Moreover, it is critical that these services exist in the community for everyone, not just offenders, and that supports not be withdrawn from others in need and merely redirected to those who have come in contact with the criminal justice system. Additional, specialized resources and programs are needed to reduce the risk of arrest for people with mental illnesses and the recidivism of those who have encountered the criminal justice system.

B. Bazelon Center Analysis and Recommendations

This paper reflects the assessments of the Bazelon Center's study and highlights issues for communities to consider when choosing to implement a mental health court. It also encourages a broader range of diversion programs as alternatives or supplements to mental health courts.

These recommendations are designed to ensure that if mental health courts are used, they are part of a broad-based approach and operate with policies and procedures that protect the individual rights of defendants who come before them.

The best approach to the problem of criminalization is to create a comprehensive system of prevention and intervention. Mental health courts may provide immediate relief to criminal justice institutions, but alone they cannot solve the underlying systemic problems that cause people with mental illnesses to be arrested and incarcerated in disproportionate numbers.

Furthermore, without careful consideration of several factors discussed in this report, reliance on mental health courts carries significant risks for individuals with mental illnesses.

1. The Role of Mental Health Courts

From the criminal law perspective, two rationales underlie the therapeutic court approach: first, to protect the public by addressing the mental illness that contributed to the criminal act, thereby reducing recidivism, and second, to recognize that criminal sanctions, whether intended as punishments or deterrents, are neither effective nor morally appropriate when mental illness is a significant cause of the criminal act. The goals of mental health courts, then, are: 1) to break the cycle of worsening mental illness and criminal behavior that begins with the failure of the community mental health system and is accelerated by the inadequacy of treatment in prisons and jails; and 2) to provide effective treatment options instead of the usual criminal sanctions for offenders with mental illnesses.

Breaking the cycle of repeated contact with the criminal or juvenile justice systems must start with expanded and more focused community-based services and supports. As currently configured in many communities, public mental health services are substantially targeted at prioritized populations: people exiting state psychiatric institutions, people regarded as being at risk of admission to these facilities, people in crisis and people whose treatment is governed by court orders. Individuals not falling into a defined priority group may find very limited services available to them. Improving access to meaningful services and supports will inevitably reduce the number of incidents between individuals with mental illnesses and the law enforcement and justice systems. Furthermore, such access is critical to the effectiveness of any diversion program directed toward people who have mental illnesses, including mental health courts.

Communities should ensure that criminal justice systems have a range of choices for diversion and disposition. Effective police diversion programs that prevent arrest for minor offenses and lead instead to services and supports are the first step in such a continuum. Various effective strategies then exist for people who have committed more serious offenses, including programs to reintegrate into the community those who have served time in jail or prison. The proper role of courts in this continuum is to address the needs of those who cannot, because of the nature of their offense, be diverted without arrest or at pre-booking or arraignment, but for whom punishment through incarceration is not appropriate.

While most specialty mental health courts handle only defendants charged with minor offenses, several court-based alternative disposition programs focus on individuals with serious felony charges. Sometimes, individuals who have already received a sentence to jail or prison are offered mental health services as a likely more effective option.

The Bazelon Center strongly believes that all courts, including mental health courts, following the approaches outlined here, can accommodate people with mental illnesses and achieve successful outcomes for them without compromising public safety *if* they function within a broader program of system reform.

2. The Operation of Mental Health Courts

Each mental health court is unique. Some have a single judge who presides over a mental health court held once or twice a week or as often as necessary. Eligible defendants usually include people who appear to have a mental illness; some courts also include people with developmental disabilities or head injuries. The courts typically have special court or pretrial-services personnel who are responsible for developing treatment plans and dedicated probation officers who monitor defendants' compliance with the plans once incorporated into court orders.

From the earliest stages of its development and continuing through implementation, a mental health court must coordinate not only with police, sheriff and prosecutors but also with state and local service systems. Only thus can a comprehensive and realistic picture be developed of how and why people with mental illnesses fall through the cracks, come in contact with law enforcement and get processed through the criminal justice system. Understanding the gaps and the reasons for these individuals' behaviors can lead to better targeted alternatives. In this regard, the participation of mental health consumers is critical. People who have "been there" can offer the most relevant perspective on how systems fail and what meaningful alternative(s) should be in place.

Of particular note to jurisdictions planning to apply for federal funds, Congress viewed coordination of services as crucial to the success of any mental health court. Specifically, Congress required both initial consultation and ongoing coordination during implementation with "all affected agencies … including the State mental health authority."

Three critical elements are needed in communities considering the establishment of mental health courts:

(1) treatment and service resources in the programs to which offenders will be referred;

(2) alternatives to arrest and diversion programs at the time of arrest, at jail before booking and at arraignment, to keep the court from being overwhelmed by individuals whose offenses are minor and to prevent its becoming a routine point of entry to mental health services for individuals whose real problem is the limited availability of help through more appropriate channels; and

(3) court procedures that do not have the effect of making a mental health court more coercive than a standard criminal court or more damaging to a defendant's future prospects for housing, employment and healthcare.

3. Mental Health Court Procedures

Mental health courts have a separate docket with a judge, prosecutors and defense attorneys who all have training in dealing with defendants with mental illnesses, who are familiar with existing service resources, and who are willing to work together with defendants and service providers to get the proper services for each defendant. Beyond these basic principles, every mental health court needs to put a number of procedures in place to ensure a fair balance between defendants' constitutional rights to trial and legal counsel and the protection of public safety and public health. Even existing mental health courts are not static; procedures and practices tend to be modified over time. While the small number of mental health courts and their evolving nature preclude definitive conclusions, the Bazelon Center's review does provide a glimpse of significant factors and trends relating to important procedural issues that any community will need to address if it chooses to establish a mental health court:

Voluntary Transfer into the Mental Health Court

It is crucial from the outset that transfer to the mental health court be entirely voluntary. Otherwise, singling out defendants with mental illnesses for separate and different treatment by the courts would violate the equal protection guarantee of the 14th Amendment and would likely violate the 6th Amendment right to a trial by jury and the prohibition against discrimination by a state program found in the Americans with Disabilities Act.

Truly voluntary transfers to mental health courts entail much more than a simple declaration by the defendant. On its face, a defendant's selection of a therapeutic court over one structured around determining guilt and meting out punishment would appear an obvious choice. In fact, as explained below, mental health courts have their own risks, sometimes subtle, that a defendant needs to understand in order to make an informed decision. According to the CSG report, "Defense attorneys should present all possible consequences to their clients when discussing options for the resolution of the case."

For example, a mental health court may function as a coercive agent in many ways similar to the controversial intervention of outpatient commitment, compelling an individual to participate in treatment under threat of court sanctions. However, the services available to the individual may be only those offered by a system that has already failed to help. Too many public mental health systems offer little more than medication and very occasional therapy. As with outpatient commitment, almost all mental health court orders require the individual to "follow the treatment plan." That plan may include little beyond medication and do nothing to address the factors associated with the criminal contact or the individual's need for housing or other healthcare or vocational services. Obviously, a defendant should be fully informed of such factors and, in the alternative, of the potential outcomes of a conventional criminal hearing.

Some defendants, and their attorneys, may feel it would be more in the person's interest to go before a conventional criminal hearing. These situations should be assessed on an individual basis. According to the CSG report: "On the one hand, the attorney has an obligation to reduce the defendant's possible exposure to sanctioning by the criminal justice system by removing him or her as quickly as possible from its jurisdiction. On the other hand, the attorney may recognize that the defendant will continue to be rearrested if his or her mental health needs are not addressed."

Further complicating the voluntary election of mental health court involvement is the fact that such decisions are made when the defendant is likely to be under considerable stress, having been arrested and taken into custody, and perhaps having spent some time in a jail cell, often without treatment of any kind.

Right to Withdraw

Defendants in mental health courts have come to the attention of the legal system because they have been charged with criminal conduct, not because they have met criteria for involuntary treatment. To ensure that mental health courts and the services they may initiate are truly voluntary, it is important for defendants to be allowed to withdraw and have their cases heard in criminal court without prejudice. In some courts, a defendant pleading guilty knows ahead of time what his or her sentence would be before choosing whether to participate in a mental health court. While the defendant's decision to opt for a hearing in a mental health court, as described above, is more complex than might first appear and has some attendant risks, 56 percent of the courts providing the Bazelon Center with information on this factor do not allow a defendant to reverse his or her decision and to withdraw from the mental health court program without prejudice. Of the courts that do permit this option, about half impose some restriction—for example, making withdrawal without prejudice available only with a 30-day time limit or only when program participation is not a condition of probation. The other half employ an approach supported by the Bazelon Center; they provide an unrestricted right for defendants to have their cases re-heard in criminal court without prejudice. It has also been suggested that people who voluntarily withdraw or "fail" in treatment monitored by mental health courts should be given credit for time "served" in the mental health court program; no court in the survey reported that it was utilizing this approach.

Appointment of Counsel

As a practical matter, mental health courts provide a form of pretrial diversion, most likely at or soon after the arraignment stage. A defendant who accepts transfer into a mental health court will be effectively waiving the right to a trial. It is the court's responsibility to ensure that the waiver of such a basic right is both voluntary and chosen with a realistic understanding of the legal consequences of the decision. The most reliable way to ensure that the waiver is both voluntary and informed is to provide defense counsel as soon as the defendant is identified as a candidate for the mental health court. The American Bar Association Standards Relating to Providing Defense Services state that "[c]ounsel should be provided to the accused as soon as feasible and, in any event, after custody begins, at appearance before a committing magistrate, or when charges are filed, whichever occurs earliest."

It is particularly important for an individual with a mental illness to have access to an advocate. Knowing that his or her advocate is participating in each step of the legal process can significantly improve the defendant's understanding of the process and the chance of success in the diversion program. The presence of defense counsel also helps with a number of court procedures, including obtaining authorization from the defendant to make available privileged information that may be used for a more positive outcome and limiting disclosure of private treatment information about the defendant. All of the courts on which the Bazelon Center has information provide for defense counsel, and at least one of the courts ensures that trained clinicians from the public defenders office assess offenders at the time of the bail hearing to determine whether they should be considered for the mental health court. For representation to be meaningful, defense counsel must have a background in mental health issues and in communicating with individuals who may be in crisis, an understanding of how the jurisdiction's public mental health system operates, resources that enable the attorney to actively participate in or challenge development of a treatment plan, and enough time to spend with the defendant for adequate representation.

Plea Requirement

Of the courts studied, approximately half require guilty or no contest pleas as a condition of participation. Some courts utilize a pre-adjudication model whereby charges are suspended or held in abeyance as the individual participates in treatment. More than a third of the courts surveyed allow for dismissal of the charges or expungement after successful completion of treatment. In most cases, dismissal of charges is not automatic and an individual must request expungement of the record, which is at best a cumbersome and difficult process. Furthermore, it is unclear what "successful completion of treatment" means, given that serious mental illnesses, by definition, are long term and often require many years of services and supports. Moreover, several courts retain participants' records of conviction.

The argument put forward by those who favor requiring a plea is that it is an effective form of coercion to increase treatment compliance. Beyond the irony of requiring an individual to follow a treatment plan developed by a mental health system with its own history of failures and which indeed may have placed the individual at risk of arrest in the first place, there are important reasons not to require a guilty plea:

- A guilty plea adds a conviction to the individual's record, making it harder to get or keep the housing and employment that are so crucial to effective mental health treatment, community tenure and management of a long-term psychiatric disability. One out of four of the courts surveyed report that the individual will have a record of conviction even if the course of court supervision is successfully completed.

- Pressuring a defendant with a mental illness into a guilty plea continues (and even exacerbates) the existing disparities between arrest rates and subsequent jail time for individuals with mental illnesses compared to other defendants.

- If a defendant without a mental illness would typically have charges dismissed, it is discriminatory to require a person with a mental illness to plead guilty in order to access services and supports.

Mental health courts are intended as an alternative to a traditional trial, but they should not be more punitive. If a guilty plea is required, a defendant should be given information that would allow him or her to weigh the likely jail or prison time associated with a conviction against the scope and duration of treatment that would be monitored by a mental health court. For individuals opting for mental health court, a guilty plea should be dismissed upon successful completion of a defined period of monitoring by the court.

Types of Offenses Covered

Half of all arrests of people with mental illnesses are for nonviolent crimes such as trespassing or disorderly conduct. While it would appear reasonable and fair to divert the least serious offenses before reaching the court, most of the early mental health courts focus primarily on misdemeanor cases. It is important to divert such cases, both to avoid overwhelming the criminal justice system and to prevent use of the court as a pathway to services, for example, for people who are homeless or temporarily incapacitated and in need of treatment.

- Mental health courts should focus their resources on individuals who are not considered appropriate for other types of diversion, either pre-booking or at arraignment.

- Of the courts studied, half limit eligibility to defendants with misdemeanor charges and half accept people charged with felonies, at least under certain circumstances.

- Eighty percent of the courts allow for cases involving violent acts, although 40 percent require some special process before these cases are accepted—for example, the victim's consent or a review of the specific charges.

- Twenty percent of the courts studied apply a blanket exclusion of defendants who have a history of violent behavior.

Based on Bazelon Center interviews with court personnel, mental health courts appear to be gradually expanding their jurisdiction to accept people charged with more serious offenses. This is a positive trend, reflecting the most appropriate use of mental health courts. Individuals with mental illnesses who are charged with more serious offenses are likely to be the least suited to the pre-booking diversion programs the Bazelon Center recommends as companions to mental health courts. To avoid becoming the entry point for people abandoned by the mental health system, mental health courts should close their doors to people charged with minor misdemeanors, as does the Brooklyn Mental Health Court, which handles only felonies.

Avoiding Court Involvement Through Services

Many encounters between people with serious mental illnesses and the police should not result in arrest, let alone court appearance and detention. For example, homeless people engaging in minor "crimes of survival" associated with living on the streets should not be arrested. According to the CSG report, "It is particularly important ... that mental illness itself not be used as a reason to detain a defendant in a case where a defendant with no mental illness facing similar charges and with a similar criminal record would likely be released." Accomplishing this will require collaboration between law enforcement and the mental health system. A far more effective solution for many is a law enforcement diversion program, using trained officers backed up by readily accessible mental health services and coupled with a deliberate effort to address mental health system reform. However, 50 percent of the courts included in the Bazelon Center survey operate in isolation without any defined pre-booking diversion program.

The CSG report includes examples of post-booking diversion programs and practices that do not utilize the mental health court model:

- The Mental Health Diversion Program, Jefferson County, Kentucky, serves nonviolent defendants charged with either misdemeanors or felonies who suffer from chronic mental illnesses and have a history of treatment for mental illness. Defendants who are placed in pretrial diversion undergo intensive treatment for a period of six months to one year. Upon successful completion, the charges are dismissed.

- In the Lane County, Oregon drug court, a mental health specialist trained to deal with cooccurring disorders is assigned to the drug court in the dual role of case manager and court liaison to assist with defendants who have co-occurring disorders.

- Project Link, Monroe County, New York, has developed a close working relationship with the probation department to identify offenders most in need of mental health services. It has a mobile treatment team consisting of a psychiatrist, nurse practitioner and five culturally diverse case workers who are available 24 hours a day to focus on 40 of the most serious cases.

- The Nathaniel Project in New York, New York, run by the Center for Alternative Sentencing and Employment Services, has established a dispositional alternative for people charged with serious offenses. The project is a two-year intensive case management and community supervision alternative-to-incarceration program for prisonbound defendants with serious mental illnesses. It targets defendants who have been indicted on a felony charge, including violent offenses, most of whom are homeless and suffer from co-occurring substance abuse disorders. Forensic Clinical Coordinators, who are masters-level mental health professionals and have expertise in negotiating the criminal justice system, create a comprehensive plan for community treatment. Starting work with participants prior to release, the project creates a seamless transition to community care. Once released, program participants are closely monitored and engaged in appropriate supervised community-based housing and treatment. Participants are required to attend periodic court progress dates. Charges are dismissed upon successful completion of the program.

- The Nathaniel Project has also developed a program that seeks to prevent a probation revocation by offering intensive treatment rather than incarceration for those who violate probation conditions. It targets offenders with mental illnesses who have violated conditions of probation. Case managers are clinically trained professionals with caseloads of only 10. Staff assist participants in obtaining medication, housing and other services, including day treatment, psychosocial clubhouse, vocational training and job placement.

Scope and Length of Judicial Supervision

One of the fundamental aspects of a mental health court is that the court maintains jurisdiction over the defendant while in services. Usually, mental health courts require the individual to "complete" a period of treatment. The Bazelon Center study found that the scope and duration of mental health courts' supervision varied from court to court. Even within a court, though, there may be significant variation.

- Most courts lack any written procedures, so uncertainty is great and the outcome depends on the judge's decision. In several courts the length of supervision is not specified, but is decided on a case-by-case basis. However, several courts place specific limits, generally from one to two years.

- In at least 40 percent of the courts reporting, the limits of court supervision significantly exceed the possible length of incarceration or probation for the offense.

Such policies likely discourage many individuals with mental illnesses from transferring their cases to the mental health courts.

The duration of the court's supervision of treatment should be based on the individual's treatment plan, but should never exceed the typical sentence and probationary period for the underlying criminal charge. To do so would compound the discriminatory inequities people with mental illnesses already face in the criminal justice system. While individuals with mental illnesses may require long-term services and supports, it is unnecessary and inappropriate for the court to continue to supervise such services beyond the typical period of court supervision for the underlying offense. It is the task of the mental health system to engage its clients in needed service programs, not to cede this function to criminal courts.

Accordingly, the court should carefully limit the scope and duration of its supervision. Conditions of release should be individualized, the least restrictive necessary and reasonably calculated to accomplish the court's goal, which is to reduce the likelihood that the person will recidivate. It is inappropriate and demeaning for the court to maintain protracted supervision based on the individual's mental illness, not on alleged criminal activity.

Sanctions for Non-Compliance

The performance standards of the National Association of Pretrial Services Agencies state that diversion conditions should be clearly written in a service plan signed by the defendant. This plan should detail what action could be taken in response to the individual's failure to comply with conditions, so that individuals know exactly what is expected of them. At the same time, the plan must consider the nature of serious mental illnesses. According to the CSG report, "it must be recognized that decompensation and other setbacks are common occurrences for people under treatment for mental illness as the attending mental health clinician seeks the most appropriate treatment." Moreover, "over-burdening defendants with mental illness with extraneous conditions of release raises the possibility that they will be unable to handle them and will fail to meet their requirements." The Bazelon Center found that courts use an array of mechanisms as sanctions for non-compliance with a service plan:

- Thirty-six percent of the courts reported that non-compliance is handled via adjustments in services.

- At least 27 percent try lectures, more frequent court appearances and increased judicial persuasion.

- Sixty-four percent of mental health courts reporting, however, use jail time as a sanction and 18 percent reported that the individual may be dropped from the program, actions that may be particularly unhelpful if the issue is one of normal relapse and the ups and downs of recovery from mental illness.

If the goal is to lessen the incarceration of people with mental illnesses, then using incarceration as punishment is a perversion of the whole idea of mental health courts. According to the CSG report: "Before imposing punitive sanctions for non-compliance, the court should conclude that the defendant was capable of complying but chose not to." This finding requires careful investigation. Mental health treatment is much more difficult to quantify than drug abuse treatment, which has easily defined measures of compliance and where non-compliance itself is a crime. The success of mental health services is gauged in outcomes, not adherence to a specific plan of care. Setbacks may have no relation to the individual's desire to comply with court orders or adherence with a treatment program. In fact, for many individuals with mental illnesses, various treatment and service options must be tried before an appropriate and effective service plan is established. In fact, "the key ... is to identify first the offender's individual needs and then identify the services in the community that can meet those needs."

When individuals run into difficulties while in a services program operating in collaboration with the court, the court should explore the causes. Noncompliance should be assessed in order to determine "whether any noncompliance with diversion conditions ... was willful, was a symptom of the mental health illness or was an indication of the need to change the treatment plan." These factors should be carefully considered before any sanctions are contemplated.

Often, "a more appropriate response would be to modify the treatment plan rather than to seek the revocation of [diversion]."

Case managers or social workers can be particularly helpful in monitoring treatment and coordinating services across various providers and systems, especially if they take a proactive approach, rather than just reacting to compliance problems.

Accountability of Mental Health Providers

Too often, the criminalization of defendants with mental illnesses begins with the failure of mental health programs to meet these individuals' needs or to accept them into services because they have difficult problems (such as co-occurring substance abuse) or because they already have a criminal record. Solving the problem, in the context of a mental health court, should begin with service providers' active participation in the mental health court plan and in the processing of individual cases moving through the court. This should include conducting assessments, designing person-centered service plans that seek to engage people in treatment that encompasses their own life goals (e.g., employment), and accepting responsibility for implementing the plan, in collaboration with the individual, once the defendant is referred by the court.

If the court is to be responsible for continuing supervision of the offender, including the possibility of applying sanctions for any type of noncompliance with the service plan, the court must also have the power to ensure that service providers are delivering appropriate services to defendants who are making a genuine effort to participate in their service plan. However, 63 percent of the courts reporting indicated that they have no authority to hold mental health providers accountable. The best ways to exercise this authority will depend on local circumstances, but may include the court's contempt powers, writs of mandamus or control over funds targeted toward service diversion plans.

Seventy percent of the courts reporting indicated that they have access to some, albeit limited, services beyond what the mental health system customarily offers. Vastly preferable would be better services integrated in the mainstream mental health system, rather than court oversight of a parallel system for offenders. Mental health systems should not be allowed to abdicate their role and their responsibilities on behalf of people with mental health care needs.

Medical Privacy

To work effectively, mental health courts often require medical and psychiatric treatment information about defendants, both as part of the disposition of a case and for ongoing monitoring. All of the courts surveyed reported some provisions to safeguard the privacy of information about defendants, for example, limiting discussion of clinical information in open court or delegating maintenance of clinical information to case managers and keeping the court record to a minimum. Use of treatment information in a criminal proceeding raises questions of doctor-patient privilege, and disclosing medical information in open court raises serious privacy concerns. Ensuring the early appointment of defense counsel can help to solve some of these problems by using defense counsel as a filter or reporting point for any potentially privileged treatment information. Mental health courts can address the privacy concern with rules that keep the medical information out of the public record of the proceedings and through sidebar or chamber conversations for sensitive discussions. They can also protect individual privacy with rules that limit judges' and prosecutors' access to the specific information they need to know to make their decisions.

Intended and Unintended Consequences

Typically, the genesis of mental health courts can be traced to concerns by local judges, attorneys and criminal justice personnel that people with mental illnesses were being wrongly subjected to arrest and incarceration. Their goal is to ensure not only that these individuals are diverted from the correctional system, but also that beneficial services are made available.

Mental health courts should be evaluated carefully to determine whether these objectives are, in fact, being met. For example, courts should ascertain whether individuals under their supervision are being rearrested and whether services are working to improve the individual's quality of life.

Furthermore, given that mental health courts are largely reactive to failing mental health systems,the evaluation should also consider whether reform efforts are underway by the public mental health system toward identifying and making services available to people with mental illnesses who are at risk of arrest. There is an inherent risk that any court-based diversion program, if not accompanied by such reforms and an effective pre-booking diversion program, might lead law enforcement officers to arrest someone with a mental illness in the expectation that this will lead to the provision of services. However, as stated above (and by the CSG), individuals with mental illnesses should not be arrested in situations where someone without a mental illness would not be. It is therefore important to also include arrest data in these evaluations. Finally, the court should create a mechanism for stakeholders, including people with mental illnesses, to have a say about its operations and to play an active role in the evaluation process.

No rational purpose is served by the current system. Public safety is not protected when people who have mental illnesses are needlessly arrested for nuisance crimes or when the mental illness at the root of a criminal act is exacerbated by a system designed for punishment, not treatment.

Individual rights are violated when people with mental illnesses are denied treatment and subjected to more frequent arrests and harsher sentences than other offenders. And beyond the trauma of arrest and incarceration are the unintended collateral consequences, such as social stigmatization based on a criminal record and the resulting denial of housing or employment or treatment services, even if charges are dropped.

The criminal and juvenile justice systems are not the appropriate "front door" to access mental health care. The factors that determine whether someone who has demonstrated problematic behavior enters the criminal justice system or the mental health system are often capricious rather than objective. For example, police officers may find it easier to process someone through the criminal justice system than to navigate the hurdles that mental health consumers routinely face to obtain services through the public mental health system. Ironically, community mental health programs often refuse to serve the very individuals who are most likely to benefit from their intervention and who are least appropriate for prosecution: those who have engaged in misdemeanors and who have low priority within mental health systems because they are not at risk of involuntary psychiatric hospitalization.

Perversely, the drift of people with mental illnesses into the criminal justice system has benefited public mental health systems by shifting their financial burden for "hard to serve" groups to the budgets of state corrections departments. As a result, taxpayers' resources are wasted on expensive and counter-productive incarceration instead of financing more appropriate and effective community mental health and supportive services. Police, court and jail personnel are forced to devote inordinate amounts of time to arresting, processing and incarcerating individuals with mental illnesses, a process that also diverts their attention from more serious crimes, defendants and inmates.

To eliminate the unnecessary and harmful criminalization of people with mental illnesses, communities must address the causes of the problem, not just its symptoms. The substantial gaps in effective community services are the root of the problem and addressing them must be the first step toward its solution. Training court personnel and law enforcement officers to enable them to make better informed decisions about people with mental illnesses and about new and existing treatment resources is also critical. Both of these steps can have a major impact on the presence of people with mental illnesses in the criminal justice system, even without creating a formal mental health court. Communities looking to create or expand court-based diversion programs should consider the wide range of existing programs, such as the examples listed above.

Jurisdictions that do create specialized mental health courts will have far more success and will better serve the cause of justice if they include treatment and diversion programs as part of a broad package of systemic reform.

If communities do choose to set up mental health courts, they should be aware of the need to focus on the final outcome, successful reintegration into the community and reduced recidivism. These outcomes are more likely to be achieved if the court focuses on ensuring the success of community services and avoids actions that hinder reintegration, such as insisting on guilty pleas that lead to denial of housing or employment.

Conclusion

This article described the Bazelon Center's study review of mental health court and its recommendation for reform. It analyzed the potential problems and benefits posed by these alternative courts and concluded that they should be used, if at all, with great caution for individual rights and only when defendants face significant jail or prison sentences and when part of a broad reform of the community mental health system. Specialty mental health courts, when used for more serious offenses and responsive to the issues raised in this paper, can play a productive role in a comprehensive strategy to break the cycle of poor treatment, worsening mental illness, escalating criminal behavior and increasing arrest and incarceration. But court-based diversion, whether through specialty mental health courts or through regular criminal courts, is not a panacea for addressing the needs of the growing number of people with mental illnesses who come in contact with the criminal justice system. Rather, it should be seen as but one part of the solution.

Certainly, not every crime committed by an individual diagnosed with a mental illness is attributable to disability or to the failure of public mental health. But homelessness, unemployment and a lack of access to meaningful treatment services have clearly put many people with mental illnesses at risk of arrest. The Bazelon Center for Mental Health Law strongly endorses efforts to address these root causes of criminalization, recognizing at the same time that this will require a fundamental change in the mental health systems that have so tragically deviated from their goal of promoting community living with dignity. Yet in large measure the reforms proposed to date come from the criminal justice sector, which finds itself both ill-equipped to address the needs of people with mental illnesses and alarmed about the *de facto* role of jails and prisons as today's psychiatric institutions. Mental health systems, even while attempting to address the criminalization of the populations they are charged with serving, have not typically originated reform efforts. For this reason, it is important to build any reforms in such a way as not to bypass the mental health and other service systems or allow them to shirk their responsibilities. Every effort should be made to assist people with serious mental illnesses before they come to the attention of law enforcement and to identify and address system failures that result in their inappropriate arrest or incarceration for minor offenses.

Innovation and, above all, a dedication to reform are necessary to address the growing problem of criminalization from both a public safety and a public health point of view. Communities that are committed to change, where mental health and criminal justice interests work collaboratively on solutions, can find cost-effective and just ways to reverse the present trend of neglected lives and wasted resources.

* * *

Questions for Discussion

1. Do you think that mental health courts are important? Why or why not? Are there any located in your city or state? If so, what are their features? If not, are any efforts underway to establish one?

2. What do you think of the different features of the mental health courts that were reviewed in this article?

For Further Reading

Eric Trupin and Henry Richards, *Seattle's Mental Health Courts: Early Indicators of Effectiveness*, 26 International Journal of Law and Psychiatry 33 (2003), retrieved May 15, 2012 at http://www.floridatac.org/files/document/Trupin_IJLP_Jan03.pdf.

Michael J. Finkle, Russell Kurth, et al., "Competency courts: a creative solution for restoring competency to the competency process," 27 Behavioral Sciences & the Law 767 (2009).

Discussion 17

Prisoners with Disabilities

Recommended Background Reading

Pennsylvania Dept of Corrections v. Yeskey, 524 U.S. 206 (1998).
Barnes v. Gorman, 536 U.S. 181 (2002).

Readings for Class Discussion

The following is information provided to prisoners by the ACLU. Footnotes have been omitted.

Know Your Rights: Legal Rights of Disabled Prisoners
ACLU National Prison Project

Important Note: The law is always evolving. If you have access to a prison law library, it is a good idea to confirm that the cases and statutes cited below are still good law. Updated 11/05 (prior to the ADA Amendments Act).

Statutes protecting disabled prisoners

Prisoners are protected by § 504 of the Rehabilitation Act of 1973, 29 U.S.C. § 794(a), and by Title II of the Americans with Disabilities Act, 42 U.S.C. § 12131, et seq. The Rehabilitation Act was created to apply to federal executive agencies, including the Bureau of Prisons, and to any program that receives federal funding. The ADA was created to regulate state and local government programs, even those that do not receive federal funding.

The Supreme Court recently held in *Goodman v. Georgia* that Title II of the ADA validly abrogates state sovereign immunity — as least insofar as it creates a private cause of action for damages for conduct that actually violates the Fourteenth Amendment. In the prison context, this means that a disabled prisoner who is incarcerated in state prison may sue the state for monetary damages under the ADA based on conduct that independently violates the Due Process Clause of the Fourteenth Amendment (incorporating the Eighth Amendment's prohibition on cruel and unusual punishment). Thus, although the ADA arguably prohibits a broader swath of state conduct than what is barred by the Eighth Amendment, it remains an unsettled question whether disabled prisoners can seek damages for conduct that violates the ADA but not the Constitution.

269

Applying these statutes in the prison context

Courts analyze the ADA and Rehabilitation Act in basically the same way. If the ADA applies, it should be interpreted to give disabled people at least as many rights as the earlier Rehabilitation Act. Thus, disabled prisoners may use cases about the Rehabilitation Act to help them interpret the ADA.

How do you define disability?

The ADA defines "disability" as:

> (A) a physical or mental impairment that substantially limits one or more of the major life activities of such individual; (B) a record of such an impairment; or (C) being regarded as having such an impairment.

A "physical or mental impairment" could include hearing and vision problems, mental illness, physical disabilities, certain diseases, or many other conditions. "Major life activities" may include many private or public activities, such as seeing, hearing, reproduction, working, walking or movement. For ADA purposes, a physical impairment substantially limits major life activities only if it prevents or severely restricts the individual from performing tasks of central importance to daily life. [Editors' note: the ADAAA explicity overrules this idea.]

"Substantially limited" means that the person's participation in the activity is significantly restricted. The restriction does not need to completely prevent the disabled person from participating in the activity, but it must do more than merely cause him or her to participate in a different manner. If a disability is corrected to the point that it does not substantially limit a major life activity, it no longer counts as a disability under the ADA.

Courts usually look at the facts of each lawsuit to decide if a person is disabled according to the ADA and Rehabilitation Act. For example, the Supreme Court has said that a person infected with HIV (human immunodeficiency virus), the virus that causes AIDS, may be disabled even if that person does not have any symptoms of the disease. On the other hand, a person with impaired vision in one eye is disabled only if his vision substantially limits participation in a major life activity.

Enforcing your legal rights

Title II of the ADA states:

> [N]o qualified individual with a disability shall, by reason of such disability, be excluded from participation in or be denied the benefits of the services, programs, or activities of a public entity, or be subjected to discrimination by any such entity.

To bring a lawsuit under the ADA and/or the Rehabilitation Act, disabled prisoners must show: (1) that they are disabled within the meaning of the statutes, (2) that they are "qualified" to participate in the program, and (3) that they are excluded from, are not allowed to benefit from, or have been subjected to discrimination in the program because of their disability. Under the Rehabilitation Act, prisoners must also show that the prison officials or the governmental agency named as defendants receive federal funding.

Courts generally require factual evidence that shows the prisoners are qualified for the programs, sought participation, and were denied entry based upon their disabilities. Disabled prisoners are "qualified" to participate in a program under the ADA and the Rehabilitation Act if they meet the program requirements.

Which rights can be enforced?

Disabled prisoners have sued to get equal access to facilities, programs and services. For example, inmates and arrestees have sued to be able to use prison showers and toilets and to be protected from injury or the risk of injury.

Deaf and hearing-impaired prisoners have won cases to get sign language interpreters for disciplinary hearings, classification decisions, HIV-AIDS counseling, and educational and vocational programs.

Disabled prisoners have challenged inadequate medical care and prison officials' failure to provide them with medical supplies or devices such as wheelchairs or canes. These cases may combine ADA claims with arguments that prison officials have violated the Eighth Amendment of the U.S. Constitution by being deliberately indifferent to prisoners' serious medical needs.

Disabled prisoners have challenged their confinement in isolation and segregation units under the ADA and the Rehabilitation Act. In one case, for example, the Seventh Circuit ruled that prison officials discriminated against a quadriplegic prisoner in Indiana who was housed in an infirmary unit for over one year and was thereby denied access to the dining hall, recreation area, visiting, church, work, transitional programs and the library. However, some courts have upheld policies segregating HIV-positive prisoners because of the risk or perceived risk of transmission.

Limitations on these rights

Prison officials are not required to provide accommodations that impose "undue financial and administrative burdens" or require "a fundamental alteration in the nature of [the] program." Prison officials are also allowed to discriminate if the disabled inmates' participation would pose "significant health and safety risks" or a "direct threat" to others. Finally, some courts have said that prison officials can discriminate against disabled prisoners as long as the discriminatory policies serve "legitimate penological interests."

Alternatives to the ADA and Rehabilitation Act

Disabled prisoners may make claims for relief based on the United States Constitution either in addition to, or instead of, ADA and Rehabilitation Act claims. The Eighth Amendment prohibits any form of cruel or unusual punishment. For example, federal or state prison officials violate the Eighth Amendment when staff members are deliberately indifferent to the serious medical needs of prisoners, including the special requirements of disabled inmates.

The Fifth and Fourteenth Amendments prohibit government officials from depriving persons of life, liberty or property without "due process" of law, and the Fourteenth Amendment requires that all citizens receive the "equal protection" of the law. Thus, prison officials may violate the Constitution if they discriminate against disabled inmates on the basis of their disabilities. However, to win an equal protection claim, disabled persons must prove that there is no legitimate government reason for the discriminatory policy. This is a very difficult standard for prisoners to meet because courts generally give prison officials wide discretion in administering correctional facilities.

Finally, the laws of some states may provide different or greater legal rights than the federal laws discussed in this information sheet. Disabled prisoners should investigate this possibility before bringing suit.

* * *

Questions for Discussion

1. Did the ADA Amendments Act make any changes that would affect the substance of this article? Has the U.S. Supreme Court decided any cases that would impact the substance of this article?

2. Does your state provide broader protections to prisoners with disabilities than the ADA does?

———————

The following is a more recent article about reasonable accommodation requests by prisoners and arrestees. Footnotes have been omitted.

Expecting the Unreasonable:
Why a Specific Request Requirement for ADA Title II
Discrimination Claims Fails to Protect Those Who
Cannot Request Reasonable Accommodations

David A. Maas, Harvard Law & Policy Review, February 28, 2011

Introduction

Persons with disabilities can pose complex challenges to law enforcement officers charged with keeping the peace. Police officers are often the first responders to persons with mental disabilities in crisis. These problematic, high-stakes encounters have drastically increased in frequency as a result of the gradual shift from institutional to community-based care. The difficulties associated with this integration process have been exacerbated by insufficient funding for outpatient support services. To make matters worse, many mental or developmental disabilities when untreated can produce behaviors that aggravate officers or members of the public. Some scholars have even argued that our laws have effectively criminalized the symptoms of disabilities. As a result, persons with disabilities are in a vulnerable position: they need a robust set of protections in place to provide some measure of security and predictability in their interactions with law enforcement. This article analyzes how the Americans with Disabilities Act ("ADA") can help bring stability and justice to the interactions between law enforcement officers and persons with disabilities.

Part I describes how most courts have correctly reached the conclusion that law enforcement activities are covered by the ADA. Although there has been limited resistance to this doctrinal development, the plain language of the statute and the legislative history both support the prevailing jurisprudence. As the federal courts have addressed an increasing number of ADA cases brought by arrestees with disabilities, judges have generally succeeded in effectuating the remedial purpose of the ADA. However, Part II identifies one place where the judiciary has gotten it wrong. Under Title II of the ADA, persons with disabilities are entitled to reasonable modifications to a public entity's services, programs, and activities to avoid discrimination. The Eleventh Circuit has held that to state a claim for failure to provide reasonable modifications, a plaintiff must have made a specific request for accommodation. Part II discusses how a "specific request" requirement is itself discriminatory because it fails to protect persons who cannot articulate their need for reasonable accommodations.

This article argues that the ADA places an affirmative duty on law enforcement agencies to provide reasonable modifications in their policies and procedures. To satisfy this antidiscrimination command of Title II of the ADA, law enforcement officers should receive training in the provision of reasonable accommodations. Part III explores some of the issues that surround police interactions with persons with disabilities and discusses how those issues have precipitated innovative training programs. Many disability rights groups have already pushed for better police training, and many have succeeded at the local and even state level. Using those successful efforts as a model, Part IV proposes a national mandate solidifying the affirmative duty to provide reasonable accommodations in law enforcement activities. This article submits two model regulations for the Department of Justice ("DOJ") to consider issuing pursuant to its ADA Title II authority. The first clarifies that persons with disabilities are entitled to reasonable accommodations even absent a specific request. The second attempts to consolidate and nationalize the scattered local programs that provide training to law enforcement officers for their inevitable interactions with persons with disabilities. Finally, Part IV suggests that the DOJ issue tailored guidance for law enforcement agencies, setting out examples and best practices for the provision of reasonable accommodations to persons with mental and developmental disabilities.

I. Why the ADA Covers Law Enforcement Activities

When a unanimous Supreme Court decided *Pennsylvania Department of Corrections v. Yeskey*, it opened the floodgates for prison inmates with disabilities seeking to vindicate their rights in federal court under the ADA. Given the penal system's well-documented inadequacies in fairly and equitably treating persons with disabilities, *Yeskey* was a watershed decision for disability rights advocates. In the wake of *Yeskey*, plaintiffs were finally able to remedy ADA violations against incarcerated persons with disabilities. However, *Yeskey* left unanswered whether ADA protections extend to arrestees and pre-trial detainees.

The ADA prohibits a "public entity" from discriminating against a qualified individual with a disability on account of that disability. To state a claim under Title II, a plaintiff must allege that (1) he is a qualified individual with a disability, (2) who was excluded from participation in or denied the benefits of a public entity's services, programs, or activities, and (3) such exclusion, denial of benefits, or discrimination was by reason of a disability. Courts have agreed that a law enforcement agency constitutes a "public entity." The only point of contention about the ADA's coverage of arrestees is whether an arrest—or any other law enforcement activity—constitutes a "benefit" of a public entity's services, programs or activities. Without guidance from the Supreme Court, the lower courts have generally answered this question in the affirmative, finding that qualified arrestees and pre-trial detainees with disabilities are covered under Title II of the ADA.

Shortly after *Yeskey* was decided, the Eighth Circuit set a strong precedent when it held that arrestees and pre-trial detainees are not overlooked by the ADA. In *Gorman v. Bartch*, a paraplegic man was arrested and transported in a vehicle not equipped for wheelchairs; he fell from a bench in the vehicle and suffered a serious injury that required surgery. The court allowed the plaintiff's Title II claim to proceed based on the plain language of the statute and a judicious application of the Supreme Court's holding in *Yeskey*. With a few exceptions, the lower courts have to come to this sensible conclusion that arrestees are entitled to ADA protection, including reasonable accommodations. However, the existing jurisprudence has not fully addressed all of the complicated and sensitive issues that arise in the interactions between persons with disabilities and law enforcement. In particular, courts have not grappled with the reality that many persons with disabilities are incapable of articulating their needs to police officers.

II. The Specific Request Requirement: ADA Jurisprudence Gone Awry

This article focuses on an issue that has given the courts trouble: whether persons with disabilities must make specific requests for modifications to state discrimination claims for failure to provide reasonable accommodations. A Title II claim for compensatory relief requires a showing of discrimination. A plaintiff can proceed on theories of (1) intentional discrimination, (2) disparate treatment, or (3) failure to make reasonable accommodations. The first two types of discrimination claims—intentional misconduct and disparate treatment—are more easily identifiable. But some forms of discrimination can come in the form of *normal* treatment, when special treatment is necessary. The failure to provide reasonable accommodations embodies this kind of latent discrimination, and the justice system must be more vigilant to protect against it.

The ADA provides this extra security by placing an affirmative duty on law enforcement agencies and other public entities to provide reasonable accommodations. The ADA expressly provides that it is discriminatory when an entity fails to "take such steps as may be necessary to ensure that no individual with a disability is excluded, denied services, segregated or otherwise treated differently than other individuals because of the absence of auxiliary aids and services." As the Fifth Circuit stated, a "plain reading of the ADA evidences that Congress intended to impose an affirmative duty on public entities to create policies or procedures to prevent discrimination based on disability." This positive duty is not an entirely new or extraordinary burden on law enforcement agencies: it is functionally similar to the policing requirements set forth by the Supreme Court in *Miranda v. Arizona*. An *unconditional* duty to provide accommodations would present problems. It would interfere with an officer's ability to protect public safety, and officers also might have difficulty identifying disabilities. However, the ADA addresses these concerns by (1) requiring only *reasonable* modifications, and (2) providing a defense for modifications that fundamentally alter the nature of an activity.

Furthermore, courts have already developed public-safety and exigent-circumstances exceptions to the anti-discrimination command of the ADA. For example, the Fifth Circuit held that "Title II does not apply to an officer's on-the-street responses to reported disturbances or other similar incidents, whether or not those calls involve subjects with mental disabilities, prior to the officer's securing the scene and ensuring that there is no threat to human life." This narrow exception allows officers to function in their law enforcement capacity without the unreasonable burden of proactively accommodating persons with disabilities. The courts are well suited to develop and refine the contours of these exceptions in the time-honored common-law tradition.

Unfortunately, some courts have restricted the availability of discrimination claims based on the failure to provide reasonable accommodations. The Eleventh Circuit held in *Rylee v. Chapman* that "[i]n cases alleging a failure to make reasonable accommodations, the defendant's duty to provide a reasonable accommodation is not triggered until the plaintiff makes a '*specific demand*' for an accommodation." In *Rylee*, bad facts resulted in bad law and a dangerous precedent for persons with disabilities. The plaintiff, a man with a hearing impairment, filed suit alleging intentional discrimination under Title II of the ADA based on his treatment during an arrest, booking, interrogation, and appearance hearing. He was arrested after his son and wife called 911 and reported that Rylee had physically assaulted and threatened to kill his wife. In the course of that 911 call, Rylee's wife had informed officers that Rylee did not know sign language but could read lips when spoken to slowly. During Rylee's arrest, he made no specific request for accommodations and the officers did not provide an interpreter or communicate in writing. While being booked, Rylee requested to communicate in writing, and the booking officer complied. The court found that Rylee could not state an ADA Title II discrimination claim because he had not articulated any specific request for accommodation that the police officers had failed to provide during his arrest.

The court in *Rylee* took this highly unfavorable set of facts and drove the doctrine of ADA Title II discrimination in the wrong direction. The court supported its reasoning by citing an Eleventh Circuit case, *Gaston v. Bellingrath Gardens & Home, Inc.*, which it used to justify the invocation of a "specific demand" requirement. The court's reliance on *Gaston*, an ADA Title I employment discrimination case, was misguided. Even if requiring a specific request was legitimate under the ADA in the employment context, the court should not have imported it into Title II's coverage of law enforcement activities. Persons with disabilities seeking accommodations in the employment context generally have the time and resources to organize and articulate requests; in contrast, during arrests, interrogations, and other pressured law enforcement activities, persons with disabilities lack the time to collect their thoughts or seek outside assistance. The specific request requirement fails to protect fairly and adequately persons with disabilities during interactions with law enforcement.

The *Rylee* decision effectively dismembers the anti-discrimination power of Title II of the ADA. Persons with mental and developmental disabilities in particular could be left without a cause of action under this narrow reading of the statute. The lower courts should revisit and reinterpret the definition of discrimination to resolve the Eleventh Circuit's flawed framing of the doctrine.

III. The Challenges of Training Law Enforcement: State and Local Solutions

If courts confirm that law enforcement agencies have an affirmative duty to provide accommodations, the question becomes how agencies can feasibly train police officers to comply. This question has already been answered in part by proactive measures taken on the state and local level. Since the Supreme Court decided *Olmstead v. L.C.*, more and more persons with disabilities are becoming active members of mainstream society. As a result of this deinstitutionalization process, persons with disabilities are interacting with law enforcement on a more consistent basis. Persons with mental and developmental disabilities are particularly prone to interactions with law enforcement officers, in part because some symptoms can provoke police encounters. The sheer number of police interactions is not the only challenge. The vast array of disabilities makes the project of training and sensitizing law enforcement officers to the particularized needs of every kind of disability virtually impossible. Moreover, some disabilities manifest themselves in behaviors that are difficult to detect, understand, and control. These obstacles have not stopped local and state movements from succeeding in training law enforcement officers.

Perhaps the most famous local law enforcement training program is Memphis, Tennessee's Crisis Intervention Team ("CIT"). The program began before the enactment of the ADA in response to the tragic shooting of a mentally ill person by a police officer. The Memphis CIT operates by specially training a small unit of police personnel who are dispatched to any calls that involve persons with mental illnesses. Regular patrol officers receive basic training on how to handle these complicated interactions and benefit from their cooperative work with the CIT members. The Memphis CIT model has spread to other cities, often after an unfortunate interaction between law enforcement and a person with a disability. For example, Chicago has adopted a similar CIT program that promotes training and awareness through cooperative ventures with groups like The Autism Program of Illinois. The cooperation and support of disability rights groups minimizes the financial burden on law enforcement agencies and allows persons with disabilities to have a voice in the training programs. Local CIT programs have proven very successful; they provide model policies for other law enforcement agencies seeking to introduce training programs. Moreover, some states have taken more concrete legislative steps to ensure appropriate training of law enforcement. These measures are the result of targeted advocacy; their successes showcase the viability and importance of a national mandate. The spread of training programs should not depend on local tragedies that mobilize advocates.

The absence of a federal directive leaves persons with mental and developmental disabilities especially at risk. All disabilities present challenges, but mental and developmental disabilities "present a particular challenge in the context of police encounters, where mis-understood, socially atypical behavior may result in a dangerous situation for both the officer and the individual." The ADA should not deny protection to persons with disabilities who require more nuanced accommodations. The ADA was not intended to create a hierarchy of persons with disabilities or provide tiered protections based on the ease of accommodation. The success of state and local movements should signal to the courts and the DOJ that a national mandate is timely, feasible, and commanded by the ADA.

IV. Nationalizing the Solution: Proposed New and Amended Regulations for the Department of Justice

The U.S. Department of Justice serves as the congressionally-mandated enforcer of Title II of the ADA. In this capacity, the DOJ has issued regulations "to effectuate subtitle A of title II of the [ADA], which prohibits discrimination on the basis of disability by public entities." The ADA and the DOJ regulations both require a public entity to "make reasonable modifications in policies, practices, or procedures when the modifications are necessary to avoid discrimination on the basis of disability, unless the public entity can demonstrate that making the modifications would fundamentally alter the nature of the service, program, or activity." Thus, the plain language of the existing DOJ regulation places the burden on a public entity to make reasonable modifications unless the entity can raise a fundamental alteration defense. The dangerous, misguided, and judicially created "specific request" requirement is contrary to the DOJ's existing regulations. The DOJ should clarify that there is an affirmative duty on law enforcement agencies to provide reasonable accommodations by amending the existing regulation.

The DOJ should also consider issuing new, tailored regulations that provide more specific guidance to law enforcement agencies in the training of police officers. The proposed model regulations for law enforcement agencies appended to this article contain a number of important elements: (1) a general duty to train, (2) with all deliberate speed, and (3) an undue burden defense. The general duty to train flows directly from the affirmative duty to provide reasonable accommodations. Officers must be able to recognize and understand a broad spectrum of disabilities before they can know when to make ac-commodations proactively. Training programs will empower the police with the knowledge necessary to avoid inadvertent discrimination. The proposed regulations also set forth that training shall proceed with all deliberate speed. This language, inherited from the Supreme Court's school-desegregation jurisprudence, is not new to disability law. The inclusion of a flexible but still exacting time mandate will give teeth to these new regulations while recognizing that some law enforcement agencies are better equipped than others to implement new training procedures.

The proposed regulations also contain an undue burden defense. Comprehensive training of police officers will be a substantial financial and administrative burden to law enforcement agencies. Under the DOJ's existing Title II regulations, the undue burden defense is limited to the accessibility section. If the DOJ attaches a similar defense to these targeted regulations for law enforcement activities, it will address the possibility of unwieldy costs. An unconditional affirmative duty on law enforcement to train officers in the provision of reasonable modifications for all disabilities would be unfeasible. However, comprehensive training of law enforcement officers is not necessary to establish an enforceable baseline standard of training that the judiciary can refine over time on a case by case basis. The purpose of these regulations is to motivate training regimes that eventually set a minimum standard that persons with disabilities can expect in their interactions with law enforcement.

Law enforcement agencies would also benefit from a set of DOJ provisions addressing mental and developmental disabilities. Persons with mental and developmental disabilities pose a unique set of challenges for law enforcement; without specific protections, this class will remain vulnerable to discrimination and reckless ignorance. These individuals can face substantial hurdles in overcoming discrimination: many do not know their rights and cannot communicate their needs. As a result, they are at the mercy of a system that does not proactively accommodate them.

The ADA commands particularized protections for the provision of reasonable accommodations in law enforcement activities. Persons with mental and developmental disabilities require more than simple modifications, translators, or physical assistance. The DOJ has set an example by issuing a detailed and constructive set of guidelines for law enforcement officers interacting with persons who have hearing impairments. In that document, the DOJ provides not only a well-articulated set of requirements for law enforcement officers but also a useful set of "Practical Suggestions for Communicating Effectively." In the practical suggestions section, the DOJ sets forth the everyday ways in which law enforcement officers can provide reasonable accommodations for persons with hearing impairments. Some of these may seem obvious, like "try to converse in a well-lit area" or "face the person and do not turn away while speaking." However, they serve two important purposes: (1) they help remedy institutional ignorance about persons with disabilities; and (2) they provide a standard of care for persons with disabilities to expect. The DOJ should provide similar guidance for accommodating persons with mental and developmental disabilities such that those persons can expect a baseline standard of care in their interactions with law enforcement.

If the DOJ can mobilize a task force to create this tailored guidance, law enforcement agencies can integrate the guidance into their training programs. Eventually, disability training will become a small subset of the multifaceted law enforcement training procedures. As disability training continues to develop and spread, it will infuse the law enforcement system with institutional knowledge about persons with disabilities. This knowledge will foster sensitivity to the needs of persons with disabilities and should help reduce the frequency of tragic encounters. Thus, although there will be significant startup costs to a national training mandate, there will be counterbalancing benefits including the vindication of the rights of this marginalized group.

Conclusion

The growing population of persons with disabilities living in community settings presents significant challenges to law enforcement. The inadequacy of outpatient services often results in persons with disabilities receiving improper or insufficient treatment. These systemic failures leave persons with mental disabilities susceptible to committing crimes or otherwise encountering law enforcement officers. Although the ADA covers arrestees, there is no particularized framework set out to protect persons with disabilities in these dangerous and high-stakes situations. The goal of this article is not to suggest that police forces are acting with discriminatory animus against persons with disabilities. Instead, this article is intended to motivate a discussion about the best way to effectuate the ADA's protections in the context of law enforcement activities. Police officers must receive notice and training before we can expect them appropriately to modify policies and procedures for persons with disabilities. Until there is a more robust set of protections in place, persons with disabilities remain vulnerable. The DOJ should remedy this systemic weakness by issuing new and amended regulations that solidify the ADA's protection of law enforcement activities and nationalize the police training movement.

APPENDIX 1: Proposed Model Regulations

Proposal 1: Amendment of Existing Regulation to Correct the Specific Request Requirement

28 C.F.R. § 35.130 General prohibitions against discrimination.

...

(7) A public entity shall make reasonable modifications in policies, practices, or procedures when the modifications are necessary to avoid discrimination on the basis of disability, unless the public entity can demonstrate that making the modifications would fundamentally alter the nature of the service, program, or activity. When reasonable modifications are necessary to avoid discrimination, a public entity shall make these modifications regardless of whether persons with disabilities specifically articulate a request for accommodation.

Proposal 2: New Regulation Tailored for Law Enforcement Agencies

28 C.F.R. § 35.XXX—Additional Requirements for Law Enforcement Agencies

(a) A law enforcement agency shall make reasonable modifications in policies, practices, or procedures when the modifications are necessary to avoid discrimination on the basis of disability. When reasonable modifications are necessary to avoid discrimination, a law enforcement agency shall make these modifications regardless of whether persons with disabilities specifically articulate a request for accommodation. A law enforcement agency shall take all reasonable steps to train officers in the provision of reasonable modifications for persons with disabilities.

(b) Law enforcement agencies should proceed with all deliberate speed in training officers in the provision of reasonable modifications to persons with disabilities. The reasonableness of a law enforcement agency's training program depends on the following non-exhaustive list of considerations: (1) the population of a law enforcement agency's jurisdiction; (2) the number of persons with disabilities in a law enforcement agency's jurisdiction; (3) the financial and administrative burdens of training, including the availability of outside support in training; (4) the number of officers in a law enforcement agency; (5) a law enforcement agency's history of interactions with persons with disabilities; and (6) the length of time elapsed since the effective date of this section.

(c) This section does not require a law enforcement agency to take any action that it can demonstrate would result in a fundamental alteration in the nature of a service, program, or activity, or in undue financial or administrative burdens. In those circumstances where personnel of the law enforcement agency believe that the proposed action would fundamentally alter the service, program, or activity, or would result in undue financial or administrative burdens, a law enforcement agency has the burden of proving that compliance with 35.XXX(a) or (b) of this section would result in such alteration or burdens.

(d) Nothing in this section shall be construed to limit a state or local government or law enforcement agency from maintaining a training program that exceeds the minimum standards required by this section.

* * *

Questions for Discussion

1. Do you agree with the conclusions and proposed solutions in this article? What other ideas do you have about these issues?

2. What types of accommodations can you imagine an arrestee requesting? What types of accommodations might a prisoner with a disability seek?

The following is a fact sheet prepared by National Disability Rights Network.

Youths With Disabilities in the Juvenile Justice System Fact Sheet
September 2007

In 2000, more than 30 million youth were under juvenile court jurisdiction; 80% of involved youth were between the ages of 10 and 15.[1]

A disproportionate number of youth with mental health, substance use, cognitive, developmental, learning, and other disabilities come into contact with juvenile justice (JJ) systems. Between 50 and 75% of incarcerated youth have diagnosable mental health problems.[2] Having a disability is a risk factor for contact with the JJ system.[3]

Some 33.4% of incarcerated youth have an identified special education disability, compared to roughly 10% of the general education population. This includes only those who have been identified.[4]

In one study of detainees at a large metropolitan juvenile detention center, among detainees who had major mental health impairments and associated functional impairments, only 15.4% of those youth received any treatment while in the detention center, and only 8.1% received treatment in the community by the time of disposition or within 6 months, whichever came first.[5]

Some children and youth in detention facilities have not committed any offense. For example, two thirds of detention facilities have reported holding children, sometimes as

---

1. Juvenile Court Statistics 2000-Report (2004). NCJJ/OJJDP, available at: http://www.ncjrs.gov/pdffiles1/ojjdp/209736.pdf.

2. With regard to mental health disabilities, see Mental Health Needs of Youth and Young Offenders: Issues & Facts. Coalition for Juvenile Justice (2000), available at: http://www.juvjustice.org/factsheet_8.html.

3. A Shortage of Mental Health Services Drives Inappropriate Placements in Juvenile Detention, M. Sage, Focal Point, Vol. 20, No. 2 (Summer, 2006), available at: http://www.rtc.pdx.edu/PDF/fpS0609.pdf.

4. IDEA and the Juvenile Justice System: A Factsheet (April 2005), available at: http://www.neglected-delinquent.org/nd/resources/spotlight/spotlight200503f.asp.

5. Detecting Mental Disorder in Juvenile Detainees: Who Receives Services, Linda A. Teplin, et al. 95(10) Am. J. Public Health 1773 (Oct., 2005), available at: http://www.ajph.org/cgi/content/abstract/95/10/1773.

young as seven, who are waiting for a mental health placement. A 2004 report to Congress documented that about 7% of youth in detention were there for this purpose.[6]

"Delinquent" behaviors may be directly related to an unknown, untreated, or inappropriately treated disability. Identifying disabilities and providing timely access to appropriate treatment and services can prevent further and future contact with the JJ system.[7]

Youth in the JJ system are "disproportionately minority, impoverished, and poorly educated, and many lack social networks—characteristics known to limit the type and scope of mental health services provided to youth."[8]

Juvenile Justice agencies report a lack of expertise, staffing, and training to care adequately for emotionally challenged youth.[9]

* * *

Questions for Discussion

1. How do issues for incarcerated juveniles with disabilities differ from incarcerated adults with disabilities?

2. What can be done to increase diagnosis and treatment of mental health disorders in juveniles?

For Further Reading

Shook v. The Board of County Commissioners of the County of El Paso, 543 F.3d 597 (10th Cir. 2008). Prisoners in the El Paso County jail brought suit based on deliberate indifference to their mental health needs; the court upheld the district court's denial of class certification.

Fisher, Jennifer. *The Americans with Disabilities Act: Correcting Discrimination of Persons with Mental Disabilities in the Arrest, Post-Arrest, and Pretrial Processes*, 23 Law & Ineq. 157 (2005).

---

6. Incarceration of youth who are waiting for community mental health services in the United States. U.S. Congress (2004). House of Representatives Committee on Governmental Reform. http://www.senate.gov/~govt-aff/_files/040707juvenilereport.pdf.

7. "[C]riminality in juveniles is almost always the product of the child's untreated social, mental or education problems." An Evaluation of the Youth Advocacy Project (May 2001), The Spangenberg Group, available at: http://www.abanet.org/legalservices/downloads/sclaid/indigentdefense/mayapreport.pdf.

8. Psychiatric Disorders of Youth in Detention. Teplin, L.A. et al (2006), OJJDP Juvenile Justice Bulletin, at p. 13; available at: http://www.ncjrs.gov/pdffiles1/ojjdp/210331.pdf.

9. Annual Report 2006, Federal Advisory Committee on Juvenile Justice, available at: http://www.ncjrs.gov/pdffiles1/ojjdp/218367.pdf.

Discussion 18

The Death Penalty and Intellectual Disability

Recommended Background Reading

Penry v. Lynaugh, 492 U.W. 302 (1989).

————

Readings for Class Discussion

This is a case about executing people with "mental retardation." Due to the length of the case, the footnotes and appendices have been removed, but they also deserve study and discussion.

Atkins v. Virginia
SUPREME COURT OF THE UNITED STATES
536 U.S. 304 (2002)

JUDGES: STEVENS, J., delivered the opinion of the Court, in which O'CONNOR, KENNEDY, SOUTER, GINSBURG, and BREYER, JJ., joined. REHNQUIST, C. J., filed a dissenting opinion, in which SCALIA and THOMAS, JJ., joined. SCALIA, J., filed a dissenting opinion, in which REHNQUIST, C. J., and THOMAS, J., joined.

JUSTICE STEVENS delivered the opinion of the Court.

Those mentally retarded persons who meet the law's requirements for criminal responsibility should be tried and punished when they commit crimes. Because of their disabilities in areas of reasoning, judgment, and control of their impulses, however, they do not act with the level of moral culpability that characterizes the most serious adult criminal conduct. Moreover, their impairments can jeopardize the reliability and fairness of capital proceedings against mentally retarded defendants. Presumably for these reasons, in the 13 years since we decided *Penry v. Lynaugh*, 492 U.S. 302, 106 L. Ed. 2d 256, 109 S. Ct. 2934 (1989), the American public, legislators, scholars, and judges have deliberated over the question whether the death penalty should ever be imposed on a mentally retarded criminal. The consensus reflected in those deliberations informs our answer to the question presented by this case: whether such executions are "cruel and unusual punishments" prohibited by the Eighth Amendment to the Federal Constitution.

I

Petitioner, Daryl Renard Atkins, was convicted of abduction, armed robbery, and capital murder, and sentenced to death. At approximately midnight on August 16, 1996, Atkins and William Jones, armed with a semiautomatic handgun, abducted Eric Nesbitt, robbed him of the money on his person, drove him to an automated teller machine in his pickup truck where cameras recorded their withdrawal of additional cash, then took him to an isolated location where he was shot eight times and killed.

Jones and Atkins both testified in the guilt phase of Atkins' trial. Each confirmed most of the details in the other's account of the incident, with the important exception that each stated that the other had actually shot and killed Nesbitt. Jones' testimony, which was both more coherent and credible than Atkins', was obviously credited by the jury and was sufficient to establish Atkins' guilt. At the penalty phase of the trial, the State introduced victim impact evidence and proved two aggravating circumstances: future dangerousness and "vileness of the offense." To prove future dangerousness, the State relied on Atkins' prior felony convictions as well as the testimony of four victims of earlier robberies and assaults. To prove the second aggravator, the prosecution relied upon the trial record, including pictures of the deceased's body and the autopsy report.

In the penalty phase, the defense relied on one witness, Dr. Evan Nelson, a forensic psychologist who had evaluated Atkins before trial and concluded that he was "mildly mentally retarded." His conclusion was based on interviews with people who knew Atkins, a review of school and court records, and the administration of a standard intelligence test which indicated that Atkins had a full scale IQ of 59.

At the sentencing phase, Dr. Nelson testified: "[Atkins'] full scale IQ is 59. Compared to the population at large, that means less than one percentile.... Mental retardation is a relatively rare thing. It's about one percent of the population." According to Dr. Nelson, Atkins' IQ score "would automatically qualify for Social Security disability income." Dr. Nelson also indicated that of the over 40 capital defendants that he had evaluated, Atkins was only the second individual who met the criteria for mental retardation. He testified that, in his opinion, Atkins' limited intellect had been a consistent feature throughout his life, and that his IQ score of 59 is not an "aberration, malingered result, or invalid test score."

The jury sentenced Atkins to death, but the Virginia Supreme Court ordered a second sentencing hearing because the trial court had used a misleading verdict form. At the re-sentencing, Dr. Nelson again testified. The State presented an expert rebuttal witness, Dr. Stanton Samenow, who expressed the opinion that Atkins was not mentally retarded, but rather was of "average intelligence, at least," and diagnosable as having antisocial personality disorder. The jury again sentenced Atkins to death.

The Supreme Court of Virginia affirmed the imposition of the death penalty. Atkins did not argue before the Virginia Supreme Court that his sentence was disproportionate to penalties imposed for similar crimes in Virginia, but he did contend "that he is mentally retarded and thus cannot be sentenced to death." The majority of the state court rejected this contention, relying on our holding in *Penry*. 260 Va. at 387, 534 S.E.2d at 319. The Court was "not willing to commute Atkins' sentence of death to life imprisonment merely because of his IQ score."

Justice Hassell and Justice Koontz dissented. They rejected Dr. Samenow's opinion that Atkins possesses average intelligence as "incredulous as a matter of law," and concluded that "the imposition of the sentence of death upon a criminal defendant who has the mental age of a child between the ages of 9 and 12 is excessive." In their opinion, "it is indefensible to conclude that individuals who are mentally retarded are not to some degree less culpable for their criminal acts. By definition, such individuals have substantial limitations not shared by the general population. A moral and civilized society diminishes itself if its system of justice does not afford recognition and consideration of those limitations in a meaningful way." *Dissent*

Because of the gravity of the concerns expressed by the dissenters, and in light of the dramatic shift in the state legislative landscape that has occurred in the past 13 years, we granted certiorari to revisit the issue that we first addressed in the *Penry* case. 533 U.S. 976, 150 L. Ed. 2d 805, 122 S. Ct. 24 (2001).

II

The Eighth Amendment succinctly prohibits "excessive" sanctions. It provides: "Excessive bail shall not be required, nor excessive fines imposed, nor cruel and unusual punishments inflicted." In *Weems v. United States*, 217 U.S. 349, 54 L. Ed. 793, 30 S. Ct. 544 (1910), we held that a punishment of 12 years jailed in irons at hard and painful labor for the crime of falsifying records was excessive. We explained "that it is a precept of justice that punishment for crime should be graduated and proportioned to the offense." Id., at 367. We have repeatedly applied this proportionality precept in later cases interpreting the Eighth Amendment. See *Harmelin v. Michigan*, 501 U.S. 957, 997–998, 115 L. Ed. 2d 836, 111 S. Ct. 2680 (1991) (KENNEDY, J., concurring in part and concurring in judgment); see also id., at 1009–1011 (White, J., dissenting). Thus, even though "imprisonment for ninety days is not, in the abstract, a punishment which is either cruel or unusual," it may not be imposed as a penalty for "the 'status' of narcotic addiction," *Robinson v. California*, 370 U.S. 660, 666–667, 8 L. Ed. 2d 758, 82 S. Ct. 1417 (1962), because such a sanction would be excessive. As Justice Stewart explained in *Robinson*: "Even one day in prison would be a cruel and unusual punishment for the 'crime' of having a common cold." Id., at 667.

A claim that punishment is excessive is judged not by the standards that prevailed in 1685 when Lord Jeffreys presided over the "Bloody Assizes" or when the Bill of Rights was adopted, but rather by those that currently prevail. As Chief Justice Warren explained in his opinion in *Trop v. Dulles*, 356 U.S. 86, 2 L. Ed. 2d 630, 78 S. Ct. 590 (1958): "The basic concept underlying the Eighth Amendment is nothing less than the dignity of man.... The Amendment must draw its meaning from the evolving standards of decency that mark the progress of a maturing society." Id., at 100–101. *Current standards*

Proportionality review under those evolving standards should be informed by " 'objective factors to the maximum possible extent,' " see *Harmelin*, 501 U.S. at 1000 (quoting *Rummel v. Estelle*, 445 U.S. 263, 274–275, 63 L. Ed. 2d 382, 100 S. Ct. 1133 (1980)). We have pinpointed that the "clearest and most reliable objective evidence of contemporary values is the legislation enacted by the country's legislatures." *Penry*, 492 U.S. at 331, 106 L. Ed. 2d 256, 109 S. Ct. 2934. Relying in part on such legislative evidence, we have held that death is an impermissibly excessive punishment for the rape of an adult woman, *Coker v. Georgia*, 433 U.S. 584, 593–596, 53 L. Ed. 2d 982, 97 S. Ct. 2861 (1977), or for a defendant who neither took life, attempted to take life, nor intended to take life, *Enmund v. Florida*, 458 U.S. 782, 789–793, 73 L. Ed. 2d 1140, 102 S. Ct. 3368 (1982). In *Coker*, we focused primarily on the then-recent legislation that had been enacted in response to our decision 10 years earlier in *Furman v. Georgia*, 408 U.S. 238, 33 L. Ed. 2d 346, 92 S. Ct. 2726 (1972) (*per curiam*), to support the conclusion that the "current judgment," though "not wholly unanimous," weighed very heavily on the side of rejecting capital punishment as a "suitable penalty for raping an adult woman." *Coker*, 433 U.S. at 596. The "current legislative judgment" relevant to our decision in *Enmund* was less clear than in *Coker* but "nevertheless weighed on the side of rejecting capital punishment for the crime at issue." *Enmund*, 458 U.S. at 793.

We also acknowledged in *Coker* that the objective evidence, though of great importance, did not "wholly determine" the controversy, "for the Constitution contemplates that in the end our own judgment will be brought to bear on the question of the acceptability of the death penalty under the Eighth Amendment." 433 U.S. at 597. For example, in *Enmund*, we concluded by expressing our own judgment about the issue:

> For purposes of imposing the death penalty, Enmund's criminal culpability must be limited to his participation in the robbery, and his punishment must be tailored to his personal responsibility and moral guilt. Putting Enmund to death to avenge two killings that he did not commit and had no intention of committing or causing does not measurably contribute to the retributive end of ensuring that the criminal gets his just desserts. This is the judgment of most of the legislatures that have recently addressed the matter, and we have no reason to disagree with that judgment for purposes of construing and applying the Eighth Amendment. 458 U.S. at 801.

Thus, in cases involving a consensus, our own judgment is "brought to bear," *Coker*, 433 U.S. at 597, by asking whether there is reason to disagree with the judgment reached by the citizenry and its legislators.

Guided by our approach in these cases, we shall first review the judgment of legislatures that have addressed the suitability of imposing the death penalty on the mentally retarded and then consider reasons for agreeing or disagreeing with their judgment.

III

The parties have not called our attention to any state legislative consideration of the suitability of imposing the death penalty on mentally retarded offenders prior to 1986. In that year, the public reaction to the execution of a mentally retarded murderer in Georgia apparently led to the enactment of the first state statute prohibiting such executions. In 1988, when Congress enacted legislation reinstating the federal death penalty, it expressly provided that a "sentence of death shall not be carried out upon a person who is mentally retarded." In 1989, Maryland enacted a similar prohibition. It was in that year that we decided *Penry*, and concluded that those two state enactments, "even when added to the 14 States that have rejected capital punishment completely, do not provide sufficient evidence at present of a national consensus." 492 U.S. at 334, 106 L. Ed. 2d 256, 109 S. Ct. 2934.

Much has changed since then. Responding to the national attention received by the Bowden execution and our decision in *Penry*, state legislatures across the country began to address the issue. In 1990 Kentucky and Tennessee enacted statutes similar to those in Georgia and Maryland, as did New Mexico in 1991, and Arkansas, Colorado, Washington, Indiana, and Kansas in 1993 and 1994. In 1995, when New York reinstated its death penalty, it emulated the Federal Government by expressly exempting the mentally retarded. Nebraska followed suit in 1998. There appear to have been no similar enactments during the next two years, but in 2000 and 2001 six more States—South Dakota, Arizona, Connecticut, Florida, Missouri, and North Carolina—joined the procession. The Texas Legislature unanimously adopted a similar bill, and bills have passed at least one house in other States, including Virginia and Nevada.

It is not so much the number of these States that is significant, but the consistency of the direction of change. Given the well-known fact that anticrime legislation is far more popular than legislation providing protections for persons guilty of violent crime, the large number of States prohibiting the execution of mentally retarded persons (and the complete absence of States passing legislation reinstating the power to conduct such executions) provides powerful evidence that today our society views mentally retarded offenders as categorically less culpable than the average criminal. The evidence carries even greater force when it is noted that the legislatures that have addressed the issue have voted overwhelmingly in favor of the prohibition. Moreover, even in those States that allow the execution of mentally retarded offenders, the practice is uncommon. Some States, for example New Hampshire and New Jersey, continue to authorize executions, but none have been carried out in decades. Thus there is little need to pursue legislation barring the execution of the mentally retarded in those States. And it appears that even among those States that regularly execute offenders and that have no prohibition with regard to the mentally retarded, only five have executed offenders possessing a known IQ less than 70 since we decided *Penry*. The practice, therefore, has become truly unusual, and it is fair to say that a national consensus has developed against it.

To the extent there is serious disagreement about the execution of mentally retarded offenders, it is in determining which offenders are in fact retarded. In this case, for instance, the Commonwealth of Virginia disputes that Atkins suffers from mental retardation. Not all people who claim to be mentally retarded will be so impaired as to fall within the range of mentally retarded offenders about whom there is a national consensus. As was our approach in *Ford v. Wainwright*, with regard to insanity, "we leave to the States the task of developing appropriate ways to enforce the constitutional restriction upon its execution of sentences." 477 U.S. 399, 405, 416–417, 91 L. Ed. 2d 335, 106 S. Ct. 2595 (1986).

[handwritten margin note: Determination of intellectual disability is where the disagreement is]

IV

This consensus unquestionably reflects widespread judgment about the relative culpability of mentally retarded offenders, and the relationship between mental retardation and the penological purposes served by the death penalty. Additionally, it suggests that some characteristics of mental retardation undermine the strength of the procedural protections that our capital jurisprudence steadfastly guards.

As discussed above, clinical definitions of mental retardation require not only subaverage intellectual functioning, but also significant limitations in adaptive skills such as communication, self-care, and self-direction that became manifest before age 18. Mentally retarded persons frequently know the difference between right and wrong and are competent to stand trial. Because of their impairments, however, by definition they have diminished capacities to understand and process information, to communicate, to abstract from mistakes and learn from experience, to engage in logical reasoning, to control impulses, and to understand the reactions of others. There is no evidence that they are more likely to engage in criminal conduct than others, but there is abundant evidence that they often act on impulse rather than pursuant to a premeditated plan, and that in group settings they are followers rather than leaders. Their deficiencies do not warrant an exemption from criminal sanctions, but they do diminish their personal culpability.

In light of these deficiencies, our death penalty jurisprudence provides two reasons consistent with the legislative consensus that the mentally retarded should be categorically excluded from execution. First, there is a serious question as to whether either justification that we have recognized as a basis for the death penalty applies to mentally retarded

[handwritten margin note: Basis for D.P. retribution deterrence]

offenders. *Gregg v. Georgia*, 428 U.S. 153, 183, 49 L. Ed. 2d 859, 96 S. Ct. 2909 (1976), identified "retribution and deterrence of capital crimes by prospective offenders" as the social purposes served by the death penalty. Unless the imposition of the death penalty on a mentally retarded person "measurably contributes to one or both of these goals, it 'is nothing more than the purposeless and needless imposition of pain and suffering,' and hence an unconstitutional punishment." *Enmund*, 458 U.S. at 798.

With respect to retribution—the interest in seeing that the offender gets his "just desserts"— the severity of the appropriate punishment necessarily depends on the culpability of the offender. Since *Gregg*, our jurisprudence has consistently confined the imposition of the death penalty to a narrow category of the most serious crimes. For example, in *Godfrey v. Georgia*, 446 U.S. 420, 64 L. Ed. 2d 398, 100 S. Ct. 1759 (1980), we set aside a death sentence because the petitioner's crimes did not reflect "a consciousness materially more 'depraved' than that of any person guilty of murder." Id., at 433. If the culpability of the average murderer is insufficient to justify the most extreme sanction available to the State, the lesser culpability of the mentally retarded offender surely does not merit that form of retribution. Thus, pursuant to our narrowing jurisprudence, which seeks to ensure that only the most deserving of execution are put to death, an exclusion for the mentally retarded is appropriate.

With respect to deterrence—the interest in preventing capital crimes by prospective offenders—"it seems likely that 'capital punishment can serve as a deterrent only when murder is the result of premeditation and deliberation,'" *Enmund*, 458 U.S. at 799. Exempting the mentally retarded from that punishment will not affect the "cold calculus that precedes the decision" of other potential murderers. *Gregg*, 428 U.S. at 186. Indeed, that sort of calculus is at the opposite end of the spectrum from behavior of mentally retarded offenders. The theory of deterrence in capital sentencing is predicated upon the notion that the increased severity of the punishment will inhibit criminal actors from carrying out murderous conduct. Yet it is the same cognitive and behavioral impairments that make these defendants less morally culpable—for example, the diminished ability to understand and process information, to learn from experience, to engage in logical reasoning, or to control impulses—that also make it less likely that they can process the information of the possibility of execution as a penalty and, as a result, control their conduct based upon that information. Nor will exempting the mentally retarded from execution lessen the deterrent effect of the death penalty with respect to offenders who are not mentally retarded. Such individuals are unprotected by the exemption and will continue to face the threat of execution. Thus, executing the mentally retarded will not measurably further the goal of deterrence.

The reduced capacity of mentally retarded offenders provides a second justification for a categorical rule making such offenders ineligible for the death penalty. The risk "that the death penalty will be imposed in spite of factors which may call for a less severe penalty," *Lockett v. Ohio*, 438 U.S. 586, 605, 57 L. Ed. 2d 973, 98 S. Ct. 2954 (1978), is enhanced, not only by the possibility of false confessions, but also by the lesser ability of mentally retarded defendants to make a persuasive showing of mitigation in the face of prosecutorial evidence of one or more aggravating factors. Mentally retarded defendants may be less able to give meaningful assistance to their counsel and are typically poor witnesses, and their demeanor may create an unwarranted impression of lack of remorse for their crimes. As *Penry* demonstrated, moreover, reliance on mental retardation as a mitigating factor can be a two-edged sword that may enhance the likelihood that the aggravating factor of future dangerousness will be found by the jury. 492 U.S. at 323–325, 106 L. Ed. 2d 256, 109 S. Ct. 2934. Mentally retarded defendants in the aggregate face a special risk of wrongful execution.

Our independent evaluation of the issue reveals no reason to disagree with the judgment of "the legislatures that have recently addressed the matter" and concluded that death is not a suitable punishment for a mentally retarded criminal. We are not persuaded that the execution of mentally retarded criminals will measurably advance the deterrent or the retributive purpose of the death penalty. Construing and applying the Eighth Amendment in the light of our "evolving standards of decency," we therefore conclude that such punishment is excessive and that the Constitution "places a substantive restriction on the State's power to take the life" of a mentally retarded offender. *Ford*, 477 U.S. 399, at 405, 91 L. Ed. 2d 335, 106 S. Ct. 2595.

The judgment of the Virginia Supreme Court is reversed and the case is remanded for further proceedings not inconsistent with this opinion.

It is so ordered.

CHIEF JUSTICE REHNQUIST, with whom JUSTICE SCALIA and JUSTICE THOMAS join, dissenting.

The question presented by this case is whether a national consensus deprives Virginia of the constitutional power to impose the death penalty on capital murder defendants like petitioner, i.e., those defendants who indisputably are competent to stand trial, aware of the punishment they are about to suffer and why, and whose mental retardation has been found an insufficiently compelling reason to lessen their individual responsibility for the crime. The Court pronounces the punishment cruel and unusual primarily because 18 States recently have passed laws limiting the death eligibility of certain defendants based on mental retardation alone, despite the fact that the laws of 19 other States besides Virginia continue to leave the question of proper punishment to the individuated consideration of sentencing judges or juries familiar with the particular offender and his or her crime.

I agree with JUSTICE SCALIA, (dissenting opinion), that the Court's assessment of the current legislative judgment regarding the execution of defendants like petitioner more resembles a post hoc rationalization for the majority's subjectively preferred result rather than any objective effort to ascertain the content of an evolving standard of decency. I write separately, however, to call attention to the defects in the Court's decision to place weight on foreign laws, the views of professional and religious organizations, and opinion polls in reaching its conclusion. The Court's suggestion that these sources are relevant to the constitutional question finds little support in our precedents and, in my view, is antithetical to considerations of federalism, which instruct that any "permanent prohibition upon all units of democratic government must [be apparent] in the operative acts (laws and the application of laws) that the people have approved." *Stanford v. Kentucky*, 492 U.S. 361, 377, 106 L. Ed. 2d 306, 109 S. Ct. 2969 (1989) (plurality opinion). The Court's uncritical acceptance of the opinion poll data brought to our attention, moreover, warrants additional comment, because we lack sufficient information to conclude that the surveys were conducted in accordance with generally accepted scientific principles or are capable of supporting valid empirical inferences about the issue before us.

In making determinations about whether a punishment is "cruel and unusual" under the evolving standards of decency embraced by the Eighth Amendment, we have emphasized that legislation is the "clearest and most reliable objective evidence of contemporary values." *Penry v. Lynaugh*, 492 U.S. 302, 331, 106 L. Ed. 2d 256, 109 S. Ct. 2934 (1989). See also *McCleskey v. Kemp*, 481 U.S. 279, 300, 95 L. Ed. 2d 262, 107 S. Ct. 1756 (1987). The reason we ascribe primacy to legislative enactments follows from the constitutional role legislatures play in expressing policy of a State. " 'In a democratic society legislatures, not courts, are constituted to respond to the will and consequently the moral values of the people.'" *Gregg v. Georgia*, 428 U.S. 153, 175–176, 49 L. Ed. 2d 859, 96 S. Ct. 2909 (1976) (joint opinion of Stewart, Powell, and STEVENS, JJ.) (quoting *Furman v. Georgia*, 408 U.S. 238, 383, 33 L. Ed. 2d 346, 92 S. Ct. 2726 (1972) (Burger, C. J., dissenting)). And because the specifications of punishments are "peculiarly questions of legislative policy," *Gore v. United States*, 357 U.S. 386, 393, 2 L. Ed. 2d 1405, 78 S. Ct. 1280 (1958), our cases have cautioned against using "'the aegis of the Cruel and Unusual Punishment Clause'" to cut off the normal democratic processes, *Gregg*, supra, at 176 (quoting *Powell v. Texas*, 392 U.S. 514, 533, 20 L. Ed. 2d 1254, 88 S. Ct. 2145 (1968) (plurality opinion)).

Our opinions have also recognized that data concerning the actions of sentencing juries, though entitled to less weight than legislative judgments, "'is a significant and reliable index of contemporary values,'" *Coker v. Georgia*, 433 U.S. 584, 596, 53 L. Ed. 2d 982, 97 S. Ct. 2861 (1977) (plurality opinion) (quoting *Gregg*, supra, at 181), because of the jury's intimate involvement in the case and its function of "'maintaining a link between contemporary community values and the penal system,'" *Gregg*, supra, at 181 (quoting *Witherspoon v. Illinois*, 391 U.S. 510, 519, 20 L. Ed. 2d 776, 88 S. Ct. 1770, 46 Ohio Op. 2d 368, n. 15 (1968)). In *Coker*, 433 U.S. at 596–597, for example, we credited data showing that "at least 9 out of 10" juries in Georgia did not impose the death sentence for rape convictions. And in *Enmund v. Florida*, 458 U.S. 782, 793–794, 73 L. Ed. 2d 1140, 102 S. Ct. 3368 (1982), where evidence of the current legislative judgment was not as "compelling" as that in *Coker* (but more so than that here), we were persuaded by "overwhelming [evidence] that American juries ... repudiated imposition of the death penalty" for a defendant who neither took life nor attempted or intended to take life.

In my view, these two sources — the work product of legislatures and sentencing jury determinations — ought to be the sole indicators by which courts ascertain the contemporary American conceptions of decency for purposes of the Eighth Amendment. They are the only objective indicia of contemporary values firmly supported by our precedents. More importantly, however, they can be reconciled with the undeniable precepts that the democratic branches of government and individual sentencing juries are, by design, better suited than courts to evaluating and giving effect to the complex societal and moral considerations that inform the selection of publicly acceptable criminal punishments.

In reaching its conclusion today, the Court does not take notice of the fact that neither petitioner nor his amici have adduced any comprehensive statistics that would conclusively prove (or disprove) whether juries routinely consider death a disproportionate punishment for mentally retarded offenders like petitioner. Instead, it adverts to the fact that other countries have disapproved imposition of the death penalty for crimes committed by mentally retarded offenders. I fail to see, however, how the views of other countries regarding the punishment of their citizens provide any support for the Court's ultimate determination. While it is true that some of our prior opinions have looked to "the climate of international opinion," *Coker*, 433 U.S. at 596, n. 10, to reinforce a conclusion regarding evolving standards of decency, see *Thompson v. Oklahoma*, 487 U.S. 815, 830, 101 L. Ed. 2d 702, 108 S. Ct. 2687 (1988) (plurality opinion); *Enmund*, 458 U.S. at 796–797, n. 22 (1982); *Trop v. Dulles*, 356 U.S. 86, 102–103, 2 L. Ed. 2d 630, 78 S. Ct. 590 (1958) (plurality opinion); we have since explicitly rejected the idea that the sentencing practices of other countries could "serve to establish the first Eighth Amendment prerequisite, that [a] practice is accepted among our people." *Stanford*, 492 U.S. at 369, n. 1 (emphasizing that "American conceptions of decency ... are dispositive").

Stanford's reasoning makes perfectly good sense, and the Court offers no basis to question it. For if it is evidence of a national consensus for which we are looking, then the viewpoints of other countries simply are not relevant. And nothing in *Thompson, Enmund, Coker,* or *Trop* suggests otherwise. *Thompson, Enmund,* and *Coker* rely only on the bare citation of international laws by the *Trop* plurality as authority to deem other countries' sentencing choices germane. But the *Trop* plurality—representing the view of only a minority of the Court—offered no explanation for its own citation, and there is no reason to resurrect this view given our sound rejection of the argument in *Stanford*.

To further buttress its appraisal of contemporary societal values, the Court marshalls public opinion poll results and evidence that several professional organizations and religious groups have adopted official positions opposing the imposition of the death penalty upon mentally retarded offenders (citing Brief for American Psychological Association et al. as Amici Curiae; Brief for American Association on Mental Retardation et al. as Amici Curiae; noting that "representatives of widely diverse religious communities ... reflecting Christian, Jewish, Muslim, and Buddhist traditions ... 'share a conviction that the execution of persons with mental retardation cannot be morally justified'"; and stating that "polling data shows a widespread consensus among Americans ... that executing the mentally retarded is wrong"). In my view, none should be accorded any weight on the Eight Amendment scale when the elected representatives of a State's populace have not deemed them persuasive enough to prompt legislative action. In *Penry*, 492 U.S. at 334–335, 106 L. Ed. 2d 256, 109 S. Ct. 2934, we were cited similar data and declined to take them into consideration where the "public sentiment expressed in [them]" had yet to find expression in state law. See also *Stanford*, 492 U.S. at 377 (plurality opinion) (refusing "the invitation to rest constitutional law upon such uncertain foundations" as "public opinion polls, the views of interest groups, and the positions adopted by various professional organizations"). For the Court to rely on such data today serves only to illustrate its willingness to proscribe by judicial fiat—at the behest of private organizations speaking only for themselves—a punishment about which no across-the-board consensus has developed through the workings of normal democratic processes in the laboratories of the States.

Even if I were to accept the legitimacy of the Court's decision to reach beyond the product of legislatures and practices of sentencing juries to discern a national standard of decency, I would take issue with the blind-faith credence it accords the opinion polls brought to our attention. An extensive body of social science literature describes how methodological and other errors can affect the reliability and validity of estimates about the opinions and attitudes of a population derived from various sampling techniques. Everything from variations in the survey methodology, such as the choice of the target population, the sampling design used, the questions asked, and the statistical analyses used to interpret the data can skew the results. See, e.g., R. Groves, Survey Errors and Survey Costs (1989); 1 C. Turner & E. Martin, Surveying Subjective Phenomena (1984).

The Federal Judicial Center's Reference Manual on Scientific Evidence 221–271 (1994) and its Manual for Complex Litigation § 21.493 pp. 101–103 (3d ed. 1995), offer helpful suggestions to judges called upon to assess the weight and admissibility of survey evidence on a factual issue before a court. Looking at the polling data (reproduced in the Appendix to this opinion) [Editor's note: Appendix is not included.] in light of these factors, one cannot help but observe how unlikely it is that the data could support a valid inference about the question presented by this case. For example, the questions reported to have been asked in the various polls do not appear designed to gauge whether the respondents might find the death penalty an acceptable punishment for mentally retarded offenders in rare cases. Most are categorical (e.g., "Do you think that persons convicted of murder who are mentally retarded should or should not receive the death penalty?"), and, as such, would not elicit whether the respondent might agree or disagree that all mentally retarded people by definition can never act with the level of culpability associated with the death penalty, regardless of the severity of their impairment or the individual circumstances of their crime. Second, none of the 27 polls cited disclose the targeted survey population or the sampling techniques used by those who conducted the research. Thus, even if one accepts that the survey instruments were adequately designed to address a relevant question, it is impossible to know whether the sample was representative enough or the methodology sufficiently sound to tell us anything about the opinions of the citizens of a particular State or the American public at large. Finally, the information provided to us does not indicate why a particular survey was conducted or, in a few cases, by whom, factors which also can bear on the objectivity of the results. In order to be credited here, such surveys should be offered as evidence at trial, where their sponsors can be examined and cross-examined about these matters.

There are strong reasons for limiting our inquiry into what constitutes an evolving standard of decency under the Eighth Amendment to the laws passed by legislatures and the practices of sentencing juries in America. Here, the Court goes beyond these well-established objective indicators of contemporary values. It finds "further support to [its] conclusion" that a national consensus has developed against imposing the death penalty on all mentally retarded defendants in international opinion, the views of professional and religious organizations, and opinion polls not demonstrated to be reliable. Believing this view to be seriously mistaken, I dissent.

JUSTICE SCALIA, with whom the CHIEF JUSTICE and JUSTICE THOMAS join, dissenting.

Today's decision is the pinnacle of our Eighth Amendment death-is-different jurisprudence. Not only does it, like all of that jurisprudence, find no support in the text or history of the Eighth Amendment; it does not even have support in current social attitudes regarding the conditions that render an otherwise just death penalty inappropriate. Seldom has an opinion of this Court rested so obviously upon nothing but the personal views of its members.

I

I begin with a brief restatement of facts that are abridged by the Court but important to understanding this case. After spending the day drinking alcohol and smoking marijuana, petitioner Daryl Renard Atkins and a partner in crime drove to a convenience store, intending to rob a customer. Their victim was Eric Nesbitt, an airman from Langley Air Force Base, whom they abducted, drove to a nearby automated teller machine, and forced to withdraw $200. They then drove him to a deserted area, ignoring his pleas to leave him unharmed. According to the co-conspirator, whose testimony the jury evidently credited, Atkins ordered Nesbitt out of the vehicle and, after he had taken only a few steps, shot him one, two, three, four, five, six, seven, eight times in the thorax, chest, abdomen, arms, and legs.

The jury convicted Atkins of capital murder. At resentencing (the Virginia Supreme Court affirmed his conviction but remanded for resentencing because the trial court had used an improper verdict form, 257 Va. 160, 179, 510 S.E.2d 445, 457 (1999)), the jury heard extensive evidence of petitioner's alleged mental retardation. A psychologist testified that petitioner was mildly mentally retarded with an IQ of 59, that he was a "slow learner," App. 444, who showed a "lack of success in pretty much every domain of his life," id., at 442, and that he had an "impaired" capacity to appreciate the criminality of his conduct and to conform his conduct to the law, id., at 453. Petitioner's family members offered additional evidence in support of his mental retardation claim (e.g., that petitioner is a "follower," id., at 421). The State contested the evidence of retardation and presented testimony of a psychologist who found "absolutely no evidence other than the IQ score ...

indicating that [petitioner] was in the least bit mentally retarded" and concluded that petitioner was "of average intelligence, at least." Id., at 476.

The jury also heard testimony about petitioner's 16 prior felony convictions for robbery, attempted robbery, abduction, use of a firearm, and maiming. Id., at 491–522. The victims of these offenses provided graphic depictions of petitioner's violent tendencies: He hit one over the head with a beer bottle, id., at 406; he slapped a gun across another victim's face, clubbed her in the head with it, knocked her to the ground, and then helped her up, only to shoot her in the stomach, id., at 411–413. The jury sentenced petitioner to death. The Supreme Court of Virginia affirmed petitioner's sentence. 260 Va. 375, 534 S.E.2d 312 (2000).

II

As the foregoing history demonstrates, petitioner's mental retardation was a central issue at sentencing. The jury concluded, however, that his alleged retardation was not a compelling reason to exempt him from the death penalty in light of the brutality of his crime and his long demonstrated propensity for violence. "In upsetting this particularized judgment on the basis of a constitutional absolute," the Court concludes that no one who is even slightly mentally retarded can have sufficient "moral responsibility to be subjected to capital punishment for any crime. As a sociological and moral conclusion that is implausible; and it is doubly implausible as an interpretation of the United States Constitution." *Thompson v. Oklahoma*, 487 U.S. 815, 863–864, 101 L. Ed. 2d 702, 108 S. Ct. 2687 (1988) (SCALIA, J., dissenting).

Under our Eighth Amendment jurisprudence, a punishment is "cruel and unusual" if it falls within one of two categories: "those modes or acts of punishment that had been considered cruel and unusual at the time that the Bill of Rights was adopted," *Ford v. Wainwright*, 477 U.S. 399, 405, 91 L. Ed. 2d 335, 106 S. Ct. 2595 (1986), and modes of punishment that are inconsistent with modern "standards of decency," as evinced by objective indicia, the most important of which is "legislation enacted by the country's legislatures," *Penry v. Lynaugh*, 492 U.S. 302, 330–331, 106 L. Ed. 2d 256, 109 S. Ct. 2934 (1989).

The Court makes no pretense that execution of the mildly mentally retarded would have been considered "cruel and unusual" in 1791. Only the severely or profoundly mentally retarded, commonly known as "idiots," enjoyed any special status under the law at that time. They, like lunatics, suffered a "deficiency in will" rendering them unable to tell right from wrong. 4 W. Blackstone, Commentaries on the Laws of England 24 (1769) (hereinafter Blackstone); see also *Penry*, 492 U.S. 302, at 331–332, 106 L. Ed. 2d 256, 109 S. Ct. 2934 ("The term 'idiot' was generally used to describe persons who had a total lack of reason or understanding, or an inability to distinguish between good and evil"); id., 492 U.S. at 333, 106 L. Ed. 2d 256, 109 S. Ct. 2934 (citing sources indicating that idiots generally had an IQ of 25 or below, which would place them within the "profound" or "severe" range of mental retardation under modern standards); 2 A. Fitz-Herbert, Natura Brevium 233B (9th ed. 1794) (originally published 1534) (An idiot is "such a person who cannot account or number twenty pence, nor can tell who was his father or mother, nor how old he is, etc., so as it may appear that he hath no understanding of reason what shall be for his profit, or what for his loss"). Due to their incompetence, idiots were "excused from the guilt, and of course from the punishment, of any criminal action committed under such deprivation of the senses." 4 Blackstone 25; see also *Penry*, 492 U.S. at 331, 106 L. Ed. 2d 256, 109 S. Ct. 2934. Instead, they were often committed to civil confinement or made wards of the State, thereby preventing them from "going loose, to the terror of the king's subjects." 4 Blackstone 25; see also S. Brakel, J. Parry, & B. Weiner, The Mentally Disabled and the Law 12–14 (3d ed. 1985); 1 Blackstone 292–296; 1 M. Hale, Pleas of the Crown 33 (1st Am. ed. 1847). Mentally retarded offenders with less severe impairments—those who were not "idiots"—suffered criminal prosecution and punishment, including capital punishment. See, e.g., I. Ray, Medical Jurisprudence of Insanity 65, 87–92 (W. Overholser ed. 1962) (recounting the 1834 trial and execution in Concord, New Hampshire, of an apparent "imbecile"—imbecility being a less severe form of retardation which "differs from idiocy in the circumstance that while in [the idiot] there is an utter destitution of every thing like reason, [imbeciles] possess some intellectual capacity, though infinitely less than is possessed by the great mass of mankind"); A. Highmore, Law of Idiocy and Lunacy 200 (1807) ("The great difficulty in all these cases, is to determine where a person shall be said to be so far deprived of his sense and memory as not to have any of his actions imputed to him: or where notwithstanding some defects of this kind he still appears to have so much reason and understanding as will make him accountable for his actions …").

The Court is left to argue, therefore, that execution of the mildly retarded is inconsistent with the "evolving standards of decency that mark the progress of a maturing society." *Trop v. Dulles*, 356 U.S. 86, 101, 2 L. Ed. 2d 630, 78 S. Ct. 590 (1958) (plurality opinion) (Warren, C. J.). Before today, our opinions consistently emphasized that Eighth Amendment judgments regarding the existence of social "standards" "should be informed by objective factors to the maximum possible extent" and "should not be, or appear to be, merely the subjective views of individual Justices." *Coker v. Georgia*, 433 U.S. 584, 592, 53 L. Ed. 2d 982, 97 S. Ct. 2861 (1977) (plurality opinion); see also *Stanford*, supra, at 369; *McCleskey v. Kemp*, 481 U.S. 279, 300, 95 L. Ed. 2d 262, 107 S. Ct. 1756 (1987); *Enmund v. Florida*, 458 U.S. 782, 788, 73 L. Ed. 2d 1140, 102 S. Ct. 3368 (1982). "First" among these objective factors are the "statutes passed by society's elected representatives," *Stanford v. Kentucky*, 492 U.S. 361, 370, 106 L. Ed. 2d 306, 109 S. Ct. 2969 (1989); because it "will rarely if ever be the case that the Members of this Court will have a better sense of the evolution in views of the American people than do their elected representatives," *Thompson*, supra, at 865 (SCALIA, J., dissenting).

The Court pays lipservice to these precedents as it miraculously extracts a "national consensus" forbidding execution of the mentally retarded, ante, at 12, from the fact that 18 States—less than half (47%) of the 38 States that permit capital punishment (for whom the issue exists)—have very recently enacted legislation barring execution of the mentally retarded. Even that 47% figure is a distorted one. If one is to say, as the Court does today, that all executions of the mentally retarded are so morally repugnant as to violate our national "standards of decency," surely the "consensus" it points to must be one that has set its righteous face against all such executions. Not 18 States, but only seven—18% of death penalty jurisdictions—have legislation of that scope. Eleven of those that the Court counts enacted statutes prohibiting execution of mentally retarded defendants convicted after, or convicted of crimes committed after, the effective date of the legislation; those already on death row, or consigned there before the statute's effective date, or even (in those States using the date of the crime as the criterion of retroactivity) tried in the future for murders committed many years ago, could be put to death. That is not a statement of absolute moral repugnance, but one of current preference between two tolerable approaches. Two of these States permit execution of the mentally retarded in other situations as well: Kansas apparently permits execution of all except the severely mentally retarded; New York permits execution of the mentally retarded who commit murder in a correctional facility. N.Y. Crim. Proc. Law § 400.27(12)(d) (McKinney 2001); N.Y. Penal Law § 125.27 (McKinney 202).

But let us accept, for the sake of argument, the Court's faulty count. That bare number of States alone—18—should be enough to convince any reasonable person that no "national consensus" exists. How is it possible that agreement among 47% of the death penalty jurisdictions amounts to "consensus"? Our prior cases have generally required a much higher degree of agreement before finding a punishment cruel and unusual on "evolving standards" grounds. In *Coker*, 433 U.S. at 595–596, we proscribed the death penalty for rape of an adult woman after finding that only one jurisdiction, Georgia, authorized such a punishment. In *Enmund*, 458 U.S. at 789, we invalidated the death penalty for mere participation in a robbery in which an accomplice took a life, a punishment not permitted in 28 of the death penalty States (78%). In *Ford*, 477 U.S. at 408, we supported the common-law prohibition of execution of the insane with the observation that "this ancestral legacy has not outlived its time," since not a single State authorizes such punishment. In *Solem v. Helm*, 463 U.S. 277, 300, 77 L. Ed. 2d 637, 103 S. Ct. 3001 (1983), we invalidated a life sentence without parole under a recidivist statute by which the criminal "was treated more severely than he would have been in any other State." What the Court calls evidence of "consensus" in the present case (a fudged 47%) more closely resembles evidence that we found inadequate to establish consensus in earlier cases. *Tison v. Arizona*, 481 U.S. 137, 154, 158, 95 L. Ed. 2d 127, 107 S. Ct. 1676 (1987), upheld a state law authorizing capital punishment for major participation in a felony with reckless indifference to life where only 11 of the 37 death penalty States (30%) prohibited such punishment. *Stanford*, 492 U.S. at 372, upheld a state law permitting execution of defendants who committed a capital crime at age 16 where only 15 of the 36 death penalty States (42%) prohibited death for such offenders.

Moreover, a major factor that the Court entirely disregards is that the legislation of all 18 States it relies on is still in its infancy. The oldest of the statutes is only 14 years old; five were enacted last year; over half were enacted within the past eight years. Few, if any, of the States have had sufficient experience with these laws to know whether they are sensible in the long term. It is "myopic to base sweeping constitutional principles upon the narrow experience of [a few] years." *Coker*, 433 U.S. at 614 (Burger, C. J., dissenting); see also *Thompson*, 487 U.S. at 854–855 (O'CONNOR, J., concurring in judgment).

The Court attempts to bolster its embarrassingly feeble evidence of "consensus" with the following: "It is not so much the number of these States that is significant, but the consistency of the direction of change." But in what other direction could we possibly see change? Given that 14 years ago all the death penalty statutes included the mentally retarded, any change (except precipitate undoing of what had just been done) was bound to be in the one direction the Court finds significant enough to overcome the lack of real consensus. That is to say, to be accurate the Court's "consistency-of-the-direction-of-change" point should be recast into the following unimpressive observation: "No State has yet undone its exemption of the mentally retarded, one for as long as 14 whole years." In any event, reliance upon "trends," even those of much longer duration than a mere 14 years, is a perilous basis for constitutional adjudication, as JUSTICE O'CONNOR eloquently explained in *Thompson*:

> In 1846, Michigan became the first State to abolish the death penalty.... In succeeding decades, other American States continued the trend towards abolition.... Later, and particularly after World War II, there ensued a steady and dramatic decline in executions.... In the 1950's and 1960's, more States abolished or radically restricted capital punishment, and executions ceased completely for several years beginning in 1968....

> In 1972, when this Court heard arguments on the constitutionality of the death penalty, such statistics might have suggested that the practice had become a relic, implicitly rejected by a new societal consensus.... We now know that any inference of a societal consensus rejecting the death penalty would have been mistaken.

But had this Court then declared the existence of such a consensus, and outlawed capital punishment, legislatures would very likely not have been able to revive it. The mistaken premise of the decision would have been frozen into constitutional law, making it difficult to refute and even more difficult to reject.

487 U.S. at 854–855.

Her words demonstrate, of course, not merely the peril of riding a trend, but also the peril of discerning a consensus where there is none.

The Court's thrashing about for evidence of "consensus" includes reliance upon the margins by which state legislatures have enacted bans on execution of the retarded. Ante, at 11. Presumably, in applying our *Eighth Amendment* "evolving-standards-of-decency" jurisprudence, we will henceforth weigh not only how many States have agreed, but how many States have agreed by how much. Of course if the percentage of legislators voting for the bill is significant, surely the number of people represented by the legislators voting for the bill is also significant: the fact that 49% of the legislators in a State with a population of 60 million voted against the bill should be more impressive than the fact that 90% of the legislators in a state with a population of 2 million voted for it. (By the way, the population of the death penalty States that exclude the mentally retarded is only 44% of the population of all death penalty States. U.S. Census Bureau, Statistical Abstract of the United States 21 (121st ed. 2001).) This is quite absurd. What we have looked for in the past to "evolve" the Eighth Amendment is a consensus of the same sort as the consensus that adopted the Eighth Amendment: a consensus of the sovereign States that form the Union, not a nose count of Americans for and against.

Even less compelling (if possible) is the Court's argument, that evidence of "national consensus" is to be found in the infrequency with which retarded persons are executed in States that do not bar their execution. To begin with, what the Court takes as true is in fact quite doubtful. It is not at all clear that execution of the mentally retarded is "uncommon," ibid., as even the sources cited by the Court suggest, (citing D. Keyes, W. Edwards, & R. Perske, People with Mental Retardation are Dying Legally, 35 Mental Retardation (Feb. 1997) (updated by Death Penalty Information Center; available at http://www.advocacyone.org/deathpenalty.html) (June 12, 2002) (showing that 12 States executed 35 allegedly mentally retarded offenders during the period 1984–2000)). See also Bonner & Rimer, *Executing the Mentally Retarded Even as Laws Begin to Shift*, N. Y. Times, Aug. 7, 2000 p. A1 (reporting that 10% of death row inmates are retarded). If, however, execution of the mentally retarded is "uncommon"; and if it is not a sufficient explanation of this that the retarded comprise a tiny fraction of society (1% to 3%), Brief for American Psychological Association et al. as Amici Curiae 7; then surely the explanation is that mental retardation is a constitutionally mandated mitigating factor at sentencing, *Penry*, 492 U.S. at 328, 106 L. Ed. 2d 256, 109 S. Ct. 2934. For that reason, even if there were uniform national sentiment in favor of executing the retarded in appropriate cases, one would still expect execution of the mentally retarded to be "uncommon." To adapt to the present case what the Court itself said in *Stanford*, 492 U.S. at 374: "It is not only possible, but overwhelmingly probable, that the very considerations which induce [today's majority] to believe that death should never be imposed on [mentally retarded] offenders ... cause prosecutors and juries to believe that it should rarely be imposed."

But the Prize for the Court's Most Feeble Effort to fabricate "national consensus" must go to its appeal (deservedly relegated to a footnote) to the views of assorted professional and religious organizations, members of the so-called "world community," and respondents to opinion polls. I agree with the CHIEF JUSTICE, (dissenting opinion), that the views of professional and religious organizations and the results of opinion polls are irrelevant. Equally irrelevant are the practices of the "world community," whose notions of justice are (thankfully) not always those of our people. "We must never forget that it is a Constitution for the United States of America that we are expounding.... Where there is not first a settled consensus among our own people, the views of other nations, however enlightened the Justices of this Court may think them to be, cannot be imposed upon Americans through the Constitution." *Thompson*, 487 U.S. at 868–869, n. 4 (SCALIA, J., dissenting).

III

Beyond the empty talk of a "national consensus," the Court gives us a brief glimpse of what really underlies today's decision: pretension to a power confined neither by the moral sentiments originally enshrined in the Eighth Amendment (its original meaning) nor even by the current moral sentiments of the American people. "The Constitution," the Court says, "contemplates that in the end our own judgment will be brought to bear on the question of the acceptability of the death penalty under the Eighth Amendment" (quoting *Coker*, 433 U.S. at 597). (The unexpressed reason for this unexpressed "contemplation" of the Constitution is presumably that really good lawyers have moral sentiments superior to those of the common herd, whether in 1791 or today.) The arrogance of this assumption of power takes one's breath away. And it explains, of course, why the Court can be so cavalier about the evidence of consensus. It is just a game, after all. "In the end," it is the feelings and intuition of a majority of the Justices that count—"the perceptions of decency, or of penology, or of mercy, entertained ... by a majority of the small and unrepresentative segment of our society that sits on this Court." *Thompson*, 487 U.S. at 873 (SCALIA, J., dissenting).

The genuinely operative portion of the opinion, then, is the Court's statement of the reasons why it agrees with the contrived consensus it has found, that the "diminished capacities" of the mentally retarded render the death penalty excessive. The Court's analysis rests on two fundamental assumptions: (1) that the Eighth Amendment prohibits excessive punishments, and (2) that sentencing juries or judges are unable to account properly for the "diminished capacities" of the retarded. The first assumption is wrong, as I explained at length in *Harmelin v. Michigan*, 501 U.S. 957, 966–990, 115 L. Ed. 2d 836, 111 S. Ct. 2680 (1991) (opinion of SCALIA, J.). The Eighth Amendment is addressed to always-and-everywhere "cruel" punishments, such as the rack and the thumbscrew. But where the punishment is in itself permissible, "the Eighth Amendment is not a ratchet, whereby a temporary consensus on leniency for a particular crime fixes a permanent constitutional maximum, disabling the States from giving effect to altered beliefs and responding to changed social conditions." Id., at 990. The second assumption—inability of judges or juries to take proper account of mental retardation—is not only unsubstantiated, but contradicts the immemorial belief, here and in England, that they play an indispensable role in such matters:

> It is very difficult to define the indivisible line that divides perfect and partial insanity; but it must rest upon circumstances duly to be weighed and considered both by the judge and jury, lest on the one side there be a kind of inhumanity towards the defects of human nature, or on the other side too great an indulgence given to great crimes....

1 Hale, Pleas of the Crown, at 30.

Proceeding from these faulty assumptions, the Court gives two reasons why the death penalty is an excessive punishment for all mentally retarded offenders. First, the "diminished capacities" of the mentally retarded raise a "serious question" whether their execution contributes to the "social purposes" of the death penalty, *viz.*, retribution and deterrence. Ante, at 13–14. (The Court conveniently ignores a third "social purpose" of the death penalty—"incapacitation of dangerous criminals and the consequent prevention of crimes that they may otherwise commit in the future," *Gregg v. Georgia*, 428 U.S. 153, 183, n. 28, 49 L. Ed. 2d 859, 96 S. Ct. 2909 (1976) (joint opinion of Stewart, Powell, and Stevens, JJ.). But never mind; its discussion of even the other two does not bear analysis.) Retribution is not advanced, the argument goes, because the mentally retarded are no more culpable than the average murderer, whom we have already held lacks sufficient culpability to warrant the death penalty, see *Godfrey v. Georgia*, 446 U.S. 420, 433, 64 L. Ed. 2d 398, 100 S. Ct. 1759 (1980) (plurality opinion). Who says so? Is there an established correlation between mental acuity and the ability to conform one's conduct to the law in such a rudimentary matter as murder? Are the mentally retarded really more disposed (and hence more likely) to commit willfully cruel and serious crime than others? In my experience, the opposite is true: being childlike generally suggests innocence rather than brutality.

Assuming, however, that there is a direct connection between diminished intelligence and the inability to refrain from murder, what scientific analysis can possibly show that a mildly retarded individual who commits an exquisite torture-killing is "no more culpable" than the "average" murderer in a holdup-gone-wrong or a domestic dispute? Or a moderately retarded individual who commits a series of 20 exquisite torture-killings? Surely culpability, and deservedness of the most severe retribution, depends not merely (if at all) upon the mental capacity of the criminal (above the level where he is able to distinguish right from wrong) but also upon the depravity of the crime—which is precisely why this sort of question has traditionally been thought answerable not by a categorical rule of the sort the Court today imposes upon all trials, but rather by the sentencer's weighing of the circumstances (both degree of retardation and depravity of crime) in the particular case. The fact that juries continue to sentence mentally retarded offenders to death for extreme crimes shows that society's moral outrage sometimes demands execution of retarded offenders. By what principle of law, science, or logic can the Court pronounce that this is wrong? There is none. Once the Court admits (as it does) that mental retardation does not render the offender morally blameless, there is no basis for saying that the death penalty is never appropriate retribution, no matter how heinous the crime. As long as a mentally retarded offender knows "the difference between right and wrong," only the sentencer can assess whether his retardation reduces his culpability enough to exempt him from the death penalty for the particular murder in question.

As for the other social purpose of the death penalty that the Court discusses, deterrence: That is not advanced, the Court tells us, because the mentally retarded are "less likely" than their non-retarded counterparts to "process the information of the possibility of execution as a penalty and ... control their conduct based upon that information." Of course this leads to the same conclusion discussed earlier—that the mentally retarded (because they are less deterred) are more likely to kill—which neither I nor the society at large believes. In any event, even the Court does not say that all mentally retarded individuals cannot "process the information of the possibility of execution as a penalty and ... control their conduct based upon that information"; it merely asserts that they are "less likely" to be able to do so. But surely the deterrent effect of a penalty is adequately vindicated if it successfully deters many, but not all, of the target class. Virginia's death penalty, for example, does not fail of its deterrent effect simply because some criminals are unaware that Virginia has the death penalty. In other words, the supposed fact that some retarded criminals cannot fully appreciate the death penalty has nothing to do with the deterrence rationale, but is simply an echo of the arguments denying a retribution rationale, discussed and rejected above. I am not sure that a murderer is somehow less blameworthy if (though he knew his act was wrong) he did not fully appreciate that he could die for it; but if so, we should treat a mentally retarded murderer the way we treat an offender who may be "less likely" to respond to the death penalty because he was abused as a child. We do not hold him immune from capital punishment, but require his background to be considered by the sentencer as a mitigating factor. *Eddings v. Oklahoma*, 455 U.S. 104, 113–117, 71 L. Ed. 2d 1, 102 S. Ct. 869(1982).

The Court throws one last factor into its grab bag of reasons why execution of the retarded is "excessive" in all cases: Mentally retarded offenders "face a special risk of wrongful execution" because they are less able "to make a persuasive showing of mitigation," "to give meaningful assistance to their counsel," and to be effective witnesses. "Special risk" is pretty flabby language (even flabbier than "less likely") — and I suppose a similar "special risk" could be said to exist for just plain stupid people, inarticulate people, even ugly people. If this unsupported claim has any substance to it (which I doubt) it might support a due process claim in all criminal prosecutions of the mentally retarded; but it is hard to see how it has anything to do with an Eighth Amendment claim that execution of the mentally retarded is cruel and unusual. We have never before held it to be cruel and unusual punishment to impose a sentence in violation of some other constitutional imperative.

Today's opinion adds one more to the long list of substantive and procedural requirements impeding imposition of the death penalty imposed under this Court's assumed power to invent a death-is-different jurisprudence. None of those requirements existed when the Eighth Amendment was adopted, and some of them were not even supported by current moral consensus. They include prohibition of the death penalty for "ordinary" murder, *Godfrey*, 446 U.S. at 433, for rape of an adult woman, *Coker*, 433 U.S. at 592, and for felony murder absent a showing that the defendant possessed a sufficiently culpable state of mind, *Enmund*, 458 U.S. at 801; prohibition of the death penalty for any person under the age of 16 at the time of the crime, *Thompson*, 487 U.S. at 838 (plurality opinion); prohibition of the death penalty as the mandatory punishment for any crime, *Woodson v. North Carolina*, 428 U.S. 280, 305, 49 L. Ed. 2d 944, 96 S. Ct. 2978 (1976) (plurality opinion), *Sumner v. Shuman*, 483 U.S. 66, 77–78, 97 L. Ed. 2d 56, 107 S. Ct. 2716 (1987); a requirement that the sentencer not be given unguided discretion, *Furman v. Georgia*, 408 U.S. 238, 33 L. Ed. 2d 346, 92 S. Ct. 2726 (1972) (per curiam), a requirement that the sentencer be empowered to take into account all mitigating circumstances, *Lockett v. Ohio*, 438 U.S. 586, 604, 57 L. Ed. 2d 973, 98 S. Ct. 2954 (1978) (plurality opinion), *Eddings v. Oklahoma*, supra, at 110; and a requirement that the accused receive a judicial evaluation of his claim of insanity before the sentence can be executed, *Ford*, 477 U.S. at 410–411 (plurality opinion). There is something to be said for popular abolition of the death penalty; there is nothing to be said for its incremental abolition by this Court.

This newest invention promises to be more effective than any of the others in turning the process of capital trial into a game. One need only read the definitions of mental retardation adopted by the American Association of Mental Retardation and the American Psychiatric Association (set forth in the Court's opinion) to realize that the symptoms of this condition can readily be feigned. And whereas the capital defendant who feigns insanity risks commitment to a mental institution until he can be cured (and then tried and executed), *Jones v. United States*, 463 U.S. 354, 370, 77 L. Ed. 2d 694, 103 S. Ct. 3043, and n. 20 (1983), the capital defendant who feigns mental retardation risks nothing at all. The mere pendency of the present case has brought us petitions by death row inmates claiming for the first time, after multiple habeas petitions, that they are retarded. See, e.g., *Moore v. Texas*, 535 U.S. 1044, 152 L. Ed. 2d 668, 122 S. Ct. 1814 (2002) (SCALIA, J., dissenting from grant of applications for stay of execution).

Perhaps these practical difficulties will not be experienced by the minority of capital-punishment States that have very recently changed mental retardation from a mitigating factor (to be accepted or rejected by the sentencer) to an absolute immunity. Time will tell—and the brief time those States have had the new disposition in place (an average of 6.8 years) is surely not enough. But if the practical difficulties do not appear, and if the other States share the Court's perceived moral consensus that all mental retardation renders the death penalty inappropriate for all crimes, then that majority will presumably follow suit. But there is no justification for this Court's pushing them into the experiment—and turning the experiment into a permanent practice—on constitutional pretext. Nothing has changed the accuracy of Matthew Hale's endorsement of the common law's traditional method for taking account of guilt-reducing factors, written over three centuries ago:

> [Determination of a person's incapacity] is a matter of great difficulty, partly from the easiness of counterfeiting this disability ... and partly from the variety of the degrees of this infirmity, whereof some are sufficient, and some are insufficient to excuse persons in capital offenses....
>
> Yet the law of England hath afforded the best method of trial, that is possible, of this and all other matters of fact, namely, by a jury of twelve men all concurring in the same judgment, by the testimony of witnesses..., and by the inspection and direction of the judge.
>
> 1 Hale, Pleas of the Crown, at 32–33.

I respectfully dissent.

* * *

Questions for Discussion

1. Which opinion do you think gets it right—the majority, or one of the dissents? Which arguments did you find compelling on each side?

2. Do you think that there should be special death penalty jurisprudence for people with intellectual disabilities? Psychiatric illnesses? Do you think that national consensus should be considered as a factor in judicial decisions? Do you think courts or legislatures should make decisions about punishment?

3. Does your state allow executions? If so, does your state law have any exceptions for people with intellectual disabilities?

For Further Reading

Nava Feldman, *Application of Constitutional Rule of Atkins v. Virginia, 536 U.S. 304, 122 S. Ct. 2242, 153 L. Ed. 2d 335 (2002), that Execution of Mentally Retarded Persons Constitutes 'Cruel and Unusual Punishment' in Violation of Eighth Amendment*, 122 A.L.R.5th 14.

Discussion 19

Drugs, Alcohol & Disability

Recommended Background Reading

"What are an Employer's Obligations to Alcoholic Employees?" retrieved May 15, 2012
at http://library.findlaw.com/1999/Apr/1/128935.html.

"Module 101: Disabilities and Alcohol Use Disorders," National Institute of Health,
retrieved May 15, 2012 at http://pubs.niaaa.nih.gov/publications/Social/Module10I
Disabilities/Module10I.html.

Readings for Class Discussion

The following are the major statutory provisions of the Americans with Disabilities
Act regarding drug and alcohol use.

42 USC § 12114

(a) Qualified individual with a disability

For purposes of this subchapter, the term "qualified individual with a disability" shall
not include any employee or applicant who is currently engaging in the illegal use of
drugs, when the covered entity acts on the basis of such use.

(b) Rules of construction

Nothing in subsection (a) of this section shall be construed to exclude as a qualified
individual with a disability an individual who—

(1) has successfully completed a supervised drug rehabilitation program and is no
longer engaging in the illegal use of drugs, or has otherwise been rehabilitated
successfully and is no longer engaging in such use;

(2) is participating in a supervised rehabilitation program and is no longer engaging
in such use; or

(3) is erroneously regarded as engaging in such use, but is not engaging in such use;
except that it shall not be a violation of this chapter for a covered entity to adopt or
administer reasonable policies or procedures, including but not limited to drug

testing, designed to ensure that an individual described in paragraph (1) or (2) is no longer engaging in the illegal use of drugs.

(c) Authority of covered entity

A covered entity—

(1) may prohibit the illegal use of drugs and the use of alcohol at the workplace by all employees;

(2) may require that employees shall not be under the influence of alcohol or be engaging in the illegal use of drugs at the workplace;

(3) may require that employees behave in conformance with the requirements established under the Drug-Free Workplace Act of 1988 (41 U.S.C. 701 et seq.);

(4) may hold an employee who engages in the illegal use of drugs or who is an alcoholic to the same qualification standards for employment or job performance and behavior that such entity holds other employees, even if any unsatisfactory performance or behavior is related to the drug use or alcoholism of such employee; and

(5) may, with respect to Federal regulations regarding alcohol and the illegal use of drugs, require that—

(A) employees comply with the standards established in such regulations of the Department of Defense, if the employees of the covered entity are employed in an industry subject to such regulations, including complying with regulations (if any) that apply to employment in sensitive positions in such an industry, in the case of employees of the covered entity who are employed in such positions (as defined in the regulations of the Department of Defense);

(B) employees comply with the standards established in such regulations of the Nuclear Regulatory Commission, if the employees of the covered entity are employed in an industry subject to such regulations, including complying with regulations (if any) that apply to employment in sensitive positions in such an industry, in the case of employees of the covered entity who are employed in such positions (as defined in the regulations of the Nuclear Regulatory Commission); and

(C) employees comply with the standards established in such regulations of the Department of Transportation, if the employees of the covered entity are employed in a transportation industry subject to such regulations, including complying with such regulations (if any) that apply to employment in sensitive positions in such an industry, in the case of employees of the covered entity who are employed in such positions (as defined in the regulations of the Department of Transportation).

(d) Drug testing

(1) In general

For purposes of this subchapter, a test to determine the illegal use of drugs shall not be considered a medical examination.

(2) Construction

Nothing in this subchapter shall be construed to encourage, prohibit, or authorize the conducting of drug testing for the illegal use of drugs by job applicants or employees or making employment decisions based on such test results.

(e) Transportation employees

Nothing in this subchapter shall be construed to encourage, prohibit, restrict, or authorize the otherwise lawful exercise by entities subject to the jurisdiction of the Department of Transportation of authority to —

(1) test employees of such entities in, and applicants for, positions involving safety-sensitive duties for the illegal use of drugs and for on-duty impairment by alcohol; and

(2) remove such persons who test positive for illegal use of drugs and on-duty impairment by alcohol pursuant to paragraph (1) from safety-sensitive duties in implementing subsection (c) of this section.

* * *

Questions for Discussion

1. Do you believe that these policies, as outlined in this statute, are fair? Are there changes you might make?

2. What cases have explored the nexus between alcoholism and disability? Illegal drugs and disability?

The following is an article by the U.S. Commission on Civil Rights.

Sharing the Dream: Is the ADA Accommodating All? Substance Abuse under the ADA

It has been reported that 10 percent to 25 percent of the American population is "sometimes on the job under the influence of alcohol or some illicit drug."[1] The social and economic costs of substance abuse in America are staggering. In a report issued in 1998 by the National Institute on Alcohol Abuse and Alcoholism and the National Institute on Drug Abuse, it is estimated that the cost of alcohol and drug abuse for 1995 was $276.4 billion, of which $166.5 billion was for alcohol abuse and $109.8 billion was for drug abuse.[2]

Title I of the Americans with Disabilities Act[3] specifically permits employers to ensure that the workplace is free from the illegal use of drugs and the use of alcohol, and to

---

1. *See* Federico E. Garcia, "The Determinants of Substance Abuse in the Workplace," *Social Science Journal*, vol. 33 (1996), pp. 55, 56. *See also* National Institute on Alcohol Abuse and Alcoholism, U.S. Department of Health and Human Services, *Sixth Special Report to the U.S. Congress on Alcohol and Health*, no. 22 (1987).

2. The main components of the estimated costs of alcohol abuse include health care expenditures (12.3 percent); productivity losses due to premature death (21.2 percent); productivity impairment due to alcohol-related illness (45.7 percent); and property and administrative costs of alcohol-related motor vehicle crashes (9.2 percent). The main components of the estimated costs of drug abuse include health care expenditures (10.2 percent); lost productivity of incarcerated perpetrators of drug-related crimes (18.3 percent); lost legitimate production due to drug-related crime careers (19.7 percent); other costs of drug-related crime, including police, legal, and corrections services, federal drug traffic control, and property damage (18.4 percent); and impaired productivity due to drug-related illness (14.5 percent). National Institute on Alcohol Abuse and Alcoholism (NIAAA) and the National Institute on Drug Abuse (NIDA), *The Economic Costs of Alcohol and Drug Abuse in the United States*, May 13, 1998.

3. 42 U.S.C. §§ 12111–12117 (1994).

comply with other federal laws and regulations regarding drug and alcohol use. At the same time, the ADA provides limited protection from discrimination for recovering drug abusers and for alcoholics.[4]

The following is an overview of the current legal obligations for employers and employees:

- An individual who is currently engaging in the illegal use of drugs is not an "individual with a disability" when the employer acts on the basis of such use.

- An employer may not discriminate against a person who has a *history* of drug addiction but who is not currently using drugs and who has been rehabilitated.

- An employer may prohibit the illegal use of drugs and the use of alcohol at the workplace.

- It is not a violation of the ADA for an employer to give tests for the illegal use of drugs.

- An employer may discharge or deny employment to persons who currently engage in the illegal use of drugs.

- Employees who use drugs or alcohol may be required to meet the same standards of performance and conduct that are set for other employees.

- Employees may be required to follow the Drug-Free Workplace Act of 1988 and rules set by federal agencies pertaining to drug and alcohol use in the workplace.[5]

WHEN ARE DRUG USERS COVERED UNDER THE ADA?

The ADA provides that any employee or job applicant who is "currently engaging" in the illegal use of drugs is not a "qualified individual with a disability."[6] Therefore, an employee who illegally uses drugs—whether the employee is a casual user or an addict— is not protected by the ADA if the employer acts on the basis of the illegal drug use.[7] As a result, an employer does not violate the ADA by uniformly enforcing its rules prohibiting

---

4. 42 U.S.C. §§ 12111–12117.

5. Equal Employment Opportunity Commission, Technical Assistance Manual on the Employment Provisions (Title I) of the Americans with Disabilities Act § 8.2, January 1992 (hereafter cited as EEOC Technical Assistance Manual on the ADA).

6. 42 U.S.C. § 12114(a) (1994); 29 C.F.R. § 1630.3(a) (1999). *See, e.g., Shafer v. Preston Mem'l Hosp. Corp.*, 107 F.3d 274 (4th Cir. 1997) (current illegal drug user is not covered). Ellen Weber, director of the national office of the Legal Action Center, a law and policy office that specializes in alcohol, drug, and AIDS issues, said in her testimony before the Commission that prior to passage of the ADA, individuals with current drug problems were protected under the Rehabilitation Act against discrimination to the extent they could perform their jobs. "[The] decision to eliminate coverage," Ms. Weber testified, "was based on nothing other than the pure political decision that nobody wanted to appear soft on drugs...." Ellen Weber, testimony before the U.S. Commission on Civil Rights, hearing, Washington, D.C., Nov. 12–13, 1998, transcript, p. 25 (hereafter cited as Hearing Transcript). Ms. Weber argued that this change in the law "did nothing more than ... deter some individuals from getting into treatment and driving the problem underground in an effort to hide that problem from an employer." Ibid., pp. 25–26.

7. Under the ADA, "illegal use" is broader than just the use of drugs that are commonly viewed as illegal. It includes the use of illegal drugs that are controlled substances (e.g., cocaine) as well as the illegal use of prescription drugs that are controlled substances (e.g., Valium). For example, in *Nielsen v. Moroni Feed Co.*, 162 F.3d 604, 611, fn. 12 (10th Cir. 1998), the court stated there "is no doubt that, under the ADA, illegal drug use includes the illegal misuse of pain-killing drugs which are controlled by prescription as well as illegal street drugs like cocaine."

employees from illegally using drugs.[8] However, "qualified individuals" under the ADA include those individuals:

- who have been successfully rehabilitated and who are no longer engaged in the illegal use of drugs;[9]

- who are currently participating in a rehabilitation program and are no longer engaging in the illegal use of drugs;[10] and

- who are regarded, erroneously, as illegally using drugs.[11]

A former drug *addict* may be protected under the ADA because the addiction may be considered a substantially limiting impairment.[12] However, according to the EEOC Technical Assistance Manual on the ADA, a former *casual* drug user is not protected:

> [A] person who casually used drugs illegally in the past, but did not become addicted is not an individual with a disability based on the past drug use. In order for a person to be "substantially limited" because of drug use, s/he must be addicted to the drug.[13]

What Is a "Current" Drug User?

The definition of "current" is critical because the ADA only excludes someone from protection when that person is a "current" user of illegal drugs. In her testimony before the Commission, Nancy Delogu, counsel to the Institute for a Drug-Free Workplace,[14] stated, "There is insufficient law on the issue right now and it is causing great difficulty for employers to determine exactly when they may take discipline against an employee."[15]

Mark Rothstein, professor of law and director of the Health, Law and Policy Institute at the University of Houston, concurred with Ms. Delogu, testifying before the

---

8. EEOC Technical Assistance Manual on the ADA §8.3. *See, e.g., Wood v. Indianapolis Power & Light*, 2000 U.S. App. LEXIS 1769 (7th Cir. 2000), No. 99-1652 (meter reader who tested positive for cocaine and marijuana use was not protected by the ADA).

9. 42 U.S.C. §12114(b) (1994).

10. 42 U.S.C. §12114(b) (1994). A "rehabilitation program" may include inpatient, outpatient, or employee assistance programs, or recognized self-help programs such as Narcotics Anonymous. EEOC Technical Assistance Manual on the ADA §8.5.

11. 42 U.S.C. §12114(b). *See Ackridge v. Dep't of Human Servs., City of Philadelphia*, 3 AD Cases (BNA) 575, 576 (E.D. Pa. 1994), in which the plaintiff claimed that she was discriminated against because she was incorrectly regarded as an alcoholic and/or a substance abuser. In dicta, the court noted that if the plaintiff was in fact regarded as a drug abuser (and if she was not using drugs), or if she was regarded as an alcoholic, she might have a valid ADA claim. *Id.* at 576. *See also* EEOC Technical Assistance Manual on the ADA, which states that "tests for illegal use of drugs may reveal the presence of lawfully-used drugs. If a person is excluded from a job because the employer erroneously 'regarded' him/her to be an addict currently using drugs illegally when a drug test revealed the presence of a lawfully prescribed drug, the employer would be liable under the ADA." Ibid. at §8.9.

12. *See* EEOC Technical Assistance Manual on the ADA §8.5. *See also Hartman v. City of Petaluma*, 841 F. Supp. 946, 949 (N.D. Cal. 1994) (there must be "some indicia of dependence" to be considered substantially limiting a major life activity).

13. EEOC Technical Assistance Manual on the ADA §8.5.

14. The Institute for a Drug-Free Workplace, a nonprofit corporation, was established in 1989 as an independent private sector coalition. Its membership includes major employers and employer organizations, including leading American companies in petrochemical, manufacturing, high technology, construction, pharmaceutical, hospitality, retail, and transportation industries. The institute is active on legislative, legal, and regulatory issues at the federal, state, and local levels. *See 1999–2000 Guide to State and Federal Drug-Testing Laws*, by Mark A. de Bernardo and Nancy N. Delogu, published by the Institute for a Drug-Free Workplace, Washington, D.C.

15. Nancy Delogu Testimony, Hearing Transcript, p. 12.

Commission that the EEOC should "engage in some sort of interpretive statement" and, after consulting with experts in the rehabilitation community, could offer guidance that would be very helpful to employers in this area such as stating a particular length of time that an individual must be stable and making progress or require certification of an individual who had a substance abuse problem from some professional that they were making good progress before they would be covered [by the ADA], because … employers are having a difficult time making a determination. The courts have been reluctant to set out specific time periods, and this is an area that has caused a great deal of concern.[16]

The EEOC has defined "current" to mean that the illegal drug use occurred "recently enough" to justify the employer's reasonable belief that drug use is an ongoing problem.[17] The EEOC Technical Assistance Manual on the ADA provides the following guidance:

- If an individual tests positive on a drug test, he or she will be considered a current drug user, so long as the test is accurate.

- Current drug use is the illegal use of drugs that has occurred recently enough to justify an employer's reasonable belief that involvement with drugs is an ongoing problem.

- "Current" is not limited to the day of use, or recent weeks or days, but is determined on a case-by-case basis.[18]

The Circuit Courts of Appeals have held that a person can still be considered a current user even if he or she has not used drugs for a number of weeks or even months. For example, in *Zenor v. El Paso Healthcare Systems, Ltd.*,[19] the court held that the employee, a pharmacist, was a "current" user because he had used cocaine five weeks prior to his notification that he was going to be discharged. In *Salley v. Circuit City Stores, Inc.*,[20] the court noted that it knew of "no case in which a three-week period of abstinence has been considered long enough to take an employee out of the status of 'current' user."[21]

In *Shafer v. Preston Memorial Hospital Corp.*,[22] the court considered the ADA claim of a nurse who was stealing medication to which she had become addicted.[23] While the hospital investigated the matter, the nurse was put in drug rehabilitation.[24] The day after she finished her inpatient drug rehabilitation, she was notified that she had been terminated for "gross misconduct involving the diversion of controlled substances."[25]

In concluding that the plaintiff was still a "current" illegal drug user, the court noted that "the ordinary or natural meaning of the phrase 'currently using drugs' does not require that a drug user have a heroin syringe in his arm or a marijuana bong to his mouth at the exact moment contemplated."[26] Rather, according to the court, someone is a "current"

---

16. Mark Rothstein Testimony, Hearing Transcript, p. 17.
17. *See* 29 C.F.R. § 1630.3, app. at 357 (1999).
18. EEOC Technical Assistance Manual on the ADA § 8.3.
19. 176 F.3d 847, 867 (5th Cir. 1999).
20. 160 F.3d 977 (3d Cir. 1998).
21. *Id.* at 980.
22. 107 F.3d 274 (4th Cir. 1997).
23. *Id.* at 275.
24. *Id.*
25. *Id.*
26. *Id.* at 278.

user if he or she illegally used drugs "in a periodic fashion during the weeks and months prior to discharge."[27]

Can Enrolling in a Rehabilitation Program Provide ADA Protection?

A question sometimes arises as to whether a drug addicted employee who breaks the company rules can, before being disciplined, enroll in a supervised drug rehabilitation program, and then claim ADA protection as a former drug addict who no longer illegally uses drugs. In her testimony before the Commission, Nancy Delogu stated:

> It is causing great difficulty for employers to determine exactly when they may take discipline against an employee who may have had a disciplinary problem, tests positive or admits to a substance abuse problem, comes into rehabilitation for maybe 30 days. The employer waits until the employee returns to the work force and then says, "All right, now we're going to talk about the problems we have," and the employee says, "Hey, I'm disabled, I'm now covered by the ADA...." This provision actually serves as something of a disincentive to employers to offer rehabilitation and other services to employees before addressing any substantive performance problems.[28]

The EEOC Technical Assistance Manual on the ADA states that such claims made by an applicant or employee will not be successful:

> An applicant or employee who tests positive for an illegal drug cannot immediately enter a drug rehabilitation program and seek to avoid the possibility of discipline or termination by claiming s/he is now in rehabilitation and is no longer using drugs illegally. A person who tests positive for illegal use of drugs is not entitled to the protection that may be available to former users who have been or are in rehabilitation.[29]

Notwithstanding the EEOC's clear language, employees still attempt to use the argument in courts. When they do, the employer will argue — and usually with success — that the employee is a "current" user despite his or her recent admission into a drug rehabilitation program.[30]

For example, in *Collings v. Longview Fibre Co.*,[31] the employer fired several employees for using illegal drugs at the facility.[32] In their ADA lawsuit, seven of the eight plaintiffs said they had either completed drug rehabilitation programs or were in the process of rehabilitation at the time they were fired, so they were not "current" users.[33] Some of the plaintiffs even took drug tests shortly after they were discharged to prove they were not currently using illegal drugs.[34]

The court said "current" use was not limited to the use of drugs "on the day of, or within a matter of days or weeks before" the employment action in question.[35] Rather, said the court, the provision is intended to apply "to the illegal use of drugs that has occurred

---

27. *Id.*
28. Delogu Testimony, Hearing Transcript, p. 12.
29. EEOC Technical Assistance Manual on the ADA § 8.3.
30. *See* Cong. Rep. 336, 101st Cong. 2d Sess. (1990).
31. 63 F.3d 828 (9th Cir. 1995), *cert. denied*, 516 U.S. 1048 (1996).
32. *Id.* at 830.
33. *Id.* at 833.
34. *Id.*
35. *Id.*

recently enough to indicate that the individual is actively engaged in such conduct."[36] The plaintiffs were held to be "current" users and, despite the fact that they had entered or had completed a drug rehabilitation program, were not protected by the ADA.[37]

Reasonable Accommodation for Drug Addicts

The duty to provide reasonable accommodations to qualified individuals with disabilities is considered one of the most important statutory requirements of the ADA.[38] If a recovering drug addict is not currently illegally using drugs, then he or she may be entitled to reasonable accommodation. This would generally involve a modified work schedule so the employee could attend Narcotics Anonymous meetings or a leave of absence so the employee could seek treatment.[39]

WHEN ARE ALCOHOL USERS COVERED UNDER THE ADA?

Individuals who abuse alcohol may be considered disabled under the ADA if the person is an alcoholic or a recovering alcoholic.[40] Courts have usually held that alcoholism is a covered disability. For example, in *Williams v. Widnall*,[41] the court flatly stated, without discussion, that alcoholism "is a covered disability."[42]

Some courts have questioned whether alcoholism should automatically be designated as a covered disability. For example, in *Burch v. Coca-Cola*,[43] the court held that alcoholism is not a per se disability and found that the plaintiff's alcoholism was not a covered disability because it did not substantially limit any of his major life activities.[44] Similarly, in *Wallin v. Minnesota Department of Corrections*,[45] the court suggested that it would analyze alcoholism on a case-by-case basis and noted that the plaintiff had not presented evidence "that his alcoholism impaired a major life activity."[46] Moreover, both *Burch* and

---

36. *Id.*

37. Similarly, in *McDaniel v. Mississippi Baptist Med. Ctr.*, 877 F. Supp. 321 (S.D. Miss. 1994), *aff'd*, 74 F.3d 1238 (5th Cir. 1995), the plaintiff had illegally used drugs and entered a drug treatment center prior to his termination. The court held that even though the plaintiff had entered treatment, he still was not protected by the ADA because he had not been drug free for a "considerable length" of time. In this case, the plaintiff said that he had not used drugs for only a few weeks.

38. Employers do not have to provide an accommodation that causes an "undue hardship," meaning significant difficulty or expense. The analysis used to determine undue hardship focuses on the particular employer's resources, and on whether the accommodation is unduly extensive, substantial, or disruptive, or would fundamentally alter the nature or operation of the business. 42 U.S.C. § 12111(10) (1994); 29 C.F.R. § 1630.2(p) (1999). Another defense to an allegation of discrimination is "direct threat," meaning a significant risk to the health or safety of others that cannot be eliminated by reasonable accommodation. *See* 42 U.S.C. § 12111(3); 29 C.F.R. §§ 1630.2(r), 1630.15(b)(2).

39. *See* 42 U.S.C. § 12111(9) (1994); 29 C.F.R. § 1630.2(o)(2) (1999).

40. *See, e.g., Adamczyk v. Baltimore County*, No. 97-1240, 1998 U.S. App. LEXIS 1331 (4th Cir. 1998) (alcoholism is covered under the Rehabilitation Act); *Mararri v. WCI Steel, Inc.*, 130 F.3d 1180, 1185 (6th Cir. 1997) (the ADA "treats drug addiction and alcoholism differently").

41. 79 F.3d 1003 (10th Cir. 1996). *See also Adamczyk v. Baltimore County*, 1998 U.S. App. LEXIS 1331 (4th Cir. 1998) (alcoholism is covered under the Rehabilitation Act); *Miners v. Cargill Communications, Inc.*, 113 F.3d 820 (8th Cir. 1997), *cert. denied*, 118 S. Ct. 441 (1997) (where plaintiff could show she was regarded as being an alcoholic, she was "disabled within the meaning of the ADA"); Office of the Senate Sergeant-at-Arms v. Office of Senate Fair Employment Practices, 95 F.3d 1102 (Fed. Cir. 1996) ("it is well-established that alcoholism meets the definition of a disability").

42. 79 F.3d 1003 (10th Cir. 1996).

43. 119 F.3d 305 (5th Cir. 1997), *cert. denied*, 118 S. Ct. 871 (1998).

44. *Id.* at 322.

45. 153 F.3d 681 (8th Cir. 1998).

46. *Id.* at 686.

Wallin are consistent with the United States Supreme Court's ruling in *Sutton v. United Airlines, Inc.*,[47] which stated clearly that an "individualized inquiry" will be conducted to determine whether an impairment "substantially limits" a major life activity. As the Court explained in *Sutton*:

> A "disability" exists only where an impairment "substantially limits" a major life activity, not where it "might," "could," or "would" be substantially limiting if corrective measures were not taken. Second, because subsection (A) [of 42 U.S.C. § 12102(2)] requires that disabilities be evaluated "with respect to an individual" and be determined based on whether an impairment substantially limits the individual's "major life activities," the question whether a person has a disability under the ADA is an individualized inquiry.[48] [Editor's note: *Sutton* has been overruled, and language in the ADAA states that plaintiffs are considered in their uncorrected states.]

Even though courts may determine that alcoholism is a covered disability, the law makes it clear that employers can enforce rules concerning alcohol in the workplace. The ADA provides that employers may:

- prohibit the use of alcohol in the workplace;[49]

- require that employees not be under the influence of alcohol in the workplace;[50] and

- hold an employee with alcoholism to the same employment standards to which the employer holds other employees even if the unsatisfactory performance or behavior is related to the alcoholism.[51]

The EEOC Technical Assistance Manual giving further guidance on the ADA provides that employers are free to "discipline, discharge or deny employment to an alcoholic whose use of alcohol adversely affects job performance or conduct to the extent that s/he is not 'qualified.'"[52] The manual elaborates with the following example:

> If an individual who has alcoholism often is late to work, or is unable to perform the responsibilities of his/her job, an employer can take disciplinary action on the basis of the poor job performance and conduct. However, an employer may not discipline an alcoholic employee more severely than it does other employees for the same performance or conduct.[53]

For example, if an alcoholic employee and a non-alcoholic employee are caught having a beer on the loading dock, the employer cannot fire the alcoholic employee while giving the other employee only a written warning.[54] In *Flynn v. Raytheon Co.*,[55] the court dealt with this precise issue. It held that even though an employer can enforce its rules against intoxication on the job, it could not selectively enforce its rules in a way that treats

---

47. 119 S. Ct. 2139, 527 U.S. 471 (1999).
48. 119 S. Ct. at 2142.
49. 42 U.S.C. § 12114. *See Walker v. Consol. Biscuit Co.*, 522 U.S. 1028 (1997) (the court held that the employer could terminate an employee for violating its rule prohibiting employees from being under the influence of alcohol in the workplace).
50. 42 U.S.C. § 12114 (1994).
51. 42 U.S.C. § 12114 (1994).
52. EEOC Technical Assistance Manual on the ADA § 8.4.
53. Ibid.
54. Ibid.
55. 868 F. Supp. 383 (D. Mass. 1994); *aff'd* 94 F.3d 640 (1st Cir. 1996).

alcoholics more harshly.[56] In short, whatever policies the employer enacts must be uniformly applied.[57]

Reasonable Accommodation for Alcoholics

The duty to provide reasonable accommodations to qualified individuals with disabilities is considered one of the most important statutory requirements of the ADA.[58] Reasonable accommodation for an alcoholic would generally involve a modified work schedule[59] so the employee could attend Alcoholics Anonymous meetings, or a leave of absence[60] so the employee could seek treatment. In *Schmidt v. Safeway, Inc.*,[61] for example, the court held that the employer must provide a leave of absence so the employee could obtain medical treatment for alcoholism.[62]

The ADA does not require an employer to provide an alcohol rehabilitation program or to offer rehabilitation in lieu of disciplining an employee for alcohol-related misconduct or performance problems. In Senate proceedings, Senator Daniel Coats (R-IN) asked Senator Tom Harkin (D-IA), the ADA's chief sponsor, "Is the employer under a legal obligation under the act to provide rehabilitation for an employee who is using ... alcohol?" In response, Senator Harkin stated, "No, there is no such legal obligation."[63] The Senate report echoes Senator Harkin's response that reasonable accommodation "does not affirmatively require that a covered entity must provide a rehabilitation program or an opportunity for rehabilitation ... for any current employee who is [an] alcoholic against whom employment-related actions are taken" for performance or conduct reasons.[64]

The EEOC has held that "federal employers are no longer required to provide the reasonable accommodation of 'firm choice' under Section 501 of the Rehabilitation Act."[65] "Firm choice" generally entails a warning to employees with alcohol-related employment problems that they will be disciplined if they do not receive alcohol treatment. The EEOC's rationale is that the Rehabilitation Act was amended in 1992 to apply ADA standards, and that the ADA does not require an employer to excuse misconduct for poor performance, even if it is related to alcoholism. In EEOC's "Enforcement Guidance on Reasonable Accommodation and Undue Hardship" statement, the EEOC reiterated that an employer "has no obligation to provide 'firm choice' or a 'last chance agreement' as a reasonable accommodation."[66]

---

56. *See also Miners v. Cargill Communications, Inc.*, 113 F.3d 820 (8th Cir. 1997), *cert. denied*, 118 S. Ct. 441 (1997), in which the court found that evidence of inconsistent enforcement of a policy concerning alcohol use (e.g., not enforcing the policy against management employees) was relevant in showing discrimination against an employee "regarded as" being an alcoholic.

57. EEOC Technical Assistance Manual on the ADA § 8.7.

58. *See* the preceding discussion under "Reasonable Accommodation for Drug Addicts" in this chapter.

59. 42 U.S.C. § 12111(9) (1994); 29 C.F.R. § 1630.2(o)(2) (1999).

60. 42 U.S.C. § 12111(9); 29 C.F.R. § 1630.2(o)(2).

61. 864 F. Supp. 991 (D. Ore. 1994).

62. *Id.* at 996.

63. 135 CONG. REC. S10777 (daily ed. Sept. 7, 1989).

64. S. REP. NO. 101-116 (1989).

65. *See Johnson v. Babbitt.* Pet. No. 03940100, MSPB No. SF-0752-93-0613-I-1 (EEOC 3/28/96).

66. *See* Equal Employment Opportunity Commission, "Enforcement Guidance on Reasonable Accommodation and Undue Hardship," no. 915.002 (Mar. 1, 1999). *See also Adamczyk v. Baltimore County*, 1998 U.S. App. LEXIS 1331 (4th Cir. 1998), where the employer fired a police officer for misconduct allegedly caused by alcoholism, and the employer was not required to permit the officer to seek treatment before taking adverse action.

Moreover, an employer is generally not required to provide leave to an alcoholic employee if the treatment would appear to be futile. For example, in *Schmidt v. Safeway, Inc.*,[67] the court said an employer would not be required "to provide repeated leaves of absence (or perhaps even a single leave of absence) for an alcoholic employee with a poor prognosis for recovery."[68] And in *Fuller v. Frank*,[69] the court held that the employer was not required to give an alcoholic employee another leave of absence when alcohol treatment had repeatedly failed in the past.[70]

Finally, an employer generally has no duty to provide an accommodation to an employee who has not asked for an accommodation and who denies having a disability. In *Larson v. Koch Refining Co.*,[71] the court dealt with this precise issue and held that the employer had no obligation to provide accommodation to an employee with alcoholism when the employee did not ask for an accommodation, and in fact expressly denied having an alcohol problem.[72]

Blaming Misconduct on Alcoholism

Courts routinely hold that employees cannot blame misconduct on alcoholism. For example, in *Renaud v. Wyoming Department of Family Services*,[73] the court noted that even if alcoholism is assumed to be a disability, the ADA distinguishes between alcoholism and alcoholism-related misconduct.[74] The court determined that the employer could lawfully terminate the employee (a school superintendent) for coming to work drunk, even though he claimed the conduct resulted from his alcoholism.[75]

In *Labrucherie v. Regents of the University of California*,[76] the court stated it was not discriminatory to fire an employee because he was incarcerated after his third arrest for drunk driving.[77] The court noted that "a termination based on *misconduct stemming from a disability*, rather than the disability itself, is valid."[78]

Likewise, in *Maddox v. University of Tennessee*,[79] the university fired an assistant football coach after his third arrest for drunk driving.[80] During the arrest, the assistant coach was combative and would not take a Breathalyzer test.[81] The employee claimed that he was discriminated against based on his alcoholism because his drunk driving was a result of the alcoholism.[82] The court agreed with the university that the misconduct could be

---

67. 864 F. Supp. 991 (D. Ore. 1994).

68. *Id.* at 997.

69. 916 F.2d 558, 562 (9th Cir. 1990).

70. Similarly, in *Evans v. Fed. Express Corp.*, 133 F.3d 137 (1st Cir. 1998), the court held that the employer was not required to provide a second leave of absence to an employee for substance abuse treatment. The court noted, "It is one thing to say that further treatment made medical sense, and quite another to say that the law required the company to retain [the employee] through a succession of efforts."

71. 920 F. Supp. 1000 (D. Minn. 1995).

72. *Id.* at 1006.

73. 203 F.3d 723 (10th Cir. 2000).

74. *Id.* at 730.

75. *Id.* at 730–731.

76. 1997 U.S. app. LEXIS 17755 (9th Cir. 1997).

77. *Id.* at *3.

78. *Id.*

79. 62 F.3d 843 (6th Cir. 1995).

80. *Id.* at 845.

81. *Id.*

82. *Id.*

separated from the alcoholism and that the assistant coach was properly terminated due to the misconduct.[83]

It is clear that an employer does not, as a reasonable accommodation, have to forgive misconduct because the misconduct resulted from alcoholism. In *Flynn v. Raytheon Co.*,[84] the lower court noted that an employee who broke the company's policy prohibiting being under the influence of alcohol in the workplace cannot "belatedly avail himself of the reasonable accommodation provisions" of the ADA to escape discipline for his misconduct.[85] The First Circuit also noted that the ADA "does not require an employer to rehire a former employee who was lawfully discharged for disability-related failures to meet its legitimate job requirements."[86]

DIRECT THREAT POSED BY SUBSTANCE ABUSE

The defense of "direct threat" is one that is raised frequently by employers in dealing with issues of substance abuse. The ADA defines direct threat as "a significant risk to the health or safety of others that cannot be eliminated by reasonable accommodation."[87] The ADA permits employers to require, as a job qualification, that an individual not "pose a direct threat to the health or safety of other individuals in the workplace."[88] Moreover, an employer may institute such a requirement even if an employer's reliance on such a qualification might "screen out or tend to screen out or otherwise deny a job or benefit to an individual with a disability."[89]

The determination that an individual with a disability poses a direct threat shall be based on an individualized assessment of the individual's present ability to safely perform the essential functions of the job.[90] In determining whether an individual would pose a direct threat, the factors to be considered include:

- the duration of the risk;
- the nature and severity of the potential harm;
- the likelihood that the potential harm will occur; and
- the imminence of the potential harm.[91]

Evidence used in making the determination may include information from the individual, including the individual's experience in previous similar situations, and the

---

83. Other courts, too, have held that an employer may terminate an employee because of improper conduct, even if the conduct is a direct result of alcoholism. In *Williams v. Widnall*, 79 F.3d 1003 (10th Cir. 1996), it was held that an employer lawfully fired an employee because of his threatening conduct, even though the conduct may have been a result of alcoholism. And in *Newland v. Dalton*, 81 F.3d 904 (9th Cir. 1996), it was held that an employer lawfully fired an employee because of a "drunken rampage," even if it was related to alcoholism.

84. 868 F. Supp. 383 (D. Mass. 1994), *aff'd*, 94 F.3d 640 (1st Cir. 1996).

85. *Id.* at 387.

86. *Id.*

87. 42 U.S.C. § 12111(3) (1994).

88. 42 U.S.C. § 12113(b) (1994). An employer is also permitted to require that an individual not pose a direct threat of harm to his or her own safety or health. *See* 29 C.F.R. § 1630.2(r), app. at 356 (1999).

89. 42 U.S.C. § 12113(a) (1994).

90. 29 C.F.R. § 1630.2(r) (1999). The regulations state that the assessment shall be based on a medical judgment that relies on the most "current" medical knowledge and/or on the "best available objective evidence."

91. 29 C.F.R. § 1630.2(r) (1999).

opinions of doctors, rehabilitation counselors, or physical therapists who have expertise in the specific disability or who have direct knowledge of the individual.[92]

Moreover, the EEOC has emphasized, in its Interpretive Guidance on Title I of the ADA, that an employer may not deny employment to an individual with a disability "merely because of a slightly increased risk. The risk can only be considered when it poses a significant risk, i.e., high probability of substantial harm; a speculative or remote risk is insufficient."[93]

EEOC v. Exxon Corporation

In *EEOC v. Exxon Corporation*,[94] the courts were forced to analyze the ADA's "direct threat"[95] defense and how it interacts with the "business necessity"[96] defense. With respect to substance abuse and the ADA, courts have generally recognized an employer's prerogative to formulate and rely upon safety-based job qualifications, even though they may screen out individuals with disabilities.

In *Exxon*, the EEOC brought suit against Exxon on behalf of several employees,[97] alleging that the company's blanket policy of prohibiting individuals who have ever been treated for drug or alcohol abuse from working in safety-sensitive "designated positions"[98] (approximately 10 percent of Exxon's positions) violated the ADA.[99] The EEOC argued that the company's policy was invalid on its face because it did not provide, as mandated

---

92. 29 C.F.R. § 1630.2(r), app. at 356 (1999).

93. 29 C.F.R. § 1630.2(r), app. at 356 (1999). *See also* EEOC Technical Assistance Manual on the ADA § 8.7, which states: "An employer cannot prove a 'high probability' of substantial harm simply by referring to statistics indicating the likelihood that addicts or alcoholics in general have a specific probability of suffering a relapse. A showing of 'significant risk of substantial harm' must be based upon an assessment of the particular individual and his/her history of substance abuse and the specific nature of the job to be performed."

94. 967 F. Supp. 208 (N.D. Tex. 1997); *reversed and remanded in* 203 F.3d 871 (5th Cir. 2000).

95. The ADA defines direct threat as "a significant risk to the health or safety of others that cannot be eliminated by reasonable accommodation." *EEOC v. Exxon*, 967 F. Supp. 210. *See* 42 U.S.C. § 12111(3) (1994).

96. The ADA states: "It may be a defense to a charge of discrimination under this Act that an alleged application of qualification standards, tests, or selection criteria that screen out or tend to screen out or otherwise deny a job or benefit to an individual with a disability has been shown to be job related and consistent with business necessity, and such performance cannot be accomplished by reasonable accommodation, as required under this title." *Id.* at 210. *See* 42 U.S.C. § 12113(a) (1994).

97. 967 F. Supp. 209–10. The named plaintiffs were two Exxon employees who had been working as flight engineers but were demoted in 1994 to mechanics when they were asked whether they had a history of drug or alcohol abuse. Salvatore Filippone, who was in his late 40s, had been convicted of abusing a prescription drug when he was 19 years old. He went into rehabilitation, never abused drugs again, and in 1983 joined Exxon, where he was responsible for monitoring aircraft systems during flight, according to EEOC documents filed in federal court. Glenn Hale, who went into treatment for alcohol abuse in 1985, was hired by Exxon as a flight engineer in 1988. He abstained from drinking and never had a relapse, according to the EEOC court filing. *Id.*

98. *Id.* at 210. The company defined a "designated position" as one in which failure could cause a catastrophic incident, and for which the employee plays a key and direct role with either no direct or very limited supervision. *Id.*

99. *Id.* at 209–10. Exxon adopted its substance abuse policy after the Exxon Valdez ran aground in Alaska and dumped 11 million gallons of oil into the Prince William Sound. The company, eager to avoid another Valdez disaster, applied the policy to plant operators, drivers, and ships' mates after news reports surfaced that the captain of the Valdez, Joseph Hazelwood, had been drinking and that Exxon officials knew he had sought treatment for his drinking problem four years before the accident. Mr. Hazelwood was later cleared by a jury of intoxication charges. *See Seahawk Seafoods, Inc. v. Alyeska Pipeline Serv. Co.*, 206 F.3d 900 (9th Cir. 2000); *State v. Hazelwood*, 946 P.2d 875 (Alaska 1997).

by ADA regulations, for an "individualized assessment" of whether former drug abusers were qualified to work in any of the designated safety-sensitive positions.[100]

The company countered by claiming that the ADA does not require an individualized assessment of an employee's risk of relapse where such an assessment would be impractical or impossible.[101] The company argued that the risk of relapse for rehabilitated substance abusers is too great to permit them to work in the designated safety-sensitive positions, and that the inability to predict a relapse makes individualized assessments futile.[102]

The U.S. District Court found that the ADA permits an exception to the individualized assessment ordinarily required under the law.[103] The court relied on the ADA's emphasis on protecting employers from the risks posed by recently rehabilitated employees, and on other employment discrimination statutes that permit blanket exclusions where safety is an issue and the employer has reason to believe that all of the disqualified employees would be unable to perform safely.[104]

In its appeal, the EEOC relied on its Interpretive Guidance to argue that employers must meet the direct threat defense:

> With regard to safety sensitive requirements that screen out or tend to screen out an individual with a disability or a class of individuals with disabilities, an employer must demonstrate that the requirement, as applied to the individual, satisfies the "direct threat" standard ... in order to show that the requirement is job-related and consistent with a business necessity.[105]

The Fifth Circuit Court of Appeals examined the text of the ADA and held while "direct threat" focuses on the individual employee and examines the specific risk posed by the employee's disability, "business necessity" addresses whether the qualification standard can be justified as an across-the-board requirement.[106] The court determined that while Exxon's "blanket" across-the-board policy might exclude individuals with disabilities without an individualized analysis as to whether they could perform the essential functions of the position, this exclusion was appropriate if the employer could demonstrate that it is justified by business necessity.[107]

The *Exxon* case generated significant debate during the Commission's ADA hearing. Nancy Delogu, counsel to the Institute for a Drug-Free Workplace, said it was important to resolve the issue. She testified:

---

100. *See* 29 C.F.R. § 1630.2(r), app. at 356 (1999), which states, "Determining whether an individual poses a significant risk of substantial harm to others must be made on a case by case basis."

101. 967 F. Supp. 210.

102. *Id.*

103. *Id.* at 214.

104. These statutes included the Rehabilitation Act, the Age Discrimination in Employment Act (ADEA), and Title VII "because these statutes are similar in purpose to the ADA and have often been relied upon in interpreting the ADA." *Id.* at 212. *See Buchanan v. City of San Antonio*, 85 F.3d 196, 200 (5th Cir. 1996); *Daigle V. Liberty Life Ins. Co.*, 70 F.3d 394, 396 (5th Cir. 1995). The court noted that Rehabilitation Act case law "is especially persuasive given that the ADA is modeled after the Rehabilitation Act and Congress has directed that the two acts' judicial and agency standards be harmonized." 967 F. Supp. 212.

105. 203 F.3d 871, 873 (5th Cir. 2000).

106. *Id.* at 874.

107. *Id.* The court stated: "We have found nothing in the statutory language, legislative history or case law that persuades that the direct threat provision addresses safety-based qualification standards in cases where an employer has developed a standard applicable to all employees of a given class. We hold that an employer need not proceed under the direct threat provision of § 12113(b) in such cases but rather may defend the standard as a business necessity." *Id.* at 874.

Alcoholism and substance abuse are chronic conditions for which the risk of relapse cannot be well ... predicted. And for certain very, very highly safety-sensitive positions, those which have no ... direct supervision and for which a lapse in judgment could lead to a catastrophic error, employers wish to be able to exclude those employees from those positions. Whether they're required to transfer them to another position would certainly be something open to a policy debate, but currently this is quite a concern.[108]

Kenneth Collins, formerly the manager of the Employee Assistance Program at Chevron Corporation and currently vice president for Value Options, the nation's second largest provider of behavioral health care services, testified that the Chevron Corporation conducted a study on accident rates of its workers.[109] The study concluded that workers who had completed Employee Assistance Program-monitored substance abuse rehabilitation had no more on-the-job or off-the-job accidents than did the "regular" Chevron population.[110] Mr. Collins testified:

It certainly is my position based on my experience and the research done within Chevron and at other similar oil companies who have tightly structured employee assistance programs that, in fact, you can return individuals to highly safety-sensitive positions and not expose the company to increased risks of accidents or errors in judgment. But that is premised on having a rigorous follow-up program [which involves weekly follow-up testing].[111]

The *Exxon* case suggests that an employer should carefully consider the context in which medical guidelines will be used; i.e., will medical guidelines be used as a basis for formulating job qualifications for safety-based reasons, or will they be used to assess, during a medical examination, whether an individual poses a direct threat. The ruling in *Exxon* suggests that an employer's reliance on medical guidelines may be more defensible when they are used to formulate a broad-based qualification than to assess an individual case.

Some experts suggest that partly because of the publicity surrounding notorious cases like *Exxon*, companies can become too quick to designate a position as "safety sensitive." Mark Rothstein, professor of law and director of the Health, Law and Policy Institute at the University of Houston, testified before the Commission that some employers have indeed been overly inclusive in the process of determining which positions are safety sensitive:

I think some employers have an overly broad view of what a safety-sensitive position is and have ... declared many jobs permanently unavailable to individuals who have ever had any sort of substance abuse problem, no matter

---

108. Delogu Testimony, Hearing Transcript, p. 14. Ms. Delogu testified later in the hearing that employers should not "be able to exclude all former substance abusers for some very broad and undefined categories of safety-sensitive jobs. I do believe, however, ... that there should be a mechanism for those very safety-critical positions to make this exception." Ibid., pp. 39–40.

109. Kenneth Collins Testimony, Hearing Transcript, p. 16.

110. Ibid.

111. Ibid. *See also* testimony of Dr. Joseph Autry, the acting deputy administrator in the Substance Abuse and Mental Health Services Administration of the Department of Health and Human Services, who also emphasized the importance of follow-up treatment: "Increasingly research is indicating that relapse prevention following treatment and drug testing or alcohol testing are probably the most important things in keeping someone drug and alcohol free as they return to the workplace.... There needs to be ongoing rehabilitation, if you will, or relapse prevention, interventions, coupled with testing in order to maintain sobriety or to be drug free." Joseph Autry Testimony, Hearing Transcript, pp. 35–36.

how many years in the past. And I think that these policies are not substantiated by the scientific evidence and I think are directly counter to the purposes of the ADA.[112]

Mr. Rothstein testified that while he thought a blanket policy was "understandable" in the *Exxon* case, he thought it "ill-advised" to adopt a "basically irrebuttable presumption" that anyone who has ever had a substance abuse problem should be barred for his or her lifetime from engaging in an activity that the employer deems to be safety sensitive.[113] To illustrate his point, Mr. Rothstein referred to the case of *Knox County Education Association v. Knox County Board of Education*.[114]

In *Knox County*, the Sixth Circuit upheld the drug testing of school personnel, including principals, teachers, aides, secretaries, and bus drivers, on the ground that because these individuals play a unique role in the lives of children, all the positions were deemed to be safety sensitive, including the people who worked in the office.[115] Mr. Rothstein testified:

> It seems to me that if you broaden the concept of safety sensitive as far as that court and applied it in the workplace, now you're basically saying that anyone who ever had a minor substance abuse problem in college 25 or 30 years ago, they're now barred from who knows how many jobs. That strikes me as not being based on any good facts or any good policy.[116]

Ellen Weber, director of the national office of the Legal Action Center, a law and policy office that specializes in alcohol, drug, and AIDS issues, concurred with Mr. Rothstein. She testified before the Commission, "We ... agree to a great extent with ... what Mr. Rothstein has said with regard to the issues of employers overly expanding the list of safety-sensitive jobs to which people are rejected from blanketly."[117]

PRE-EMPLOYMENT INQUIRIES ABOUT DRUG AND ALCOHOL USE

An employer may make certain pre-employment, pre-offer inquiries regarding use of alcohol or the illegal use of drugs.[118] An employer may ask whether an applicant drinks alcohol or whether he or she is currently using drugs illegally.[119] However, an employer may not ask whether an applicant is a drug abuser or alcoholic, or inquire whether he or she has ever been in a drug or alcohol rehabilitation program.[120] Indeed, the EEOC has provided extensive guidance of what can and cannot be asked through its Enforcement Guidance titled "Pre-employment Disability-Related Questions and Medical Examinations."[121]

After a conditional offer of employment, an employer may ask any question concerning past or present drug or alcohol use as long as it does so for all entering employees in the

---

112. Rothstein Testimony, Hearing Transcript, p. 19.

113. Ibid., p. 32.

114. 158 F.3d 361 (6th Cir. 1998), *cert. denied*, 120 S. Ct. 46 (1999).

115. *Id.* at 363. *But see Chandler v. Miller*, 520 U.S. 305 (1997), in which the Supreme Court held that a Georgia policy requiring all candidates for public office to submit to drug tests violated the Fourth Amendment's requirement that a search be justified either by particularized suspicion or by "special needs" beyond crime detection.

116. Rothstein Testimony, Hearing Transcript, p. 31. Mr. Rothstein testified later in the hearing that "drug testing, where necessary, should be limited to the smallest group of people possible, not demonstrated as a badge that the company disapproves of illicit substances." Ibid., p. 41.

117. Ellen Weber Testimony, Hearing Transcript, p. 21.

118. EEOC Technical Assistance Manual on the ADA §8.8.

119. Ibid.

120. Ibid.

121. "Pre-employment Disability-Related Questions and Medical Examinations" was issued by the EEOC on Oct. 10, 1995.

same job category.[122] The employer may not, however, use such information to exclude an individual with a disability, on the basis of a disability, unless it can show that the reason for exclusion is job related and consistent with business necessity, and that legitimate job criteria cannot be met with a reasonable accommodation.[123]

DRUG TESTING

An employer may conduct tests to detect illegal use of drugs.[124] The ADA does not prohibit, require, or encourage drug tests. Drug tests are not considered medical examinations, and an *applicant* can be required to take a drug test before a conditional offer of employment has been made.[125] An *employee* also can be required to take a drug test, whether or not such a test is job related and necessary for the business.[126]

An employer may refuse to hire an applicant or may discharge or discipline an employee based upon a test result that indicates the illegal use of drugs. The employer may take these actions even if an applicant or employee claims that he or she recently stopped illegally using drugs.[127]

Tests for illegal use of drugs also may reveal the presence of lawfully used drugs, i.e., prescription medications. If a person is excluded from a job because the employer erroneously "regarded" him or her to be a drug abuser, currently using drugs illegally, and a drug test revealed the presence of a lawfully prescribed drug, the employer would be liable under the ADA.[128] There was testimony at the Commission's ADA hearing to suggest that this problem should be examined more closely to see if it is leading to costly and unnecessary litigation in the workplace. Nancy Delogu told the Commission:

> With drug abuse in the workplace and the number of individuals who are subject to drug testing, anyone who ever has a positive drug test, theoretically, can claim to be perceived as disabled by his or her employer or would-be employer. As a result, many cases have been brought, and many which are quite frivolous based on a positive drug test. The employer is going to do whatever they are going to do and then the employee says, "Well you saw me as disabled and I'm going to sue." Unfortunately, that's an issue of fact that requires usually lengthy discovery and litigation costs before that can be resolved.[129]

To avoid such potential liability, the employer would have to determine whether the individual was using a legally prescribed drug. An employer may not ask what prescription drugs an individual is taking before making a conditional job offer; however, an employer may validate a positive test result by asking about an applicant's lawful use of drugs or for other possible explanations for the positive test result. Alternatively, the EEOC Technical Assistance Manual on the ADA suggests:

> [O]ne way to avoid liability is to conduct drug tests after making an offer, even though such tests may be given at anytime under the ADA. Since applicants who test positive for illegal drugs are not covered by the ADA, an employer can withdraw an offer of employment on the basis of illegal drug use.[130]

---

122. EEOC Technical Assistance Manual on the ADA § 8.8.
123. Ibid.
124. Ibid. § 8.9.
125. Ibid.
126. Ibid.
127. Ibid.
128. Ibid. §§ 8.6, 8.9.
129. Delogu Testimony, Hearing Transcript, p. 13.
130. EEOC Technical Assistance Manual on the ADA § 8.9.

Mark Rothstein, professor of law and director of the Health, Law and Policy Institute at the University of Houston, endorses this EEOC recommendation. He testified at the Commission's ADA hearing:

> This is a problem that can be avoided very simply by employers who defer drug testing until the post-offer stage, that is the pre-placement stage when there are no restrictions on inquiries regarding medical conditions or substances that could cause cross-reactivity. The reason that many employers don't want to ... defer the testing until the post-offer stage is they think it's cheaper to screen out workers or potential workers on the basis of a positive drug test than it is to review their résumés and applications and references and to actually look at the individual. And that may well be true, but I think that's a rather unconvincing reason to me, at least, for subjecting individuals to this violation of their privacy that Congress otherwise said was impermissible.[131]

If the results of a drug test indicate the presence of a lawfully prescribed drug, such information must be kept confidential, in the same way as any medical record. If the results reveal information about a disability in addition to information about drug use, the disability-related information is to be treated as a confidential medical record.[132]

OTHER LAWS AND REGULATIONS CONCERNING DRUGS AND ALCOHOL

The ADA does not interfere with an employer's ability to comply with other federal laws and regulations concerning the use of drugs and alcohol, including the Drug-Free Workplace Act of 1988; regulations applicable to particular types of employment, such as law enforcement positions; regulations of the Department of Transportation for airline employees, interstate motor carrier drivers, and railroad engineers; and regulations for safety-sensitive positions established by the Department of Defense and the Nuclear Regulatory Commission. Employers may continue to require that their applicants and employees comply with such federal laws and regulations.[133]

* * *

Questions for Discussion

1. Which aspects of this area of law might prove complex for an employer to understand?

2. What policy concerns can you identify after reading this article?

3. How might the ADAAA impact the findings in this article?

For Further Reading

"Drugs and Alcohol under the ADA/HR Made Simple," retrieved May 15, 2012 at http://blog.hrsentry.com/2008/11/19/drugs-and-alcohol-under-the-ada/.

---

131. Rothstein Testimony, Hearing Transcript, pp. 18–19.
132. EEOC Technical Assistance Manual on the ADA § 8.9. For example, if drug test results indicate that an individual is HIV positive, or that a person has epilepsy or diabetes because use of a related prescribed medicine is revealed, this information must remain confidential. Ibid.
133. Ibid. § 8.10.

Discussion 20

Employment Law Overview: Disability Discrimination from 3,000 Feet

Recommended Background Reading

ADA Amendments Act, 42 USC § 12101-12102.

Readings for Class Discussion

The following article, prepared by the Job Accommodation Network (JAN), a service of the U.S. Department of Labor's Office of Disability, gives an overview of the ADA Amendments Act.

Accommodation and Compliance Series:
The ADA Amendments Act of 2008
I. BACKGROUND

On January 1, 2009, the Americans with Disabilities Act Amendments Act (ADAAA) of 2008 went into effect, making some major changes to the way the definition of disability was interpreted in the past. The changes apply to both the ADA and the Rehabilitation Act. Very few people argue that these changes were not needed—the courts had interpreted the definition of disability so narrowly that hardly anyone could meet it—but the challenge now is understanding what the changes are and who is covered as of January 1, 2009.

In the ADAAA, Congress expressly gave the Equal Employment Opportunity Commission (EEOC) the authority to revise its regulations regarding the definition of disability to make them consistent with the Act's purpose. On March 25, 2011, the EEOC issued long-awaited final regulations. These regulations apply to title I of the ADA and section 501 of the Rehabilitation Act. These are effective as of May 24, 2011.

The following provides an overview of the changes made to the definition of disability under the ADAAA and the regulations and accompanying interpretive guidance (appendix).

II. OVERALL PURPOSE

According to Congress, the ADAAA was passed "to carry out the ADA's objectives of providing 'a clear and comprehensive national mandate for the elimination of discrimination' by reinstating a broad scope of protection to be available under the ADA." In other words, the purpose of the original ADA was to eliminate discrimination. However, if hardly anyone was covered, then hardly anyone was actually being protected from discrimination. So, in the ADAAA, Congress fixed the definition of disability to cover more people and as a result, prevent more discrimination. That means that employers should no longer be focusing so much on who has a disability, but instead should be focusing on making accommodations and avoiding discrimination.

III. DEFINITION OF DISABILITY

A. Basic Three-Part Definition Will Stay the Same

Definition: Disability.

(1) Disability.— The term 'disability' means, with respect to an individual—

   (A) a physical or mental impairment that substantially limits one or more major life activities of such individual;

   (B) a record of such an impairment; or

   (C) being regarded as having such an impairment.

The ADAAA did not change the actual definition of disability—the definition is exactly the same as it was. What *did* change is the meaning of some of the words used in the definition and the way those words are to be applied to individuals.

B. Definition of Impairment is the Same

Definition: Impairment

(1) Any physiological disorder or condition, cosmetic disfigurement, or anatomical loss affecting one or more body systems, such as neurological, musculoskeletal, special sense organs, respiratory (including speech organs), cardiovascular, reproductive, digestive, genitourinary, immune, circulatory, hemic, lymphatic, skin, and endocrine; or

(2) Any mental or psychological disorder, such as an intellectual disability (formerly termed "mental retardation"), organic brain syndrome, emotional or mental illness, and specific learning disabilities.

The ADAAA did not change the definition of impairment, but the ADAAA regulations *did* add references to the immune system and the circulatory system because both are mentioned in the definition of "major bodily functions" and the EEOC wanted to be consistent.

The term "impairment" does not include physical characteristics such as eye color, hair color, left-handedness, or height, weight, or muscle tone that are within "normal" range and are not the result of a physiological disorder; characteristic predisposition to illness or disease; pregnancy; common personality traits such as poor judgment or a quick temper where these are not symptoms of a mental or psychological disorder; or environmental, cultural, or economic disadvantages such as poverty, lack of education, or a prison record.

C. Major Life Activities Expanded to Include Bodily Functions

Definition: Major Life Activities

Major life activities include, but are not limited to:

Caring for oneself, performing manual tasks, seeing, hearing, eating, sleeping, walking, standing, sitting, reaching, lifting, bending, speaking, breathing, learning, reading, concentrating, thinking, communicating, interacting with others, and working; and

The operation of a major bodily function, including functions of the immune system, special sense organs and skin; normal cell growth; and digestive, genitourinary, bowel, bladder, neurological, brain, respiratory, circulatory, cardiovascular, endocrine, hemic, lymphatic, musculoskeletal, and reproductive functions. The operation of a major bodily function includes the operation of an individual organ within a body system.

In the past, there was some debate over what activities were considered "major life activities" for ADA purposes, but one of the most confusing issues was whether someone with a medical condition that only affected internal functions would be covered. Conditions such as gastrointestinal disorders, cancer, sleep disorders, and heart disease often only affect bodily functions without producing any outward limitations and courts grappled with whether bodily functions were classified as major life activities. Now Congress has cleared up the confusion by specifically stating in the ADAAA that bodily functions are indeed major life activities.

For example, a person with insulin-dependent diabetes will most likely be covered under the first part of the new definition of disability because endocrine system function is definitely considered a major life activity as of January 1, 2009.

Note that the lists provided in the definition of major life activity are not exhaustive; they are just examples of some of the activities that can be considered.

D. Substantially Limits, Nine Rules to Follow

Definition: No Specific Definition, Follow Nine Rules of Construction.

In the ADAAA, Congress expressly directed the EEOC to revise its regulations regarding the definition of substantially limits. In the past, the EEOC regulations had defined substantially limits as "significantly restricted," but Congress told the EEOC, that is too high a standard—go back and make it an easier standard to meet. In the final regulations, the EEOC did not specifically define substantially limits, but instead provided guidance referred to as "rules of construction."

The following rules of construction come from the EEOC's final regulations, which are linked from http://www.eeoc.gov/laws/statutes/adaaa_info.cfm.

1. A Lot More Individuals Will Be Substantially Limited

The term "substantially limits" shall be construed broadly in favor of expansive coverage, to the maximum extent permitted by the terms of the ADA. "Substantially limits" is not meant to be a demanding standard.

2. Comparison is to Most People in the General Population

An impairment is a disability if it substantially limits the ability of an individual to perform a major life activity as compared to most people in the general population. An impairment need not prevent, or significantly or severely restrict, the individual from performing a major life activity in order to be considered substantially limiting.

The comparison to most people in the general population continues to mean a comparison to other people in the general population, not a comparison to those similarly situated. For example, the ability of an individual with an amputated limb to perform a major life activity is compared to other people in the general population, not to other amputees.

3. Assessing Whether Individual is Substantially Limited Should Be Quick

The primary focus under the ADA now should be whether employers have complied with their obligations and whether discrimination has occurred, not whether an individual's impairment substantially limits a major life activity. Accordingly, determining whether an impairment substantially limits a major life activity should be done quickly and should not demand extensive analysis.

4. Disability is Still Determined on a Case-By-Case Basis

The determination of whether an impairment substantially limits a major life activity still requires an individualized assessment. However, in making this assessment, substantially limits should be considered a much lower standard than it was prior to the ADAAA. Even with this lower standard, not every impairment will constitute a disability.

5. Scientific, Medical, or Statistical Evidence Usually Not Required

The comparison of an individual's performance of a major life activity to the performance of the same major life activity by most people in the general population usually will not require scientific, medical, or statistical analysis. Nothing prohibits the presentation of scientific, medical, or statistical evidence to make such a comparison where appropriate.

6. Mitigating Measures Will Not Be Considered

Definition: Mitigating Measures, Things Such As:

(i) Medication, medical supplies, equipment, or appliances, low-vision devices (defined as devices that magnify, enhance, or otherwise augment a visual image, but not including ordinary eyeglasses or contact lenses), prosthetics including limbs and devices, hearing aid(s) and cochlear implant(s) or other implantable hearing devices, mobility devices, and oxygen therapy equipment and supplies;

(ii) Use of assistive technology;

(iii) Reasonable accommodations or "auxiliary aids or services,"

(iv) Learned behavioral or adaptive neurological modifications; or

(v) Psychotherapy, behavioral therapy, or physical therapy.

Except:

The ameliorative effects of the mitigating measures of ordinary eyeglasses or contact lenses shall be considered in determining whether an impairment substantially limits a major life activity.

When determining whether a person is substantially limited in a major life activity, we ignore the beneficial effects of mitigating measures except ordinary eyeglasses or contact lens. In the past, the U.S. Supreme Court held the opposite, that you do not ignore mitigating measures. This holding resulted in a lot of people not being covered by the ADA—people with conditions such as epilepsy, diabetes, and mental illness, who controlled their symptoms through measures like medication, good diet, and regular sleep. Prior to the Supreme Court holding, few people questioned whether individuals with these types of conditions had disabilities, but after the holding it was clear that many of them did not, at least not under the ADA definition. The ADAAA rejected the Supreme Court's holding regarding the use of mitigating measures.

For example, a person with epilepsy who takes medication to control her seizures will most likely be covered under the first part of the new definition of disability because we will consider what her limitations would be without her medication.

And note that the ADAAA states that the ameliorative (i.e., beneficial) effects of mitigating measures are ignored; if the mitigating measure itself causes any limitations, then those will be considered.

Evidence showing that an impairment would be substantially limiting without mitigating measures could include evidence of limitations that a person experienced prior to using a mitigating measure, evidence concerning the expected course of a particular disorder absent mitigating measures, or readily available and reliable information of other types.

7. Episodic or in Remission, Limitations Will Be Considered As if Active

In the past, a person whose condition was in remission or whose limitations came and went might not have been covered by the ADA, depending on how long that person's limitations were in an active state. This meant that a person with, for example, mental illness, might not be entitled to accommodations in the workplace when his condition was active because he did not meet the ADA's definition of disability.

Now the fact that the periods during which an episodic impairment is active and substantially limits a major life activity may be brief or occur infrequently is no longer relevant to determining whether the impairment substantially limits a major life activity. For example, a person with post-traumatic stress disorder who experiences intermittent flashbacks to traumatic events is substantially limited in brain function and thinking.

Other examples of conditions that may be episodic or go into remission include epilepsy, multiple sclerosis, cancer, hypertension, diabetes, asthma, major depressive disorder, bipolar disorder, and schizophrenia.

8. Only One Major Life Activity Needs to be Substantially Limited

The ADAAA states that an impairment need only substantially limit one major life activity to be considered a disability under the ADA. For example, an individual with diabetes is substantially limited in endocrine function and thus an individual with a disability under the first prong of the definition. He need not also show that he is substantially limited in eating to qualify for coverage under the first prong. An individual whose normal cell growth is substantially limited due to lung cancer need not also show that she is substantially limited in breathing or respiratory function. And an individual with HIV infection is substantially limited in the function of the immune system, and therefore is an individual with a disability without regard to whether his or her HIV infection substantially limits him or her in reproduction.

9. Six Month Time Frame Does Not Apply

The six-month "transitory" part of the "transitory and minor" exception to "regarded as" coverage does not apply to the "actual disability" prong or the "record of" prong. The effects of an impairment lasting or expected to last fewer than six months can be substantially limiting within the meaning of this section.

For example, if an individual has a back impairment that results in a 20-pound lifting restriction that lasts for several months, he is substantially limited in the major life activity of lifting, and therefore covered under the first prong of the definition of disability. At the same time, "[t]he duration of an impairment is one factor that is relevant in determining whether the impairment substantially limits a major life activity. Impairments that last only for a short period of time are typically not covered, although they may be covered if sufficiently severe."

E. Predictable Assessments

Putting all this together, the individualized assessment of some kinds of impairments will virtually always result in a determination of disability. The following impairments are examples from the regulations of impairments that should be easily found to be substantial limiting a major life activity:

- Deafness substantially limits hearing.
- Blindness substantially limits seeing.
- An intellectual disability (formerly mental retardation) substantially limits brain function.
- Partially or completely missing limbs or mobility impairments requiring the use of a wheelchair substantially limit musculoskeletal function.
- Autism substantially limits brain function.
- Cancer substantially limits normal cell growth.
- Cerebral palsy substantially limits brain function.
- Diabetes substantially limits endocrine function.
- Epilepsy substantially limits neurological function.
- Human Immunodeficiency Virus (HIV) infection substantially limits immune function.
- Multiple sclerosis substantially limits neurological function.
- Muscular dystrophy substantially limits neurological function.
- Major depressive disorder, bipolar disorder, post-traumatic stress disorder, obsessive compulsive disorder, and schizophrenia substantially limit brain function.

F. Condition, Manner, or Duration

For conditions that are not so obviously disabilities, the EEOC regulations state that in determining whether an individual is substantially limited in a major life activity, it may be useful in appropriate cases to consider, as compared to most people in the general population, the condition under which the individual performs the major life activity; the manner in which the individual performs the major life activity; and/or the duration of time it takes the individual to perform the major life activity, or for which the individual can perform the major life activity. However, the regulations no longer include the additional list of "substantial limitation" factors contained in the previous version of the regulations (i.e., the nature and severity of the impairment, duration or expected duration of the impairment, and actual or expected permanent or long-term impact of or resulting from the impairment).

Consideration of facts such as condition, manner, or duration may include, among other things, consideration of the difficulty, effort, or time required to perform a major life activity; pain experienced when performing a major life activity; the length of time a major life activity can be performed; and/or the way an impairment affects the operation of a major bodily function.

G. Record of a Disability

An individual has a record of a disability if the individual has a history of, or has been misclassified as having, a mental or physical impairment that substantially limits one or more major life activities. The terms "substantially limits" and "major life activity" under the record of prong of the definition of disability are the same terms used in the "actual disability" prong as described in C and D above.

An individual with a record of a substantially limiting impairment may be entitled, absent undue hardship, to a reasonable accommodation if needed and related to the past disability. For example, an employee with an impairment that previously limited, but no longer substantially limits, a major life activity may need leave or a schedule change to permit him or her to attend follow-up or "monitoring" appointments with a health care provider.

H. Regarded As Is Very Broad, No Substantially Limits Requirement

Definition: Regarded As.

"(A) An individual meets the requirement of 'being regarded as having such an impairment' if the individual establishes that he or she has been subjected to an action prohibited under this Act because of an actual perceived physical or mental impairment whether or not the impairment limits or is perceived to limit a major life activity.

(B) Regarded as does not apply to impairments that are transitory and minor. A transitory impairment is an impairment with an actual or expected duration of 6 months or less."

The ADAAA makes regarded as coverage under the ADA very broad. To be covered, an individual only has to establish that an employer discriminated against him because of a medical condition, whether he actually has one or the employer just thought he did. He does not have to meet the substantially-limited-in-a-major-life activity standard. One exception under regarded as is that impairments that are transitory (lasting or expected to last 6 months or less) *and* minor, are not covered. Arguably, impairments that are transitory or minor, but not both, will be covered.

For example, if an employer denies employment to a job applicant solely because the applicant has had back problems in the past, without looking at whether he can safely perform the job, the applicant will most likely be covered under the regarded as part of the definition.

Congress broadened coverage under the regarded as part of the definition to help address the prejudice, antiquated attitudes, and the failure to remove societal and institutional barriers that still exist.

IV. REASONABLE ACCOMMODATION

The ADAAA did not change the definition of reasonable accommodation. However, the Act does clarify that only individuals who meet the first (actual disability) and second (record of a disability) parts of the definition are entitled to accommodations; individuals who only meet the third part (regarded as) are not entitled to accommodations. Even though the definition did not change, it is clear that with a broader definition of disability, more focus will be placed on providing reasonable accommodations.

Another thing to keep in mind is the flexibility built into the reasonable accommodation obligation under the ADA. For example:

- employers can choose among effective accommodation options and do not always have to provide the requested accommodation,
- employers do not have to provide accommodations that pose an undue hardship,
- employers do not have to provide as reasonable accommodation personal use items needed in accomplishing daily activities both on and off the job,
- employers do not have to make an accommodation for an individual who is not otherwise qualified for a position, and
- employers do not have to remove essential functions, create new jobs, or lower productions standards as an accommodation.

For more information, see Reasonable Accommodation and Undue Hardship under the ADA at http://www.eeoc.gov/policy/docs/accommodation.html.

V. PRACTICAL TIPS

What does all this mean to employers? The following are some practical tips for applying the ADAAA in the workplace:

A. Get Past the Definition of Disability

First and foremost, with the new, broader definition of disability, employers should no longer be spending a lot of time analyzing whether employees meet the definition of disability. Employers can still require medical documentation when an employee requests an accommodation and the disability and/or need for accommodation are not obvious, but the documentation related to determining whether someone has a disability should not be extensive. Instead, the focus should be on the accommodation, whether it is reasonable, whether it can be provided without an undue hardship, and whether there are other accommodations that can be considered.

B. Do Not Confuse the Definition of Disability and Accommodation

Remember that the definition of disability is an impairment that substantially limits at least one major life activity and the ADAAA has a list of things that are considered major life activities. This list includes things like sleeping; reproducing; eating; normal cell growth; and digestive, bowel, and bladder functioning. These major life activities are not normally things that employers relate to the workplace or job performance so the question many employers have is whether they have any obligation to accommodate employees who are substantially limited in any of these activities. The answer is yes.

And here is why. Once an employer establishes that an employee is substantially limited in *any* major life activity, then the employer has established that the employee has a disability and is entitled to an accommodation for *any* limitations associated with the disability. The accommodation does not have to be for the limitation that established disability, it can be for any limitation associated with the disability, whether substantial or not.

For example, an employee has breast cancer and establishes that she has a disability by showing that she is substantially limited in the major life activity of normal cell growth. However, she needs an accommodation related to typing because she has some swelling in her right arm because of the treatment she is receiving for her cancer. Even though she is not substantially limited in the use of her arm and hand, she is still entitled to an accommodation for typing because the limitation is related to her disability.

C. Make Decisions That Are Job-Related and Consistent with Business Necessity

As mentioned previously, the ADAAA broadens the definition of disability and places the focus on the actions taken by employers. One problem employers can have is making assumptions or comments about employees' medical conditions, which could lead employees to believe that decisions were made on the basis of their real or perceived disabilities, even if that is not the case. To help avoid this problem, employers should focus on any performance or conduct problems that employees have and apply their policies in a uniform manner rather than assuming that a medical problem or disability is contributing to or causing the problem. In general, it is the employee's responsibility to let the employer know that a conduct or performance problem is disability-related and to request an accommodation to overcome the problem so there is usually no reason for an employer to bring up medical issues first.

For more information, see The ADA: Applying Performance and Conduct Standards to Employees with Disabilities at http://www.eeoc.gov/facts/performance-conduct.html.

Also, when making decisions such as who to hire or promote, focus on qualifications for the job, not on perceptions about someone's disability or need for accommodation.

D. Train Frontline Supervisors and Managers

No amount of preparation will be effective unless employers train their frontline managers and supervisors because the frontline usually has the most contact with employees on a day to day basis. If nothing else, employers should train their frontline to refrain from mentioning medical conditions unless relevant, to recognize accommodation requests, and to remember who to contact for assistance (many employers, as part of their accommodation procedures, appoint a responsible person to handle accommodation requests, keep confidential medical information, and help avoid discriminatory employment decisions).

Another important reason to train frontline supervisors and manages is to help reduce retaliation claims. The frontline needs to understand that making negative or derogatory remarks in response to an accommodation request can be considered retaliation.

E. Document Actions and Decisions

Because the focus of the ADA has shifted away from the definition of disability and toward whether employers complied with their obligations, documentation of actions and decisions can be very important if an employee alleges discrimination. In the past, many such allegations were never looked at because the employee could not meet the narrow definition of disability. Now, especially with the broad coverage under the regarded as part of the definition, most cases will hinge on whether an employer discriminated. Therefore, employers should keep accurate records because it can be difficult to remember what happened without good recordkeeping and written records are generally considered more reliable than memory alone.

Another important aspect of documentation is effective communication with employees. Many problems occur because employers do not let employees know, for example, how their performance needs to improve, the status of their accommodation requests, or why an accommodation request was denied. Employees need to be informed so they can have the opportunity to address performance problems or suggest alternative accommodation options.

* * *

Questions for Discussion

1. What do you think of the various changes to the statute? Which problems do you think these changes might help solve? Which problems do you think these changes might create?

2. What do you think of the article's advice to employers? What training will employers need about the amendments?

The following article talks about implementing a national employment policy beyond the confines of the ADA. While parts of the article are now outdated (for example, the British quota system was replaced with a job subsidy program some years ago), the article still provides an excellent basis for discussion. Footnotes have been removed.

Beyond the Americans with Disabilities Act:
A National Employment Policy for People with Disabilities

Mark C. Weber,* 46 Buffalo L. Rev. 123 (1998)

Introduction

Of all the personal narratives about individuals with disabilities and employment, one of the most revealing is that of the well-dressed business traveler, sitting in an airport in her wheelchair with a styrofoam cup full of coffee in her hand. Along comes another traveler, who smiles at her, and then drops a quarter into the cup.

The story is hardly the most outrageous example of mistreatment of persons with disabilities. After all, the person dropping the quarter into the cup caused no physical harm beyond the splashing; in fact, he was motivated by human sympathy and genuinely wanted to help. More telling about the story is its illustration of the stereotyped assumption that a person with a disability in an airport is begging, not working, and needs a contribution (a very small one, in this case) to survive.

The prevalence of the assumption is not an insurmountable problem. As time goes on, if persons with disabilities are integrated into the working economy, the would-be patron will observe the difference and change attitudes. What is more vexing is that at present, for all too many persons with disabilities, the assumption is true. Persons with disabilities are not working in the numbers that they want to be, or in the numbers that reflect their representation in the national population. As a result, they are disproportionately poor and very much dependent on private and public subsidies.

Both discriminatory exclusion and limits on competitiveness stemming from disability itself prevent people with disabilities from working. Discrimination comes in the form of the stereotypes held by the donor of the quarter, and in other more and less subtle forms. Competitive limits consist of the difficulties that physical and mental disabilities impose on an individual vying for employment in the marketplace. Even without discrimination, persons who have impairments in their abilities to do major functions of life will be at a disadvantage selling their time to employers.

The purpose of this Article is to demonstrate the need for a national employment policy for persons with disabilities, and to sketch the outlines of such a policy. The need arises from poverty and unemployment caused by discrimination and competitive disadvantage. Existing legal remedies embodied in the Americans with Disabilities Act and other laws, though beneficial, do not eliminate the problem; despite existing education and training efforts, unemployment and poverty linger.

A more effective solution lies beyond the Americans with Disabilities Act. The remedy for continuing conscious and unconscious discrimination is to supplement existing nondiscrimination law with strengthened affirmative action obligations to hire and promote persons with disabilities, and to expand those obligations from federal agencies and contractors to the rest of American employers. Given the economic limits that disabilities impose, however, such measures will not be sufficient. The solution for competitive disadvantage is an even more ambitious program consisting of non-remedial employment setasides, first by government, but ultimately by all employers. Together these steps will constitute the beginnings of an effective national employment policy for persons with disabilities.

---

* Professor, DePaul University College of Law. B.A. Columbia, 1975; J.D. Yale, 1978.

This Article brings together a number of the disparate strands in the legal literature on disability and develops several themes the literature has left unexplored and unconnected. Commentaries on the existing affirmative action provisions of the Rehabilitation Act are sparse, and do not consider the possibility of the extending the provisions to nonfederal employment. Comparative law sources note that European countries and Japan compel employers to hire specified percentages of persons with disabilities. Some of the authorities have suggested that a comparable American program would be desirable. Nevertheless, no source has fully examined the justifications for such a plan and answered the likely objections to it. For their part, the sources discussing the European quota programs do not draw any connections to existing American affirmative action provisions.

In the flush of excitement over the passage of the Americans with Disabilities Act, most commentators focused on the specific provisions of the Act; the topics of federal affirmative action programs and setasides along European lines have been neglected. Nevertheless, even the most optimistic commentators on the new federal law tempered their enthusiasm with the recognition that its antidiscrimination measures would leave many persons with disabilities out of the work force and, consequently, out of most of economic life in America. Similarly, prominent authorities on the Rehabilitation Act have noted that even if that law were to be interpreted properly and enforced aggressively, huge gaps in employment and other aspects of economic participation would remain.

Part I of this Article describes the unemployment and consequent poverty of the bulk of the population with disabilities. It traces the conditions to continuing discrimination — particularly unconscious discrimination and stereotypes — as well as to the competitive limits imposed by physical and mental impairments. Part II discusses the inadequacy of existing measures to improve the employment picture for persons with disabilities. Part III describes the role that affirmative action should play in combating discrimination, discussing the proper interpretation of existing affirmative action statutes and proposing steps to promote their enforceability and expansion to the parts of the national economy they do not now cover. Part IV addresses employment problems other than discrimination, proposing a regime of nonremedial setasides of jobs, by the national government, other governmental employers, and ultimately by private industry.

I. The Economic Exclusion of Persons with Disabilities

People with disabilities exist on the margins of American economic life, largely outside of the world of work and with little disposable income. Discrimination is to blame, but real limits on economic competitiveness play a role as well.

A. Poverty, Work, and People with Disabilities

People with disabilities are poor. Of adults with disabilities, fifty-nine percent live in households with earnings of $ 25,000 or less, while for adults without disabilities, less than forty percent do. The poverty rate for adults with disabilities is three times that of the rest of the population. The explanation for the poverty is obvious: persons with disabilities are not employed. Only thirty-one percent of persons with disabilities age 16 to 64 work part- or full-time; this number has actually decreased since 1986.

People with disabilities want to work. A survey cited in the legislative history of the Americans with Disabilities Act reported that two-thirds of working age persons with disabilities who do not have jobs say that they want to work. A more recent survey by the Harris polling organization reported that of persons who identified themselves as having disabilities who were not working and were ages 16 to 64, seventy-nine percent said that they would prefer to be working.

The most obvious reason that people with disabilities need to work is the money. Although the Social Security Disability Insurance and Supplemental Security Income programs guarantee a subsistence income to persons with total, long-term disabilities, only employment gives individuals enough money to participate fully in the life of the community. Within the world of work, the monetary advantage lies with jobs from ordinary employers. Employment in the general workforce yields far greater monetary benefits than work in sheltered workshops, even when the additional costs of job-coaching or otherwise supporting the individual are subtracted from the worker's salary.

Work, however, gives rewards beyond its wages. It brings the individual an identity, a niche in society, and sources of friendship and social support. Work contributes to self-esteem by conferring a sense of mastery over the environment and reaffirming to the worker that he or she is making a contribution to society. One's sense of self-worth is enhanced by the knowledge that one has succeeded at work and by others' recognition of that success. Work helps individuals order their lives; those who are chronically unemployed frequently experience attitudinal deterioration even when they have adequate economic resources.

The presence of persons with disabilities in the workplace also benefits society as a whole. First, exposure to human beings who do not in all ways conform to the norm is crucial to dispelling myths about individuals with disabilities. Individuals who are not in the workplace and other places where people carry on business and recreational activities are not part of the consciousness of those who are there. In a real sense, people with disabilities who are not integrated into society are invisible to the rest of society. This invisibility fosters social attitudes of fear and condescension. Integration fosters realistic attitudes, demonstrating that persons with disabilities are not threatening, helpless, or evil. Society at large benefits when false fears die out and truth prevails.

Second, persons who are employed contribute to the social product of the economy and pay tax dollars into the treasury rather than drawing subsistence payments from the government or insurers. Although relief programs provide benefits that are much smaller than incomes from employment, their cost to society as a whole is huge. The cost of maintaining persons who are now thirty-five years old on Supplemental Security Income or Social Security Disability Insurance and associated medical and other benefits for the rest of their lives is slightly more than one trillion dollars. The government spends thirty billion dollars a year on these benefits; roughly the same amount is spent on medical assistance for persons with disabilities. After reciting these figures, an evaluation specialist for the United States Department of Health and Human Services concluded: "It costs a lot of money to dribble out sub-poverty level benefits to a substantial number of people for a long period of time. Were we a private insurer, we would be … trying to reduce the likelihood of our having to spend all that money." Paid employment for individuals with disabilities is the solution.

B. Reasons for Exclusion from Employment

What keeps people with disabilities out of the working economy is a combination of discrimination on the part of employers and difficulties with being fully competitive even when no discrimination takes place.

1. Discrimination. In employment, as in other fields of human endeavor, persons with disabilities have been the object of fear and hostility. In the first half of this century, with the Eugenics movement still strong, hospitals and doctors routinely denied children with severe disabilities necessary medical treatment, leaving them to die. More recently, people with disabilities have been kept from employment, recreation, transportation, and shopping, simply because they were different from others. Potential employers have more negative

attitudes about persons with disabilities than about ethnic minorities, elderly job applicants, or ex-convicts. Some employer conduct is based on predictions that consumers harbor prejudice or stereotypes, but employers in fact possess less favorable attitudes about how consumers will react to employees with disabilities than the consumers themselves do. Prejudice starts at a young age. Attitudinal surveys show that children with disabilities are the least-liked and the lowest in social prestige among their classmates.

It was not until 1973 that the City of Chicago repealed its ordinance prohibiting persons who were "deformed" and "unsightly" from exposing themselves to public view on the streets. The spirit of the ordinance, however, lives on elsewhere. In the mass products liability trial concerning birth defects said to result from fetal exposure to the anti-nausea drug Bendectin, the judge excluded all plaintiffs with visible deformities from the courtroom, on the ground that their appearance might excite passions against the defendant. What Jacobus tenBroek termed "the right to live in the world" was thus taken away from human beings who suffered disabling injuries on the grounds that their very disabilities were too horrible to be on display. The essence of invidious discrimination is being treated worse than others because of a trait that one has no control over and that has no just relation to the entitlement at issue. Few things could be more unfair than being excluded from the judicial proceeding that could bring closure to a personal disaster on the ground that the disaster left one unfit to be in the presence of justice.

Not all disability discrimination is intentional. Much is the result of unconscious attitudes or unexamined stereotypes. Unintentional discrimination is pervasive. Stereotypes and prejudices grow easily in the absence of day-to-day contact with human beings who are different. Research shows that employers who have no employees with disabilities have more negative attitudes towards workers with disabilities than those who have moderate or large numbers. Many courts and commentators have observed that discrimination against persons with disabilities stems as much from ignorance, fear, or a misplaced concern for the persons' well-being as from intentional discrimination.

Statistics about complaints filed with the Equal Employment Opportunity Commission support the inference that stereotypes now keep many individuals with disabilities out of the workplace. The vast bulk of complaints are filed by those who already are, or recently were, employed. The two forms of disability discrimination that lead the statistics are those related to back problems and mental health problems. Both forms of disability are ones that are frequently not visible when the employee is hired. More obvious forms of disability, such as mobility impairments, are far behind, an indication that the individuals never made it through the employer's door. This subtle discrimination will be difficult to overcome.

2. Limits on Economic Competitiveness. A disability means a limit on major life activity. Not all disabilities prevent persons from achieving full economic productivity, but most do. Bertrand Russell once observed that all human work consists of altering the position of matter relative to other matter, or directing other people to do so. Limits on the ability to move, to carry, to push, to pull, all make an individual less competitive than an individual who does not have those limits, as do any limits on mental or communicative powers that prevent an individual from being as effective as others in directing production processes. Although technological advances will provide more employment opportunities for persons with disabilities whose intelligence and education place them above or on a par with other persons, they will exacerbate the difficulties of those persons with limits on mental and some sensory capacities.

These facts bear out the proposition that disability is largely socially determined. In a society in which few could read and reading was unimportant to most economic activity, persons with dyslexia were not disabled. In some future society in which machines do all the physical labor, those with physical impairments will not have a disability. But in society as it is now constituted, either mental or physical disability makes a potential job candidate less desirable than a candidate who does not have the disability, when all other characteristics of the applicants are the same.

II. The Inadequacy of Present Efforts to Combat Economic Exclusion of Persons with Disabilities

Neither existing antidiscrimination laws nor existing educational and training efforts have succeeded in bringing persons with disabilities into the economic mainstream. An examination of these measures shows that there is little reason to expect that they will be fully successful in that regard.

A. The Marginal Role of Antidiscrimination Measures

Commentators have praised the Americans with Disabilities Act for its bans on intentional discrimination, screening, segregation, and failure to provide reasonable accommodation. These praises, however, are merited only if the Americans with Disabilities Act is fully enforced as written. There remains the possibility that the Act will not be fully enforced. The Act requires employers to conduct themselves to the detriment of their economic self-interest. Unlike Title VII of the Civil Rights Act of 1964, which requires merely that employers behave rationally by hiring the candidate who can do the job most effectively and cheaply irrespective of race, religion, national origin or sex, the Americans with Disabilities Act requires employers to lay out greater costs for the group of workers it protects than for the individuals who are competing with them. The costs generally are modest, but they do exist.

To change the calculus of employers' self-interest, managers will need to be convinced that the risks of liability outweigh the economic costs of compliance with the law. It is unclear whether and when awards of damages will create this shift. Some authorities have expressed pessimism about voluntary compliance with the Act, citing empirical evidence that neither employers nor persons with disabilities know about the legal standards, that some subgroups of persons with disabilities tend to be passive regarding legal rights matters, and that attitudinal change among employers takes time. Others have stressed that employers view the law favorably and are complying voluntarily, but these sources tend to draw from limited samples. Broader samplings reveal widespread ignorance of the law and the absence of expectations by employers that they will hire more employees with disabilities as a result of the Act. Statistical evidence on the success of the law to date remains equivocal.

Stereotyping is particularly hard to overcome. Attitudes about disability and employment are notoriously difficult to change. Although law influences attitudes, the influence may take significant time to manifest itself in social conduct. If prejudices keep individuals with disabilities away from those without them, the very stereotypes that led to the exclusion are unlikely to be challenged.

Even if the Act is fully enforced, the beneficiaries will not be all persons with disabilities. They will be those persons whose work is superior to that of other job candidates once the reasonable accommodations have been put into place, or those who overcompensate for their disabilities or who do not really have disabilities but are merely perceived as disabled or stereotyped as disabled. The fact, however, is that a disability is a disability. It limits one's ability to do something important. Limits on workplace productivity are an inherent part of many disabling conditions.

For this reason, although the Americans with Disabilities Act can be expected to promote the employment and general integration of persons with disabilities, expectations should not be too high. The effect of the Act is marginal, in a rather literal sense of the term. Employers are still able to hire any employee without a disability who can do the essential functions of a job marginally better than a person with a disability can, as long as that person has received reasonable accommodations. If the law is followed, the employees with disabilities who will benefit will be those who were marginally superior in the first place (but whose superiority was ignored because of prejudice or stereotyping) and those who become marginally superior to employees without disabilities because of the forced provision of reasonable accommodations. Although the employer is not permitted to count the cost of the accommodation in considering the marginal superiority or inferiority of the job candidate with a disability, that candidate will still need to be superior to get the job.

B. Limits on the Potential of Education and Rehabilitation

Reformers once had hopes that education for persons with disabilities would pull them into the mainstream of American society, both by providing them the skills to succeed in the workplace and by exposing persons without disabilities to the reality that persons with disabilities are human beings who deserve full integration. In the nearly twenty years of legally mandated education for all children with disabilities, however, reformers' expectations have diminished.

The Supreme Court was the first to prick the balloon. In *Board of Education v. Rowley*, the Court's first decision under the Education for All Handicapped Children Act of 1975, the Court read the Act's requirement that children with disabilities be afforded an "appropriate" education as guaranteeing nothing more than meaningful "access" to education. Educational programs would be approved if they conferred "some benefit"; they need not afford the child with a disability an opportunity to achieve as much of his or her potential as the child without disabilities would be permitted to achieve.

Although subsequent judicial decisions bolstered reformers' hopes, the reality of daily decision making under the special education laws should keep anyone from setting those hopes too high. School authorities tend to place a child into a disability category and adjust the expectations for the child's achievement accordingly, even though the federal law calls for an individualized education for children with disabilities. Parents, for their part, are reluctant to confront school authorities and demand what their children need, or they are ground down by the system if they make the attempt.

Empirical evidence confirms this discouraging impression. Clearly, the educational state of children with disabilities is dramatically better than it was before the Education for All Handicapped Children Act. Equally clearly, students with disabilities have not made the educational gains that would enable large numbers to compete on an even plane for scarce employment opportunities. Students with disabilities have lower grades than those without disabilities; more than two-thirds of those who complete four years of high school fail one or more courses. A disproportionate share of students with disabilities drop out of high school; many of these students stay four or more years but fail to obtain enough credits to graduate. The proportion of individuals with disabilities who attend college is less than one-third of that of individuals who do not have disabilities. Limits on educational opportunity tend to apply to all disabilities, not just to mental retardation or other disabilities that might be expected to impose limits on success in school. Indeed, some students without disabilities have been harmed by being misclassified as children with disabilities and shunted into low expectations programs in which they are segregated from other children.

Compounding this difficulty is the failure of employment services for adults with disabilities to reach those with the greatest need for them. The problem, frequently described as "creaming," is that rehabilitation services agencies, looking for quick success, tend to give services to those persons with disabilities who have the least severe problems, and hence are most likely to be able to move into competitive employment with the lowest expenditure of resources. Although the solution that Congress has adopted—giving statutory priority to persons with severe disabilities—has promise, the breadth of the definition of severe disability creates enough discretionary decision making that the legislative end may be frustrated.

The candidate with a disability must be superior to other candidates (once reasonable accommodations are provided) in order to get the job. But the road to superiority is difficult, with limited opportunities for training and education. Then the candidate must overcome subtle forms of discrimination as well as the underlying disability itself. Small wonder that so many persons with disabilities lack employment.

III. The Role of Affirmative Action in Combating Unconscious Discrimination and Stereotyping

The exclusion from the workplace of persons with disabilities, and its likely intractability in the face of existing antidiscrimination measures, suggest that more aggressive efforts are needed. To succeed, the efforts will need to be directed against both of the problems that lead to economic exclusion: discrimination—especially unconscious discrimination—and the limits on competitiveness imposed by the disability itself. Only by addressing these problems will the United States move from a narrow policy likely to be effective only against certain kinds of discrimination to a true national employment policy for persons with disabilities. The first step, that of dealing with unconscious discrimination, entails the clarification and strengthening of affirmative action in employment for persons with disabilities.

A. The Analogy from Affirmative Action to Remedy Race Discrimination to Affirmative Action for Persons with Disabilities

Affirmative action is most familiar as a remedy for employment discrimination on grounds of race or sex. Some efforts placed under the rubric of affirmative action are modest and noncontroversial, such as expanding the pool of applicants for hiring and promotion by outreach efforts and reviewing ordinary employment qualifications to determine whether they are actually necessary for the performance of the job. In recent years, these efforts have frequently been reclassified as simple avoidance of disparate impact discrimination rather than affirmative action. The more controversial aspects of affirmative action are making radical changes in job qualification standards as well as setting numerical hiring or promotion goals for underrepresented groups and taking whatever steps are needed to find qualified members of the groups to meet those goals.

Advocates of affirmative action advance two justifications for intrusive measures such as numerical targets. The first is that the employer or its industry has discriminated against the underrepresented group in the past. Since the particular victims are unlikely to be found or are no longer in a position to benefit from the relief, jobs for members of the same underrepresented group are the next best form of relief. An affirmative action plan, though frequently voluntary, carries a justification similar to that of the relief that courts provide when evidence at trial shows pervasive, long-term discrimination that has yielded dramatic underrepresentation of racial minorities or women.

The second justification for applying numerical systems is as a means of combating present-day unconscious, undetectable, or otherwise intractable discrimination. The affirmative action plan is designed to produce a workplace that is as it would be in the absence of discrimination. If there would be no reason to expect women or racial minorities to shun the employer or particular job classifications, or to fail to obtain the qualifications for the job, then the numbers in the job should be comparable to those in the relevant labor market. Numerical hiring targets force the employer to produce that result.

Both justifications for affirmative action apply to persons with disabilities. First, the legacy of discrimination against persons with disabilities is long and virulent; the discrimination has been illegal, depending on the employer, for as long as twenty-three years. Particular employers may or may not have paper records of excluding persons with disabilities. Exclusion is so pervasive, however, that records should not be expected to exist. Everyone knew that people who had physical or mental disabilities were not welcome, so none applied. One is reminded of the schoolmaster's explanation to Stephen Dedalus in Ulysses that the best means to avoid the scourge of anti-Semitism is to keep Jews from entering the country.

Second, unconscious and hidden discrimination against persons with disabilities is widespread. The attitudes that persons with disabilities are repugnant or evil are not overcome in a day. The widespread use of subjective decision making in hiring and promotion gives free rein to subtle and not-so-subtle prejudices against persons with disabilities.

Disability is different from race, of course, in that for many disabling conditions the disability is not a characteristic that is part of one's genetic code or one handed down from parent to child; nor is disability linked to the "peculiar institution" of chattel slavery. The need for affirmative efforts, however, still applies. In the first place, it is a remedy provided to the closest available group of persons for the wrongs suffered by others who are similar in a relevant respect. It is thus comparable to affirmative action in race contexts as well as to cypres remedies in trust adjudication and their modern analogues in class actions when the actual persons who were harmed cannot be found.

Second, by guaranteeing that workers with disabilities are on the job, it alleviates the legacy of discrimination. The long period in which persons with disabilities have been excluded from the workplace affects the attitudes of personnel managers, supervisors, and co-workers, making it more difficult for a person with disabilities to make it inside the employer's doors, and, if there, to stay. When someone who has long been invisible suddenly materializes, others can be expected to act as though they have seen a ghost. Placing people with disabilities at the workplace breaks the pattern of exclusion.

Affirmative action on the basis of race has been the subject of immense controversy. Many find the use of racial classifications distasteful, and fear that continued classification of Americans on the ground of race will have lasting negative effects. They emphasize that racial classifications are properly suspect, because race rarely correlates to any characteristic that anyone has any business considering in employment decisions or governmental choices. Supporters of affirmative action counter that there is no other effective mechanism to eliminate the effects of prior overt discrimination and current hidden discrimination. They argue that use of racial classifications in order to end racial subordination is not the same as using the classifications to perpetuate it.

Whatever one's position on this controversy might be, none of the arguments against affirmative action on the basis of race apply to affirmative action on the basis of disability. Ability classifications are unavoidable in the world of work, and do correlate to relevant job classifications. Disability classifications do not always carry stigma or set off alarms concerning invidious treatment: although government conduct has harmed those with disabilities in many instances, government has also established a long tradition of benign social welfare programs for those with disabilities. Finally, it is impossible to deny that for disability, if for no other characteristic, perfectly equal treatment can constitute discrimination. For example, a rule that all persons, whether blind or not, must take a written admissions test for law school is discriminatory. In the example, some unequal treatment for blind persons — use of braille or oral tests or another form of adaptation — is plainly required in order to avoid invidious discrimination. Once the need for different treatment is recognized, affirmative action for persons with disabilities emerges as one of many forms of different treatment that might be needed to achieve equality. By contrast, many critics of affirmative action on the basis of race declare that they would countenance no form of different treatment for different races, ever.

As a statutory and constitutional matter, affirmative action on behalf of persons with disabilities is a much simpler question than affirmative action on behalf of racial minorities. Title VII of the Civil Rights Act of 1964 bars discrimination on account of race and sex irrespective of the race or sex of the person being discriminated against. Thus whites and males whose job opportunities have been diminished by affirmative action programs have been able to sue their employers under the statute. Similarly, the Constitution affords heightened scrutiny when anyone — of whatever race — is disadvantaged because of his or her color. By contrast, the Americans with Disabilities Act prohibits discrimination against qualified individuals with disabilities, conferring no enforceable obligations on employers or other covered entities to avoid discrimination against persons who do not have disabilities. Under constitutional principles, absence of disability is not a suspect classification, and no elevated scrutiny applies when a disadvantage is attached to that status.

B. Distinguishing Affirmative Action from Reasonable Accommodation

Affirmative action differs from reasonable accommodation in both degree and character. As for degree, the employer engaged in affirmative action must take extraordinary measures to eliminate barriers to employability, and must be willing to give significant accommodations that impose some degree of hardship on ordinary operations. By contrast, an employer providing reasonable accommodation for otherwise qualified persons with disabilities must modify rules, practices, and physical environments only up to the point where it begins to suffer from undue hardship.

The character of affirmative action also differs from that of reasonable accommodation. Reasonable accommodation makes the person without the disability the norm. The employer makes modest departures from the rules or the environment to accommodate the person who is considered different. This able-bodied orientation has two effects: identification of the person with a disability as different, and a corresponding limit on the steps that the employer must take to depart from the standard of nondisability.

The first effect is the "dilemma of difference" described by Professor Martha Minow, but it appears here in a particularly insoluble form: all efforts to benefit the person with a disability inevitably identify that person as different from everyone else. The effort to make the person equal contributes to the perception that the person is not. The second effect, the limit on reasonable accommodation, inheres in the term "reasonable" as well as in the idea that the necessary steps are merely an "accommodation" from the nondisabled norm. Reasonable accommodation does not require a reorienting of the world around the person with a disability or an attempt to make the environment confer an equal benefit on all persons. It stops at the point of that which can be done without undue financial hardship or basic changes in the operation of the enterprise.

Affirmative action, though still marking persons with disabilities as different, pushes past the limits of "reasonable" accommodation. The employer must do more than bend rules. Moreover, to the extent that the affirmative action efforts simply increase numbers of persons with disabilities at the job site, the viewpoint of supervisors and coworkers has to shift to one in which persons with disabilities are part of the working world. Necessity may cause further invention in job routines to allow workers with disabilities to succeed. Social perspectives may shift with the shift in the means of production.

Although mandatory accommodation that far exceeds reasonable standards or imposes an undue hardship might have some of the same effects as setasides or other measures traditionally associated with affirmative action, reasonable accommodation has both a different justification and a different effect than traditional affirmative action programs. Reasonable accommodations equalize the position of the person with the disability and the competitors for employment or other benefits. Unlike affirmative action, the reasonable accommodations are not necessarily remedial and do not specifically address the problem of unconscious discrimination. The operation of the regime is also different. As noted, under a system of accommodations, the person with a disability must still demonstrate superiority under conventional measures (with the accommodation, of course) in order to get the job. Under a setaside designed to remedy prior discrimination or present unconscious discrimination, that is not necessarily the case. In order to meet a numerical goal, an employer can be required to take an individual who can do the job even if he or she is not the candidate it would otherwise choose.

Affirmative action obligations are not limitless. If affirmative action is conceived as a remedy for past or present discrimination, the nature of the violation should determine the scope of the remedy. For affirmative action programs involving job targets, the targets themselves act as a proxy for what the hiring rate would be under ideal conditions. It may be difficult to determine what the hiring rates for persons with disabilities would be in the absence of discrimination, but statistics about qualified individuals with disabilities in the local economy could form the starting point, just as they do in plans to remedy race and sex discrimination.

For efforts that do not entail numerical targets, other outside limits might apply. For example, in suits brought under the affirmative action provisions currently applicable to federal agencies, the court in granting relief is to take into account the cost and the availability of alternatives. Although the relief may exceed what would be required under the duty of reasonable accommodation, it would remain less than what would work severe economic harm on the employer.

C. Existing Affirmative Action Efforts for Persons with Disabilities

The provisions of federal legislation requiring affirmative action on behalf of persons with disabilities apply to employment in federal agencies and federal contractors. Sections 501 (federal agencies) and 503 (federal contractors) were part of the original nondiscrimination title of the Rehabilitation Act of 1973, which also includes section 504, a general prohibition of disability discrimination on the part of federal grantees. The original regulations promulgated under section 504 by what was then the United States Department of Health, Education and Welfare imposed an obligation on the grantees to afford reasonable accommodation in employment, while at the same time barring disparate treatment, unnecessary practices with a disparate impact, and segregation.

Congress intended sections 501 and 503 to confer duties greater than section 504's reasonable accommodation duty on federal agencies and federal contractors. One important piece of evidence for this proposition is the passage of all of the sections at the same time. When Congress wanted to create a simple prohibition on discrimination, it knew how to do so: no individual "shall, solely by reason of her or his disability, be excluded from the participation in, be denied the benefits of, or be subjected to discrimination under any program or activity...." Congress used much different language in creating the affirmative action obligations of federal agencies:

> Each department, agency, and instrumentality ... in the executive branch shall ... submit ... an affirmative action program plan for the hiring, placement, and advancement of individuals with disabilities.... Such plan shall include a description of the extent to which and methods whereby the special needs of employees who are individuals with disabilities are being met.... Such plan must provide sufficient assurances, procedures and commitments to provide adequate hiring, placement, and advancement opportunities....

Congress did not even include federal agencies in the nondiscrimination provision of section 504 until 1978. But when the Congress did place federal instrumentalities under section 504 at that time, it left the affirmative action provision intact, even though the Department of Health, Education, and Welfare had adopted regulations explicitly prescribing reasonable accommodation duties as part of the nondiscrimination obligation for entities covered by section 504.

A basic principle of statutory construction is that every provision of a statute is to be given some meaning; readings finding surplusage are to be avoided. To give the affirmative action provision meaning, it has to carry obligations different from the reasonable accommodation obligations of section 504. Significantly, it was in the same 1978 enactment that Congress explicitly provided that the affirmative action provision applicable to federal agencies would be enforceable in court under the same procedures as those used for Title VII of the Civil Rights Act of 1964. Thus at the same time Congress recognized the different, higher, obligations imposed on federal agencies and contractors, it made the higher obligations directly enforceable against the agencies.

A second persuasive piece of evidence is that when Congress passed the Americans with Disabilities Act, extending the reasonable accommodation duties imposed on federal grantees in the Rehabilitation Act to those parts of the United States economy not already covered, it again left the affirmative action language of sections 501 and 503 undisturbed. The Americans with Disabilities Act takes the language of the section 504 regulations and codifies the obligations against overt discrimination, disparate impact discrimination, segregation, and failure to provide reasonable accommodation found there. It does not, however, borrow the affirmative action language from sections 501 and 503, preserving a distinction between the more limited obligations of reasonable accommodation applicable to all employment and the greater obligations of affirmative action applicable to employment by federal agencies and contractors. The actions of Congress based on a given understanding of a law passed earlier lend force to that understanding of the earlier law's meaning.

A final indicator of congressional intent is a portion of the Rehabilitation Act Amendments of 1992 concerning section 504 and the employment title of the Americans with Disabilities Act. Although these amendments deal primarily with the federal state vocational rehabilitation services program, they include a provision declaring standards used to determine whether an employment activity violates the Rehabilitation Act will be same as those for determining violations of the employment title of the Americans with Disabilities Act. The statute, however, explicitly excepts affirmative action complaints from the uniform standards. Congress thus recognized a uniform definition of reasonable accommodation and other duties found in the Rehabilitation Act and the Americans with Disabilities Act, but also recognized that more could be demanded of federal agencies and contractors under the affirmative action provisions.

Nevertheless, false uniformity of rules is a difficult temptation to resist, particularly for judges and regulators. Almost from the start, court decisions and regulations have tried to equate reasonable accommodation and affirmative action obligations, despite Congress' intentions. Illustrating this false equation is a government publication describing section 503 and 504. The pamphlet reads: "Section 503 calls for 'affirmative action.' Section 504 calls for 'non-discrimination.' In practicality, there's little difference in how they affect you in employment.... These ... programs boil down to this fact: Employers covered by either of them no longer may screen out handicapped people simply because of their disabilities." The Americans with Disabilities Act, following the regulations promulgated under section 504, defines screening as a component of prohibited discrimination under that statute. Affirmative action goes far beyond the obligation not to impose discriminatory screens.

The Equal Employment Opportunity Commission also appears to have missed the distinction. Its regulations promulgated pursuant to section 501 are essentially identical to the substantive provisions governing section 504. The regulations under section 503 are primarily procedural, but to the extent they have a substantive content, it resembles that of the section 504 rules. Since Congress did not amend section 504 to explicitly bar federal agencies from discriminating on the basis of disability until five years after section 501 passed, the regulators were apparently concerned with establishing a construction of section 501 that entailed a general nondiscrimination obligation, including the duty to provide reasonable accommodation. This preoccupation seems to have kept them from making the distinction between the lower obligations of accommodation under section 504 and the higher ones under section 501. In an early administrative decision, the agency nonetheless applied a high standard of accommodation to federal employers.

There is little excuse for the mistaken identity given the Supreme Court case law on section 504 of the Rehabilitation Act. The Supreme Court's first case under the section 504 spelled out the distinction between reasonable accommodation and affirmative action. *Southeastern Community College v. Davis* upheld a decision of a community college not to modify its nurses' training program to permit a student who was deaf to complete the clinical portion of the work. The Court noted that section 504 required some accommodations, but argued that the requested accommodation would amount to affirmative action, and that affirmative action was more than Congress wished to force upon states and localities. In making the argument, the Court contrasted the limited duty of reasonable accommodation with the greater, affirmative action obligations imposed on federal agencies by section 501. By using section 501 as a foil for section 504, the Court established that the accommodations required under section 501's affirmative action regime are greater than the reasonable accommodations required under section 504.

In 1985, in *Alexander v. Choate*, the Court responded to criticism of Davis's characterization of extensive accommodation efforts as "affirmative action." The Court upheld an annual limit on days of Medicaid-covered hospitalization, which was said to have a greater negative impact on persons with disabilities than on persons without disabilities, and which lacked a justification to make it superior to other forms of budget control with a lesser impact. In discussing *Davis*'s language about accommodations and affirmative action, the Court said that the case meant to exclude from the requirements of section 504 only fundamental alterations in programs. This interpretation left unchanged the basic reasoning of *Davis* that affirmative action obligations under section 501 carry an obligation to do more to accommodate individuals with disabilities than do the obligations of section 504.

The better reasoned decisions of the lower courts hold federal agencies sued under section 501 to standards higher than the section 504 standards of reasonable accommodation. An example is Judge Pollak's decision in *Taylor v. Garrett*. In Taylor, the court found that a Navy rigger who because of a back injury could no longer do the essential functions of his original job could be entitled to reclassification into a permanent light duty job, an accommodation the Navy had refused to provide. The court emphasized that section 501 places higher standards on a federal agency than section 504 places on a federal grantee. Looking to the Supreme Court precedent that contrasted section 504 and section 501 as well as to commentary on section 501, the court concluded that the elevated obligation imposed by section 501 could require an agency to consider an employee's fitness to perform jobs other than that which the employee previously occupied. The limit of required accommodation would be that a worker need not be placed in a position if the worker could not perform its essential functions; in the section 501 context, that would constitute undue hardship for the employer.

Some cases overturning agency or lower court decisions rejecting plaintiffs' requests for particular accommodations rely heavily on precedent from courts applying ordinary reasonable accommodation obligations, but they nonetheless state that an elevated duty to accommodate exists under section 501. Still other courts reject requests for accommodations while nevertheless recognizing that federal agencies are under greater duties to accommodate by virtue of the affirmative action provision.

Unfortunately, other judicial opinions are hardly faithful in observing the distinction between affirmative action and reasonable accommodation obligations under existing law. One court has suggested that the sole difference between section 501 and 504 causes of action is that the burden of persuasion rests on the employer in an affirmative action case but on the employee with a reasonable accommodation case. This charges affirmative action with a meaning somewhat stronger than that of reasonable accommodation as the term has been interpreted by a few cases applying section 504, but it makes the term indistinguishable from reasonable accommodation as it is interpreted by other courts and as it is codified in Title I of the Americans with Disabilities Act, which places the burden on the employer. Making affirmative action overlap in this fashion is not true to the congressional intention to have affirmative action be a higher obligation than reasonable accommodation.

Even more erroneous in its approach is the recent decision *Fedro v. Reno*, in which the court, following the decisions of various cases interpreting section 504, ruled that the obligation of reasonable accommodation did not include the duty to place a former deputy marshal who had contacted hepatitis while on the job in an alternative position in which the risk of contamination of others from his blood would not be significant. The employee proposed that he be placed in a full-time job combining two part-time positions as a background investigator. The court conceded that the proposal was both feasible and cheaper to the government than providing workers compensation to the employee, but said there was no obligation to provide it. Judge Ilana Rovner protested in a partial dissent that the court was wrong to rely thoughtlessly on precedent under section 504 when section 501 affords federal employees "substantially greater rights." The duty under the law to become a model employer of persons with disabilities entails the obligation to make substantial changes and fundamental alterations in programs. Reassignment is part of the federal government's "affirmative obligation to expand the employment opportunities available" to workers with disabilities.

The *Fedro* majority is not an isolated opinion. Other courts have also equated reasonable accommodation and affirmative action obligations, usually without any discussion whether the federal agency is under a higher standard. Some commentary interpreting this caselaw has similarly underplayed the difference between affirmative action under section 501 and reasonable accommodation.

D. Strengthening Existing Affirmative Action Obligations

Strengthening current affirmative action efforts will help American society address the problems of past and present disability discrimination, especially unconscious discrimination. The first step to strengthening existing affirmative action law is for courts in their decisions and the EEOC in its regulations to recognize the higher obligations that sections 501 and 503 impose on federal agencies and contractors. Courts need to appreciate the wisdom of cases such as *Taylor v. Garrett* and apply similar interpretations to section 501 cases coming before them. The EEOC should take a page from the courts and replace its existing section 501 and 503 regulations with provisions that recognize the elevated duties federal agencies and contractors are under.

As a second step, the language that the regulators adopt should more explicitly embrace numerical employment goals. In combating disability discrimination, as in combating discrimination based on race and sex, the one form of affirmative action that is most likely to be successful is the use of employment targets, both for entry-level jobs and promotions. Persons with disabilities cannot show their abilities unless they are present in the workplace. All the obvious ingredients for greater success in the workplace are already present: The Americans with Disabilities Act already requires employers to review job qualifications to eliminate those that discriminate against persons with disabilities; many employers say that they are engaging in outreach and recruitment activities; persons with disabilities want to work. Yet persons with disabilities are still not in jobs. To overcome the subtle and less-subtle discrimination that remains as a barrier, numerical targets are needed.

While goals and timetables have long been part of federal equal employment opportunity regulations promulgated under Title VII of the Civil Rights Act of 1964, which forbids racial, ethnic, religious, and sex discrimination, the regulations promulgated under section 501 have no comparable requirements and are all but identical to the nondiscrimination regulations promulgated under section 504. The section 503 regulations are almost totally procedural, dealing with complaint processing rather than with the actual content of what is required from federal contractors in the way of affirmative activity. Once again, goals and timetables escape mention. Regulations comparable to those that exist for Title VII should be adopted for sections 501 and 503.

Clear regulations requiring goals and timetables would strengthen federal affirmative action efforts. The adequacy of affirmative action plans adopted by agencies and contractors could be measured against the steps called for in the goals and timetables regulations. Individuals suing in court or employers defending there could point to compliance or noncompliance with the standards. Of course, the standards must retain some flexibility for particular circumstances, but they need be no more vague than the ordinary standard of reasonable accommodation is. The elevated duty of reasonable accommodation that applies under the affirmative action obligation must also remain somewhat vague because of the variety of circumstances that both employees and employers may find themselves in.

A third step to enhance the enforceability of the affirmative action obligation that applies to federal contractors would be enacting a private right of action. Although the statute is phrased in mandatory terms, the present consensus of the courts is that it confers no right of action on which the aggrieved employee or job candidate can sue. Unlike its counterpart requiring affirmative action by federal agencies, section 501, the federal contractor provision is not included in the remedies section of Title V of the Rehabilitation Act. The legislative history of the 1992 Rehabilitation Act Amendments affirms the ability of individuals to sue to enforce section 504, the general nondiscrimination provision, against federal agencies, but does not extend the cause of action to persons suing contractors, leaving the employees of federal contractors without a remedy. A cause of action against federal contractors by their employees and applicants would create no more problems than does the parallel action that exists against the federal agencies. It would go far in alleviating the current situation in which the right to affirmative action efforts lacks any reliable remedy.

E. Expanding Affirmative Action for Persons with Disabilitiess

While affirmative action should be strengthened where it currently applies, it should also be expanded to areas in which it does not. Unconscious discrimination and the legacy of past discriminatory practices are hardly unique to federal agencies and federal contractors. The two logical expansions of affirmative action for persons with disabilities are imposing the obligation on state and local governmental entities, and imposing the obligation on private employers.

1. Affirmative Action by State and Local Government. It would take only a slight modification of the existing statute to impose the same affirmative action obligations on state and local government that now apply to federal agencies. State and local government currently employ 15.5 million Americans, more workers than those employed in the manufacturing of durable goods and roughly twice the number of those employed in the manufacture of nondurable goods. Thus requiring states and localities to engage in affirmative action would have a significant impact on the employment of persons with disabilities. State and local governments are responsible for the legislation that has been most oppressive and discriminatory towards persons with disabilities. They continue to labor under the effects of past discriminatory practices; as is the case with other employers, their employment decisions are subject to unconscious or other undetectable discrimination. Accordingly, the same affirmative action requirements that apply to the federal government should apply to them. The adequacy of their efforts should be measured by the same standards, both with respect to the accommodation they offer and the goals and timetables they establish and fulfill.

The step proposed here is not without precedent. An affirmative action obligation applies to all state and local educational agencies that receive federal funding for special education of children with disabilities. The obligation extends to the employment of individuals with disabilities, and requires actions beyond what section 504 or the Americans with Disabilities Act would otherwise entail. This requirement has not given rise to widespread dissatisfaction or reports that it is not workable.

The measure would be well within congressional authority to enforce the Fourteenth Amendment to the United States Constitution. The Amendment compels states to provide the equal protection of the law to all persons within their jurisdiction; persons with disabilities receive the benefit of the equal protection clause, just as everyone else does. Congress has authority to enforce the Amendment with appropriate legislation. This power is exceedingly broad, and does not depend on any finding by the judiciary or another body that the evil proscribed by the legislation violates the Amendment. As previously noted, since the absence of disability is not a suspect classification, no heightened constitutional scrutiny applies. The Supreme Court has ruled that congressional action to enforce the Fourteenth Amendment is able to override any restrictions on federal court remedies that would otherwise apply under sovereign immunity principles embodied in the Eleventh Amendment.

2. Affirmative Action by Private Employers. Private employers, too, should be subject to affirmative action obligations. Congressional action to elevate the duty of reasonable accommodation and to impose goals and timetables would not be an easy political achievement, but the likelihood of success is fair. An exhaustive study of the legislative process that led to the Americans with Disabilities Act commented that the proponents of the law could have enacted a stricter law, given the high level of support that they had for the measure that passed. For advocates of disability rights, the Act is an example of compromising too easily. While the vagaries of congressional politics are beyond the scope of this paper, affirmative action measures are a worthy legislative goal.

The reason that affirmative action by private employers is worthy is the same reason that federal action is justified and states and localities' obligations ought to be enhanced. Persons with disabilities need employment both from government and from the private sector to overcome poverty and integrate themselves into society as a whole. Private employers have been guilty of discriminating against persons with disabilities in the past, and they will continue to do so in subtle ways in the future unless more aggressive steps are taken.

Congress has the power to impose affirmative action obligations on private employers under its authority to regulate interstate commerce. While the power may not extend to some of the very smallest entities whose actions have no effect whatsoever on interstate economic activity, it is extremely broad with respect to any business conduct. It was broad enough to permit Congress to enact the Civil Rights Act of 1964, whose provisions cover employers with as few as fifteen employees, and which compels affirmative action under a variety of circumstances. It would permit the legislation proposed here.

IV. Beyond Affirmative Action: Nonremedial Setasides in
Public and Private Employment

A strengthened regime of affirmative action would be effective at combating the conscious and unconscious discrimination that keeps qualified individuals with disabilities out of work and in poverty. But more than discrimination stands in the way of economic self-sufficiency for persons whose disabilities are real and severe, as opposed to perceived or mild. Many disabilities, particularly mobility limits and serious sensory deficits, do in fact make it more difficult for the persons with them to compete in the workplace. This does not make the individuals productively useless or unable to contribute economically. But it does mean that more than antidiscrimination efforts will be needed to achieve the employment of this group.

Nonremedial setasides are needed to make a significant impact on the employment of persons with more severe disabilities. Nonremedial setasides entail reserving a certain percentage of jobs, or of jobs within a given classification, for persons whose disabilities reach a defined level of severity. Setasides of this type go beyond affirmative action in degree, and are different in character. Even when affirmative action includes numerical targets for hiring, the plan remains a means to avoid discrimination, albeit by a somewhat wider berth than might be required by rules that lack the numerical goals. Nonremedial employment setasides are something more. At the risk of sounding facetious, the something might be termed "unreasonable accommodation," the limit of which goes beyond undue hardship to include hardship that, though real, is "due" in order to finally integrate persons with more severe disabilities into the American workplace.

A. Nonremedial Setasides in Federal Employment

Nothing would be more due than for the federal government, the "model employer" of persons with disabilities, to adopt nonremedial setasides, reserving percentages of jobs for persons with serious disabilities. Persons with disabilities would contribute to the efforts of the government, while no longer requiring the welfare outlays that the federal government provides. No problem could be anticipated with the constitutionality of a law of this type. Minimal scrutiny applies to federal social and economic legislation, and federal hiring can be used to serve any national priority Congress chooses.

B. Nonremedial Setasides in Employment by State and Local Governments Receiving Federal Funds

Next in line after federal government are state governmental agencies that receive federal money. These entities ought to join in the effort to bring persons with disabilities into the economic mainstream. Like the federal government, these governments will benefit by the product of the persons at work and by the reduction in the need for welfare assistance. Percentage setasides that would apply to the states would be modeled on those made applicable to the federal government. The size of the agency and the nature of its work would need to be considered in calibrating the obligation to be imposed.

Some doubts may be raised concerning the constitutionality of this measure. In *New York v. United States*, the Supreme Court ruled that Congress could not impose obligations on state governments without their consent; the Commerce Clause of Article I and the Tenth Amendment forbid "commandeering" state governments for federal purposes. To do so diminishes the accountability of federal and state decision making, for voters are unable to determine whether to blame their congressional or state representatives for bad legislative choices.

The *New York v. United States* Court, however, carefully distinguished conditional spending from direct imposition of duties. In an unbroken line of cases from *Steward Machine Co. v. Davis* to *South Dakota v. Dole*, the Supreme Court has established that Congress may place conditions on funding that it provides to states.

Congress does not evade accountability when it employs conditional spending measures. The state or local official who is taken to task for following the federal directive can properly blame Congress, and Congress has no credible means for shifting the blame back to the states. Of course, state and local officials can be — and should be — taken to task for the decision they themselves make: to take the money under the federal conditions or to forego it.

Using the conditional spending power sidesteps the problems that might be present were Congress to impose setaside obligations on states and localities by fiat under Commerce Clause or Fourteenth Amendment authority. However, if nonremedial setaside requirements were imposed on private business, they could be imposed on state and local agencies that do not receive federal funding. *New York v. United States* distinguished cases such as *Garcia v. San Antonio Metropolitan Transit Authority*, which upheld the application of minimum wage laws to state employees, on the grounds that rules that apply uniformly to both state governments and private businesses do not exceed Congress' Commerce Clause powers.

C. Nonremedial Setasides in Private Employment

It took nearly twenty years for the United States to impose the same disability discrimination provisions on private employers as it had imposed on public employers receiving federal money. The failure to cover private employment prevented meaningful progress from being made with respect to eliminating discrimination in the economy as a whole. In order to have a real policy of promoting employment for persons with disabilities, setasides would need to be extended to private employment, where new legislation should put them into place.

Much of the rest of the industrialized world imposes quotas on private industry to force businesses to hire persons with disabilities. Austria requires employers with twenty-five or more employees to hire at least one person certified as having a disability for each twenty-five employees. France makes firms with more than ten workers allocate ten percent of vacancies to persons with disabilities; employers with at least twenty workers must have full or part-time employees with disabilities totaling six percent of their workers. Germany has a six percent quota for hiring persons with severe disabilities, and imposes it on all public and private employers; those workers are specially protected against termination of employment once they have served a probationary period. Luxembourg forces employers with fifty or more employees to reserve two percent of staff positions for workers with disabilities.

In the Netherlands, companies negotiate their standards, but the government may compel the employment of between three percent and seven percent persons with disabilities if a firm's voluntary performance is not satisfactory. In Spain, two percent of jobs are reserved for workers with disabilities in companies with more than fifty employees. The United Kingdom has a three percent quota for workers certified as having a disability for all employers with twenty or more workers. Japan has an employment quota for persons with disabilities of 1.5% for profit-making businesses and 1.8 to 1.9% for public entities and nonprofit organizations.

Some flexibility exists in most of these countries for firms to make payments to the government if they do not meet their quotas in a given month. In some countries, subsidies are available for specialized equipment or other additional costs of hiring persons with disabilities.

The presence of these programs elsewhere in the world proves a number of points about setaside programs for persons with disabilities. First and most obviously, placing such a system into effect in the United States will not cause us to suffer competitive disadvantage in the world economy. We would merely be doing what our competitors now do. We may lose some modest advantage we currently have, but other countries will not be able to gain any special edge over us. Moreover, strictly in monetary terms, we will gain the value of the product of the persons added to the workforce, their taxes, and the public savings from their decreased need for welfare assistance. Where appropriate, portions of these resources might be reallocated to enhance the competitiveness of businesses threatened by foreign competition.

Second, it is workable to shift the costs of employment of persons with disabilities to private employers. Placing the costs on the private sector spurs economic actors to develop the lowest cost means of accomplishing the job. Problems of defining disability, financing costs, and policing compliance, though they may be quite real, have not proved severe enough to cause the European countries or Japan to abandon their initiatives.

Third, imposing the costs on business is legitimate, by the standards of global economic fairness. It might be argued that setaside programs for persons with disabilities are unfair to business by charging them the entire cost of fixing a social problem they did not create. However, the question of who bears the cost of disability is an open one. Majoritarian processes of government are right to modify existing entitlements when doing so will best accomplish social objectives, particularly in a situation such as this one in which the employers, by definition, have a monopoly on the scarce commodity of employment. The burden imposed is a measured one, and is likely to be kept modest both for political reasons and in order to allow the employers to stay profitably in business and thus provide the needed jobs.

All of this is not to argue that nonremedial setasides will solve the dilemma of difference by shifting the national view of what is disability and what is not. A workable program of setasides will need definitions of disability and will classify individuals accordingly. Employees without disabilities are highly likely to consider the individuals freshly hired to satisfy the quota as something other, and quite possibly something lesser, than themselves.

Two compensations will exist, however. The first is the sheer fact of exposure. Being exposed to the reality that persons with disabilities are in the world and part of it should, over time, bring changes in the way others view reality. The modifications in physical space and workplace routines that employers will find it economical to undertake should aid this process.

The second compensation is, frankly, compensation. Nothing so much affects one's acceptance by others as one's economic status, and although workers whose disabilities limit their marginal product will be at the lower end of the wage scale, they will be on a much higher economic plane than they are now. Workers whose disabilities are unrelated to success at work will gain entry-level jobs and the opportunity to prove themselves over time. The economic improvement should translate into improvement in how individuals are treated.

An additional objection to nonremedial setasides is that they will lead to featherbedding or make-work jobs that contribute little to the employer's product and provide no opportunity for advancement. But the economic incentive for employers is to gain whatever marginal contribution the employee can make, and not to leave the employee idle. Employers are the ones in the best position to determine exactly how to achieve the maximum benefit. Workers with more severe impairments may be limited in their opportunities to advance, but it is to be hoped that as workers with disabilities become more of an ordinary part of the work experience, those with the capacity to rise will do so. The employer will have the incentive to undertake changes in the work settings and practices so as to maximize the economic contribution of the workers who are there.

Commentators have proposed other strategies for enhancing the employment opportunities of persons with disabilities. Some propose full or partial subsidies for employers' voluntary modifications of workplaces and workplace routines. Tax incentives exist to defray some of the cost of accommodations, but with all of today's competing demands for government aid, subsidies are unlikely to increase. Significantly, European countries, which typically tax citizens and businesses at a much higher rate than the United States does and spend proportionally more government money on social programs, impose the costs of employing persons with disabilities on employers. Subsidies are frequently present, but they defray only a fraction of the employers' costs.

As with nonremedial setasides to be applied to federal and state governmental agencies, regulations would need to embody flexibility and attention to the nature of the enterprise being regulated. In particular, the regulations would need to establish rating mechanisms for the severity of the disability of persons hired, to keep employers from creaming off persons with the least serious disabilities and counting them towards their setasides in a manner that is equal to that used for persons with much greater severity of disability.

Just as the Commerce Clause is the simplest ground on which to uphold the constitutionality of affirmative action efforts imposed on private employers, so to would it be for nonremedial setasides. The same principles would all apply, as would the basic principle that absence of disability is not a suspect classification triggering heightened scrutiny. Although not in the form of a tax, a regulation of the type proposed is not much different from a tax, or from minimum employee benefits such as family medical leave or minimum wage. Real costs are being placed on employers, but for a valid social goal. Real costs are already imposed on employers under the duty to provide reasonable accommodations, and although the proposed measure will entail greater costs, quotas along European models are not high enough to produce serious economic discomfort for employers. Special hardship exceptions could be created were there a serious risk of this result.

Conclusion

The steps proposed in this Article represent the beginning of a true employment policy for persons with disabilities, as opposed to the present patchwork of antidiscrimination laws with limited affirmative action requirements, limited educational and rehabilitation services, and subsistence welfare. Proper interpretation and broader application of affirmative action efforts are needed to complete the work of eliminating discrimination and its effects, but nonremedial setasides will be needed to bring persons with disabilities into the working economy and out of poverty and dependency. The steps proposed here take persons with disabilities seriously as members and potential members of the working community.

* * *

Questions for Discussion

1. Will the ADA Amendments help alleviate some of the problems mentioned in this article?

2. What can be done to increase the employment rate of people with disabilities? What suggestions in this article do you think should be implemented? What other suggestions do you have?

3. What do you think of affirmative action in general? What do you think of it in this context?

4. What do you think of the idea of setasides in private businesses?

For Further Reading

The U.S. Equal Opportunities Commission, "Facts About the Americans with Disabilities Act," retrieved June 11, 2012 at http://www.eeoc.gov/facts/fs-ada.html.

Edward J. McGraw, "Compliance Costs of the Americans with Disabilities Act," 18 Del. J. Corp. L. 521 (1993).

Discussion 21

Then Who *Was*
Disabled under the ADA?

Recommended Background Reading

Sutton v. United Airlines, 527 U.S. 471 (1999).

Toyota v. Williams, 534 U.S. 184 (2002).

The ADA Amendments Act, ("ADAAA"), 42 USCA § 12101 et seq.

Readings for Class Discussion

This 2007 decision may have been one that led many people to ask, "Who is protected under the ADA anymore?"

Littleton v. Wal-Mart

In the United States Court of Appeals
for the Eleventh Circuit
No. 05-12770
Appeal from the United States District Court
for the Northern District of Alabama
(May 11, 2007)

Before BIRCH and BLACK, Circuit Judges, and MILLS, District Judge.

PER CURIAM:

Charles Irvin Littleton, Jr. appeals the district court's order granting Wal-Mart Store, Inc. summary judgment on his failure-to-hire disability discrimination claim under the Americans with Disabilities Act ("ADA"), 42 U.S.C. §§ 12112, 12132.

Littleton claims that the district court erred in finding that he was not disabled under the ADA because his permanent condition of mental retardation limits one or more of his major life activities, namely (1) learning, (2) thinking, (3) communicating, (4) social interaction, and (5) working. We assume the parties' familiarity with the facts and procedural history of this case.

I. BACKGROUND

On appeal, Littleton claims that there is at least a genuine issue of material fact tending to show that his mental retardation substantially limited him as to certain major life activities. Regarding the major life activities of learning, thinking, communicating and social interaction, Littleton contends that the district court failed to consider the following evidence in the light most favorable to him: (1) testimony from his job coach and mother concerning his limited ability to think and communicate; (2) Wal-Mart personnel manager Marlene Barcanic's awareness of Littleton's limitations and need for assistance during the interview process; (3) observations of Wal-Mart interviewers that Littleton displayed poor interpersonal skills and a lack of enthusiasm about the job; and (4) his deposition testimony, which showed that he had limited cognitive abilities and difficulty navigating the interview process. Based on these factors, Littleton argues that a reasonable jury could infer that he is disabled under the ADA.

Charles Irvin Littleton, Jr. is a 29-year-old man who was diagnosed with mental retardation as a young child. Littleton receives social security benefits because of his disability and lives at home with his mother. He graduated from high school in 1994 with a certificate in special education. Throughout his working life, Littleton has been a client of various state agencies and public service organizations. He was referred to Carolyn Agee, an employment coordinator with the Alabama Independent Living Center. They attempted to secure employment for Littleton as a cart-push associate with a Wal-Mart Store in Leeds, Alabama. Littleton claims that Barcanic, the personnel manager at that store, initially said that Agee could accompany him in the interview. Upon arrival at the store, however, Agee was not allowed to accompany Littleton in the interview. The interview did not go well and Littleton was not offered a position.

II. DISCUSSION

"We review de novo a district court's ruling on summary judgment, applying the same legal standards as the district court." *Matthews v. Crosby*, 480 F.3d 1265, 1268 (11th Cir. 2007) (citation omitted). The Court views the evidence in the light most favorable to the nonmoving party. *Id.* at 1269. Summary judgment is appropriate if the evidence shows that "there is no genuine issue as to any material fact and that the moving party is entitled to a judgment as a matter of law." Fed. R. Civ. P. 56(c).

To establish a prima facie case of disability discrimination under the ADA, a plaintiff must show (1) that he has a disability; (2) he is a qualified individual; and (3) he was discriminated against because of his disability. See *Cleveland v. Home Shopping Network, Inc.*, 369 F.3d 1189, 1193 (11th Cir. 2004). If Littleton establishes a prima facie case, a presumption of discrimination arises and the burden shifts to Wal-Mart to proffer a legitimate, nondiscriminatory reason for the employment action. *Id.* If Wal-Mart meets its burden, then Littleton must show that the proffered reason is a pretext for discrimination. *Id.*

The ADA defines "disability" as "(A) a physical or mental impairment that substantially limits one or more of the major life activities of such individual; (B) a record of such impairment; or (C) being regarded as having such an impairment." 42U.S.C. § 12102(2). To prove that he is disabled due to an impairment, a plaintiff must prove that the impairment, as personally suffered by him, substantially limits a major life activity. See *Pritchard v. Southern Co. Services*, 92 F.3d 1130, 1132 (11th Cir. 1996) (citing 29 C.F.R. § 1630.2(j) (App.)). Under the "regarded as" prong of section 12102(2)(c), an individual is "disabled" if his employer perceives him as having an ADA-qualifying disability. See *Carruthers v. BSA Advertising*, Inc., 357 F.3d 1213, 1216 (11th Cir. 2004).

Littleton asserts that: (1) he is substantially limited in the major life activities of learning, thinking, communicating, social interaction and working; and (2) Wal-Mart perceived him as being substantially limited in working, communicating, and social interaction. Courts look to the ADA's implementing regulations to determine the functions that qualify as "major life activities." We are mindful that the Supreme Court has stated that the term "disability" is to be "interpreted strictly to create a demanding standard for qualifying as disabled." See *Carruthers*, 357 F.3d at 1216 (quoting *Toyota Motor Mfg., Ky., Inc. v. Williams*, 534 U.S. 184, 197 (2002)). The regulations provide that mental retardation qualifies as a "mental impairment." See 29 C.F.R. § 1630.2(h)(2). Major life activities include "functions such as caring for oneself, performing manual tasks, walking, seeing, hearing, speaking, breathing, learning, and working." See 29 C.F.R. § 1630.2(i). This court has not determined whether thinking, communicating and social interaction constitute "major life activities" under the ADA.

In his appellate brief Littleton asserts that the district court did not consider evidence pertaining to limitations on his ability to think and communicate. After reviewing the record, however, we conclude that Littleton failed to argue before the district court that there were any limitations on his ability to think and communicate, nor did he contend he was substantially limited as to any other alleged major life activity. This is true even though Wal-Mart asserted that it was entitled to summary judgment because Littleton could not establish a prima facie case under the ADA, in that he was unable to show he was substantially limited in any major life activity. Because Littleton produced no evidence on this point, the district court properly concluded that "Wal-Mart is entitled to judgment as a matter of law here because there is no evidence to support Littleton's necessary contention that his retardation substantially limits him in one or more major life activities." See, e.g., *Williams*, 534 U.S. at 195 ("Merely having an impairment does not make one disabled for purposes of the ADA. Claimants also need to demonstrate that the impairment limits a major life activity.").

We generally do not consider issues that were not raised before the district court. See *Narey v. Dean*, 32 F.3d 1521, 1526–27 (11th Cir. 1994). Even if the issue was properly raised, we conclude that Wal-Mart is still entitled to summary judgment because Littleton has failed to produce any evidence that his mental impairment substantially limited any major life activities.

As for the major life activity of working, "[t]he term substantially limits means significantly restricted in the ability to perform either a class of jobs or a broad range of jobs in various classes as compared to the average person having comparable training, skills and abilities. The inability to perform a single, particular job does not constitute a substantial limitation in the major life activity of working." See 29 C.F.R. § 1630.2(j)(3)(i). Littleton, his mother and Agee all testified that there are no jobs he cannot perform because of any alleged disability. Accordingly, Littleton has not shown that he is substantially limited in this major life activity.

"Learning" is also a major life activity, see 29 C.F.R. § 1630.2(i), so we must determine whether there is a genuine issue of material fact regarding whether Littleton's ability to learn is substantially limited by his mental retardation. Wal-Mart acknowledges that Littleton's mental retardation is a permanent condition, which is a factor that courts consider in determining whether an individual is substantially limited in a major life activity. See 29 C.F.R. § 1630.2(j)(2)(ii)-(iii).

After graduating from high school with a certificate in special education, Littleton attended a technical college and majored in mechanical maintenance. The record shows that Littleton is able to read and comprehend and is able to perform various types of jobs.

It is apparent that Littleton is somewhat limited in his ability to learn because of his mental retardation. However, he has pointed to no evidence which would create a genuine issue of material fact regarding whether he was substantially limited in the major life activity of learning because of his mental retardation. It is unclear whether thinking, communicating and social interaction are "major life activities" under the ADA. We acknowledge that a review of Littleton's deposition testimony is not inconsistent with his assertion that he sometimes has difficulty thinking or communicating. Even if thinking and communicating are major life activities, however, Littleton has not shown that he is substantially limited in those activities.

As Wal-Mart contends, moreover, the fact that Littleton drives a car might be determined to be inconsistent with his assertion that his abilities to think and learn are substantially limited. Additionally, Littleton's mother and Agee testified that Littleton is capable of being interviewed for a job without any accommodation, is "very verbal," and would not need a job coach to communicate effectively with other people in the workforce. This bolsters Wal-Mart's contention that any difficulty Littleton has with communicating does not appear to be a substantial limitation.

We do not doubt that Littleton has certain limitations because of his mental retardation. In order to qualify as "disabled" under the ADA, however, Littleton has the burden of proving that he actually is, is perceived to be, or has a record of being substantially limited as to "major life activities" under the ADA. 42 U.S.C. §§ 12102(2)(A), 12112(a), 12132; see also *Hilburn v. Murata Electronics North America, Inc.*, 181 F.3d 1220, 1227 (11th Cir. 1997). Assuming that thinking, communicating and social interaction are "major life activities" under the ADA, we conclude that Littleton has failed to create a genuine issue of material fact that he is substantially limited in those pursuits. Thus he has failed to assert a prima facie case of discrimination under the ADA.

We AFFIRM the district court's entry of summary judgment in favor of Wal-Mart.

* * *

Questions for Discussion

1. What do you think of the "major life activities" analysis in this opinion? How might this case have come down if it had been brought after the ADAAA?

2. Did the holdings in *Sutton v. United Airlines* and *Toyota v. Williams* mandate the result in this case?

3. Why are "failure to hire" cases so difficult for plaintiffs to prove?

For Further Reading

Steny L. Hoyer, "Not Exactly What We Intended, Justice O'Connor," *Wash. Post*, Jan 20, 2002, at B01.

Charles Lane, "O'Connor Criticizes Disabilities Law as Too Vague," *Wash. Post*, Mar 15, 2002, at A02.

Discussion 22

Supported Employment &
Sheltered Workshops

Recommended Background Reading

42 USC sec. 12112.

"What is Supported Employment?" United Cerebral Palsy, retrieved May 15, 2012 at http://affnet.ucp.org/ucp_channeldoc.cfm/1/17/107/107-107/1701.

Zana Marie Lutfiyya, Pat Rogan, and Bonnie Shoultz, "Supported Employment: A Conceptual Overview." Center on Human Policy/Research and Training Center on Community Integration, Syracuse University, retrieved May 15, 2012 at http://thechp.syr.edu/workovw.htm.

Readings for Class Discussion

The following case attempts to differentiate between supported employment and reasonable accommodation. Do you agree with the reasoning? The outcome? The discourse?

Hertz v. Arkay

United States District Court, E.D. Michigan
No. 96-72421
1998 U.S. Dist. LEXIS 58 (E.D. Mich., Jan. 6, 1998)

FEIKENS, District J.

I. Background

Chief Justice Earl Warren would often ask when judging a case: "Is it fair, is it just?" That question must be asked in this case. The Equal Employment Opportunity Commission (EEOC) and Arkay, Inc. (Arkay), a federally-funded entity which supplies job coaches to assist handicapped persons, have combined in this suit to seek sanctions against the Hertz Corporation (Hertz). They now have been joined by several groups, Disability Rights Advocates and Michigan Protection and Advisory Services, as amici, who support that effort. With this array, one must ask what it is in this case that brings the EEOC and these rights advocate agencies together to pursue this matter.

One need not look far. Arkay, Inc. is the motivator.

Arkay has an appealing approach. It seeks out employers, like Hertz, and makes a proposal: that if the employer will hire a handicapped person, it (Arkay) will provide a job coach, free of charge, to the employer, who will assist the handicapped person in doing some work for the employer. Arkay is paid for these efforts by federal government funding.

This is what happened in this case. In early 1994, Arkay went to Hertz and pointed out to it that at its rental car operations at Detroit Metropolitan Airport, it could hire two handicapped persons (mentally retarded) who could work a limited number of hours each day (approximately four hours—the record is not clear), and they would be trained and assisted by two job coaches provided by Arkay. It is clear in the record that these handicapped persons (Donald Klem and Kenneth Miller) would not be able to do the intended work, picking up trash in the Hertz parking lot, without training by and the actual supervision of the job coaches.

Hertz agreed, and the venture started. But it soon went awry. It appears that the job coaches furnished by Arkay had other distracting interests.

One day (the record is not clear if this was the first time, or the only time), the job coaches had Mr. Klem and Mr. Miller seated in the back seat of a car while they, a man and a woman, according to current jargon, were "making out" in the front seat. It is not clear from the record just what was going on.[1] Hertz claims that four or five of its supervisors saw rather passionate lovemaking, while EEOC and Arkay claim the two were exchanging gifts and thanking each other with kisses.

When the event in the car was observed by the Hertz supervisors, the job coaches were ordered off the premises and the jobs of Messrs. Klem and Miller were terminated. What happened next is that Arkay went to the EEOC and claimed that a violation of the Americans With Disabilities Act (ADA) had occurred and EEOC had better do something about it.

This suit followed.

Plaintiff's major contention is that Hertz, having hired Messrs. Klem and Miller, now have a continuing duty to employ them, and that Hertz must provide reasonable accommodation to continue their training and employment. That reasonable accommodation, EEOC argues, would require Hertz to find other job coaches to train and supervise Mr. Klem and Mr. Miller.

When Arkay first approached Hertz, and asked it to hire Mr. Klem and Mr. Miller, Hertz had no legal obligation to do so. See *Reigel v. Kaiser Foundation Health Plan of N.C.*, 859 F.Supp. 963 (E.D.N.C.1994).

When it did hire these men, it was essential that they be accompanied, while being trained and working on Hertz's premises, to be supervised by competent job coaches. Arkay committed itself to provide this important accommodation; it was the essential element, the consideration for the contract.

That employment contract was breached by Arkay because of the conduct of its incompetent job coaches.

In this bizarre situation, EEOC, Arkay and the amici now seek to impose a legal obligation on Hertz that they say is compelled by 42 U.S.C. § 12112(ADA). Their complaint

---

1. The female participant is still employed with Arkay. The male participant was apparently married at the time. The female participant downplayed the incident, saying that she and her paramour were merely engaged in a "prolonged hug." The male participant was apparently never deposed.

"relates solely to Hertz's failure to reasonably accommodate Klem and Miller…." This alleged failure to so accommodate, they claim, is discrimination.

Now to the facts that are not in dispute.

This case has its origins in defendant Hertz's April 1994 decision to contract with Arkay, Inc., for an employment service for individuals with developmental disabilities.[2] Arkay representative Susan Skibo contacted Hertz as to the possibility of employing Arkay personnel. Ms. Skibo eventually contacted Keith Lamb, one of Hertz's senior station managers at its Detroit Metropolitan Airport location, and outlined to him the arrangement that Arkay wanted to structure with Hertz: in exchange for Hertz's provision of menial tasks for Arkay's developmentally handicapped individuals, Arkay promised to provide job coaches to train them, to closely supervise them and, if necessary, tend to any of their medical needs. If Hertz would agree to employ and pay the handicapped individuals, Arkay would provide and pay the job coaches.

Mr. Lamb expressed some misgivings, but promised to speak to his supervisor, Gary Wellman, about Arkay's proposal. Mr. Lamb spoke with Mr. Wellman and told him that, in light of litter problems Hertz had on its premises, Arkay's proposal "might be something that would be good to try." (Lamb dep. at 15). Mr. Wellman, in turn, took the matter to his supervisor, Michael Kieleszewski, who sought and then obtained permission from Hertz Headquarters to accept Arkay's offer.[3]

The term "'supported employment,' which has been applied to a wide variety of programs to assist individuals with severe disabilities in both competitive and non-competitive employment, is not synonymous with reasonable accommodation." The Interpretative Guidance to Reg. 29 CFR 1630.9 states that an example of supported employment might include providing "a temporary job coach to assist in the training of a qualified individual with a disability…." Before Messrs. Klem and Miller could be hired, however, Hertz had to make additional accommodations. First, Hertz agreed to waive its usual application and interview process. Hertz also allowed Messrs. Klem and Miller to take a paid half-hour break, even though their shift lasted only four hours. Most important, Hertz allowed Messrs. Klem and Miller to have supportive "job coaches."

The record also indicates that Hertz did not hold Messrs. Klem and Miller to the higher standards of its other employees. On one occasion, Mr. Lamb saw Mr. Klem spit on the floor inside Hertz's car return building, an area used by Hertz customers. Mr. Lamb did not discipline Mr. Klem; he wanted to give Mr. Klem an opportunity to adjust to his new environment. Mr. Miller and Mr. Klem also were not held to the attendance standards of other employees. Mr. Lamb testified that the pair missed work without penalty. Deposition testimony also raises serious questions whether, even with a job coach, Mr. Klem could perform the essential functions of his job. Both Mr. Lamb and one of Mr. Klem's job coaches testified as to incidents in which Mr. Klem spent part of a workday staring at airplanes overhead and refused orders from his job coach to do his job.

---

2. Arkay is funded, at least in part, by Medicaid. Arkay is funded by Medicaid in an arrangement that it has with Wayne Community Living Services (WCLS), and that entity works with and through Arkay to provide supported employment for mentally retarded persons. The record indicates that on behalf of WCLS, Arkay entered into this employment agreement with Hertz, which Arkay states in its Answer to Hertz's Third-Party Complaint against it, Para. 9, would be on a trial basis.

3. Prior to accepting Arkay's offer, Hertz had no employees assigned specifically to cleaning the parking lot. Hertz created positions for Messrs. Klem and Miller to do this. The positions have not been filled since Mr. Klem's and Mr. Miller's employment was terminated.

Hertz did accommodate to this. Hertz claims, however, that it could not tolerate problems created by the job coaches assigned to Messrs. Klem and Miller. The first job coach that Arkay sent was "mean" to Messrs. Klem and Miller. Hertz requested that this coach be replaced. Arkay granted this request and, for a time, provided a job coach that met Hertz's expectations. This second job coach was subsequently replaced by another coach who, on June 7, 1994, was involved in the incident which precipitated the termination of Hertz's relationship with Arkay.

To this incident, Hertz's response was swift. One of its managers confronted the job coaches and promptly told them to leave Hertz property. Hertz then contacted Arkay and severed its relationship with that company. Even though, at that point, it could have easily have done so, Arkay refused to turn Messrs. Klem and Miller over to another job agency performing the same function that Arkay performed.[4] Instead, Arkay threatened to, and eventually did, contact EEOC and induced it to institute this action. The record is not clear that Arkay ever informed Wayne Community Living Services, of this situation, or that Arkay received WCLS's consent to secure other job coaches, i.e., organizations that, like Arkay, could have provided this type of employment support to Messrs. Klem and Miller.

II. Analysis

The comment of Judge Richard Posner in Vande Zande v. State of Wisc. Dept. of Admin., 44 F.3d 538 (7th Cir.1995), is instructive:

> [I]f the employer ... bends over backwards to accommodate a disabled worker— goes farther than the law requires—... it must not be punished for its generosity by being deemed to have conceded the reasonableness of so far reaching an accommodation. That would hurt rather than help disabled workers.

While, as is pointed out hereinafter, EEOC cannot even come close to establishing a prima facie case of disability discrimination against Hertz, this is a case in which there is no discrimination whatever.[5] The teaching of the ancient fable is instructive: It took a child to point out to the crowd admiring what they thought was an ornately dressed emperor riding a horse, that the emperor had no clothes on at all.

EEOC's position fits that fable. One wonders why that agency is unable to see clearly what it is attempting to claim. Hertz should be complimented for what it tried to do here—not sued. How does EEOC expect to further the goal of assisting handicapped persons that employers will hire if it seeks to punish them for their generosity?

Putting that aside for the moment, and taking on EEOC's argument that it has here a prima facie case, EEOC cannot and does not establish a prima facie case of discrimination required by ADA. *Monette v. Electronic Data Systems Corp.*, 90 F.3d 1173 (6th Cir.1996), teaches that, to establish a prima facie case, a plaintiff must show that 1) he or she is disabled, 2) is otherwise qualified for the job, with or without "reasonable" accommodation, 3) suffered an adverse employment decision, 4) the employer knew or had reason to know

[handwritten margin note: Prima Facia elements to discrim]

---

4. Two Hertz managers, Gary Wellman and Michael Kieleszewski, testified that, had Arkay made such an offer, they would have considered extending the employment of Messrs. Klem and Miller.

5. In cases brought under Title VII of the Civil Rights Act of 1964 (see 42 U.S.C. § 2000e-2(a)(1)), once an employer proffers a legitimate, nondiscriminatory reason for a challenged employment decision, as Hertz has done in this case, the *McDonnell-Douglas* burden shifting framework becomes irrelevant; the only thing left to be decided is the ultimate question: whether defendant engaged in discrimination. See *St. Mary's Honor Society v. Hicks*, 509 U.S. 502, 510–512, 113 S.Ct. 2742, 2748–2750, 125 L.Ed.2d 407 (1993). The same reasoning applies to claims of discrimination brought under ADA.

of his or her disability, and 5) after rejection or termination the position remained open, or the disabled individual was replaced.

It is clear that plaintiff does not and cannot establish factor 2). Messrs. Klem and Miller are not qualified for the job because accommodation to permit them to function was not provided by Arkay (or anyone else). It is not the duty, obligation or responsibility of Hertz to provide job coaches, either on a temporary basis or on a permanent basis, to train and supervise these handicapped individuals.

It is also clear that after Messrs. Klem and Miller were terminated due to Arkay's breach of the trial arrangement, that these positions [Klem's and Miller's] did not remain open. These positions ceased when the arrangement failed. It is also clear that they [Klem and Miller] were not replaced.

The result in this case was not brought about by Hertz. Arkay and, perhaps, Wayne Community Living Services had a responsibility for "picking up the pieces," and should have initiated a reopening of the arrangement with Hertz. The record indicates that had Arkay "made such an offer, Hertz would have seriously considered extending the employment" of Mr. Klem and Mr. Miller.

But, even more important, the position of the EEOC is troublesome. This case should not have been brought against Hertz; EEOC's focus was misplaced. EEOC should have advised Arkay that this was not a case of discrimination against handicapped persons but rather a breakdown in Arkay's procedures in affording assistance to handicapped people.

Even EEOC's Interpretative Guidance stands in its way. The guidelines provide at 29 CFR 1630.9 that:

> The term "supported employment," which has been applied to a wide variety of programs to assist individuals with severe disabilities in both competitive and non-competitive employment is not synonymous with reasonable accommodation. Examples of supported employment include modified training materials, re-structuring essential functions to enable an individual to perform a job, or hiring an outside professional ("job coach") to assist in job training. Whether a particular form of assistance would be required as a reasonable accommodation must be determined on an individualized, case by case basis without regard to whether that assistance is referred to as "supported employment." For example, an employer, under certain circumstances, may be required to provide modified training materials or a temporary "job coach" to assist in the training of a qualified individual with a disability as a reasonable accommodation.[6]

If a temporary job coach providing job training to a qualified individual may be a reasonable accommodation, the clear implication is that a full-time job coach providing more than training to unqualified Individuals is not. Caselaw supports this view. *Ricks v. Xerox Corp.*, 877 F.Supp. 1468 (D.Kan.1995), is on point. In that case, the district court ruled that an employee's request for a full-time "helper" to assist in the performance of the essential functions of his job was unreasonable as a matter of law. A similar result

---

6. There is no dispute here that the role of the job coaches in this case went far beyond that of "job training." The record reflects that the coaches supervised, disciplined, and assisted in the performance of work. In addition, Arkay representative Susan Skibo testified that neither Mr. Klem nor Mr. Miller had ever worked without the full-time assistance of a job coach. Ms. Skibo further testified that they would always need this full-time assistance. Finally, while there is an issue of fact with regard to whether Messrs. Klem and Miller were qualified individuals, the fact that they required full-time assistance for more than job training moots, for purposes of summary judgment, the factual dispute.

was reached *in Gilbert v. Frank*, 949 F.2d 637 (C.A.2 1991), in which the U.S. Court of Appeals for the Second Circuit held that it was unreasonable to have two people performing the same tasks normally performed by one. Insisting that Messrs. Miller and Klem have a full-time job coach to assist in the performance of job duties on a permanent basis is, likewise, unreasonable.

Neither party disputes that Hertz had no initial obligation to hire Messrs. Klem and Miller. See *Reigel*, supra, at 963, 973: "[The ADA] cannot be construed to require an employer to make fundamental or substantial modifications in its operations to assure every disabled individual the benefit of employment."

EEOC, in the face of this precedent and in spite of its inability to point to any case mandating that a full-time job coach is a reasonable accommodation, advances the incredible argument that, because Hertz could have obtained a job coach for Messrs. Klem and Miller at no cost to itself, the provision of a job coach is a per se reasonable accommodation, and must be provided.

Plaintiff seeks to establish an expanded liability for putative employers who consider hiring handicapped persons, i.e., that once an employer evidences an intent to and does provide employment for a handicapped person with support for that person of a job coach, it is obligated to continue that relationship in perpetuity and without regard to any event(s) that make that employment relationship untenable. The ADA does not require this.

III. Conclusion

The motion brought by Hertz for summary judgment is GRANTED.

IT IS SO ORDERED.

Questions for Discussion

1. Why do you think the EEOC made the argument it did? Do you think their argument may have had merit?

2. What discourse in the case might seem problematic to a disability rights advocate?

3. Is it fair that Klem and Miller lost their jobs due to the actions of their job coaches?

———————

The following case is an example of a victory for a supported employee.

Perkl v. CEC Entertainment, Inc.

United States District Court, W.D. Wisconsin
No. 98-C-698-X
March 14, 2000

CROCKER, Magistrate J.

This civil action for monetary damages and equitable relief is before the court following a trial in which a jury found that defendant CEC Entertainment, Inc. intentionally discriminated against plaintiff-intervenor Donald Perkl by terminating his employment because he was disabled, in violation of Title I of the Americans With Disabilities Act, 42 U.S.C. §§ 12111–12117. The jury awarded Perkl $70,000 in compensatory damages and $13 million in punitive damages, although the total award is statutorily capped at $300,000. Before the court is defendant's motion for judgment as a matter of law, plaintiff

EEOC's motion for equitable relief] and costs and Perkl's motion for entry of judgment, attorneys fees, costs and equitable relief.

Notwithstanding the huge damages verdict and the plaintiffs' claim of complete and total victory, the jury just as easily could have found for CEC on all issues. The outcome on both liability and damages hinged on the credibility of one or two key witnesses for each side. The jury chose to believe plaintiffs' witnesses, which was its prerogative. As discussed below, the evidence was sufficient to support the jury's determination that Perkl was a qualified individual and that CEC discriminated against him because of his disability when it fired him. Accordingly, I am denying CEC's motion for judgment as a matter of law.

The damages verdict is a closer call. Although I have some reservations which I discuss below, I am upholding the jury's verdict on both compensatory and punitive damages.

As for equitable relief, I am not providing much more than the parties have agreed to in their post-verdict negotiations. Because CEC has made Perkl an unconditional offer of re-employment, I am ordering CEC to reinstate Perkl to his former position at the Madison Chuck E. Cheese's restaurant, and I am denying Perkl's request for front pay. Perkl shall be awarded prejudgment interest on his back pay award.

As for costs, I am awarding the EEOC its costs in the amount of $7,615.84. I am staying final action on Perkl's request for attorneys fees and costs pending the provision of some additional information material to my decision. I am declining to establish the supplemental needs trust requested by Perkl as unnecessary.

Evidence Adduced at Trial

For the purpose of deciding CEC's motion for judgment as a matter of law, I am synopsizing the evidence adduced at trial:

CEC is a nationwide restaurant chain that operates under the name of Chuck E. Cheese's. In 1998, CEC had revenues of $379.4 million and net income of $33.7 million. CEC's restaurants are run by managers, who oversee the day-to-day operations of the store, who are in turn supervised by general managers, who are in turn supervised by area or district managers. District managers supervise the operations of several Chuck E. Cheese restaurants in a particular region. In January 1997, Donald Creasy became the district manager of the Chuck E. Cheese's restaurant in Madison.

On Creasy's first visit to the Madison restaurant, he observed that it was dirty and disorganized and that there was a lack of leadership by the management staff. That day, Creasy had a conversation with Sharon Fitch, the restaurant's general manager, regarding the need for her to give checklists to her employees to ensure they were all doing their jobs.

At a later visit to the Madison restaurant, Creasy found the situation essentially unchanged from his first visit. He again spoke with Fitch about the need for checklists. He also spoke to both Fitch and Brea Wittwer, another manager, about their need to implement a "close-to-open" policy, a practice whereby tasks such as vacuuming, cleaning bathrooms, sweeping and mopping the kitchen were completed by the evening crew while the restaurant was closing so that the restaurant would be ready to open without additional work the next morning. Creasy also told Fitch and Wittwer that they should reassign one of the employees, Jason Martin, to perform more cleaning duties in lieu of the kitchen prep tasks he was doing. At the time, Martin's responsibilities were taking out trash, washing windows, picking up the parking lot and doing some kitchen preparation work, including breaking up chunks of pizza cheese.

On March 17, 1997, Wittwer hired plaintiff Donald Perkl to perform janitorial duties at the restaurant. Perkl is a mentally retarded, autistic and nonverbal man who communicates through the use of picture cards. He was referred to Chuck E. Cheese's by Madison Packaging & Assembly, a community vocational rehabilitation program that provides a variety of services to people with and without disabilities, including work assessments, supported employment in the form of job coaches and community placements. Wittwer hired Perkl to replace Janice Oliver, another developmentally disabled individual whose employment at Chuck E. Cheese's had been supported by Madison Packaging & Assembly.

Perkl had over six years' experience working at a sheltered workshop at Madison Packaging & Assembly, where he performed light assembly and packaging tasks. He also had worked in the community in a supported employment position as a janitor at Northwest Fabrics in 1996. Perkl's case workers told Wittwer that Northwest Fabrics had been happy with Perkl's performance but his job had been terminated in December 1996 because the company hired an outside janitorial service. Wittwer hired Perkl with the understanding that he would be working with a job coach funded by Dane County.

The role of a job coach is to assist in teaching the disabled individual the tasks that he is expected to perform, provide on-site supervision during the early phases of the individual's employment, monitor the employee's progress and serve as a liaison between the employee and the employer. In theory, the job coach is supposed to "fade" over time; in other words, to provide less and less support as the individual becomes more independent on the job. The job coach also keeps case notes that record the individual's progress on the job.

Perkl worked at Chuck E. Cheese's from 8 a.m. to noon, Monday through Friday. His job duties consisted of various cleaning tasks, including mopping the floors, vacuuming carpets and cleaning the bathrooms. Perkl was accompanied on the job every day by a job coach.

Creasy happened to be visiting the restaurant on March 18, 1997, Perkl's first day of work and he saw Perkl working. Creasy asked Wittwer who he was and Wittwer explained that Perkl was mentally retarded and nonverbal and that she had just hired him; Creasy then told Wittwer to fire him. At trial, Wittwer testified that Creasy told her about an incident that had occurred in a Chuck E. Cheese's restaurant in California that had involved a developmentally disabled employee and said that it was now defendant's policy not to hire "those kind of people." Fitch testified that Creasy had made a similar statement about Oliver, the mentally retarded woman whom Perkl had replaced.

In his testimony at trial, Creasy agreed that he questioned why Wittwer hired Perkl, but stated that it was not because Perkl was disabled. He testified that he questioned Wittwer's decision to hire Perkl because there was not a position available for him; namely, the restaurant already had Jason Martin whom Creasy believed should perform custodial duties in the store. Creasy also testified that he told Wittwer that the tasks that Perkl was performing should have been done at closing time instead of in the mornings and that an additional employee was not needed at that time of the year because sales were starting to decline.

Wittwer asked Creasy if she could have a couple of weeks to see what she could do with Perkl; Creasy agreed. After Creasy left the restaurant that day, Wittwer wrote and sent a letter via facsimile to Leslie Crim in the human resources department at defendant's headquarters in Dallas, Texas. The letter stated, in part:

I hired a 50-year-old man yesterday who happens to be autistic and has a diagnosis of mental retardation. He works with job coaches who are fully trained and cost us nothing. He started today and will be doing all of our cleaning and maintenance. Our district manager wants me to fire him because, we don't need "those kind of people" working for us. Can someone please help me with this situation, so we can at least give this guy a chance? We are an equal opportunity employer, are we not?

Crim received Wittwer's letter and faxed a copy of it to Creasy and Creasy's boss, Regional Vice President Gary Spring. Crim did not call Wittwer. Hearing no response from Crim, Wittwer telephoned Spring a few days later. Wittwer testified that she told Spring about Creasy's discriminatory remark and that Creasy wanted her to fire Perkl. According to Wittwer, Spring told her that the decision whether or not to fire Perkl was hers to make. Spring acknowledged that he never asked Wittwer any questions about the incident or conducted any investigation into Wittwer's complaint.

Between March 18, 1997 to April 7, 1997, Creasy visited the Madison restaurant on various occasions and observed Perkl working. According to Creasy, on each of these occasions, Perkl was vacuuming after the restaurant had opened for business. Creasy testified that he addressed this concern with Wittwer. However, Wittwer testified that she did not recall a time when Perkl vacuumed the carpets after the restaurant had opened and she did not recall having any conversation with Creasy regarding Perkl's work performance.

On April 7, 1997, after Perkl's shift had ended, Creasy contacted Madison Packaging & Assembly and informed the receptionist that Perkl's services would not be needed for the rest of the summer. Wittwer testified that Dave Lemanski, Perkl's case manager at Madison Packaging & Assembly, telephoned the restaurant about five minutes later. According to Wittwer, Creasy refused to take the call; instead, he directed Wittwer to take the call and to tell Lemanski that she had decided to terminate Perkl. Although Creasy testified that he did at some point speak with Lemanski and explain the reasons for terminating Perkl, Lemanski testified that he never spoke with Creasy about Perkl.

On April 9, 1997, two days after Perkl's termination, Lemanski faxed a letter to Creasy requesting his presence at a meeting on April 25, 1997, at the Madison Chuck E. Cheese's restaurant to discuss Perkl's termination. Although Creasy testified that he did not see the fax until April 12 or 13, 1997, a copy of the fax somehow made its way to Crim in Dallas by April 10, because on that day, Crim wrote a letter to Lemanski in which she indicated that she had received a copy of it. In her letter, Crim stated that she did not understand what Lemanski's connection was to Perkl, and that, in order to protect the privacy of its employees, the company would not discuss any employee matters with someone "who has not identified themselves as a legitimate representative of the employee." Crim also stated in the letter that she had instructed Creasy and Wittwer not to discuss the matter with anyone and that there would be no meeting on April 25.

Lemanski did not receive Crim's letter until April 14, 1997. Meanwhile, on April 10, 1997, he attempted to reach Crim by telephone to discuss Perkl's termination. Lemanski left two messages for Crim; she did not return his calls that day. The next day, April 11, 1997, Lemanski obtained the number for Dick Frank, defendant's chief executive officer. Lemanski called Frank and left a message; Frank returned the call within half an hour. Lemanski explained that he was calling about Perkl's termination and that he had not gotten any response from Creasy or the human resources department. Frank assured Lemanski that the company would investigate the matter.

Frank then spoke with Crim, who told him about Lemanski's letter of April 9, 1997, and her response of April 10, 1997, regarding the company's need to understand Lemanski's role in the situation before it discussed Perkl's employment with him. Frank viewed Crim's response as appropriate because he shared her concerns about Lemanski's connection to Perkl.

On April 14, 1997, Lemanski sent a letter to Frank in which he enclosed a copy of Wittwer's March 18, 1997, fax to Crim. Lemanski also provided information that clarified his relationship to Perkl. Crim attempted to contact Lemanski on April 17, 1997, but Lemanski did not return her calls. Lemanski testified that, by that time, attorney Monica Murphy was involved in the case on Perkl's behalf and he thought it was more appropriate for her to deal with the situation.

At trial, Creasy gave three reasons for firing Perkl: no position was available; the restaurant's sales were starting to decline and labor costs were high; and that, in failing to get the carpets cleaned before the restaurant opened, Perkl was not meeting Creasy's performance standards. Creasy denied that he fired Perkl because he was disabled.

Plaintiffs presented only one witness, Perkl's foster mother Linnel Thomas, in support of Perkl's claim for compensatory damages. Perkl has lived with Thomas, her husband and her two children for four years. Thomas testified that Perkl communicates with her by nodding yes or no in response to her questions or by pointing at pictures in his communication book. Thomas testified that Perkl was very excited and happy when he got the job at Chuck E. Cheese's. He showed Thomas and her family his uniform and jumped up and down so high that his head hit the ceiling. Thomas testified that she knew that Perkl was very happy working at Chuck E. Cheese's because he expressed that to her and because he would get up and ready for work in the morning on his own.

Thomas testified that Perkl came home early on the day he was terminated and went immediately to his room without communicating with anyone. She testified that, from his demeanor and body language, she could tell that something bad had happened to him; in her words, Perkl was "devastated." Thomas spoke with Wittwer and Lemanski that same day and learned about Perkl's termination. She testified that she then went in to talk to Perkl who indicated that someone at Chuck E. Cheese's had told him that he was being let go from his job. Thomas testified that from that day to the present, Perkl has been less attentive to his personal hygiene, fails to get up on his own in the morning, has less interest in participating in social activities or family activities and lost 11 pounds. She testified that Perkl's doctor has not diagnosed Perkl with depression and Perkl does not take any medication for depression. Thomas testified that, although Perkl subsequently obtained another job in the community, he did not express the same joy as when he got the job at Chuck E. Cheese's. According to Thomas, Perkl is still puzzled about why he got fired and worries that it will happen again.

CEC presented Dr. Hugh Johnston, a psychiatrist at the University of Wisconsin Medical School who testified as an expert on the issue of Perkl's emotional distress. Dr. Johnston had conducted an independent medical examination of Perkl prior to trial and had videotaped his interview with Perkl (although CEC did not play the video at trial). Dr. Johnston opined that although Perkl was able to experience emotional distress to the same degree as anyone else, Perkl was not currently suffering from any emotional distress whatsoever and it was unlikely that he had ever suffered any emotional distress as a result of having been fired from Chuck E. Cheese.

ANALYSIS

I. *Defendant's Rule 50 Motion for Judgment as a Matter of Law*

As the Court of Appeals for the Seventh Circuit has noted, attacking a jury verdict is a hard row to hoe. *Sheehan v. Donlen Corp.*, 173 F.3d 1039, 1043 [79 Fair Empl. Prac.

Cas. (BNA) 540] (7th Cir. 1999). The court's inquiry on a motion for judgment as a matter of law "is limited to whether the evidence presented, combined with all reasonable inferences permissibly drawn therefrom, is sufficient to support the verdict when viewed in the light most favorable to the party against whom the motion is directed." *Id.* (quoting *Emmel v. Coca-Cola Bottling Co. of Chicago*, 95 F.3d 627, 629 [72 Fair Empl. Prac. Cas. (BNA) 1811] (7th Cir. 1996) (internal citations omitted)). The jury verdict must stand unless defendant can show that no rational jury could have brought in a verdict against it. *EEOC v. G-K-G, Inc.*, 39 F.3d 740, 745 [66 Fair Empl. Prac. Cas. (BNA) 344] (7th Cir. 1994). CEC has not made that showing here.

A. Qualified Individual with a Disability

Before an employer can be held liable for discrimination in violation of the Americans with Disabilities Act, the employee must demonstrate that he was a "qualified individual with a disability." 42 U.S.C. § 12112(a). A "qualified individual with a disability" is defined in relevant part as: "an individual with a disability who, with or without reasonable accommodation, can perform the essential functions of the employment position that such individual holds or desires." 42 U.S.C. § 12111(9).

To make this showing, a plaintiff must meet two criteria. First, he must show that he satisfied the prerequisites of his position by possessing "the requisite skill, experience, education and other job-related requirements." *Ross v. Indiana State Teacher's Ass'n Insurance Trust*, 159 F.3d 1001, 1013 [8 Am. Disabilities Cas. (BNA) 1273] (7th Cir. 1998); *Weiler v. Household Finance Corp.*, 101 F.3d 519, 524 [6 Am. Disabilities Cas. (BNA) 106] (7th Cir. 1996); 29 C.F.R. app. § 1630.2(m). Second, he must establish that he can perform the "essential functions" of such a position with or without accommodation. *Id.*

The ADA defines an "essential function" as a "fundamental" job duty of the employment position the individual with a disability holds; it excludes functions that are "marginal." 29 C.F.R. § 1630.2(n). The essential functions inquiry includes an assessment of whether the employee was capable of performing his work in accordance with the employer's performance standards. *See Hedberg v. Indiana Bell Telephone Co.*, 47 F.3d 928, 934 [4 Am. Disabilities Cas. (BNA) 65] (7th Cir. 1995) (an "employer may fire the employee because he cannot perform his job adequately, i.e., he is not a 'qualified individual' within the meaning of the ADA"); 29 C.F.R. app. § 1630 (ADA is intended to enable disabled persons to compete in workforce according to same performance standards and requirements that employers expect of persons who are not disabled).

Pointing out that the court may not "second-guess" the employer's judgment in describing the essential requirements for the job, *see DePaoli v. Abbott Laboratories*, 140 F.3d 668, 674 [7 Am. Disabilities Cas. (BNA) 1828] (7th Cir. 1998), CEC contends that it is entitled to judgment as a matter of law because plaintiffs failed to prove that Perkl was meeting Creasy's bona fide performance expectations. CEC argues that Creasy presented unrebutted testimony that one of the essential functions of Perkl's job was to finish vacuuming before the restaurant opened and that he observed Perkl vacuuming after opening on three occasions.

However, the jury also heard Wittwer, a manager at the restaurant and Perkl's immediate supervisor, testify that Perkl performed his job well and that she could not recall any time when he was vacuuming after the restaurant had opened, nor did she recall a time that Creasy had spoken to her about Perkl's work. In addition, Kristin Thielig, one of Perkl's job coaches, testified that he performed his work satisfactorily on each of the six occasions that she accompanied him on the job. Thielig also testified that vacuuming was the first task Perkl would do when he arrived at work in the morning and that, when she was there, he never took two hours to finish vacuuming. Granted, Thielig's testimony is of limited weight because she did not accompany Perkl every day that he worked, but it bolsters Wittwer's testimony that Perkl was performing his job satisfactorily.

Plaintiffs also presented the deposition testimony of Stephanie Henry, a general manager for defendant, who testified that, before firing an employee for performance problems, a manager will typically give the employee a warning or some sort of notice that his performance is deficient before considering termination. It is undisputed that Perkl never received any warnings before his termination. In light of this testimony, the jury was entitled to conclude that Perkl could perform the essential functions of the job.

Moreover, even though Creasy's testimony that Perkl was vacuuming after opening on three occasions was not refuted directly, the jury was not required to believe it. *See Kasper v. Saint Mary of Nazareth Hospital*, 135 F.3d 1170, 1173 (7th Cir. 1998). It is clear from the jury's verdict that it did not find Creasy to be a credible witness. The outcome of this case depended largely on who won the swearing contest between Creasy and Wittwer. The jury's verdict demonstrates that it generally disbelieved Creasy's story; therefore, it could also have disbelieved him when he said that he observed Perkl vacuuming after the restaurant had opened.

Or perhaps the jury concluded that Creasy's asserted expectation that Perkl would have the vacuuming done before the restaurant opened was not bona fide, a conclusion that would have been easy to draw once the jury concluded that Creasy had in fact made a discriminatory remark about mentally retarded people. We can only speculate as to what the jury was thinking, but the point remains that under either scenario the evidence is sufficient to support the jury's conclusion that Perkl was a qualified individual with a disability.

B. Discrimination

CEC also contends that the evidence is insufficient to support the jury's finding that defendant terminated Perkl because of his disability. CEC argues that the unrefuted evidence shows that the reason Creasy fired Perkl was because another maintenance worker did not fit within the plan that Creasy had for the Madison restaurant, which was to implement a close-to-open policy and reassign Martin to solely custodial duties. Defendant points out that both Creasy and Fitch testified that Creasy had these goals for the restaurant before Perkl was hired.

Plaintiffs contend that they presented evidence from which the jury could conclude that Creasy's asserted reasons for terminating Perkl were a pretext for discrimination. As evidence that the close-to-open rationale was phony, plaintiffs point to memoranda that Creasy had written to Fitch in the weeks prior to Perkl's employment regarding items that needed to be cleaned or improved at the Madison restaurant and which contain no mention of implementing the "close-to-open" system. They also note that, even if the close-to-open system had been implemented, Perkl was not given the option of working in the evening. Plaintiffs also cite the testimony of defense witness Michael O'Leary, who replaced Fitch as general manager of the Madison restaurant. O'Leary testified that he allowed one of his employees to vacuum in the morning. Plaintiffs offer this as proof that the close-to-open system was never implemented. As for CEC's claim that Martin was performing Perkl's job duties, plaintiffs point out that Perkl was hired to replace Oliver, who had previously been doing maintenance chores; that Martin was a kitchen worker whose duties did not overlap with Perkl's; and that Martin did not begin to do any of Perkl's duties until after Perkl was fired.

It would be difficult to sustain the jury's verdict if plaintiffs' case rested solely on a pretext theory. Fitch, who was plaintiffs' witness, acknowledged that Creasy had spoken to her about implementing the close-to-open policy and about reassigning Martin's job duties before Perkl was hired. The fact that Martin was not performing Perkl's job duties at the time Perkl was hired does not refute Creasy's testimony regarding Martin, for Creasy did not testify that Martin was performing the same tasks as Perkl; he testified that he told the managers at the Madison restaurant that they *should* have Martin do more custodial duties instead of the kitchen prep tasks that he was doing. Creasy testified that the cooks could do their own preparation work. The reason Martin was not doing Perkl's duties at the time of Perkl's employment was because the managers at the restaurant did not follow Creasy's wishes; it does not refute Creasy's testimony that he believed Martin could have and should have been performing Perkl's job.

Plaintiffs are also on soft ground in the pretext department with respect to their attack on Creasy's close-to-open justification for firing Perkl. Contrary to plaintiffs' assertion, O'Leary testified that at the time he took over for Fitch as the general manager of the Madison restaurant, Creasy had begun to implement the close-to-open system. O'Leary testified that the close-to-open system is defendant's policy for all its restaurants and that he had no problem making the system work in the Madison restaurant. O'Leary testified that under the close-to-open system, the bathrooms and other areas of the restaurant were cleaned in the evening. The only exception was vacuuming, which O'Leary allowed to be done for an hour each morning by a disabled employee. O'Leary's testimony, which was unrebutted, supports the legitimacy of Creasy's expressed desire to implement the close-to-open system in the Madison restaurant.

On the other hand, Creasy may have undercut his own credibility on this point by providing too many questionable reasons for firing Perkl. At trial, Creasy testified that another reason he fired Perkl was because sales were starting to decline at the restaurant and the restaurant's labor costs were high. However, Wittwer, Fitch, and Henry, all former assistant managers for CEC, testified that they were not aware of a case in which CEC terminated an employee because of a decline in sales; rather, the usual practice was to cut back hours. CEC's regional vice president Spring also testified that he was not aware of any employee other than Perkl who was terminated for sales reasons. This evidence was sufficient to cast a doubt upon Creasy's "sales decline" justification; if the jury suspected Creasy was lying about one reason, it could reasonably conclude that he was lying about them all.

The heart of plaintiffs' case, however, was the direct evidence of discrimination, namely Creasy's alleged statement to Wittwer that she should fire Perkl because CEC did not hire "those kind of people." If the jury believed that Creasy made the statement, then it could reasonably infer that Creasy's decision to fire Perkl was motivated by discriminatory animus and not by his asserted management goals for the restaurant. Wittwer's testimony and the letter she faxed to Crim the next day provided evidence sufficient to allow the jury to conclude that Creasy made the statement. Moreover, Fitch testified that Creasy had made a similar statement about Oliver. The jury obviously believed Wittwer and may well have believed Fitch. Because there was a reasonable basis for the jury's verdict, it shall stand. *Knox v. State of Indiana*, 93 F.3d 1327, 1332 [71 Fair Empl. Prac. Cas. (BNA) 1519] (7th Cir. 1996).

CEC argues that Wittwer's recollection of Creasy's discriminatory statement is implausible because Creasy and Wittwer both testified that Perkl's disability is not obvious from his appearance, and it was undisputed that Creasy had not spoken to Perkl before he told Wittwer to fire him. However, Creasy's testimony at trial counters this assertion. Creasy testified that upon seeing Perkl, he asked Wittwer who he was and Wittwer explained that Perkl was autistic, mentally retarded and nonverbal and that she had just hired him to do maintenance. Also, Wittwer testified that Perkl was working with his job coach the first time Creasy saw him.

CEC also argues that Creasy's alleged statement cannot be viewed as evincing a discriminatory intent when both Wittwer and Fitch admitted on cross-examination that they could not be certain what Creasy meant by the statement and when neither asked Creasy to explain it. CEC made this same argument to the jury during closing argument, but the jury didn't buy it. Creasy denied making the statement, so the jury never heard him explain what he meant by it. CEC's decision to deny that Creasy ever made the statement while also arguing that Wittwer and Fitch didn't know what Creasy meant when he said it might have seemed like a necessary tactic at the time, but it also might have helped galvanize the jury for Perkl and against CEC. Once the jury concluded that Creasy had made the statement, it was up to the jury to infer from the circumstances in which the statement was made whether it was discriminatory and the extent to which the statement bore on Creasy's decision to fire Perkl.

Wittwer testified that when Creasy started talking about "those kind of people" he related an incident that had occurred in a California Chuck E. Cheese's restaurant that had involved a developmentally disabled person. From this, the jury could reasonably infer that by "those kind of people," Creasy was referring to the developmentally disabled. "[A] remark need not explicitly refer to the plaintiff's protected status ... for a reasonable jury to conclude that it is direct evidence of illegal motivation based on that status." *Sheehan*, 173 F.3d at 1044–45 (observing that reasonable jury could conclude that supervisor's statement to employee known to be pregnant that she was being fired so that she could "spend more time at home with her children" reflected unlawful motivations because "it invoked widely understood stereotypes the meaning of which is hard to mistake").

Moreover, even if the jury *might* have concluded rationally that Creasy's statement could be construed innocently, it was not *required* to do so. *See, e.g., Sheehan*, 173 F.3d at 1045 (rational jury need not have accepted defendant's explanation that plaintiff's supervisor was joking when she told plaintiff: "If you have another baby, I'll invite you to stay home"; "Oh, my God, she's pregnant again"; and, "Gina, you're not coming back after this baby."); *EEOC v. Century Broadcasting Corp.*, 957 F.2d 1446, 1457 [58 Fair Empl. Prac. Cas. (BNA) 696] (7th Cir. 1992) (supervisor's statements that radio station wanted "new young sound" would support conclusion of age discrimination, even though remarks might reasonably be subject to "innocent" interpretation).

CEC also argues that the three weeks that elapsed between the alleged remark and Perkl's termination removes any inference of discrimination. *See Kennedy v. Schoenberg, Fisher & Newman, Ltd.*, 140 F.3d 716, 723 [78 Fair Empl. Prac. Cas. (BNA) 346] (7th Cir.), *cert. denied* [525 U.S. 870], 119 S. Ct. 167 [81 Fair Empl. Prac. Cas. (BNA) 1472, 142 L. Ed. 2d 136] (1998) (to rise to level of direct evidence of discrimination, "isolated comments must be contemporaneous with the discharge or causally related to the discharge decision making process.") (quoting *Geier v. Medtronic, Inc.*, 99 F.3d 238, 242 [72 Fair Empl. Prac. Cas. (BNA) 249] (7th Cir. 1996)). I disagree. Three weeks is a relatively short time period between the remark and Perkl's termination. Moreover, Creasy's statement was causally related to Perkl's discharge: it was made at the restaurant, while Perkl was working, in the context of Creasy's disappointment with Wittwer that she had hired Perkl. The evidence was sufficient to support a nexus between the remark and Perkl's discharge. *Compare Kennedy*, 140 F.3d at 724 (supervisor's alleged comment to plaintiff that, "if you were my wife, I would not want you working after having children," did not support inference of discriminatory intent where comment was made at least five months before plaintiff's termination and occurred in casual setting unrelated to discussions regarding issues that led to plaintiff's dismissal); *Geier*, 99 F.3d at 242 (supervisor's isolated comments did not constitute direct evidence of pregnancy discrimination because they were made one year prior to plaintiff's termination and in setting unrelated to discussions of plaintiff's work performance); *McCarthy v. Kemper Life Ins. Companies*, 924 F.2d 683, 686–87 [55 Fair Empl. Prac. Cas. (BNA) 115] (7th Cir. 1991) (racial remarks made two years before plaintiff's discharge not probative of discrimination).

Because there was more than one conclusion that could be drawn from the evidence, CEC's motion for judgment as a matter of law shall be denied. *See Emmel*, 95 F.3d at 636 (motion for judgment as matter of law should be granted only when there can be but one conclusion from evidence); *Kasper*, 135 F.3d at 1173 ("When a case turns on credibility, neither side is entitled to judgment as a matter of law unless objective evidence shows that it would be unreasonable to believe a critical witness for one side").

C. Compensatory damages

CEC contends that Thomas's testimony is insufficient to support the jury's determination that Perkl was entitled to compensatory damages. Pointing to Thomas's testimony regarding Perkl's ability to communicate, CEC suggests that Perkl's failure to testify on his own behalf or to call a medical expert to corroborate Thomas's testimony regarding the emotional distress he suffered precludes any award of compensatory damages as a matter of law. CEC asserts that it is not aware of any case in the Seventh Circuit or elsewhere in which the court upheld an award of damages for emotional distress in a discrimination case when neither the plaintiff nor a doctor testified about the alleged damages. In fact, argues CEC, the Court of Appeals for the Seventh Circuit reviews critically even those cases in which the plaintiff testifies regarding his emotional distress when no corroborating evidence is offered. From this, CEC suggests that the least that a discrimination victim must do to prove emotional distress, at least in the Seventh Circuit, is to testify on his own behalf regarding any emotional distress that he allegedly suffered as a result of the discrimination.

It is true that, unlike cases involving physical injuries, a victim of discrimination is not presumed to have suffered emotional distress merely from the fact that discrimination occurred: a plaintiff must actually prove that he suffers from emotional distress and that the discrimination caused that distress. *United States v. Balistrieri*, 981 F.2d 916, 931 (7th Cir. 1992). It is also true that, in certain instances, an injured party's testimony about emotional distress may of itself support an award for nonpecuniary loss. *See Merriweather v. Family Dollar Stores of Ind., Inc.*, 103 F.3d 576, 580 [76 Fair Empl. Prac. Cas. (BNA) 1251] (7th Cir. 1996); *Avitia v. Metropolitan Club of Chicago*, 49 F.3d 1219, 1227–29 [2 Wage & Hour Cas. 2d (BNA) 993] (7th Cir. 1995). However, I disagree with CEC's claim that these cases impose some sort of bright-line, minimum quantum of proof requiring a plaintiff to testify on his own behalf in order to recover nonpecuniary damages.

Like CEC, I have not uncovered a case in which damages for emotional distress in a discrimination case were awarded in the absence of testimony from the injured plaintiff. However, in *Carey v. Piphus*, 435 U.S. 247, 55 L. Ed. 2d 252, 98 S. Ct. 1042 (1978), the Supreme Court expressed the general rule governing damages for emotional distress: "Although essentially subjective, genuine injury in this respect may be evidenced by one's conduct and observed by others. Juries must be guided by appropriate instructions, and an award of damages must be supported by competent evidence concerning the injury." *Id.* at 264 n.20. Having carefully reviewed *Merriweather*, *Avitia*, and other similar cases from the Seventh Circuit involving emotional distress claims, I conclude that Perkl's failure to testify does not bar him from recovering nonpecuniary damages. Although no case is directly on point — because in each case the plaintiff testified about emotional distress — I find nothing in these cases to suggest that a plaintiff *must* take the stand in order to recover such damages, so long as the evidence that is presented meets the competency standard of *Carey v. Piphus.*

Generally speaking, the most competent evidence of the emotional distress suffered by a plaintiff will come from the plaintiff himself, who is in the best position to describe the emotional pain he suffered and to link it to the discrimination. That may not always be the case, however, such as in a case like this where the plaintiff is mentally retarded and has a limited ability to communicate even simple concepts, much less an abstract, subjective concept like emotional distress.

As noted in *Carey*, evidence that a plaintiff suffered emotional distress may include the testimony of others who observed the plaintiff. Here, Perkl's foster mother of four years testified regarding negative changes in Perkl's demeanor and behavior after his termination. Defendant's expert, Dr. Johnston, agreed that evidence of changes in Perkl's behavior would be relevant to determining whether he suffered emotional distress. This testimony was sufficient to support the jury's conclusion that Perkl had suffered emotional distress as a result of losing his job at Chuck E. Cheese's.

Although some of Thomas's testimony regarding her understanding of the events surrounding Perkl's testimony was inconsistent with the evidence presented during the liability phase of the trial, that is not a reason to set aside the jury's award. CEC was free to expose this inconsistency during cross-examination, which it did, and in closing arguments, which it did not.

Clearly, the jury concluded that any inconsistencies between Thomas's testimony and the other evidence — including Dr. Johnston's opinion — were insignificant to the emotional distress question. Viewing the evidence in the light most favorable to the plaintiff, I cannot say that the jury's conclusion that Perkl suffered emotional distress was unreasonable.

This is as good a point as any to observe that CEC made a tactical decision during the damages phase not to call Perkl to the stand as an adverse witness, or to seek admission of his videotaped interview with Dr. Johnston. Clearly it was Perkl's burden to prove that he had suffered emotional distress, and CEC had no burden to disprove this contention. And perhaps CEC's tactical decision will ultimately prove correct if the court of appeals decides that Thomas's testimony just didn't get Perkl over the hump on compensatory damages.

But CEC had these options available to it in order to bolster Dr. Johnston's testimony and to let the jury get a closer look at Perkl and his demeanor so that the jury could assess the degree of emotional distress Perkl was experiencing now and had experienced in the past. If Dr. Johnston was correct, then Perkl's testimony, either live or taped, would not have supported his claim of emotional distress. Having foregone these evidentiary options, CEC is not in quite so strong a position to quibble over the persuasiveness of Thomas's unequivocal testimony. *Cf. Avitiano*, 49 F.3d at 1228 (even where defendant had no ability to refute a claim of emotional distress because it was so minimally supported as to defy rebuttal, it was proper for the jury to consider the claim).

A more difficult question is whether the evidence supports the amount of $70,000 that the jury awarded to Perkl for emotional distress. CEC contends that a remittitur of the amount of compensatory damages is warranted because the jury's award of $70,000 was not connected rationally to the evidence and is not comparable to awards made in similar cases. *See Riemer*, 148 F.3d 800, 808 [8 Am. Disabilities Cas. (BNA) 440] (7th Cir. 1998) (quoting *EEOC v. AIC Security Investigations, Inc.*, 55 F.3d 1276, 1285 [4 Am. Disabilities

Cas. (BNA) 693] (7th Cir. 1995)) (when reviewing a compensatory damages award, court must consider whether the award is "monstrously excessive," whether there is no rational connection between the award and the evidence and whether the award is roughly comparable to awards made in similar cases).

Before considering the merits of defendant's arguments, I must first address the EEOC's claim that CEC has waived its right to remittitur by failing to bring a motion for a new trial under Fed. R. Civ. P. 59(a). It is clear that CEC has not waived its right to request a new trial, for such a motion need not be filed until 10 days after judgment has been entered and judgment has not yet been entered in this case. Fed. R. Civ. P. 59(e). However, I agree with the EEOC that it is more appropriate to consider defendant's excessive damages claim in the context of a Rule 59 motion for a new trial, even though it may not be improper to consider it at this stage. *See Central Office Telephone, Inc. v. American Telegram & Telegraph Co.*, 108 F.3d 981, 993 (9th Cir. 1997), *rev'd on other grounds*, 524 U.S. 214, 141 L. Ed. 2d 222, 118 S. Ct. 1956 (1998) (court's reduction of damages on motion for judgment as matter of law did not appear to conflict with Seventh Amendment). That said, because I conclude that the damages awarded in this case were not excessive, I will address CEC's request for a reduced damages award at this juncture even though it may be premature.

CEC argues that the award is not connected rationally to the evidence because the evidence regarding Perkl's emotional distress consisted solely of Thomas's uncorroborated and conclusory testimony. CEC compares this case to *Avitia*, 49 F.3d 1219, a case in which the sole evidence of the plaintiff's emotional distress consisted of his answer to a single question in which his lawyer asked him how he felt when he was fired. Plaintiff responded that he felt like the Sears Tower was falling on top of him, that he was speechless, that he had cried and that he felt like he had been tossed like a "piece of garbage." He testified that "until now I can feel that." *Id.* at 1227. Finding it plausible that, after working for the same employer for 13 years plaintiff would have been deeply distressed by what he regarded as an unjust and unjustified discharge, the court ruled that some amount of damages was appropriate. *Id.* at 1229.

Noting that plaintiff found a replacement job within three months of his discharge, the court concluded that his brief testimony did not sufficiently prove such deep upset that would justify an award of $21,000. Accordingly, the court found that a remittitur of half the award ($10,500) was necessary. *Id.* at 1229–30. *See also Biggs v. Village of Dupo*, 892 F.2d 1298, 1304–05 (7th Cir. 1990) (finding claimant's "conclusory" testimony "that he was affected emotionally by being fired, and that he was concerned over 'the idea of my family going through it'" insufficient to sustain award for emotional distress); *Nekolny v. Painter*, 653 F.2d 1164, 1172–73 (7th Cir. 1981) (evidence of emotional distress offered by three different claimants was insufficient where one stated merely he was "very depressed," another that she was "a little despondent," and third that he was "completely humiliated").

In the instant case, Thomas provided specific testimony regarding objective, observable changes in Perkl's behavior before and after his termination from Chuck E. Cheese's. From Thomas's detailed descriptions of Perkl's behavior, the jury could rationally conclude that Perkl was severely hurt by losing his job. It was not necessary for plaintiffs to prove that Perkl understood that his firing was discriminatory in order to recover damages for emotional distress, so long as the evidence linked Perkl's mental anguish to defendant's wrongful termination. *See Riemer*, 148 F.3d at 808 (upholding award of $45,582 to ADA plaintiff for emotional distress and mental anguish where plaintiff testified that, due to employer's discriminatory reassignment, he was at home only on weekends, that his long absences led to frequent arguments with his wife, and that these problems caused him to feel "stressed out" because he felt there was nothing he could do to improve his home life other than quit his job).

Moreover, the jury was entitled to consider how much the job meant to Perkl when determining the appropriate amount of damages. *See EEOC v. AIC Security Investigations, Ltd.*, 55 F.3d 1276, 1286–87 [4 Am. Disabilities Cas. (BNA) 693] (7th Cir. 1995) (finding evidence sufficient to support jury's award of $50,000 to ADA plaintiff, noting that plaintiff almost never took vacations, often put his job before his family and plaintiff's job was one of the "major defining aspects of his life"). Thomas testified that Perkl literally jumped for joy and hit his head on the ceiling when he first told her family about his job at Chuck E. Cheese's, that he showed off his uniform proudly and that he was eager and ready to go to work every morning. She also testified that Perkl did not express the same joy when he obtained different jobs in the community after he was fired from Chuck E. Cheese's. The jury reasonably could have concluded — and, I infer, *did* conclude — that Perkl's distress over losing his job at Chuck E. Cheese's was greater than that suffered by the ordinary victim of a wrongful discharge. *Cf. AIC Security*, 55 F.3d at 1286 (noting that emotional burden on plaintiff, who was dying of cancer and who perceived himself as unable to provide adequately for his family, was "considerably greater" than that suffered by ordinary victim of wrongful discharge).

Of course, not all of the evidence supports the jury's award. Perkl worked at Chuck E. Cheese's for only three weeks, he has no dependents and, contrary to his assertions, he was not terminated in a humiliating or demeaning manner or subjected to such treatment when he worked at Chuck E. Cheese's. *See Balistreri*, 981 F.2d at 932 ("The more inherently degrading or humiliating the defendant's action is, the more reasonable it is to infer that a person would suffer humiliation or distress from that action"). Dr. Johnston testified that it was unlikely that Perkl had ever experienced any severe distress from his termination, although I infer that the jury gave no credence to Dr. Johnston's opinions.[1]

I must take all of the relevant circumstances into account to ensure that the emotional distress award is commensurate to the damage actually caused. *See Avitia*, 49 F.3d at 1229. Having done so, I decline to order a remittitur on the basis of lack of evidence. To most people, losing a minimum pay job cleaning toilets at a pizza franchise would be viewed as a minor inconvenience and nothing more. But for Perkl, it was much, much more. Through no fault of his own, Perkl's disabilities have rendered him unable to savor many of the joys and pleasures the world has to offer. There was uncontradicted evidence that the job at Chuck E. Cheese's was the be-all and end-all for Perkl. The jury was within its discretion to take this into account in awarding an amount significantly higher than it would have awarded the average Chuck E. Cheese "cast member" who lost such a job after three weeks of part time work.

Even so, CEC contends that $70,000 is out of line with other awards in the Seventh Circuit for emotional distress, noting that the highest awards in the circuit have been around $50,000. *See Riemer*, 148 F.3d at 809 (upholding award of $45,582 under ADA for emotional distress and inconvenience resulting from wrongful reassignment); *AIC*

---

1. While Dr. Johnston could have anticipated the possibility that the jury would reject his opinion as to the quantity and quality of Perkl's emotional distress, I doubt that any scientific professional could have anticipated the lambasting Dr. Johnston took in the local press, which distilled his opinion down to a sound byte and then pilloried him for his insensitivity.

Madison is a tough town in which to advocate unpopular positions; former Mayor Paul Soglin has likened it to sticking your tongue in a toaster.

Security, 55 F.3d at 1286 (upholding award of $50,000); *Fleming v. County of Kane*, 898 F.2d 553, 561–62 (7th Cir. 1990) (upholding award of $40,000 under 42 U.S.C. § 1983 for emotional distress resulting from wrongful termination); *Webb v. City of Chester*, 813 F.2d 824, 836–37 [43 Fair Empl. Prac. Cas. (BNA) 507] (7th Cir. 1987) (reviewing cases and concluding that damages for claims under 42 U.S.C. § 1983 resulting from illegitimate firings "ranged from a low of $500 to a high of over $50,000"); *Ramsey v. American Air Filter Co.*, 772 F.2d 1303, 1313 [38 Fair Empl. Prac. Cas. (BNA) 1612] (7th Cir. 1985) (holding that $35,000 was an appropriate award for emotional harm suffered as a result of discriminatory treatment and termination).

Admittedly, the $70,000 awarded in this case is on the high side, and I appreciate that this court must not be casual with other people's money. *See Avitia*, 49 F.3d at 1229. However, in affirming the award in *AIC Security*, the court observed that some of the awards in earlier cases had occurred several years ago; if adjusted to their current value, they would be "considerably greater" as a result of the changing value of money over time. *Id.*, 55 F.3d at 1286. Taking such a consideration into account, I conclude that the jury's award of $70,000 to Perkl is "roughly comparable" to awards made in similar cases.

D. Punitive Damages

Under the ADA and the Civil Rights Act of 1991, plaintiffs who prevail on a claim of intentional discrimination may recover punitive damages against an employer if the plaintiff demonstrates that the employer "engaged in a discriminatory practice or discriminatory practices with malice or with reckless indifference to the federally protected rights of an aggrieved individual." 42 U.S.C. § 1981a(b)(1). This standard requires the plaintiff to show more than merely intentional discrimination under the ADA. *Kolstad v. American Dental Association*, 527 U.S. 526, 119 S. Ct. 2118, 2124 [79 Fair Empl. Prac. Cas. (BNA) 1697, 144 L. Ed. 2d 494] (1999). However, the Supreme Court has rejected the conclusion that an additional showing of "egregious conduct" is required. Rather, the Court stated that "[t]he terms 'malice' and 'reckless' ultimately focus on the actor's state of mind." 119 S. Ct. at 2124. This state of mind requirement "pertain[s] to the employer's knowledge that it may be acting in violation of federal law, not its awareness that it is engaging in discrimination." *Id.* Although not required, "egregious or outrageous acts may serve as evidence supporting an inference of the requisite 'evil motive.'" *Id.* at 2126.

CEC contends that the evidence adduced at trial was insufficient to support the jury's conclusion that CEC acted with malice or reckless indifference to Perkl's federal rights. I disagree. As discussed previously, the jury acted within its prerogatives by concluding that Creasy intentionally discriminated against Perkl when he fired him. Because Creasy's conduct occurred during the scope of his employment as a district manager for CEC, the jury properly imputed Creasy's acts to CEC. Indeed, CEC ultimately stood by Creasy and declined to have the court instruct the jury on *Kolstad*'s "good faith" defense to the imposition of punitive damages; such an instruction would have allowed CEC to argue that Creasy had acted inconsistently with CEC's good faith efforts to prevent discrimination in the workplace. *See Kolstad*, 119 S. Ct. at 2129.

As noted previously, under *Kolstad*, plaintiffs did not need to show that the circumstances surrounding Perkl's termination were egregious; all that had to be shown was that Creasy terminated Perkl "in the face of a perceived risk that [his] actions [would] violate federal law." *Kolstad*, 119 S. Ct. at 2125. There was ample evidence adduced at trial to support a conclusion that Creasy was well aware of the ADA's prohibitions at the time he fired Perkl, including Creasy's testimony that defendant has a policy against discrimination and promotes the hiring of disabled individuals. Moreover, CEC did not contend that Creasy was unaware of the ADA or that he discriminated with the belief that such discrimination was lawful. *See id.* at 2125. Under these circumstances, the jury's determination that CEC was liable for punitive damages was proper.

Citing cases from the Seventh Circuit, CEC argues that plaintiffs needed to show something more, such as the involvement of upper management or that CEC had a pattern of flouting the law, in order to recover punitive damages. *See, e.g., Lindale v Tokheim Corp.,* 145 F.3d 953 [76 Fair Empl. Prac. Cas. (BNA) 1858] (7th Cir. 1998) (punitive damages may not be awarded in "garden-variety" disparate treatment case involving middle-level supervisor unless there are aggravating circumstances); *Tincher v. Wal-Mart Stores, Inc.,* 118 F.3d 1125, 1134 [74 Fair Empl. Prac. Cas. (BNA) 1503] (7th Cir. 1997) (employee's failure to show that employer acted egregiously in terminating her because of her religious beliefs precluded award of punitive damages). To the extent these cases suggest that there must be aggravating circumstances before punitive damages may be awarded, they appear to be invalidated by *Kolstad.* In any event, even if these authorities remain good law in light of *Kolstad,* I conclude that there was evidence of such factors in this case to support the jury's punitive damages award. Foremost was the lack of any response to Wittwer's fax from CEC's human resources department or from Spring, a fact from which the jury could choose to infer that CEC's human resources department and Creasy's boss cared little about Perkl's rights, or more generally, about preventing discrimination in the workplace. Even though Perkl had not actually been terminated at that time, the jury was entitled to view CEC's failure to investigate Wittwer's allegations as evidence that it did not care about what happened to Perkl, or about whether one of its managers was discriminating against disabled employees.

Moreover, there was evidence from which the jury could have concluded that CEC's post-termination investigation was equally sub-par. Wittwer testified that she spoke with Crim after Perkl's termination and reminded Crim about her March 18, 1997, fax regarding Creasy's "those kind of people" remark about Perkl; however, Crim indicated that she had never received Wittwer's fax. At trial, the evidence showed that Crim had in fact received Wittwer's fax. Nonetheless, Crim did not at that time or at any time ask Wittwer to explain in more detail the circumstances surrounding Creasy's alleged remarks. According to Wittwer, Crim told her not to speak with Lemanski and that there would be no meeting at the restaurant as Lemanski had requested. Wittwer also testified that Crim asked her questions about who Dave Lemanski was. From this, the jury could have inferred that Crim's purported reluctance to talk to Lemanski until after he had clarified in writing his relationship to Perkl was not worthy of credence, when she presumably had obtained or could have obtained this information from Wittwer. Granted, the jury could have concluded that CEC's response was slow and cautious but not obstructionist; but the jury obviously did *not* conclude this, and the jury was not *required* to conclude this.

Finally, at the time of trial, Creasy was still employed by CEC as a district manager and had not been disciplined. CEC had a reason for this: its CEO, Dick Frank, testified that he had trouble believing that Creasy had ever made the alleged remark about "those kind of people." But once the jury concluded that Creasy *had* made the remark, it would most likely conclude that CEC's failure to discipline Creasy flouted CEC's obligations to Perkl under the ADA. Given the size of the jury's award, I surmise that's exactly the conclusion that the jury drew. Viewing all of this evidence and the inferences therefrom in the light most favorable to plaintiff, I conclude that the evidence reasonably supports the jury's award of punitive damages.

A more difficult question is whether the amount of punitive damages awarded is excessive. When answering this question, the court looks to the amount of punitive damages remaining after reducing the jury's award to the statutory cap and subtracting any amount awarded for compensatory damages. *See, e.g.*, *AIC Security*, 55 F.3d at 1287; *Hennessy v. Penril Datacomm Networks, Inc.*, 69 F.3d 1344, 1356 [69 Fair Empl. Prac. Cas. (BNA) 398] (7th Cir. 1995). Applying that procedure in this case, the punitive damages award under scrutiny is $230,000.

This is less than 2% of what the jury deemed appropriate: the jury, acting without knowledge of the cap, awarded $13 million in punitive damages, which would be about 39% of one year's net income for CEC. With this as context, the following discussion has an air of artificiality to it. How can we realistically discuss where this award should fit on the 0 to $300,000 spectrum when $12,770,000 of the award has already been excised? The breathtaking magnitude of an eight-figure punitive damages award demonstrates that the jury wanted to send CEC a loud, clear message. Having worked with the jurors through the entire trial, I found them all to be attentive, intelligent, thoughtful, and rational. No evidence was introduced at trial that was inflammatory or unfairly prejudicial. I see no basis to conclude the jury ignored the evidence, disobeyed the court's instructions, acted with passion rather than reason, or otherwise abandoned its duty to provide a just verdict.[2]

This is not to say that the $13,000,000 verdict would necessarily stand if it were before the court, but it's not before the court: we've already had a de facto remittitur of 98.23% of the award. To argue over the fraction that remains could be viewed as denigrating the jury's very function in this trial. That being said, to end the analysis on this note would be to court reversal on appeal, so I will apply the case law to determine whether the remaining $230,000 in punitive damages should be reduced further still. I conclude that it should not.

In *BMW of North America, Inc. v. Gore*, 517 U.S. 559, 134 L. Ed. 2d 809, 116 S. Ct. 1589 (1996), the court identified three guideposts for evaluating the excessiveness of a punitive damages award: (1) the degree of reprehensibility of the defendant's conduct, (2) the proportion of punitive damages to compensatory damages, and (3) the relation of the damage award to other statutory remedies available to redress similar wrongful acts. *Id.* at 575–83. Although the court in *BMW* was concerned about "constitutional" reasonableness in light of due process considerations of fair notice, other courts, including the Seventh Circuit, appear to have relied upon *BMW* to analyze damage awards that do not necessarily implicate due process. *See, e.g.*, *Deters v. Equifax*, 202 F.3d 1262, 2000 WL 121273, *7 [81 Fair Empl. Prac. Cas. (BNA) 1577] (10th Cir. Feb. 1, 2000) (analyzing punitive damages awarded in sexual harassment claim in light of *BMW* factors); *Pavon v. Swift Transportation Co., Inc.*, 192 F.3d 902, 909–910 [80 Fair Empl. Prac. Cas. (BNA) 1557] (9th Cir. 1999) (utilizing *BMW* guideposts in race discrimination case); *Jonasson v. Lutheran Child and Family Servs.*, 115 F.3d 436, 441 [73 Fair Empl. Prac. Cas. (BNA) 1662] (7th Cir. 1997) (observing that district court committed no error in reviewing damage award in sexual harassment case pursuant to *BMW* guideposts); *Lawyer v. 84 Lumber Co.*, 991 F. Supp. 973, 976–77 [76 Fair Empl. Prac. Cas. (BNA) 832] (N.D. Ill. 1997) (utilizing *BMW* guideposts to evaluate reasonableness of punitive damages award in race discrimination case).

The punitive damages award in this case is within the second and third guideposts of *BMW*, which overlap somewhat. By virtue of the statutory cap, the ratio of punitive damages to compensatory damages is a little more than three to one; if back pay is counted

---

2. There was one instance where the EEOC defied my specific order and attempted to demonstrate that CEC's employee manual violated the ADA, but I struck the question and admonished the jury.

as part of the compensatory damages, the ratio is less than three to one. The Seventh Circuit has held this ratio is appropriate, or at least permissible, in most cases. *See, e.g., AIC Security*, 55 F.3d at 1287. As the court observed in *AIC Security*, "statutes routinely provide for double and treble damages awards to deter and punish." *Id.* For instance, the ADEA provides for double damages in cases of willful violations. 29 U.S.C. § 626(b).

The most difficult factor is the third guidepost, the degree of reprehensibility of defendant's conduct. CEC contends that an award at the statutory limit should be reserved only for the most egregious cases, and that this is not that type of case. In support of its claim, CEC relies on *Hennessy*, 69 F.3d 1344, a sex and pregnancy discrimination case in which the Court of Appeals for the Seventh Circuit stated that punitive damages awards in the amount of the statutory cap should be "reserved for egregious cases." *Id.* at 1355. The evidence showed that plaintiff's supervisor had propositioned plaintiff about a year before he became her boss; when he became her boss, he gave her a more negative evaluation than had plaintiff's previous supervisor; upon learning that plaintiff was pregnant, he expressed surprise, stating that he believed her to be a "career woman"; he sent critical memoranda about her to others at the company while at the same time reassured plaintiff "not to worry" about her probationary status; and the company's president did not want to hire women in the sales field because they get pregnant. *Id.* at 1354. The jury did not award any compensatory damages but awarded punitive damages of $300,000, which the trial court reduced to the statutory cap of $100,000. On review of the punitive damages award, the court found that the evidence was sufficient to support the jury's award of punitive damages but the case was not "so egregious that an award at 100 percent of what can legally be awarded against a company of [defendant's] size is appropriate." *Id.* at 1356. The court remanded the case to the trial court to determine what "smaller figure" of damages was appropriate.

It is questionable whether *Hennessy* is controlling authority in light of *Kolstad*, for it seems to conflict with *Kolstad's* holding that a showing of egregiousness is not required in order for a plaintiff to recover punitive damages. On the other hand, the opinion in *Kolstad* addresses only the circumstances under which punitive damages may be awarded; it does not foreclose CEC's contention that the amount of punitive damages awarded should approach the statutory cap only in the most egregious cases.

This case, which involved an isolated instance of discrimination by a single supervisor, is not at the "most egregious" end of the spectrum. I am nonetheless declining to reduce Perkl's damages recovery to an amount lower than the statutory cap, notwithstanding *Hennessy*. First, *Hennessy* is distinguishable in that the jury in that case did not award the plaintiff any compensatory damages and the punitive damages were therefore "100 percent" of the allowable statutory damages. In contrast, the jury awarded Perkl $70,000 in compensatory damages and therefore the entire award in this case does not consist solely of punitive damages. Here, the punitive damages award is only 77 percent of the total allowable award for a defendant of CEC's size.

Second, the degree of reprehensibility of CEC's conduct is only one of the factors to be considered in evaluating a punitive damages award. *See BMW, supra.* As noted previously, an award of punitive damages that is less than three times the amount of Perkl's compensatory damages is reasonable in light of the second and third guideposts of *BMW*. Moreover, the Seventh Circuit has stated that "[w]e will set aside a jury's award of punitive damages only if we are certain that it exceeds what is necessary to serve the objectives of deterrence and punishment." *AIC Security*, 55 F.3d at 1287 (citing *Bogan v. Stroud*, 958 F.2d 180, 185 (7th Cir. 1992)). A relevant consideration in determining whether a punitive damages award serves these objectives is the wealth of the corporation. *Id.; see also* H.R. No. 102-40(I), P.L. 102-166, *reprinted in* 1991 U.S.C.C.A.N. 2, 549, 611 (recognizing that juries may properly take defendant's financial standing into account when awarding damages under Civil Rights Act of 1991 in order to ensure effective deterrence). Assuming that a wealthy corporation and a corporation of lesser worth engage in the same type of misconduct, common sense dictates that it will take a larger punitive damages award to deter the wealthy corporation from future misconduct.

CEC had gross revenues of over $379 million and net profits of over $33 million. *Cf. AIC Security*, 55 F.3d at 1287 (sustaining punitive damages award of $150,000 where defendant employed over 300 employees and had gross yearly revenues of "several million" dollars). Although the size and to some extent the wealth of a defendant is taken into account by the statutory caps, it is not improper to consider the wealth of the defendant when evaluating whether a punitive damages award within the relevant provision is excessive. Given the size and wealth of the defendant in this case, I conclude that an award at the statutory limit does not exceed the bounds of reasonableness.

Finally, as noted at the outset of this discussion, the primary responsibility for deciding the appropriate amount of punitive damages rests with the jury. *AIC Security*, 55 F.3d at 1287. As two courts of appeals have concluded, "[n]othing in the language of [42 U.S.C. § 1981a] suggests that the cap on damages is intended to diminish the jury's role in assessing punitive damages or to alter the standard for judicial review of such awards." *Luciano v. Olsten Corp.*, 110 F.3d 210, 220–21 [73 Fair Empl. Prac. Cas. (BNA) 722] (2d Cir. 1997); *see also Deters*, 2000 WL 121273 at *7. With due respect to the Seventh Circuit's opinion in *Hennessy*, if a trial court must recalibrate the jury's award in every case by using the statutory cap as an endpoint, there would appear to be little point in allowing the jury to assess punitive damages.

Therefore, given the jury's view that CEC's conduct was egregious and that a significant amount of damages was required to punish it and to deter it and others from engaging in such discriminatory conduct in the future, in addition to the other factors just discussed, I decline to order a remittitur of the jury's award below the statutory cap.

E. Constitutionality of the Statutory Cap on Damages

Perkl devotes the last 1 1/2 pages of his brief to his contention that imposing a damages cap violates his right to equal protection. Perkl argues generally that the caps are unfair because they impose limits on the amount that a disabled individual can recover that do not apply to others. For example, Perkl argues, a successful race discrimination plaintiff may pursue remedies under 42 U.S.C. § 1981 that are not subject to any cap. Perkl also refers obliquely to the Seventh Amendment right to trial by jury, arguing that the caps limit the jury's ability to assess damages.

Perkl's argument is woefully underdeveloped. Engaging in an equal protection analysis of legislation is hardly a rote exercise. For starters, it requires identification of the standard of scrutiny to which the legislation is subject, an analysis that Perkl has not undertaken. Nor has he cited to a single case that might illuminate the legal underpinnings of his claim. Perkl's Seventh Amendment argument is no more than a passing reference.

The law of this circuit is unequivocal:

> We repeatedly have made clear that perfunctory and undeveloped arguments, and arguments that are unsupported by pertinent authority, are waived (even where those arguments raise constitutional issues). A party urging us to reverse a district court's judgment has an obligation to argue why we should reverse that judgment, and to cite appropriate authority to support that argument. "The premise of our adversarial system is that appellate courts do not sit as self-directed

boards of legal inquiry and research, but essentially as arbiters of legal questions presented and argued by the parties before them." *Carducci v. Regan*, 230 U.S. App. D.C. 80, 714 F.2d 171, 177 (D.C. Cir. 1983) (Scalia, J.). It is not this court's responsibility to research and construct the parties' arguments.

United States v. Lanzotti, 205 F.3d 951, 2000 WL 157484, *5 (7th Cir. 2000) (citations omitted). This reasoning applies with equal force to undeveloped arguments made at the district court level. Accordingly, Perkl has waived his constitutional challenge to the statutory caps.

That said, even if this court were to consider his arguments, they have little merit. Although there is limited authority on the constitutionality of Title VII's damages caps, the authority that exists favors constitutionality of the caps. *Means v. Shyam Corp.*, 44 F. Supp. 2d 129, 131–33 (D. N.H. 1999); *Passantino v. Johnson & Johnson Consumer Prods., Inc.*, 982 F. Supp. 786, 788 [77 Fair Empl. Prac. Cas. (BNA) 275] (W.D. Wash. 1997). In *Means*, the court reviewed the legislative history of the Civil Rights Act of 1991 and concluded that Congress' decision to treat employment discrimination victims differently than other tort victims was rationally related to Congress' interests in deterring frivolous suits and avoiding ruinous awards in certain employment discrimination actions. *Means*, 44 F. Supp. 2d at 132–33. Although *Means* is not on all fours with the instant case because the plaintiff was the victim of sexual harassment, the court's review of the legislative history and its conclusion that the statutory caps are rationally related to a valid legislative purpose appear sound.

If this court were to consider Perkl's claim on its merits, his chance of success would be slim. This goes for his Seventh Amendment claim as well. *See Davis v. Omitowoju*, 883 F.2d 1155, 1161–1165 (3rd Cir. 1989), (Reexamination Clause of Seventh Amendment does not impede federal court's post-verdict application of state statutory cap in diversity case); *Boyd v. Bulala*, 877 F.2d 1191, 1196 (4th Cir. 1989) (post-verdict application of state statutory cap in diversity case does not violate Seventh Amendment right of trial by jury); *Pierre v. Eastern Air Lines*, 152 F. Supp. 486 (D. N.J. 1957) (provisions of Warsaw Convention limiting recovery for negligence injuring passenger in international flight to sum of approximately $8,300 are not violative of constitutional guarantee of trial by jury).

In sum, there is no need to pursue this claim further. The cap stands.

II. *Plaintiffs' Motions for Injunctive and Other Equitable Relief*

The "powers, remedies, and procedures" of Title VII apply to the Americans with Disabilities Act according to 42 U.S.C. § 12117(a). Under Title VII, injunctive relief is authorized when the court finds that the defendant "has intentionally engaged in or is intentionally engaging in an unlawful employment practice…." 42 U.S.C. § 2000e-5(g). The court may enjoin further discrimination, and may order appropriate affirmative action, including equitable relief. 42 U.S.C. § 2000e-5(g)(1). Courts are given wide discretion to fashion a complete remedy, which may include injunctive relief, in order to make victims of employment discrimination whole. *See Albemarle Paper Co. v. Moody*, 422 U.S. 405, 421 [10 Fair Empl. Prac. Cas. (BNA) 1181, 45 L. Ed. 2d 280, 95 S. Ct. 2362] (1975).

Plaintiffs have asked this court to provide equitable relief by ordering that CEC:

1) Pay prejudgment interest on Perkl's back pay award;

2) Pay the sum of $9,523 to Perkl as front pay;

3) Provide ADA training to all of its managers, supervisors, trainers, recruiters and human resources personnel, with various attendant conditions;

4) Convene a formal meeting of its directors within 60 days and adopt a corporate resolution indicating that defendant is an equal opportunity employer and shall conduct its employment practices in accord with the ADA;

5) Create a written policy prohibiting disability discrimination, distribute a copy of it to all its employees within 60 days and post such policy in all of its restaurants;

6) Post a notice in all of its restaurants for three years informing its employees of this lawsuit and its outcome and further informing its employees that it may bring complaints of disability discrimination to the EEOC or to defendant's human resources department; and

7) Provide the EEOC and the Wisconsin Coalition for Advocacy with a report every six months for the next three years describing all complaints of disability discrimination made to its human resources department during the reporting period.

Plaintiffs also request the court to enter an injunction permanently enjoining defendant for three years from:

a) engaging in any employment practice that discriminates on the basis of disability or violating the ADA in any respect;

b) failing to promptly investigate and respond to any and all complaints of disability discrimination; and

c) asking applicants for employment about potential disabilities or handicaps; and

d) following its "Six Traits of a Winner" or "Six Traits of a Star" hiring policy.

I consider these requests in turn.

A. Interest on Back Pay

The parties have stipulated that Perkl should be awarded $9,657 in back pay and that he should be awarded prejudgment interest on that amount. However, the parties disagree as to the proper rate at which the interest should be calculated. CEC and the EEOC agree that the prejudgment interest should be calculated using a prime interest rate of 8.5 percent, but Perkl argues that I should apply an annual rate of 12 percent interest as is required by Wisconsin law. In federal cases, the court is to use the prime rate, compounded monthly, to calculate prejudgment interest. *See Partington v. Broyhill Furniture Industries, Inc.*, 999 F.2d 269, 274 [62 Fair Empl. Prac. Cas. (BNA) 534] (7th Cir. 1993). The amount should be calculated up to the date of the entry of judgment and should not stop at the date of the verdict, as defendant has proposed. I leave it to the parties to compute the proper interest in accordance with this order.

B. Reinstatement vs. Front Pay

Reinstatement is among the remedies that a court may order under Title VII. 42 U.S.C. § 2000e-5(g)(1). In cases where reinstatement is unavailable, front pay may be awarded as a substitute remedy. *Williams v. Pharmacia, Inc.*, 137 F.3d 944, 951–952 [76 Fair Empl. Prac. Cas. (BNA) 310] (7th Cir. 1998) (citing cases from other circuits with approval). Front pay has been described as "a monetary award equal to the gain [the plaintiff] would have obtained if reinstated." *Id.* (citing *Tobey v. Extel/JWP, Inc.*, 985 F.2d 330, 332 [61 Fair Empl. Prac. Cas. (BNA) 69] (7th Cir. 1993)).

Generally, front pay is awarded as a substitute remedy only when reinstatement is inappropriate, such as when "there [is] no position available or the employer-employee relationship [is] pervaded by hostility." *Id.* (citation omitted). The friction between employer and employee arising from the litigation process itself is an insufficient reason to deny reinstatement. *Hutchison v. Amateur Electronic Supply, Inc.*, 42 F.3d 1037, 1046 [66 Fair Empl. Prac. Cas. (BNA) 1275] (7th Cir. 1994). Whether reinstatement is an appropriate remedy is a fact-intensive inquiry that varies depending on the circumstances of each case.

An employee's refusal to accept a reasonable offer of reinstatement tolls the employer's liability for back pay and front pay. *Graefenhain v. Pabst Brewing Co.*, 870 F.2d 1198, 1203 [49 Fair Empl. Prac. Cas. (BNA) 829] (7th Cir. 1989). In determining whether the employee's refusal was reasonable, "the trial court must consider the circumstances under which the offer was made or rejected, including the terms of the offer and the reasons for refusal." *Id.* (quoting *Claiborne v. Illinois Central Railroad*, 583 F.2d 143, 153 [18 Fair Empl. Prac. Cas. (BNA) 536] (5th Cir. 1978)). "An offer of reinstatement tolls the accrual of damages only if it 'afford[s] the claimant virtually identical promotional opportunities, compensation, job responsibilities, working conditions and status.'" *Id.* (quoting *Rasimas v. Michigan Dep't of Mental Health*, 714 F.2d 614, 624 [32 Fair Empl. Prac. Cas. (BNA) 688] (6th Cir. 1983)).

CEC has offered to reinstate Perkl. When the instant motion went under advisement, the terms of CEC's offer were inked in an affidavit from William Gilow, the current general manager of the Chuck E. Cheese's restaurant in Madison, who averred that Perkl is welcome to work at the Madison restaurant at a rate comparable to other employees, and that Gilow "will work to accommodate his schedule and arrange for him to have four hours a day if that is what he desires." Dkt. # 215, Ex. B. Perkl and the EEOC responded that CEC's offer of reinstatement was inadequate because CEC had merely offered Perkl re-employment and did not offer to reinstate him to his former janitorial position and did not even identify any jobs that it was contemplating assigning to Perkl.

In a letter dated February 2, 2000, CEC clarified its offer, stating that if Perkl wants to return to Chuck E. Cheese in a maintenance capacity, CEC will make a maintenance position available at the Madison restaurant, and that Perkl may begin immediately or whenever he is ready to return. Dkt. # 234. CEC also stated that it will work with Perkl to accommodate him if he wants to try other duties at the restaurant.

Perhaps Perkl has already accepted CEC's offer. The offer is reasonable and there are no other factors militating against reinstatement. The offer is unconditional and provides Perkl the opportunity to return to what was described at trial as his "dream job" at a higher rate of pay. I disagree with Perkl's claim that he would be returning to a hostile environment if he returned to the Madison Chuck E. Cheese's restaurant. The key figure in the controversy, district manager Donald Creasy, is no longer assigned to the Madison restaurant and there is little if any evidence of any animosity by CEC towards Perkl or his job coaches. Perkl got along fine with most of the employees the last time he worked at CEC and there is no reason to think that this will change. As noted previously, the fact that Perkl was Chuck E. Cheese's opponent in this litigation is an insufficient reason to deny reinstatement. Because reinstatement is appropriate, Perkl's request for front pay will be denied.

C. Corporate Resolution & Certification of Court's Judgment

CEC has agreed that, within 60 days of this order, it will convene a formal meeting of its board of directors to adopt a corporate resolution reconfirming that is an equal opportunity employer and that its employment practices will be conducted in accord with the requirements of the ADA. CEC has agreed that it will communicate the resolution orally and in writing to all company managers, trainers and human resources personnel. Additionally, CEC has agreed to file an authenticated copy of the resolution with the Clerk of Court and to provide the EEOC with a copy. CEC further agrees that, upon compliance with each provision of this court's judgment, it will certify such compliance to the EEOC.

However, CEC objects to providing the Wisconsin Coalition for Advocacy ("WCA") with a copy of its corporate resolution or certification of compliance, on the ground that WCA is not a party to this lawsuit. WCA is a federally-funded advocacy and protection agency for persons with developmental disabilities; WCA also employs Monica Murphy, Perkl's attorney and guardian ad litem. As such, argue plaintiffs, WCA is well-suited to oversee CEC's compliance with the ADA. The EEOC argues that CEC's resistance to providing WCA with a copy of its corporate resolution makes little sense in light of the fact that CEC's shares are publicly traded and a copy of the resolution will be on file with the court. Rather, argues the EEOC, CEC's stance with respect to WCA evinces CEC's hostility towards the principles and purposes of WCA and suggests a lack of remorse.

The EEOC is overreacting. The WCA is not a party to this lawsuit. Although WCA is a public advocacy and protection agency and it no doubt had a public agenda when it first got involved in this case, WCA's ultimate role in *this* lawsuit was to represent Perkl's private interests. Even if it were proper for WCA to assume an oversight role, there is no need for double agency oversight of CEC in this case. WCA is not entitled to CEC's resolution or certification of CEC's compliance.

D. Proposed Training

Plaintiffs have asked that the court require CEC to provide training on the ADA under the following conditions: 1) all managers, supervisors, trainers, recruiters and human resource personnel receive the training; 2) the training be conducted by one or more outside trainers chosen by CEC; 3) the training be conducted on an annual basis for the next three years; 4) the training last a minimum of two hours each training session; 5) the EEOC and the WCA approve the selection of the outside consultant, be informed at least thirty days in advance of each training session and be provided with an outline of the training to be given and copies of all of the handouts; and 6) all costs associated with the training be paid by CEC.

CEC has agreed to perform this training, but requests certain modifications. First, CEC agrees to present the training to all its district managers, regional managers, trainers, recruiters and human resource personnel every year, and to present it to its store managers during the annual manager conferences. CEC notes that the annual conferences are mandatory for store managers except for those managers excused from attending for good cause. CEC asserts that it will provide these excused managers with the handouts from the ADA training.

The EEOC responds that, under CEC's proposal, a newly-hired or promoted store manager could be employed for several months without receiving ADA training, or, if excused for good cause, might never receive anything except the handouts. A better alternative, suggests the EEOC, would be to require CEC to provide videotaped training on the ADA to new store managers when they are hired in addition to providing it at the annual managers' meeting.

The EEOC's suggestion is a reasonable compromise between the plaintiffs' interest in ensuring that all of CEC's managers receive ADA training in a timely fashion and CEC's apparent concern about its ability to comply with an annual training requirement for its store managers. CEC already provides videotaped training to its new employees during orientation that covers sexual harassment. Requiring CEC also to provide ADA training to new managers at this time would not be unduly burdensome. Accordingly, I will order that individuals who are hired into positions as store managers who are not able to attend an annual manager conference within 45 days from the date of hire, and those managers who are excused from attending the annual manager conference, be required to receive specific training on the ADA within 45 days of the date on which they are hired or excused from the annual manager conference, whichever the case may be. CEC may choose the format for this training.

CEC agrees that a two-hour presentation on discrimination is appropriate, but contends that it should be a split session providing one hour of training about the ADA and another hour about race, gender, age and religious discrimination. CEC asserts that a two-hour presentation on the ADA alone is simply too long to present to hundreds of store managers. Plaintiffs respond that one hours' worth is insufficient to provide any meaningful training on the ADA, particularly "[g]iven the ignorance regarding the ADA and its requirements displayed during trial by all levels of Chuck E' Cheese's management …". EEOC's Reply Brief, Dkt. # 232 at 10.

I agree with CEC. Because the ADA's provisions governing discrimination in employment share many features with Title VII, one hour of training focusing on the special requirements of the ADA would be sufficient when combined with another hour of training covering other types of discrimination. In fact, I'll take it a step further: although this particular case was about the ADA, I hesitate to order CEC to give particular prominence to the ADA relative to other antidiscrimination laws that are equally important and with which CEC employees should be equally well versed. I will order that CEC provide two hours of annual training on antidiscrimination law which shall educate CEC employees as to the essential elements of the federal laws prohibiting discrimination on the basis of age, disability, gender, national origin, race, and religion.

Finally, for the reasons discussed previously, I am not requiring CEC to obtain the approval of its trainer from the WCA.

E. Written Policy Prohibiting Disability Discrimination

In accordance with plaintiffs' request, CEC has agreed to adopt within 60 days of this order a written policy prohibiting disability discrimination, which it will distribute to all its employees and managers. CEC will post a copy of the policy immediately after its adoption at all of its restaurants in a place where employee notices are customarily posted for six months, and will take reasonable steps to ensure that the policy is not obstructed by any other document, posting or paper. CEC avers that it will publish the policy in the next edition of its employee handbook, "Chuck E. Today," which it will distribute on an unspecified date during the calendar year 2000.

Unsatisfied, the EEOC responds that CEC has had ample time since the jury verdict to update its handbook and there is no reason for any further delay. It would have been helpful if CEC would have explained why it needs more than 60 days to update its handbook; on the other hand, CEC's agreement to distribute a copy of the policy to all of its employees and managers and to post notice of the new policy as soon as it is adopted indicates that CEC is not trying to avoid informing its employees of the policy. Accordingly, I will grant CEC's request in part and order that the updated handbook containing the new policy must be distributed by the time the six-month posting period expires, which would be no more than eight months from the date of this order.

F. Posting of Notice

Plaintiffs request that CEC be ordered to post a notice informing its employees of the outcome of this lawsuit, the relief ordered and the employee's right to bring any complaints of disability discrimination to CEC's human resources department or the EEOC. CEC objects to the notice as unnecessary in light of its agreement to adopt and disseminate a written policy against disability discrimination. CEC also points out that there is no evidence that Perkl or any other employee was hampered in his or her ability to bring a discrimination complaint.

I agree. Such a notice is overkill. As the EEOC itself points out, federal law already requires CEC to display a poster informing its employees of their rights under the federal anti-discrimination laws. 42 U.S.C. §2000e-10; 29 C.F.R. §1601.30. Moreover, CEC has agreed to adopt a policy against disability discrimination and to distribute it to all of its employees and to provide ADA training to its managers, supervisors, trainers, recruiters and human resources personnel.

In this respect, this case differs from *EEOC v. AIC Security Investigations, Ltd.*, 823 F. Supp. 571 [2 Am. Disabilities Cas. (BNA) 890] (N.D. Ill. 1993), *aff'd in part, rev'd in part on other grounds*, 55 F.3d 1276 [4 Am. Disabilities Cas. (BNA) 693] (7th Cir. 1995), a case in which the district court ordered the defendant to post a notice much like the one at issue here but did not order the company to provide ADA training or adopt any policy against discrimination. Moreover, the discriminatory termination decision in that case was made by the company's sole owner, whose testimony demonstrated lack of remorse and "a cynical attitude towards the judicial process as well as the purposes and intent of the [ADA]." *Id.*, 823 F. Supp. at 578. Where the owner, the discriminator, and the highest-ranking decision-maker at the company were one in the same and accountable to no one, it made sense to require the posting of the notice proposed by the EEOC. Here, however, where a publicly-held company, through its chief executive officer, has expressed remorse for its actions and has agreed to other injunctive measures designed to prevent future incidents of disability discrimination, the posting of such a notice is unnecessary.

G. Report of Complaints

The EEOC's proposed judgment contains a requirement that, every six months for the next three years, CEC shall provide the EEOC with all complaints of disability discrimination reported to CEC's human resources department. I am not inclined to require this because the substantial burden outweighs the marginal benefit. True, CEC screwed up its handling of Wittwer's faxed complaint in this case, but CEC is now painfully aware of the costs resulting from such mistakes and has committed to correcting its procedures to prevent similar problems in the future.

This is not a situation where there was an absence of institutional procedures for handling complaints, or a widespread pattern of neglect in implementing those procedures. Frank, the CEO, personally involved himself in Perkl's case when Lemanski telephoned him, although his subordinates ultimately appear to have dropped the ball. In any event, Frank took the stand at trial and promised to fix whatever was broken. I had no reason to doubt these averments at the time, and the jury's subsequent $13 million verdict undoubtedly has focused Frank's attention even more keenly on the task at hand. EEOC oversight of CEC's procedures is not necessary in this case.

H. Permanent Injunction

Plaintiffs request a permanent injunction restraining CEC from:

1) Engaging in any employment practice that discriminates on the basis of disability;

2) Violating the Americans with Disabilities Act in any and all respects;

3) Failing to promptly investigate and respond to any and all complaints of disability discrimination;

4) Asking applicants for employment about potential disabilities or handicaps; and

5) Following its "Six Traits of a Winner" or "Six Traits of a Star" hiring policy.

Defendant objects to all but the last request, averring that it has already abandoned the "six traits" policy.

Under Title VII, injunctive relief is not limited to those cases in which a pattern or practice of discrimination was shown but is authorized once the court finds that the defendant intentionally engaged in an unlawful employment practice. 42 U.S.C. § 2000e-5(g)(1); *EEOC v. Ilona of Hungary, Inc.*, 108 F.3d 1569, 1578 [73 Fair Empl. Prac. Cas. (BNA) 528] (7th Cir. 1997). Moreover, injunctive relief is appropriate even where there is no evidence of discrimination going beyond the particular claimant's case if circumstances suggest that discriminatory conduct could persist in the future. *Id.* at 1578–79.

As noted in the previous section, I conclude that the circumstances of this case indicate that CEC's discriminatory conduct is not likely to persist in the future. CEC has agreed to provide training to its employees, adopt a corporate policy against disability discrimination and to notify its employees of the policy. Moreover, CEC has suffered im-measurable damage to its reputation as a result of the publicity generated by this case and the jury's enormous award of punitive damages. Although CEC's investigation into Creasy's remarks and his termination of Perkl was lackluster, there was no evidence adduced at trial to suggest that CEC is a corporation that flouts its obligations or is unconcerned about complying with laws prohibiting discrimination. To the contrary, the evidence at trial demonstrated that CEC has a positive record for hiring disabled employees, including employees with developmental disabilities. Perkl's case appears to have been the exception, not the rule. The EEOC essentially conceded as much in a post trial interview, contending simply that CEC's record of hiring other disabled workers did not provide a sufficient defense to the charge that CEC discriminated against a particular employee. *Jury Awards $13 Million to Mentally Retarded Man...*, 35 Fair Employment Practices Reporter (BNA), No. 886 at 144 (Nov. 25, 1999).

In light of these factors, I find that Creasy's continued employment with the company is not by itself a sufficient reason to grant the injunction. Plaintiffs' request for an injunction will be denied.

As for plaintiffs' request that CEC be enjoined from asking applicants for employment about potential disabilities or handicaps, it is beyond the scope of this lawsuit. This was an unlawful termination case, not an unlawful hiring case. Plaintiffs' victory in this lawsuit does not grant the EEOC an unfettered license to correct any and all perceived evils on its list of CEC's alleged shortcomings. The equitable relief to which CEC has voluntarily agreed more than covers its bill in Perkl's case. Accordingly, this portion of plaintiff's requested injunction is also denied.

III. *Establishment of a Trust*

Perkl, through his guardian ad litem and attorney, asks this court to establish a sup-plemental or special needs trust for him and to order that the proceeds from this litigation be deposited in the trust. Perkl asserts that he receives Supplemental Security Income and Medical Assistance through the federal Medicaid program and benefits under the Community Integration Program, a state medical assistance waiver program. Perkl asserts that he uses these benefits to cover the cost of his supported employment and vocational programming, his transportation and his adult family home, and that he could lose his eligibility for these benefits as a result of the substantial sum of damages he will receive. CEC opposes this request for a variety of reasons.

In 1993, as part of the Omnibus Budget Reconciliation Act, Congress exempted the assets in what are known as "supplemental needs trusts" from those assets and resources that are counted for the purposes of determining an individual's eligibility for Medicaid assistance. Pub. L. 103-66, § 13611(b), *codified at* 42 U.S.C. § 1396p(d)(4)(A). "Supplemental needs trust" is the term commonly used to describe a trust that is established for the benefit of a disabled person and that is intended to supplement public benefits without increasing countable assets and resources so as to disqualify the individual from public benefits. *See* Jill S. Gilbert, *Using Trusts in Planning for Disabled Beneficiaries*, Wisconsin Lawyer (Feb. 1997); *Sullivan v. County of Suffolk*, 174 F.3d 282, 284 (2nd Cir. 1999).

Under the relevant federal statutory provision, disabled persons under the age of 65 remain eligible for ongoing Medicaid assistance in spite of funds held in a supplemental needs trust, so long as the trust contains a provision that provides that any funds remaining in the trust upon the death of the individual shall be used to pay back any Medicaid assistance paid on behalf of the individual. 42 U.S.C. § 1396p(d)(4)(A); *Norwest Bank of North Dakota, N.A. v. Doth*, 159 F.3d 328, 330 (8th Cir. 1998). In Wisconsin, the creation of such trusts is authorized by Wis. Stat. § 701.06(5m), which provides that a trust "that is established for the benefit of an individual who has a disability which has continued or can be expected to continue indefinitely, substantially impairs the individual from adequately providing for his or her own care or custody, and constitutes a substantial handicap to the afflicted individual" is exempt from claims for public support if the trust does not result in ineligibility for public assistance. Wis. Stat. § 701.06(5m); *see also* Wis. Stat. § 49.454(4).

Plaintiffs argue that this court has the inherent authority to order that Perkl's monetary award be deposited into a supplemental needs trust if it finds that it is in Perkl's best interests to do so. However, plaintiffs do not ask this court simply to order that the funds be deposited into a trust that already exists, but are asking the court to establish the trust. Recognizing that I may indeed have the authority to establish such a trust and that such a trust appears to be in Perkl's best interests, I am nonetheless declining to enter plaintiff-intervenor's proposed order. Under 42 U.S.C. § 1396p(d)(4)(A), Perkl's parent or guardian can establish such a trust.

To ensure that Perkl's eligibility for benefits is not unfairly compromised by the award in this case, I will order CEC to make a lump sum payment to Monica Murphy, as guardian ad litem for Donald Perkl. Murphy can retain the funds in her IOLTA account until such a trust has been established.

IV. Plaintiff-Intervenor's Attorney Fees and Costs

Perkl seeks an award of $97,714.50 in attorney fees and $24,275.19 in costs. The Americans with Disabilities Act provides for an award of reasonable attorneys fees, litigation expenses and costs to "the prevailing party, other than the United States." CEC has crafted some novel arguments challenging the fee request filed by plaintiff-intervenor's counsel, Monica Murphy. First, CEC argues that Murphy cannot recover for any time she expended on this lawsuit prior to the time that Murphy became Perkl's guardian ad litem in August 1999. I granted Murphy's request to become Perkl's guardian ad litem after the parties discovered that Alice Perkl, Perkl's mother and the initial intervening plaintiff, was mistaken in her belief that she was Perkl's guardian. CEC argues that Donald Perkl, not Alice Perkl, was the "prevailing party" and therefore Donald Perkl cannot recover fees for any work performed by Murphy in her capacity as Alice Perkl's attorney.

Second, CEC argues that Murphy cannot recover any fees that occurred *after* she became Perkl's guardian ad litem because she was acting as an attorney at the same time. According to CEC, Murphy "began to represent herself in the litigation," and, as such, was like a pro se litigant who may not recover fees in a civil rights action. *See Kay v. Ehrler*, 499 U.S. 432 [55 Fair Empl. Prac. Cas. (BNA) 737, 113 L. Ed. 2d 486, 111 S. Ct. 1435] (1991) (attorney who represents himself in successful civil rights action may not be awarded "a reasonable attorney's fee as part of the costs" under 42 U.S.C. § 1988).

CEC's arguments are nimble but unpersuasive. First, as Perkl argues, his interests and no one else's were at stake throughout this entire litigation. Alice Perkl never had a separate claim and was merely intervening on behalf of her son, whom she mistakenly believed was her ward. The fact that Alice Perkl was mistaken about her legal status was a technicality that had no material bearing on the manner in which Murphy litigated this case, which was always with an eye on Donald Perkl's interests.

CEC's second argument is also a nonstarter, for it relies on the faulty premise that, as guardian ad litem, Murphy was representing herself. To the contrary, Murphy was appointed to represent Perkl's best interests, not her own. *See* Fed. R. Civ. P. 17(c) (infant or incompetent person who does not have duly appointed representative may sue by a next friend or guardian ad litem). Donald Perkl was in the beginning, is now and ever shall be the real party in interest in this lawsuit. Moreover, it is not inappropriate for an individual to serve the dual roles of attorney and guardian ad litem for an incompetent client. *See, e.g., Kollsman v. Cohen*, 996 F.2d 702, 706 (4th Cir. 1993). A guardian ad litem's fees may be taxed as costs under Fed. R. Civ. P. 54(d), so long as those costs do not include services the guardian ad litem performed in her role as an attorney to the incompetent. *Id*. Time spent by the guardian ad litem in her role as an attorney are treated like any other attorney fees, and may be shifted in accordance with any applicable fee-shifting statute. *Id*.

Thus, although Murphy cannot obtain a double recovery, CEC is liable one way or another for the time she spent on this case, either as costs for her services as guardian ad litem under Fed. R. Civ. P. 54(d), or as attorney fees under 42 U.S.C. § 2000e-5.

This segues into Perkl's actual request. He seeks an award of attorney fees for 501.90 hours of work performed by Murphy at a rate of $175, and 73.20 hours of work performed by attorney Jodi Hanna at a rate of $135. Like Murphy, Hanna is a staff attorney for the Wisconsin Coalition for Advocacy. CEC objects to the fee request as unreasonable.

The court's determination of reasonableness is guided by the Supreme Court's decision in *Hensley v. Eckerhart*, 461 U.S. 424, [31 Fair Empl. Prac. Cas. (BNA) 1169, 76 L. Ed. 2d 40, 103 S. Ct. 1933] (1983). Under *Hensley*, "[t]he most useful starting point for determining the amount of a reasonable fee is the number of hours reasonably expended on the litigation multiplied by a reasonable hourly rate", 461 U.S. at 433, to arrive at what is commonly referred to as the "lodestar." The party seeking the fee award bears the burden of proving the reasonableness of the hours worked and the hourly rates claimed. *See Hensley*, 461 U.S. at 433, 103 S. Ct. 1933. Furthermore, the district court has an obligation to "exclude from this initial fee calculation hours that were not 'reasonably expended'" on the litigation. *Id*. at 434. The district court may then increase or reduce the modified lodestar amount by considering a variety of factors, *see id*. at 434–35, the most important of which is the "degree of success obtained." *Id*. at 436.

CEC raises specific objections to only a few line items on Murphy and Hanna's billing statements. First, it objects to time spent by Hanna accompanying Murphy to expert depositions at which the EEOC's attorneys were also present. This is a reasonable objection. It was unnecessary for both Murphy *and* Hanna to attend the depositions of Dr. Peter Blanck and Dr. Johnston, when the EEOC also sent its attorneys. Deducting the time spent on these activities results in a reduction of 15.2 hours. Similarly, given the fact that there were already three attorneys on board, it was unnecessary for Hanna to work on plaintiffs' *Daubert* motion to exclude Dr. Johnston's testimony. Deducting the time spent by Hanna on the motion results in an additional reduction of 4 hours.

Defendant next objects to time spent by Murphy and Hanna meeting with affiants who were intended to rebut Dr. Johnston's report. I agree that these fees must be disallowed because they were not reasonably expended on the litigation. As I explained when I disallowed the witnesses, the time to name such experts had long since passed. From Hanna's and Murphy's billing statements, I have computed the time spent relating to the preparation of these affidavits to be 4.5 hours by Hanna and 14.8 hours by Murphy. Perkl's fee request will be reduced accordingly. In addition, I am disallowing another 8 hours claimed by Hanna for "witness prep" on October 30 and 31, on the assumption that these unnamed witnesses were the putative rebuttal experts. If I have erred in my assumption, Perkl may provide documentation on this point when he submits the other supplementary materials I am requesting, as will be explained below.

I am rejecting CEC's objection to Murphy's time spent "correcting errors" she made regarding Perkl's guardianship status. The mistake was not Murphy's fault; she, like everyone else who was acquainted with Perkl, including Alice Perkl herself, believed that Alice Perkl was Donald's legal guardian. Indeed, much of the time spent by Murphy to rectify the situation was prompted by CEC, which smelled blood and moved in for the kill. The time Murphy spent on this issue is compensable.

Next, CEC argues generally that the fee request is unreasonable because most of the work on Perkl's behalf was performed by the two attorneys from the EEOC, Laurie Vasichek and Barbara Henderson, who each played a larger role than Murphy in preparing and trying this case. *See AIC Security*, 55 F.3d at 1288 (trial court acted within its discretion by reducing a fee request by 50% after finding that EEOC attorneys handled the bulk of the trial and the preparation of such). Perkl responds that CEC should count its blessings: but for the EEOC's assistance, Perkl's attorneys would have spent substantially more time and money on this case, greatly increasing the final cost to CEC.

Perkl has the better argument here, but CEC is entitled to some small measure of relief. From my constant interaction with the lawyers in this case during pretrial hearings and motions practice, and during the trial itself, I have no trouble concluding that Murphy pulled her own weight. The plaintiffs had clearly apportioned the work between the EEOC and Murphy, so that each had specific responsibilities both before and during trial.

That being said, although Murphy was by no means a fifth wheel on the truck, many of her briefs and arguments on behalf of Perkl essentially duplicated the EEOC's work. While I appreciate that lawyers don't like to leave any stone unturned and that no one likes to miss a motion hearing, in this case the EEOC's and Perkl's interests were essentially identical. It should have been clear to both sides by our third or fourth hearing that one lawyer could adequately brief and argue most of plaintiffs' joint positions on the disputes brought to the court's attention.

Additionally, I did not realize until the post trial motions that Perkl had a *fourth* lawyer, Ms. Hanna, working with Murphy at the WCA in addition to the EEOC's two attorneys, Ms. Henderson and Ms. Vasichek. This was overkill. Three attorneys were more than enough for this case, particularly where two of them had available the relatively vast resources of the EEOC.

Taking all of this into account, I conclude that a 5% discount, in the fashion of *AIC Security*, is appropriate here. I will cut 5% from the otherwise allowable fees claimed by Murphy and Hanna.

CEC's only remaining objection to Perkl's attorney fee request is that a number of the entries on Murphy's time log are vague, but CEC does not specifically identify any such entry. Counsel who oppose fees have a "responsibility to state objections with particularity and clarity." *Hutchison*, 42 F.3d at 1048 (quoting *Ohio-Sealy Mattress Mfg. Co. v. Sealy Inc.*, 776 F.2d 646, 664 (7th Cir. 1985)). I have independently reviewed the fee statements of Hanna and Murphy and find that the entries are sufficiently detailed to permit review.

Having completed that review, I conclude that with the exceptions noted above, the hours spent and the hourly rates requested are reasonable. Therefore, accounting for the deductions previously discussed, Perkl shall be awarded attorney fees for 487.1 hours of work performed by Monica Murphy at a rate of $175 and 41.5 hours of work performed by Jodi Hanna at a rate of $135, less five percent, for a total of $86,302.87.

As for costs, CEC objects to Perkl's claim for $2,000 for a "trust drafting fee" and to the $406.51 claim for two "trial team dinners." These objections are well-founded. Although, as noted previously, it is probably in Perkl's best interests to have the proceeds from this lawsuit deposited into a supplemental needs trust, Perkl can obtain this same relief without this court's intervention and without shifting this cost to CEC. Moreover, Murphy has not provided any documentation to show that a $2,000 flat fee for the drafting of the trust (which was drafted by a private attorney named Roy Froemming) is reasonable.

Not much needs to be said about the dinners, one of which cost nearly $350. They are not allowed. Murphy's decision to treat the team to a fancy meal gets put on her tab, not CEC's.

Beyond CEC's objections to Perkl's requested costs, I have my own concerns. Perkl seeks reimbursement for $15,333.38 in "expenses," which he supports with a ledger sheet from WCA. According to the ledger sheet, the $15,333.38 sum includes approximately $7,500 paid as salaries and wages to various WCA staff, including one staff attorney. It also includes approximately $400 in payroll taxes and benefits. Perkl has not explained why these items, which appear to be part of WCA's overhead costs, are reimbursable as part of the costs of this litigation. To the extent that some of these costs represent attorney fees, there is no indication that the unnamed staff attorneys actually worked on this case; moreover, there is no itemized account of the hours spent by these attorneys. Accordingly, unless Perkl can provide clarification, all of these "costs" will be denied.

The ledger raises other concerns. It shows $1,389.75 under the category of "Travel-Staff"; however, on a separate itemized list, Attachment B, Perkl requests reimbursement for travel expenses totaling $1,054. Additionally, the ledger reports $2,878 in expenses for legal computer and online research; however, Attachment B requests reimbursement for WESTLAW in the amount of $2,022.79. Finally, the ledger includes $3,167 for "litigation expenses," but Perkl fails to itemize or describe with any particularity the nature of such expenses.

I will give Perkl until March 28, 2000 to respond to my concerns about his requested costs. Perkl should explain the discrepancies between the WCA ledger sheet and Attachment B, provide a detailed itemization of the $3,167 requested for "litigation expenses" and, to the extent I am correct that some of the requested costs constitute WCA's overhead, provide authority in support of his claim that such expenses are allowable as costs. CEC shall have until that same date, March 28, 2000 to object to the reasonableness of the itemized fees and expenses requested by Perkl for work relating to post-judgment motions. I will reserve entering judgment on Perkl's request for attorney fees and costs until I have had the opportunity to consider the additional submissions from the parties.

ORDER

For the reasons discussed above, it is ORDERED that the motion of defendant CEC Entertainment, Inc., for judgment as a matter of law is DENIED.

It is FURTHER ORDERED that the motions of plaintiff Equal Employment Opportunity Commission and plaintiff-intervenor Donald Perkl for entry of judgment, equitable and injunctive relief and attorney fees and costs are GRANTED IN PART and DENIED IN PART as specifically detailed in the judgment of the court issued herewith.

Questions for Discussion

1. Can this case be reconciled with the *Hertz* case? What are the similarities and differences between the cases?

2. What do you think were the facts that really defined this decision?

3. What do you think of the statutory cap on damages under the ADA?

4. What did you think of the relief requested by the plaintiffs? What did you think of the court's decision regarding the different types of relief?

———————

The following is an article discussing sheltered workshops. What competing policies do you see? What do you think the best resolution to the situation is?

Sheltered Workshops Pay Equal to Sweatshops, Says Group

Dave Reynolds, *Inclusion Daily Express*

LAWRENCE, KS, Feb. 9, 2004 — Few people know that, here in the United States, thousands of employees perform menial tasks — day after day — for just pennies an hour. Their work goes by the name of "productivity" or "piece-work."

The practice is entirely legal and tax dollars have been supporting much of it since the 1930s. In fact, the U.S. Department of Defense, along with other federal, state and local agencies, provide and pay for much of the work through contracts with employment agencies.

The pay scale is called "sub-minimum wage," and the vast majority of those who receive these below-minimum wages are people with developmental disabilities.

Those who receive it are told they are lucky they to get that. Sub-minimum wage is determined by a formula which measures how fast the average trained, "non-disabled" worker would perform a certain job or assemble a certain item. Then the worker with a disability is timed doing the same work. The speed with which that person does the work, compared to the "non-disabled" or "100 percent" worker, determines how much the worker is paid. In theory, a person with a disability who works half as quickly would receive half the pay of a "normal" worker without a disability.

It's not uncommon for a person to work 40 hours for just a few bucks.

Some advocates in Kansas, which has the lowest state minimum wage in the U.S., want to see that change.

"It has become a sweatshop kind of thing," Greg Jones, director of advocacy for an independent living center in Lawrence, told the Journal-World. "We allow this stuff to happen right here under our very nose and we call it OK."

While the federal minimum wage is $5.15 per hour, the minimum wage varies from state to state, and even from city to city. The state of Washington's minimum wage — the highest in the country — is $7.16 an hour. The minimum wage in Kansas is just $2.65.

Jones and other critics point out that most of the work is overseen by employment service providers that contract with governments, non-profits and commercial businesses for the "piece-work." Most of those providers also receive government funds to serve their clients — the workers themselves.

"At the same time community service providers are selling the services of people with disabilities at a very substandard rate, these providers are bilking Medicaid waivers of Kansas a daily rate between $32 and $82.54 to keep these people out of their homes for five hours a day, as they perform demeaning tasks for little or no pay," Jones said.

Mr. Jones and others are supporting a bill in the Kansas legislature that would increase the state's minimum wage to $7.50 an hour by Jan. 1, 2007.

"Kansans with disabilities want to work and will work, but they need a fair and decent wage to make that transition attractive," said Shannon Jones, executive director of the Statewide Independent Living Council of Kansas.

Questions for Discussion

1. Does your state have sheltered workshops? What kind of pay scales do they have?

2. Do you think sheltered workshops are better than the alternatives, or do you think they are unacceptable? What is being done to phase out sheltered workshops in favor of regular jobs?

For Further Reading and Viewing

"Great Hires," retrieved May 15, 2012 at http://www.youtube.com/watch?v=VPXiIYz4uw0. A short video about supported employment.

"Hiring Disabled Workers is Good for Business, Companies Say," retrieved May 15, 2012 at http://www.freeenterprise.com/article/hiring-disabled-workers-is-good-for-business-companies-say.

Discussion 23

Disability Harassment and Misconduct at Work

Recommended Background Reading

Maddox v. University of Tennessee, 62 F.3d 843 (6th Cir. 1995).

Humphrey v. Memorial Hospitals Ass'n, 239 F.3d 1128 (9th Cir. 2001).

Readings for Class Discussion

How much harassment can a workplace dish out before it is liable? This case examines the connection between disability and constructive discharge.

McKelvey v. United States Army

450 Fed. Appx. 532 (6th Cir. 2011)

ON APPEAL FROM THE UNITED STATES DISTRICT COURT FOR THE EASTERN DISTRICT OF MICHIGAN

SUTTON, Circuit Judge.

James McKelvey, an Army veteran, lost his right hand and suffered other serious injuries trying to defuse a roadside bomb in Iraq. Without question, the Nation owes him considerable gratitude and respect for his service and sacrifice. The more difficult question is whether it also owes him nearly $4.4 million in front pay because, upon returning home and securing a civilian job with the Army, he faced a work environment so hostile that he had no realistic option but to quit. We conclude that the district court did not abuse its discretion in declining to order that remedy and instead requiring the Army to make good on reinstating McKelvey to a job with higher pay.

I.

McKelvey was attempting to defuse a roadside bomb in Iraq in February 2004 when it exploded. McKelvey lost his right hand in the incident and sustained injuries to his left hand, an eye and his lungs. After recovering at a base in Germany and at Walter Reed

Army Medical Center, McKelvey moved back to Michigan, and in February 2006 he accepted a position as an operations specialist first at Selfridge Air National Guard Base and eventually at the Detroit Arsenal. McKelvey's new job did not go well. Although his account of what transpired differs in some respects from the Secretary's, we must adopt his version of events at this stage of the litigation. *See Ford v. County of Grand Traverse*, 535 F.3d 483, 494 (6th Cir. 2008). In March or April 2006, one of McKelvey's coworkers told him that his supervisor, Alan Parks, was "going around telling everybody you're all f****d up from the war, you're a piece of s***, that he should have never hired you, you're worthless." R.102 at 63. Parks did not assign McKelvey enough work to keep him busy, even though his coworkers were "slammed" with work. R.102 at 66–67. And the work Parks did assign tended toward the menial. When one employee asked for help moving some boxes, Parks "kind of chuckled and he [said] ... 'I'll send McKelvey down. He's worthless anyhow. I'll send the cripple down to you.'" R.98 at 21.

Other colleagues were equally abusive. One, Maurice "Bud" Spaulding, got "pretty indignant" about the fact that McKelvey had a handicapped parking permit even though he was not mobility-impaired, and would sometimes call McKelvey "lefty" or "cripple." R.102 at 64–65. McKelvey initially took these comments to be poor attempts at humor, and he asked Parks's supervisor, Deputy Garrison Commander Robert Graves, to suggest to Parks and Spaulding that they tone it down.

That did not happen. Between June and August 2006, the comments "changed in tone. They didn't seem like they were meant to be a joke, and they were coming more frequently than previously." R.102 at 70. Parks and Spaulding regularly called McKelvey a "f***ing cripple" and became "agitated" with him for no apparent reason. R.102 at 70. Parks continued to assign McKelvey less work than his colleagues. In August or September, McKelvey complained again to Graves about his work environment, but nothing changed. Around this time, McKelvey also sought help from Mark Lewis, the office's Equal Employment Opportunity counselor, who encouraged him to file a formal complaint, but McKelvey preferred to try to work things out on his own. McKelvey began applying for other jobs in the federal government, but could not find any in Michigan.

Things got worse. By September and October, the workplace abuse "picked up a lot," with the taunting and name-calling becoming a weekly occurrence. R.102 at 80–81. At one point, Parks sought out McKelvey to ask him to destroy boxes of paper in an industrial shredder. McKelvey said he was not comfortable putting his only good hand into the machine, which prompted Parks to call him a "f***ing cripple" and walk out of the room. R.102 at 81–82. Parks also excluded McKelvey from a meeting about a planning exercise that McKelvey was supposed to coordinate. When McKelvey scheduled another appointment in December with Lewis to file a formal complaint, Lewis told him that "things aren't going to change" and suggested McKelvey find an attorney. R.102 at 86. After McKelvey filed his complaint, Parks and Spaulding "stopped calling [him] names," and Parks attempted to include McKelvey in more meetings. R.103 at 16–17.

In mid-January 2007, McKelvey met with Lieutenant Colonel Kevin Austin, the garrison commander. Austin told McKelvey, "[All] I can tell you is if you don't like the way you're being treated, go find another job." R.102 at 92. McKelvey was still trying to do just that. In late January he met with Jason Bradley, a human resources specialist, to see if a new civilian job with the Army had opened up, but the only ones available were an out-of-state position and a job as a security guard, which would have entailed taking a pay cut and carrying a gun, which McKelvey could not realistically do. When the Oakland County Sheriff's Department offered him a job, McKelvey took it and resigned his position at the armory on February 16, 2007. According to McKelvey, he would have left much sooner, but stayed because he "ha[d] a wife and child to take care of." R.103 at 31.

In October 2007, McKelvey sued the Secretary in district court, alleging the Army had discriminated against him based on his disability in violation of the Rehabilitation Act of 1973, 29 U.S.C. § 791 *et seq.* After discovery, the district court granted summary judgment to the Secretary on one of McKelvey's claims (failure to make reasonable accommodations), and McKelvey voluntarily dismissed a second claim (retaliation). His remaining claims (hostile work environment and constructive discharge) went to trial. The jury ruled for McKelvey on both claims, awarding no compensatory damages on the hostile-work-environment claim but $4,388,302 in front pay on the constructive-discharge claim. After trial, the Secretary filed motions under Federal Rules of Civil Procedure 50 and 59 for judgment as a matter of law on the constructive-discharge claim and to vacate the award of front pay. The district court granted both motions, holding that McKelvey had presented insufficient evidence to sustain a finding of constructive discharge and, in the alternative, that the proper remedy for a constructive discharge would be an order reinstating McKelvey to a job at the armory, not front pay.

II.

McKelvey first argues that the district court should not have granted the Secretary's motion for judgment as a matter of law on his constructive-discharge claim. We agree. Judgment as a matter of law is appropriate only when "reasonable minds could come to but one conclusion, in favor of the moving party." *Noble v. Brinker Int'l, Inc.*, 391 F.3d 715, 720 (6th Cir. 2004). Reasonable jurors could have gone either way on this issue.

An employer is liable for constructive discharge when it coerces an employee to leave by creating "working conditions so intolerable that a reasonable person would have felt compelled to resign." *Pa. State Police v. Suders*, 542 U.S. 129, 147 (2004). The test deliberately "sets a high bar," as the law generally expects employees to remain on the job while pursuing relief from harassment. *Porter v. Erie Foods, Int'l*, 576 F.3d 629, 639–40 (7th Cir. 2009). To determine whether that standard is met, we consider the following factors relevant, singly or in combination: (1) demotion; (2) reduction in salary; (3) reduction in job responsibilities; (4) reassignment to menial or degrading work; (5) reassignment to work under a younger supervisor; (6) badgering, harassment, or humiliation by the employer calculated to encourage the employee's resignation; or (7) offers of early retirement or continued employment on terms less favorable than the employee's former status. *Logan v. Denny's, Inc.*, 259 F.3d 558, 569 (6th Cir. 2001).

McKelvey presented evidence about three of these factors: a lack of job responsibilities relative to his colleagues, assignment to menial work and harassment. Yet the crux of this claim turns on the harassment McKelvey endured. McKelvey presented evidence that Parks and Spaulding repeatedly called him, among other derogatory things, "all f***ed up," "a piece of s***," "worthless," and "a f***ing cripple." R.98 at 21; R.102 at 63, 64–65, 70, 81–82. Repeated over the course of nine months, this constant stream of invective could sustain a finding of constructive discharge. It is "sever[e]" and "humiliating," not a collection of "mere offensive utterance[s]." *Goldmeier v. Allstate Ins. Co.*, 337 F.3d 629, 635 (6th Cir. 2003). It is the sort of "repeated … taunting" that goes beyond what one finds in even an ordinary hostile work environment. *Lifton v. Bd. of Educ. of Chicago*, 416 F.3d 571, 578 (7th Cir. 2005); *see also Chertkova v. Conn. Gen. Life Ins. Co.*, 92 F.3d 81, 89 (2d Cir. 1996). Other federal courts have determined that an employer may be held liable for constructive discharge when a supervisor repeatedly calls a disabled employee a "cripple." *See Vasquez v. Atrium, Inc.*, No. 00-1265PHXLOA, 2002 WL 818066, at *6 (D.

Ariz. Apr. 24, 2002); *Metzgar v. Lehigh Valley Hous. Auth.*, No. 98-CV-3304, 1999 WL 562756, at *1–3 (E.D. Pa. July 27, 1999).

But, the Secretary maintains, McKelvey waited too long to leave: even if this work environment became so intolerable that it effectively would have compelled a reasonable employee to resign, that is not what McKelvey did. He did not leave until February 2007, roughly two months later, by which time conditions had improved. This argument has some force. Plaintiffs alleging constructive discharge must establish that "the working environment *at the time of their resignation*" forced them to quit. *Baugham v. Battered Women, Inc.*, 211 F. App'x 432, 440 (6th Cir. 2006). The question is whether, given the totality of the circumstances, the employee left "within a reasonable time after last being the subject of discrimination." *Smith v. Bath Iron Works Corp.*, 943 F.2d 164, 167 (1st Cir. 1991). The premise of a constructive-discharge claim is that conditions were so bad that the plaintiff was essentially fired—and people who are fired do not remain on the job for an extended period of time.

Had McKelvey stayed at the armory much longer than he did, we would be reluctant to uphold a constructive-discharge finding. But a rational jury could have concluded that McKelvey was still constructively discharged when he resigned in February 2007. McKelvey resigned two months after filing his formal complaint, one month after meeting with Lieutenant Colonel Austin to air his grievances, and just two and a half weeks after meeting with Bradley to look for other jobs. This gap is too short for us to say as a matter of law that McKelvey's workplace was no longer intolerable, and is shorter than the gaps in cases where an employee's delay in leaving precluded a finding of constructive discharge. *See, e.g., Geisler v. Folsom*, 735 F.2d 991, 992–93, 996 (6th Cir. 1984) (employee did not resign until seven months after conditions had improved); *Coffey v. Chattanooga-Hamilton County Hosp. Auth.*, No. 98-6230, 1999 WL 824870, at *3 (6th Cir. Oct. 6, 1999) (same); *Poland v. Chertoff*, 494 F.3d 1174, 1185 (9th Cir. 2007) (eight months); *Jeanes v. Allied Life Ins. Co.*, 300 F.3d 938, 943 (8th Cir. 2002) (six months); *Bath Iron Works*, 943 F.2d at 167 (same); *Jett v. Dallas Indep. Sch. Dist.*, 798 F.2d 748, 755–56 (5th Cir. 1986) (five months), *aff'd in part and remanded in part on other grounds*, 491 U.S. 701 (1989). Other courts have permitted findings of constructive discharge despite time lapses as long as or longer than the one in this case. *See, e.g., Wallace v. City of San Diego*, 479 F.3d 616, 627 (9th Cir. 2007) (three months); *Williams v. W.G. Johnson & Son, Inc.*, No. 1:08-cv-00235, 2010 WL 5583107, at *6 (N.D. Fla. Nov. 15, 2010) (47 days).

Along with the relatively short interlude between the last discrete act of discrimination and McKelvey's departure, other facts supported the jury's verdict. There had been no change in personnel at the armory that would lead McKelvey to believe that the improved work environment was anything more than a temporary respite. This sets his case apart from others where an employee's delay in leaving proved fatal to a constructive-discharge claim. *See Geisler*, 735 F.2d at 996 (finding no constructive discharge in part because discriminatory supervisor had left before the plaintiff's resignation); *Steiner v. Showboat Operating Co.*, 25 F.3d 1459, 1465 (9th Cir. 1994) (same). And McKelvey had good reason to believe his work environment would not improve: Lewis, the employment counselor, had told him as much, and Austin, the garrison commander, had told McKelvey that if he didn't like the way he was being treated, his only option was to find another job. On this record, the jury permissibly concluded that, when McKelvey left the armory in February 2007, a reasonable person in his position would have felt forced to quit.

III.

But that does not mean McKelvey is entitled to nearly $4.4 million in front pay. After the verdict, the district court granted the Secretary's motion to alter or amend the judgment, and determined that an order of reinstatement (requiring the Secretary to give McKelvey his job back, with improved working conditions and higher pay), rather than front pay, was the appropriate remedy. "While the determination of the precise amount of an award of front pay is a jury question, the initial determination of the propriety of an award of front pay is a matter for the court." *Arban v. West Pub. Corp.*, 345 F.3d 390, 406 (6th Cir. 2003). We review a district court's decision to deny front pay for an abuse of discretion, *id.*, and conclude that there was none here.

McKelvey's argument that it was an abuse of discretion for the district court not to order front pay faces several hurdles. Reinstatement "is the presumptively favored equitable remedy" when an employee is improperly discharged, so it "should be granted in the ordinary case." *Roush v. KFC Nat'l Mgmt. Co.*, 10 F.3d 392, 398 (6th Cir. 1993). And while we have in the past *upheld* district courts' awards of front pay, McKelvey has cited no case (nor are we aware of any) in which this court has held that a district court abused its discretion in *declining* to award front pay.

McKelvey has not shown why this case should be the first. In deciding whether to award front pay, district courts must consider several factors, including "an employee's duty to mitigate, the availability of employment opportunities, the period within which one by reasonable efforts may be re-employed, the employee's work and life expectancy, [and] the discount tables to determine the present value of future damages." *Id.* at 399. These factors counsel against an award of front pay here. McKelvey can be reinstated to work at the armory quickly, without disrupting operations and without displacing another employee. In point of fact, the Army continues to offer him a position at the armory at a higher salary than he was earning before and under new supervisors. McKelvey's relatively young age, 38, likewise suggests that front pay is not appropriate, since it requires highly speculative projections about his earning capacity and about employment decisions decades into the future. *See Davis v. Combustion Eng'g, Inc.*, 742 F.2d 916, 923 (6th Cir. 1984).

McKelvey offers two main arguments in response. The first is that we have sometimes observed that even though reinstatement is the preferred remedy, "it is not appropriate where the plaintiff has found other work." *Arban*, 345 F.3d at 406. But McKelvey's new job does not on its own mean the district court abused its discretion in declining to award front pay. Even if a plaintiff chooses not to seek reinstatement, "she [is] not automatically entitled to an award of front pay." *Roush*, 10 F.3d at 398. The district court still must apply the relevant factors, which, we repeat, support the court's decision not to award front pay in this case.

That brings us to McKelvey's second argument: that reinstatement is inappropriate because returning to his old workplace would be too traumatic. But, as the district court noted, "such feelings likely exist in every discrimination case," and are mitigated here by the fact that, were McKelvey to return to the armory, his supervisors and four of his six co-workers would be new, with no connection to the harassment he suffered. R.87 at 9–10; *see also Farber v. Massillon Bd. of Educ.*, 917 F.2d 1391, 1396 (6th Cir. 1990) (grounds for not ordering reinstatement "must be more compelling than the personal preferences and distrusts which accompanied the initial discriminatory activity"). At the end of the day, McKelvey's arguments at best suggest it is possible the district court would not have abused its discretion had it ordered front pay. *See Fuhr v. School Dist. of Hazel Park*, 364 F.3d 753, 761 (6th Cir. 2004). They do not show that the district court abused its discretion by *not* ordering front pay.

IV.

For these reasons, we reverse the district court's grant of judgment as a matter of law to the Secretary on McKelvey's constructive-discharge claim, and we affirm the district court's alternative conclusion that reinstatement, rather than front pay, is the appropriate prospective remedy. We remand the case to the district court for proceedings consistent with this opinion, including a calculation of the amount McKelvey should receive in back pay for the period of time between his discharge and the Secretary's offer of reinstatement. *See Madden v. Chattanooga City Wide Serv. Dep't,* 549 F.3d 666, 678–79 (6th Cir. 2008); *Suggs v. ServiceMaster Educ. Food Mgmt.,* 72 F.3d 1228, 1233 (6th Cir. 1996).

* * *

Questions for Discussion

1. Why is reinstatement a problematic remedy in this type of case?

2. What did you think about whether the plaintiff should have been awarded front pay?

3. What do you think of constructive discharge as a legal claim? What other policy issues do you see in this case? How much unfriendly language should an employee be required to endure? What about a student?

When can an employer terminate an employee for alleged misconduct? This case tackles that question.

Gambini v. Total Renal Care Inc.

486 F.3d 1087 (9th Cir. 2007).

Before ALFRED T. GOODWIN and ALEX KOZINSKI, Circuit Judges, and MILTON I. SHADUR, Senior District Judge.

OPINION

Stephanie Gambini ("Gambini") appeals the district court's denial of her renewed motion, alternatively seeking judgment as a matter of law and a new trial, following a jury verdict in favor of her former employer Total Renal Care, Inc., d/b/a DaVita, Inc. ("DaVita"). Gambini originally brought suit in Pierce County Superior Court in Tacoma, Washington, charging that DaVita had discriminated against her in violation of the Washington Law Against Discrimination ("Washington Law," Wash. Rev.Code §§ 49.60.010 to 49.60.401) and the Family Medical Leave Act ("FMLA," 29 U.S.C. §§ 2601 to 2654). DaVita then timely removed the case to the United States District Court for the Western District of Washington, where DaVita prevailed at trial. We affirm as to Gambini's FMLA claim, but reverse and remand as to her Washington Law claim.

Background

In November 2000 Gambini began working as a contracts clerk at DaVita, a company that provides dialysis to renal patients. It is undisputed that Gambini had a history of health problems that predated her employment at DaVita. After several months at DaVita she began to experience depression and anxiety, and in April 2001 she experienced an emotional breakdown at work. Gambini eventually met with a mental health provider at the community health clinic and was told that her symptoms were consistent with bipolar disorder.

Upon returning to work several days later, Gambini informed her supervisor Robin Warren ("Warren") that she was seeking medical treatment for bipolar disorder. When Warren was promoted in May 2001, DaVita replaced her with Carrie Bratlie ("Bratlie"), who became Gambini's new direct supervisor. Gambini also told Bratlie that she was suffering from bipolar disorder and requested several accommodations. In addition, Gambini told her co-workers that she was experiencing mood swings, which she was addressing with medications, and asked that they not be personally offended if she was irritable or short with them. Gambini privately divulged to Bratlie that she was seeing a therapist and struggling with some medication issues.

Gambini's bipolar symptoms grew more severe in April 2002—she found herself increasingly irritable and easily distracted and began to have a hard time concentrating or assigning priorities as between her tasks. Gambini admitted to a fellow co-worker, who also suffered from bipolar disorder, that she was struggling to perform her job because of her symptoms. That co-worker recommended that Gambini seek treatment from psychiatric nurse practitioner Bobbie Fletcher ("Fletcher"), who confirmed Gambini's bipolar disorder based on Gambini's "short fuse," high energy, and propensity to exhibit anger and irritability.

During that period Gambini's current and former supervisors, Warren and Bratlie, convened to discuss Gambini's attitude and what they perceived as her poor job performance. Their meeting culminated in a decision to deliver a written performance improvement plan to Gambini at a later meeting that would include Bratlie, Gambini, and Gina Lovell ("Lovell"), the Supervisor of Payor Contracting. Accordingly, on July 11, 2002 Bratlie emailed Gambini, requesting that she come to Bratlie's office without indicating any specific purpose for the meeting.

Upon arriving at Bratlie's office Gambini was already agitated because she did not know the purpose of the meeting or why Lovell was in attendance. When Bratlie presented Gambini with the improvement plan, the first sentence of which stated, "[Gambini's] attitude and general disposition are no longer acceptable in the SPA department," Gambini began to cry. Reading the remainder of the document did not alleviate Gambini's symptoms—instead she found her face growing hot and felt a tightening feeling in her chest, as well as short ness of breath and shaking. When she had finished reading the performance plan, Gambini threw it across the desk and in a flourish of several profanities expressed her opinion that it was both unfair and unwarranted. Before slamming the door on her way out, Gambini hurled several choice profanities at Bratlie. There is a dispute about whether during her dramatic exit Gambini warned Lovell and Bratlie that they "will regret this," but Bratlie did observe Gambini kicking and throwing things at her cubicle after the meeting. Back at her cubicle, Gambini tried unsuccessfully to call Fletcher to tell her about how upset the meeting made her feel and about her ensuing suicidal thoughts.

Gambini reported for work the next morning and received a return phone call from Fletcher who, alarmed about Gambini's suicidal thoughts, told Gambini to go directly to the hospital. Gambini told Bratlie that she needed to check into the hospital, and Bratlie asked Gambini's boyfriend Todd DeMille ("DeMille") to pick her up and take her to the hospital. When DeMille arrived, Bratlie gave him FMLA forms for Gambini to fill out. She also signed the personnel change notice for Gambini's leave request. Gambini went straight from work to St. Joseph's Hospital, where her bipolar diagnosis was reconfirmed.

On July 16 DaVita provisionally approved Gambini's request for FMLA leave, subject to medical certification from her health care provider. Additionally, DaVita's human resource generalist Mara McLemore ("McLemore") began an investigation into the July

11 meeting with Gambini by interviewing Gambini's supervisors. During the investigation McLemore asked Bratlie via email about Gambini's expected date of return. During the same time frame several employees sent emails to McLemore stating concerns about Gambini's outburst. For example, one employee specifically requested that Gambini be prevented from returning to work.

On the following business day, McLemore and Bratlie called Gambini on her cell phone to tell her that her employment was being terminated. Three days later Gambini sent DaVita a letter stating that her behavior during the July 11 meeting was a consequence of her bipolar disorder and asking DaVita to reconsider its decision to terminate her. When DaVita refused to reconsider, Gambini filed this action, which proceeded to trial in December 2004.

At trial Gambini objected to the district court's substantive jury instructions on each of her legal claims. After a seven-day jury trial, the jury returned a verdict in favor of DaVita on all claims. After the trial court denied her post-trial alternative motion, Gambini filed a timely appeal to this court, challenging the giving of several jury instructions as well as the failure to give her proffered Instructions 11, 12, 21, 26, 27, 30 and 33.

Standard of Review

Where a challenge to jury instructions is at issue, "prejudicial error results when, looking to the instructions as a whole, the substance of the applicable law was not fairly and correctly covered" (*Swinton v. Potomac Corp.*, 270 F.3d 794, 802 (9th Cir.2001), quoting earlier caselaw (internal citations omitted)). Where an error is merely harmless, reversal is not required (*Wall Data Inc. v. Los Angeles County Sheriff's Dep't*, 447 F.3d 769, 784 (9th Cir.2006)). As *Wall Data Inc.* teaches, "We review a district court's formulation of civil jury instructions for an abuse of discretion," and "[w]e review de novo whether a jury instruction misstates the law." Here analysis reveals that the trial court committed reversible error when it refused to give Gambini's Prop. Instr. 26 because it failed "fairly and adequately" to cover the issues presented and to state the law correctly, and because it was ultimately misleading. And because the case will have to be retried, we address other questioned instructions as well.

Swinton, 270 F.3d at 805–06 (quoting earlier caselaw, with internal citations omitted) reconfirmed the standard for evaluating a verdict where the jury has been given an incorrect instruction:

> An error in instructing the jury in a civil case requires reversal unless the error is more probably than not harmless. While this standard of review is less stringent than review for harmless error in a criminal case, it is more stringent than review for sufficiency of the evidence in which we view the evidence in the light most favorable to the prevailing party. In reviewing a civil jury instruction for harmless error, the prevailing party is not entitled to have disputed factual questions resolved in his favor because the jury's verdict may have resulted from a misapprehension of law rather than from factual determinations in favor of the prevailing party.

That yardstick will be applied in our review of the actual and proposed jury instructions at issue on this appeal.

Instructions Regarding Gambini's Disparate Treatment Claim

Instruction as to Conduct Resulting from Disability

Gambini submitted and the trial court denied Prop. Instr. 26:

Conduct resulting from a disability is part of the disability and not a separate basis for termination.

We conclude (1) that the district court abused its discretion when it declined to give that instruction and (2) that such exclusion was not harmless error.

Most significantly, the Washington Supreme Court has itself enunciated the rule embodied in that instruction. On that score *Riehl v. Foodmaker, Inc.*, 152 Wash.2d 138, 94 P.3d 930, 938 (2004) (en banc) has stated explicitly:

Conduct resulting from the disability is part of the disability and not a separate basis for termination.

In so doing *Riehl* drew on our own holding *in Humphrey v. Memorial Hospitals Ass'n*, 239 F.3d 1128, 1139–40 (9th Cir.2001), which in the context of the Americans With Disabilities Act ("ADA") similarly articulated that "conduct resulting from a disability is considered part of the disability, rather than a separate basis for termination." As a practical result of that rule, where an employee demonstrates a causal link between the disability-produced conduct and the termination, a jury must be instructed that it may find that the employee was terminated on the impermissible basis of her disability.

Because of the Washington Supreme Court's express reliance on *Humphrey*, we may properly look to that decision in applying the Washington Law. Indeed, the facts in *Humphrey* are substantially analogous to Gambini's situation, and we held there (239 F.3d at 1140) that a jury could reasonably find the "requisite causal link between" the symptoms of obsessive compulsive disorder and Humphrey's inability to conform her behavior to her employer's expectations of punctuality and attendance, so that she was fired because of her disability.

As we have said, that principle has been adhered to by the Washington Supreme Court, again in analogous circumstances. In *Riehl*, 94 P.3d at 938 an employer terminated and refused to rehire an employee who began to suffer from depression and posttraumatic stress disorder ("PTSD") after approximately five years of service. Evidence that the employee's mental disability motivated the adverse employment action included his supervisor's written comments about the employee's personality change after his illness, which "suggest[ed] he was not the same as the 'old [Riehl]'" (id.). In light of his favorable performance reviews and promotions within the company (id. at 937), the supervisor's comments "suggest that [the employer's] decision to fire and/or not rehire Riehl was based on Riehl's personality difference, which may have been caused by his disability" (id. at 938). In fact, when Riehl was terminated he was told that the decision was not based on his performance (id. at 938).

Hence the court held that a jury could reasonably find that the mental disability was a "substantial factor" in the adverse employment actions, making the critical point that under Washington law a plaintiff need not prove that the impermissible basis for the adverse employment action—mental disability—was itself "the determining factor" (id. at 936). As *Mackay v. Acorn Custom Cabinetry, Inc.*, 127 Wash.2d 302, 898 P.2d 284, 288 (1995) (en banc) explains:

Washington's disdain for discrimination would be reduced to mere rhetoric if this court were to require proof that one of the attributes enumerated in [the antidiscrimination statute] was a "determining factor" in the employer's adverse employment decision.

Thus a decision motivated even in part by the disability is tainted and entitles a jury to find that an employer violated antidiscrimination laws.

Failure to have instructed the jury on that score plainly requires reversal. At trial Gambini presented evidence that DaVita signed an interrogatory response, which stated that one of the reasons it terminated Gambini was because she had "frightened her co-workers with her violent outbursts," as "documented by emails to the People Services Department." Her "violent outbursts," like Humphrey's obsessive rituals or Riehl's subdued personality, were arguably symptomatic of her bipolar disorder. Gambini had informed her supervisors about her condition and kept them apprised of her medication issues and the various accommodations she thought might reduce the chances of an outburst at work. When her temper erupted during the July 11 meeting, Gambini was in the throes of a medication change, which heightened the volatility of the mood swings that she and her health care providers were trying to get under control.

Under all the circumstances it was surely permissible for a properly instructed jury to review the events culminating in the July 11 meeting and Gambini's eventual termination and to conclude that it was her personality and not her work product that motivated DaVita. In fact, the very first sentence of the written performance improvement plan that Bratlie presented to Gambini on July 11 stated, "[Gambini's] attitude and general disposition are no longer acceptable in the SPA department." It is undisputed that people who suffer from bipolar disorder struggle to control their moods, which may vacillate wildly from deep depressions to wild frenzies of hypomania. Hence the record is replete with examples of how Gambini's bipolar disorder manifested itself through her irritability, her "short fuse" and her sometimes erratic emotions.

Accordingly the jury was entitled to infer reasonably that her "violent outburst" on July 11 was a consequence of her bipolar disorder, which the law protects as part and parcel of her disability. In those terms, if the law fails to protect the manifestations of her disability, there is no real protection in the law because it would protect the disabled in name only. As *School Board of Nassau County, Florida v. Arline*, 480 U.S. 273, 279, 107 S.Ct. 1123, 94 L.Ed.2d 307 (1987) instructs, the disability discrimination laws are necessary because Congress acknowledged that "the American people are simply unfamiliar with and insensitive to the difficulties confront[ing] individuals with handicaps."

Gambini was therefore entitled to have the jury instructed that if it found that her conduct at issue was caused by or was part of her disability, it could then find that one of the "substantial reasons" she was fired was her bipolar condition. Rejection of that instruction cannot be labeled a "harmless error" under the *Swinton* standard.

In its petition for rehearing, which has been joined by an amicus brief, DaVita argues that "[n]either the *Riehl* nor *Humphrey* Courts state or imply that arguably disabled employees are entitled to absolute protection regardless of their transgressions against the employer, let alone more protection than would be afforded a non-disabled employee for the same misconduct." But the law often does provide more protection for individuals with disabilities. Unlike other types of discrimination where identical treatment is the gold standard, identical treatment is often not equal treatment with respect to disability discrimination—see, e.g., *Holland v. Boeing Co.*, 90 Wash.2d 384, 583 P.2d 621, 623 (1978) (en banc) ("Identical treatment may be a source of discrimination in the case of the handicapped, whereas different treatment may eliminate discrimination against the handicapped and open the door to employment opportunities."). That's why the ADA and Washington Law require employers to make reasonable accommodations for disabilities.

That said, requiring Prop. Instr. 26 in no way provides employees with absolute protection from adverse employment actions based on disability-related conduct. Under the ADA a plaintiff must still establish that she is "an individual with a disability who, with or without reasonable accommodation, can perform the essential functions of the employment position that such individual holds or desires" (42 U.S.C. § 12111(8)). Washington Law has a similar provision: "[T]he prohibition against discrimination because of such disability shall not apply if the particular disability prevents the proper performance of the particular worker involved" (Wash. Rev.Code § 49.60.180(1)). Even if a plaintiff were to establish that she's qualified, under the ADA the defendant would still be entitled to raise a "business necessity" or "direct threat" defense against the discrimination claim (see 42 U.S.C. § 12113(a)-(b)). Defendant may also raise the defense that the proposed reasonable accommodation poses an undue burden (see id. § 12111(10)). Here DaVita would be able to raise any analogous defenses available to it under Washington Law. Our holding is thus far less controversial and sweeping than DaVita and the amici proclaim.

Failure To Offer Instruction on "Direct Threat" Defense

Another instruction refused by the district court was one on the "direct threat" doctrine, codified in the ADA's statutory text at 42 U.S.C. § 12111(3), which provides a defense to employers who terminate an otherwise protected employee because she poses a threat to the health or safety of other individuals in the workplace. In the ADA context *Morton v. United Parcel Service, Inc.*, 272 F.3d 1249, 1259 (9th Cir.2001) described the doctrine as "a very narrow permission to employers to exclude individuals with disabilities not for reasons related to performance of their jobs, but because their mere presence would endanger others with whom they work and whom they serve." Gambini tendered her Prop. Instr. 30 to address that subject.

To be sure, we have said in such cases as *Sharpe v. AT&T Co.*, 66 F.3d 1045, 1050 (9th Cir.1995), there citing *Clarke v. Shoreline Sch. Dist.*, 106 Wash.2d 102, 720 P.2d 793, 806 (1986):

Washington courts look to federal discrimination law to interpret their own discrimination law.

But because the Washington Law does not contain an explicit counterpart to the ADA's "direct threat" provision and its implementing regulation, the possible incorporation of such a defense into the state's jurisprudence poses an unresolved question.

Most importantly, that is a question that would be inappropriate for us to resolve in the context of this appeal. Even under the federal statutory scheme, that issue becomes relevant if the employer's defense puts the issue into play, and here DaVita did not do so. Instead the heart of DaVita's defense was its claim that Gambini "lost her job because of misconduct."

Because DaVita did not invoke the "direct threat" concept to justify its termination of Gambini, the latter cannot force it to defend a theory that it chose not to pursue. We cannot find the trial court committed error by refusing to include an instruction on this uninvoked defense.

FMLA Instructions

Instructions as to FMLA Interference

As for her FMLA interference claim, Gambini asserts that the trial court erroneously gave Instr. 21:

Plaintiff claims that defendant interfered with her FMLA rights. In order for the plaintiff to establish a violation of the FMLA, she must prove all of the following elements by a preponderance of the evidence:

(1) plaintiff was eligible for leave under the Family Medical Leave Act;

(2) plaintiff had a bipolar condition and it constituted a "serious health condition;"

(3) plaintiff gave defendant appropriate notice of her need to be absent from work; and

(4) Plaintiff's FMLA leave was a negative factor in defendant's decision to terminate her.

According to Gambini, she simply had to prove that DaVita interfered with her FMLA leave without also having to offer any proof about DaVita's motive. Prop. Instr. 11, which was refused by the trial court, spoke only in these terms:

She has the burden of proving by a preponderance of the evidence that (1) she was entitled to FMLA leave and (2) DaVita interfered with, restrained or denied her FMLA rights.

Under the FMLA "employees who must be absent from work because of their own illness, to care for family members who are ill, or to care for new babies" are provided job security (*Bachelder v. Am. W. Airlines, Inc.*, 259 F.3d 1112, 1119 (9th Cir.2001)). *Bachelder*, id., reminds us that "[t]he FMLA was the culmination of several years of negotiations in Congress to achieve a balance that reflected the needs of both employees and their employers," and the result is that "the Act entitles covered employees up to twelve weeks of leave each year for their own illnesses and guarantees them reinstatement after exercising their leave rights." Thus the statute "creates two interrelated, substantive employee rights: first, the employee has a right to use a certain amount of leave for protected reasons, and second, the employee has a right to return to his or her job or an equivalent job after using protected leave" (id. at 1122). Though the FMLA generally confers the right to reinstatement, an employer may still terminate an employee during her leave if the employer would have made the same decision had the employee not taken leave (29 U.S.C. §2614(a); 29 C.F.R. §825.216(a)(1)).

Gambini objects to Instr. 21 because she contends that it fails to instruct the jury accurately that DaVita had the burden of proving that her federally-protected leave was not a factor in its decision to terminate her employment. But DaVita offered unrefuted evidence that it would have terminated Gambini for her conduct regardless of whether she had taken her FMLA leave. There was no evidence whatever that DaVita would have retained Gambini had she remained at work after the July 11 altercation. *Mockler v. Multnomah County*, 140 F.3d 808, 812–13 (9th Cir.1998) held that a jury verdict could not be tainted by an erroneous instruction on a burden of proof where the prevailing party's evidence was undisputed. Similarly, any arguable error in instructing as to the burden of proof would be harmless indeed in light of DaVita's uncontroverted evidence that it would have fired Gambini for her conduct regardless of her leave status.

Instructions as to Failure To Reinstate After FMLA Leave of Absence

Gambini also takes issue with the trial court's failure to give this Prop. Instr. 12 as to DaVita's liability for failure to reinstate her after her period of FMLA leave:

If you find Ms. Gambini was entitled to FMLA leave, DaVita can avoid liability for interfering, denying or restraining her rights under the FMLA by not reinstating her to her former position after leave only if it can demonstrate, by a preponderance of the evidence, that it would have discharged Ms. Gambini for a lawful reason wholly unrelated to her FMLA leave.

Rejecting that proposal, the trial court instead issued Instr. 24: Under the FMLA, after the period of qualified leave expires, the employee generally is entitled to be reinstated to the former position or an equivalent one with the same benefits and terms of employment that existed before the employee took the leave. However the FMLA does not protect an employee from discipline or discharge for conduct that violates company policy.

As above, Gambini argues that Instr. 24 misstates the law because it does not require DaVita to prove that her discharge was not motivated by her FMLA leave. Again because of the uncontradicted evidence that DaVita terminated Gambini for conduct unrelated to her FMLA leave, any putative error as to allocating the burden of proof was harmless, and Wall Data Inc., 447 F.3d at 784 has held that reversal is not required where an error is merely harmless.

Instructions as to Obligation To Accommodate Disability

Finally, Gambini contends that the trial court instructed the jury erroneously on her failure-to-accommodate claim when this Instr. 15 was accepted over her objection:

An employer is not required to accommodate an employee's disability if it would impose an undue hardship on the operation of the employer's business. The defendant has the burden of proving that an accommodation would impose an undue hardship on the defendant.

As Gambini would have it, her Prop. Instrs. 21 and 33 should have gone to the jury instead:

Prop. Instr. 21: The law does not require an employee to prove that a particular form of accommodation is certain or even likely to be successful in order for it to be a reasonable accommodation. As long as a reasonable accommodation available to an employer could plausibly have enabled a disabled employee to adequately perform her job, the employer is liable for failing to attempt that accommodation.

Prop. Instr. 33: An employer is not required to accommodate an employee's disability if it would impose an undue hardship on the operation of the employer's business. DaVita has the burden of proving that an accommodation would impose an undue hardship.

An accommodation will be considered an undue hardship on the conduct of the employer's business only if the cost or difficulty is unreasonably high in view of the size of the employer's business, the value of the employee's work, whether the cost can be included in planned remodeling or maintenance, and the requirements of contracts.

We reject Gambini's contention. *Morton*, 272 F.3d at 1252 has expressed the operative rule in much the same way as Instr. 15: It is an act of discrimination to fail reasonably to accommodate a qualified employee with a disability unless the employer can show that such an accommodation would impose an undue hardship.

Thus the instruction tracked the nature of the defendant's burden precisely as the law directs.

Despite that direct parallel, Gambini argues that Instr. 15 is misleading on the premise that the jury would "have no way of knowing that a plaintiff need prove only that a proposed accommodation would plausibly have enabled her to perform the essential functions of her job." Gambini contends that the jury would apply the general instructions as to the preponderance of the evidence standard to Instr. 15 and falsely assume that Gambini had a duty to prove "any accommodation she proposed to DaVita was likely to succeed on a more probable than not basis."

We disagree. Instr. 15 not only states the law accurately but it nowhere says (or even implies) that Gambini had to make any quantum showing as to the likely success of her suggested accommodation. While Instr. 15 does not expressly define what constitutes "undue hardship," Prop. Instr. 33 does not offer particularly helpful guidance to the jury, because it generally tracks Wash. Admin. Code § 162-22-075, which sets forth the relevant factors for evaluating a claim of undue hardship where an employer will be subject to the costs of remodeling to accommodate physical disabilities. That statutory section is silent as to accommodations for mental disabilities and thus provides no aid to the evaluation of Gambini's claim. Moreover, on remand the jury will be instructed that Gambini's disability-related misconduct is protected under Washington Law, rendering Prop. Instr. 33 unnecessary. In sum, the failure to give either Prop. Instr. 21 or Prop. Instr. 33 cannot be labeled as error because the jury was specifically instructed that DaVita had the burden of proving that Gambini's requested reasonable accommodation created an undue hardship.

Conclusion

Because the only purported errors ascribed to the verdict on Gambini's FMLA claim relate to jury instructions and because we have rejected those challenges, we affirm as to that claim. But as to Gambini's claim under Washington Law, the error in instructing the jury that we have identified here infected the verdict on that claim, requiring a remand for a new trial rather than the entry of a judgment in Gambini's favor as a matter of law.

AFFIRMED in part and REVERSED and REMANDED in part.

* * *

Questions for Discussion

1. Did the court reach the right decision here? Is this the majority view in the circuits?

2. What did you think of the proposed jury instructions in this case?

3. How do the ADA and FMLA interact?

4. How much workplace misconduct should an employer be required to tolerate, even if the employee does have a disability?

For Further Reading

Leah C. Meyers, "Disability Harassment: How Far Should the ADA Follow in the Footsteps of Title VII?" 17 *BYU J. Pub. L.* 265 (2003).

Sharlott K. Thompson, "Hostile Work Environment: Disability Harassment Under the ADA." 73 *UMKC L. Rev.* 715 (2005).

"Man Sues in 27 cent dispute," retrieved May 15, 2012 at http://community.seattletimes. nwsource.com/archive/?date=19980502&slug=2748387. A person with a disability sues after being fired for "stealing" a salad from his workplace.

Simone Baribeau, "Dwarfs Better Off Tossed Than Jobless, Florida Republican Says," retrieved May 15, 2012 at http://mobile.bloomberg.com/news/2011-10-06/dwarfs-are-better-off-tossed-than-jobless-florida-republican-workman-says.

Discussion 24

Public Transit

Recommended Background Reading

42 USC 12132, 12141, and 12142.

Kinney v. Yerusalim, 9 F.3d 1067 (3d Cir. 1993).

_____

Readings for Class Discussion

The following is an article by John Hockenberry, a reporter with National Public Radio.

Public Transit

John Hockenberry

If you use a wheelchair and you want to avoid cabs in New York City, you can pay ten thousand dollars a year in parking to have your own car, or you can try your luck at public transit. There are para-transit wheelchair vans which are bookable far in advance. Then there is the subway, which has only twenty elevator sites out of hundreds of stations. And there are the buses.

The buses in New York have wheelchair lifts, and if the driver is carrying a key to operate the lift, and the lift has been serviced recently, and the bus is not too crowded, and the driver notices you at the stop, then you have a chance of getting a ride. Because the fare box is at the front of the bus and the lift is at the back, you can ask the driver to put your bus token into the box, but he will refuse. "I'm not allowed to touch your money," is what they usually say, and so they hand you instead a self-addressed stamped envelope for you to mail a check for a dollar and twenty-five cents to the Transit Authority. The bus lifts are better than nothing, except that when the city buys new buses, the new wheelchair lifts don't work properly, so there is a period of months when a bus drives up and the driver shrugs and says that his bus is one of the new ones. Only in New York would the new buses be the ones you can count on not to work.

Attempting to use public transit involves taking the risk of finding no bus lift, no elevator, or that either one will stop working while you are in the middle of using it. The transit system in New York sometimes seems like an elaborate trap for people in wheelchairs, lured like mice to cheese with promises of accessible transportation. For years, in New York's Herald Square there were signs indicating an accessible subway station with an elevator. The space for the elevator was a large cube covered with plywood that looked as though it hadn't been disturbed for years. Wheelchair signs had arrived before the elevators, but that didn't keep the Transit Authority from putting the signs up even when there was no way to use the train at this stop. While they waited for the long-delayed elevator, the Transit Authority covered the little wheelchair symbols on the Herald Square subway station to prevent confusion. Today the elevator works, but the signs for it are still covered. The Transit Authority apparently wants it to be a surprise.

When I returned to New York City from the Middle East in 1990, I lived in Brooklyn, just two blocks from the Carroll Street subway stop on the F train. It was not accessible, and as there appeared to be no plans to make it so, I didn't think much about the station. When I wanted to go into Manhattan I would take a taxi, or I would roll up Court Street to the walkway entrance to the Brooklyn Bridge and fly into the city on a ribbon of oak planks suspended from the bridge's webs of cable that appeared from my wheelchair to be woven into the sky itself. Looking down, I could see the East River through my wheelchair's spokes. Looking up, I saw the clouds through the spokes of the bridge. It was always an uncommon moment of physical integrity with the city that ended when I came to rest at the traffic light on Chambers Street, next to City Hall.

It was while rolling across the bridge one day that I remembered a promise to Donna, my physical therapist, how I would one day ride the rapid transit trains in Chicago. Pumping my arms up the incline of the bridge toward Manhattan and then coasting down the other side in 1990, I imagined that I would be able physically to accomplish everything I had theorized about the subway in Chicago in those first days of being a paraplegic back in 1976. In the Middle East I had climbed many stairways and hauled myself and the chair across many filthy floors on my way to interviews, apartments, and news conferences. I had also lost my fear of humiliation from living and working there. I was even intrigued with the idea of taking the train during the peak of rush hour when the greatest number of people of all kinds would be underground with me.

I would do it just the way I had told Donna back in the rehab hospital. But this time I would wire myself with a microphone and a miniature cassette machine to record everything that happened along the way. Testing my old theory might make a good commentary for an upcoming NPR radio program about inaccessibility. Between the Carol Street Station and City Hall there were stairs leading in and out of the stations as well as to transfer from one line to another inside the larger stations. To get to Brooklyn Bridge/City Hall, I would make two transfers, from the F to the A, then from the A to the 5, a total of nearly 150 stairs.

I rolled up to the Brooklyn Carroll Street stop on the F train carrying a rope, a backpack, and wired for sound. Like most of the other people on the train that morning I was on my way to work. Taking the subway was how most people crossed the East River, but it would have been hard to come up with a less practical way, short of swimming, for a paraplegic to cover the same distance. Fortunately I had the entire morning to kill. I was confident that I had the strength for it, and unless I ended up on the tracks, I felt sure that I could get out of any predicament I found myself in, but I was prepared for things to be more complicated. As usual, trouble would make the story more interesting.

The Carroll Street subway station has two staircases. One leads to the token booth, where the fare is paid by the turnstiles at the track entrance; the other one goes directly down to the tracks. Near the entrance is a newsstand. As I rolled to the top of the stairs, the man behind the counter watched me closely and the people standing around the newsstand stopped talking. I quickly climbed out of my chair and down onto the top step.

I folded my chair and tied the length of rope around it, attaching the end to my wrist. I moved down to the second step and began to lower the folded chair down the steps to the bottom. It took just a moment. Then, one at a time, I descended the first flight of stairs with my backpack and seat cushion in my lap until I reached a foul-smelling landing below street level. I was on my way. I looked up. The people at the newsstand who had been peering sheepishly down at me looked away. All around me, crowds of commuters with briefcases and headphones walked by, stepping around me without breaking stride. If I had worried about anything associated with this venture it was that I would just be in the way, but I was invisible.

I slid across the floor to the next flight of stairs, and the commuters arriving at the station now came upon me suddenly from around a corner. Still, they expressed no surprise and neatly moved over to form an orderly lane on the side of the landing opposite me as I lowered my chair once again to the bottom of the stairs where the token booth was.

With an elastic cord around my legs to keep them together and more easily moved (an innovation I hadn't thought of back in rehab), I continued down the stairs, two steps at a time, reaching the chair at the bottom of the steps. I stood it up, unfolded it, and did a two-armed, from-the-floor lift back onto the seat. My head rose out of the sea of commuter legs, and I took my place in the subway token line.

"You know, you get half-price," the tinny voice through the bullet-proof glass told me, as though this were compensation for the slight inconvenience of having no ramp or elevator. There next to his piles of tokens the operator had a stack of official half-price certificates for the disabled users. He seemed thrilled to have a chance to use them. "No thanks, the tokens are fine." I bought two, rolled through the rickety gate next to the turnstiles and to the head of the next set of stairs. I could hear the trains rumbling below.

I got down on the floor again, and began lowering the chair. I realized that getting the chair back up again was not going to be as simple as this lowering maneuver. Most of my old theory about riding the trains in Chicago had pertained to getting up to the tracks, because the Chicago trains are elevated. Down was going well, as I expected, but up might be more difficult.

Around me walked the stream of oblivious commuters. Underneath their feet, the paper cups and straws and various other bits of refuse they dropped were too soiled by black subway filth to be recognizable as having any connection at all to their world above. Down on the subway floor they seemed evil, straws that could only have hung from diseased lips, plastic spoons that could never have carried anything edible. Horrid puddles of liquid were swirled with chemical colors, sinister black mirrors in which the bottoms of briefcases sailed safely overhead like rectangular airships. I was freshly showered, with clean white gloves and black jeans, but in the reflection of one of these puddles I too looked as foul and discarded as the soda straws and crack vials. I looked up at the people walking by, stepping around me, or watching me in their peripheral vision. By virtue of the fact that my body and clothes were in contact with places they feared to touch, they saw and feared me much as they might fear sudden assault by a mugger. I was just like the refuse, irretrievable, present only as a creature dwelling on the rusty edge of a dark drain. By stepping around me as I slid, two steps at a time down toward the tracks, they created a quarantined space, just for me, where even the air seemed depraved.

I rolled to the platform to wait for the train with the other commuters. I could make eye contact again. Some of the faces betrayed that they had seen me on the stairs by showing relief that I had not been stuck, or worse, living there. The details they were too afraid to glean back there by pausing to investigate, they were happy to take now as a happy ending which got them off the hook. They had been curious as long as they didn't have to act on what they learned. As long as they didn't have to act, they could stare.

I had a speech all prepared for the moment anyone asked if I needed help. I felt a twinge of satisfaction over having made it to the tracks without having to give it. My old theory, concocted while on painkillers in an intensive care unit in Pennsylvania, had predicted that I would make it. I was happy to do it all by myself. Yet I hadn't counted on being completely ignored. New York was such a far cry from the streets of Jerusalem, where Israelis would come right up to ask you how much you wanted for your wheelchair, and Arabs would insist on carrying you up a flight of stairs whether you wanted to go or not.

I took the F train to the Jay Street-Borough Hall station. The train ride was exhilarating. I had a dumb smile on my face as I realized that the last subway ride I had taken was in February 1976, when I went from Garfield on the Dan Ryan train in Chicago to Irving Park on the north side to visit a friend. The Chicago trains had a green ambient light from the reflection off the industrial paint on all the interior surfaces. The New York trains were full of yellows and oranges. But the motion and the sound of the train was familiar. The experience was completely new and just as completely nostalgic.

The Jay Street station was a warren of tunnels and passageways with steps in all of them. To get to the A train track for the ride into Manhattan I had to descend a flight of stairs to the sub-platform; then, depending on which direction I was going, ascend another stairway to the tracks. Because it was a junction for three subway lines, there was a mix of people rushing through the station in all directions, rather than the clockwork march of white office-garbed commuters from Brooklyn Heights and Carroll Gardens on their way to midtown.

I rolled to the stairs and descended into a corridor crowded with people coming and going. "Are you all right?" A black lady stopped next to my chair. She was pushing a stroller with two seats, one occupied by a little girl, the other empty, presumably for the little boy with her, who was standing next to a larger boy. They all beamed at me, waiting for further orders from Mom.

"I'm going down to the A train," I said. "I think I'll be all right, if I don't get lost."

"You sure you want to go down there?" She sounded as if she was warning me about something. "I know all the elevators from having these kids," she said. "They ain't no elevator on the A train, young man." Her kids looked down at me as if to say, "What can you say to that?" I told her that I knew there was no elevator, and that I was just seeing how many stairs there were between Carroll Street and City Hall. "I can tell you, they's lots of stairs." As she said good-bye, her oldest boy looked down at me as if he understood exactly what I was doing, and why. "Elevators smell nasty," he said.

Once on the A train I discovered at the next stop that I had chosen the wrong side of the platform and was going away from Manhattan. If my physical therapist, Donna, could look in on me at this point in my trip, she might be a bit more doubtful about my theory than I was. By taking the wrong train I had probably doubled the number of stairs I would have to climb.

I wondered if I could find a station not too far out where the platform was between the tracks, so that all I had to do was roll to the other side and catch the inbound train. The subway maps gave no indication of this, and the commuters I attempted to query on the subject simply ignored me or seemed not to understand what I was asking. Another black lady with a large shopping bag and a brown polka-dotted dress sitting in a seat across the car volunteered that Franklin Avenue was the station I wanted. "No stairs there," she said.

At this point, every white person I had encountered had ignored me or pretended that I didn't exist, while every black person who came upon me had offered to help without being asked. I looked at the tape recorder in my jacket to see if it was running. It was awfully noisy in the subway, but if any voices at all were recorded, this radio program was going to be more about race than it was about wheelchair accessibility. It was the first moment that I suspected the two were deeply related in ways I have had many occasions to think about since.

At Franklin Avenue I crossed the tracks and changed direction, feeling for the first time that I was a part of the vast wave of migration in and out of a Manhattan that produced the subway, all the famous bridges, and a major broadcast industry in traffic reporting complete with network rivals and local personalities who have added words like "rubbernecking" to the language. I rolled across the platform like any other citizen and onto the train with ease. As we pulled away from the station, I thought how much it would truly change my life if there was a way around the stairs, and I could actually board the subway anywhere without having to be Sir Edmund Hillary.

The incoming trains were more crowded in the last minutes of the morning rush, and back at the Jay Street station there was a roar of people rushing to catch that lucky train that might make them not late after all. As I was sliding my folded chair toward the steps down to the platform, a young black man with a backward baseball cap walked right up to me out of the crowds. "I can carry the chair, man," he said. "Just tell me where you want me to set it back up." I looked at him. He was thin and energetic, and his suggestion was completely sensible. I didn't feel like giving him my speech about how I didn't need any help. "Take it to the Manhattan-bound A train," I said. "I'll be right behind you."

One train went by in the time it took to get up the flight of stairs, but going up was still much easier than I had imagined. My legs dragged along cooperatively just as my theory had predicted. At trackside, the boy with my chair had unfolded it and was sitting in it, trying to balance on two wheels. A friend of his, he explained, could do wheelies ever since he had been shot in the back during a gang shooting. "Your chair has those big-ole' wheels," he said, commenting on the large-diameter bicycle wheels I used, as if to explain why he was having some trouble keeping his balance. "I never seen those kinda wheels," he said as I hopped back into the chair.

As the train approached, he asked me for some cash. I thought that I must be some kind of idiot to go through all this and end up spending more to get into Manhattan than anyone else on the subway that day. The smallest bill I had was a five. I handed it over to him and boarded the train, laughing to myself at the absolute absurdity of it all. When I looked up, I could see commuters looking up from their newspapers. They cautiously regarded my laughing, as though I had just come from a rubber room at Bellevue Hospital. I let out a loud, demented shriek, opening my eyes as wide as I could. The heads bobbed quickly back behind the newsprint.

On the last flight of stairs leading onto City Hall Plaza at Centre Street and Chambers, the commuters in suits poured into the passageway from six trains. There was not a lot of space, and people began to trip over me. One gray-suited man in headphones carrying a gym bag nearly fell down, but he caught himself and swore as he scrambled up to street level, stepping on one of my hands in the process. A tall black man in a suit holding his own gym bag picked up my chair and started to carry it up the stairs. In a dignified voice he said, "I know you're okay, right?" I nodded.

Behind him a Puerto Rican mother with two identically dressed daughters in fluffy flowered skirts with full slips holding corsages offered to take my backpack and cushion up to the top so that I could haul myself without worrying about keeping track of the loose things. At the top, as I unfolded the wheelchair, the mother told me that she was on her way to get married at the Manhattan municipal building. Her two daughters were bridesmaids. She said she was going to put on her wedding dress, which she had in her gym bag, in the ladies' room before the ceremony. I wished her good luck and hopped back up into the chair as the commuters streamed by. It was a familiar place, the same spot I always rolled to so effortlessly off the Brooklyn Bridge.

I turned to roll away and noticed that the two little girls had come back. In unison they said, "We will pray for Jesus to bring back your legs, mister." "Thank you," I said. As though I had just given them each a shiny new quarter, they ran back to their mother, who was waiting for them with her hand outstretched to take them across busy Center Street. It was not the sort of thing I ever cared to hear people say, but after the ordeal of the subway, and the icy silence of what had seemed like every white person I met, I didn't mind at all. For once, I looked forward to riding home in a cab.

Since 1976 I had imagined the trip on the subway. I knew it was possible, while my physical therapist back in Michigan had known it would be utterly impractical as a form of transportation. We were both right, but neither of us could have imagined the America I found down there. The New York subway required only a token to ride, but on each person's face was the ticket to where they were all really going, the places they thought they never had to leave, the people they thought they never had to notice, or stop and apologize for stepping on them. Without knowing it, I had left that America behind long ago. I discovered it alive and well on the F train.

* * *

Questions for Discussion

1. What did you think of Hockenberry's attempt to ride the inaccessible subway? What did you think of other people's responses to him? If you had crossed his path during this endeavor, what might your reaction have been? Why?

2. What do you think Hockenberry was hoping to learn from this endeavor? What other things do you think he ended up learning?

3. What accessible and inaccessible places have you noticed as you have traveled? What accessibility features have you noticed with regards to public transportation? Do you think our current system of public transit provides "good enough" accessibility? Why or why not? How could we, as a society, improve physical accessibility? Stricter laws? Better enforcement? More awareness?

Mean Streets

Ed Eames,* *Ragged Edge Online*, Issue 5, September 2001

Sitting around the large conference table in Room 4017 in Fresno's City Hall on March 16, we heard the usual topics discussed. Little did we realize when Elias Gutierrez, with palpable fear in his voice, again noted the danger he faced on a daily basis traversing the

---

* Ed Eames is Chair of the Fresno Americans with Disabilities Act Advisory Council.

streets of our city, that two days later he would be the victim of the city's lack of concern and wanton disregard for the safety of its citizens.

Most of the regulars were at the meeting. There were people from the Fresno Center for Independent Living, The National Federation of the Blind and the California Access Network. As chair of the Advisory Council, I was delighted to welcome several new wheelchair users to the group. In addition to disabled members of the community, representatives of the Fresno city administration were present.

Dr. Bob Quesada, Deputy City Manager, acting as liaison between the city and the Advisory Council, sat on my right. Scattered around the table were representatives of the Fire Department, Convention Center, Public Works and Traffic Engineering. The Fire Department reported that of the more than 1,000 fire hydrants inspected in the last month, none were in violation of the minimum mandated clear path of travel of 48 inches.

The Convention Center representative indicated the water fountain had been lowered to the required height and the women's toilet was being renovated to meet codes. Traffic engineering spokesperson reported on traffic signals where the crossing time had been extended to give pedestrians a fighting chance to get across the street. The Public Works representative talked about the proposed installation of audible pedestrian signals at several high-traffic pedestrian crosswalks.

Gutierrez, a member of the Advisory Council for more than a year, pressed the city representatives on what they were doing to remove parked cars blocking the sidewalks in his neighborhood. These vehicles were forcing him out into the street on a major road leading to the airport, he said, and he had had several near-accidents.

He was told that the area in question was a county pocket within Fresno, and the city could do nothing about ticketing the drivers or removing the cars.

We all joined Gutierrez in expressing our dismay at this impasse. The discussion then turned to the lack of curb ramps in the city. Once again Gutierrez spoke, telling of his inability to get to bus stops because of the lack of curb ramps. All Fresno city buses are equipped with wheelchair lifts, he said—but what use were they when you couldn't get to them because you couldn't get up or down the sidewalks? Others voiced the same complaint.

Ever since joining the Advisory Council, Gutierrez had been complaining about the lack of sidewalks and curb ramps in Fresno. He had been forced into the streets to travel from his home to stores, recreation centers and friends' homes.

Gutierrez was foretelling his own death.

Two days after the meeting—on Sunday, March 18—the 60-year-old activist was killed when he was struck by a car as he was traveling in his power wheelchair next to the curb on Palm Avenue near Cornell.

That evening, Fresno television stations broadcast the image of an overturned wheelchair on the sidewalk of Palm, and a single shoe in the street. It made a profound emotional impact.

The news report that night did not mention Gutierrez by name. We didn't know until the Fresno Bee published his name in a follow-up story the next day that the man killed had been our Elias Gutierrez.

Learning of his death, I became depressed, as did most of the Advisory Council members.

The motorist who killed Gutierrez admitted he was driving 40 miles an hour on a local street when he decided to switch lanes. The 40 miles an hour was the posted speed limit, even though it was a residential area. The motorist had not seen the wheelchair until it was too late.

For years, members of the Advisory Council had been exhorting city traffic engineers to lower speed limits and prolong crossing times at traffic signals. The city would always respond that our needs as pedestrians had to be balanced with the needs of motorists who had to get where they were going as quickly as possible. We were continually told that any increase in time for motorists at red lights would lead to more road rage, resulting in even more violence against pedestrians and other drivers. Our right to safe passage seemed never to enter the equation.

Gutierrez's daughter arrived in Fresno several days later to go over his things. She told me that in his journals Gutierrez constantly wrote of the fear he felt every time he went out in his wheelchair.

For many of us, depression soon turned to anger when we learned that the motorist who killed Gutierrez was being only cited for driving without a license. Had Gutierrez been nondisabled, his death would have been considered manslaughter, we felt sure.

Enraged by the incident and the manner in which it was being treated, we scheduled a public meeting on May 2. The city would have to answer some questions.

Our press conference May 1 had been planned to coincide with a City Council meeting. The four local network affiliates and the Fresno bilingual TV station all covered our statements, weaving in footage of the spot where Gutierrez was killed. The coverage helped spread the word about the next day's event.

The public meeting the following day was packed. Gutierrez's daughter from Connecticut and his former wife from New Mexico were there as well.

Calling the meeting to order, I asked the group for a moment of silence in tribute to our dead activist. I had given considerable thought to what I wanted to see accomplished in this session. I wanted the city to know we would not let this incident go unnoticed. I wanted members of the disabled community to seize the opportunity to express their fears, hopes and anger in the presence of city officials and the press. I wanted to begin the development of a plan of action to avoid a repetition of this tragedy. As I sat in the seat reserved for the President of Fresno City Council, I thought about how unresponsive this body had been to the needs of Gutierrez and other wheelchair users.

When Sgt. Jim Lusk of the Traffic Division confirmed that driver had merely been cited — for driving without a license — disabled people demanded to know why charges of vehicular or involuntary manslaughter had not been lodged. Lusk said it might take up to six months to complete the investigation; it would then be up to the district attorney's office whether to press manslaughter charges. We were dismayed to hear the police say they had no idea as to the whereabouts of the driver.

We were told that since 1992 fewer than 400 corners in the city had been retrofitted with curb ramps. We learned the city had written to the Department of Justice in 1996 requesting an exemption from the ADA Title II mandate requiring curbs be ramped! The city had told DOJ there were more than 10,000 corners in Fresno needing curb ramps; despite this, a spokesperson said the Fresno Public Works Department was asking the city for only $175,000 for the next fiscal year — to install 130 ramps.

We disabled people were stunned. We felt betrayed by the city.

The meeting wasn't just about curb ramps. City officials were asked about increased time for pedestrians to cross at traffic lights, installing audible pedestrian signals, removing barriers on sidewalks, providing access over railroad crossings. An amazing number of wheelchair pedestrians told the meeting that they, too had been involved in accidents, or nearly missed being hit. Over and over we heard, "We need sidewalks! We need ramps! We need time to get across streets!"

Our anger was permeating the chamber. A city staffer said he "sympathized with the plight of wheelchair users." "We don't want sympathy, we want action!" an Advisory Council member roared back.

Something had to be done, we all agreed, to avoid a repetition of the events leading to Gutierrez' death. The city had to lower speed limits. It had to install curb ramps. It had to increase pedestrian street crossing time at traffic signals. It had to enforce the laws about cars and obstacles obstructing sidewalks.

At an emotional budget hearing held on June 5, members of the Advisory Council urged the City Council to allocate $500,000 for cutting curbs, up from the $175,000 that had been sought. When the final budget was adopted, the recommended $500,000 allocation for curb ramps had been reduced to $225,000.

In July, the Fresno police department finished its investigation of the incident. They found the driver was going 48 mph and was at fault for not having a clear view of the road on the right when he decided to pass the car in front of him. They recommended to the district attorney that vehicular manslaughter charges be lodged against the driver.

A county-wide campaign is underway to pass a half-cent sales tax to appropriate funds for transportation. As a member of the Steering Committee convened to plan expenditures of the new tax income, I am working to include funding for audible pedestrian signals, sidewalk curb cuts, longer crossing time at signals and pedestrian overpasses at high traffic intersections—so members of the Fresno disabled community will have a fighting chance to stay alive.

* * *

Questions for Discussion

1. Does your city do a good job of having curb cuts and accessible travel paths, or does your city have "mean streets"? What can be done to remedy the issue?

2. Should the ADA (or state or local laws) require cities to cut all curbs, even those that adjoin older streets? Why or why not?

The following is a settlement agreement between a disability coalition and a city. The complaint and answer from the litigation are also available at http://www.ccdconline.org/case/documents/07-28-2009/complaint-2.

Colorado Cross-Disability Coalition v. City of Colorado Springs

Settlement Agreement

1. Introduction

SETTLEMENT AGREEMENT

1.1. This Settlement Agreement ("Agreement") is entered into by and between the City of Colorado Springs ("City") and the Colorado Cross-Disability Coalition ("CCDC") (collectively, "the Parties").

1.2. CCDC is a nonprofit, statewide corporation whose members are persons with disabilities and their nondisabled allies.

1.3. The City operates the Front Range Express ("FREX"), an over-the-road commuter bus service between Fountain, Colorado, and downtown Denver, Colorado.

1.4. FREX is operated by Professional Transit Management ("PTM"), with which the City contracts. PTM also operates the City's local bus service in the Colorado Springs area, "Springs Transit."

1.5. CCDC has members who are disabled, who use wheelchairs for mobility, and who have used, or attempted to use, FREX. CCDC also has members who are disabled, who have vision impairments, and who use or have attempted to use FREX, and who have used or attempted to use FREX's website, www.frontrangeexpress.com.

1.6. CCDC has brought suit in the United States District Court for the District of Colorado, Civil Action No. 04-CV-2621 EWN (CBS) ("Lawsuit"), in which they allege that the City violated Title II of the Americans with Disabilities Act ("ADA"), 42 U.S.C. § 12131 et seq., and the Rehabilitation Act, 29 U.S.C. § 701 et seq. One of the issues in the Lawsuit is whether the City engaged in "good faith efforts" to purchase accessible buses and coaches, as that term is defined by ADA regulations.

1.7. From its inception, five of FREX's nine coaches or buses in operation at any time were not wheelchair-accessible. With the planned implementation of three additional accessible coaches by July 31, 2005, five of FREX's twelve coaches or buses in operation at any time will not be wheelchair-accessible.

1.8. The parties now wish to settle the Lawsuit, and thereby effect a complete resolution and settlement of all claims, disputes and controversies relating in any way to FREX, including any allegation made by CCDC in the Lawsuit.

1.9. CCDC represents that, during the course of the Lawsuit, it has raised ADA and Rehabilitation Act claims, both formally and informally, both in writing and verbally, regarding the accessibility of FREX buses and coaches, the accessibility of FREX services, the accessibility of FREX's website, www.frontranizeexpress.com, and FREX's operations, conditions, policies and practices it has believed to be (or has been) in violation of the ADA and the Rehabilitation Act during the period commencing three years before the filing of the Lawsuit and continuing during the pendency of the Lawsuit.

1.10. The City has denied and continues to deny any and all liability in the Lawsuit. By entering into this Agreement, the City does not admit any impropriety, wrongdoing or liability of any kind whatsoever, including any as to the claims raised in the Lawsuit, and on the contrary, expressly denies same. The City has entered into this Agreement in the furtherance of its objective to make FREX as accessible as possible for the public, including persons with disabilities, and for the purpose of avoiding the expense, inconvenience, distraction and delay of the Lawsuit, without admitting any wrongdoing or liability whatsoever.

1.11. By entering into this Agreement, the Parties do not intend to create third party beneficiaries. No individual, organization or combination thereof shall have any right to bring any action or commence any proceeding for any alleged violation of this Agreement. Only CCDC Counsel and the City shall have the authority to enforce this Agreement.

2. Conditions precedent to this Settlement Agreement

2.1. This Agreement shall be conditioned upon, and shall be effective only upon, the occurrence of all the following events:

2.1.1. This Settlement Agreement must be signed by all of the Parties to this Settlement Agreement, each signature verified by a Notary Public.

2.1.2. The attorneys in the Lawsuit for CCDC and the City must sign a Stipulation for Dismissal with Prejudice (Exhibit A hereto) and file it with the Court, along with a proposed Order of Dismissal with Prejudice (Exhibit B hereto).

2.1.3. The Court must sign an order dismissing the Lawsuit with prejudice, the said order to be substantially in the form of the proposed Order of Dismissal with Prejudice (Exhibit B).

2.2. The effective date of this Settlement Agreement shall be the date when all of the above conditions have been satisfied and all of the above events have occurred. Assuming that this Agreement has become effective, the measures, steps and requirements set forth in Sections 5 through 11 of this Agreement, inclusive, shall be implemented by the City on or before August 31, 2005, unless another deadline is specifically set forth with regard to a specific measure, step or requirement set forth herein, in which event the other deadline will apply.

3. Definitions [editors' note: definitions were removed]

4. Wheelchair-Accessible Vehicles

4.1. Within thirty (30) days immediately following the Court's dismissal of the Lawsuit with prejudice, the City shall arrange for FREX's exclusive use one of Springs Transit's used accessible buses or coaches, in addition to FREX's current fleet.

4.2. On or before November 30, 2005, the City shall have one of the nonaccessible coaches in FREX's current fleet retrofitted with a wheelchair lift and put into use in FREX's operations.

4.3. In the event that the City purchases any new or used coach or bus for FREX's use during the demonstration project period, the coach or bus will have a wheelchair lift, whether installed originally or retrofitted.

5.1. FREX's coaches and buses, supplemented with any wheelchair-accessible coach or bus as provided in Section 4 above, shall be assigned to the FREX ride schedule so that rides or trips spaced throughout the day will have wheelchair-accessible coaches or buses. The Parties agree that Exhibit C attached hereto reflects such a mutually-agreed upon schedule with rides or trips with wheelchair-accessible coaches or buses spaced throughout the day, and that this schedule will be implemented by the City and PTM upon the effective date of this Agreement and continuing indefinitely thereafter.

5.2. All literature or other communications disseminated to the public regarding FREX's trip or ride schedule shall reflect, with asterisks, those specific FREX trips or runs that will have wheelchair-accessible coaches or buses.

5.3. The City and/or PTM shall make information on those specific FREX trips or runs that will have wheelchair-accessible coaches or buses available on the FREX website, www.frontrangeexpress.com, visually and in a format accessible to individuals with vision impairments. The Parties agree that the compliance with the changes to the FREX website set forth in Section 12 shall be sufficient.

5.4. All literature disseminated to the public regarding FREX's schedule shall contain the following or similar language: "FREX is a demonstration project. Although the City of Colorado Springs hopes that all FREX buses some day will be wheelchair-accessible, at this time, not all of FREX's coaches are wheelchair-accessible. In consultation with the disabled community, FREX's schedule has been arranged so that regularly scheduled trips throughout the day will be made with wheelchair accessible vehicles. Those trips are designated with asterisks (*)." Similar language shall also be included, both visually and in a format accessible to individuals with vision impairments, in the FREX website,www.frontrangeexpress.com. The Parties agree that the compliance with the changes to the FREX website set forth in Section 12 shall be sufficient.

5.5. The Parties further agree that nothing herein shall be interpreted as limiting or restricting in any way the exclusive right of City management and/or PTM management to modify or change the FREX trip or ride schedule; however, with any modification or change in the FREX trip or ride schedule, the requirements regarding scheduling above shall be observed, and wheelchair-accessible coaches or buses shall be assigned so that the rides or trips with lift-equipped coaches or buses will be spaced throughout the day. In particular, alternating FREX trips running northbound to Denver each morning, during the peak period, starting with the first north-bound trip to Denver, will have a coach or bus with a wheelchair lift. All but one of the north-bound FREX trips to Denver during the non-peak period each day will have a coach or bus with a wheelchair lift. Alternating FREX trips running south-bound from Denver each evening, during the peak period, including the last south-bound trip from Denver, will have a coach or bus with a wheelchair lift. The last north-bound and the last south-bound FREX trip for each day will have a coach or bus with a wheelchair lift.

6.1. Before a FREX coach or bus leaves the garage to transport passengers, the operator will cycle the lift to ensure that it is operational. Each operator will fill out an entry in the DOT book verifying that the lift was cycled and that the lift worked. If CCDC Counsel so requests, and articulates a reasonable factual basis for believing that a bus lift has not been cycled or that a FREX coach or bus with an inoperative lift has knowingly been sent to transport passengers, the pertinent DOT books for that coach or bus will be made available to CCDC Counsel for inspection. For the purpose of the previous sentence, a CCDC member's inability to board a FREX coach or bus because the lift is inoperative shall be sufficient as a "reasonable factual basis" for the inspection of DOT books for that particular coach or bus.

6.2. If a lift is discovered to be inoperative, on the next business day after the discovery, FREX will repair the lift and put one of the spare accessible buses into service. If a lift cannot be repaired, it will be replaced. If a lift is inoperative three times in a subsequent six week period, it will be replaced.

6.3. If an operator reports that a lift is inoperative when it is later shown to be working, (1) the driver will be retrained by an instructor or supervisor on the operation of lifts, and (2) two unannounced monitoring tests of the operator will be conducted within two weeks of retraining. Copies of the documents referred to in this Section relating to such a driver's report of an inoperative lift later shown to be working will be made available to CCDC Counsel upon request, but such requests will be made no more frequently than once each calendar quarter.

6.4. To help identify operators who are not reporting inoperative wheelchair lifts and operators who claim that lifts are inoperative when they are in fact operational, the City and/or PTM will compare all customer reports of inoperative lifts with driver defect forms and dispatch logs to determine if a Report Failure has occurred. This comparison will occur within two weeks of receipt of a customer report of an inoperative wheelchair lift. Any driver who is found not to be reporting inoperative wheelchair lifts or who claims that lifts are inoperative when they are in fact operational will be subject to the requirements of Section 6.3. Copies of the documents referred to in this Section relating to such a driver's improper reporting will be made available to CCDC Counsel upon request.

6.5. If an operator tells a passenger who uses a wheelchair that a lift is inoperative, the operator will attempt to work the lift if requested to do so by the passenger.

7. Service Violations

7.1. The City and PTM will use coaches and buses with inoperative lifts only on the day that the inoperative lift is discovered. The City and PTM will not put a coach or bus with an inoperative lift into service on any day subsequent to the day that the inoperative lift is discovered unless such lift has been repaired. If CCDC Counsel so requests, and articulates a reasonable factual basis for believing that a particular coach or bus has had recurring problems with inoperative wheelchair lifts, records of maintenance and repair on the wheelchair lift on that coach or bus shall be made available to CCDC Counsel for inspection. For the purpose of the previous sentence, CCDC members' inability to board a FREX coach or bus because the lift is inoperative (1) on two consecutive days, or (2) on three or more different days, shall be sufficient as a "reasonable factual basis" for the inspection of the lift maintenance and repair records for that coach or bus.

7.2. The City and PTM will repair, or have repaired, any inoperative wheelchair lift as promptly as possible.

8. Special Requests for Accessible Vehicles on Trips Not Scheduled to be Accessible

8.1. FREX shall include the following statement in its trip schedule brochures and other communications regarding its trip schedule, "Passengers using wheelchairs who want to ride FREX on a trip not scheduled to have a wheelchair-accessible coach or bus may request that a wheelchair accessible vehicle be assigned to the desired trip, by telephoning FREX at 719-385-7401, during the hours of Monday through Friday, 8:00 a.m. to 5:00 p.m. (excluding holidays)." FREX will attempt to accommodate all such requests, but will take requests on a first come, first served basis. The Parties understand that FREX will be more likely to accommodate such requests if notice is provided as far in advance as possible, and a statement to this effect shall be included in its trip schedule brochures and other communications regarding its trip schedule.

8.2. When a passenger using a wheelchair telephones FREX to request wheelchair-accessible transportation on a FREX trip not scheduled to have a wheelchair-accessible coach or bus, FREX and/or PTM shall use its available resources to arrange for a wheelchair-accessible coach, bus or vehicle for the passenger for the desired trip. Such arrangements may involve traveling with or without other passengers. However, the Parties recognize and agree that, if FREX receives such requests after the limits of FREX resources have been reached, FREX will not be able to provide such arrangements.

...

9. Alternative Transportation When Vehicles on Trips Scheduled to be Accessible are Not Accessible

9.1. When a rider using a wheelchair cannot board a FREX coach or bus on a FREX trip scheduled to have a wheelchair-accessible coach or bus, because of an inoperative accessibility device, because the coach or bus does not have a lift, because the coach or bus is too full to allow a rider using a wheelchair on the coach or bus, or because all securement locations in the coach or bus are occupied, and either the next FREX coach or bus (1) is not scheduled to arrive for more than 30 minutes, or (2) is not then expected to arrive for more than 30 minutes, the City and PTM will provide the passenger with alternative transportation, as set forth in Section 9.2 below. Before any arrangements for such alternative transportation are made, the individual using a wheelchair will be informed by the driver, dispatcher and/or other FREX employees of the expected time of the next available accessible FREX coach or bus at that stop.

9.2. In their exclusive discretion, the City and PTM may provide this alternative transportation in various forms, including but not limited to:

9.2.1. Sending to the passenger another FREX coach, bus or other vehicle with a wheelchair lift from Colorado Springs, Colorado;

9.2.2. Sending to the passenger another FREX coach, bus or other vehicle with a wheelchair lift, in the field along the FREX route;

9.2.3. Commencing within six (6) weeks of the effective date of this Agreement and continuing thereafter during the term of this Agreement, hiring the services of a taxicab company, a transit company, or a paratransit company, to pick up the passenger using a wheelchair and to transport him or her some or all of the way to the passenger's destination, or to the FREX stop closest to the passenger's destination, at the operator's exclusive discretion. In this event, the passenger will be required to pay the applicable FREX fare for the FREX trip scheduled to have a wheelchair accessible coach or bus, and the City will pay any additional expense or fare.

9.3. The parties agree that the alternative transportation provided to the passenger using a wheelchair may involve a combination of the above forms of alternative transportation, including combinations that would require the passenger using a wheelchair to change vehicles during his or her trip, and that FREX may require the passenger to change vehicles during his or her trip. The preceding sentence shall not require the passenger to transfer between vehicles more than once.

9.4. If the alternative transportation is that described in Section 9.2.3 above, the call to arrange such alternative transportation will be made by FREX immediately following the instruction of the passenger using a wheelchair. If a passenger in a wheelchair is provided with alternative transportation that includes the mode described in Section 9.2.3 above, the alternative transportation shall not increase the travel time required of the passenger, more than 30 minutes beyond the time that would have been required, if the passenger had boarded the coach or bus that was assigned to the FREX trip that was scheduled to have been wheelchair-accessible.

10. Securement

10.1. FREX passengers who use wheelchairs may choose whether they wish to be secured. FREX will not refuse transportation on the ground that a passenger in a wheelchair elects to ride unsecured.

10.2. When a passenger in a wheelchair is boarding a FREX coach or bus, the operator will ask whether the passenger wants to be secured. If a passenger in a wheelchair states that he or she does not want to be secured, the operator will respect that decision without question or comment. If a passenger in a wheelchair states that he or she prefers to be secured, the operator will secure the wheelchair.

10.3. Operators will allow passengers in wheelchairs to secure and unsecure themselves if the passengers so desire and indicate to the operators.

11. Training

FREX operators will be trained and instructed to stop at any FREX-designated pick up point where a passenger using a wheelchair is located. If the coach or bus driven by the operator does not have a lift, the operator shall inform the passenger using the wheelchair of that fact, and of the estimated time of arrival of the next regularly-scheduled FREX coach or bus with a lift. The operator shall also discuss alternative transportation, as provided in Section 9.1 above, with the passenger.

12. Website

12.1. Within twenty (20) days of the effective date of this Agreement, the City will provide Ramp WEB with a copy of the FREX website, www.frontrangeexpress.com. RampWEB will then manipulate the copy of the FREX website to make the changes set forth below, and shall then return to the City the copy with the changes. Within thirty (30) days of receipt of the copy from Ramp WEB, the City and/or PTM will then make the following changes in the actual FREX website.

12.1.1. On the page for FREX service to Fountain, when an image of the route map appears, alternative text, "Route Map for Fountain," will be inserted.

12.1.2. On each web page that requires that an applet, plug-in or other application be present on the client system to interpret page content, a link to the Adobe Acrobat reader will be provided.

12.1 3. Titles of pages, including the titles of the pages for Fountain, Colorado Springs, Monument, Castle Rock, Ride Guide, Map/Times, Contact, DIA Connection, FREX Alerts, Free Wireless Internet Service, Buy Bus Tickets, will be made more descriptive of the content of the pages.

12.1.4. Links, including links on the page for Castle Rock, will be made more descriptive of the content of the linked page.

12.1.5. A fare table with specific headers, row and column indicators, that is readable by a screen reader user, will be inserted.

12.1.6. Text equivalents for the images of a FREX bus, the WIFI icon, and a FREX pass, will be inserted.

12.1.7. On the Ride Guide page, the content of the pdf document will be made available in HTML format.

12.1.8. Information regarding discounted fares for disabled passengers will be made available on additional pages of the website.

12.1.9. Each of the various fields of the FREX form used for registering to receive FREX Alerts will be defined, labeled and associated.

12.1.10. On all pages, skip navigation links will be added to skip over the repetitive navigation links. This change will be made to the FREX template so that future page will automatically include this change.

12.1.11. All pages will be given descriptive page titles.

12.1.12. On each page that has a link to a PDF document, a link to the Adobe Acrobat reader will be provided.

12.1.13. Links will be made more descriptive. External links will warn user that they are leaving the FREX site by adding a title attribute that states "link to external site" or an icon that is included in the link to let users know that it is an external link.

12.1.14. All images that have no alternative text will be given the appropriate alt text. All images with alternative text will be evaluated and modified as necessary.

12.1.15. Equivalent text will be provided within the page content for each of the maps on the Fountain, Colorado Springs, Monument, Castle Rock and Denver pages.

12.1.16. The fields on the FREX alerts registration will be labeled and associated with the appropriate entry box.

12.1.17. An explicit link to buy bus tickets will be added to the tickets page. The table on the tickets page will be put into table format with appropriate column and row headers defined.

12.1.18. Headings will be added to the dates on the updates page.

12.1.19. Row and column headers will be fixed on the times page.

12.1.20. Ride Guide will be put into HTML format.

12.1.21. On the transit links page, the text "PublicTransportation—WhereverLifeTakesYou" needs to be in sentence form without the spaces. Also the list items on this page will be made into HMTL list items.

12.1.22. The row and column headers will be added to the table on the DIA connection page.

12.1.23. The address for FREX will be added to the contact page.

12.2. In the event that the City or PTM has questions regarding the changes set forth in Section 12.1 above, Ramp WEB personnel will provide consultation by telephone to the City and/or PTM with regard to such changes.

12.3. Ramp WEB will spend whatever time is necessary to make the changes and will provide up to four hours of consultation indicated above. RampWEB's total charges for this project shall not exceed Two Thousand Dollars ($2,000.00).

...

13. Contractors

The City will require its contractors, including PTM, to abide by the terms of this Agreement, including without limitation the terms relating to documentation and monitoring.

14. Attorney Fees and Costs

14.1. The City shall pay CCDC Counsel the sum of One Hundred Thousand Dollars and No Cents ($100,000.00), representing their reasonable attorney fees and costs through the Court's dismissal of the Lawsuit with prejudice. The City shall make such payment within ten business (10) days of the effective date of this Agreement by delivering to the Colorado Cross-Disability Coalition a check in the amount of One Hundred Thousand Dollars and No Cents ($100,000.00), made payable to the Colorado Cross-Disability Coalition and Fox & Robertson, P.C.

14.2. The payment provided in Section 14.1 above will be in full and complete satisfaction of any and all claims for attorney fees, litigation expenses, including expert witness fees, and costs under federal or state law that CCDC, CCDC members, or CCDC Counsel have against the City in connection with this matter, with the exception of fees and costs described in Section 15.5 below.

15. Dispute Resolution. Any dispute between or among the City, CCDC or CCDC Counsel regarding an alleged breach of this Agreement shall be subject to the following dispute resolution process:

15.1. The party asserting that a breach has been committed shall give prompt written notice to the party allegedly committing the breach at the address(es) set forth in Section 19.1. The parties expressly agree that electronic mail shall not be deemed sufficient written notice for purposes of this Section 15.1. In no event will a party asserting that a breach has been committed be permitted to invoke this Dispute Resolution Procedure after seven business days following the term of this Agreement have elapsed; if a party asserting that a breach has been committed does not invoke the Dispute Resolution Process within seven business days following the last day of the term of this Agreement, the party will have waived such claims.

15.2. Within one calendar week of receipt of the notice provided in Section 15.1, CCDC Counsel and a representative of the City shall confer in person or by telephone and attempt to resolve the dispute.

15.3. If the meet and confer process provided in Section 15.2 does not resolve the dispute, the dispute shall be mediated before a neutral third party mutually agreed to by the party asserting that a breach has been committed and the party allegedly committing the breach.

15.4. If mediation does not resolve the dispute, the dispute shall be submitted to the United States District Court for the District of Colorado.

15.5. If the dispute is submitted to the United States District Court for the District of Colorado, and if CCDC proves that the City has breached this Agreement, CCDC shall be deemed a "prevailing plaintiff" under the Americans with Disabilities Act, and, as such, will be awarded reasonable attorneys' fees and costs incurred in connection with the unsuccessful mediation and the subsequent litigation proceedings, to the extent provided under the Americans with Disabilities Act and other statutory and case law applicable to ADA cases. If the dispute is submitted to the United States District Court for the District of Colorado, and if CCDC does not prove that the City has breached this Agreement, the City may be awarded reasonable attorneys' fees and costs in connection with the unsuccessful mediation and the subsequent litigation proceedings, to the extent provided under the Americans with Disabilities Act and other statutory and case law applicable to ADA cases.

15.6. The parties agree that the Court in the Lawsuit may reserve continuing jurisdiction over the enforcement of the terms of this Agreement, until the Term of this Agreement (as provided in Section 16) expires.

16. Term of Agreement. Assuming this Agreement becomes effective, the term of this Agreement shall commence upon the Parties' filing of Exhibit A with the Court, and shall continue until the earlier of (a) the termination of the FREX demonstration project, or (b) September 30, 2007.

17. Release

17.1. Assuming this Agreement becomes effective, effective upon the Parties' filing of Exhibit A with the Court, CCDC, on behalf of itself and its executors, successors, heirs, assigns, agents and representatives, in consideration of the relief set forth herein, the sufficiency of which is expressly acknowledged, do fully and finally release, acquit, waive and discharge the City, the City's contractors, including but not limited to PTM, and their respective parent and subsidiary corporations, and each of their respective present, former or future directors, officers, shareholders, owners, managers, supervisors, employees, partners, consultants, attorneys, agents and representatives, and their respective successors, heirs and assigns (collectively, "Releasees"), from the Released Claims as defined in Section 17.2 below.

17.2. For purposes of Section 17 1 above, the Released Claims are any and all actions, causes of action, claims, charges, demands, losses, damages, judgments, liens, indebtedness and liabilities of every kind and character, for injunctive relief, declaratory relief, damages, and costs and attorneys' fees, whether known or unknown, suspected or unsuspected, arising under the Americans with Disabilities Act, as amended, 42 U.S.C. § 12131 et sec., the Rehabilitation Act, 29 U.S.C. § 701 et seq., federal regulations, Colorado statutory law, Colorado regulations, Colorado common law, all other Colorado legal or equitable law, and county or municipal ordinances, regulations, standards or other law regarding access for persons with disabilities to public transportation, whether known or unknown, suspected or unsuspected, asserted or unasserted in the Lawsuit, that CCDC may have or claim to have, in any way relating to or arising out of FREX, FREX's operations, FREX's coaches or buses, or the FREX website, www.frontrangeexpress.com, prior to the Parties' filing of Exhibit A with the Court, and, if the City is in compliance with this

Agreement, the accessibility of FREX, FREX's operations, FREX's coaches or buses, or the FREX website, www.frontrangeexpress.com, in the future, during the term of this Agreement.

17.3. Effective upon the Parties' filing of Exhibit A with the Court, CCDC, on behalf of any and all individuals who are or were members of CCDC at any time on or after October 1, 2004, and their respective executors, successors, heirs, assigns, agents and representatives, in consideration of the relief set forth herein, the sufficiency of which is expressly acknowledged, do fully and finally release, acquit, waive and discharge the City, the City's contractors, including but not limited to PTM, and their respective parent and subsidiary corporations, and each of their respective present, former or future directors, officers, shareholders, owners, managers, supervisors, employees, partners, consultants, attorneys, agents and representatives, and their respective successors, heirs and assigns (collectively, "Releasees"), from the Released Claims as defined in Section 17.4 below.

17.4. For purposes of Section 17.3 above, the Released Claims are any and all actions, causes of action, claims, charges, demands, losses, damages, judgments, liens, indebtedness and liabilities of every kind and character, for injunctive relief, declaratory relief, and costs and attorneys' fees related to such claims, whether known or unknown, suspected or un-suspected, arising under the Americans with Disabilities Act, as amended, 42 U.S.C. § 12131 et seg, the Rehabilitation Act, 29 U.S.C. § 701 et seq., federal regulations, Colorado statutory law, Colorado regulations, Colorado common law, all other Colorado legal or equitable law, and county or municipal ordinances, regulations, standards or other law regarding access for persons with disabilities to public transportation, whether known or unknown, suspected or unsuspected, asserted or unasserted in the Lawsuit, that a CCDC member may have or claim to have, in any way relating to or arising out of FREX, FREX's operations, FREX's coaches or buses, or the FREX website, www.frontrangeexpress.com, prior to the Parties' filing of Exhibit A with the Court, and, if the City is in compliance with this Agreement, the accessibility of FREX, FREX's operations, FREX's coaches or buses, or the FREX website, www.frontrangeexpress.com, during the term of this Agreement.

17.5. Assuming this Agreement becomes effective, CCDC covenants that it will not file suit, on its behalf or on behalf of its members or anyone else, relating to the accessibility of FREX, FREX's operations, FREX's coaches or buses, or the FREX website, www.fron-trangeexpress.com, for injunctive relief or attorney fees and costs under any statute regarding access for persons with disabilities to public transportation against any contractor of the City, including PTA, that operates in compliance with this Agreement.

17.6. CCDC hereby warrants to the City that it has not assigned or transferred to any person or entity any portion of any of the Released Claims that are released, waived and discharged in Section 17 above.

17.7. Nothing in this Section 17 shall prevent or preclude any Party from seeking to enforce this Agreement.

. . .

19.3. No term or provision of this Settlement Agreement may be modified or extinguished, in whole or in part, except by a writing which is dated and signed by (1) CCDC, and (2) the City's Transportation Services Manager, the City Attorney or a majority of the members of City Council of the City, at that point in time. No waiver of any of the provisions or conditions of this Settlement Agreement or of any of the rights, powers or privileges of a party hereto shall be effective or binding unless in writing and signed by the party claimed to have given or consented to such waiver. No representative, agent or employee of the City other than the City's Transportation Services Manager, the City Attorney or a majority of the members of City Council of the City, at that point in time, has authority to sign such a waiver.

19.4. Nothing in this Agreement shall bar or preclude the City, of its own volition, pursuant to government directive, or otherwise, from taking further steps or implementing further measures, above and beyond the specific requirements of this Agreement, to enhance further the accessibility of FREX, FREX's operations, FREX's coaches or buses, or the FREX website, www.frontrangeexpress.com.

19.5. The Parties acknowledge that they discussed this Settlement Agreement with their respective attorneys in the Lawsuit before signing this Settlement Agreement, that they were represented by their attorneys in the Lawsuit in the negotiation and preparation of this Settlement Agreement, that they have carefully read and understand each of the terms of this Settlement Agreement, and that they have knowingly and voluntarily signed this Settlement Agreement as their own free act, without coercion or duress.

19.6. Each of the Parties to this Settlement Agreement forever waives all rights to assert that this Settlement Agreement was the result of a mistake of law or fact.

19.7. Each party to this Settlement Agreement acknowledges and stipulates that the compromise and settlement which form the basis of this Settlement Agreement have been arrived at after thorough bargaining and negotiation and represent a final mutually agreeable compromise of matters provided herein. The Settlement Agreement shall not be construed more strictly against one party than another merely by virtue of the fact that it may have been prepared by counsel for one of the parties, it being recognized that, because of the arm's-length negotiations between the parties, both parties hereto have contributed substantially and materially to the preparation of the Agreement.

19.8. The headings contained in this Settlement Agreement are for convenience only, do not constitute part of the Settlement Agreement and shall not limit, be used to interpret or otherwise affect in any way the provisions of the Settlement Agreement.

19.9. This Settlement Agreement shall be governed and construed in accordance with the laws of Colorado, without regard to its conflict of laws principles.

19.10. If any provision or any part of this Settlement Agreement shall at any time be held unlawful, or inconsistent with applicable law, in whole or in part, under any federal, state, county, municipal or other law, ruling or regulation, then the remaining provisions of this Settlement Agreement shall remain effective and enforceable.

19.11. If the terms of this Settlement Agreement are challenged by any individual or entity not a party to the Agreement, or if any individual or entity not a party to this Agreement asserts that FREX's operations as required under the terms of this Agreement are in violation of the Americans with Disabilities Act and/or the Rehabilitation Act, CCDC acknowledges and agrees that it will cooperate in defending the reasonableness and fairness of the terms of this Agreement.

IN WITNESS THEREOF, and intending to be legally bound, the parties have executed this Settlement Agreement.

* * *

Questions for Discussion

1. What other cases have been litigated about inoperative bus lifts? What other settlements about inaccessible buses have you heard about in the media? What should be the penalties for inoperative bus lifts? For drivers that refuse to stop for wheelchair users?

2. What did you think about the provisions requiring changes to the website? What did you think of the "release" provisions?

3. What did you think of the settlement provisions as a whole?

———

For Further Reading and Viewing

Fell v. Spokane Paratransit, 128 Wash.2d 618 (1996). Case about the legal differences between fixed route and paratransit, containing some interesting discourse.

"City Agrees Teen Can Use Wheelchair in Streets," retrieved May 15, 2012 at http://www.mnddc.org/news/inclusion-daily/2003/10/102203iaaccadv.htm. An article about a teenager who got ticketed for riding his motorized wheelchair in the street.

www.adapt.org is the website for ADAPT, a group of disability activists who often focus their efforts on improving main line bus service. Check out videos of their various protests on www.youtube.com.

de Montalambert, Hugues. *Invisible*. An artist becomes blind as a result of an assault, but he continues traveling around the world.

Discussion 25

Restaurants, Hotels, Theme Parks, and More: Access to Places of Public Accommodation

Recommended Background Reading

ADA Title III, 42 U.S.C. 12101, 12112, 12113, and accompanying regulations, 28 C.F.R. 36.202, 203.

"Disabilities Act Prompts Flood of Suits Some Cite as Unfair," *New York Times*, retrieved May 15, 2012 at http://www.nytimes.com/2012/04/17/nyregion/lawyers-find-obstacles-to-the-disabled-then-find-plaintiffs.html?_r=1&nl=todaysheadlines&emc=edit_th_20120417.

PGA Tour, Inc. v. Casey Martin, 121 S.Ct. 1897 (2001).

Readings for Class Discussion

The following is a an opinion and order about lack of appropriate service at a drive-through.

Bunjer v. McDonald's
985 F. Supp 165 (D.D.C. 1997)

The opinion of the court was delivered by: SPORKIN

MEMORANDUM OPNION

This matter is before the Court on Count I of Plaintiff's Second Amended Complaint. Plaintiff seeks injunctive relief pursuant to Title III of the Americans with Disabilities Act ("ADA"), 42 U.S.C. 12101 et seq. In addition, Plaintiff's complaint alleged in Counts II, III, IV and V that Defendants are liable for assault and battery, false arrest, false imprisonment, and intentional infliction of emotional distress. The case went to trial before a jury on Counts II through V. Simultaneously, the Court heard Count I, the ADA claim. At the conclusion of Plaintiff's case, Defendants moved pursuant to Fed. R. Civ.

P. 50 for judgment as a matter of law as to all of Plaintiff's causes of action. The Court dismissed three of Plaintiff's causes of action. See Memorandum Opinion of December 22, 1997. The cause of action for intentional infliction of emotional distress went to the jury, which rendered a verdict in favor of the Plaintiff for $1500. The Court reserved its decision on the ADA cause of action. After the conclusion of the trial, the Court held an additional hearing on the matter. Below, the Court will address Plaintiff's ADA claim and set forth its findings of fact and conclusions of law.

I. FINDINGS OF FACT

On May 21, 1995, Plaintiff Bunjer attempted to place an order at the drive-through facility of Defendants' McDonald's restaurant, located at 75 New York Avenue, N.E., Washington, D.C. The drive-through facility required the customer to order from a displayed menu through a speaker before proceeding to the window to pay for the food. Plaintiff, who is deaf, could not place his order in this manner. He drove directly to the drive-through window and attempted to place his order (which consisted of a Big Mac, french fries, and a large Sprite) by writing it down on a piece of paper. His order was initially refused, and he was told to park his car and come inside to place the order. Plaintiff insisted upon being treated like everyone else by being served at the window. Because of the back-up of persons in automobiles waiting behind Plaintiff, the Defendants' employees in charge of the drive-through eventually decided to serve Plaintiff. Plaintiff stated that he observed that the employees were snickering as they brought his order to the window. He testified that he was given the wrong change and warm water with a white substance instead of Sprite.

Plaintiff went inside the restaurant to complain about not receiving the correct change and drink. Once in the restaurant, the employees ignored him. When he placed his order on the counter, some of the drink spilled on the counter. Officer Jed Worrell, an off-duty police Metropolitan Police Department officer who was employed by Defendants to serve as a part-time security guard at their McDonald's restaurant, attempted to communicate with Plaintiff. He saw that Plaintiff was displeased with his treatment and told the McDonald's personnel to refund Plaintiff's money. When Officer Worrell saw that Plaintiff did not accept the refund and continued to be irate, he ordered Plaintiff to leave the premises. When Plaintiff refused to leave, Officer Worrell forcibly restrained and arrested him.

Plaintiff was taken to the local precinct and held in custody for approximately six hours. He posted twenty-five dollars for collateral and was released in the early morning hours of May 22, 1995. Plaintiff took a cab back to the McDonald's restaurant to retrieve his car. Upon reaching the restaurant, Plaintiff discovered that his car keys had not been returned to him. After a short conversation with the employees of the McDonald's restaurant, Plaintiff went home. Subsequently, he hired a locksmith to let him into his car. In connection with the incident, Plaintiff was arrested, spent six hours in custody, and incurred expenses ($25 for collateral, $40 for the cab fare, and $60 for the locksmith).

II. CONCLUSIONS OF LAW

Title III of the ADA, 42 U.S.C. sec 12101 et. seq., mandates that disabled people be provided equal access to public accommodations. A place of public accommodation, such as a restaurant, is required by the ADA to "take such steps as may be necessary to ensure that no individual with a disability is excluded, denied services, segregated or otherwise treated differently than other individuals because of the absence of auxiliary aids and services ..." 42 U.S.C. § 12182(b)(2)(A)(iii). Failure to do so constitutes discrimination within the meaning of the ADA, for which an individual may seek injunctive relief. 42 U.S.C. § 12188(a).

In this case, the Court finds that the Defendants' drive-through facility discriminates against the deaf and those with hearing impairments. Under the current system, deaf and hearing impaired patrons have no way to make use of the drive-through facility. There is an easy way to make provision for these patrons. All that needs to be done is for the restaurant to put up a sign at the initial speaker/menu point instructing deaf patrons to proceed directly to the window to have their orders filled.

Additionally, the employees of Defendant's McDonald's franchise were inadequately trained to deal with the special needs of deaf and hearing impaired patrons. Defendants' McDonald's restaurant is located in close proximity to Gallaudet University, the foremost national university devoted entirely to the deaf and the hearing impaired. Defendant William Edwards testified that because of its location near the university, his McDonald's franchise typically serves about twenty-five deaf persons per day. Despite the numerous deaf patrons at the restaurant, Defendant has in place no policies or training to instruct employees about the special needs of such customers. The circumstances in this case illustrate that the employees of Defendants' restaurant were far from capable of dealing effectively with deaf patrons. Had Defendants provided adequate training to their employees, the offensive treatment of the Plaintiff that occurred in this case might have been avoided. Accordingly, the Court will order Defendants to implement policies and provide training for their employees to accommodate the deaf and hearing impaired. Although the injunction will be limited to Defendants' McDonald's franchise, see *Marshall v. Goodyear Tire & Rubber Co.*, 554 F.2d 730, 733 (5th Cir. 1977) ("[A] nationwide or companywide injunction is appropriate only when the facts indicate a company policy or practice in violation of the statute."), the Court hopes that it will serve as a "wake-up call" for the national McDonald's Corporation to put in place training and other appropriate procedures for dealing with the deaf and the hearing impaired. It was conceded at trial that the parent McDonald's Corporation provides no training to its own employees or its franchise proprietors with respect to dealing with the deaf and hearing impaired.

Finally, the Court will order that the Defendants maintain records of incidents such as the one in this case. The Defendants could not identify the employees on duty at the time of the incident. The Court cannot understand why no records were kept regarding an incident that resulted in an arrest of a patron on the premises. The Court will require Defendants' employees to maintain records of all incidents involving hearing impaired persons. The Court wants to ensure that no person with a hearing disability be denied reasonable accommodations and that the Defendants will put in place effective means for communicating with such persons.

An appropriate order and judgment and injunction accompanies this opinion.

12/23/97

Stanley Sporkin

United States District Judge

ORDER AND JUDGMENT AND INJUNCTION

On December 19, 1997, the jury rendered a verdict in the above-captioned matter. It is hereby

ORDERED that judgment in the amount of $1500 plus costs be entered in favor of the Plaintiff. It is further

ORDERED that Defendants, their officers, agents, servants, employees, attorneys, and those persons in active concert or participation with them who receive actual notice of the order by personal service or otherwise be PERMANENTLY ENJOINED from discriminating against persons who are hearing disabled in the use of Defendants' facilities. It is further

ORDERED that Defendants shall be required to make available to hearing impaired customers access to the drive-through facility that is open to all customers, including, but not limited to placing a sign at the initial point of the drive-through facility to indicate to deaf and hearing impaired customers that they can proceed directly to the drive-through window to place their orders. It is further

ORDERED that once at that facility, Defendants shall provide hearing disabled persons with access to appropriate writing instruments to write down their order. It is further

ORDERED that Defendants shall establish written policies and establish a training program to deal effectively with the needs of deaf and hearing impaired customers. It is further

ORDERED that Defendants maintain records of incidents involving a disruption in service with respect to hearing disabled patrons. Said records shall include, but are not limited to, the name, phone number, and address of the hearing impaired customer; the date of the incident; the nature and resolution of the incident; and the names of the supervisor and all employees involved. Said records shall be maintained for a period of at least five years. It is further

ORDERED that the Court will retain jurisdiction of this matter to order such other and further relief as may be necessary to carry out this order.

12/23/97

* * *

Questions for Discussion

1. As a policy matter, should corporations be held liable for unacceptable actions of their employees, or should the individual employees be liable instead?

2. Do you think that the plaintiff was "made whole" in this case?

3. What other accessibility issues might apply to drive-throughs? To restaurants in general? What other pieces have you seen in the media about restaurant accessibility?

———————

The following is an article about Clint Eastwood's role as an ADA defendant.

The Clint Eastwood Verdict Makes My Day

John M. Williams, October 6, 2000, Businessweek.com*

A jury has found in the actor's favor, and that sends a strong signal about the Disabilities Act: It's a good law, but don't misuse it

Famed film star Clint Eastwood couldn't have scripted it better himself. On Sept. 29, a U.S. District Court in San Jose, Calif., ruled that the Academy Award-winning director

———————

* http://www.businessweek.com/bwdaily/dnflash/oct2000/nf2000106_353.htm.

and actor wasn't liable for damages in a case filed against him by Diane zum Brunnen. A resident of Alameda, Calif., zum Brummen alleged that Eastwood's Carmel Mission Ranch Inn violated title III of the Americans with Disabilities Act (see BW Online, 5/10/00, "Now, Dirty Harry Is Gunning for the ADA") and 5/17/00, "Clint Eastwood Explains His Beef with the ADA").

Disregarding a closing argument from zum Brunnen's attorney that compared her to Rosa Parks, the five-man and three-woman civil jury found the disabled woman had suffered no harm at Eastwood's inn. The jury did find Eastwood guilty only of two minor violations—lack of a wheelchair-accessible ramp and not having a sign to point disabled patrons to wheelchair-accessible bathrooms. Eastwood has long since remedied both of these situations.

The verdict makes my day. Many in the disability community have voiced outrage over this outcome. As anyone who reads this column knows, I strongly support the ADA. I believe every building and bathroom should be accessible to the disabled. Access to public and private buildings is a right, and it should be protected.

That said, I also believe that sometimes attorneys and people with disabilities abuse the ADA. The Eastwood case is one of these instances—and never should have gone to court. Furthermore, I believe these ill-advised lawsuits do far more harm than good by frightening business owners, encouraging expensive litigation, and making cooperation on compliance far more difficult to achieve.

The battle between Dirty Harry and zum Brunnen, who has muscular dystrophy, started when she and her husband arrived on a Sunday afternoon in January, 1996, to spend the night at Eastwood's inn. According to documents filed in the case, the couple didn't have a reservation and learned the only room for wheelchair users was occupied. They stayed for dinner. Afterward, Mrs. zum Brunnen claimed she was directed to an inaccessible bathroom. There was a wheelchair-accessible bathroom closer than the bathroom to which she said she had been directed, but no one told her about it, according to filings submitted in the case.

NO ANSWER. The zum Brunnens left the hotel and sent several letters to Eastwood complaining about the inaccessible bathroom. When the letters went unanswered, on Jan. 21, 1997, zum Brunnen's attorney, Paul Rein, who has initiated more than 20 ADA cases, filed a federal suit against Eastwood. John Burris was brought in for the trial. He specializes in litigating complaints of ADA violations and believed Eastwood had broken the law. "There was a clear violation of the rules when Mrs. zum Brunnen visited, and Mr. Eastwood, as owner of the Mission Ranch, is responsible for the violations of those rules," said Burris during the trial.

For more than two years after the complaint had been filed, zum Brunnen and her attorney sought a cash settlement from Eastwood. Last spring, Eastwood told a congressional committee that zum Brunnen wanted an out-of-court settlement of $576,000. It wouldn't have been her first. Previously, zum Brunnen had won an ADA lawsuit filed against Mendocino's historic Heritage House Hotel, which paid $20,000 to her and $48,000 to her lawyer. In that case, zum Brunnen complained that a doorway was too narrow and an ocean-front path too rough for her wheelchair.

Not only did Eastwood refuse to settle but he also turned the case into a media war and a four-year legal slugfest. "I'm doing this to help protect small-business people from the same kind of lawsuit," he told this columnist before the trial. Eastwood's attorneys warned him that if he fought the case in court, he could end up stuck paying $1 million worth of zum Brunnen's legal bills. Under the law, the complainant's attorneys in ADA cases can collect their legal fees from the other side if they win. This double-whammy is why businesses often settle out of court rather than fight.

During the trial, Eastwood's attorney, Chuck Keller, told the jury that zum Brunnen may not have even visited the hotel. "There are many discrepancies in her story, and there is a lack of corroboration," Keller said. "For zum Brunnen to win, she must prove that she visited Mission Ranch as a bona fide guest, not on a pretext, setting the stage for this lawsuit." For her part, zum Brunnen had pledged to give her legal winnings to charity.

READY TO APPEAL. The jury took only five hours to deliberate — and it came down squarely on Dirty Harry's side. "The verdict was correct. I hope I set an example for other small businesses to follow," said Eastwood, adding he would have appealed if he had lost. And he's right on the money. All along, Eastwood says that he has supported the ADA's access requirements and continues to. And the facts support him: Eastwood's hotel did have a wheelchair-accessible bathroom and a wheelchair-accessible room. When notified of existing problems, he fixed them, as mandated by the law. And zum Brunnen's offer to settle for nearly a half-million dollars seems excessive to this columnist in light of the circumstances.

By standing up and taking the case to trial, Eastwood sent the right message. Since Congress passed the ADA in 1990, the disabled community has filed thousands of lawsuits against businesses, most of which have been settled out of court. The vast majority of ADA lawsuits have rightfully served as a last resort to force business owners to put in place legally mandated equal-access provisions. And this strong legal crowbar has played a major role in literally opening doors to the disabled across this country.

But the outcome of this trial should serve both as a warning to trial lawyers and a wake-up call to businesses, especially small ones. The ADA is a landmark law. People with disabilities should resort to it as a legal weapon only after they truly have been denied access and have exhausted all other remedies. And small-business owners should understand that they have rights and recourse to reasonable remedies under the ADA, too. Lawyers who knowingly — and repeatedly — misuse the ADA to try to collect cash settlements should be dealt with by the American Bar Assn.

At the end of the trial, zum Brunnen's attorney declared that the case was a victory for the disabled by raising awareness of the issues. It sure did, in more ways than he realizes.

* * *

Questions for Discussion

1. Should business owners be allowed a window of time to comply with the ADA after an individual has a complaint? Why or why not?

2. Does it do disservice to the disability community for individuals to sue multiple business owners for alleged ADA violations, or should this be a commonly accepted practice?

3. What do you think of the discourse in this article?

The following is an article in a Pennsylvania newspaper, *The Morning Call*, about litigation brought against an amusement park.

Discrimination Lawsuit Filed against Dorney

Shannon P. Duffy, *The Morning Call*, December 16, 1994

When Edward Dzura of Quakertown took his son, Edward Jr., to Dorney Park on Aug. 13, they planned to start off the way they always did—going round and round on the carousel.

But before they got to ride, they got a different kind of runaround, Dzura Sr. said yesterday.

Park workers noticed that Edward Dzura Jr., 33, has Down syndrome, so they said he would have to pass a "test" before he boarded any rides. As Dzura Sr. described it, the carousel operator approached them as they were waiting in line and "in a loud voice, she said, 'Is he retarded?'"

When he answered yes, Dzura Sr. said, he was sent to the public relations office where he was asked a series of "silly questions" about his son—whether he could walk, talk, climb, follow directions—and once again was forced to answer in front of a crowd.

After securing a piece of paper that entitled them to enter any ride they wished—something Dzura Sr. said he and his son had never needed before as season-pass holders—the carousel operator did not even look at it.

Feeling singled out and discriminated against, father and son boarded just one ride and left. "My son knew ... he knew he was being demeaned," Dzura Sr. said.

Yesterday, the Dzuras filed a class-action federal lawsuit against the park under the Americans with Disabilities Act.

The suit seeks no money—just an injunction prohibiting the park from discriminating against the disabled.

Park spokesman Bernard Bonuccelli said he could not answer any questions because park officials have not yet seen the suit.

Attorney Stefan Presser of the Americans Civil Liberties Union said Dzura Jr. "lives on his own, attends karate classes, and has a job" and should not have been singled out for an evaluation.

"This nation made a commitment with the passing of the Americans with Disabilities Act that disabled persons were not to be discriminated against, that they were not to be treated in this fashion," Presser said.

At a press conference to announce the filing of the suit, Dzura Sr. said he told park workers they were being discriminatory.

"It surprised me to no end and I said, 'This has never happened. This is discrimination. You can't do things like this.' I objected strenuously, but it didn't do any good," Dzura said.

Attorney Stephen Gold, who specializes in disability law, said, "We're seeing another form of hatred against people with disabilities."

Under the act, Gold said, "if a person is a safety threat to others—not to himself—that is the only way they can impose different eligibility criteria. What this says is that if a person with a disability wants to take a chance on a ride, they're going to be treated equally as everyone else."

Gold said he did not believe that the park was truly worried about disabled people getting hurt on rides.

"This wasn't a safety issue. This was purely he looked different, he talked different, he looked disabled."

Presser agreed. "This is not a reasonable business rule designed to protect the park, but may, in fact, be just rank prejudice. Some people are looking at other people's physical appearances and they're concerned about the impact that may have on other people's enjoyment of the park."

* * *

Questions for Discussion

1. Are you surprised that something like this still happens in modern times?

2. What would the Dzuras likely have had to prove as elements of this lawsuit? What would the park have been likely to argue?

2. Should business owners be held to a different standard if one of their policies is discriminatory vs. if one of their policies is incorrectly applied by an employee?

3. Should damages for emotional distress be available in a case like this? Are they?

For Further Reading

"Disabled patrons file suit against Fort Lauderdale Museum of Art over Tut," retrieved May 15, 2012 at http://www.disabilityrights.org/306.htm.

"Disabled, and Shut Out at the Gym," retrieved May 15, 2012 at http://www.disability rights.org/306.htm.

"Wheelchairs in the Wilderness," *The Christian Science Monitor*, retrieved May 15, 2012 at http://www.csmonitor.com/2005/1003/p09s01-coop.html.

"In NYC, the show goes on, and so does the discrimination," retrieved May 15, 2012 at www.raggededgemagazine.com/departments/news/000469.html.

Discussion 26

Service Animals

Recommended Background Reading

Crowder v. Kitagawa, 81 F.3d 1480 (1996).

Readings for Class Discussion

The following is the new regulation, promulgated by the Department of Justice in 2011, defining the term "service animal." This definition is substantially different than the prior definition. The prior definition of "service animal" was "any guide dog, signal dog, or other animal individually trained to do work or perform tasks for the benefit of an individual with a disability."

28 CFR 36.104 (Americans with Disabilities Act's New Definition of Service Animal as of 2010)

Service animal means any dog that is individually trained to do work or perform tasks for the benefit of an individual with a disability, including a physical, sensory, psychiatric, intellectual, or other mental disability. Other species of animals, whether wild or domestic, trained or untrained, are not service animals for the purposes of this definition. The work or tasks performed by a service animal must be directly related to the individual's disability. Examples of work or tasks include, but are not limited to, assisting individuals who are blind or have low vision with navigation and other tasks, alerting individuals who are deaf or hard of hearing to the presence of people or sounds, providing non-violent protection or rescue work, pulling a wheelchair, assisting an individual during a seizure, alerting individuals to the presence of allergens, retrieving items such as medicine or the telephone, providing physical support and assistance with balance and stability to individuals with mobility disabilities, and helping persons with psychiatric and neurological disabilities by preventing or interrupting impulsive or destructive behaviors. The crime deterrent effects of an animal's presence and the provision of emotional support, well-being, comfort, or companionship do not constitute work or tasks for the purposes of this definition.

* * *

Questions for Discussion

1. Why do you think this change was made? What can you learn about the history of this change? Who do you think is impacted by this change?

2. Which definition do you think is better, and why?

The following is a U.S. Department of Justice publication about service animals, found at http://www.ada.gov/service_animals_2010.htm.

ADA 2010 Revised Requirements
U.S. Department of Justice
Civil Rights Division
Disability Rights Section

Service Animals

The Department of Justice published revised final regulations implementing the Americans with Disabilities Act (ADA) for title II (State and local government services) and title III (public accommodations and commercial facilities) on September 15, 2010, in the Federal Register. These requirements, or rules, clarify and refine issues that have arisen over the past 20 years and contain new, and updated, requirements, including the 2010 Standards for Accessible Design (2010 Standards).

Overview

This publication provides guidance on the term "service animal" and the service animal provisions in the Department's new regulations.

- Beginning on March 15, 2011, only dogs are recognized as service animals under titles II and III of the ADA.

- A service animal is a dog that is individually trained to do work or perform tasks for a person with a disability.

- Generally, title II and title III entities must permit service animals to accompany people with disabilities in all areas where members of the public are allowed to go.

How "Service Animal" Is Defined

Service animals are defined as dogs that are individually trained to do work or perform tasks for people with disabilities. Examples of such work or tasks include guiding people who are blind, alerting people who are deaf, pulling a wheelchair, alerting and protecting a person who is having a seizure, reminding a person with mental illness to take prescribed medications, calming a person with Post Traumatic Stress Disorder (PTSD) during an anxiety attack, or performing other duties. Service animals are working animals, not pets. The work or task a dog has been trained to provide must be directly related to the person's disability. Dogs whose sole function is to provide comfort or emotional support do not qualify as service animals under the ADA.

This definition does not affect or limit the broader definition of "assistance animal" under the Fair Housing Act or the broader definition of "service animal" under the Air Carrier Access Act.

Some State and local laws also define service animal more broadly than the ADA does. Information about such laws can be obtained from the State attorney general's office.

Where Service Animals Are Allowed

Under the ADA, State and local governments, businesses, and nonprofit organizations that serve the public generally must allow service animals to accompany people with disabilities in all areas of the facility where the public is normally allowed to go. For example, in a hospital it would be inappropriate to exclude a service animal from areas such as patient rooms, clinics, cafeterias, or examination rooms. However, it may be appropriate to exclude a service animal from operating rooms or burn units where the animal's presence may compromise a sterile environment.

Service Animals Must Be Under Control

Under the ADA, service animals must be harnessed, leashed, or tethered, unless these devices interfere with the service animal's work or the individual's disability prevents using these devices. In that case, the individual must maintain control of the animal through voice, signal, or other effective controls.

Inquiries, Exclusions, Charges, and Other Specific Rules Related to Service Animals

- When it is not obvious what service an animal provides, only limited inquiries are allowed. Staff may ask two questions: (1) is the dog a service animal required because of a disability, and (2) what work or task has the dog been trained to perform. Staff cannot ask about the person's disability, require medical documentation, require a special identification card or training documentation for the dog, or ask that the dog demonstrate its ability to perform the work or task.

- Allergies and fear of dogs are not valid reasons for denying access or refusing service to people using service animals. When a person who is allergic to dog dander and a person who uses a service animal must spend time in the same room or facility, for example, in a school classroom or at a homeless shelter, they both should be accommodated by assigning them, if possible, to different locations within the room or different rooms in the facility.

- A person with a disability cannot be asked to remove his service animal from the premises unless: (1) the dog is out of control and the handler does not take effective action to control it or (2) the dog is not housebroken. When there is a legitimate reason to ask that a service animal be removed, staff must offer the person with the disability the opportunity to obtain goods or services without the animal's presence.

- Establishments that sell or prepare food must allow service animals in public areas even if state or local health codes prohibit animals on the premises.

- People with disabilities who use service animals cannot be isolated from other patrons, treated less favorably than other patrons, or charged fees that are not charged to other patrons without animals. In addition, if a business requires a deposit or fee to be paid by patrons with pets, it must waive the charge for service animals.

- If a business such as a hotel normally charges guests for damage that they cause, a customer with a disability may also be charged for damage caused by himself or his service animal.

- Staff are not required to provide care or food for a service animal.

Miniature Horses

In addition to the provisions about service dogs, the Department's revised ADA regulations have a new, separate provision about miniature horses that have been individually trained to do work or perform tasks for people with disabilities. (Miniature horses generally range in height from 24 inches to 34 inches measured to the shoulders and generally weigh between

70 and 100 pounds.) Entities covered by the ADA must modify their policies to permit miniature horses where reasonable. The regulations set out four assessment factors to assist entities in determining whether miniature horses can be accommodated in their facility. The assessment factors are (1) whether the miniature horse is housebroken; (2) whether the miniature horse is under the owner's control; (3) whether the facility can accommodate the miniature horse's type, size, and weight; and (4) whether the miniature horse's presence will not compromise legitimate safety requirements necessary for safe operation of the facility.

* * *

Questions for Discussion

1. Enforcers of the Fair Housing Act have not changed to the new, more restrictive definition of "service animal." Why do you think the definition of "service animal" should be interpreted so differently under two civil rights statutes (ADA and FHA)? Does this make sense?

2. What did you think of the other policies set forth in this article? What media coverage have you seen about service animals?

The following is a case about service animals and condominiums.

Overlook Mutual Homes, Inc. v. Spencer

666 F. Supp. 2d 850 (2009); 2009 U.S. Dist. LEXIS 105100

UNITED STATES DISTRICT COURT FOR THE SOUTHERN DISTRICT OF OHIO, WESTERN DIVISION

OPINION BY: WALTER HERBERT RICE

This litigation arises out of the efforts of Vickie and Joey Spencer (collectively the "Spencers") to keep a dog in their dwelling at the residences managed by Plaintiff Overlook Mutual Homes, Inc. ("Overlook"). Overlook is a mutual housing corporation, which is operated by its members, all of whom are residents living at the property owned by Overlook. The members operate Overlook through an elected Board of Trustees ("Board"), which is authorized to adopt rules and regulations. One of those rules, the no pet rule, prohibits members/residents from having pets, except for service animals which are necessary to accommodate a resident's disability.

In April, 2007, after other residents had complained about the noise made by a barking dog in the Spencer's dwelling, Overlook provided written warning to them that they were with violating the no pet rule. In response, Vickie Spencer submitted an affidavit, stating that the dog had been permanently removed. Subsequently, however, she visited the Miami Valley Fair Housing Center ("MVFHC"), which resulted in its President, Jim McCarthy ("McCarthy"), writing a letter to Overlook, under date of August 1, 2007. Therein, McCarthy requested a reasonable accommodation on behalf of the Spencers, to permit Lynsey [their daughter] to keep Scooby.[1] McCarthy explained that Lynsey was currently receiving psychological counseling and that her psychologist had recommended that Lynsey have a companion/service dog to facilitate her treatment. McCarthy also

---

1. The dog is a neutered, male Cockapoo named Scooby. A Cockapoo is a "designer dog" created by breeding an American or English Cocker Spaniel with a Poodle, usually of the miniature or toy variety.

enclosed a statement from Miriam Hoefflin ("Hoefflin"), Lynsey's treating psychologist, indicating that, as a result of her assessment and counseling of Lynsey, she had recommended that the child "have a service dog to facilitate treatment."

John Folkerth ("Folkerth"), an attorney representing Overlook in this litigation, responded to McCarthy's letter. In particular, Folkerth set forth therein his reasons for being skeptical of Vickie Spencer's assertion that her daughter needed to keep the dog as a service animal. He also indicated that, if Lynsey was disabled and in need of a service animal, Overlook would be willing to engage in a dialogue to determine whether a reasonable accommodation could be provided. In addition, Folkerth stated that Vickie Spencer would be required to fill out a form, seeking a waiver of the no pet rule and requested all manner of information concerning Lynsey's asserted disability and need for the dog as a service animal. He requested that the information be provided in two weeks and that, in the meantime, Overlook would refrain from initiating eviction proceedings against the Spencers. Thereafter, Vickie Spencer filled out an Overlook request for accommodation form, asserting that the dog was necessary to ameliorate her daughter's disability, which she described as anxiety disorder and neurological and emotional conditions. McCarthy also provided some additional information concerning Lynsey's disability and her need for the dog as a reasonable accommodation.

On September 10, 2007, Folkerth wrote back to McCarthy, indicating that the information McCarthy had provided was not sufficient to permit Overlook's Trustees to determine whether Lynsey was disabled as defined by law and whether the accommodation requested was appropriate or necessary. Folkerth also included releases for Lynsey's medical and psychological records maintained by Hoefflin. In addition, he stated that, depending upon the content of the released records, additional information could be required and cautioned that if signed releases were not returned, the Trustees would file suit to obtain those records. On September 25, 2007, Michael Allen ("Allen"), the attorney representing the Spencers in this litigation, wrote to Folkerth in response, explaining that he had been retained by Vickie Spencer and the MVFHC in the matter of the request for a reasonable accommodation on behalf of Lynsey and that, while concerned about the failure of Overlook to grant same, he was most disturbed by the invasiveness of the inquiry into her medical records, which Folkerth had proposed. To bridge their differences, Allen suggested that he and Folkerth conduct a conference call with Hoefflin, during which Folkerth could ask the treating psychologist questions about why the dog was necessary to afford Lynsey the equal opportunity of enjoying the Spencers' unit at Overlook. Allen also indicated that Hoefflin would be on vacation and could not participate in a conference call until October 10, 2007, and that he would be available for such a conference call during the afternoons of October 10th, 11th and 12th. There is no evidence that the conference call proposed by Allen ever took place. Overlook initiated this litigation on October 17, 2007.

In its Complaint against Vickie Spencer, Overlook requests that this Court enter relief, declaring the following, to wit: 1) that it must be provided with the medical and counseling records maintained by Hoefflin, in order to permit it to determine whether Lynsey is disabled within the meaning of the law; 2) that its request for records maintained by Hoefflin is not in violation of federal or state law prohibiting housing discrimination; 3) that, upon Vickie Spencer's failure to provide those records, it was not obligated to waive its no pet rule and could enforce same; and 4) that the dog, Scooby, is not a service animal as defined by law and does not qualify as a reasonable accommodation for purposes of waiving its no pet rule.

Vickie Spencer, joined by her husband Joey, responded to Overlook's Complaint, by, inter alia, asserting a Counterclaim. In that pleading, the Spencers have set forth the following claims for relief, to wit: 1) a claim that Overlook has violated the Fair Housing

Act ("FHA"), 42 U.S.C. §3601, et seq., by enforcing the no pet rule and failing to make a reasonable accommodation of that rule;[2] 2) a claim under Ohio's fair housing statute, §4112.02(H) of the Ohio Revised Code, setting forth similar allegations against Overlook, and, in addition, alleging the making of impermissible inquiries on the basis of disability and coercing, intimidating and interfering with the Spencers because of their advocacy of disability rights; and 3) a claim of negligence under the common law of Ohio. The Spencers request injunctive relief; compensatory, statutory and punitive damages; and costs, including reasonable attorney's fees.

This case is now before the Court on Overlook's Motion for Summary Judgment. As a means of analysis, the Court will initially set forth the procedural standards it must apply whenever it rules on a motion for summary judgment, following which it will turn to the parties' arguments in support of and in opposition to the instant such motion.

. . .

With its motion, Overlook has set forth three arguments in support of its request for summary judgment, to wit: 1) that it is permitted to set pet policies for its tenants and to obtain the information necessary to evaluate the appropriateness of a tenant's request for a waiver of the no pet rule; 2) that an animal must have individual training to qualify as a "service animal" under the federal definition of that term (id. at 12–13); and 3) that it is entitled to summary judgment on the Spencers' negligence claim (id. at 13–15). As a means of analysis, the Court will address those three arguments in the above order.

A. Overlook Is Permitted to Set Pet Policies for its Tenants and to Obtain the Information Necessary to Evaluate the Appropriateness of a Tenant's Request for a Waiver of the No Pet Rule

As indicated, the Spencers allege that Overlook has violated 42 U.S.C. §3604(f)(3), by failing allow them to keep Scooby. "To prevail on a claim under 42 U.S.C. §3604(f)(3), a plaintiff must prove all of the following elements: (1) that the plaintiff or his associate is handicapped within the meaning of 42 U.S.C. §3602(h); (2) that the defendant knew or should reasonably be expected to know of the handicap; (3) that accommodation of the handicap may be necessary to afford the handicapped person an equal opportunity to use and enjoy the dwelling; (4) that the accommodation is reasonable; and (5) that defendant refused to make the requested accommodation." *DuBois v. Association of Apartment Owners of 2987 Kalakaua*, 453 F.3d 1175, 1179 (9th Cir. 2006), cert. denied, 549 U.S. 1216, 127 S. Ct. 1267, 167 L. Ed. 2d 92 (2007). The Sixth Circuit, however, has held that an accommodation must be necessary. See *Howard v. City of Beavercreek*, 276 F.3d 802, 806 (6th Cir. 2002) (noting that "'the concept of necessity requires at a minimum the showing that the desired accommodation will affirmatively enhance a disabled plaintiff's quality of life by ameliorating the effects of the disability'") (quoting *Bronk v. Ineichen*, 54 F.3d 425, 429 (7th Cir. 1995)). Thus, the third above-quoted element has been effectively modified by the Sixth Circuit to replace the "may be" with "is."

Parenthetically, the Spencers' claim under §4112.02(H) includes allegations that Overlook violated that statute by making impermissible inquiries on the basis of disability and coercing, intimidating and interfering with the Spencers because of their advocacy

---

2. The FHA makes it unlawful to discriminate on the basis of handicap and defines discrimination to include "a refusal to make reasonable accommodations in rules, policies, practices, or services, when such accommodations may be necessary to afford such person equal opportunity to use and enjoy a dwelling." 42 U.S.C. §3604(f)(3)(B).

of disability rights. Since those aspects of the Spencers' Ohio statutory claim have been omitted from the Final Pretrial Conference Order, they have been waived.

Overlook contends that it is entitled to summary judgment, because it is permitted to set pet policies for its tenants and to obtain the information necessary to evaluate the appropriateness of a tenant's request for a waiver of the no pet rule. This Court will decline to enter summary judgment in favor of Overlook on this proposition. Initially, this Court cannot agree with Overlook that it is free to set pet policies for its tenants. On the contrary, such policies must comply with the FHA. Given that Overlook has failed to demonstrate that the evidence does not raise a genuine issue of material fact as to whether its no pet policy, as applied to the Spencers, violates the FHA, that question will be resolved by the jury after the presentation of the evidence.

For two reasons, the Court denies Overlook's request for summary judgment, on the basis that it was permitted to obtain information necessary to evaluate the appropriateness of a tenant's request for a waiver of the no pet rule. First, the Spencers have not alleged that Overlook violated the FHA by requesting information concerning Lynsey's disability and need for Scooby. Although they initially alleged that Overlook's request for such information violated § 4112.02(H), such a claim is not included in their claims that have been identified in the Final Pretrial Statement. Therefore, that claim has been waived. Given that the Spencers are not alleging that Overlook violated either the federal or state statute by requesting such information, the Court questions whether Overlook's request for declaratory relief on that question presents an actual controversy. Until it is satisfied that Overlook's claim in that regard presents such a controversy, this Court will not proceed to trial on such a claim, let alone enter judgment in favor of Overlook on it.

Second, the Department of Housing and Urban Development ("HUD") and the Department of Justice ("DOJ") indicated in their Joint Statement on Reasonable Accommodations under the FHA that the provider of housing is entitled to obtain only that information necessary to determine whether the requested accommodation is necessary because of a disability. Construing the evidence most strongly in favor of the Spencers, the Court concludes that there is a genuine issue of material fact on the issue of whether the information sought by Overlook was necessary. Overlook initiated this litigation without taking advantage of the Spencers' offer to allow its counsel to participate in a conference call with their counsel and Hoefflin, Lynsey's treating psychologist. During that conference call, Overlook's counsel would have been permitted to question Hoefflin on Lynsey's disability and her need for Scooby. Consequently, there is a genuine issue of material fact as to whether Overlook was offered the opportunity to obtain the necessary information, an opportunity which it unilaterally chose to disregard.

Accordingly, the Court rejects Overlook's contention that it is entitled to summary judgment, because it is permitted to set pet policies for its tenants and to obtain the information necessary to evaluate the appropriateness of a tenant's request for a waiver of the no pet rule.

B. An Animal Must Have Individual Training to Qualify as a "Service Animal" under the Federal Definition of that Term

While this proposition is phrased somewhat abstractly, Overlook contends that it is entitled to summary judgment on the Spencer's claim under the FHA, because Scooby is not a "service animal." Although that term is not to be found in the FHA or in regulations interpreting that statute,[3] Overlook contends that this Court must apply that term and

---

3. A regulation adopted by HUD, a federal agency charged with enforcing the FHA, provides in relevant part:

its definition found in regulations adopted to enforce a different statute, the Americans with Disabilities Act (ADA), 42 U.S.C. § 12101, et seq. In particular, "service animal" is defined in 28 CFR § 36.104, as:

> any guide dog, signal dog, or other animal individually trained to do work or perform tasks for the benefit of an individual with a disability, including, but not limited to, guiding individuals with impaired vision, alerting individuals with impaired hearing to intruders or sounds, providing minimal protection or rescue work, pulling a wheelchair, or fetching dropped items. [Editor's note: this definition has now been changed as noted above in this chapter.]

The Spencers have not challenged Overlook's assertion that Scooby will qualify as a "service animal," under the ADA regulation, only if he was individually trained. Moreover, as Overlook argues, the uncontroverted evidence, Vickie Spencer's responses to its interrogatories, demonstrates that Scooby was not individually trained. Nevertheless, the Spencers argue that Overlook is not entitled to summary judgment on this point, because it is not necessary for Scooby to be a service animal, in order to qualify as a reasonable accommodation under the FHA. For reasons which follow, this Court agrees with the Spencers and, thus, rejects Overlook's argument that it is entitled to summary judgment on all claims under the FHA because Scooby was not individually trained, as is required of service animals under the regulations adopted to enforce a different statute, the ADA.

In support of this premise, Overlook places primary reliance upon *In re Kenna Homes Co-op. Corp.*, 210 W.Va. 380, 557 S.E.2d 787 (2001). Therein, the West Virginia Supreme Court addressed the issue of whether an animal had to qualify as a service animal under the regulations governing the ADA, in order to constitute a reasonable accommodation under the FHA. The West Virginia Supreme Court concluded that only a service animal could qualify as a reasonable accommodation under the FHA, writing:

> In sum, we hold that the Federal Fair Housing Act, 42 U.S.C. §§ 3601 to 3631, … require[s] that a service animal be individually trained and work for the benefit of a disabled person in order to be considered a reasonable accommodation of that person's disability. A person claiming the need for an alleged service animal as a reasonable accommodation of his or her disability has the burden of proving these requirements. Further, under the Federal Fair Housing Act, 42 U.S.C. §§ 3601 to 3631…, a landlord or person similarly situated may require a disabled tenant who asserts the need to keep an alleged service animal to show that the animal is properly trained; to produce in writing the formal assertion of the trainer that the animal has been so trained; and to present a statement from a licensed physician specializing in the field of [the] subject disability which certifies that the alleged service animal is necessary to ameliorate the effects of the tenant's disability. *Id.* at 392–93, 557 S.E.2d at 799–800. In *Prindable v. Association of*

(a) It shall be unlawful for any person to refuse to make reasonable accommodations in rules, policies, practices, or services, when such accommodations may be necessary to afford a handicapped person equal opportunity to use and enjoy a dwelling unit, including public and common use areas.

(b) The application of this section may be illustrated by the following examples:

Example (1): A blind applicant for rental housing wants live in a dwelling unit with a seeing eye dog. The building has a no pets policy. It is a violation of § 100.204 for the owner or manager of the apartment complex to refuse to permit the applicant to live in the apartment with a seeing eye dog because, without the seeing eye dog, the blind person will not have an equal opportunity to use and enjoy a dwelling.

24 CFR § 100.204.

Apartment Owners of 2987 Kalakuna, 304 F. Supp. 2d 1245 (D.Hawaii 2003), affirmed on other grounds sub nom., *DuBois v. Association of Apartment Owners
of 2987 Kalakaua*, 453 F.3d 1175 (9th Cir. 2006), cert. denied, 549 U.S. 1216,
127 S. Ct. 1267, 167 L. Ed. 2d 92 (2007), the District Court followed Kenna
Homes and held that an animal did not constitute a reasonable accommodation
under the FHA, unless it had been individually trained. 304 F. Supp.2d at 1256.

In opposition, the Spencers contend that reasonable accommodations under the FHA
are not limited to animals which qualify as service animals; rather, they contend that such
animals include emotional support animals, the function which Scooby was fulfilling
with Lynsey. The Spencers point out that the only place in the regulations adopted to
enforce the ADA, in which service animals are discussed, other than the above quoted
definition of that term, is 28 CFR § 36.302(c), which generally provides that a public accommodation "shall modify policies, practices, or procedures to permit the use of a service
animal by an individual with a disability." The FHA, in contrast with the ADA, does not
regulate disability discrimination by public accommodations and in places of public accommodation. Rather, the FHA, inter alia, makes it illegal to discriminate against
handicapped individuals in providing housing. 42 U.S.C. § 3604(f)(1). Simply stated,
there is a difference between not requiring the owner of a movie theater to allow a customer
to bring her emotional support dog, which is not a service animal, into the theater to
watch a two-hour movie, an ADA-type issue, on one hand, and permitting the provider
of housing to refuse to allow a renter to keep such an animal in her apartment in order
to provide emotional support to her and to assist her to cope with her depression, an
FHA-type issue, on the other.

Based upon the foregoing alone, this Court would conclude that accommodations under
the FHA regarding animals are not limited to service animals. However, additional indicia
demonstrate that the two federal agencies charged with enforcing that statute, HUD and
the DOJ, take the opposite position from that advocated herein by Overlook. For instance,
HUD recently revised its regulations concerning pet ownership by the elderly and persons
with disabilities residing in HUD-assisted, public housing. See Pet Ownership for the Elderly
and Persons with Disabilities, 73 F.R. 63834–38 (October 27, 2008). The revised regulation
excludes from HUD's regulations prohibiting pet ownership in public housing "animals that
are used to assist, support, or provide service to persons with disabilities." 24 CFR § 5.303.
HUD has explained that the revised rule applies not just to service animals, as defined by
the regulations implementing the ADA, but also to support and therapy animals. 73 F.R.
63834. Such animals are defined to include those "providing emotional support to persons
who have a disability related need for such support." Id. As can be seen, HUD has declined
to limit its regulation on keeping animals to those that have been individually trained, unlike
the regulations implementing the ADA. HUD explained its reasons for doing so:

> Finally, the Department believes that removing the animal training requirement
> ensures equal treatment of persons with disabilities who need animals in housing
> as a reasonable accommodation, for a wide variety of purposes. While many
> animals are trained to perform certain tasks for persons with disabilities, others
> do not need training to provide the needed assistance. For example, there are
> animals that have an innate ability to detect that a person with a seizure disorder
> is about to have a seizure and can let the individual know ahead of time so that
> the person can prepare. This ability is not the result of training, and a person
> with a seizure disorder might need such an animal as a reasonable accommodation
> to his/her disability. Moreover, emotional support animals do not need training
> to ameliorate the effects of a person's mental and emotional disabilities. Emotional

support animals by their very nature, and without training, may relieve depression and anxiety, and/or help reduce stress-induced pain in persons with certain medical conditions affected by stress.

Proposed elimination of training component is inconsistent with the regulations implementing the Americans with Disabilities Act. Several commenters wrote that the applicable definition of the term "service animal" is contained in the Department of Justice regulations implementing the Americans with Disabilities Act (ADA) (42 U.S.C. 12101 et seq.). The commenters wrote that HUD regulations have never specifically defined the term "service animal." Under the ADA regulations at 28 CFR 36.104, a service animal is defined as an animal "individually trained" to do work or perform tasks for the benefit of an individual with a disability. The commenters wrote that this definition covers both ADA claims and claims under Section 504, which HUD is responsible for enforcing. Also according to the commenters, by eliminating the training requirement, the proposed rule contradicts the ADA definition.

The Department [HUD] does not agree that the definition of the term "service animal" contained in the Department of Justice regulations implementing the ADA should be applied to the Fair Housing Act and Section 504. The ADA governs the use of animals by persons with disabilities primarily in the public arena. There are many areas where the ADA and the Fair Housing Act and Section 504 contain different requirements. For example, accessibility is defined differently under the ADA than under the Fair Housing Act and Section 504.

The Fair Housing Act and HUD's Section 504 regulations govern the use of animals needed as a reasonable accommodation in housing. HUD's regulations and policies pertaining to reasonable accommodation were constructed specifically to address housing and, furthermore, were enacted prior to the development and implementation of the ADA regulations. Thus, the requirements for assistance/service animals must be evaluated in the appropriate context of housing, and are independent of the ADA regulations that were formulated to meet the needs of persons with disabilities in a different context and were adopted subsequent to HUD's regulations.

There is a valid distinction between the functions animals provide to persons with disabilities in the public arena, i.e., performing tasks enabling individuals to use public services and public accommodations, as compared to how an assistance animal might be used in the home. For example, emotional support animals provide very private functions for persons with mental and emotional disabilities. Specifically, emotional support animals by their very nature, and without training, may relieve depression and anxiety, and help reduce stress-induced pain in persons with certain medical conditions affected by stress. Conversely, persons with disabilities who use emotional support animals may not need to take them into public spaces covered by the ADA.

Id. at 63836. Although the revised rule applies only to HUD-assisted public housing, as opposed applying to housing generally, as does the FHA, the rationale in support thereof is equally applicable to all types of housing regulated by the FHA.

In addition, subsequent to the decision of the West Virginia Supreme Court in *Kenna Homes*, the DOJ, in conjunction with HUD, brought an action against that entity, alleging that it had violated the FHA by implementing a rule which limited the types of dogs residents could keep to dogs that were trained and certified for a particular disability, a rule which had the effect of denying a mentally impaired resident the ability to keep a dog which provided emotional support. *United States v. Kenna Homes Cooperative Corp. Kenna Homes* and the Government subsequently entered into a consent decree, under which the former agreed to adopt an exception to any rule preventing residents from keeping pets, by permitting disabled residents to have service animals or emotional support animals. An emotional support animal was defined as an animal, "the presence of which ameliorates the effects of a mental or emotional disability." *Id.*

In sum, this Court concludes that the types of animals that can qualify as reasonable accommodations under the FHA include emotional support animals, which need not be individually trained. Accordingly, the Court rejects Overlook's assertion that it is entitled to summary judgment, because Scooby was not so trained.

C. Negligence

Overlook moves for summary judgment on the Spencers' negligence claim, arguing that it is entitled to same because it has not taken action against the Spencers, pending disposition of Vickie Spencer's request for a waiver of the no pet rule. As a consequence, Overlook's argument continues, the Spencers have not suffered any harm. Based upon Vickie Spencer's declaration and other evidence before the Court, this Court concludes that the evidence raises a genuine issue of material fact as to whether the Spencers have suffered harm. Overlook, acting through its counsel, has raised the specter of evicting the Spencers for violating the no pet policy. In her declaration, Vickie Spencer states that she and her husband have lost sleep and suffered anxiety as a result of feeling that they will lose their home over the presence of Scooby.

Alternatively, Overlook argues that it is entitled to summary judgment on this claim, because it did not owe the Spencers a duty, a fundamental element of any claim of negligence. In particular, relying on *Kenna Homes*, Overlook contends that in determining whether a duty exists, its Board of Trustees was required to consider the interests of other tenants, who chose to live in a pet free environment, as well as the damage that can be caused by "[e]ven the most carefully controlled and well behaved pets." Simply stated, in the absence of Ohio authority to the contrary, this Court cannot conclude that the duty required in an Ohio negligence claim cannot be based on a violation of the FHA and Ohio's statutory counterpart, §4112.02(H). This Court notes that Ohio courts have frequently recognized that a negligence claim can be based upon a violation of other anti-discrimination provisions of §4112.02.

Accordingly, the Court rejects Overlook's request for summary judgment on the Spencers' negligence claim.

Based upon the foregoing, the Court overrules Overlook's Motion for Summary Judgment.

* * *

Questions for Discussion

1. Can you see yourself practicing in this area of law? Would you rather represent the service animal owner or the landlord? If you were a judge in this case, would you find this case interesting, or think it was a waste of time?

2. What if a particular service animal in a condo complex is noisy? What if neighbors are allergic to dogs and the dog frequents the common areas such as the clubhouse? What does the Fair Housing Act say about such situations?

The following case tackles the issue of service animals in places of public accommodation.

DiLorenzo v. Costco Wholesale Corp.
515 F.Supp.2d 1187 (W.D.Wash.) (2007)

ORDER

This matter comes before the Court on Defendant's Motion for Summary Judgment, Plaintiff's Response (Dkt. No. 46-1), and Defendant's Reply. Having considered the papers submitted by the parties and determined that oral argument is unnecessary, the Court hereby finds and rules as follows.

I. BACKGROUND

Plaintiff alleges that she is a disabled individual who suffers from a variety of ailments arising after her service in the armed forces. With the support of her treating psychologist, Plaintiff began to employ the assistance of a dog, who Plaintiff asserts is "a service animal trained to assist her in resisting and responding to the difficulties raised by her conditions." Plaintiff acquired the dog, a pug named Dilo, in approximately March 2004, when it was an untrained eight month-old puppy. Plaintiff's claims arise from interactions with Costco store employees on two separate shopping trips with Dilo in her company. First, on or around April 30, 2004, Plaintiff entered Defendant's Bellingham warehouse and informed an employee at the entrance that Plaintiff was accompanied by an animal that was in the process of being trained as a "service animal." At that time Dilo was about twelve weeks old and was not wearing any accessory indicating he was a service animal. Plaintiff was asked to proceed to a podium where she was given copies of Costco's Service Animal Policy and a Department of Justice Business Brief on service animals. Plaintiff showed an employee at the podium a copy of a letter from her psychologist, which briefly described her disabilities and attested to Plaintiff's suitability for owning a service animal. Plaintiff did not leave a copy of the letter or any other information about herself for future reference, nor did the employee ask her to do so.

On a second visit to the Bellingham warehouse on July 3, 2004, Dilo was wearing a vest that read "service dog in training." Defendant's employee described the vest as being, at least in part, "homemade." Plaintiff, her husband and Dilo entered the warehouse unmolested and while shopping in the meat section, Plaintiff began to carry Dilo in her arms to avoid injury to the dog from the crowd of shopping carts. (Pl.'s Dep. 111:4-14. Prior to reaching the cash registers, Plaintiff was approached by store manager Adele Wolcott, who asked Plaintiff on whose behalf the dog acted as a service animal, as well as what task it performed. Plaintiff responded that Dilo was hers and that he "alert[ed] [her] to—for spells." Ms. Wolcott then walked away and Plaintiff proceeded through the check-out line. While approaching the warehouse exit, Plaintiff and her party were confronted by Ms. Wolcott and Ken Burnham, another manager, who asked to speak with her. According to Plaintiff, Ms. Wolcott said she believed the dog belonged to Plaintiff's husband, apparently because he had brought Dilo into the warehouse on a previous occasion. Ms. Wolcott also asserted that the dog's vest was not "regulation." Finally, Ms. Wolcott objected to the fact that Plaintiff had carried the dog around the warehouse. The tone of this interaction, according to Plaintiff, was not "nice," but rather "inappropriate … loud … embarrassing … humiliating … degrading." At that point, Burnham informed Plaintiff that companion animals were not allowed in the warehouse and that in the future Plaintiff could "sit in [her] car with [her] dog." Plaintiff asserts that

Defendant's employees' actions constituted harassment, as they were, in her words, accusing her of being a "liar." Plaintiff also claims that the encounter may have created the false impression for passers-by, some of whom may have been acquaintances, that she was suspected of shoplifting. Feeling uncomfortable, Plaintiff took note of Ms. Wolcott and Mr. Burnham's contact information and left the warehouse.

According to the parties, each made subsequent attempts to contact the other to follow up on the July 3, 2004 incident. Plaintiff claims she left several messages with Costco employees which were never returned. Defendant's lawyer sent, and Plaintiff did receive, a letter asking her to provide further information about her dog's training and the tasks it performs. The purpose of the letter was to "determine whether the dog was a bona fide service animal." Plaintiff never responded to this letter and claims that it constituted further harassment.

Finally, from the available record, it appears that Costco may have deviated from its policies regarding service animals at the time. Plaintiff asserts, and Defendant does not clearly refute, that the relevant policy stated that service animals visually identifiable as such would not be subject to further scrutiny. Furthermore, no distinction was drawn between service animals and service animals in-training. The foregoing set of events is the basis upon which Plaintiff brings her claims under state and federal law, each of which the Court addresses below in turn.

II. DISCUSSION

A. Standard of Review [Editor's note: discussion of summary judgment standard omitted.]

B. Americans with Disabilities Act ("ADA") Claim

Plaintiff's second cause of action alleges that Defendant failed to comply with its obligations as a public accommodation under the ADA. Title III of the ADA states that "[n]o individual shall be discriminated against on the basis of disability in the full and equal enjoyment of the goods, services, facilities, privileges, advantages, or accommodations of any place of public accommodation ..." 42 U.S.C. § 12182(a). The statute further instructs the Attorney General to issue regulations implementing the non-transportation provisions of the ADA. 42 U. S.C. § 12186(b). Accordingly, the Department of Justice ("DOJ") regulations state that:

> A public accommodation shall make reasonable modifications in policies, practices, or procedures, when the modifications are necessary to afford goods, services, facilities, privileges, advantages, or accommodations to individuals with disabilities, unless the public accommodation can demonstrate that making the modifications would fundamentally alter the nature of the goods, services, facilities, privileges, advantages, or accommodations.

28 C.F.R. § 36.302(a). With regard to service animals in particular, the regulations state: "Generally, a public accommodation shall modify policies, practices, or procedures to permit the use of a service animal by an individual with a disability." Id. at § 36.302(c)(1). Furthermore, a "service animal" is defined as:

> [a]ny guide dog, signal dog, or other animal individually trained to do work or perform tasks for the benefit of an individual with a disability, including, but not limited to, guiding individuals with impaired vision, alerting individuals with impaired hearing to intruders or sounds, providing minimal protection or rescue work, pulling a wheelchair, or fetching dropped items. [Editor's note: this definition has now been changed as noted above in this chapter.]

Id. at § 36.104. Furthermore, as the "agency directed by Congress to issue implementing regulations, to render technical assistance, and to enforce Title III in court, the Department's views are entitled to deference." *Bragdon v. Abbott*, 524 U.S. 624, 646, 118 S. Ct. 2196, 141 L. Ed. 2d 540 (1998) (internal citations omitted).

In her second cause of action, Plaintiff asserts that Defendant discriminated against her in violation of the ADA by failing or refusing "to modify its policies, practices and procedures when such modifications were necessary" to allow her access to its goods, services, facilities, privileges, advantages, and accommodations. Such modification, she asserts, should have included making allowance for her service animal, which helped her cope with the consequences of her disability. Defendant responds by asserting that Plaintiff's dog was not a service animal under the governing regulations at the time in question, and that in any case, Plaintiff refused to respond to a reasonable inquiry which would have allowed Costco to determine the dog's qualifications.

It is not entirely clear what specific acts or omissions by Defendant form the basis of Plaintiff's ADA claim. The Amended Complaint cites the statutory language regarding the obligation of a public accommodation to make "reasonable modifications" to its polices, but does not describe what Defendant specifically did or failed to do. The modification sought cannot be to have allowed entry into the warehouse with her dog, because she was admitted on every occasion in question. In her deposition testimony, Plaintiff states that the conduct she deemed illegal was the "harassment" of being questioned about her dog on July 3, 2004. While this may not serve as the operative legal statement of her claim, her response brief does little to clarify the matter, as it simply quotes provisions of the ADA without any discussion of how they apply to the facts of this case. Under these circumstances, the Court interprets Plaintiff's ADA claim as challenging the legitimacy of the inquiry about her dog's qualifications, in so far as it may have impeded her "full and equal enjoyment" of Defendant's facilities. 42 U.S.C. § 12182(a). Since Defendant indicated in its letter that Plaintiff would need to respond to further questioning before being admitted with her dog in the future, the analysis necessarily includes the legitimacy of this further inquiry subsequent to the July 3, 2004 encounter.

Once Plaintiff's claim is understood in this way, there are two issues raised by the parties that confuse the question before the Court. First, Plaintiff's emphasis on Costco's service animal policy is misplaced for the purposes of the ADA analysis. That is, the question of Costco's compliance with its own policy does not obviate the fundamental inquiry into whether its actions violated the statute. Whether a given policy sets forth standards of conduct within statutory bounds is a question of facial validity, which in the case of Costco's service dog policy, was upheld in *Grill v. Costco Wholesale Corp.*, 312 F. Supp. 2d 1349 (W.D. Wash. 2004). The existence of a legal policy notwithstanding, a public accommodation can still act in a manner that violates the ADA, which is precisely the question raised in this case. Either way, Costco does not violate the ADA simply by violating its own policy.

Second, Defendant's emphasis on Dilo's lack of qualifications as a service dog at the time in question does not address the entire issue. That is because a violation of the statute can occur by virtue of the manner by which an inquiry is conducted. As discussed in *Grill*, cited by Defendant, the DOJ has issued guidance as to what constitutes a legitimate inquiry as to a particular animal's qualifications. See *Grill*, 312 F. Supp. 2d at 1352. It appears that Costco employees were aware of such limitations based on Ms. Wolcott's deposition testimony, in which she stated that "[w]e cannot ask their disability, but Costco does have the right to ask them what function the animal does perform." Thus, Defendant does not defeat Plaintiff's ADA claim by simply showing that Dilo was not a bona fide service animal at the time of the inquiry, since the manner in which it went about verifying such a fact could have violated the law.

Plaintiff's ADA claim ultimately depends on whether Defendant exceeded the parameters of a legitimate inquiry in confronting Plaintiff about her dog. That Costco had a right to make an inquiry in the first place cannot seriously be questioned. This follows from DOJ interpretations regarding "legitimate inquiry," the *Grill* case, as well as common sense. In operating its business, Costco has the authority to exclude ordinary pets from its facilities, and yet must also comply with federal anti-discrimination law, which under most circumstances includes permitting service animals into its warehouses. Given these two co-existing conditions, an occasion for some kind of inquiry is bound to arise. In *Grill*, the court examined the limitations on inquiry about service animal's qualifications, citing a DOJ business brief providing that a "[b]usiness may ask if an animal is a service animal or ask what tasks the animal has been trained to perform, but cannot require special ID cards for the animal or ask about the person's disability." *Grill*, 312 F. Supp. 2d at 1352. This is referred to as a "task or function" inquiry and is the key method for distinguishing a service dog from a pet.

Based upon this standard, Defendant's employees did not exceed the boundaries of a permissible inquiry by their conduct on July 3, 2004. They never asked Plaintiff to state her disability, nor did they demand proof of special training. In the encounter prior to Plaintiff entering the checkout line, Ms. Wolcott made a standard "task or function" inquiry by asking whose dog it was and what task it performed. As for the content of the subsequent letter sent by Costco's attorney, it too posed standard "task or function" questions by asking who the dog was trained to assist, and what training it had received. The letter also asked whether the dog was a "seizure alert dog" or a "comfort dog." While it is not clear why these were the only available options, presumably Plaintiff could have responded that her dog was neither and it would not have disqualified Dilo as a service animal.

The fact, in and of itself, that Defendant made a second "task or function" inquiry by letter, and that Plaintiff's future admittance was apparently conditioned upon her answers is a separate question. Clearly an inquiry would cease to be legitimate if it was used to harass or discourage people with disabilities from availing themselves of public accommodation. In this way, unduly repetitive questioning, after an adequate answer has been given, could suggest a pretext for discrimination, constituting an illegitimate inquiry. However, a similar course of action to what Defendant took here has been recognized as legitimate in the housing context. In *Prindable v. Ass'n of Apartment Owners*, the court concluded that:

> In any event, there is no evidence that Defendants ever denied Plaintiffs' request for a service animal. Beginning with their response to Dr. Kalauawa's May 17, 2000 letter, the AOAO merely requested additional, appropriate information from Prindable and his treating physicians.

304 F. Supp. 2d 1245, 1260 (D. Haw. 2003). The Court finds this reasoning analogous to the present case.

Furthermore, in evaluating Defendant's conduct here, other facts surrounding the encounter cannot be ignored. The following factors, which Plaintiff has either explicitly acknowledged or not disputed, clearly raised legitimate suspicions about whether Dilo was indeed a service animal: (1) The first time Plaintiff brought her dog into the warehouse as a "service dog in training," it was an untrained twelve week-old puppy; (2) Plaintiff's husband appears to have brought Dilo into the warehouse on at least one occasion prior to July 3, 2004, claiming that it served as a "comfort animal" to him; (3) Plaintiff carried Dilo in her arms for an extended period of time while shopping on July 3, 2004; and (4) As of the date in question, Dilo was unable to independently perform his task (as a service animal) of alerting for panic attacks without prompting from Plaintiff's husband. While

Defendant's employees did not know this latter fact at the time, it is safe to say they could not witness the dog performing any task to assist Plaintiff with her disability. Under these circumstances, it was not unreasonable or illegitimate for Defendant to have expressed doubts about Dilo's status, or to have sent a follow-up letter seeking further clarification. Had Plaintiff responded by affirming that the dog was her service animal and that it was individually trained to alert her for panic and anxiety attacks, it is not clear on what basis Defendant could object in the future. As this did not occur, however, the Court concludes that Costco's actions did not exceed the boundaries of a legitimate inquiry under the ADA, and thus Defendant is entitled to judgment as a matter of law on this claim.

C. Washington Law Against Discrimination ("WLAD") claim

Similar to the anti-discrimination scheme of the ADA, Washington law protects "[t]he right to the full enjoyment of any of the accommodations, advantages, facilities, or privileges of any place of public resort, accommodation, assemblage, or amusement." WASH. REV. CODE. § 49.60.030(1)(b). Denial of "full enjoyment" under the statute includes causing someone to be "treated as not welcome, accepted, desired, or solicited." Id. at § 49.60.040(9). Furthermore, the law prohibits acts which "directly or indirectly result in … the refusing or withholding from any person the admission, patronage, custom, presence, frequenting, dwelling, staying, or lodging in any place of public resort, accommodation, assemblage, or amusement." Id. at § 49.60.215. These protections explicitly extend to "the use of a trained dog guide or service animal by a person with a disability." Id. A service animal is defined as "an animal trained for the purpose of assisting or accommodating a person's sensory, mental, or physical disability." WASH. ADMIN. CODE § 162.26.040(2). Washington state courts have recognized that disability discrimination under state law "substantially parallels federal law" on the subject, and therefore have indicated that "courts should look to interpretations of federal anti-discrimination laws, including the ADA, when applying the WLAD." Grill v. Costco Wholesale Corp., 312 F. Supp. 2d 1349, 1354 (W.D. Wash. 2004) (citing Matthews v. NCAA, 179 F. Supp. 2d 1209, 1229 (E.D. Wash. 2001).)

The circumstances under which the Court finds that Plaintiff's ADA claim fails, are equally applicable to her WLAD claim. Plaintiff presents no authority for the proposition that a different analysis governs her state law discrimination claim, such that Defendant would be subject to a different legal standard than that which obtains under the ADA for inquiring about a service animal. Having determined that Defendant did not exclude Plaintiff and her dog from their warehouse, and that it conducted a legitimate inquiry under the ADA as to whether the dog functioned as a service animal in light of circumstances that suggested otherwise, Plaintiff's WLAD claim presents no genuine issue of material fact and fails as a matter of law.

D. Negligent Infliction of Emotional Distress ("NIED") claim

Plaintiff brings a tort claim of NIED as a result of her interactions with Costco employees on her shopping trips to Defendant's Bellingham warehouse. In Washington, the tort of NIED requires a showing that (1) The defendant owed a duty of care to plaintiff, (2) Defendant breached that duty, (3) There was proximate cause between breach and damages, and (4) Damages did indeed inhere. Hunsley v. Giard, 87 Wn.2d 424, 553 P.2d 1096, 1102 (Wash. 1976). In Hunsley, the state supreme court made clear that in applying this test, "[n]ot every act which causes harm results in legal liability," since "[o]ur experience tells us that mental distress is a fact of life." Id. at 1102–03. Accordingly, a defendant's "obligation to refrain from particular conduct is owed only to those who are foreseeably endangered by the conduct and only with respect to those risks or hazards whose likelihood made the conduct unreasonably dangerous." Id. at 1103.

"Under traditional negligence principles, whether a particular class of defendants owes a duty to a particular class of plaintiffs is a question of law and depends on mixed considerations of 'logic, common sense, justice, policy, and precedent.'" *Keates v. Vancouver*, 73 Wn. App. 257, 869 P.2d 88, 92 (Wash. Ct. App. 1994) (quoting *Hartley v. State*, 103 Wn.2d 768, 698 P.2d 77, 83 (Wash. 1985)). "In deciding whether a duty is owed the primary consideration is whether the conduct in question is unreasonably dangerous." Id. at 93 (citing *Corrigal v. Ball & Dodd Funeral Home, Inc.*, 89 Wn.2d 959, 577 P.2d 580 (Wash. 1978)). "Unless the defendant's conduct is unreasonably dangerous, the defendant owes no duty." Id. (citing *Hunsley*, 553 P.2d at 1103). "Conduct is unreasonably dangerous when the risks of harm outweigh the utility of the activity." *Wells v. Vancouver*, 77 Wn.2d 800, 467 P.2d 292, 298 (Wash. 1970) (quoting *Raymond v. Paradise Unified School Dist.*, 218 Cal.App.2d 1, 31 Cal. Rptr. 847 (Dist.Ct.App.1963)).

Plaintiff's claim for NIED requires consideration of her two shopping trips in tandem. In amending the Complaint to comply with this Court's August 9, 2006 Order, Plaintiff clarified her theory that the April trip to Defendant's Bellingham warehouse, in which she furnished the letter from her psychologist, effectively put Defendant on notice that a "high likelihood [of] risk of injury would accompany any unnecessary attention to plaintiff and plaintiff's animal, and that additional public attention which might result from Defendant's public questioning would be unreasonably dangerous and would subject her to injury and damage." Essentially, Plaintiff claims that this letter made Defendant's subsequent conduct on her July visit to the warehouse "unreasonably dangerous," and therefore constituted a breach of duty. Defendant takes issue with Plaintiff's failure to leave a copy of her psychologist's letter, and furthermore asserts that "the text of the letter does not suggest anything about a heightened risk of injury to Plaintiff if Costco takes (or fails to take) any action with respect to Plaintiff."

The Court need not address whose obligation it was to give or retain a copy of the letter in April 2004, since even if Defendant was chargeable with its contents, the letter failed to indicate a "high likelihood of risk" attached to future questioning making such conduct "unreasonably dangerous." The letter from Plaintiff's psychologist is not nearly as enlightening as her amended complaint and response brief suggest. The letter explains that Plaintiff has been diagnosed with "Posttraumatic Stress Disorder and Major Depression," and states that she "would be a good candidate and responsible recipient for service dog ownership." Furthermore, it implies that she needs to feel "enhanced personal safety" and "unconditional love and devotion." Contrary to Plaintiff's assertion in the Amended Complaint, the letter does not say anything about "panic disorder." More importantly, the general description of Plaintiff's ailments could not reasonably instruct a lay person that an ordinarily unobjectionable course of conduct, an inquiry made in public space, would be "unreasonably dangerous" with regard to Plaintiff.[1] The Court need not doubt the veracity of Plaintiff's suffering to find that it would have taken more to put Defendant's employees on notice that ordinary conduct would cause extraordinary emotional harm to Plaintiff. Accordingly, this falls into the category of an act which caused harm without resulting in liability, and therefore Plaintiff's NIED claim fails as a matter of law.

---

1. Nor does the fact that Costco may have deviated from its service animal policy render its questioning an "unreasonably dangerous" act. Requiring Plaintiff to enter an unexpected conversation hardly bespeaks the kind of peril that would invoke a duty here.

E. Intentional Infliction of Emotional Distress/Outrage claim

Plaintiff also brings a claim of outrage as a consequence of her treatment by Defendant. To establish a claim for the tort of outrage, a plaintiff must show "(1) extreme and outrageous conduct, (2) intentional or reckless infliction of emotional distress, and (3) severe emotional distress on the part of the plaintiff." *Reid v. Pierce County*, 136 Wn.2d 195, 961 P.2d 333, 337 (Wash. 1998). Regarding the standard for "extreme and outrageous conduct," the Washington Supreme Court has held that "the conduct in question must be 'so outrageous in character, and so extreme in degree, as to go beyond all possible bounds of decency, and to be regarded as atrocious, and utterly intolerable in a civilized community.'" *Dicomes v. Washington*, 113 Wn.2d 612, 782 P.2d 1002, 1012 (Wash. 1989) (citing *Grimsby v. Samson*, 85 Wn.2d 52, 530 P.2d 291, 295 (1975)). "While the question of outrageousness is normally one for the jury to decide, it is for the court to make the initial determination of whether 'reasonable minds could differ on whether the conduct was sufficiently extreme to result in liability.'" *Bryant v. Country Life Ins. Co.*, 414 F. Supp. 2d 981, 1004 (W.D. Wash. 2006) (quoting *Grimsby*, 530 P.2d at 295). "Conduct which is merely insulting or annoying, or even threatening will not trigger liability." *Bryant*, 414 F. Supp. 2d at 1004.

Similar to her claim of NIED, Plaintiff bases her outrage claim upon the entire course of Defendant's conduct, in light of having presented her letter to Defendant's employees on her April visit. Not only does she claim that she should not have been questioned in the first place, she asserts that the interactions were excessively unpleasant, describing the tone struck by Defendant's employees as "inappropriate" and "loud." Furthermore, she describes Ms. Wolcott and Mr. Burnham as essentially accusing her of being a liar, and the entire transaction as creating the false impression that she was suspected of shoplifting. Finally, Plaintiff insinuates that the encounter was something tantamount to being detained. Defendant responds that its conduct was not sufficiently egregious to trigger liability under the tort of outrage.

The Court finds that there is no genuine issue of material fact as to whether Defendant's conduct met the requisite level of impropriety, even taking Plaintiff's account as true and drawing all inferences in her favor. No reasonable jury could find Defendant's conduct "so outrageous in character, and so extreme in degree, as to go beyond all possible bounds of decency, and to be regarded as atrocious, and utterly intolerable in a civilized community." *Dicomes*, 113 Wn.2d 612, 782 P.2d 1002, 1012 (Wash. 1989).

As an initial matter, making the inquiry, in itself, cannot constitute an intentional infliction of emotional distress in light of the Court's finding that Defendant was not even negligent in this regard. As for how they carried out the inquiry, it is clear that Defendant's employees did not believe Dilo functioned as a service animal. Taking Plaintiff's account as true, Ms. Wolcott and Mr. Burnham were impolite and confrontational. While this indicates that they believed Plaintiff was lying, Plaintiff acknowledges that they never called her a "liar." Similarly, Plaintiff asserts that the encounter created the false impression that she was suspected of shoplifting. Even if this is true, she also explicitly acknowledges that they never called her a "thief." Finally, Plaintiff suggests in her briefing that Defendant's employees "detain[ed]" her for questioning. However, Plaintiff concedes in her deposition that Ms. Wolcott and Mr. Burnham never said anything to indicate that she was not free to leave. While they were standing between her and the exit, she gives no indication that she could not walk out at any time, as she ultimately did.

Clearly this was not an amicable encounter, and the Court takes Plaintiff at her word that it was severely distressing to her. However Washington law requires a plaintiff to meet a high threshold to succeed on a claim of outrage, and makes clear that "[c]onduct which is merely insulting or annoying, or even threatening will not trigger liability." *Bryant*, 414 F. Supp. 2d at 1004. This is just such a case, and therefore Plaintiff's outrage claim fails.

F. Washington Consumer Protection Act ("CPA") claim

Plaintiff's fifth cause of action alleges violation of the Washington CPA. WASH. REV. CODE § 19.86.020 et seq. The parties agree that the elements of a claim under the Washington Consumer Protection Act were correctly set forth by the Washington Supreme Court in *Hangman Ridge Training Stables, Inc. v. Safeco Title Ins. Co.*, 105 Wn.2d 778, 719 P.2d 531 (Wash. 1986). This test requires, among other things, that Plaintiff show injury to her "business or property." *Id.* at 535. In her deposition testimony, Plaintiff unequivocally states that she is not claiming any harm to her business or property. In her response brief, Plaintiff confirms that damage to business or property is an essential element of a CPA claim, however she asserts that it was satisfied in this case by injury to her "daily shopping trade." In the absence of any authority that would support this apparently novel theory of harm, Plaintiff's CPA claim fails as a matter of law.

III. CONCLUSION

For the foregoing reasons, Defendant's motion for summary judgment is hereby GRANTED. Accordingly, Defendant's motions in limine, Plaintiff's response, and Defendant's reply are moot and hereby STRICKEN.

* * *

Questions for Discussion

1. What did you think about the facts in the case? Do you think that Costco treated this plaintiff poorly? What did you think of the court's reaction to the facts?

2. Would the 2010 changes to the definitions in the ADA regulations have any impact on this case?

———————

For Further Reading

Mcdonald v. Dep't of Envtl. Quality, 351 Mont. 243, 214 P.3d 749, 214 P.3d 749 (2009). Must an employer accommodate an employee's service dog by installing carpet if the dog slips and falls on the hallways?

Silver, Kate. "How Mya Saved Jacob." *Spirit* (June 2010): 102–118, also anthologized in *An Anthology of Disability Literature.*, ed. by Christy Thompson Ibrahim. True story about a war veteran whose service dog helps him with effects of PTSD.

http://www.raggededgemagazine.com/departments/spotlight/002251.html, a list of articles archived on Ragged Edge Online.

An article about a service dog with an interesting role: http://todayhealth.today.msnbc. msn.com/_news/2012/03/21/10780622-girls-best-friend-is-dog-who-carries-her-oxygen

Perry A. Zirkel, "Service Animals in Public Schools," ELA Notes, January 2011, Vol. 46, No. 1, available online.

Index